McG... ...IES

INDIAN POLITY

for

Civil Services Examinations

4th Edition

McGRAW HILL EDUCATION   WE   SERIES

WINNING EDGE

INDIAN POLITY

for

Civil Services Examinations

4th Edition

M Laxmikanth

Founder-Director,
Laxmikanth's IAS,
Hyderabad

McGraw Hill Education (India) Private Limited
NEW DELHI

McGraw Hill Education Offices

New Delhi   New York   St Louis   San Francisco   Auckland   Bogotá   Caracas
Kuala Lumpur   Lisbon   London   Madrid   Mexico City   Milan   Montreal
San Juan   Santiago   Singapore   Sydney   Tokyo   Toronto

McGraw Hill Education (India) Private Limited

Published by McGraw Hill Education (India) Private Limited
P-24, Green Park Extension, New Delhi 110 016

Indian Polity, 4/e

20th reprint 2015
DCCCRRAVRBBRC

ISBN (13): 978-1-25-906412-8
ISBN (10): 1-25-906412-3

Managing Director—*Kaushik Bellani*
Deputy General Manager—Test Prep and School: *Tanmoy Roychowdhury*
Publishing Manager—Test Prep: *K N Prakash*
Assistant Sponsoring Editor—*Bhavna Malhotra*
Asst. Manager (Developmental Editing): *Anubha Srivastava*
Asst. Manager—Production: *Medha Arora*
Production Executive: *Dharmender Sharma*
Product Specialist: *Vikas Sharma*
General Manager—Production: *Rajender P Ghansela*
Manager—Production: *Reji Kumar*

Typeset at The Composers, 260, C.A. Apt., Paschim Vihar, New Delhi 110 063 and text and cover printed at Gopsons Papers Ltd., A2&3, Sector 64, Noida

Cover Designer: K Anoop

Visit us at: www.mheducation.co.in

To
my wife
M Vidya

PREFACE TO THE FOURTH EDITION

I am pleased to place before the readers a thoroughly revised, enlarged and updated edition of this widely read book on Indian Polity.

In 2011 and 2013, the UPSC changed the pattern and syllabus of the preliminary and main examinations, respectively. In both the changes, the scope of Indian Polity has been considerably increased. Hence, this new edition of the book is more relevant now and is aimed to meet the expanded needs of the aspirants.

In the course of revision and updation of this edition of the book, the various new developments related to the subject like recent constitutional amendments, parliamentary legislations, executive decisions and supreme court judgments have been taken into account.

Changes in this Edition:
1. Addition of 8 new chapters.
2. Addition of 3 new appendices.
3. Inclusion of 2010, 2011, 2012 and 2013 preliminary questions with answers.
4. Inclusion of 2009, 2010, 2011 and 2012 mains questions.
5. Updation of the year-wise break-up of the UPSC questions in the preliminary and main examinations.
6. Inclusion of additional updated information on a number of topics.
7. List of Articles included at the end of each chapter.
8. New items included in various chapters.

New Chapters:
1. Basic Structure of the Constitution
2. Cabinet Committees
3. Parliamentary Committees
4. Parliamentary Forums
5. Central Bureau of Investigation
6. Cooperative Societies
7. Special Provisions Relating to Certain Classes
8. Electoral Reforms

New Appendices:
1. Flag Code of India
2. Allied Amending Acts at a Glance
3. Model Code of Conduct Relating to Elections

I firmly believe that this is now a very comprehensive and updated manual. It is a matter of immense satisfaction that the previous three editions of this book have received an overwhelming response from readers. I am confident that readers would continue to repose their faith in this edition as well.

Constructive comments and concrete suggestions to further improve the book are welcome and shall be gratefully acknowledged.

M. LAXMIKANTH

PREFACE TO THE FIRST EDITION

I have great pleasure in placing this book before the aspirants of the top administrative services. The book has been written to meet the growing requirements of the candidates appearing for the Civil Services Examinations (Preliminary and Main) conducted by the Union Public Service Commission. It directly and fully covers the Indian Polity section of the paper on General Studies and is also useful for certain optional subjects like Public Administration, Political Science, Law, Sociology and Anthropology.

This comprehensive volume would enable the readers to acquire a complete and detailed understanding of the subject. It covers all dimensions (constitutional, non-constitutional, political and administrative) of the subject. My first-hand experience of coaching the candidates for the Civil Services Examinations has been a great source of inspiration and has helped me immensely in writing this book.

An effort has been made to make the contents of the book relevant, authentic, and up-to-date. The constitutional provisions are explained in the light of the debates of the Constituent Assembly of India as well as the judgements of the Supreme Court and the high courts. I have also used tables to make the presentation more clear. The Appendices, provided at the end of the book, serve as a reference section.

I welcome all constructive comments and concrete suggestions from the readers of this book.

M. LAXMIKANTH

ACKNOWLEDGEMENTS

During the course of writing this book, I have received the help, encouragement and assistance from my teachers, students, family members, colleagues, friends, library staff and others. I am thankful to all of them.

I am particularly grateful to my wife Smt. M Vidya for her encouragement and support that she provided during the preparation of the book.

I am deeply indebted to the eminent political scientists and constitutional experts (Granville Austin, Moris Jones, K C Wheare, Rajni Kothari, Paul Appleby, K Santhanam, N A Palkhivala, Soli Sorabji, D D Basu, V N Shukla, M P Jain, Subhash Kashyap) and other scholars of repute whose valuable works have been highly useful in writing this book.

My thanks are also due to Mr Tanmoy Roychowdhury, Mr K N Prakash, Ms Anubha Srivastava and Ms Medha Arora of McGraw Hill Education India Private Limited for their unstinted cooperation in bringing out this updated edition on time.

M. LAXMIKANTH

Year-wise Break-up of the UPSC Marks on Indian Polity (General Studies—Mains)

Sl.No.	Year	No. of Marks Allotted
1.	1993	89
2.	1994	89
3.	1995	89
4.	1996	89
5.	1997	89
6.	1998	89
7.	1999	89
8.	2000	130
9.	2001	100
10.	2002	130
11.	2003	100
12.	2004	100
13.	2005	100
14.	2006	100
15.	2007	100
16.	2008	130
17.	2009	66
18.	2010	66
19.	2011	111
20.	2012	47

Note: In 2013, the UPSC changed the pattern and syllabus of the Main Examination. In the new scheme, a separate and full paper on "Governance, Constitution, Polity, Social Justice and International Relations" has been introduced. It carries 250 marks.

Year-Wise Break-up of the UPSC Questions on Indian Polity (General Studies—Prelims)

Sl.No.	Year	No. of Questions Asked
1.	1993	14
2.	1994	14
3.	1995	17
4.	1996	10
5.	1997	12
6.	1998	05
7.	1999	09
8.	2000	12
9.	2001	12
10.	2002	19
11.	2003	19
12.	2004	22
13.	2005	10
14.	2006	13
15.	2007	12
16.	2008	13
17.	2009	14
18.	2010	10
19.	2011	12
20.	2012	20
21.	2013	18

Note: In 2011, the UPSC changed the pattern and syllabus of the Preliminary Examination. In the new scheme, the Indian Polity section has been renamed as "Indian Polity and Governance". It covers Constitution, Political System, Panchayati Raj, Public Policy, Rights Issues, etc. Also, now each question carries two marks (previously one mark).

Year-Wise Break-up of the UPSC Questions on Indian Polity (General Studies—Prelims)

About the Civil Services Examination

The Civil Services examination comprises two successive stages:

(i) Civil Services (Preliminary) Examination (Objective Type) for the selection of candidates for Main Examination; and

(ii) Civil Services (Main) Examination (Written and Interview) for the selection of candidates for the various services and posts.

Scheme and subjects for the Preliminary and Main Examination.

A. PRELIMINARY EXAMINATION

The Examination shall comprise two compulsory Papers of 200 marks each.

Note:

(i) Both the question papers will be of the objective type (multiple choice questions).

(ii) The question papers will be set both in Hindi and English. However, questions relating to English Language Comprehension Skills of Class X level will be tested through passages from English language only without providing Hindi translation thereof in the question paper.

B. MAIN EXAMINATION

The written examination will consist of the following papers:

Qualifying Papers:

Paper A: (One of the Indian Language to be selected by the candidate from the Languages included in the Eighth Schedule to the Constitution).   **300 Marks**

Paper B: English   **300 Marks**

The papers on Indian Languages and English (Paper A and Paper B) will be of Matriculation or equivalent standard and will be of qualifying nature. The marks obtained in these papers will not be counted for ranking.

Papers to be counted for merit

Paper I: Essay   **250 Marks**

Paper II: General Studies–I   **250 Marks**
(Indian Heritage and Culture, History and Geography of the World and Society)

Paper III: General Studies –II   **250 Marks**
(Governance, Constitution, Polity, Social Justice and International Relations)

Paper IV: General Studies –III   **250 Marks**
(Technology, Economic Development, Bio-diversity, Environment, Security and Disaster Management)

Paper V: General Studies –IV   **250 Marks**
(Ethics, Integrity and Aptitude)

Paper VI: Optional Subject – Paper 1   **250 Marks**

Paper VII: Optional Subject – Paper 2   **250 Marks**
Sub Total (Written test):   **1750 Marks**
Personality Test: **275 Marks**
Grand Total: **2025 Marks**

Candidates may choose any one of the optional subjects from amongst the list of subjects given below:

List of optional subjects for Main Examination:

(i)   Agriculture
(ii)   Animal Husbandry and Veterinary Science
(iii)   Anthropology
(iv)   Botany
(v)   Chemistry
(vi)   Civil Engineering
(vii)   Commerce and Accountancy
(viii) Economics
(ix)   Electrical Engineering
(x)   Geography
(xi)   Geology
(xii)   History
(xiii) Law
(xiv)   Management
(xv)   Mathematics
(xvi)   Mechanical Engineering
(xvii) Medical Science
(xviii) Philosophy
(xix)   Physics
(xx)   Political Science and International Relations
(xxi)   Psychology
(xxii) Public Administration
(xxiii) Sociology
(xxiv) Statistics
(xxv)   Zoology
(xxvi) Literature of any one of the following

Assamese, Bengali, Bodo, Dogri, Gujarati, Hindi, Kannada, Kashmiri, Konkani, Maithili, Malayalam, Manipuri, Marathi, Nepali, Oriya, Punjabi, Sanskrit, Santhali, Sindhi, Tamil, Telugu, Urdu and English.

LIST OF TABLES

CONTENTS

PART I
Constitutional Framework

PART II
System of Government

PART III
Central Government

PART IV
State Government

PART V
Local Government

PART VI
Union Territories and Special Areas

PART VII
Constitutional Bodies

PART VIII
Non-Constitutional Bodies

PART IX
Other Constitutional Dimensions

PART X
Political Dynamics

PART XI
Working of the Constitution

PART I

CONSTITUTIONAL FRAMEWORK

1. Historical Background
2. Making of the Constitution
3. Salient Features of the Constitution
4. Preamble of the Constitution
5. Union and its Territory
6. Citizenship
7. Fundamental Rights
8. Directive Principles of State Policy
9. Fundamental Duties
10. Amendment of the Constitution
11. Basic Structure of the Constitution

Historical Background

The British came to India in 1600 as traders, in the form of East India Company, which had the exclusive right of trading in India under a charter granted by Queen Elizabeth I. In 1765, the Company, which till now had purely trading functions obtained the 'diwani' (i.e., rights over revenue and civil justice) of Bengal, Bihar and Orissa.[1] This started its career as a territorial power. In 1858, in the wake of the 'sepoy mutiny', the British Crown assumed direct responsibility for the governance of India. This rule continued until India was granted independence on August 15, 1947.

With Independence came the need of a Constitution. As suggested by M N Roy (a pioneer of communist movement in India and an advocate of Radical Democratism) in 1934, a Constituent Assembly was formed for this purpose in 1946 and on January 26, 1950, the Constitution came into being. However, various features of the Indian Constitution and polity have their roots in the British rule. There are certain events in the British rule that laid down the legal framework for the organisation and functioning of government and administration in British India. These events have greatly influenced our constitution and polity. They are explained here in a chronological order:

THE COMPANY RULE (1773–1858)

Regulating Act of 1773

This act is of great constitutional importance as (a) it was the first step taken by the British Government to control and regulate the affairs of the East India Company in India; (b) it recognised, for the first time, the political and administrative functions of the Company; and (c) it laid the foundations of central administration in India.

Features of the Act

1. It designated the Governor of Bengal as the 'Governor-General of Bengal' and created an Executive Council of four members to assist him. The first such Governor-General was Lord Warren Hastings.
2. It made the governors of Bombay and Madras presidencies subordinate to the governor-general of Bengal, unlike earlier, when the three presidencies were independent of one another.
3. It provided for the establishment of a Supreme Court at Calcutta (1774) comprising one chief justice and three other judges.
4. It prohibited the servants of the Company from engaging in any private trade or accepting presents or bribes from the 'natives'.
5. It strengthened the control of the British Government over the Company by requiring the Court of Directors (governing body of the Company) to report on its revenue, civil, and military affairs in India.

Pitt's India Act of 1784

In a bid to rectify the defects of the Regulating Act of 1773, the British Parliament passed the Amending Act of 1781, also known as the Act of Settlement.

The next important act was the Pitt's India Act[2] of 1784.

Features of the Act

1. It distinguished between the commercial and political functions of the Company.
2. It allowed the Court of Directors to manage the commercial affairs but created a new body called Board of Control to manage the political affairs. Thus, it established a system of double government.
3. It empowered the Board of Control to supervise and direct all operations of the civil and military government or revenues of the British possessions in India.

Thus, the act was significant for two reasons: first, the Company's territories in India were for the first time called the 'British possessions in India'; and second, the British Government was given the supreme control over Company's affairs and its administration in India.

Charter Act of 1833

This Act was the final step towards centralisation in British India.

Features of the Act

1. It made the Governor-General of Bengal as the Governor-General of India and vested in him all civil and military powers. Thus, the act created, for the first time, a Government of India having authority over the entire territorial area possessed by the British in India. Lord William Bentick was the first governor-general of India.
2. It deprived the governor of Bombay and Madras of their legislative powers. The Governor-General of India was given exclusive legislative powers for the entire British India. The laws made under the previous acts were called as **Regulations** while laws made under this act were called as **Acts**.
3. It ended the activities of the East India Company as a commercial body, which became a purely administrative body. It provided that the company's territories in India were held by it 'in trust for His Majesty, His heirs and successors'.

4. The Charter Act of 1833 attempted to introduce a system of open competition for selection of civil servants, and stated that the Indians should not be debarred from holding any place, office and employment under the Company. However, this provision was negated after opposition from the Court of Directors.

Charter Act of 1853

This was the last of the series of Charter Acts passed by the British Parliament between 1793 and 1853. It was a significant constitutional landmark.

Features of the Act

1. It separated, for the first time, the legislative and executive functions of the Governor-General's council. It provided for addition of six new members called legislative councillors to the council. In other words, it established a separate Governor-General's legislative council which came to be known as the Indian (Central) Legislative Council. This legislative wing of the council functioned as a mini-Parliament, adopting the same procedures as the British Parliament. Thus, legislation, for the first time, was treated as a special function of the government, requiring special machinery and special process.
2. It introduced an open competition system of selection and recruitment of civil servants. The covenanted civil service[3] was thus thrown open to the Indians also. Accordingly, the Macaulay Committee (the Committee on the Indian Civil Service) was appointed in 1854.
3. It extended the Company's rule and allowed it to retain the possession of Indian territories on trust for the British Crown. But, it did not specify any particular period, unlike the previous Charters. This was a clear indication that the Company's rule could be terminated at any time the Parliament liked.
4. It introduced, for the first time, local representation in the Indian (Central) Legislative Council. Of the six new legislative members of the governor-general's council, four members were appointed by the local (provincial) governments of Madras, Bombay, Bengal and Agra.

THE CROWN RULE (1858–1947)

Government of India Act of 1858

This significant Act was enacted in the wake of the Revolt of 1857—also known as the First War of Independence or the 'sepoy mutiny'. The act known as the **Act for the Good Government of India**, abolished the East India Company, and transferred the powers of government, territories and revenues to the British Crown.

Features of the Act

1. It provided that India henceforth was to be governed by, and in the name of, Her Majesty. It changed the designation of the Governor-General of India to that of Viceroy of India. He (viceroy) was the direct representative of the British Crown in India. Lord Canning thus became the first Viceroy of India.
2. It ended the system of double government by abolishing the Board of Control and Court of Directors.
3. It created a new office, Secretary of State for India, vested with complete authority and control over Indian administration. The secretary of state was a member of the British cabinet and was responsible ultimately to the British Parliament.
4. It established a 15-member Council of India to assist the secretary of state for India. The council was an advisory body. The secretary of state was made the chairman of the council.
5. It constituted the secretary of state-in-council as a body corporate, capable of suing and being sued in India and in England.

'The Act of 1858 was, however, largely confined to the improvement of the administrative machinery by which the Indian Government was to be supervised and controlled in England. It did not alter in any substantial way the system of government that prevailed in India[4].'

Indian Councils Act of 1861, 1892 and 1909

After the great revolt of 1857, the British Government felt the necessity of seeking the cooperation of the Indians in the administration of their country.

In pursuance of this policy of association, three acts were enacted by the British Parliament in 1861, 1892 and 1909. The Indian Councils Act of 1861 is an important landmark in the constitutional and political history of India.

Features of the Act of 1861

1. It made a beginning of representative institutions by associating Indians with the law-making process. It thus provided that the viceroy should nominate some Indians as non-official members of his expanded council. In 1862, Lord Canning, the then viceroy, nominated three Indians to his legislative council—the Raja of Benaras, the Maharaja of Patiala and Sir Dinkar Rao.
2. It initiated the process of decentralisation by restoring the legislative powers to the Bombay and Madras Presidencies. It thus reversed the centralising tendency that started from the Regulating Act of 1773 and reached its climax under the Charter Act of 1833. This policy of legislative devolution resulted in the grant of almost complete internal autonomy to the provinces in 1937.
3. It also provided for the establishment of new legislative councils for Bengal, North-Western Frontier Province (NWFP) and Punjab, which were established in 1862, 1866 and 1897 respectively.
4. It empowered the Viceroy to make rules and orders for the more convenient transaction of business in the council. It also gave a recognition to the 'portfolio' system, introduced by Lord Canning in 1859. Under this, a member of the Viceroy's council was made in-charge of one or more departments of the government and was authorised to issue final orders on behalf of the council on matters of his department(s).
5. It empowered the Viceroy to issue ordinances, without the concurrence of the legislative council, during an emergency. The life of such an ordinance was six months.

Features of the Act of 1892

1. It increased the number of additional (non-official) members in the Central and provincial legislative councils, but maintained the official majority in them.

2. It increased the functions of legislative councils and gave them the power of discussing the budget[5] and addressing questions to the executive.
3. It provided for the nomination of some non-official members of the (a) Central Legislative Council by the viceroy on the recommendation of the provincial legislative councils and the Bengal Chamber of Commerce, and (b) that of the Provincial legislative councils by the Governors on the recommendation of the district boards, municipalities, universities, trade associations, zamindars and chambers.

'The act made a limited and indirect provision for the use of election in filling up some of the non-official seats both in the Central and provincial legislative councils. The word "election" was, however, not used in the act. The process was described as nomination made on the recommendation of certain bodies[6].'

Features of the Act of 1909   This Act is also known as Morley-Minto Reforms (Lord Morley was the then Secretary of State for India and Lord Minto was the then Viceroy of India).

1. It considerably increased the size of the legislative councils, both Central and provincial. The number of members in the Central Legislative Council was raised from 16 to 60. The number of members in the provincial legislative councils was not uniform.
2. It retained official majority in the Central Legislative Council but allowed the provincial legislative councils to have non-official majority.
3. It enlarged the deliberative functions of the legislative councils at both the levels. For example, members were allowed to ask supplementary questions, move resolutions on the budget, and so on.
4. It provided (for the first time) for the association of Indians with the executive Councils of the Viceroy and Governors. **Satyendra Prasad Sinha** became the first Indian to join the Viceroy's Executive Council. He was appointed as the law member.
5. It introduced a system of communal representation for Muslims by accepting the concept of 'separate electorate'. Under this, the Muslim members were to be elected only by Muslim

voters. Thus, the Act 'legalised communalism' and Lord Minto came to be known as the **Father of Communal Electorate**.
6. It also provided for the separate representation of presidency corporations, chambers of commerce, universities and zamindars.

Government of India Act of 1919

On August 20, 1917, the British Government declared, for the first time, that its objective was the gradual introduction of responsible government in India[7].

The Government of India Act of 1919 was thus enacted, which came into force in 1921. This Act is also known as Montagu-Chelmsford Reforms (Montagu was the Secretary of State for India and Lord Chelmsford was the Viceroy of India).

Features of the Act

1. It relaxed the central control over the provinces by demarcating and separating the central and provincial subjects. The central and provincial legislatures were authorised to make laws on their respective list of subjects. However, the structure of government continued to be centralised and unitary.
2. It further divided the provincial subjects into two parts—transferred and reserved. The **transferred subjects** were to be administered by the governor with the aid of ministers responsible to the legislative Council. The **reserved subjects**, on the other hand, were to be administered by the governor and his executive council without being responsible to the legislative Council. This dual scheme of governance was known as 'dyarchy'—a term derived from the Greek word *di-arche* which means double rule. However, this experiment was largely unsuccessful.
3. It introduced, for the first time, bicameralism and direct elections in the country. Thus, the Indian Legislative Council was replaced by a bicameral legislature consisting of an Upper House (Council of State) and a Lower House (Legislative Assembly). The majority of members of both the Houses were chosen by direct election.

4. It required that the three of the six members of the Viceroy's executive Council (other than the commander-in-chief) were to be Indian.
5. It extended the principle of communal representation by providing separate electorates for Sikhs, Indian Christians, Anglo-Indians and Europeans.
6. It granted franchise to a limited number of people on the basis of property, tax or education.
7. It created a new office of the High Commissioner for India in London and transferred to him some of the functions hitherto performed by the Secretary of State for India.
8. It provided for the establishment of a public service commission. Hence, a Central Public Service Commission was set up in 1926 for recruiting civil servants[8].
9. It separated, for the first time, provincial budgets from the Central budget and authorised the provincial legislatures to enact their budgets.
10. It provided for the appointment of a statutory commission to inquire into and report on its working after ten years of its coming into force.

Simon Commission In November 1927 itself (i.e., 2 years before the schedule), the British Government announced the appointment a seven-member statutory commission under the chairmanship of Sir John Simon to report on the condition of India under its new Constitution. All the members of the commission were British and hence, all the parties boycotted the commission. The commission submitted its report in 1930 and recommended the abolition of dyarchy, extension of responsible government in the provinces, establishment of a federation of British India and princely states, continuation of communal electorate and so on. To consider the proposals of the commission, the British Government convened three round table conferences of the representatives of the British Government, British India and Indian princely states. On the basis of these discussions, a 'White Paper on Consitutional Reforms' was prepared and submitted for the consideration of the Joint Select Committee of the British Parliament. The recommendations of this committee were incorporated (with certain changes) in the next Government of Inida Act of 1935.

Communal Award In August 1932, Ramsay MacDonald, the British Prime Minister, announced a scheme of representation of the minorities, which came to be known as the Communal Award. The award not only continued separate electorates for the Muslims, Sikhs, Indian Christians, Anglo-Indians and Europeans but also extended it to the depressed classes (scheduled castes). Gandhiji was distressed over this extension of the principle of communal representation to the depressed classes and undertook fast unto death in Yeravada Jail (Poona) to get the award modified. At last, there was an agreement between the leaders of the Congress and the depressed classes. The agreement, known as Poona Pact, retained the Hindu joint electorate and gave reserved seats to the depressed classes.

Government of India Act of 1935

The Act marked a second milestone towards a completely responsible government in India. It was a lengthy and detailed document having 321 Sections and 10 Schedules.

Features of the Act

1. It provided for the establishment of an All-India Federation consisting of provinces and princely states as units. The Act divided the powers between the Centre and units in terms of three lists—**Federal List** (for Centre, with 59 items), **Provincial List** (for provinces, with 54 items) and the Concurrent List (for both, with 36 items). Residuary powers were given to the Viceroy. However, the federation never came into being as the princely states did not join it.
2. It abolished dyarchy in the provinces and introduced 'provincial autonomy' in its place. The provinces were allowed to act as autonomous units of administration in their defined spheres. Moreover, the Act introduced responsible governments in provinces, that is, the governor was required to act with the advice of ministers responsible to the provincial legislature. This came into effect in 1937 and was discontinued in 1939.
3. It provided for the adoption of dyarchy at the Centre. Consequently, the federal subjects

were divided into reserved subjects and transferred subjects. However, this provision of the Act did not come into operation at all.

4. It introduced bicameralism in six out of eleven provinces. Thus, the legislatures of Bengal, Bombay, Madras, Bihar, Assam and the United Provinces were made bicameral consisting of a legislative council (upper house) and a legislative assembly (lower house). However, many restrictions were placed on them.

5. It further extended the principle of communal representation by providing separate electorates for depressed classes (scheduled castes), women and labour (workers).

6. It abolished the Council of India, established by the Government of India Act of 1858. The secretary of state for India was provided with a team of advisors.

7. It extended franchise. About 10 per cent of the total population got the voting right.

8. It provided for the establishment of a Reserve Bank of India to control the currency and credit of the country.

9. It provided for the establishment of not only a Federal Public Service Commission but also a Provincial Public Service Commission and Joint Public Service Commission for two or more provinces.

10. It provided for the establishment of a Federal Court, which was set up in 1937.

Indian Independence Act of 1947

On February 20, 1947, the British Prime Minister Clement Atlee declared that the British rule in India would end by June 30,1948; after which the power would be transferred to responsible Indian hands. This announcement was followed by the agitation by the Muslim League demanding partition of the country. Again on June 3, 1947, the British Government made it clear that any Constitution framed by the Constituent Assembly of India (formed in 1946) cannot apply to those parts of the country which were unwilling to accept it. On the same day (June 3, 1947), Lord Mountbatten, the viceroy of India, put forth the partition plan, known as the **Mountbatten Plan**. The plan was accepted by the Congress and the Muslim League. Immediate effect was given to the plan by enacting the Indian Independence Act[9] (1947).

Features of the Act

1. It ended the British rule in India and declared India as an independent and sovereign state from August 15,1947.

2. It provided for the partition of India and creation of two independent dominions of India and Pakistan with the right to secede from the British Commonwealth.

3. It abolished the office of viceroy and provided, for each dominion, a governor-general, who was to be appointed by the British King on the advice of the dominion cabinet. His Majesty's Government in Britain was to have no responsibility with respect to the Government of India or Pakistan.

4. It empowered the Constituent Assemblies of the two dominions to frame and adopt any constitution for their respective nations and to repeal any act of the British Parliament, including the Independence act itself.

5. It empowered the Constituent Assemblies of both the dominions to legislate for their respective territories till the new constitutions were drafted and enforced. No Act of the British Parliament passed after August 15, 1947 was to extend to either of the new dominions unless it was extended thereto by a law of the legislature of the dominion.

6. It abolished the office of the secretary of state for India and transferred his functions to the secretary of state for Commonwealth Affairs.

7. It proclaimed the lapse of British paramountcy over the Indian princely states and treaty relations with tribal areas from August 15,1947.

8. It granted freedom to the Indian princely states either to join the Dominion of India or Dominion of Pakistan or to remain independent.

9. It provided for the governance of each of the dominions and the provinces by the Government of India Act of 1935, till the new Constitutions were framed. The dominions were however authorised to make modifications in the Act.

10. It deprived the British Monarch of his right to veto bills or ask for reservation of certain bills for his approval. But, this right was reserved

for the Governor-General. The Governor-General would have full power to assent to any bill in the name of His Majesty.

11. It designated the Governor-General of India and the provincial governors as constitutional (nominal) heads of the states. They were made to act on the advice of the respective council of ministers in all matters.

12. It dropped the title of Emperor of India from the royal titles of the king of England.

13. It discontinued the appointment to civil services and reservation of posts by the secretary of state for India. The members of the civil services appointed before August 15, 1947 would continue to enjoy all benefits that they were entitled to till that time.

At the stroke of midnight of 14–15 August, 1947, the British rule came to an end and power was transferred to the two new independent Dominions of India and Pakistan[10]. Lord Mountbatten became the first governor-general of the new Dominion of India. He swore in Jawaharlal Nehru as the first prime minister of independent India. The Constituent Assembly of India formed in 1946 became the Parliament of the Indian Dominion.

Table 1.1 *Interim Government (1946)*

Sl. No.	Members	Portfolios Held
1.	Jawaharlal Nehru	External Affairs & Commonwealth Relations
2.	Sardar Vallabhbhai Patel	Home, Information & Broadcasting
3.	Dr. Rajendra Prasad	Food & Agriculture
4.	Dr. John Mathai	Industries & Supplies
5.	Jagjivan Ram	Labour
6.	Sardar Baldev Singh	Defence
7.	C.H. Bhabha	Works, Mines & Power
8.	Liaquat Ali Khan	Finance
9.	Abdur Rab Nishtar	Posts & Air
10.	Asaf Ali	Railways & Transport
11.	C. Rajagopalachari	Education & Arts
12.	I.I. Chundrigar	Commerce
13.	Ghaznafar Ali Khan	Health
14.	Joginder Nath Mandal	Law

Note: The members of the interim government were members of the Viceroy's Executive Council. The Viceroy continued to be the head of the Council. But, Jawaharlal Nehru was designated as the Vice-President of the Council.

Table 1.2 *First Cabinet of Free India (1947)*

Sl. No.	Members	Portfolios Held
1.	Jawaharlal Nehru	Prime Minister; External Affairs & Commonwealth Relations; Scientific Research
2.	Sardar Vallabhbhai Patel	Home, Information & Broadcasting; States

(Contd.)

Sl. No.	Members	Portfolios Held
3.	Dr. Rajendra Prasad	Food & Agriculture
4.	Maulana Abul Kalam Azad	Education
5.	Dr. John Mathai	Railways & Transport
6.	R.K. Shanmugham Chetty	Finance
7.	Dr. B.R. Ambedkar	Law
8.	Jagjivan Ram	Labour
9.	Sardar Baldev Singh	Defence
10.	Raj Kumari Amrit Kaur	Health
11.	C.H. Bhabha	Commerce
12.	Rafi Ahmed Kidwai	Communication
13.	Dr. Shyam Prasad Mukherji	Industries & Supplies
14.	V.N. Gadgil	Works, Mines & Power

NOTES AND REFERENCES

1. The Mughal Emperor, Shah Alam, granted 'Diwani' to the Company after its victory in the Battle of Buxar (1764).

2. It was introduced in the British Parliament by the then Prime Minister, William Pitt.

3. At that time, the Civil Services of the company were classified into covenanted civil services (higher civil services) and uncovenanted civil services (lower civil services). The former was created by a law of the Company, while the later was created otherwise.

4. Subhash C. Kashyap, *Our Constitution,* National Book Trust, Third Edition, 2001, P. 14.

5. The system of Budget was introduced in British India in 1860.

6. V. N. Shukla, *The Constitution of India*, Eastern Book Company, Tenth Edition, 2001, P. A-10.

7. The declaration thus stated: 'The policy of His Majesty's Government is that of the increasing association of Indians in every branch of the administration, and the gradual development of self-government institutions, with a view to the progressive realisation of responsible government in India as an integral part of the British Empire'.

8. This was done on the recommendation of the Lee Commission on Superior Civil Services in India (1923–24).

9. The Indian Independence Bill was introduced in the British Parliament on July 4, 1947 and received the Royal Assent on July 18, 1947. The act came into force on August 15, 1947.

10. The boundaries between the two Dominions were determined by a Boundary Commission headed by Radcliff. Pakistan included the provinces of West Punjab, Sind, Baluchistan, East Bengal, North-Western Frontier Province and the district of Sylhet in Assam. The referendum in the North-Western Frontier Province and Sylhet was in favour of Pakistan.

Making of the Constitution

It was in 1934 that the idea of a Constituent Assembly for India was put forward for the first time by M. N. Roy, a pioneer of communist movement in India and an advocate of radical democratism. In 1935, the Indian National Congress (INC), for the first time, officially demanded a Constituent Assembly to frame the Constitution of India. In 1938, Jawaharlal Nehru, on behalf the INC declared that 'the Constitution of free India must be framed, without outside interference, by a Constituent Assembly elected on the basis of adult franchise'.

The demand was finally accepted in principle by the British Government in what is known as the 'August Offer' of 1940. In 1942, Sir Stafford Cripps, a member of the cabinet, came to India with a draft proposal of the British Government on the framing of an independent Constitution to be adopted after the World War II. The Cripps Proposals were rejected by the Muslim League which wanted India to be divided into two autonomous states with two separate Constituent Assemblies. Finally, a Cabinet Mission[1] was sent to India. While it rejected the idea of two Constituent Assemblies, it put forth a scheme for the Constituent Assembly which more or less satisfied the Muslim League.

COMPOSITION OF THE CONSTITUENT ASSEMBLY

The Constituent Assembly was constituted in November 1946 under the scheme formulated by the Cabinet Mission Plan. The features of the scheme were:

1. The total strength of the Constituent Assembly was to be 389. Of these, 296 seats were to be allotted to British India and 93 seats to the Princely States. Out of 296 seats allotted to the British India, 292 members were to be drawn from the eleven governors' provinces[2] and four from the four chief commissioners' provinces[3], one from each.

2. Each province and princely state (or group of states in case of small states) were to be allotted seats in proportion to their respective population. Roughly, one seat was to be allotted for every million population.

3. Seats allocated to each British province were to be decided among the three principal communities—Muslims, Sikhs and general (all except Muslims and Sikhs), in proportion to their population.

4. The representatives of each community were to be elected by members of that community in the provincial legislative assembly and voting was to be by the method of proportional representation by means of single transferable vote.

5. The representatives of princely states were to be nominated by the heads of the princely states.

It is thus clear that the Constituent Assembly was to be a partly elected and partly nominated body. Moreover, the members were to be indirectly elected by the members of the provincial assemblies, who themselves were elected on a limited franchise[4].

The elections to the Constituent Assembly (for 296 seats allotted to the British Indian Provinces) were held in July–August 1946. The Indian National Congress won 208 seats, the Muslim League 73 seats, and the small groups and independents got the remaining 15 seats. However, the 93 seats allotted to the princely states were not filled as they decided to stay away from the Constituent Assembly.

Although the Constituent Assembly was not directly elected by the people of India on the basis of adult franchise, the Assembly comprised representatives of all sections of Indian Society—Hindus, Muslims, Sikhs, Parsis, Anglo–Indians, Indian Christians, SCs, STs including women of all these sections. The Assembly included all important personalities of India at that time, with the exception of Mahatma Gandhi and M A Jinnah.

Working of the Constituent Assembly

The Constituent Assembly held its first meeting on December 9, 1946. The Muslim League boycotted the meeting and insisted on a separate state of Pakistan. The meeting was thus attended by only 211 members. *Dr Sachchidanand Sinha, the oldest member, was elected as the temporary President of the Assembly, following the French practice.*

Later, on December 11, 1946, Dr Rajendra Prasad and H C Mukherjee were elected as the President and Vice-President of the Assembly respectively. Sir B N Rau was appointed as the Constitutional advisor to the Assembly.

Objectives Resolution

On December 13, 1946, Jawaharlal Nehru moved the historic 'Objectives Resolution' in the Assembly. It laid down the fundamentals and philosophy of the constitutional structure. It read:

1. "This Constituent Assembly declares its firm and solemn resolve to proclaim India as an Independent Sovereign Republic and to draw up for her future governance a Constitution:
2. Wherein the territories that now comprise British India, the territories that now form the Indian States, and such other parts of India as are outside India and the States as well as other territories as are willing to be constituted

into the independent sovereign India, shall be a Union of them all; and
3. wherein the said territories, whether with their present boundaries or with such others as may be determined by the Constituent Assembly and thereafter according to the law of the Constitution, shall possess and retain the status of autonomous units together with residuary powers and exercise all powers and functions of Government and administration save and except such powers and functions as are vested in or assigned to the Union or as are inherent or implied in the Union or resulting therefrom; and
4. wherein all power and authority of the Sovereign Independent India, its constituent parts and organs of Government are derived from the people; and
5. wherein shall be guaranteed and secured to all the people of India justice, social, economic and political; equality of status of opportunity, and before the law; freedom of thought, expression, belief, faith, worship, vocation, association and action, subject to law and public morality; and
6. wherein adequate safeguards shall be provided for minorities, backward and tribal areas, and depressed and other backward classes; and
7. whereby shall be maintained the integrity of the territory of the Republic and its sovereign rights on land, sea and air according to justice and the law of civilized nations; and
8. This ancient land attains its rightful and honoured place in the world and makes its full and willing contribution to the promotion of world peace and the welfare of mankind."

This Resolution was unanimously adopted by the Assembly on January 22, 1947. It influenced the eventual shaping of the constitution through all its subsequent stages. Its modified version forms the Preamble of the present Constitution.

Changes by the Independence Act

The representatives of the princely states, who had stayed away from the Constituent Assembly, gradually joined it. On April 28, 1947, representatives of the six states[5] were part of the Assembly. After the acceptance of the Mountbatten Plan of June 3, 1947 for a partition of the country, the representatives of most of the other princely states took their seats in the Assembly. The members of the Muslim League from the Indian Dominion also entered the Assembly.

The Indian Independence Act of 1947 made the following three changes in the position of the Assembly:

1. The Assembly was made a fully sovereign body, which could frame any Constitution it pleased. The act empowered the Assembly to abrogate or alter any law made by the British Parliament in relation to India.
2. The Assembly also became a legislative body. In other words, two separate functions were assigned to the Assembly, that is, making of a constitution for free India and enacting of ordinary laws for the country. These two tasks were to be performed on separate days. Thus, the Assembly became the first Parliament of free India (Dominion Legislature). Whenever the Assembly met as the Constituent body it was chaired by Dr. Rajendra Prasad and when it met as the legislative body[6], it was chaired by G V Mavlankar. These two functions continued till November 26, 1949, when the task of making the Constitution was over.
3. The Muslim League members (hailing from the areas[7] included in the Pakistan) withdrew from the Constituent Assembly for India. Consequently, the total strength of the Assembly came down to 299 as against 389 originally fixed in 1946 under the Cabinet Mission Plan. The strength of the Indian provinces (formerly British Provinces) was reduced from 296 to 229 and those of the princely states from 93 to 70. The state-wise membership of the Assembly as on December 31, 1947, is shown in Table 2.1 at the end of this chapter.

Other Functions Performed

In addition to the making of the Constitution and enacting of ordinary laws, the Constituent Assembly also performed the following functions:

1. It ratified the India's membership of the Commonwealth in May 1949.
2. It adopted the national flag on July 22, 1947.
3. It adopted the national anthem on January 24, 1950.
4. It adopted the national song on January 24, 1950.
5. It elected Dr Rajendra Prasad as the first President of India on January 24, 1950.

In all, the Constituent Assembly had 11 sessions over two years, 11 months and 18 days. The Constitution-makers had gone through the constitutions of about 60 countries, and the Draft Constitution was considered for 114 days. The total expenditure incurred on making the Constitution amounted to ₹ 64 lakh.

On January 24, 1950, the Constituent Assembly held its final session. It, however, did not end, and continued as the provisional parliament of India from January 26, 1950 till the formation of new Parliament[8] after the first general elections in 1951–52.

COMMITTEES OF THE CONSTITUENT ASSEMBLY

The Constituent Assembly appointed a number of committees to deal with different tasks of constitution-making. Out of these, eight were major committees and the others were minor committees. The names of these committees and their chairmen are given below:

Major Committees

1. Union Powers Committee – Jawaharlal Nehru
2. Union Constitution Committee – Jawaharlal Nehru
3. Provincial Constitution Committee – Sardar Patel
4. Drafting Committee – Dr. B.R. Ambedkar
5. Advisory Committee on Fundamental Rights, Minorities and Tribal and Excluded Areas – Sardar Patel. This committee had the following sub-committies:
   (a) Fundamental Rights Sub-Committee – J.B. Kripalani
   (b) Minorities Sub-Committee – H.C. Mukherjee
   (c) North-East Frontier Tribal Areas and Assam Excluded & Partially Excluded Areas Sub-Committee – Gopinath Bardoloi
   (d) Excluded and Partially Excluded Areas (Other than those in Assam) Sub-Committee – A.V. Thakkar

6. Rules of Procedure Committee – Dr. Rajendra Prasad
7. States Committee (Committee for Negotiating with States) – Jawaharlal Nehru
8. Steering Committee – Dr. Rajendra Prasad

Minor Committees

1. Committee on the Functions of the Constituent Assembly – G.V. Mavalankar
2. Order of Business Committee – Dr. K.M. Munshi
3. House Committee – B. Pattabhi Sitaramayya
4. Ad-hoc Committee on the National Flag – Dr. Rajendra Prasad
5. Special Committee to Examine the Draft Constitution – Alladi Krishnaswamy Ayyar
6. Credentials Committee – Alladi Krishnaswamy Ayyar
7. Finance and Staff Committee – Dr. Rajendra Prasad.
8. Hindi Translation Committee
9. Urdu Translation Committee
10. Press Gallery Committee
11. Committee to Examine the Effect of Indian Independence Act of 1947
12. Committee on Chief Commissioners' Provinces – B. Pattabhi Sitaramayya.
13. Commission on Linguistic Provinces
14. Expert Committee on Financial Provisions
15. *Ad-hoc* Committee on the Supreme Court – S. Varadachariar.

Drafting Committee

Among all the committees of the Constituent Assembly, the most important committee was the Drafting Committee set up on August 29, 1947. It was this committee that was entrusted with the task of preparing a draft of the new Constitution. It consisted of seven members. They were:

1. Dr B R Ambedkar (*Chairman*)
2. N Gopalaswamy Ayyangar
3. Alladi Krishnaswamy Ayyar
4. Dr K M Munshi
5. Syed Mohammad Saadullah
6. N Madhava Rau (He replaced B L Mitter who resigned due to ill-health)

7. T T Krishnamachari (He replaced D P Khaitan who died in 1948)

The Drafting Committee, after taking into consideration the proposals of the various committees, prepared the first draft of the Constitution of India, which was published in February 1948. The people of India were given eight months to discuss the draft and propose amendments. In the light of the public comments, criticisms and suggestions, the Drafting Committee prepared a second draft, which was published in October 1948.

The Drafting Committee took less than six months to prepare its draft. In all it sat only for 141 days.

ENACTMENT OF THE CONSTITUTION

Dr B R Ambedkar introduced the final draft of the Constitution in the Assembly on November 4, 1948 (first reading). The Assembly had a general discussion on it for five days (till November 9, 1948).

The second reading (clause by clause consideration) started on November 15, 1948 and ended on October 17, 1949. During this stage, as many as 7653 amendments were proposed and 2473 were actually discussed in the Assembly.

The third reading of the draft started on November 14, 1949. Dr B R Ambedkar moved a motion—'the Constitution as settled by the Assembly be passed'. The motion on Draft Constitution was declared as passed on November 26, 1949, and received the signatures of the members and the president. Out of a total 299 members of the Assembly, only 284 were actually present on that day and signed the Constitution. This is also the date mentioned in the Preamble as the date on which the people of India in the Constituent Assembly adopted, enacted and gave to themselves this Constitution.

The Constitution as adopted on November 26, 1949, contained a Preamble, 395 Articles and 8 Schedules. The Preamble was enacted after the entire Constitution was already enacted.

Dr B R Ambedkar, the then Law Minister, piloted the Draft Constitution in the Assembly. He took a very prominent part in the deliberations of the Assembly. He was known for his logical, forceful and persuasive arguments on the floor of the Assembly.

He is recognised as the 'Father of the Constitution of India'. This brilliant writer, constitutional expert, undisputed leader of the scheduled castes and the 'chief architect of the Constitution of India' is also known as a 'Modern Manu'.

ENFORCEMENT OF THE CONSTITUTION

Some provisions of the Constitution pertaining to citizenship, elections, provisional parliament, temporary and transitional provisions, and short title contained in Articles 5, 6, 7, 8, 9, 60, 324, 366, 367, 379, 380, 388, 391, 392 and 393 came into force on November 26, 1949 itself.

The remaining provisions (the major part) of the Constitution came into force on January 26, 1950. This day is referred to in the Constitution as the 'date of its commencement', and celebrated as the Republic Day.

January 26 was specifically chosen as the 'date of commencement' of the Constitution because of its historical importance. It was on this day in 1930 that *Purna Swaraj* day was celebrated, following the resolution of the Lahore Session (December 1929) of the INC.

With the commencement of the Constitution, the Indian Independence Act of 1947 and the Government of India Act of 1935, with all enactments amending or supplementing the latter Act, were repealed. The Abolition of Privy Council Jurisdiction Act (1949) was however continued.

CRITICISM OF THE CONSTITUENT ASSEMBLY

The critics have criticised the Constituent Assembly on various grounds. These are as follows:

1. *Not a Representative Body*: The critics have argued that the Constituent Assembly was not a representative body as its members were not directly elected by the people of India on the basis of universal adult franchise.
2. *Not a Sovereign Body*: The critics maintained that the Constituent Assembly was not a sovereign body as it was created by the proposals of the British Government. Further, they said that the Assembly held its sessions with the permission of the British Government.
3. *Time Consuming*: According to the critics, the Constituent Assembly took unduly long time to make the Constitution. They stated that the framers of the American Constitution took only four months to complete their work.
4. *Dominated by Congress*: The critics charged that the Constituent Assembly was dominated by the Congress party. Granville Austin, a British Constitutional expert, remarked: 'The Constituent Assembly was a one-party body in an essentially one-party country. The Assembly was the Congress and the Congress was India'[9].
5. *Lawyer–Politician Domination*: It is also maintained by the critics that the Constituent Assembly was dominated by lawyers and politicians. They pointed out that other sections of the society were not sufficiently represented. This, to them, is the main reason for the bulkiness and complicated language of the Constitution.
6. *Dominated by Hindus*: According to some critics, the Constituent Assembly was a Hindu dominated body. Lord Viscount Simon called it 'a body of Hindus'. Similarly, Winston Churchill commented that the Constituent Assembly represented 'only one major community in India'.

Table 2.1 *Statewise Membership of the Constituent Assembly of India as on December 31, 1947*

	S.No.	*Name*	*No. of Members*
A.	**Provinces (Indian Provinces)—229**		
	1.	Madras	49
	2.	Bombay	21
	3.	West Bengal	19
	4.	United Provinces	55

(Contd.)

S.No.	Name	No. of Members
5.	East Punjab	12
6.	Bihar	36
7.	C.P. and Berar	17
8.	Assam	8
9.	Orissa	9
10.	Delhi	1
11.	Ajmer-Merwara	1
12.	Coorg	1
B.	**Indian States (Princely States)—70**	
1.	Alwar	1
2.	Baroda	3
3.	Bhopal	1
4.	Bikaner	1
5.	Cochin	1
6.	Gwalior	4
7.	Indore	1
8.	Jaipur	3
9.	Jodhpur	2
10.	Kolhapur	1
11.	Kotah	1
12.	Mayurbhanj	1
13.	Mysore	7
14.	Patiala	2
15.	Rewa	2
16.	Travancore	6
17.	Udaipur	2
18.	Sikkim and Cooch Behar Group	1
19.	Tripura, Manipur and Khasi States Group	1
20.	U.P. States Group	1
21.	Eastern Rajputana States Group	3
22.	Central India States Group (including Bundelkhand and Malwa)	3
23.	Western India States Group	4
24.	Gujarat States Group	2
25.	Deccan and Madras States Group	2
26.	Punjab States Group	3

(*Contd.*)

	S.No.	Name	No. of Members
	27.	Eastern States Group I	4
	28.	Eastern States Group II	3
	29.	Residuary States Group	4
			Total 299

Table 2.2 *Sessions of the Constituent Assembly at a Glance*

Sessions	Period
First Session	9–23 December, 1946
Second Session	20–25 January, 1947
Third Session	28 April–2 May, 1947
Fourth Session	14–31 July, 1947
Fifth Session	14–30 August, 1947
Sixth Session	27 January, 1948
Seventh Session	4 November, 1948–8 January, 1949
Eighth Session	16 May–16 June, 1949
Ninth Session	30 July–18 September, 1949
Tenth Session	6–17 October, 1949
Eleventh Session	14–26 November, 1949

Note: The Assembly met once again on 24 January, 1950, when the members appended their signatures to the Constitution of India.

NOTES AND REFERENCES

1. The Cabinet Mission consisting of three members (Lord Pethick Lawrence, Sir Stafford Cripps and A V Alexander) arrived in India on March 24, 1946. The Cabinet Mission published its plan on May 16, 1946.
2. These include Madras, Bombay, U P , Bihar, Central Provinces, Orissa, Punjab, NWFP, Sindh, Bengal and Assam.
3. These include Delhi, Ajmer–Merwara, Coorg and British Baluchistan.
4. The Government of India Act of 1935 granted limited franchise on the basis of tax, property and education.
5. These include Baroda, Bikaner, Jaipur, Patiala, Rewa and Udaipur.
6. For the first time, the Constituent Assembly met as Dominion Legislature on November 17, 1947 and elected G V Mavlankar as its speaker.
7. These are West Punjab, East Bengal, NWFP, Sindh, Baluchistan and Sylhet District of Assam. A separate Constituent Assembly was set up for Pakistan.
8. The Provisional Parliament ceased to exist on April 17, 1952. The first elected Parliament with the two Houses came into being in May 1952.
9. Granville Austin, *The Indian Constitution—Cornerstone of a Nation*, Oxford, 1966, P. 8.

Salient Features of the Constitution

INTRODUCTION

The Indian Constitution is unique in its contents and spirit. Though borrowed from almost every constitution of the world, the constitution of India has several salient features that distinguish it from the constitutions of other countries.

It should be noted at the outset that a number of original features of the Constitution (as adopted in 1949) have undergone a substantial change, on account of several amendments, particularly 7th, 42nd, 44th, 73rd and 74th Amendments. In fact, the 42nd Amendment Act (1976) is known as 'Mini-Constitution' due to the important and large number of changes made by it in various parts of the Constitution. However, in the *Kesavananda Bharati* case[1] (1973), the Supreme Court ruled that the constituent power of Parliament under Article 368 does not enable it to alter the 'basic structure' of the Constitution.

SALIENT FEATURES OF THE CONSTITUTION

The salient features of the Constitution, as it stands today, are as follows:

1. Lengthiest Written Constitution

Constitutions are classified into written, like the American Constitution, or unwritten, like the British Constitution. The Constitution of India is the lengthiest of all the written constitutions of the world. It is a very comprehensive, elaborate and detailed document.

Originally (1949), the Constitution contained a Preamble, 395 Articles (divided into 22 Parts) and 8 Schedules. Presently (2013), it consists of a Preamble, about 465 Articles (divided into 25 Parts) and 12 Schedules[2]. The various amendments carried out since 1951 have deleted about 20 Articles and one Part (VII) and added about 85 Articles, four Parts (IVA, IXA, IXB and XIVA) and four Schedules (9, 10, 11 and 12). No other Constitution in the world has so many Articles and Schedules[3].

Four factors have contributed to the elephantine size of our Constitution. They are:

(a) Geographical factors, that is, the vastness of the country and its diversity.

(b) Historical factors, e.g., the influence of the Government of India Act of 1935, which was bulky.

(c) Single Constitution for both the Centre and the states except Jammu and Kashmir[4].

(d) Dominance of legal luminaries in the Constituent Assembly.

The Constitution contains not only the fundamental principles of governance but also detailed administrative provisions. Further, those matters which in other modern democratic countries have been left to the ordinary legislation or established political conventions have also been included in the constitutional document itself in India.

2. Drawn From Various Sources

The Constitution of India has borrowed most of its provisions from the constitutions of various other countries as well as from the Government of India Act[5] of 1935. Dr B R Ambedkar proudly acclaimed that the Constitution of India has been framed after 'ransacking all the known Constitutions of the World[6]'.

The structural part of the Constitution is, to a large extent, derived from the Government of India Act of 1935. The philosophical part of the Constitution (the Fundamental Rights and the Directive Principles of State Policy) derive their inspiration from the American and Irish Constitutions respectively. The political part of the Constitution (the principle of Cabinet Government and the relations between the executive and the legislature) have been largely drawn from the British Constitution[7].

The other provisions of the Constitution have been drawn from the constitutions of Canada, Australia, Germany, USSR (now Russia), France, South Africa, Japan, and so on[8].

However, the criticism that the Indian Constitution is a 'borrowed Constitution', a 'patchwork' and contains nothing new and original is unfair and illogical. This is because, the framers of the Constitution made necessary modifications in the features borrowed from other constitutions for their suitability to the Indian conditions, at the same time avoiding their faults[9].

3. Blend of Rigidity and Flexibility

Constitutions are also classified into rigid and flexible. A rigid Constitution is one that requires a special procedure for its amendment, as for example, the American Constitution. A flexible constitution, on the other hand, is one that can be amended in the same manner as the ordinary laws are made, as for example, the British Constitution.

The Constitution of India is neither rigid nor flexible but a synthesis of both. Article 368 provides for two types of amendments:

(a) Some provisions can be amended by a special majority of the Parliament, i.e., a two-third majority of the members of each House present and voting, and a majority (that is, more than 50 per cent), of the total membership of each House.

(b) Some other provisions can be amended by a special majority of the Parliament and with the ratification by half of the total states.

At the same time, some provisions of the Constitution can be amended by a simple majority of the Parliament in the manner of ordinary legislative process. Notably, these amendments do not come under Article 368.

4. Federal System with Unitary Bias

The Constitution of India establishes a federal system of government. It contains all the usual features of a federation, viz., two government, division of powers, written Constitution, supremacy of Constitution, rigidity of Constitution, independent judiciary and bicameralism.

However, the Indian Constitution also contains a large number of unitary or non-federal features, viz., a strong Centre, single Constitution, single citizenship, flexibility of Constitution, integrated judiciary, appointment of state governor by the Centre, all-India services, emergency provisions, and so on.

Moreover, the term 'Federation' has nowhere been used in the Constitution. Article 1, on the other hand, describes India as a 'Union of States' which implies two things: one, Indian Federation is not the result of an agreement by the states; and two, no state has the right to secede from the federation.

Hence, the Indian Constitution has been variously described as 'federal in form but unitary in spirit', 'quasi-federal' by K C Wheare, 'bargaining federalism' by Morris Jones, 'co-operative federalism' by Granville Austin, 'federation with a centralising tendency' by Ivor Jennings, and so on.

5. Parliamentary Form of Government

The Constitution of India has opted for the British parliamentary System of Government rather than American Presidential System of Government. The parliamentary system is based on the principle of cooperation and co-ordination between the legislative and executive organs while the presidential system is based on the doctrine of separation of powers between the two organs.

The parliamentary system is also known as the 'Westminster'[10] model of government, responsible government and cabinet government. The Constitution establishes the parliamentary system not only at the Centre but also in the states. The features of parliamentary government in India are:

(a) Presence of nominal and real executives;

(b) Majority party rule,

(c) Collective responsibility of the executive to the legislature,

(d) Membership of the ministers in the legislature,

(e) Leadership of the prime minister or the chief minister,

(f) Dissolution of the lower House (Lok Sabha or Assembly).

Even though the Indian Parliamentary System is largely based on the British pattern, there are some fundamental differences between the two. For example, the Indian Parliament is not a sovereign body like the British Parliament. Further, the Indian State has an elected head (republic) while the British State has hereditary head (monarchy).

In a parliamentary system whether in India or Britain, the role of the Prime Minister has become so significant and crucial that the political scientists like to call it a 'Prime Ministerial Government'.

6. Synthesis of Parliamentary Sovereignty and Judicial Supremacy

The doctrine of sovereignty of Parliament is associated with the British Parliament while the principle of judicial supremacy with that of the American Supreme Court.

Just as the Indian parliamentary system differs from the British system, the scope of judicial review power of the Supreme Court in India is narrower than that of what exists in US. This is because the American Constitution provides for 'due process of law' against that of 'procedure established by law' contained in the Indian Constitution (Article 21).

Therefore, the framers of the Indian Constitution have preferred a proper synthesis between the British principle of parliamentary sovereignty and the American principle of judicial supremacy. The Supreme Court, on the one hand, can declare the parliamentary laws as unconstitutional through its power of judicial review. The Parliament, on the other hand, can amend the major portion of the Constitution through its constituent power.

7. Integrated and Independent Judiciary

The Indian Constitution establishes a judicial system that is integrated as well as independent.

The Supreme Court stands at the top of the integrated judicial system in the country. Below it, there are high courts at the state level. Under a high court, there is a hierarchy of subordinate courts, that is, district courts and other lower courts. This single system of courts enforces both the central laws as well as the state laws, unlike in USA, where the federal laws are enforced by the federal judiciary and the state laws are enforced by the state judiciary.

The Supreme Court is a federal court, the highest court of appeal, the guarantor of the fundamental rights of the citizens and the guardian of the Constitution. Hence, the Constitution has made various provisions to ensure its independence—security of tenure of the judges, fixed service conditions for the judges, all the expenses of the Supreme Court charged on the Consolidated Fund of India, prohibition on discussion on the conduct of judges in the legislatures, ban on practice after retirement, power to punish for its contempt vested in the Supreme Court, separation of the judiciary from the executive, and so on.

8. Fundamental Rights

Part III of the Indian Constitution guarantees six[11] fundamental rights to all the citizens:

(a) Right to Equality (Articles 14–18),

(b) Right to Freedom (Articles 19–22),

(c) Right against Exploitation (Articles 23–24),

(d) Right to Freedom of Religion (Articles 25–28),

(e) Cultural and Educational Rights (Articles 29–30), and

(f) Right to Constitutional Remedies (Article 32).

The Fundamental Rights are meant for promoting the idea of political democracy. They operate as limitations on the tyranny of the executive and arbitrary laws of the legislature. They are justiciable in nature, that is, they are enforceable by the courts for their violation. The aggrieved person can directly go to the Supreme Court which can issue the writs of *habeas corpus, mandamus,* prohibition, *certiorari* and *quo warranto* for the restoration of his rights.

However, the Fundamental Rights are not absolute and subject to reasonable restrictions. Further, they are not sacrosanct and can be curtailed or repealed by the Parliament through a constitutional amendment act. They can also be suspended during the operation of a National Emergency except the rights guaranteed by Articles 20 and 21.

9. Directive Principles of State Policy

According to Dr B R Ambedkar, the Directive Principles of State Policy is a 'novel feature' of the Indian Constitution. They are enumerated in Part IV of the Constitution. They can be classified into three broad categories—socialistic, Gandhian and liberal–intellectual.

The directive principles are meant for promoting the ideal of social and economic democracy. They seek to establish a 'welfare state' in India. However, unlike the Fundamental Rights, the directives are non-justiciable in nature, that is, they are not enforceable by the courts for their violation. Yet, the Constitution itself declares that 'these principles are fundamental in the governance of the country and it shall be the duty of the state to apply these principles in making laws'. Hence, they impose a moral obligation on the state authorities for their application. But, the real force (sanction) behind them is political, that is, public opinion.

In the *Minerva Mills* case[12] (1980), the Supreme Court held that 'the Indian Constitution is founded on the bedrock of the balance between the Fundamental Rights and the Directive Principles'.

10. Fundamental Duties

The original constitution did not provide for the fundamental duties of the citizens. These were added during the operation of internal emergency (1975–77) by the 42nd Constitutional Amendment Act of 1976 on the recommendation of the Swaran Singh Committee. The 86th Constitutional Amendment Act of 2002 added one more fundamental duty.

The Part IV-A of the Constitution (which consists of only one Article—51-A) specifies the eleven Fundamental Duties viz., to respect the Constitution, national flag and national anthem; to protect the sovereignty, unity and integrity of the country; to

promote the spirit of common brotherhood amongst all the people; to preserve the rich heritage of our composite culture and so on.

The fundamental duties serve as a reminder to citizens that while enjoying their rights, they have also to be quite conscious of duties they owe to their country, their society and to their fellow-citizens. However, like the Directive Principles, the duties are also non-justiciable in nature.

11. A Secular State

The Constitution of India stands for a secular state. Hence, it does not uphold any particular religion as the official religion of the Indian State. The following provisions of the Constitution reveal the secular character of the Indian State:

(a) The term 'secular' was added to the Preamble of the Indian Constitution by the 42nd Constitutional Amendment Act of 1976.

(b) The Preamble secures to all citizens of India liberty of belief, faith and worship.

(c) The State shall not deny to any person equality before the law or equal protection of the laws (Article 14).

(d) The State shall not discriminate against any citizen on the ground of religion (Article 15).

(e) Equality of opportunity for all citizens in matters of public employment (Article 16).

(f) All persons are equally entitled to freedom of conscience and the right to freely profess, practice and propagate any religion (Article 25).

(g) Every religious denomination or any of its section shall have the right to manage its religious affairs (Article 26).

(h) No person shall be compelled to pay any taxes for the promotion of a particular religion (Article 27).

(i) No religious instruction shall be provided in any educational institution maintained by the State (Article 28).

(j) Any section of the citizens shall have the right to conserve its distinct language, script or culture (Article 29).

(k) All minorities shall have the right to establish and administer educational institutions of their choice (Article 30).

(l) The State shall endeavour to secure for all the citizens a Uniform Civil Code (Article 44).

The Western concept of secularism connotes a complete separation between the religion (the church) and the state (the politics). This negative concept of secularism is inapplicable in the Indian situation where the society is multireligious. Hence, the Indian Constitution embodies the positive concept of secularism, i.e., giving equal respect to all religions or protecting all religions equally.

Moreover, the Constitution has also abolished the old system of communal representation[13], that is, reservation of seats in the legislatures on the basis of religion. However, it provides for the temporary reservation of seats for the scheduled castes and scheduled tribes to ensure adequate representation to them.

12. Universal Adult Franchise

The Indian Constitution adopts universal adult franchise as a basis of elections to the Lok Sabha and the state legislative assemblies. Every citizen who is not less than 18 years of age has a right to vote without any discrimination of caste, race, religion, sex, literacy, wealth, and so on. The voting age was reduced to 18 years from 21 years in 1989 by the 61st Constitutional Amendment Act of 1988.

The introduction of universal adult franchise by the Constitution-makers was a bold experiment and highly remarkable in view of the vast size of the country, its huge population, high poverty, social inequality and overwhelming illiteracy.[14]

Universal adult franchise makes democracy broad-based, enhances the self-respect and prestige of the common people, upholds the principle of equality, enables minorities to protect their interests and opens up new hopes and vistas for weaker sections.

13. Single Citizenship

Though the Indian Constitution is federal and envisages a dual polity (Centre and states), it provides for only a single citizenship, that is, the Indian citizenship.

In countries like USA, on the other hand, each person is not only a citizen of USA but also a citizen of the particular state to which he belongs. Thus,

he owes allegiance to both and enjoys dual sets of rights—one conferred by the National government and another by the state government.

In India, all citizens irrespective of the state in which they are born or reside enjoy the same political and civil rights of citizenship all over the country and no discrimination is made between them excepting in few cases like tribal areas, Jammu and Kashmir, and so on.

Despite the constitutional provision for a single citizenship and uniform rights for all the people, India has been witnessing the communal riots, class conflicts, caste wars, linguistic clashes and ethnic disputes. This means that the cherished goal of the Constitution-makers to build an united and integrated Indian nation has not been fully realised.

14. Independent Bodies

The Indian Constitution not only provides for the legislative, executive and judicial organs of the government (Central and state) but also establishes certain independent bodies. They are envisaged by the Constitution as the bulworks of the democratic system of Government in India. These are:

(a) Election Commission to ensure free and fair elections to the Parliament, the state legislatures, the office of President of India and the office of Vice-president of India.

(b) Comptroller and Auditor-General of India to audit the accounts of the Central and state governments. He acts as the guardian of public purse and comments on the legality and propriety of government expenditure.

(c) Union Public Service Commission to conduct examinations for recruitment to all-India services[15] and higher Central services and to advise the President on disciplinary matters.

(d) State Public Service Commission in every state to conduct examinations for recruitment to state services and to advice the governor on disciplinary matters.

The Constitution ensures the independence of these bodies through various provisions like security of tenure, fixed service conditions, expenses being charged on the Consolidated Fund of India, and so on.

15. Emergency Provisions

The Indian Constitution contains elaborate emergency provisions to enable the President to meet any extraordinary situation effectively. The rationality behind the incorporation of these provisions is to safeguard the sovereignty, unity, integrity and security of the country, the democratic political system and the Constitution.

The Constitution envisages three types of emergencies, namely:

(a) National emergency on the ground of war or external aggression or armed rebellion[16] (Article 352);

(b) State emergency (President's Rule) on the ground of failure of Constitutional machinery in the states (Article 356) or failure to comply with the directions of the Centre (Article 365); and

(c) Financial emergency on the ground of threat to the financial stability or credit of India (Article 360).

During an emergency, the Central Government becomes all-powerful and the states go into the total control of the centre. It converts the federal structure into a unitary one without a formal amendment of the Constitution. This kind of transformation of the political system from federal (during normal times) to unitary (during emergency) is a unique feature of the Indian Constitution.

16. Three-tier Government

Originally, the Indian Constitution, like any other federal constitution, provided for a dual polity and contained provisions with regard to the organisation and powers of the Centre and the states. Later, the 73rd and 74th Constitutional Amendment Acts (1992) have added a third-tier of government (i.e., local) which is not found in any other Constitution of the world.

The 73rd Amendment Act of 1992 gave constitutional recognition to the panchayats (rural local governments) by adding a new Part IX[17] and a new Schedule 11 to the Constitution. Similarly, the 74th Amendment Act of 1992 gave constitutional. recognition to the municipalities (urban local governments) by adding a new Part IX-A[18] and a new Schedule 12 to the Constitution.

Table 3.1 *The Constitution of India at a Glance*

Parts	Subject Matter	Articles Covered
I	The Union and its territory	1 to 4
II	Citizenship	5 to 11
III	Fundamental Rights	12 to 35
IV	Directive Principles of State Policy	36 to 51
IV-A	Fundamental Duties	51-A
V	The Union Government	52 to 151
	Chapter I – The Executive	52 to 78
	Chapter II – Parliament	79 to 122
	Chapter III – Legislative Powers of President	123
	Chapter IV – The Union Judiciary	124 to 147
	Chapter V – Comptroller and Auditor-General of India	148 to 151
VI	The State Governments	152 to 237
	Chapter I – General	152
	Chapter II – The Executive	153 to 167
	Chapter III – The State Legislature	168 to 212

(Contd.)

Parts	Subject Matter	Articles Covered
	Chapter IV – Legislative Powers of Governor	213
	Chapter V – The High Courts	214 to 232
	Chapter VI – Subordinate Courts	233 to 237
VIII	The Union Territories	239 to 242
IX	The Panchayats	243 to 243-O
IX-A	The Municipalities	243-P to 243-ZG
IX-B	The Co-operative Societies	243-ZH to 243-ZT
X	The Scheduled and Tribal Areas	244 to 244-A
XI	Relations between the Union and the States	245 to 263
	Chapter I – Legislative Relations	245 to 255
	Chapter II – Administrative Relations	256 to 263
XII	Finance, Property, Contracts and Suits	264 to 300-A
	Chapter I – Finance	264 to 291
	Chapter II – Borrowing	292 to 293
	Chapter III – Property, Contracts, Rights, Liabilities, Obligations and Suits	294 to 300
	Chapter IV – Right to Property	300-A
XIII	Trade, Commerce and Intercourse within the Territory of India	301 to 307
XIV	Services under the Union and the States	308 to 323
	Chapter I – Services	308 to 314
	Chapter II – Public Service Commissions	315 to 323
XIV-A	Tribunals	323-A to 323-B
XV	Elections	324 to 329-A
XVI	Special Provisions relating to Certain Classes	330 to 342
XVII	Official Language	343 to 351
	Chapter I – Language of the Union	343 to 344
	Chapter II – Regional Languages	345 to 347
	Chapter III—Language of the Supreme Court, High Courts, and so on	348 to 349
	Chapter IV—Special Directives	350 to 351
XVIII	Emergency Provisions	352 to 360
XIX	Miscellaneous	361 to 367
XX	Amendment of the Constitution	368
XXI	Temporary, Transitional and Special Provisions	369 to 392
XXII	Short title, Commencement, Authoritative Text in Hindi and Repeals	393 to 395

Note: Part VII (dealing with Part-B states) was deleted by the 7th Amendment Act (1956). On the other hand, both Part IV-A and Part XIV-A were added by the 42nd Amendment Act (1976), while Part IX-A was added by the 74th Amendment Act (1992), and Part IX-B was added by the 97th Amendment Act (2011).

Table 3.2 *Important Articles of the Constitution at a Glance*

Articles	Deals with
1	Name and territory of the Union
3	Formation of new states and alteration of areas, boundaries or names of existing states
13	Laws inconsistent with or in derogation of the fundamental rights
14	Equality before law
16	Equality of opportunity in matters of public employment
17	Abolition of untouchability
19	Protection of certain rights regarding freedom of speech, etc.
21	Protection of life and personal liberty
21A	Right to elementary education
25	Freedom of conscience and free profession, practice and propagation of religion
30	Right of minorities to establish and administer educational institutions
31C	Saving of laws giving effect to certain directive principles
32	Remedies for enforcement of fundamental rights including writs
38	State to secure a social order for the promotion of welfare of the people
40	Organisation of village panchayats
44	Uniform civil code for the citizens
45	Provision for early childhood care and education to children below the age of 6 years.
46	Promotion of educational and economic interests of scheduled castes, scheduled tribes and other weaker sections
50	Separation of judiciary from executive
51	Promotion of international peace and security
51A	Fundamental duties
72	Power of president to grant pardons, etc., and to suspend, remit or commute sentences in certain cases
74	Council of ministers to aid and advise the president
78	Duties of prime minister as respects the furnishing of information to the president, etc.
110	Definition of Money Bills
112	Annual financial statement (Budget)
123	Power of president to promulgate ordinances during recess of Parliament
143	Power of president to consult Supreme Court
155	Appointment of governor
161	Power of governor to grant pardons, etc., and to suspend, remit or commute sentences in certain cases
163	Council of ministers to aid and advise the governor
167	Duties of chief minister with regard to the furnishing of information to governor, etc.
169	Abolition or creation of legislative councils in states
200	Assent to bills by governor (including reservation for President)
213	Power of governor to promulgate ordinances during recess of the state legislature

(Contd.)

Articles	Deals with
226	Power of high courts to issue certain writs
239AA	Special provisions with respect to Delhi
249	Power of Parliament to legislate with respect to a matter in the State List in the national interest
262	Adjudication of disputes relating to waters of inter-state rivers or river valleys
263	Provisions with respect to an inter-state council
265	Taxes not to be imposed save by authority of law
275	Grants from the Union to certain states
280	Finance Commission
300	Suits and proceedings
300A	Persons not to be deprived of property save by authority of law (Right to property)
311	Dismissal, removal or reduction in rank of persons employed in civil capacities under the Union or a state.
312	All-India Services
315	Public service commissions for the Union and for the states
320	Functions of Public service commissions
323-A	Administrative tribunals
324	Superintendence, direction and control of elections to be vested in an Election Commission
330	Reservation of seats for scheduled castes and scheduled tribes in the House of the People
335	Claims of scheduled castes and scheduled tribes to services and posts
352	Proclamation of Emergency (National Emergency)
356	Provisions in case of failure of constitutional machinery in states (President's Rule)
360	Provisions as to financial emergency.
365	Effect of failure to comply with, or to give effect to, directions given by the Union (President's Rule)
368	Power of Parliament to amend the Constitution and procedure therefor
370	Temporary provisions with respect to the state of Jammu and Kashmir

Table 3.3 *Schedules of the Constitution at a Glance*

Numbers	Subjext Matter	Articles Covered
First Schedule	1. Names of the States and their territorial jurisdiction.	1 and 4
	2. Names of the Union Territories and their extent.	
Second Schedule	Provisions relating to the emoluments, allowances, privileges and so on of:	59, 65, 75, 97, 125, 148, 158, 164, 186 & 221
	1. The President of India	
	2. The Governors of States	
	3. The Speaker and the Deputy Speaker of the Lok Sabha	
	4. The Chairman and the Deputy Chairman of the Rajya Sabha	

(Contd.)

Numbers	Subjext Matter	Articles Covered
	5. The Speaker and the Deputy Speaker of the Legislative Assembly in the states	
	6. The Chairman and the Deputy Chairman of the Legislative Council in the states	
	7. The Judges of the Supreme Court	
	8. The Judges of the High Courts	
	9. The Comptroller and Auditor-General of India	
Third Schedule	Forms of Oaths or Affirmations for:	75, 84, 99, 124, 146, 173, 188 and 219
	1. The Union ministers	
	2. The candidates for election to the Parliament	
	3. The members of Parliament	
	4. The judges of the Supreme Court	
	5. The Comptroller and Auditor-General of India	
	6. The state ministers	
	7. The candidates for election to the state legislature	
	8. The members of the state legislature	
	9. The judges of the High Courts	
Fourth Schedule	Allocation of seats in the Rajya Sabha to the states and the union territories.	4 and 80
Fifth Schedule	Provisions relating to the administration and control of scheduled areas and scheduled tribes.	244
Sixth Schedule	Provisions relating to the administration of tribal areas in the states of Assam, Meghalaya, Tripura and Mizoram.	244 and 275
Seventh Schedule	Division of powers between the Union and the States in terms of List I (Union List), List II (State List) and List III (Concurrent List). Presently, the Union List contains 100 subjects (originally 97), the state list contains 61 subjects (originally 66) and the concurrent list contains 52 subjects (originally 47).	246
Eighth Schedule	Languages recognized by the Constitution. Originally, it had 14 languages but presently there are 22 languages. They are: Assamese, Bengali, Bodo, Dogri (Dongri), Gujarati, Hindi, Kannada, Kashmiri, Konkani, Mathili (Maithili), Malayalam, Manipuri, Marathi, Nepali, Oriya, Punjabi, Sanskrit, Santhali, Sindhi, Tamil, Telugu and Urdu. Sindhi was added by the 21st Amendment Act of 1967; Konkani, Manipuri and Nepali were added by the 71st Amendment Act of 1992; and Bodo, Dongri, Maithili and Santhali were added by the 92nd Amendment Act of 2003.	344 and 351

(Contd.)

Numbers	Subjext Matter	Articles Covered
Ninth Schedule	Acts and Regulations (originally 13 but presently 282)[19] of the state legislatures dealing with land reforms and abolition of the zamindari system and of the Parliament dealing with other matters. This schedule was added by the 1st Amendment (1951) to protect the laws included in it from judicial scrutiny on the ground of violation of fundamental rights. However, in 2007, the Supreme Court ruled that the laws included in this schedule after April 24, 1973, are now open to judicial review.	31-B
Tenth Schedule	Provisions relating to disqualification of the members of Parliament and State Legislatures on the ground of defection. This schedule was added by the 52nd Amendment Act of 1985, also known as Anti-defection Law.	102 and 191
Eleventh Schedule	Specifies the powers, authority and responsibilities of Panchayats. It has 29 matters. This schedule was added by the 73rd Amendment Act of 1992.	243-G
Twelfth Schedule	Specifies the powers, authority and responsibilities of Municipalities. It has 18 matters. This schedule was added by the 74th Amendment Act of 1992.	243-W

Table 3.4 *Sources of the Constitution at a Glance*

	Sources	Features Borrowed
1.	Government of India Act of 1935	Federal Scheme, Office of governor, Judiciary, Public Service Commissions, Emergency provisions and administrative details.
2.	British Constitution	Parliamentary government, Rule of Law, legislative procedure, single citizenship, cabinet system, prerogative writs, parliamentary privileges and bicameralism.
3.	US Constitution	Fundamental rights, independence of judiciary, judicial review, impeachment of the president, removal of Supreme Court and high court judges and post of vice-president.
4.	Irish Constitution	Directive Principles of State Policy, nomination of members to Rajya Sabha and method of election of president.
5.	Canadian Constitution	Federation with a strong Centre, vesting of residuary powers in the Centre, appointment of state governors by the Centre, and advisory jurisdiction of the Supreme Court.
6.	Australian Constitution	Concurrent List, freedom of trade, commerce and inter-course, and joint sitting of the two Houses of Parliament.
7.	Weimar Constitution of Germany	Suspension of Fundamental Rights during Emergency.
8.	Soviet Constitution (USSR, now Russia)	Fundamental duties and the ideal of justice (social, economic and political) in the Preamble.
9.	French Constitution	Republic and the ideals of liberty, equality and fraternity in the Preamble.
10.	South African Constitution	Procedure for amendment of the Constitution and election of members of Rajya Sabha.
11.	Japanese Constitution	Procedure established by Law.

NOTES AND REFERENCES

1. *Kesavananda Bharati* v. *State of Kerala,* (1973)
2. For details on Parts, important Articles and Schedules, see Tables 3.1, 3.2 and 3.3 at the end of this chapter.
3. The American Constitution originally consisted of only 7 Articles, the Australian 128, the Chinese 138, and the Canadian 147.
4. The State of Jammu and Kashmir has its own Constitution and thus, enjoys a special status by virtue of Article 370 of the Constitution of India.
5. About 250 provisions of the 1935 Act have been included in the Constitution.
6. *Constituent Assembly Debates,* Volume VII, P. 35–38.
7. P M Bakshi, *The Constitution of India*, Universal, Fifth Edition, 2002, P. 4.
8. See Table 3.4 at the end of this chapter.
9. In this context, Dr B R Ambedkar said: 'One likes to ask whether there can be anything new in a Constitution framed at this hour in the history of the world. More than hundred years have rolled over when the first written Constitution was drafted. It has been followed by many countries reducing their constitutions to writing. What the scope of a constitution should be has long been settled. Similarly, what are the fundamentals of a constitution are recognised all over the world. Given these facts, all Constitutions in their main provisions must look similar. The only new things if there can be any, in a Constitution framed so late in the day are the variations made to remove the faults and to accommodate it to the needs of the country. The charge of producing a blind copy of the Constitutions of other countries is based, I am sure, on an inadequate study of the Constitution. As to the accusation that the draft Constitution. has produced a good part of the provisions of the Government of India Act, 1935, I make no apologies. There is nothing to be ashamed of in borrowing. It involves no plagiarism. Nobody holds any patent rights in the fundamental ideas of a Constitution'. (*Constituent Assembly Debates,* Volume VII, p. (35–38).

10. Westminster is a place in London where the British Parliament is located. It is often used as a symbol/synonym of the British Parliament.
11. Originally, the Constitution provided for seven Fundamental Rights. However, the Right to Property (Article 31) was deleted from the list of Fundamental Rights by the 44th Amendment Act of 1978. It is made a legal right under Article 300-A in Part XII of the constitution.
12. *Minerva Mills* v. *Union of India,* (1980).
13. The 1909, 1919, and 1935 Acts provided for communal representation.
14. Even in the western countries, the right to vote was extended only gradually. For example, USA gave franchise to women in 1920, Britain in 1928, USSR (now Russia) in 1936, France in 1945, Italy in 1948 and Switzerland in 1971.
15. At present, there are three All-India services, namely Indian Administrative Service (IAS), Indian Police Service (IPS) and Indian Forest Service (IFS). In 1947, Indian Civil Service (ICS) was replaced by IAS and the Indian Police (IP) was replaced by IPS and were recognised by the Constitution as All-India Services. In 1963, IFS was created and it came into existence in 1966.
16. The 44th Amendment Act (1978) has replaced the original term 'internal disturbance' by the new term 'armed rebellion'.
17. Part IX of the Constitution provides for a three-tier system of panchayati raj in every state, that is, panchayats at the village, intermediate and district levels.
18. Part IX-A of the Constitution provides for three types of municipalities in every state, that is, nagar panchayat for a transitional area, municipal council for a smaller urban area and municipal corporation for a larger urban area.
19. Though the last entry is numbered 284, the actual total number is 282. This is because, three entries (87,92 and 130) have been deleted and one entry is numbered as 257-A.

Preamble of the Constitution

The American Constitution was the first to begin with a Preamble. Many countries, including India, followed this practice. The term 'preamble' refers to the introduction or preface to the Constitution. It contains the summary or essence of the Constitution. N A Palkhivala, an eminent jurist and constitutional expert, called the Preamble as the 'identity card of the Constitution.'

The Preamble to the Indian Constitution is based on the 'Objectives Resolution', drafted and moved by Pandit Nehru, and adopted by the Constituent Assembly[1]. It has been amended by the 42nd Constitutional Amendment Act (1976), which added three new words—socialist, secular and integrity.

TEXT OF THE PREAMBLE

The Preamble in its present form reads:

"We, THE PEOPLE OF INDIA, having solemnly resolved to constitute India into a SOVEREIGN *SOCIALIST SECULAR* DEMOCRATIC REPUBLIC and to secure to all its citizens:

JUSTICE, Social, Economic and Political;

LIBERTY of thought, expression, belief, faith and worship;

EQUALITY of status and of opportunity; and to promote among them all;

FRATERNITY assuring the dignity of the individual and the unity *and integrity* of the Nation;

IN OUR CONSTITUENT ASSEMBLY this twenty-sixth day of November, 1949, do HEREBY ADOPT, ENACT AND GIVE TO OURSELVES THIS CONSTITUTION".

INGREDIENTS OF THE PREAMBLE

The Preamble reveals four ingredients or components:

1. Source of authority of the Constitution: The Preamble states that the Constitution derives its authority from the people of India.
2. Nature of Indian State: It declares India to be of a sovereign, socialist, secular democratic and republican polity.
3. Objectives of the Constitution: It specifies justice, liberty, equality and fraternity as the objectives.
4. Date of adoption of the Constitution: It stipulates November 26, 1949 as the date.

KEY WORDS IN THE PREAMBLE

Certain key words—Sovereign, Socialist, Secular, Democratic, Republic, Justice, Liberty, Equality and Fraternity—are explained as follows:

1. Sovereign

The word 'sovereign' implies that India is neither a dependency nor a dominion of any other nation, but an independent state[2]. There is no authority above it, and it is free to conduct its own affairs (both internal and external).

Though in 1949, India declared the continuation of her full membership of the Commonwealth of Nations and accepted the British Crown as the head of the Commonwealth, this extra-constitutional declaration does not affect India's sovereignty in any manner[3]. Further, India's membership of the United Nations Organisation (UNO) also in no way constitutes a limitation on her sovereignty[4].

Being a sovereign state, India can either acquire a foreign territory or cede a part of its territory in favour of a foreign state.

2. Socialist

Even before the term was added by the 42nd Amendment in 1976, the Constitution had a socialist content in the form of certain Directive Principles of State Policy. In other words, what was hitherto implicit in the Constitution has now been made explicit. Moreover, the Congress party itself adopted a resolution[5] to establish a 'socialistic pattern of society' in its Avadi session as early as in 1955 and took measures accordingly.

Notably, the Indian brand of socialism is a 'democratic socialism' and not a 'communistic socialism' (also known as 'state socialism') which involves the nationalisation of all means of production and distribution and the abolition of private property. Democratic socialism, on the other hand, holds faith in a 'mixed economy' where both public and private sectors co-exist side by side[6]. As the Supreme Court says, 'Democratic socialism aims to end poverty, ignorance, disease and inequality of opportunity[7]. Indian socialism is a blend of Marxism and Gandhism, leaning heavily towards Gandhian socialism'[8].

The new economic policy (1991) of liberalisation, privatisation and globalisation has, however, diluted the socialist credentials of the Indian State.

3. Secular

The term 'secular' too was added by the 42nd Constitutional Amendment Act of 1976. However,

as the Supreme Court said in 1974, although the words 'secular state'[9] were not expressly mentioned in the Constitution, there can be no doubt that Constitution-makers wanted to establish such a state and accordingly Articles 25 to 28 (guaranteeing the fundamental right to freedom of religion) have been included in the constitution.

The Indian Constitution embodies the positive concept of secularism ie, all religions in our country (irrespective of their strength) have the same status and support from the state[10].

4. Democratic

A democratic[11] polity, as stipulated in the Preamble, is based on the doctrine of popular sovereignty, that is, possession of supreme power by the people.

Democracy is of two types—direct and indirect. In direct democracy, the people exercise their supreme power directly as is the case in Switzerland. There are four devices of direct democracy, namely, **Referendum, Initiative, Recall** and **Plebiscite**[12]. In indirect democracy, on the other hand, the representatives elected by the people exercise the supreme power and thus carry on the government and make the laws. This type of democracy, also known as representative democracy, is of two kinds—parliamentary and presidential.

The Indian Constitution provides for representative parliamentary democracy under which the executive is responsible to the legislature for all its policies and actions. Universal adult franchise, periodic elections, rule of law, independence of judiciary, and absence of discrimination on certain grounds are the manifestations of the democratic character of the Indian polity.

The term 'democratic' is used in the Preamble in the broader sense embracing not only political democracy but also social and economic democracy.

This dimension was stressed by Dr. Ambedkar in his concluding speech in the Constituent Assembly on November 25, 1949, in the following way:

"Political democracy cannot last unless there lies at the base of it social democracy. What does social democracy mean ? It means a way of life which recognises liberty, equality and fraternity. The principles of liberty, equality and fraternity are not to be treated as separate items in a trinity. They form a union of trinity in the sense that to divorce one from the other is to defeat the very purpose of democracy. Liberty cannot be divorced from equality, equality cannot be divorced from liberty. Nor can liberty and equality be divorced from fraternity. Without equality, liberty would produce the supremacy of the few over the many. Equality without liberty, would kill individual initiative".[12a]

In the same context, the Supreme Court observed in 1997 that: "The Constitution envisions to establish an egalitarian social order rendering to every citizen social, economic and political justice in a social and economic democracy of the Bharat Republic".

5. Republic

A democratic polity can be classified into two categories—monarchy and republic. In a monarchy, the head of the state (usually king or queen) enjoys a hereditary position, that is, he comes into office through succession, eg, Britain. In a republic, on the other hand, the head of the state is always elected directly or indirectly for a fixed period, eg, USA.

Therefore, the term 'republic' in our Preamble indicates that India has an elected head called the president. He is elected indirectly for a fixed period of five years.

A republic also means two more things: one, vesting of political sovereignty in the people and not in a single individual like a king; second, the absence of any privileged class and hence all public offices being opened to every citizen without any discrimination.

6. Justice

The term 'justice' in the Preamble embraces three distinct forms—social, economic and political, secured through various provisions of Fundamental Rights and Directive Principles.

Social justice denotes the equal treatment of all citizens without any social distinction based on caste, colour, race, religion, sex and so on. It means absence of privileges being extended to any particular section of the society, and improvement in the conditions of backward classes (SCs, STs and OBCs) and women.

Economic justice denotes the non-discrimination between people on the basis of economic factors. It involves the elimination of glaring inequalities in wealth, income and property. A combination of social justice and economic justice denotes what is known as 'distributive justice'.

Political justice implies that all citizens should have equal political rights, equal access to all political offices and equal voice in the government.

The ideal of justice—social, economic and political—has been taken from the Russian Revolution (1917).

7. Liberty

The term 'liberty' means the absence of restraints on the activities of individuals, and at the same time, providing opportunities for the development of individual personalities.

The Preamble secures to all citizens of India liberty of thought, expression, belief, faith and worship, through their Fundamental Rights, enforceable in court of law, in case of violation.

Liberty as elaborated in the Preamble is very essential for the successful functioning of the Indian democratic system. However, liberty does not mean 'license' to do what one likes, and has to be enjoyed within the limitations mentioned in the Constitution itself. In brief, the liberty conceived by the Preamble or fundamental rights is not absolute but qualified.

The ideals of liberty, equality and fraternity in our Preamble have been taken from the French Revolution (1789–1799).

8. Equality

The term 'equality' means the absence of special privileges to any section of the society, and the provision of adequate opportunities for all individuals without any discrimination.

The Preamble secures to all citizens of India equality of status and opportunity. This provision embraces three dimensions of equality—civic, political and economic.

The following provisions of the chapter on Fundamental Rights ensure civic equality:

(a) Equality before the law (Article 14).
(b) Prohibition of discrimination on grounds of religion, race, caste, sex or place of birth (Article 15).

(c) Equality of opportunity in matters of public employment (Article 16).

(d) Abolition of untouchability (Article 17).

(e) Abolition of titles (Article 18).

There are two provisions in the Constitution that seek to achieve political equality. One, no person is to be declared ineligible for inclusion in electoral rolls on grounds of religion, race, caste or sex (Article 325). Two, elections to the Lok Sabha and the state assemblies to be on the basis of adult suffrage (Article 326).

The Directive Principles of State Policy (Article 39) secures to men and women equal right to an adequate means of livelihood and equal pay for equal work.

9. Fraternity

Fraternity means a sense of brotherhood. The Constitution promotes this feeling of fraternity by the system of single citizenship. Also, the Fundamental Duties (Article 51-A) say that it shall be the duty of every citizen of India to promote harmony and the spirit of common brotherhood amongst all the people of India transcending religious, linguistic, regional or sectional diversities.

The Preamble declares that fraternity has to assure two things—the dignity of the individual and the unity and integrity of the nation. The word 'integrity' has been added to the preamble by the 42nd Constitutional Amendment (1976).

According to K M Munshi, a member of the Drafting Committee of the Constituent Assembly, the phrase 'dignity of the individual' signifies that the Constitution not only ensures material betterment and maintain a democratic set-up, but that it also recognises that the personality of every individual is sacred. This is highlighted through some of the provisions of the Fundamental Rights and Directive Principles of State Policy, which ensure the dignity of individuals. Further, the Fundamental Duties (Article 51A) also protect the dignity of women by stating that it shall be the duty of every citizen of India to renounce practices derogatory to the dignity of women, and also makes it the duty of every citizen of India to uphold and protect the sovereignty, unity and integrity of India.

The phrase 'unity and integrity of the nation' embraces both the psychological and territorial dimensions of national integration. Article 1 of the Constitution describes India as a 'Union of States' to make it clear that the states have no right to secede from the Union, implying the indestructible nature of the Indian Union. It aims at overcoming hindrances to national integration like communalism, regionalism, casteism, linguism, secessionism and so on.

SIGNIFICANCE OF THE PREAMBLE

The Preamble embodies the basic philosophy and fundamental values—political, moral and religious—on which the Constitution is based. It contains the grand and noble vision of the Constituent Assembly, and reflects the dreams and aspirations of the founding fathers of the Constitution. In the words of Sir Alladi Krishnaswami Iyer, a member of the Constituent Assembly who played a significant role in making the Constitution, 'The Preamble to our Constitution expresses what we had thought or dreamt so long'.

According to K M Munshi, a member of the Drafting Committee of the Constituent Assembly, the Preamble is the 'horoscope of our sovereign democratic republic'.

Pandit Thakur Das Bhargava, another member of the Constituent Assembly, summed up the importance of the Preamble in the following words: 'The Preamble is the most precious part of the Constitution. It is the soul of the Constitution. It is a key to the Constitution. It is a jewel set in the Constitution. It is a proper yardstick with which one can measure the worth of the Constitution'.

Sir Ernest Barker, a distinguished English political scientist, paid a glowing tribute to the political wisdom of the authors of the Preamble. He described the Preamble as the 'key-note'[13] to the Constitution. He was so moved by the text of the preamble that he quoted[14] it at the opening of his popular book, *Principles of Social and Political Theory* (1951).

M Hidayatullah, a former Chief Justice of India, observed, 'Preamble resembles the Declaration of Independence of the United States of America, but is more than a declaration. It is the soul of our

Constitution, which lays down the pattern of our political society. It contains a solemn resolve, which nothing but a revolution can alter[15].

PREAMBLE AS PART OF THE CONSTITUTION

One of the controversies about the Preamble is as to whether it is a part of the Constitution or not.

In the *Berubari Union*[16] case (1960), the Supreme Court said that the Preamble shows the general purposes behind the several provisions in the Constitution, and is thus a key to the minds of the makers of the Constitution. Further, where the terms used in any article are ambiguous or capable of more than one meaning, some assistance at interpretation may be taken from the objectives enshrined in the Preamble. Despite this recognition of the significance of the Preamble, the Supreme Court specifically opined that Preamble is *not* a part of the Constitution.

In the *Kesavananda Bharati* case[17] (1973), the Supreme Court rejected the earlier opinion and held that Preamble *is* a part of the Constitution. It observed that the Preamble is of extreme importance and the Constitution should be read and interpreted in the light of the grand and noble vision expressed in the Preamble. In the *LIC of India* case[18] (1995) also, the Supreme Court again held that the Preamble is an integral part of the Constitution.

Like any other part of the Constitution, the Preamble was also enacted by the Constituent Assembly, but, after the rest of the Constitution was already enacted. The reason for inserting the Preamble at the end was to ensure that it was in conformity with the Constitution as adopted by the Constituent Assembly. While forwarding the Preamble for votes, the president of the Constituent Assembly said, 'The question is that Preamble stands part of the Constitution'[19]. The motion was then adopted. Hence, the current opinion held by the Supreme Court that the Preamble is a part of the Constitution, is in consonance with the opinion of the founding fathers of the Constitution.

However, two things should be noted:

1. The Preamble is neither a source of power to legislature nor a prohibition upon the powers of legislature.
2. It is non-justiciable, that is, its provisions are not enforceable in courts of law.

AMENDABILITY OF THE PREAMBLE

The question as to whether the Preamble can be amended under Article 368 of the Constitution arose for the first time in the historic case of *Kesavananda Bharati (1973)*. It was urged that the Preamble cannot be amended as it is not a part of the Constitution. The petitioner contended that the amending power in Article 368 cannot be used to destroy or damage the basic elements or the fundamental features of the Constitution, which are enshrined in the Preamble.

The Supreme Court, however, held that the Preamble is a part of the Constitution. The Court stated that the opinion tendered by it in the *Berubari Union (1960)* in this regard was wrong, and held that the Preamble can be amended, subject to the condition that no amendment is done to the 'basic features'. In other words, the Court held that the basic elements or the fundamental features of the Constitution as contained in the Preamble cannot be altered by an amendment under Article 368[20].

The Preamble has been amended only once so far, in 1976, by the 42nd Constitutional Amendment Act, which has added three new words—Socialist, Secular and Integrity—to the Preamble. This amendment was held to be valid.

NOTES AND REFERENCES

1. Moved by Nehru on December 13, 1946 and adopted by the Constituent Assembly on January 22, 1947.
2. Till the passage of the Indian Independence Act, 1947, India was a dependency (colony) of the British Empire. From August 15, 1947 to January 26, 1950, India's political status was that of a dominion in the British Commonwealth of Nations. India ceased to be a British dominion on January 26, 1950, by declaring herself a sovereign republic. However, Pakistan continued to be a British Dominion until 1956.

3. To dispel the lurking fears of some members of the Constituent Assembly, Pandit Nehru said in 1949 thus: 'We took pledge long ago to achieve *Purna Swaraj*. We have achieved it. Does a nation lose its independence by an alliance with another country? Alliance normally means commitments. The free association of the sovereign Commonwealth of Nations does not involve such commitments. Its very strength lies in its flexibility and its complete freedom. It is well-known that it is open to any member-nation to go out of the commonwealth if it so chooses'. He further stated, 'It is an agreement by free will, to be terminated by free will'.

4. India became a member of the UNO in 1945.

5. The Resolution said: 'In order to realise the object of Congress and to further the objectives stated in the Preamble and Directive Principles of State Policy of the Constitution of India, planning should take place with a view to the establishment of a socialistic pattern of society, where the principal means of production are under social ownership or control, production is progressively speeded up and there is equitable distribution of the national wealth'.

6. The Prime Minister, Indira Gandhi, said, 'We have always said that we have our own brand of socialism. We will nationalise the sectors where we feel the necessity. Just nationalisation is not our type of socialism'.

7. *G.B. Pant University of Agriculture and Technology v. State of Uttar Pradesh* (2000).

8. *Nakara v. Union of India* (1983).

9. On the basis of the attitude of the state towards religion, three types of states can be conceived of:
   (a) *Atheistic State:* The state is anti-religion and hence, condemns all religions.
   (b) *Theocratic State:* The state is pro-religion and hence, declares one particular religion as the state religion, as for example, Nepal, Bangladesh, Burma, Sri Lanka, Pakistan, and so on.
   (c) *Secular State:* The state is neutral in the matter of religion and hence, does not uphold any particular religion as the state religion, as for example, USA and India.

G S Pande, *Constitutional Law of India*, Allahabad Law Agency, eighth edition, 2002, P. 222.

10. The then Union Law Minister, H R Gokhale defined this concept as: 'There will be freedom, liberty of faith and worship, whatever religion you belong to. The State will not have anything to do, as a state, with any religion excepting to treat every religion equally, but the State will not have any foundation of religion'. Similarly, P B Gajendragadkar, a former Chief Justice of India, defined secularism as in the Indian Constitution in the following way: 'The State does not owe loyalty to any particular religion as such: it is not irreligious or anti-religious; it gives equal freedom to all religions'.

11. The term 'democracy' is derived from two Greek words, namely, *Demos* and *Kratia* meaning 'People' and 'rule' respectively.

12. *Referendum* is a procedure whereby a proposed legislation is referred to the electorate for settlement by their direct votes.
    Initiative is a method by means of which the people can propose a bill to the legislature for enactment.
    Recall is a method by means of which the voters can remove a representative or an officer before the expiry of his term, when he fails to discharge his duties properly.
    Plebiscite is a method of obtaining the opinion of people on any issue of public importance. It is generally used to solve the territorial disputes.

12a. B. Shiva Rao, *The Framing of Indian Constitution: Select Documents*, Volume IV, P. 944.

13. He said that the Preamble of the Indian Constitution states 'in a brief and pithy form the argument of much of the book; and it may accordingly serve as a key-note'.

14. He wrote: 'I am all the more moved to quote it because I am proud that the people of India should begin their independent life by subscribing to the principles of a political tradition which we in the west call western, but which is now something more than the western'.

15. M Hidayatullah, *Democracy in India and the Judicial Process,* p. 51.
16. Reference by the President of India under Article 143 of the Constitution on the implementation of the Indo-Pakistan agreement relating to Berubari union and exchange of enclaves (1960).
17. *Kesavananda Bharati* v. *State of Kerala* (1973).
18. *LIC of India* v. *Consumer Education and Research Centre* (1995).
19. *'Constituent Assembly Debates'*, Volume 10, P. 450–456.
20. The Court observed, 'The edifice of our Constitution is based upon the basic elements mentioned in the Preamble. If any of these elements are removed, the structure will not survive and it will not be the same Constitution or it cannot maintain its identity. An amending power cannot be interpreted so as to confer power on the Parliament to take away any of these fundamental and basic characteristics of the polity'.

Union and its Territory

Articles 1 to 4 under Part-I of the Constitution deal with the Union and its territory.

UNION OF STATES

Article 1 describes India, that is, Bharat as a 'Union of States' rather than a 'Federation of States'. This provision deals with two things: one, name of the country, and two, type of polity.

There was no unanimity in the Constituent Assembly with regard to the name of the country. Some members suggested the traditional name (Bharat) while other advocated the modern name (India). Hence, the Constituent Assembly had to adopt a mix of both ('India, that is, Bharat')

Secondly, the country is described as 'Union' although its Constitution is federal in structure. According to Dr B R Ambedkar, the phrase 'Union of States' has been preferred to 'Federation of States' for two reasons: one, the Indian Federation is not the result of an agreement among the states like the American Federation; and two, the states have no right to secede from the federation. The federation is an Union because it is indestructible. The country is an integral whole and divided into different states only for the convenience of administration[1].

According to Article 1, the territory of India can be classified into three categories:

1. Territories of the states
2. Union territories

3. Territories that may be acquired by the Government of India at any time.

The names of states and union territories and their territorial extent are mentioned in the first schedule of the Constitution. At present, there are 28 states and 7 union territories. The provisions of the Constitution pertaining to the states are applicable to all the states (except Jammu and Kashmir)[2] in the same manner. However, the special provisions (under Part XXI) applicable to the States of Maharashtra, Gujarat, Nagaland, Assam, Manipur, Andhra Pradesh, Sikkim, Mizoram, Arunanchal Pradesh and Goa override the general provisions relating to the states as a class. Further, the Fifth and Sixth Schedules contain separate provisions with respect to the administration of scheduled areas and tribal areas within the states.

Notably, the 'Territory of India' is a wider expression than the 'Union of India' because the latter includes only states while the former includes not only the states but also union territories and territories that may be acquired by the Government of India at any future time. The states are the members of the federal system and share a distribution of powers with the Centre. The union territories and the acquired territories, on the other hand, are directly administered by the Central government.

Being a sovereign state, India can acquire foreign territories according to the modes recognised by international law, i.e., cession (following treaty, purchase, gift, lease or plebiscite), occupation (hitherto unoccupied by a recognised ruler), conquest or subjugation. For example, India acquired several foreign territories such as Dadra and Nagar Haveli; Goa, Daman and Diu; Puducherry; and Sikkim since the commencement of the Constitution. The acquisition of these territories are discussed later in this chapter.

Article 2 empowers the Parliament to 'admit into the Union of India, or establish, new states on such terms and conditions as it thinks fit'. Thus, Article 2 grants two powers to the Parliament: (a) the power to admit into the Union of India new states; and (b) the power to establish new states. The first refers to the admission of states which are already in existence while the second refers to the establishment of states which were not in existence before. Notably, Article 2 relates to the admission or establishment of new states that are not part of the Union of India. Article 3, on the other hand, relates to the formation of or changes in the existing states of the Union of India. In other words, Article 3 deals with the internal readjustment *inter* se of the territories of the constituent states of the Union of India.

Parliament's Power to Reorganise the States

Article 3 authorises the Parliament to:
  (a) form a new state by separation of territory from any state or by uniting two or more states or parts of states or by uniting any territory to a part of any state,
  (b) increase the area of any state,
  (c) diminish the area of any state,
  (d) alter the boundaries of any state, and
  (e) alter the name of any state.

However, Article 3 lays down two conditions in this regard: one, a bill contemplating the above changes can be introduced in the Parliament only with the prior recommendation of the President; and two, before recommending the bill, the President has to refer the same to the state legislature concerned for expressing its views within a specified period.

Further, the power of Parliament to form new states includes the power to form a new state or union territory by uniting a part of any state or union territory to any other state or union territory[3].

The President (or Parliament) is not bound by the views of the state legislature and may either accept or reject them, even if the views are received in time. Further, it is not necessary to make a fresh reference to the state legislature every time an amendment to the bill is moved and accepted in Parliament[4]. In case of a union territory, no reference need be made to the concerned legislature to ascertain its views and the Parliament can itself take any action as it deems fit.

It is thus clear that the Constitution authorises the Parliament to form new states or alter the areas, boundaries or names of the existing states without their consent. In other words, the Parliament can redraw the political map of India according to its will. Hence, the territorial integrity or continued existence of any state is not guaranteed by the Constitution. Therefore, India is rightly described as 'an indestructible union of destructible states'. The Union government can destroy the states whereas the state governments cannot destroy the Union. In USA, on the other hand, the territorial integrity or continued existence of a state is guaranteed by the Constitution. The American Federal government cannot form new states or alter the borders of existing states without the consent of the states concerned. That is why the USA is described as 'an indestructible union of indestructible states.'

Moreover, the Constitution (Article 4) itself declares that laws made for admission or establishment of new states (under Article 2) and formation of new states and alteration of areas, boundaries or names of existing states (under Articles 3) are not to be considered as amendments of the Constitution under Article 368. This means that such laws can be passed by a simple majority and by the ordinary legislative process.

Does the power of Parliament to diminish the areas of a state (under Article 3) include also the power to cede Indian territory to a foreign country? This question came up for examination before the Supreme Court in a reference made by the President in 1960. The decision of the Central government to cede part of a territory known as Berubari Union (West Bengal) to Pakistan led to political agitation and controversy and thereby necessitated the Presidential reference. The Supreme Court held that the power of Parliament to diminish the area of a state (under Article 3) does not cover cession of Indian territory to a foreign country. Hence, Indian territory can be ceded to a foreign state only by amending the Constitution under Article 368. Consequently, the 9th Constitutional Amendment Act (1960) was enacted to transfer the said territory to Pakistan.

On the other hand, the Supreme Court in 1969 ruled that, settlement of a boundary dispute between India and another country does not require a constitutional amendment. It can be done by executive action as it does not involve cession of Indian territory to a foreign country.

EVOLUTION OF STATES AND UNION TERRITORIES

Integration of Princely States

At the time of independence, India comprised two categories of political units, namely, the British provinces (under the direct rule of British government) and the princely states (under the rule of native princes but subject to the paramountcy of the British Crown). The Indian Independence Act (1947) created two independent and separate dominions of India and Pakistan and gave three options to the princely states viz., joining India, joining Pakistan or remaining independent. Of the 552 princely states situated within the geographical boundaries of India, 549 joined India and the remaining 3 (Hyderabad, Junagarh and Kashmir) refused to join India. However, in course of time, they were also integrated with India—Hyderabad by means of police action, Junagarh by means of referendum and Kashmir by the Instrument of Accession.

In 1950, the Constitution contained a four-fold classification of the states of the Indian Union—Part A, Part B, Part C and Part D State[5]. In all, they numbered 29. Part-A states comprised nine erstwhile governor's provinces of British India. Part-B states consisted of nine erstwhile princely states with legislatures. Part-C states consisted of erstwhile chief commissioner's provinces of British India and some of the erstwhile princely states. These Part-C states (in all 10 in number) were centrally administered. The Andaman and Nicobar Islands were kept as the solitary Part-D state.

Dhar Commission and JVP Committee

The integration of princely states with the rest of India has purely an ad hoc arrangement. There has been a demand from different regions, particularly South India, for reorganisation of states on linguistic basis. Accordingly, in June 1948, the Government of India appointed the Linguistic Provinces Commission under the chairmanship of S K Dhar to examine the feasibility of this. The commission submitted its report in December 1948 and recommended the reorganisation of states on the basis of administrative convenience rather than linguistic factor. This created much resentment and led to the appointment of another Linguistic Provinces Committee by the Congress in December 1948 itself to examine the whole question afresh. It consisted of Jawaharlal Nehru, Vallahbhai Patel and Pattabhi Sitaramayya and hence, was popularly known as JVP Committee[6]. It submitted its report in April 1949 and formally rejected language as the basis for reorganisation of states.

However, in October 1953, the Government of India was forced to create the first linguistic state, known as Andhra state, by separating the Telugu speaking areas from the Madras state. This followed a prolonged popular agitation and the death of Potti Sriramulu, a Congress person of standing, after a 56-day hunger strike for the cause.

Fazl Ali Commission

The creation of Andhra state intensified the demand from other regions for creation of states on linguistic basis. This forced the Government of India to appoint (in December 1953) a three-member States Reorganisation Commission under the chairmanship of Fazl Ali to re-examine the whole question. Its other two members were K M Panikkar and H N Kunzru. It submitted its report in September 1955 and broadly accepted language as the basis of reorganisation of states. But, it rejected the theory of 'one language–one state'. Its view was that the unity of India should be regarded as the primary consideration in any redrawing of the country's political units. It identified four major factors that can be taken into account in any scheme of reorganisation of states:

(a) Preservation and strengthening of the unity and security of the country.

(b) Linguistic and cultural homogeneity.

(c) Financial, economic and administrative considerations.

(d) Planning and promotion of the welfare of the people in each state as well as of the nation as a whole.

The commission suggested the abolition of the four-fold classification of states under the original Constitution and creation of 16 states and 3 centrally administered territories. The Government of India accepted these recommendations with certain minor modifications. By the States Reorganisation Act (1956) and the 7th Constitutional Amendment Act (1956), the distinction between Part-A and Part-B states was done away with and Part-C states were abolished. Some of them were merged with adjacent states and some other were designated as union territories. As a result, 14 states and 6 union territories were created on November 1, 1956.[7]

New States and Union Territories Created After 1956

Even after the large-scale reorganisation of the states in 1956, the political map of India underwent continuous change due to the pressure of popular agitations and political conditions. The demand for the creation of some more states on the basis of language or cultural homogeneity resulted in the bifurcation of existing states.

Maharashtra and Gujarat In 1960, the bilingual state of Bombay was divided[8] into two separate states—Maharashtra for Marathi-speaking people and Gujarat for Gujarati-speaking people. Gujarat was established as the 15th state of the Indian Union.

Dadra and Nagar Haveli The Portuguese ruled this territory until its liberation in 1954. Subsequently, the administration was carried on till 1961 by an administrator chosen by the people themselves. It was converted into a union territory of India by the 10th Constitutional Amendment Act, 1961.

Goa, Daman and Diu India acquired these three territories from the Portuguese by means of a police action in 1961. They were constituted as a union territory by the 12th Constitutional Amendment Act, 1962. Later, in 1987, Goa was conferred a state-

hood.[9] Consequently, Daman and Diu was made a separate union territory.

Puducherry The territory of Puducherry comprises the former French establishments in India known as Puducherry, Karaikal, Mahe and Yanam. The French handed over this territory to India in 1954. Subsequently, it was administered as an 'acquired territory', till 1962 when it was made a union territory by the 14th Constitutional Amendment Act.

Nagaland In 1963, the State of Nagaland was formed[10] by taking the Naga Hills and Tuensang area out of the state of Assam. This was done to satisfy the movement of the hostile Nagas. However, before giving Nagaland the status of the 16th state of the Indian Union, it was placed under the control of governor of Assam in 1961.

Haryana, Chandigarh and Himachal Pradesh In 1966, the State of Punjab was bifurcated[11] to create Haryana, the 17th state of the Indian Union, and the union territory of Chandigarh. This followed the demand for a separate 'Sikh Homeland' *(Punjabi Subha)* raised by the Akali Dal under the leadership of Master Tara Singh. On the recommendation of the Shah Commission (1966), the punjabi-speaking areas were constituted into the unilingual state of Punjab, the Hindi-speaking areas were constituted into the State of Haryana and the hill areas were merged with the adjoining union territory of Himachal Pradesh. In 1971, the union territory of Himachal Pradesh was elevated[12] to the status of a state (18th state of the Indian Union).

Manipur, Tripura and Meghalaya In 1972, the political map of Northeast India underwent a major change.[13] Thus, the two Union Territories of Manipur and Tripura and the Sub-State of Meghalaya got statehood and the two union territories of Mizoram and Arunachal Pradesh (originally known as North-East Frontier Agency—NEFA) came into being. With this, the number of states of the Indian Union increased to 21 (Manipur 19th, Tripura 20th and Meghalaya 21st). Initially, the 22nd Constitutional Amendment Act (1969) created Meghalaya as an 'autonomous state' or 'sub-state' within the state of Assam with its own legislature and council of ministers. However, this did not satisfy the aspirations of the people of Meghalaya. The union territories of

Mizoram and Arunachal Pradesh were also formed out of the territories of Assam.

Sikkim Till 1947, Sikkim was an Indian princely state ruled by Chogyal. In 1947, after the lapse of British paramountcy, Sikkim became a 'protectorate' of India, whereby the Indian Government assumed responsibility for the defence, external affairs and communications of Sikkim. In 1974, Sikkim expressed its desire for greater association with India. Accordingly, the 35th Constitutional Amendment Act (1974) was enacted by the parliament. This amendment introduced a new class of statehood under the constitution by conferring on Sikkim the status of an 'associate state' of the Indian Union. For this purpose, a new Article 2A and a new schedule (Tenth Schedule conseriving the terms and conditions of association) were inserted in the Constitution. This experiment, however, did not last long as it could not fully satisfy the aspirations of the people of Sikkim. In a referendum held in 1975, they voted for the abolition of the institution of Chogyal and Sikkim becoming an integral part of India. Consequently, the 36th Constitutional Amendment Act (1975) was enacted to make Sikkim a full-fledged state of the Indian Union (the 22nd state). This amendment amended the First and the Fourth Schedules to the Constitution and added a new Article 371-F to provide for certain special provisions with respect to the administration of Sikkim. It also repealed Article 2A and the Tenth Schedule that were added by the 35th Amendment Act of 1974.

Mizoram, Arunachal Pradesh and Goa In 1987, three new States of Mizoram,[14] Arunachal Pradesh [15] and Goa[16] came into being as the 23rd, 24th and 25th states of the Indian Union respectively. The Union Territory of Mizoram was conferred the status of a full state as a sequel to the signing of a memorandum of settlement (Mizoram Peace Accord) in 1986 between the Central government and the Mizo National Front, ending the two-decade-old insurgency. Arunachal Pradesh had also been a union territory from 1972. The State of Goa was created by separating the territory of Goa from the Union Territory of Goa, Daman and Diu.

Chhattisgarh, Uttarakhand and Jharkhand In 2000, three more new States of Chhattisgarh,[17] Uttarakhand[18] and Jharkhand[19] were created out of the territories of Madhya Pradesh, Uttar Pradesh and Bihar respectively. These became the 26th, 27th and 28th states of the Indian Union respectively. Thus, the number of states and union territories increased from 14 and 6 in 1956 to 28 and 7 in 2000 respectively.[20]

Change of Names The names of some states and union territories have also been changed. The United Provinces was the first state to have a new name. It was renamed 'Uttar Pradesh' in 1950. In 1969, Madras was renamed[21] 'Tamil Nadu'. Similarly, in 1973, Mysore was renamed[22] 'Karnataka'. In the same year, Laccadive, Minicoy and Amindivi Islands were renamed[23] 'Lakshadweep'. In 1992, the Union Territory of Delhi was redesignated as the National Capital Territory of Delhi (without being conferred the status of a full-fledged state) by the 69th Constitutional Amendment Act, 1991.[24] In 2006, Uttaranchal was renamed[25] as 'Uttarakhand'. In the same year, Pondicherry was renamed[26] as 'Puducherry'. In 2011, Orissa was renamed[27] as 'Odisha'.

Table 5.1 *Territory of India in 1950*

States in Part-A	States in Part-B	States in Part-C	States in Part-D
1. Assam	1. Hyderabad	1. Ajmer	1. Andaman and Nicobar Islands
2. Bihar	2. Jammu and Kashmir	2. Bhopal	
3. Bombay	3. Madhya Bharat	3. Bilaspur	
4. Madhya Pradesh	4. Mysore	4. Cooch-Behar	
5. Madras	5. Patiala and East Punjab	5. Coorg	
6. Odisha	6. Rajasthan	6. Delhi	
7. Punjab	7. Saurashtra	7. Himachal Pradesh	

(Contd.)

States in Part-A	States in Part-B	States in Part-C	States in Part-D
8. United Provinces	8. Travancore-Cochin	8. Kutch	
9. West Bengal	9. Vindhya Pradesh	9. Manipur	
		10. Tripura	

Table 5.2   *Territory of India in 1956*

States	Union Territories
1. Andra Pradesh	1. Andaman and Nicobar Islands
2. Assam	2. Delhi
3. Bihar	3. Himachal Pradesh
4. Bombay	4. Laccadive, Minicoy and Amindivi Islands
5. Jammu and Kashmir	5. Manipur
6. Kerala	6. Tripura
7. Madhya Pradesh	
8. Madras	
9. Mysore	
10. Odisha	
11. Punjab	
12. Rajasthan	
13. Uttar Pradesh	
14. West Bengal	

Table 5.3   *Territory of India in 2002*

States	Union Territories
1. Andhra Pradesh	1. Andaman and Nicobar Islands
2. Arunachal Pradesh	2. Chandigarh
3. Assam	3. Dadra and Nagar Haveli
4. Bihar	4. Daman and Diu
5. Chhattisgarh	5. Delhi (National Capital Territory)

States	Union Territories
6. Goa	6. Lakshadweep
7. Gujarat	7. Puducherry
8. Haryana	
9. Himachal Pradesh	
10. Jammu and Kashmir	
11. Jharkhand	
12. Karnataka	
13. Kerala	
14. Madhya Pradesh	
15. Maharashtra	
16. Manipur	
17. Meghalaya	
18. Mizoram	
19. Nagaland	
20. Odisha	
21. Punjab	
22. Rajasthan	
23. Sikkim	
24. Tamil Nadu	
25. Tripura	
26. Uttarakhand	
27. Uttar Pradesh	
28. West Bengal	

(Contd.)

Table 5.4 *Articles Related to Union and its Territory at a Glance*

Article No.	Subject-matter
1.	Name and territory of the Union
2.	Admission or establishment of new states
2A.	Sikkim to be associated with the Union—(Repealed)
3.	Formation of new states and alteration of areas, boundaries or names of existing states
4.	Laws made under Articles 2 and 3 to provide for the amendment of the First and the Fourth Schedules and supplemental, incidental and consequential matters.

NOTES AND REFERENCES

1. *Constituent Assembly Debates*, volume 7, P, 43.
2. The State of Jammu and Kashmir enjoys a special position by virtue of Article 370 of the Indian Constitution. It has its own separate State Constitution.
3. Added by the 18th Constitutional Amendment Act of 1966.
4. *Babulal* v. *State of Bombay* (1960).
5. See Table 5.1 at the end of this chapter.
6. It had no chairman or convenor.
7. See Table 5.2 at the end of this chapter.
8. By the Bombay Reorganisation Act, 1960.
9. By the Goa, Daman and Diu Reorganisation Act, 1987.
10. By the State of Nagaland Act, 1962, with effect from December 1, 1963.
11. By Punjab Reorganisation Act, 1966.
12. By the State of Himachal Pradesh Act, 1970, with effect from January 25, 1971.
13. By the North-Eastern Areas (Reorganisation) Act, 1971, with effect from January 21, 1972.
14. By the State of Mizoram Act, 1986, with effect from February 20, 1987.
15. By the State of Arunachal Pradesh Act, 1986, with effect from February 20, 1987.
16. By the Goa, Daman and Diu Reorganisation Act, 1987.
17. By the Madhya Pradesh Reorganisation Act, 2000.
18. By the Uttar Pradesh Reorganisation Act, 2000.
19. By the Bihar Reorganisation Act, 2000.
20. See Table 5.3 at the end of this chapter.
21. By the Madras State (Alteration of Name) Act, 1968, with effect from January 14, 1969.
22. By the Mysore State (Alteration of Name) Act, 1973.
23. By the Laccadive, Minicoy and Amindivi Islands (Alteration of Name) Act, 1973.
24. With effect from February 1, 1992.
25. By the Uttaranchal (Alteration of Name) Act, 2006.
26. By the Pondicherry (Alteration of Name) Act, 2006.
27. By the Orissa (Alteration of Name) Act, 2011.

Citizenship

MEANING AND SIGNIFICANCE

Like any other modern state, India has two kinds of people—citizens and aliens. Citizens are full members of the Indian State and owe allegiance to it. They enjoy all civil and political rights. Aliens, on the other hand, are the citizens of some other state and hence, do not enjoy all the civil and political rights. They are of two categories—friendly aliens or enemy aliens. Friendly aliens are the subjects of those countries that have cordial relations with India. Enemy aliens, on the other hand, are the subjects of that country that is at war with India. They enjoy lesser rights than the friendly aliens, eg, they do not enjoy protection against arrest and detention (Article 22).

The Constitution confers the following rights and privileges on the citizens of India (and denies the same to aliens):

1. Right against discrimination on grounds of religion, race, caste, sex or place of birth (Article 15).
2. Right to equality of opportunity in the matter of public employment (Article 16).
3. Right to freedom of speech and expression, assembly, association, movement, residence and profession (Article 19).
4. Cultural and educational rights (Articles 29 and 30).
5. Right to vote in elections to the Lok Sabha and state legislative assembly.
6. Right to contest for the membership of the Parliament and the state legislature.
7. Eligibility to hold certain public offices, that is, President of India, Vice-President of India, judges of the Supreme Court and the high courts, governor of states, attorney general of India and advocate general of states.

Along with the above rights, the citizens also owe certain duties towards the Indian State, as for example, paying taxes, respecting the national flag and national anthem, defending the country and so on.

In India both a citizen by birth as well as a naturalised citizen are eligible for the office of President while in USA, only a citizen by birth and not a naturalised citizen is eligible for the office of President.

CONSTITUTIONAL PROVISIONS

The Constitution deals with the citizenship from Articles 5 to 11 under Part II. However, it contains neither any permanent nor any elaborate provisions in this regard. It only identifies the persons who became citizens of India at its commencement (i.e., on January 26, 1950). It does not deal with the problem of acquisition or loss of citizenship subsequent to its commencement. It empowers the Parliament to enact a law to provide for such matters and any other matter relating to citizenship. Accordingly, the Parliament has enacted the Citizenship Act, 1955, which has been amended in 1986, 1992, 2003 and 2005.

According to the Constitution, the following four categories of persons became the citizens of India at its commencement i.e., on 26 January, 1950:

1. A person who had his domicile in India and also fulfilled any one of the three conditions, viz., if he was born in India; or if either of his parents was born in India; or if he has been ordinarily resident in India for five years immediately before the commencement of the Constitution, became a citizen of India (Article 5).

2. A person who migrated to India from Pakistan became an Indian citizen if he or either of his parents or any of his grandparents was born in undivided India and also fulfilled any one of the two conditions viz., in case he migrated to India before July 19, 1948[1], he had been ordinarily resident in India since the date of his migration; or in case he migrated to India on or after July 19, 1948, he had been registered as a citizen of India. But, a person could be so registered only if he had been resident in India for six months preceding the date of his application for registration (Article 6).

3. A person who migrated to Pakistan from India after March 1, 1947, but later returned to India for resettlement could become an Indian citizen. For this, he had to be resident in India for six months preceding the date of his application for registration[2] (Article 7).

4. A person who, or any of whose parents or grandparents, was born in undivided India but who is ordinarily residing outside India shall become an Indian citizen if he has been registered as a citizen of India by the diplomatic or consular representative of India in the country of his residence, whether before or after the commencement of the Constitution. Thus, this provision covers the overseas Indians who may want to acquire Indian citizenship (Article 8).

To sum up, these provisions deal with the citizenship of (a) persons domiciled in India; (b) persons migrated from Pakistan; (c) persons migrated to Pakistan but later returned; and (d) persons of Indian origin residing outside India.

The other constitutional provisions with respect to the citizenship are as follows:

1. No person shall be a citizen of India or be deemed to be a citizen of India, if he has voluntarily acquired the citizenship of any foreign state (Article 9).

2. Every person who is or is deemed to be a citizen of India shall continue to be such citizen, subject to the provisions of any law made by Parliament (Article 10).

3. Parliament shall have the power to make any provision with respect to the acquisition and termination of citizenship and all other matters relating to citizenship (Article 11).

CITIZENSHIP ACT, 1955

The Citizenship Act (1955) provides for acquisition and loss of citizenship after the commencement of the Constitution. This Act has been amended so far four times by the following Acts:

1. The Citizenship (Amendment) Act, 1986.
2. The Citizenship (Amendment) Act, 1992.
3. The Citizenship (Amendment) Act, 2003.
4. The Citizenship (Amendment) Act, 2005.

Originally, the Citizenship Act (1955) also provided for the Commonwealth Citizenship. But, this provision was repealed by the Citizenship (Amendment) Act, 2003.

Acquisition of Citizenship

The Citizenship Act of 1955 prescribes five ways of acquiring citizenship, viz, birth, descent, registration, naturalisation and incorporation of territory:

1. By Birth   A person born in India on or after 26th January 1950 but before 1st July 1987 is a citizen of India by birth irrespective of the nationality of his parents.

A person born in India on or after 1st July 1987 is considered as a citizen of India only if either of his parents is a citizen of India at the time of his birth.

Further, those born in India on or after 3rd December 2004 are considered citizens of India only if both of their parents are citizens of India or one of whose parents is a citizen of India and the other is not an illegal migrant at the time of their birth.

The children of foreign diplomats posted in India and enemy aliens cannot acquire Indian citizenship by birth.

2. By Descent A person born outside India on or after 26ᵗʰ January 1950 but before 10ᵗʰ December 1992 is a citizen of India by descent, if his father was a citizen of India at the time of his birth.

A person born outside India on or after 10ᵗʰ December 1992 is considered as a citizen of India if either of his parents is a citizen of India at the time of his birth.

From 3ʳᵈ December 2004 onwards, a person born outside India shall not be a citizen of India by descent, unless his birth is registered at an Indian consulate within one year of the date of birth or with the permission of the Central Government, after the expiry of the said period. An application, for registration of the birth of a minor child, to an Indian consulate shall be accompanied by an undertaking in writing from the parents of such minor child that he or she does not hold the passport of another country.

3. By Registration The Central Government may, on an application, register as a citizen of India any person (not being an illegal migrant) if he belongs to any of the following categories, namely:-

  (a) a person of Indian origin who is ordinarily resident in India for seven years before making an application for registration;

  (b) a person of Indian origin who is ordinarily resident in any country or place outside undivided India;

  (c) a person who is married to a citizen of India and is ordinarily resident in India for seven years before making an application for registration;

  (d) minor children of persons who are citizens of India;

  (e) a person of full age and capacity whose parents are registered as citizens of India;

  (f) a person of full age and capacity who, or either of his parents, was earlier citizen of independent India, and has been residing in India for one year immediately before making an application for registration;

  (g) a person of full age and capacity who has been registered as an overseas citizen of India for five years, and who has been residing in India for one year before making an application for registration.

An applicant shall be deemed to be ordinarily resident in India if –

  (i) he has resided in India throughout the period of twelve months immediately before making an application for registration; and

  (ii) he has resided in India during the eight years immediately preceding the said period of twelve months for a period of not less than six years.

A person shall be deemed to be of Indian origin if he, or either of his parents, was born in undivided India or in such other territory which became part of India after the 15ᵗʰ August, 1947.

All the above categories of persons must take an oath of allegiance before they are registered as citizens of India. The form of the oath is as follows:

I, A/B.................... do solemnly affirm (or swear) that I will bear true faith and allegiance to the Constitution of India as by law established, and that I will faithfully observe the laws of India and fulfill my duties as a citizen of India.

4. By Naturalisation The Central Government may, on an application, grant a certificate of naturalisation to any person (not being an illegal migrant) if he possesses the following qualifications:

  (a) that he is not a subject or citizen of any country where citizens of India are prevented from becoming subjects or citizens of that country by naturalisation;

  (b) that, if he is a citizen of any country, he undertakes to renounce the citizenship of that country in the event of his application for Indian citizenship being accepted;

  (c) that he has either resided in India or been in the service of a Government in India or partly the one and partly the other, throughout the period of twelve months immediately preceding the date of the application;

  (d) that during the fourteen years immediately preceding the said period of twelve months, he has either resided in India or been in the service of a Government in India, or partly the one and partly the other, for periods amounting in the aggregate to not less than eleven years;

  (e) that he is of good character;

  (f) that he has an adequate knowledge of a language specified in the Eighth Schedule to the Constitution[3], and

(g) that in the event of a certificate of naturalisation being granted to him, he intends to reside in India, or to enter into or continue in, service under a Government in India or under an international organisation of which India is a member or under a society, company or body of persons established in India.

However, the Government of India may waive all or any of the above conditions for naturalisation in the case of a person who has rendered distinguished service to the science, philosophy, art, literature, world peace or human progress. Every naturalised citizen must take an oath of allegiance to the Constitution of India.

5. By Incorporation of Territory If any foreign territory becomes a part of India, the Government of India specifies the persons who among the people of the territory shall be the citizens of India. Such persons become the citizens of India from the notified date. For example, when Pondicherry became a part of India, the Government of India issued the Citizenship (Pondicherry) Order, 1962, under the Citizenship Act, 1955.

Loss of Citizenship

The Citizenship Act, 1955, prescribes three ways of losing citizenship whether acquired under the Act or prior to it under the Constitution, viz, renunciation, termination and deprivation:

1. By Renunciation Any citizen of India of full age and capacity can make a declaration renouncing his Indian citizenship. Upon the registration of that declaration, that person ceases to be a citizen of India. However, if such a declaration is made during a war in which India is engaged, its registration shall be withheld by the Central Government.

Further, when a person renounces his Indian citizenship, every minor child of that person also loses Indian citizenship. However, when such a child attains the age of eighteen, he may resume Indian citizenship.

2. By Termination When an Indian citizen voluntarily (consciously, knowingly and without duress, undue influence or compulsion) acquires the citizenship of another country, his Indian citizenship automatically terminates. This provision, however, does not apply during a war in which India is engaged.

3. By Deprivation It is a compulsory termination of Indian citizenship by the Central government, if:
  (a) the citizen has obtained the citizenship by fraud:
  (b) the citizen has shown disloyalty to the Constitution of India:
  (c) the citizen has unlawfully traded or communicated with the enemy during a war;
  (d) the citizen has, within five years after registration or naturalisation, been imprisoned in any country for two years; and
  (e) the citizen has been ordinarily resident out of India for seven years continuously.[4]

SINGLE CITIZENSHIP

Though the Indian Constitution is federal and envisages a dual polity (Centre and states), it provides for only a single citizenship, that is, the Indian citizenship. The citizens in India owe allegiance only to the Union. There is no separate state citizenship. The other federal states like USA and Switzerland, on the other hand, adopted the system of double citizenship.

In USA, each person is not only a citizen of USA but also of the particular state to which he belongs. Thus, he owes allegiance to both and enjoys dual sets of rights—one set conferred by the national government and another by the state government. This system creates the problem of discrimination, that is, a state may discriminate in favour of its citizens in matters like right to vote, right to hold public offices, right to practice professions and so on. This problem is avoided in the system of single citizenship prevalent in India.

In India, all citizens irrespective of the state in which they are born or reside enjoy the same political and civil rights of citizenship all over the country and no discrimination is made between them. However, this general rule of absence of discrimination is subject to some exceptions, viz,
  1. The Parliament (under Article 16) can prescribe residence within a state or union territory as a condition for certain employments or appointments in that state or union territory, or local authority or other authority within that state or union territory. Accordingly, the Parliament enacted the Public Employment

(Requirement as to Residence) Act, 1957 and thereby authorised the Government of India to prescribe residential qualification only for appointment to non-Gazetted posts in Andhra Pradesh, Himachal Pradesh, Manipur and Tripura. As this Act expired in 1974, there is no such provision for any state except Andhra Pradesh.[5]

2. The Constitution (under Article 15) prohibits discrimination against any citizen on grounds of religion, race, caste, sex or place of birth and not on the ground of residence. This means that the state can provide special benefits or give preference to its residents in matters that do not come within the purview of the rights given by the Constitution to the Indian citizens. For example, a state may offer concession in fees for education to its residents.

3. The freedom of movement and residence (under Article 19) is subjected to the protection of interests of any schedule tribe. In other words, the right of outsiders to enter, reside and settle in tribal areas is restricted. Of course, this is done to protect the distinctive culture, language, customs and manners of schedule tribes and to safeguard their traditional vocation and property against exploitation.

4. In the case of Jammu and Kashmir, the state legislature is empowered to define the persons who are permanent residents of the state and confer any special rights and privileges in matters of employment under the state government, acquisition of immovable property in the state, settlement in the state and scholarships and such other forms of aid provided by the state government.[6]

The Constitution of India, like that of Canada, has introduced the system of single citizenship and provided uniform rights (except in few cases) for the people of India to promote the feeling of fraternity and unity among them and to build an integrated Indian nation. Despite this, India has been witnessing the communal riots, class conflicts, caste wars, linguistic clashes and ethnic disputes. Thus, the cherished goal of the founding fathers and the Constitution-makers to build an united and integrated Indian nation has not been fully realised.

Table 6.1 *Comparing the PIO Card Holder and OCI*

	Elements of Comparison	Person of Indian Origin (PIO) Card Holder	Overseas Citizen of India (OCI)
1.	Who?	A person registered as PIO card holder under the Ministry of Home Affairs' scheme dated 19-08-2002.	A person registered as Overseas Citizen of India (OCI) under the Citizenship Act, 1955. The OCI scheme is operational from 02-12-2005.
2.	Who is eligible?	Any person (i) who at any time held an Indian passport; or (ii) he or either of his parents or grand parents or great grand parents was born in and was permanently resident in India as defined in the Government of India Act, 1935 and other territories that became part of India thereafter provided neither was at any time a citizen of Afghanistan, Bangladesh, Bhutan, China, Nepal, Pakistan and Sri Lanka; or (iii) he is a spouse of a citizen of India or a person of Indian origin as mentioned above.	A foreign national who (i) was eligible to become a citizen of India on 26-01-1950; or (ii) was a citizen of India on or at any time after 26-01-1950; or (iii) belonged to a territory that became part of India after 15-08-1947; or (iv) his/her children and grand children; or (v) minor children of such person. However, if the applicant had ever been a citizen of Pakistan or Bangladesh, he/she will not be eligible for OCI.

(Contd.)

	Elements of Comparison	Person of Indian Origin (PIO) Card Holder	Overseas Citizen of India (OCI)
3.	What is the Fees?	Rs.15000/- or equivalent in local currency for adults. For the children upto the age of 18 years, the fee is Rs.7500/- or equivalent in local currency.	US $ 275 or equivalent in local currency. In case of PIO card holders, it is US $ 25 or equivalent in local currency.
4.	Which nationals are eligible?	PIOs of all countries except Afghanistan, Bangladesh, Bhutan, China, Nepal, Pakistan and Sri Lanka.	PIOs of all countries except Pakistan and Bangladesh.
5.	What benefits one is entitled to?	(1) Shall not require a separate visa to visit India. (2) Will be exempt from the requirements of registration if his/her stay on any single visit in India does not exceed 180 days. In the event of continuous stay in India exceeding 180 days, he/she shall have to get himself/ herself registered within 30 days of the expiry of 180 days with the concerned FRRO/FRO. (3) Parity with NRIs in respect of all facilities available to the latter in the economic, financial and educational fields except in matters relating to the acquisition of agricultural / plantation properties. No parity shall be allowed in the sphere of political rights.	(1) A multiple entry, multi-purpose life long visa for visiting India. (2) Exemption from registration with local police authority for any length of stay in India. (3) Parity with NRIs in respect of economic, financial and educational fields except in relation to the acquisition of agricultural or plantation properties. No parity shall be allowed in the sphere of political rights.
6.	Does he/she require visa for visiting India?	Can visit India without visa for 15 years from the date of issue of PIO card.	Can visit India without visa for life long.
7.	Is he required to register with local police authorities in India?	Yes – one time when the stay in India exceeds 180 days for the first time.	No
8.	What activities can be under taken in India?	All activities except mountaineering, missionary, research work and visiting protected / restricted areas which require specific permit.	All activities except mountaineering, missionary, research work and visiting protected / restricted areas which require specific permit.
9.	How can one acquire Indian citizenship?	He/she has to reside in India for minimum 7 years before making application for granting Indian citizenship.	He/she may be granted Indian citizenship after 5 years from date of registration provided he/she stays for one year in India before making application.
10.	Can it be cancelled?	Yes – on certain grounds	Yes – on certain grounds

Note 1: The provision for Commonwealth Citizenship was omitted by the Citizenship (Amendment) Act, 2003.

Note 2: In 2011, the Government of India announced its decision to merge the PIO card and OCI card schemes into a single scheme. This new scheme is proposed to be called as the Overseas Indian Card Holders Scheme. In this regard, the Citizenship (Amendment) Bill, 2011, is under consideration of the Parliament.

Table 6.2 *Articles Related to Citizenship at a Glance*

Article No.	Subject-matter
5.	Citizenship at the commencement of the Constitution
6.	Rights of citizenship of certain persons who have migrated to India from Pakistan
7.	Rights of citizenship of certain migrants to Pakistan
8.	Rights of citizenship of certain persons of Indian origin residing outside India
9.	Persons voluntarily acquiring citizenship of a foreign State not to be citizens
10.	Continuance of the rights of citizenship
11.	Parliament to regulate the right of citizenship by law

NOTES AND REFERENCES

1. On this date, the permit system for such migration was introduced.
2. This provision refers to migration after 1 March, 1947 but before 26 January, 1950. The question of citizenship of persons who migrated after 26 January, 1950, has to be decided under the provisions of the Citizenship Act, 1955.
3. The 8th Schedule of the Constitution recognises presently 22 (originally 14) languages.
4. This will not apply if he is a student abroad, or is in the service of a government in India or an international organisation of which India is a member, or has registered annually at an Indian consulate his intention to retain his Indian citizenship.
5. By virtue of Article 371-D inserted by the 32nd Constitutional Amendment Act, 1973.
6. Article 35-A in the Constitution (Application to Jammu and Kashmir) Order, 1954. This was issued by the President of India under powers conferred on him by Article 370 of the Constitution.

Fundamental Rights

The Fundamental Rights are enshrined in Part III of the Constitution from Articles 12 to 35. In this regard, the framers of the Constitution derived inspiration from the Constitution of USA (i.e., Bill of Rights).

Part III of the Constitution is rightly described as the *Magna Carta* of India.[1] It contains a very long and comprehensive list of 'justiciable' Fundamental Rights. In fact, the Fundamental Rights in our Constitution are more elaborate than those found in the Constitution of any other country in the world, including the USA.

The Fundamental Rights are guaranteed by the Constitution to all persons without any discrimination. They uphold the equality of all individuals, the dignity of the individual, the larger public interest and unity of the nation.

The Fundamental Rights are meant for promoting the ideal of political democracy. They prevent the establishment of an authoritarian and despotic rule in the country, and protect the liberties and freedoms of the people against the invasion by the State. They operate as limitations on the tyranny of the executive and arbitrary laws of the legislature. In short, they aim at establishing 'a government of laws and not of men'.

The Fundamental Rights are named so because they are guaranteed and protected by the Constitution, which is the fundamental law of the land. They are 'fundamental' also in the sense that they are most essential for the all-round development (material, intellectual, moral and spiritual) of the individuals.

Originally, the Constitution provided for seven Fundamental Rights viz,

1. Right to equality (Articles 14–18)
2. Right to freedom (Articles 19–22)
3. Right against exploitation (Articles 23–24)
4. Right to freedom of religion (Articles 25–28)
5. Cultural and educational rights (Articles 29–30)
6. Right to property (Article 31)
7. Right to constitutional remedies (Article 32)

However, the right to property was deleted from the list of Fundamental Rights by the 44th Amendment Act, 1978. It is made a legal right under Article 300-A in Part XII of the Constitution. So at present, there are only six Fundamental Rights.

FEATURES OF FUNDAMENTAL RIGHTS

The Fundamental Rights guaranteed by the Constitution are characterised by the following:

1. Some of them are available only to the citizens while others are available to all persons whether citizens, foreigners or legal persons like corporations or companies.
2. They are not absolute but qualified. The state can impose reasonable restrictions on them. However, whether such restrictions are reasonable or not is to be decided by the courts. Thus, they strike a balance between the rights of the individual and those of the society as a whole, between individual liberty and social control.

3. Most of them are available against the arbitrary action of the State, with a few exceptions like those against the State's action and against the action of private individuals. When the rights that are available against the State's action only are violated by the private individuals, there are no constitutional remedies but only ordinary legal remedies.

4. Some of them are negative in character, that is, place limitations on the authority of the State, while others are positive in nature, conferring certain privileges on the persons.

5. They are justiciable, allowing persons to move the courts for their enforcement, if and when they are violated.

6. They are defended and guaranteed by the Supreme Court. Hence, the aggrieved person can directly go to the Supreme Court, not necessarily by way of appeal against the judgement of the high courts.

7. They are not sacrosanct or permanent. The Parliament can curtail or repeal them but only by a constitutional amendment act and not by an ordinary act. Moreover, this can be done without affecting the 'basic structure' of the Constitution. (The amendability of fundamental rights is explained in detail in Chapter 11).

8. They can be suspended during the operation of a National Emergency except the rights guaranteed by Articles 20 and 21. Further, the six rights guaranteed by Article 19 can be suspended only when emergency is declared on the grounds of war or external aggression (i.e., external emergency) and not on the ground of armed rebellion (i.e., internal emergency). (The suspension of fundamental rights during a national Emergency is explained in detail in Chapter 16).

9. Their scope of operation is limited by Article 31A (saving of laws providing for acquisition of estates, etc.), Article 31B (validation of certain acts and regulations included in the 9th Schedule) and Article 31C (saving of laws giving effect to certain directive principles).

10. Their application to the members of armed forces, para-military forces, police forces, intelligence agencies and analogous services can be restricted or abrogated by the Parliament (Article 33).

11. Their application can be restricted while martial law is in force in any area. Martial law means 'military rule' imposed under abnormal circumstances to restore order (Article 34). It is different from the imposition of national emergency.

12. Most of them are directly enforceable (self-executory) while a few of them can be enforced on the basis of a law made for giving effect to them. Such a law can be made only by the Parliament and not by state legislatures so that uniformity throughout the country is maintained (Article 35).

DEFINITION OF STATE

The term 'State' has been used in different provisions concerning the fundamental rights. Hence, Article 12 has defined the term for the purposes of Part III. According to it, the State includes the following:

(a) Government and Parliament of India, that is, executive and legislative organs of the Union government.

(b) Government and legislature of states, that is, executive and legislative organs of state government.

(c) All local authorities, that is, municipalities, panchayats, district boards, improvement trusts, etc.

(d) All other authorities, that is, statutory or non-statutory authorities like LIC, ONGC, SAIL, etc.

Thus, State has been defined in a wider sense so as to include all its agencies. It is the actions of these agencies that can be challenged in the courts as violating the Fundamental Rights.

According to the Supreme Court, even a private body or an agency working as an instrument of the State falls within the meaning of the 'State' under Article 12.

LAWS INCONSISTENT WITH FUNDAMENTAL RIGHTS

Article 13 declares that all laws that are inconsistent with or in derogation of any of the fundamental rights shall be void. In other words, it expressively provides for the doctrine of judicial review. This power has been conferred on the Supreme Court (Article 32) and the high courts (Article 226) that can declare a law unconstitutional and invalid on the ground of contravention of any of the Fundamental Rights.

The term 'law' in Article 13 has been given a wide connotation so as to include the following:

(a) Permanent laws enacted by the Parliament or the state legislatures;

(b) Temporary laws like ordinances issued by the president or the state governors;

(c) Statutory instruments in the nature of delegated legislation (executive legislation) like order, bye-law, rule, regulation or notification; and

(d) Non-legislative sources of law, that is, custom or usage having the force of law.

Thus, not only a legislation but any of the above can be challenged in the courts as violating a Fundamental Right and hence, can be declared as void.

Further, Article 13 declares that a constitutional amendment is not a law and hence cannot be challenged. However, the Supreme Court held in the *Kesavananda Bharati* case[2] (1973) that a Constitutional amendment can be challenged on the ground that it violates a fundamental right that forms a part of the 'basic structure' of the Constitution and hence, can be declared as void.

Table 7.1 *Fundamental Rights at a Glance*

Category	*Consists of*
1. Right to equality (Articles 14–18)	(a) Equality before law and equal protection of laws (Article 14). (b) Prohibition of discrimination on grounds of religion, race, caste, sex or place of birth (Article 15). (c) Equality of opportunity in matters of public employment (Article 16). (d) Abolition of untouchability and prohibition of its practice (Article 17). (e) Abolition of titles except military and academic (Article 18).
2. Right to freedom (Articles 19–22)	(a) Protection of six rights regarding freedom of: (i) speech and expression, (ii) assembly, (iii) association, (iv) movement, (v) residence, and (vi) profession (Article 19). (b) Protection in respect of conviction for offences (Article 20). (c) Protection of life and personal liberty (Article 21). (d) Right to elementary education (Article 21A). (e) Protection against arrest and detention in certain cases (Article 22).
3. Right against exploitation (Articles 23–24)	(a) Prohibition of traffic in human beings and forced labour (Article 23). (b) Prohibition of employment of children in factories, etc. (Article 24).
4. Right to freedom of religion (Article 25–28)	(a) Freedom of conscience and free profession, practice and propagation of religion (Article 25). (b) Freedom to manage religious affairs (Article 26). (c) Freedom from payment of taxes for promotion of any religion (Article 27). (d) Freedom from attending religious instruction or worship in certain educational institutions (Article 28).
5. Cultural and educational rights (Articles 29–30)	(a) Protection of language, script and culture of minorities (Article 29). (b) Right of minorities to establish and administer educational institutions (Article 30).
6. Right to constitutional remedies (Article 32)	Right to move the Supreme Court for the enforcement of fundamental rights including the writs of (i) *habeas corpus,* (ii) *mandamus,* (iii) prohibition, (iv) *certiorari,* and (v) *quo war-rento* (Article 32).

Table 7.2 *Fundamental Rights (FR) of Foreigners*

FR available only to citizens and not to foreigners	FR available to both citizens and foreigners (except enemy aliens)
1. Prohibition of discrimination on grounds of religion, race, caste, sex or place of birth (Article 15).	1. Equality before law and equal protection of laws (Article 14).
2. Equality of opportunity in matters of public employment (Article 16).	2. Protection in respect of conviction for offences (Article 20).
3. Protection of six rights regarding freedom of : (i) speech and expression, (ii) assembly, (iii) association, (iv) movement, (v) residence, and (vi) profession (Article 19).	3. Protection of life and personal liberty (Article 21).
4. Protection of language, script and culture of minorities (Article 29).	4. Right to elementary education (Article 21A).
5. Right of minorities to establish and administer educational institutions (Article 30).	5. Protection against arrest and detention in certain cases (Article 22).
	6. Prohibition of traffic in human beings and forced labour (Article 23).
	7. Prohibition of employment of children in factories etc., (Article 24).
	8. Freedom of conscience and free profession, practice and propagation of religion (Article 25).
	9. Freedom to manage religious affairs (Article 26).
	10. Freedom from payment of taxes for promotion of any religion (Article 27).
	11. Freedom from attending religious instruction or worship in certain educational institutions (Article 28).

RIGHT TO EQUALITY

1. Equality before Law and Equal Protection of Laws

Article 14 says that the State shall not deny to any person equality before the law or the equal protection of the laws within the territory of India. This provision confers rights on all persons whether citizens or foreigners. Moreover, the word 'person' includes legal persons, viz, statutory corporations, companies, registered societies or any other type of legal person.

The concept of 'equality before law' is of British origin while the concept of 'equal protection of laws' has been taken from the American Constitution. The first concept connotes: **(a)** the absence of any special privileges in favour of any person, **(b)** the equal subjection of all persons to the ordinary law of the land administered by ordinary law courts, and **(c)** no person (whether rich or poor, high or low, official or non-official) is above the law.

The second concept, on the other hand, connotes: **(a)** the equality of treatment under equal circumstances, both in the privileges conferred and liabilities imposed by the laws, **(b)** the similar application of the same laws to all persons who are similarly situated, and **(c)** the like should be treated alike without any discrimination. Thus, the former is a negative concept while the latter is a positive concept. However, both of them aim at establishing equality of legal status, opportunity and justice.

The Supreme Court held that where equals and unequals are treated differently, Article 14 does not apply. While Article 14 forbids class legislation, it permits reasonable classification of persons, objects and transactions by the law. But the classification should not be arbitrary, artificial or evasive. Rather, it should be based on an intelligible differential and substantial distinction.

Rule of Law The concept of 'equality before law' is an element of the concept of 'Rule of Law', propounded by A.V. Dicey, the British jurist. His concept has the following three elements or aspects:

(i) Absence of arbitrary power, that is, no man can be punished except for a breach of law.

(ii) Equality before the law, that is, equal subjection of all citizens (rich or poor, high or low, official or non-official) to the ordinary law of the land administered by the ordinary law courts[3].

(iii) The primacy of the rights of the individual, that is, the constitution is the result of the rights of the individual as defined and enforced by the courts of law rather than the constitution being the source of the individual rights.

The first and the second elements are applicable to the Indian System and not the third one. In the Indian System, the constitution is the source of the individual rights.

The Supreme Court held that the 'Rule of Law' as embodied in Article 14 is a 'basic feature' of the constitution. Hence, it cannot be destroyed even by an amendment.

Exceptions to Equality The rule of equality before law is not absolute and there are constitutional and other exceptions to it. These are mentioned below:

1. The President of India and the Governor of States enjoy the following immunities (Article 361):

   (i) The President or the Governor is not answerable to any court for the exercise and performance of the powers and duties of his office.

   (ii) No criminal proceedings shall be instituted or continued against the President or the Governor in any court during his term of office.

   (iii) No process for the arrest or imprisonment of the President or the Governor shall be issued from any court during his term of office.

   (iv) No civil proceedings against the President or the Governor shall be instituted during

his term of office in any court in respect of any act done by him in his personal capacity, whether before or after he entered upon his office, until the expiration of two months next after notice has been delivered to him.

2. No person shall be liable to any civil or criminal proceedings in any court in respect of the publication in a newspaper (or by radio or television) of a substantially true report of any proceedings of either House of Parliament or either House of the Legislature of a State (Article 361-A).

3. No member of Parliament shall be liable to any proceedings in any court in respect of anything said or any vote given by him in Parliament or any committee thereof (Article 105).

4. No member of the Legislature of a state shall be liable to any proceedings in any court in respect of anything said or any vote given by him in the Legislature or any committee thereof (Article 194).

5. Article 31-C is an exception to Article 14. It provides that the laws made by the state for implementing the Directive Principles contained in clause (b) or clause (c) of Article 39 cannot be challenged on the ground that they are violative of Article 14. The Supreme Court held that "where Article 31-C comes in, Article 14 goes out".

6. The foreign sovereigns (rulers), ambassadors and diplomats enjoy immunity from criminal and civil proceedings.

7. The UNO and its agencies enjoy the diplomatic immunity.

2. Prohibition of Discrimination on Certain Grounds

Article 15 provides that the State shall not discriminate against any citizen on grounds only of religion, race, caste, sex or place of birth. The two crucial words in this provision are 'discrimination' and 'only'. The word 'discrimination' means 'to make an adverse distinction with regard to' or 'to distinguish unfavourably from others'. The use of the word 'only' connotes that discrimination on other grounds is not prohibited.

The second provision of Article 15 says that no citizen shall be subjected to any disability, liability, restriction or condition on grounds only of religion, race, caste, sex, or place of birth with regard to (a) access to shops, public restaurants, hotels and places of public entertainment; or (b) the use of wells, tanks, bathing ghats, road and places of public resort maintained wholly or partly by State funds or dedicated to the use of general public. This provision prohibits discrimination both by the State and private individuals, while the former provision prohibits discrimination only by the State.

There are three exceptions to this general rule of non-discrimination:

(a) The state is permitted to make any special provision for women and children. For example, reservation of seats for women in local bodies or provision of free education for children.

(b) The state is permitted to make any special provision for the advancement of any socially and educationally backward classes of citizens or for the scheduled castes and scheduled tribes[4]. For example, reservation of seats or fee concessions in public educational institutions.

(c) The state is empowered to make any special provision for the advancement of any socially and educationally backward classes of citizens or for the scheduled castes or the scheduled tribes regarding their admission to educational institutions including private educational institutions, whether aided or unaided by the state, except the minority educational institutions.

The last provision was added by the 93rd Amendment Act of 2005. In order to give effect to this provision, the Centre enacted the Central Educational Institutions (Reservation in Admission) Act, 2006, providing a quota of 27% for candidates belonging to the Other Backward Classes (OBCs) in all central higher educational institutions including the Indian Institutes of Technology (IITs) and the Indian Institutes of Management (IIMs). In April 2008, the Supreme Court upheld the validity of both, the Amendment Act and the OBC Quota Act. But, the Court directed the central government to exclude the 'creamy layer' (advanced sections) among the OBCs while implementing the law.

Creamy Layer   The children of the following different categories of people belong to 'creamy layer' among OBCs and thus will not get the quota benefit :

1. Persons holding constitutional posts like President, Vice-President, Judges of SC and HCs, Chairman and Members of UPSC and SPSCs, CEC, CAG and so on.

2. Group 'A' / Class I and Group 'B' / Class II Officers of the All India, Central and State Services; and Employees holding equivalent posts in PSUs, Banks, Insurance Organisations, Universities etc., and also in private employment.

3. Persons who are in the rank of colonel and above in the Army and equivalent posts in the Navy, the Air Force and the Paramilitary Forces.

4. Professionals like doctors, lawyers, engineers, artists, authors, consultants and so on.

5. Persons engaged in trade, business and industry.

6. People holding agricultural land above a certain limit and vacant land or buildings in urban areas.

7. Persons having gross annual income of more than ₹4.5 lakhs or possessing wealth above the exemption limit. In 1993, when the "creamy layer" ceiling was introduced, it was ₹1 lakh. It was subsequently revised to ₹2.5 lakh in 2004 and ₹4.5 lakh in 2008. Presently (2013), the proposal to raise creamy layer ceiling to ₹6 lakh a year is under consideration of the government.

3. Equality of Opportunity in Public Employment

Article 16 provides for equality of opportunity for all citizens in matters of employment or appointment to any office under the State. No citizen can be discriminated against or be ineligible for any employment or office under the State on grounds of only religion, race, caste, sex, descent, place of birth or residence.

There are three exceptions to this general rule of equality of opportunity in public employment:

(a) Parliament can prescribe residence as a condition for certain employment or appointment in a state or union territory or local authority or other authority. As the Public Employment (Requirement as to Residence) Act of 1957 expired in 1974, there is no such provision for any state except Andhra Pradesh.[5]

(b) The State can provide for reservation of appointments or posts in favour of any backward class that is not adequately represented in the state services.

(c) A law can provide that the incumbent of an office related to religious or denominational institution or a member of its governing body should belong to the particular religion or denomination.

Mandal Commission and Aftermath In 1979, the Morarji Desai Government appointed the Second[6] Backward Classes Commission under the chairmanship of B P Mandal, a Member of Parliament, in terms of Article 340 of the Constitution to investigate the conditions of the socially and educationally backward classes and suggest measures for their advancement. The commission submitted its report in 1980 and identified as many as 3743 castes as socially and educationally backward classes. They constitute nearly 52% component of the population, excluding the scheduled castes (SCs) and the scheduled tribes (STs). The commission recommended for reservation of 27% government jobs for the Other Backward Classes (OBCs) so that the total reservation for all ((SCs, STs and OBCs) amounts to 50%.[7] It was after ten years in 1990 that the V P Singh Government declared reservation of 27% government jobs for the OBCs. Again in 1991, the Narasimha Rao Government introduced two changes: **(a)** preference to the poorer sections among the OBCs in the 27% quota, i.e., adoption of the economic criteria in granting reservation, and **(b)** reservation of another 10% of jobs for poorer (economically backward) sections of higher castes who are not covered by any existing schemes of reservation.

In the famous *Mandal* case[8] (1992), the scope and extent of Article 16(4), which provides for reservation of jobs in favour of backward classes, has been examined thoroughly by the Supreme Court. Though the Court has rejected the additional reservation of 10% for poorer sections of higher castes, it upheld the constitutional validity of 27% reservation for the OBCs with certain conditions, viz,

(a) The advanced sections among the OBCs (the creamy layer) should be excluded from the list of beneficiaries of reservation.

(b) No reservation in promotions; reservation should be confined to initial appointments only. Any

existing reservation in promotions can continue for five years only (i.e., upto 1997).

(c) The total reserved quota should not exceed 50% except in some extraordinary situations. This rule should be applied every year.

(d) The 'carry forward rule' in case of unfilled (backlog) vacancies is valid. But it should not violate 50% rule.

(e) A permanent statutory body should be established to examine complaints of over-inclusion and under-inclusion in the list of OBCs.

With regard to the above rulings of the Supreme Court, the government has taken the following actions:

(a) Ram Nandan Committee was appointed to identify the creamy layer among the OBCs. It submitted its report in 1993, which was accepted.

(b) National Commission for Backward Classes was established in 1993 by an act of Parliament. It considers inclusions in and exclusions from the lists of castes notified as backward for the purpose of job reservation.

(c) In order to nullify the ruling with regard to reservation in promotions, the 77th Amendment Act was enacted in 1995. It added a new provision in Article 16 that empowers the State to provide for reservation in promotions of any services under the State in favour of the SCs and STs that are not adequately represented in the state services. Again, the 85th Amendment Act of 2001 provides for 'consequential seniority' in the case of promotion by virtue of rule of reservation for the government servants belonging to the SCs and STs with retrospective effect from June 1995.

(d) The ruling with regard to backlog vacancies was nullified by the 81st Amendment Act of 2000. It added another new provision in Article 16 that empowers the State to consider the unfilled reserved vacancies of a year as a separate class of vaccancies to be filled up in any succeeding year or years. Such class of vacancies are not to be combined with the vacancies of the year in which they are being filled up to determine the ceiling of 50% reservation on total number of vacancies of that year. In brief, it ends the 50% ceiling on reservation in backlog vacancies.

(e) The 76th Amendment Act of 1994 has placed the Tamil Nadu Reservations Act[9] of 1994 in the Ninth Schedule to protect it from judicial review as it provided for 69 per cent of reservation, far exceeding the 50 per cent ceiling.

4. Abolition of Untouchability

Article 17 abolishes 'untouchability' and forbids its practice in any form. The enforcement of any disability arising out of untouchability shall be an offence punishable in accordance with law.

In 1976, the Untouchability (Offences) Act, 1955 has been comprehensively amended and renamed as the Protection of Civil Rights Act, 1955 to enlarge the scope and make penal provisions more stringent. The act defines civil right as any right accruing to a person by reason of the abolition of untouchability by Article 17 of the Constitution.

The term 'untouchability' has not been defined either in the Constitution or in the Act. However, the Mysore High Court held that the subject matter of Article 17 is not untouchability in its literal or grammatical sense but the 'practice as it had developed historically in the country'. It refers to the social disabilities imposed on certain classes of persons by reason of their birth in certain castes. Hence, it does not cover social boycott of a few individuals or their exclusion from religious services, etc.

Under the Protection of Civil Rights Act (1955), the offences committed on the ground of untouchability are punishable either by imprisonment up to six months or by fine upto ₹500 or both. A person convicted of the offence of 'untouchability' is disqualified for election to the Parliament or state legislature. The act declares the following acts as offences:

(a) preventing any person from entering any place of public worship or from worshipping therein;

(b) justifying untouchability on traditional, religious, philosophical or other grounds;

(c) denying access to any shop, hotel or places of public entertainment;

(d) insulting a person belonging to scheduled caste on the ground of untouchability;

(e) refusing to admit persons in hospitals, educational institutions or hostels established for public benefit;

(f) preaching untouchability directly or indirectly; and

(g) refusing to sell goods or render services to any person.

The Supreme Court held that the right under Article 17 is available against private individuals and it is the constitutional obligation of the State to take necessary action to ensure that this right is not violated.

5. Abolition of Titles

Article 18 abolishes titles and makes four provisions in that regard:

(a) It prohibits the state from conferring any title (except a military or academic distinction) on any body, whether a citizen or a foreigner.

(b) It prohibits a citizen of India from accepting any title from any foreign state.

(c) A foreigner holding any office of profit or trust under the state cannot accept any title from any foreign state without the consent of the president.

(d) No citizen or foreigner holding any office of profit or trust under the State is to accept any present, emolument or office from or under any foreign State without the consent of the president.

From the above, it is clear that the hereditary titles of nobility like Maharaja, Raj Bahadur, Rai Bahadur, Rai Saheb, Dewan Bahadur, etc, which were conferred by colonial States are banned by Article 18 as these are against the principle of equal status of all.

In 1996[10], the Supreme Court upheld the constitutional validity of the National Awards—Bharat Ratna, Padma Vibhushan, Padma Bhushan and Padma Sri. It ruled that these awards do not amount to 'titles' within the meaning of Article 18 that prohibits only hereditary titles of nobility. Therefore, they are not violative of Article 18 as the theory of equality does not mandate that merit should not be recognised. However, it also ruled that they should not be used as suffixes or prefixes to the names of awardees. Otherwise, they should forfeit the awards.

These National Awards were instituted in 1954. The Janata Party government headed by Morarji Desai discontinued them in 1977. But they were again revived in 1980 by the Indira Gandhi government.

Right to Freedom

1. Protection of Six Rights

Article 19 guarantees to all citizens the six rights. These are:

(i) Right to freedom of speech and expression.
(ii) Right to assemble peaceably and without arms.
(iii) Right to form associations or unions or co-operative societies.[10a]
(iv) Right to move freely throughout the territory of India.
(v) Right to reside and settle in any part of the territory of India.
(vi) Right to practice any profession or to carry on any occupation, trade or business.

Originally, Article 19 contained seven rights. But, the right to acquire, hold and dispose of property was deleted by the 44th Amendment Act of 1978.

These six rights are protected against only state action and not private individuals. Moreover, these rights are available only to the citizens and to shareholders of a company but not to foreigners or legal persons like companies or corporations, etc.

The State can impose 'reasonable' restrictions on the enjoyment of these six rights only on the grounds mentioned in the Article 19 itself and not on any other grounds.

Freedom of Speech and Expression   It implies that every citizen has the right to express his views, opinions, belief and convictions freely by word of mouth, writing, printing, picturing or in any other manner. The Supreme Court held that the freedom of speech and expression includes the following:

(a) Right to propagate one's views as well as views of others.
(b) Freedom of the press.
(c) Freedom of commercial advertisements.
(d) Right against tapping of telephonic conversation.
(e) Right to telecast, that is, government has no monopoly on electronic media.
(f) Right against bundh called by a political party or organisation.
(g) Right to know about government activities.
(h) Freedom of silence.
(i) Right against imposition of pre-censorship on a newspaper.
(j) Right to demonstration or picketing but not right to strike.

The State can impose reasonable restrictions on the exercise of the freedom of speech and expression on the grounds of sovereignty and integrity of India, security of the state, friendly relations with foreign states, public order, decency or morality, contempt of court, defamation, and incitement to an offence.

Freedom of Assembly   Every citizen has the right to assemble peaceably and without arms. It includes the right to hold public meetings, demonstrations and take out processions. This freedom can be exercised only on public land and the assembly must be peaceful and unarmed. This provision does not protect violent, disorderly, riotous assemblies, or one that causes breach of public peace or one that involves arms. This right does not include the right to strike.

The State can impose reasonable restrictions on the exercise of right of assembly on two grounds, namely, sovereignty and integrity of India and public order including the maintenance of traffic in the area concerned.

Under Section 144 of Criminal Procedure Code (1973), a magistrate can restrain an assembly, meeting or procession if there is a risk of obstruction, annoyance or danger to human life, health or safety or a disturbance of the public tranquillity or a riot or any affray.

Under Section 141 of the Indian Penal Code, as assembly of five or more persons becomes unlawful if the object is (a) to resist the execution of any law or legal process; (b) to forcibly occupy the property of some person; (c) to commit any mischief or criminal trespass; (d) to force some person to do an illegal act; and (e) to threaten the government or its officials on exercising lawful powers.

Freedom of Association   All citizens have the right to form associations or unions or co-operative societies[10b]. It includes the right to form political parties, companies, partnership firms, societies, clubs, organisations, trade unions or any body of persons. It not only includes the right to start an association or union but also to continue with the association or union as such. Further, it covers the negative right of not to form or join an association or union.

Reasonable restrictions can be imposed on the exercise of this right by the State on the grounds of sovereignty and integrity of India, public order and morality. Subject to these restrictions, the citizens have complete liberty to form associations or unions for pursuing lawful objectives and purposes. However, the right to obtain recognition of the association is not a fundamental right.

The Supreme Court held that the trade unions have no guaranteed right to effective bargaining or right to strike or right to declare a lock-out. The right to strike can be controlled by an appropriate industrial law.

Freedom of Movement This freedom entitles every citizen to move freely throughout the territory of the country. He can move freely from one state to another or from one place to another within a state. This right underline the idea that India is one unit so far as the citizens are concerned. Thus, the purpose is to promote national feeling and not parochialism.

The grounds of imposing reasonable restrictions on this freedom are two, namely, the interests of general public and the protection of interests of any scheduled tribe. The entry of outsiders in tribal areas is restricted to protect the distinctive culture, language, customs and manners of scheduled tribes and to safeguard their traditional vocation and properties against exploitation.

The Supreme Court held that the freedom of movement of prostitutes can be restricted on the ground of public health and in the interest of public morals. The Bombay High Court validated the restrictions on the movement of persons affected by AIDS.

The freedom of movement has two dimensions, viz, internal (right to move inside the country) and external (right to move out of the country and right to come back to the country). Article 19 protects only the first dimension. The second dimension is dealt by Article 21 (right to life and personal liberty).

Freedom of Residence Every citizen has the right to reside and settle in any part of the territory of the country. This right has two parts: (a) the right to reside in any part of the country, which means to stay at any place temporarily, and (b) the right to settle in any part of the country, which means to set up a home or domicile at any place permanently.

This right is intended to remove internal barriers within the country or between any of its parts. This promotes nationalism and avoids narrow mindedness.

The State can impose reasonable restrictions on the exercise of this right on two grounds, namely,

the interest of general public and the protection of interests of any scheduled tribes. The right of outsiders to reside and settle in tribal areas is restricted to protect the distinctive culture, language, customs and manners of scheduled tribes and to safeguard their traditional vocation and properties against exploitation. In many parts of the country, the tribals have been permitted to regulate their property rights in accordance with their customary rules and laws.

The Supreme Court held that certain areas can be banned for certain kinds of persons like prostitutes and habitual offenders.

From the above, it is clear that the right to residence and the right to movement are overlapping to some extent. Both are complementary to each other.

Freedom of Profession, etc. All citizens are given the right to practise any profession or to carry on any occupation, trade or business. This right is very wide as it covers all the means of earning one's livelihood.

The State can impose reasonable restrictions on the exercise of this right in the interest of the general public. Further, the State is empowered to:

(a) prescribe professional or technical qualifications necessary for practising any profession or carrying on any occupation, trade or business; and

(b) carry on by itself any trade, business, industry or service whether to the exclusion (complete or partial) of citizens or otherwise.

Thus, no objection can be made when the State carries on a trade, business, industry or service either as a monopoly (complete or partial) to the exclusion of citizens (all or some only) or in competition with any citizen. The State is not required to justify its monopoly.

This right does not include the right to carry on a profession or business or trade or occupation that is immoral (trafficking in women or children) or dangerous (harmful drugs or explosives, etc,). The State can absolutely prohibit these or regulate them through licencing.

2. Protection in Respect of Conviction for Offences

Article 20 grants protection against arbitrary and excessive punishment to an accused person, whether citizen or foreigner or legal person like a company or a corporation. It contains three provisions in that direction:

(a) No *ex-post-facto* law: No person shall be (i) convicted of any offence except for violation of a law in force at the time of the commission of the act, nor (ii) subjected to a penalty greater than that prescribed by the law in force at the time of the commission of the act.

(b) No double jeopardy: No person shall be prosecuted and punished for the same offence more than once.

(c) No self-incrimination: No person accused of any offence shall be compelled to be a witness against himself.

An *ex-post-facto* law is one that imposes penalties restrospectively (retroactively), that is, upon acts already done or which increases the penalties for such acts. The enactment of such a law is prohibited by the first provision of Article 20. However, this limitation is imposed only on criminal laws and not on civil laws or tax laws. In other words, a civil liability or a tax can be imposed retrospectively. Further, this provision prohibits only conviction or sentence under an *ex-post-facto* criminal law and not the trial thereof. Finally, the protection (immunity) under this provision cannot be claimed in case of preventive detention or demanding security from a person.

The protection against double jeopardy is available only in proceedings before a court of law or a judicial tribunal. In other words, it is not available in proceedings before departmental or administrative authorities as they are not of judicial nature.

The protection against self-incrimination extends to both oral evidence and documentary evidence. However, it does not extend to (i) compulsory production of material objects, (ii) compulsion to give thumb impression, specimen signature, blood specimens, and (iii) compulsory exhibition of the body. Further, it extends only to criminal proceedings and not to civil proceedings or proceedings which are not of criminal nature.

3. Protection of Life and Personal Liberty

Article 21 declares that no person shall be deprived of his life or personal liberty except according to procedure established by law. This right is available to both citizens and non-citizens.

In the famous *Gopalan* case[11] (1950), the Supreme Court has taken a narrow interpretation of the Article 21. It held that the protection under Article 21 is available only against arbitrary executive action and not from arbitrary legislative action. This means that the State can deprive the right to life and personal liberty of a person based on a law. This is because of the expression 'procedure established by law' in Article 21, which is different from the expression 'due process of law' contained in the American Constitution. Hence, the validity of a law that has prescribed a procedure cannot be questioned on the ground that the law is unreasonable, unfair or unjust. Secondly, the Supreme Court held that the 'personal liberty' means only liberty relating to the person or body of the individual. But, in *Menaka* case[12] (1978), the Supreme Court overruled its judgement in the *Gopalan* case by taking a wider interpretation of the Article 21. Therefore, it ruled that the right to life and personal liberty of a person can be deprived by a law provided the procedure prescribed by that law is reasonable, fair and just. In other words, it has introduced the American expression 'due process of law'. In effect, the protection under Article 21 should be available not only against arbitrary executive action but also against arbitrary legislative action. Further, the court held that the 'right to life' as embodied in Article 21 is not merely confined to animal existence or survival but it includes within its ambit the right to live with human dignity and all those aspects of life which go to make a man's life meaningful, complete and worth living. It also ruled that the expression 'Personal Liberty' in Article 21 is of the widest amplitude and it covers a variety of rights that go to constitute the personal liberties of a man.

The Supreme Court has reaffirmed its judgement in the *Menaka* case in the subsequent cases. It has declared the following rights as part of Article 21:

(a) Right to live with human dignity.

(b) Right to decent environment including pollution free water and air and protection against hazardous industries.

(c) Right to livelihood.

(d) Right to privacy.

(e) Right to shelter.

(f) Right to health.

(g) Right to free education up to 14 years of age.
(h) Right to free legal aid.
(i) Right against solitary confinement.
(j) Right to speedy trial.
(k) Right against handcuffing.
(l) Right against inhuman treatment.
(m) Right against delayed execution.
(n) Right to travel abroad.
(o) Right against bonded labour.
(p) Right against custodial harassment.
(q) Right to emergency medical aid.
(r) Right to timely medical treatment in government hospital.
(s) Right not to be driven out of a state.
(t) Right to fair trial.
(u) Right of prisoner to have necessities of life.
(v) Right of women to be treated with decency and dignity.
(w) Right against public hanging.
(x) Right to hearing.
(y) Right to information.
(z) Right to reputation.

4. Right to Education

Article 21 A declares that the State shall provide free and compulsory education to all children of the age of six to fourteen years in such a manner as the State may determine. Thus, this provision makes only elementary education a Fundamental Right and not higher or professional education.

This provision was added by the 86th Constitutional Amendment Act of 2002. This amendment is a major milestone in the country's aim to achieve 'Education for All'. The government described this step as 'the dawn of the second revolution in the chapter of citizens' rights'.

Even before this amendment, the Constitution contained a provision for free and compulsory education for children under Article 45 in Part IV. However, being a directive principle, it was not enforceable by the courts. Now, there is scope for judicial intervention in this regard.

This amendment changed the subject matter of Article 45 in directive principles. It now reads—'The state shall endeavour to provide early childhood care and education for all children until they complete the age of six years.' It also added a new fundamental duty under Article 51A that reads—'It shall be the duty of every citizen of India to provide opportunities for education to his child or ward between the age of six and fourteen years'.

In 1993 itself, the Supreme Court recognised a Fundamental Right to primary education in the right to life under Article 21. It held that every child or citizen of this country has a right to free education until he completes the age of 14 years. Thereafter, his right to education is subject to the limits of economic capacity and development of the state. In this judgement, the Court overruled its earlier judgement (1992) which declared that there was a fundamental right to education up to any level including professional education like medicine and engineering.

In pursuance of Article 21A, the Parliament enacted the Right of Children to Free and Compulsory Education (RTE) Act, 2009. This Act seeks to provide that every child has a right to be provided full time elementary education of satisfactory and equitable quality in a formal school which satisfies certain essential norms and standards. This legislation is anchored in the belief that the values of equality, social justice and democracy and the creation of a just and humane society can be achieved only through provision of inclusive elementary education to all.[12a]

5 Protection Against Arrest and Detention

Article 22 grants protection to persons who are arrested or detained. Detention is of two types, namely, punitive and preventive. **Punitive detention** is to punish a person for an offence committed by him after trial and conviction in a court. **Preventive detention**, on the other hand, means detention of a person without trial and conviction by a court. Its purpose is not to punish a person for a past offence but to prevent him from committing an offence in the near future. Thus, preventive detention is only a precautionary measure and based on suspicion.

The Article 22 has two parts—the first part deals with the cases of ordinary law and the second part deals with the cases of preventive detention law.

(a) The first part of Article 22 confers the following rights on a person who is arrested or detained under an ordinary law:
    (i) Right to be informed of the grounds of arrest.

(ii) Right to consult and be defended by a legal practitioner.

(iii) Right to be produced before a magistrate within 24 hours, excluding the journey time.

(iv) Right to be released after 24 hours unless the magistrate authorises further detention.

These safeguards are not available to an alien or a person arrested or detained under a preventive detention law.

The Supreme Court also ruled that the arrest and detention in the first part of Article 22 do not cover arrest under the orders of a court, civil arrest, arrest on failure to pay the income tax, and deportation of an alien. They apply only to an act of a criminal or quasi-criminal nature or some activity prejudicial to public interest.

(b) The second part of Article 22 grants protection to persons who are arrested or detained under a preventive detention law. This protection is available to both citizens as well as aliens and includes the following:

(i) The detention of a person cannot exceed three months unless an advisory board reports sufficient cause for extended detention. The board is to consist of judges of a high court.

(ii) The grounds of detention should be communicated to the detenu. However, the facts considered to be against the public interest need not be disclosed.

(iii) The detenu should be afforded an opportunity to make a representation against the detention order.

Article 22 also authorises the Parliament to prescribe **(a)** the circumstances and the classes of cases in which a person can be detained for more than three months under a preventive detention law without obtaining the opinion of an advisory board; **(b)** the maximum period for which a person can be detained in any classes of cases under a preventive detention law; and **(c)** the procedure to be followed by an advisory board in an inquiry.

The 44th Amendment Act of 1978 has reduced the period of detention without obtaining the opinion of an advisory board from three to two months. However, this provision has not yet been brought into force, hence, the original period of three months still continues.

The Constitution has divided the legislative power with regard to preventive detention between the Parliament and the state legislatures. The Parliament has exclusive authority to make a law of preventive detention for reasons connected with defence, foreign affairs and the secu-rity of India. Both the Parliament as well as the state legislatures can concurrently make a law of preventive detention for reasons connected with the security of a state, the maintenance of public order and the maintenance of supplies and services essential to the community.

The preventive detention laws made by the Parliament are:

(a) Preventive Detention Act, 1950. Expired in 1969.

(b) Maintenance of Internal Security Act (MISA), 1971. Repealed in 1978.

(c) Conservation of Foreign Exchange and Prevention of Smuggling Activities Act (COFEPOSA), 1974.

(d) National Security Act (NASA), 1980.

(e) Prevention of Blackmarketing and Maintenance of Supplies of Essential Commodities Act (PBMSECA), 1980.

(f) Terrorist and Disruptive Activities (Prevention) Act (TADA), 1985. Repealed in 1995.

(g) Prevention of Illicit Traffic in Narcotic Drugs and Psychotropic Substances Act (PITNDPSA), 1988.

(h) Prevention of Terrorism Act (POTA), 2002. Repealed in 2004.

It is unfortunate to know that no democratic country in the world has made preventive detention as an integral part of the Constitution as has been done in India. It is unknown in USA. It was resorted to in Britain only during first and second world war time. In India, preventive detention existed even during the British rule. For example, the Bengal State Prisoners Regulation of 1818 and the Defence of India Act of 1939 provided for preventive detention.

Right Against Exploitation

1. Prohibition of Traffic in Human Beings and Forced Labour

Article 23 prohibits traffic in human beings, *begar* (forced labour) and other similar forms of forced labour. Any contravention of this provision shall be an offence punishable in accordance with law. This right is available to both citizens and non-citizens. It protects the individual not only against the State but also against private persons.

The expression 'traffic in human beings' include (a) selling and buying of men, women and children like goods; (b) immoral traffic in women and children, including prostitution; (c) *devadasis*; and (d) slavery. To punish these acts, the Parliament has made the Immoral Traffic (Prevention) Act[13], 1956.

The term '*begar*' means compulsory work without remuneration. It was a peculiar Indian system under which the local zamindars sometimes used to force their tenants to render services without any payment. In addition to *begar*, the Article 23 prohibits other 'similar forms of forced labour' like 'bonded labour'. The term 'forced labour' means compelling a person to work against his will. The word 'force' includes not only physical or legal force but also force arising from the compulsion of economic circumstances, that is, working for less than the minimum wage. In this regard, the Bonded Labour System (Abolition) Act, 1976; the Minimum Wages Act, 1948; the Contract Labour Act, 1970 and the Equal Remuneration Act, 1976 were made.

Article 23 also provides for an exception to this provision. It permits the State to impose compulsory service for public purposes, as for example, military service or social service, for which it is not bound to pay. However, in imposing such service, the State is not permitted to make any discrimination on grounds only of religion, race, caste or class.

2. Prohibition of Employment of Children in Factories, etc.

Article 24 prohibits the employment of children below the age of 14 years in any factory, mine or other hazardous activities like construction work or railway. But it does not prohibit their employment in any harmless or innocent work.

The Child Labour (Prohibition and Regulation) Act, 1986, is the most important law in this direction. In addition, the Employment of Children Act, 1938; the Factories Act, 1948; the Mines Act, 1952; the Merchant Shipping Act, 1958; the Plantation Labour Act, 1951; the Motor Transport Workers Act, 1951; Apprentices Act, 1961; the Bidi and Cigar Workers Act, 1966; and other similar acts prohibit the employment of children below certain age.

In 1996, the Supreme Court directed the establishment of Child Labour Rehabilitation Welfare Fund in which the offending employer should deposit a fine of ₹20,000 for each child employed by him. It also issued directions for the improvement of education, health and nutrition of children.

The Commissions for Protection of Child Rights Act, 2005 was enacted to provide for the establishment of a National Commission and State Commissions for Protection of Child Rights and Children's Courts for providing speedy trial of offences against children or of violation of child rights.

In 2006, the government banned the employment of children as domestic servants or workers in business establishments like hotels, dhabas, restaurants, shops, factories, resorts, spas, tea-shops and so on. It warned that anyone employing children below 14 years of age would be liable for prosecution and penal action.

Total Ban on Child Labour

In August 2012, the Union Cabinet approved a proposal to completely ban employment of children below 14 years in all occupations and processes.

The Child Labour (Prohibition & Regulation) Act, 1986, will be amended to incorporate the changes and will be renamed a Child and Adolescent Labour (Prohibition) Act. Giving more teeth to the Act, offences under it have been made cognizable and the punishment has been increased.

Presently, children under the age of 14 are prohibited from employment in "hazardous occupations and processes" while their conditions of work in non-hazardous occupations and processes are merely regulated.

The amendments include increasing the age of prohibition for employment of children and adolescents in hazardous occupations, such as mining, from 14 to 18. Employment of children below 14 years is presently prohibited in 18 occupations and 65 processes.

The maximum punishment for offences under the Act has been increased from one year to two years of imprisonment and from ₹20,00 to ₹50,000 fine or both. For repeated offences, it has been raised to three years of imprisonment.

RIGHT TO FREEDOM OF RELIGION

1. Freedom of Conscience and Free Profession, Practice and Propagation of Religion

Article 25 says that all persons are equally entitled to freedom of conscience and the right to freely profess, practice and propagate religion. The implications of these are:

(a) *Freedom of conscience:* Inner freedom of an individual to mould his relation with God or Creatures in whatever way he desires.

(b) *Right to profess:* Declaration of one's religious beliefs and faith openly and freely.

(c) *Right to practice:* Performance of religious worship, rituals, ceremonies and exhibition of beliefs and ideas.

(d) *Right to propagate:* Transmission and dissemination of one's religious beliefs to others or exposition of the tenets of one's religion. But, it does not include a right to convert another person to one's own religion. Forcible conversions impinge on the 'freedom of conscience' guaranteed to all the persons alike.

From the above, it is clear that Article 25 covers not only religious beliefs (doctrines) but also religious practices (rituals). Moreover, these rights are available to all persons—citizens as well as non-citizens.

However, these rights are subject to public order, morality, health and other provisions relating to fundamental rights. Further, the State is permitted to:

(a) regulate or restrict any economic, financial, political or other secular activity associated with religious practice; and

(b) provide for social welfare and reform or throw open Hindu religious institutions of a public character to all classes and sections of Hindus.

Article 25 also contains two explanations: one, wearing and carrying of *kirpans* is to be included in the profession of the Sikh religion; and two, the Hindus, in this context, include Sikhs, Jains and Buddhists.[14]

2. Freedom to Manage Religious Affairs

According to Article 26, every religious denomination or any of its section shall have the following rights:

(a) Right to establish and maintain institutions for religious and charitable purposes;

(b) Right to manage its own affairs in matters of religion;

(c) Right to own and acquire movable and immovable property; and

(d) Right to administer such property in accordance with law.

Article 25 guarantees rights of individuals, while Article 26 guarantees rights of religious denominations or their sections. In other words, Article 26 protects collective freedom of religion. Like the rights under Article 25, the rights under Article 26 are also subject to public order, morality and health but not subject to other provisions relating to the Fundamental Rights.

The Supreme Court held that a religious denomination must satisfy three conditions:

(a) It should be a collection of individuals who have a system of beliefs (doctrines) which they regard as conductive to their spiritual well-being;

(b) It should have a common organisation; and

(c) It should be designated by a distinctive name.

Under the above criteria, the Supreme Court held that the 'Ramakrishna Mission' and 'Ananda Marga' are religious denominations within the Hindu religion. It also held that Aurobindo Society is not a religious denomination.

3. Freedom from Taxation for Promotion of a Religion

Article 27 lays down that no person shall be compelled to pay any taxes for the promotion or maintenance of any particular religion or religious denomination. In other words, the State should not spend the public money collected by way of tax for the promotion or maintenance of any particular religion. This provision prohibits the State from favouring, patronising and supporting one religion over the other. This means that the taxes can be used for the promotion or maintenance of all religions.

This provision prohibits only levy of a tax and not a fee. This is because the purpose of a fee is to control secular administration of religious institutions and not to promote or maintain religion. Thus, a fee can be levied on pilgrims to provide them some special service or safety measures. Similarly, a fee can be levied on religious endowments for meeting the regulation expenditure.

4. Freedom from Attending Religious Instruction

Under Article 28, no religious instruction shall be provided in any educational institution wholly maintained out of State funds. However, this provision shall not apply to an educational institution administered by the State but established under any endowment or trust, requiring imparting of religious instruction in such institution.

Further, no person attending any educational institution recognised by the State or receiving aid out of State funds shall be required to attend any religious instruction or worship in that institution without his consent. In case of a minor, the consent of his guardian is needed.

Thus, Article 28 distinguishes between four types of educational institutions:

(a) Institutions wholly maintained by the State.
(b) Institutions administered by the State but established under any endowment or trust.
(c) Institutions recognised by the State.
(d) Institutions receiving aid from the State.

In (a) religious instruction is completely prohibited while in (b), religious instruction is permitted. In (c) and (d), religious instruction is permitted on a voluntary basis.

CULTURAL AND EDUCATIONAL RIGHTS

1. Protection of Interests of Minorities

Article 29 provides that any section of the citizens residing in any part of India having a distinct language, script or culture of its own, shall have the right to conserve the same. Further, no citizen shall be denied admission into any educational institution maintained by the State or receiving aid out of State funds on grounds only of religion, race, caste, or language.

The first provision protects the right of a group while the second provision guarantees the right of a citizen as an individual irrespective of the community to which he belongs.

Article 29 grants protection to both religious minorities as well as linguistic minorities. However, the Supreme Court held that the scope of this article is not necessarily restricted to minorities only, as it is commonly assumed to be. This is because of the use of words 'section of citizens' in the Article that include minorities as well as majority.

The Supreme Court also held that the right to conserve the language includes the right to agitate for the protection of the language. Hence, the political speeches or promises made for the conservation of the language of a section of the citizens does not amount to corrupt practice under the Representation of the People Act, 1951.

2. Right of Minorities to Establish and Administer Educational Institutions

Article 30 grants the following rights to minorities, whether religious or linguistic:

(a) All minorities shall have the right to establish and administer educational institutions of their choice.
(b) The compensation amount fixed by the State for the compulsory acquisition of any property of a minority educational institution shall not restrict or abrogate the right guaranteed to them. This provision was added by the 44th Amendment Act of 1978 to protect the right of minorities in this regard. The Act deleted the right to property as a Fundamental Right (Article 31).
(c) In granting aid, the State shall not discriminate against any educational institution managed by a minority.

Thus, the protection under Article 30 is confined only to minorities (religious or linguistic) and does not extend to any section of citizens (as under Article 29). However, the term 'minority' has not been defined anywhere in the Constitution.

The right under Article 30 also includes the right of a minority to impart education to its children in its own language.

Minority educational institutions are of three types:

(a) institutions that seek recognition as well as aid from the State;

(b) institutions that seek only recognition from the State and not aid; and

(c) institutions that neither seek recognition nor aid from the State.

The institutions of first and second type are subject to the regulatory power of the state with regard to syllabus prescription, academic standards, discipline, sanitation, employment of teaching staff and so on. The institutions of third type are free to administer their affairs but subject to operation of general laws like contract law, labour law, industrial law, tax law, economic regulations, and so on.

RIGHT TO CONSTITUTIONAL REMEDIES

A mere declaration of fundamental rights in the Constitution is meaningless, useless and worthless without providing an effective machinery for their enforcement, if and when they are violated. Hence, Article 32 confers the right to remedies for the enforcement of the fundamental rights of an aggrieved citizen. In other words, the right to get the Fundamental Rights protected is in itself a fundamental right. This makes the fundamental rights real. That is why Dr Ambedkar called Article 32 as the most important article of the Constitution—'an Article without which this constitution would be a nullity. It is the very soul of the Constitution and the very heart of it'. The Supreme Court has ruled that Article 32 is a basic feature of the Constitution. Hence, it cannot be abridged or taken away even by way of an amendment to the Constitution. It contains the following four provisions:

(a) The right to move the Supreme Court by appropriate proceedings for the enforcement of the Fundamental Rights is guaranteed.

(b) The Supreme Court shall have power to issue directions or orders or writs for the enforcement of any of the fundamental rights. The writs issued may include *habeas corpus, mandamus,* prohibition, *certiorari* and *quo-warranto.*

(c) Parliament can empower any other court to issue directions, orders and writs of all kinds.

However, this can be done without prejudice to the above powers conferred on the Supreme Court. Any other court here does not include high courts because Article 226 has already conferred these powers on the high courts.

(d) The right to move the Supreme Court shall not be suspended except as otherwise provided for by the Constitution. Thus the Constitution provides that the President can suspend the right to move any court for the enforcement of the fundamental rights during a national emergency (Article 359).

It is thus clear that the Supreme Court has been constituted as the defender and guarantor of the fundamenetal rights of the citizens. It has been vested with the 'original' and 'wide' powers for that purpose. Original, because an aggrieved citizen can directly go to the Supreme Court, not necessarily by way of appeal. Wide, because its power is not restricted to issuing of orders or directions but also writs of all kinds.

The purpose of Article 32 is to provide a guaranteed, effective, expedious, inexpensive and summary remedy for the protection of the fundamental rights. Only the Fundamental Rights guaranteed by the Constitution can be enforced under Article 32 and not any other right like non-fundamental constitutional rights, statutory rights, customary rights and so on. The violation of a fundamental right is the *sine qua non* for the exercise of the right conferred by Article 32. In other words, the Supreme Court, under Article 32, cannot determine a question that does not involve Fundamental Rights. Article 32 cannot be invoked simply to determine the constitutionality of an executive order or a legislation unless it directly infringes any of the fundamental rights.

In case of the enforcement of Fundamental Rights, the jurisdiction of the Supreme Court is original but not exclusive. It is concurrent with the jurisdiction of the high court under Article 226. It vests original powers in the high court to issue directions, orders and writs of all kinds for the enforcement of the Fundamental Rights. It means when the Fundamental Rights of a citizen are violated, the aggrieved party has the option of moving either the high court or the Supreme Court directly.

Since the right guaranteed by Article 32 (ie, the right to move the Supreme Court where a fundamental right is infringed) is in itself a fundamental right, the availability of alternate remedy is no bar to relief under Article 32. However, the Supreme Court has ruled that where relief through high court is available under Article 226, the aggrieved party should first move the high court.

Writs—Types and Scope

The Supreme Court (under Article 32) and the high courts (under Article 226) can issue the writs of *habeas corpus, mandamus,* prohibition, *certiorari* and *quo-warranto.* Further, the Parliament (under Article 32) can empower any other court to issue these writs. Since no such provision has been made so far, only the Supreme Court and the high courts can issue the writs and not any other court. Before 1950, only the High Courts of Calcutta, Bombay and Madras had the power to issue the writs. Article 226 now empowers all the high courts to issue the writs.

These writs are borrowed from English law where they are known as 'prerogative writs'. They are so called in England as they were issued in the exercise of the prerogative of the King who was, and is still, described as the 'fountain of justice'. Later, the high court started issuing these writs as extraordinary remedies to uphold the rights and liberties of the British people.

The writ jurisdiction of the Supreme Court differs from that of a high court in three respects:

1. The Supreme Court can issue writs only for the enforcement of fundamental rights whereas a high court can issue writs not only for the enforcement of Fundamental Rights but also for any other purpose. The expression 'for any other purpose' refers to the enforcement of an ordinary legal right. Thus, the writ jurisdiction of the Supreme Court, in this respect, is narrower than that of high court.
2. The Supreme Court can issue writs against a person or government throughout the territory of India whereas a high court can issue writs against a person residing or against a government or authority located within its territorial jurisdiction only or outside its territorial jurisdiction only if the cause of action arises within its territorial jurisdiction.[15] Thus, the territorial jurisdiction of the Supreme Court

for the purpose of issuing writs is wider than that of a high court.

3. A remedy under Article 32 is in itself a Fundamental Right and hence, the Supreme Court may not refuse to exercise its writ jurisdiction. On the other hand, a remedy under Article 226 is discretionary and hence, a high court may refuse to exercise its writ jurisdiction. Article 32 does not merely confer power on the Supreme Court as Article 226 does on a high court to issue writs for the enforcement of fundamental rights or other rights as part of its general jurisdiction. The Supreme Court is thus constituted as a defender and guarantor of the fundamental rights.

Now, we will proceed to understand the meaning and scope of different kinds of writs mentioned in Articles 32 and 226 of the Constitution:

Habeas Corpus

It is a Latin term which literally means 'to have the body of'. It is an order issued by the court to a person who has detained another person, to produce the body of the latter before it. The court then examines the cause and legality of detention. It would set the detained person free, if the detention is found to be illegal. Thus, this writ is a bulwark of individual liberty against arbitrary detention.

The writ of *habeas corpus* can be issued against both public authorities as well as private individuals. The writ, on the other hand, is not issued where the **(a)** detention is lawful, **(b)** the proceeding is for contempt of a legislature or a court, **(c)** detention is by a competent court, and **(d)** detention is outside the jurisdiction of the court.

Mandamus

It literally means 'we command'. It is a command issued by the court to a public official asking him to perform his official duties that he has failed or refused to perform. It can also be issued against any public body, a corporation, an inferior court, a tribunal or government for the same purpose.

The writ of *mandamus* cannot be issued **(a)** against a private individual or body; **(b)** to enforce departmental instruction that does not possess statutory force; **(c)** when the duty is discretionary and not mandatory; **(d)** to enforce a contractual obligation; **(e)** against the president of India or the state governors; and **(f)** against the chief justice of a high court acting in judicial capacity.

Prohibition

Literally, it means 'to forbid'. It is issued by a higher court to a lower court or tribunal to prevent the latter from exceeding its jurisdiction or usurping a jurisdiction that it does not possess. Thus, unlike *mandamus* that directs activity, the prohibition directs inactivity.

The writ of prohibition can be issued only against judicial and quasi-judicial authorities. It is not available against administrative authorities, legislative bodies, and private individuals or bodies.

Certiorari

In the literal sense, it means 'to be certified' or 'to be informed'. It is issued by a higher court to a lower court or tribunal either to transfer a case pending with the latter to itself or to squash the order of the latter in a case. It is issued on the grounds of excess of jurisdiction or lack of jurisdiction or error of law. Thus, unlike prohibition, which is only preventive, *certiorari* is both preventive as well as curative.

Till recently, the writ of *certiorari* could be issued only against judicial and quasi-judicial authorities and not against administrative authories. However, in 1991, the Supreme Court ruled that the *certiorari* can be issued even against administrative authorities affecting rights of individuals.

Like prohibition, *certiorari* is also not available against legislative bodies and private individuals or bodies.

Quo-Warranto

In the literal sense, it means 'by what authority or warrant'. It is issued by the court to enquire into the legality of claim of a person to a public office. Hence, it prevents illegal usurpation of public office by a person.

The writ can be issued only in case of a substantive public office of a permanent character created by a statute or by the Constitution. It cannot be issued in cases of ministerial office or private office.

Unlike the other four writs, this can be sought by any interested person and not necessarily by the aggrieved person.

ARMED FORCES AND FUNDAMENTAL RIGHTS

Article 33 empowers the Parliament to restrict or abrogate the fundamental rights of the members of armed forces, para-military forces, police forces, intelligence agencies and analogous forces. The objective of this provision is to ensure the proper discharge of their duties and the maintenance of discipline among them.

The power to make laws under Article 33 is conferred only on Parliament and not on state legislatures. Any such law made by Parliament cannot be challenged in any court on the ground of contravention of any of the fundamental rights.

Accordingly, the Parliament has enacted the Army Act (1950), the Navy Act (1950), the Air Force Act (1950), the Police Forces (Restriction of Rights) Act, 1966, the Border Security Force Act and so on. These impose restrictions on their freedom of speech, right to form associations, right to be members of trade unions or political associations, right to communicate with the press, right to attend public meetings or demonstrations, etc.

The expression 'members of the armed forces' also covers such employees of the armed forces as barbers, carpenters, mechanics, cooks, chowkidars, bootmakers, tailors who are non-combatants.

A parliamentary law enacted under Article 33 can also exclude the court martials (tribunals established under the military law) from the writ jurisdiction of the Supreme Court and the high courts, so far as the enforcement of Fundamental Rights is concerned.

MARTIAL LAW AND FUNDAMENTAL RIGHTS

Article 34 provides for the restrictions on fundamental rights while martial law is in force in any area within the territory of India. It empowers the Parliament to indemnify any government servant or any other person for any act done by him in connection with the maintenance or restoration of order in any area where martial law was in force. The Parliament

Table 7.3 *Martial Law Vs National Emergency*

Martial Law	National Emergency
1. It affects only Fundamental Rights.	1. It affects not only Fundamental Rights but also Centre–state relations, distribution of revenues and legislative powers between centre and states and may extend the tenure of the Parliament.
2. It suspends the government and ordinary law courts.	2. It continues the government and ordinary law courts.
3. It is imposed to restore the breakdown of law and order due to any reason.	3. It can be imposed only on three grounds—war, external aggression or armed rebellion.
4. It is imposed in some specific area of the country.	4. It is imposed either in the whole country or in any part of it.
5. It has no specific provision in the Constitution. It is implicit.	5. It has specific and detailed provision in the Constitution. It is explicit.

can also validate any sentence passed, punishment inflicted, forfeiture ordered or other act done under martial law in such area.

The Act of Indemnity made by the Parliament cannot be challenged in any court on the ground of contravention of any of the fundamental rights.

The concept of martial law has been borrowed in India from the English common law. However, the expression 'martial law' has not been defined anywhere in the Constitution. Literally, it means 'military rule'. It refers to a situation where civil administration is run by the military authorities according to their own rules and regulations framed outside the ordinary law. It thus imply the suspension of ordinary law and the government by military tribunals. It is different from the military law that is applicable to the armed forces.

There is also no specific or express provision in the Constitution that authorises the executive to declare martial law. However, it is implicit in Article 34 under which martial law can be declared in any area within the territory of India. The martial law is imposed under the extraordinary circumstances like war, invasion, insurrection, rebellion, riot or any violent resistance to law. Its justification is to repel force by force for maintaining or restoring order in the society.

During the operation of martial law, the military authorities are vested with abnormal powers to take all necessary steps. They impose restrictions and regulations on the rights of the civilians, can punish the civilians and even condemn them to death.

The Supreme Court held that the declaration of martial law does not *ipso facto* result in the suspension of the writ of *habeas corpus*.

The declaration of a martial law under Article 34 is different from the declaration of a national emergency under Article 352. The differences between the two are summarised in Table 7.3.

Effecting Certain Fundamental Rights

Article 35 lays down that the power to make laws, to give effect to certain specified fundamental rights shall vest only in the Parliament and not in the state legislatures. This provision ensures that there is uniformity throughout India with regard to the nature of those fundamental rights and punishment for their infringement. In this direction, Article 35 contains the following provisions:

1. The Parliament shall have (and the legislature of a state shall not have) power to make laws with respect to the following matters:

(a) Prescribing residence as a condition for certain employments or appointments in a state or union territory or local authority or other authority (Article 16).

(b) Empowering courts other than the Supreme Court and the high courts to issue directions, orders and writs of all kinds for the enforcement of fundamental rights (Article 32).

(c) Restricting or abrogating the application of Fundamental Rights to members of armed forces, police forces, etc. (Article 33).

(d) Indemnifying any government servant or any other person for any act done during the operation of martial law in any area (Article 34).

2. Parliament shall have (and the legislature of a state shall not have) powers to make laws for prescribing punishment for those acts that are declared to be offences under the fundamental rights. These include the following:

(a) Untouchability (Article 17).

(b) Traffic in human beings and forced labour (Article 23).

Further, the Parliament shall, after the commencement of the Constitution, make laws for prescribing punishment for the above acts, thus making it obligatory on the part of the Parliament to enact such laws.

3. Any law in force at the commencement of the Constitution with respect to any of the matters specified above is to continue in force until altered or repealed or amended by the Parliament.

It should be noted that Article 35 extends the competence of the Parliament to make a law on the matters specified above, even though some of those matters may fall within the sphere of the state legislatures (i.e., State List).

PRESENT POSITION OF RIGHT TO PROPERTY

Originally, the right to property was one of the seven fundamental rights under Part III of the Constitution. It was dealt by Article 19(1)(f) and Article 31. Article 19(1)(f) guaranteed to every citizen the right to acquire, hold and dispose of property. Article 31, on the other hand, guaranteed to every person, whether citizen or non-citizen, right against deprivation of his property. It provided that no person shall be deprived of his property except by authority of law. It empowered the State to acquire or requisition the property of a person on two conditions: **(a)** it should be for public purpose, and **(b)** it should provide for payment of compensation (amount) to the owner.

Since the commencement of the Constitution, the Fundamental Right to Property has been the most controversial. It has caused confrontations between the Supreme Court and the Parliament. It has led to a number of Constitutional amendments, that is, 1st, 4th, 7th, 25th, 39th, 40th and 42nd Amendments. Through these amendments, Articles 31A, 31B and 31C have been added and modified from time to time to nullify the effect of Supreme Court judgements and to protect certain laws from being challenged on the grounds of contravention of Fundamental Rights. Most of the litigation centred around the obligation of the state to pay compensation for acquisition or requisition of private property.

Therefore, the 44th Amendment Act of 1978 abolished the right to property as a Fundamental Right by repealing Article 19(1)(f) and Article 31 from Part III. Instead, the Act inserted a new Article 300A in Part XII under the heading 'Right to Property'. It provides that no person shall be deprived of his property except by authority of law. Thus, the right to property still remains a legal right or a constitutional right, though no longer a fundamental right. It is not a part of the basic structure of the Constitution.

The right to property as a legal right (as distinct from the Fundamental Rights) has the following implications:

(a) It can be regulated ie, curtailed, abridged or modified without constitutional amendment by an ordinary law of the Parliament.

(b) It protects private property against executive action but not against legislative action.

(c) In case of violation, the aggrieved person cannot directly move the Supreme Court under Article 32 (right to constitutional remedies including writs) for its enforcement. He can move the High Court under Article 226.

(d) No guaranteed right to compensation in case of acquisition or requisition of the private property by the state.

Though the Fundamental Right to Property under Part III has been abolished, the Part III still carries two provisions which provide for the guaranteed right to compensation in case of acquisition or requisition of the private property by the state. These two cases where compensation has to be paid are:

(a) When the State acquires the property of a minority educational institution (Article 30); and

(b) When the State acquires the land held by a person under his personal cultivation and the land is within the statutory ceiling limits (Article 31 A).

The first provision was added by the 44th Amendment Act (1978), while the second provision was added by the 17th Amendment Act (1964).

Further, Articles 31A, 31B and 31C have been retained as exceptions to the fundamental rights.

EXCEPTIONS TO FUNDAMENTAL RIGHTS

1. Saving of Laws Providing for Acquisition of Estates, etc.

Article 31A[16] saves five categories of laws from being challenged and invalidated on the ground of contravention of the fundamental rights conferred by Article 14 (equality before law and equal protection of laws) and Article 19 (protection of six rights in respect of speech, assembly, movement, etc.). They are related to agricultural land reforms, industry and commerce and include the following:

(a) Acquisition of estates[17] and related rights by the State;

(b) Taking over the management of properties by the State;

(c) Amalgamation of corporations;

(d) Extinguishment or modification of rights of directors or shareholders of corporations; and

(e) Extinguishment or modification of mining leases.

Article 31A does not immunise a state law from judicial review unless it has been reserved for the president's consideration and has received his assent.

This Article also provides for the payment of compensation at market value when the state acquires the land held by a person under his personal cultivation and the land is within the statutory ceiling limit.

2. Validation of Certain Acts and Regulations

Article 31B saves the acts and regulations included in the Ninth Schedule[18] from being challenged and invalidated on the ground of contravention of any of the fundamental rights. Thus, the scope of Article 31B is wider than Article 31A. Article 31B immunises any law included in the Ninth Schedule from all the fundamental rights whether or not the law falls under any of the five categories specified in Article 31A.

However, in a significant judgement delivered in January 2007, the Supreme Court ruled that there could not be any blanket immunity from judicial review of laws included in the Ninth Schedule. The court held that judicial review is a 'basic feature' of the constitution and it could not be taken away by putting a law under the Ninth Schedule. It said that the laws placed under the Ninth Schedule after April 24, 1973, are open to challenge in court if they violated fundamentals rights guaranteed under Articles 14, 15, 19 and 21 or the 'basic structure' of the constitution. It was on April 24, 1973, that the Supreme Court first propounded the doctrine of 'basic structure' or 'basic features' of the constitution in its landmark verdict in the Kesavananda Bharati Case.[19]

Originally (in 1951), the Ninth Schedule contained only 13 acts and regulations but at present (in 2013) their number is 282.[20] Of these, the acts and regulations of the state legislature deal with land reforms and abolition of the zamindari system and that of the Parliament deal with other matters.

3. Saving of Laws Giving Effect to Certain Directive Principles

Article 31C, as inserted by the 25th Amendment Act of 1971, contained the following two provisions:

(a) No law that seeks to implement the socialistic directive principles specified in Article 39(b)[21] or (c)[22] shall be void on the ground of contravention of the fundamental rights conferred by Article 14 (equality before law and equal protection of laws) or Article 19 (protection of six rights in respect of speech, assembly, movement, etc.)

(b) No law containing a declaration that it is for giving effect to such policy shall be questioned in any court on the ground that it does not give effect to such a policy.

In the *Kesavananda Bharati* case[23] (1973), the Supreme Court declared the above second provision of Article 31C as unconstitutional and invalid on the ground that judicial review is a basic feature of the Constitution and hence, cannot be taken away. However, the above first provision of Article 31C was held to be constitutional and valid.

The 42nd Amendment Act (1976) extended the scope of the above first provision of Article 31C by including within its protection any law to implement any of the directive principles specified in Part IV of the Constitution and not merely in Article 39 (b) or (c). However, this extention was declared as unconstitutional and invalid by the Supreme Court in the *Minerva Mills* case[24] (1980).

CRITICISM OF FUNDAMENTAL RIGHTS

The Fundamental Rights enshrined in Part III of the Constitution have met with a wide and varied criticism. The arguments of the critics are:

1. Excessive Limitations

They are subjected to innumerable exceptions, restrictions, qualifications and explanations. Hence, the critics remarked that the Constitution grants Fundamental Rights with one hand and takes them away with the other. Jaspat Roy Kapoor went to the extent of saying that the chapter dealing with the fundamental rights should be renamed as 'Limitaions on Fundamental Rights' or 'Fundamental Rights and Limitations Thereon'.

2. No Social and Economic Rights

The list is not comprehensive as it mainly consists of political rights. It makes no provision for important social and economic rights like right to social security, right to work, right to employment, right to rest and leisure and so on. These rights are made available to the citizens of advanced democratic countries. Also, the socialistic constitutions of erstwhile USSR or China provided for such rights.

3. No Clarity

They are stated in a vague, indefinite and ambiguous manner. The various phrases and words used in the chapter like 'public order', 'minorities', 'reasonable restriction', 'public interest' and so on are not clearly defined. The language used to describe them is very complicated and beyond the comprehension of the common man. It is alleged that the Constitution was made by the lawyers for the lawyers. Sir Ivor

Jennings called the Constitution of India a 'paradise for lawyers'.

4. No Permanency

They are not sacrosanct or immutable as the Parliament can curtail or abolish them, as for example, the abolition of the fundamental right to property in 1978. Hence, they can become a play tool in the hands of politicians having majority support in the Parliament. The judicially innovated 'doctrine of basic structure' is the only limitation on the authority of Parliament to curtail or abolish the fundamental right.

5. Suspension During Emergency

The suspension of their enforcement during the operation of National Emergency (except Articles 20 and 21) is another blot on the efficacy of these rights. This provision cuts at the roots of democratic system in the country by placing the rights of the millions of innocent people in continuous jeopardy. According to the critics, the Fundamental Rights should be enjoyable in all situations—Emergency or no Emergency.

6. Expensive Remedy

The judiciary has been made responsible for defending and protecting these rights against the interference of the legislatures and executives. However, the judicial process is too expensive and hinders the common man from getting his rights enforced through the courts. Hence, the critics say that the rights benefit mainly the rich section of the Indian Society.

7. Preventive Detention

The critics assert that the provision for preventive detention (Article 22) takes away the spirit and substance of the chapter on fundamental rights. It confers arbitrary powers on the State and negates individual liberty. It justifies the criticism that the Constitution of India deals more with the rights of the State against the individual than with the rights of the individual against the State. Notably, no democratic country in the world has made preventive detention as an integral part of their Constitutions as has been made in India.

8. No Consistent Philosophy

According to some critics, the chapter on fundamental rights is not the product of any philosophical principle. Sir Ivor Jennings expressed this view when he said that the Fundamental Rights proclaimed by the Indian Constitution are based on no consistent philosophy.[25] The critics say that this creates difficulty for the Supreme Court and the high courts in interpreting the fundamental rights.

SIGNIFICANCE OF FUNDAMENTAL RIGHTS

In spite of the above criticism and shortcomings, the Fundamental Rights are significant in the following respects:

1. They constitute the bedrock of democratic system in the country.
2. They provide necessary conditions for the material and moral protection of man.
3. They serve as a formidable bulwark of individual liberty.
4. They facilitate the establishment of rule of law in the country.
5. They protect the interests of minorities and weaker sections of society.
6. They strengthen the secular fabric of the Indian State.
7. They check the absoluteness of the authority of the government.

8. They lay down the foundation stone of social equality and social justice.
9. They ensure the dignity and respect of individuals.
10. They facilitate the participation of people in the political and administrative process.

RIGHTS OUTSIDE PART III

Besides the Fundamental Rights included in Part III, there are certain other rights contained in other parts of the Constitution. These rights are known as constitutional rights or legal rights or non-fundamental rights. They are:

1. No tax shall be levied or collected except by authority of law (Article 265 in Part XII).
2. No person shall be deprived of his property save by authority of law (Article 300-A in Part XII).
3. Trade, commerce and intercourse throughout the territory of India shall be free (Article 301 in Part XIII).
4. The elections to the Lok Sabha and the State Legislative Assembly shall be on the basis of adult suffrage (Article 326 in Part XV).

Even though the above rights are also equally justiciable, they are different from the Fundamental Rights. In case of violation of a Fundamental Right, the aggrieved person can directly move the Supreme Court for its enforcement under Article 32, which is in itself a fundamental right. But, in case of violation of the above rights, the aggrieved person cannot avail this constitutional remedy. He can move the High Court by an ordinary suit or under Article 226 (writ jurisdiction of high court).

Table 7.4 *Articles Related to Fundamental Rights at a Glance*

Article No.	Subject-matter
General	
12.	Definition of State
13.	Laws inconsistent with or in derogation of the Fundamental Rights
Right to Equality	
14.	Equality before law
15.	Prohibition of discrimination on grounds of religion, race, caste, sex or place of birth
16.	Equality of opportunity in matters of public employment

(Contd.)

Article No.	Subject-matter
17.	Abolition of untouchability
18.	Abolition of titles
Right to Freedom	
19.	Protection of certain rights regarding freedom of speech, etc.
20.	Protection in respect of conviction for offences
21.	Protection of life and personal liberty
21A.	Right to education
22.	Protection against arrest and detention in certain cases
Right against Exploitation	
23.	Prohibition of traffic in human beings and forced labour
24.	Prohibition of employment of children in factories, etc.
Right to Freedom of Religion	
25.	Freedom of conscience and free profession, practice and propagation of religion
26.	Freedom to manage religious affairs
27.	Freedom as to payment of taxes for promotion of any particular religion
28.	Freedom as to attendance at religious instruction or religious worship in certain educational institutions.
Cultural and Educational Rights	
29.	Protection of interests of minorities
30.	Right of minorities to establish and administer educational institutions
31.	Compulsory acquisition of property—(Repealed)
Saving of Certain Laws	
31A.	Saving of laws providing for acquisition of estates, etc.
31B.	Validation of certain Acts and Regulations
31C.	Saving of laws giving effect to certain directive principles
31D.	Saving of laws in respect of anti-national activities—(Repealed)
Right to Constitutional Remedies	
32.	Remedies for enforcement of rights conferred by this part
32A.	Constitutional validity of State laws not to be considered in proceedings under Article 32—(Repealed)
33.	Power of Parliament to modify the rights conferred by this part in their application to forces, etc.
34.	Restriction on rights conferred by this part while martial law is in force in any area
35.	Legislation to give effect to the provisions of this part

Notes and References

1. 'Magna Carta' is the Charter of Rights issued by King John of England in 1215 under pressure from the barons. This is the first written document relating to the Fundamental Rights of citizens.

2. *Kesavananda Bharati vs. State of Kerala,* (1973).

3. Dicey observe: "No man is above the law, but every man, whatever be his rank or condition, is subject to the ordinary law of the realm and amenable to the jurisdiction of the ordinary tribunals. Every official from the Prime Minister down to a constable or a collector of taxes, is under the same responsibility for every act done without legal justification as any other citizen". (A V Dicey, *Introduction to the Study of the Law of the Constitution,* Macmillan, 1931 Edition P. 183–191).

4. This second provision was added by the first Amendment Act of 1951.

5. By virtue of Article 371D inserted by the 32nd Amendment Act of 1973.

6. The first Backward Classes Commission was appointed in 1953 under the chairmanship of Kaka Kalelkar. It submitted its report in 1955.

7. In 1963, the Supreme Court ruled that more than 50% reservation of jobs in a single year would be unconstitutional.

8. *Indra Sawhney v. Union of India,* (1992).

9. The Tamil Nadu Backward Classes, Scheduled Castes and Scheduled Tribes (Reservation of seats in educational institutions and of appointments or posts in the services under the state) Act, 1994.

10. *Balaji Raghavan v. Union of India,* (1996).

10a. The provision for "co-operative societies" was made by the 97th Constitutional Amendment Act of 2011.

10b. Ibid

11. *A K Gopalan v. State of Madras,* (1950).

12. *Menaka Gandhi v. Union of India,* (1978).

12a. The Constitution (Eighty-sixth amendment) Act, 2002 and the Right of Children to Free and Compulsory Education Act, 2009 have come into force w.e.f. 1 April 2010.

13. Originally known as the Suppression of Immoral Traffic in Women and Girls Act, 1956.

14. In this clause, the reference to Hindus shall be construed as including a reference to persons professing the Sikh, Jaina and Buddhist religion and the reference to Hindu religious institutions shall be construed accordingly (Article 25).

15. The second provision was added by the 15th Constitutional Amendment Act of 1963.

16. Added by the 1st Constitutional Amendment Act of 1951 and amended by the 4th, 17th and 44th Amendments.

17. The expression 'estate' includes any *jagir, inam, muafi* or other similar grant, any *janmam* right in Tamil Nadu and Kerala and any land held for agricultural purposes.

18. Article 31B along with the Ninth Schedule was added by the 1st Constitutional Amendment Act of 1951.

19. *Kesavananda Bharati v. State of Kerala,* (1973).

20. Though the last entry is numbered 284, the actual total number is 282. This is because, the three entries (87, 92 and 130) have been deleted and one entry is numbered as 257A.

21. Article 39 (b) says—The State shall direct its policy towards securing that the ownership and control of the material resources of the community are so distributed as best to subserve the common good.

22. Article 39 (c) says—The state shall direct its policy towards securing that the operation of the economic system does not result in the concentration of wealth and means of production to the common detriment.

23. *Kesavananda Bharati v. State of Kerala,* (1973).

24. *Minerva Mills v. Union of India, (1980).*

25. *Sir Ivor Jennings wrote: 'A thread of nineteenth century liberalism runs through it; there are consequences of the political problems of Britain in it; there are relics of the bitter experience in opposition to British rule; and there is evidence of a desire to reform some of the social institutions which time and circumstances have developed in India. The result is a series of complex formulae, in twenty-four articles, some of them lengthy, which must become the basis of a vast and complicated case law'.*

Directive Principles of State Policy

The Directive Principles of State Policy are enumerated in Part IV of the Constitution from Articles 36 to 51[1]. *The framers of the Constitution borrowed this idea from the Irish Constitution of 1937, which had copied it from the Spanish Constitution.* Dr B R Ambedkar described these principles as 'novel features' of the Indian Constitution. The Directive Principles along with the Fundamental Rights contain the philosophy of the Constitution and is the soul of the Constitution. Granville Austin has described the Directive Principles and the Fundamental Rights as the 'Conscience of the Constitution'[2].

FEATURES OF THE DIRECTIVE PRINCIPLES

1. The phrase 'Directive Principles of State Policy' denotes the ideals that the State should keep in mind while formulating policies and enacting laws. These are the constitutional instructions or recommendations to the State in legislative, executive and administrative matters. According to Article 36, the term 'State' in Part IV has the same meaning as in Part III dealing with Fundamental Rights. Therefore, it includes the legislative and executive organs of the central and state governments, all local authorities and all other public authorities in the country.

2. The Directive Principles resemble the 'Instrument of Instructions' enumerated in the Government of India Act of 1935. In the words of Dr B R Ambedkar, 'the Directive Principles are like the instrument of instructions, which were issued to the Governor-General and to the Governors of the colonies of India by the British Government under the Government of India Act of 1935. What is called Directive Principles is merely another name for the instrument of instructions. The only difference is that they are instructions to the legislature and the executive'.

3. The Directive Principles constitute a very comprehensive economic, social and political programme for a modern democratic State. They aim at realising the high ideals of justice, liberty, equality and fraternity as outlined in the Preamble to the Constitution. They embody the concept of a 'welfare state' and not that of a 'police state', which existed during the colonial era[3]. In brief, they seek to establish economic and social democracy in the country.

4. The Directive Principles are non-justiciable in nature, that is, they are not legally enforceable by the courts for their violation. Therefore, the government (Central, state and local) cannot be compelled to implement them. Nevertheless, the Constitution (Article 37) itself says that these principles are fundamental in the governance of the country and it shall be the duty of the State to apply these principles in making laws.

5. The Directive Principles, though non-justiciable in nature, help the courts in examining and determining the constitutional validity of a law. The Supreme Court has ruled many a times that in determining the constitutional-

ity of any law, if a court finds that the law in question seeks to give effect to a Directive Principle, it may consider such law to be 'reasonable' in relation to Article 14 (equality before law) or Article 19 (six freedoms) and thus save such law from unconstitutionality.

CLASSIFICATION OF THE DIRECTIVE PRINCIPLES

The Constitution does not contain any classification of Directive Principles. However, on the basis of their content and direction, they can be classified into three broad categories, viz, socialistic, Gandhian and liberal–intellectual.

Socialistic Principles

These principles reflect the ideology of socialism. They lay down the framework of a democratic socialist state, aim at providing social and economic justice, and set the path towards welfare state. They direct the state:

1. To promote the welfare of the people by securing a social order permeated by justice—social, economic and political—and to minimise inequalities in income, status, facilities and opportunities[4] (Article 38).
2. To secure (a) the right to adequate means of livelihood for all citizens; (b) the equitable distribution of material resources of the community for the common good; (c) prevention of concentration of wealth and means of production; (d) equal pay for equal work for men and women; (e) preservation of the health and strength of workers and children against forcible abuse; and (f) opportunities for healthy development of children[5] (Article 39).
3. To promote equal justice and to provide free legal aid to the poor[6] (Article 39 A).
4. To secure the right to work, to education and to public assistance in cases of unemployment, old age, sickness and disablement (Article 41).
5. To make provision for just and humane conditions for work and maternity relief (Article 42).
6. To secure a living wage[7], a decent standard of life and social and cultural opportunities for all workers (Article 43).

7. To take steps to secure the participation of workers in the management of industries[8] (Article 43 A).
8. To raise the level of nutrition and the standard of living of people and to improve public health (Article 47).

Gandhian Principles

These principles are based on Gandhian ideology. They represent the programme of reconstruction enunciated by Gandhi during the national movement. In order to fulfil the dreams of Gandhi, some of his ideas were included as Directive Principles. They require the State:

1. To organise village panchayats and endow them with necessary powers and authority to enable them to function as units of self-government (Article 40).
2. To promote cottage industries on an individual or co-operation basis in rural areas (Article 43).
3. To promote voluntary formation, autonomous functioning, democratic control and professional management of co-operative societies[8a] (Article 43B).
4. To promote the educational and economic interests of SCs, STs, and other weaker sections of the society and to protect them from social injustice and exploitation (Article 46).
5. To prohibit the consumption of intoxicating drinks and drugs which are injurious to health (Article 47).
6. To prohibit the slaughter of cows, calves and other milch and draught cattle and to improve their breeds (Article 48).

Liberal–Intellectual Principles

The principles included in this category represent the ideology of liberalism. They direct the state:

1. To secure for all citizens a uniform civil code throughout the country (Article 44).
2. To provide early childhood care and education for all children until they complete the age of six years[9] (Article 45).
3. To organise agriculture and animal husbandry on modern and scientific lines (Article 48).
4. To protect and improve the environment and to safeguard forests and wild life[10] (Article 48 A).

5. To protect monuments, places and objects of artistic or historic interest which are declared to be of national importance (Article 49).
6. To separate the judiciary from the executive in the public services of the State (Article 50).
7. To promote international peace and security and maintain just and honourable relations between nations; to foster respect for international law and treaty obligations, and to encourage settlement of international disputes by arbitration (Article 51).

NEW DIRECTIVE PRINCIPLES

The 42nd Amendment Act of 1976 added four new Directive Principles to the original list. They require the State:

1. To secure opportunities for healthy development of children (Article 39).
2. To promote equal justice and to provide free legal aid to the poor (Article 39 A).
3. To take steps to secure the participation of workers in the management of industries (Article 43 A).
4. To protect and improve the environment and to safeguard forests and wild life (Article 48 A).

The 44th Amendment Act of 1978 added one more Directive Principle, which requires the State to minimise inequalities in income, status, facilities and opportunities (Article 38).

Again, the 86th Amendment Act of 2002 changed the subject-matter of Article 45 and made elementary education a fundamental right under Article 21 A. The amended directive requires the State to provide early childhood care and education for all children until they complete the age of six years.

The 97th Amendment Act of 2011 added a new Directive Principle relating to co-operative societies. It requires the state to promote voluntary formation, autonomous functioning, democratic control and professional management of co-operative societies (Article 43B).

SANCTION BEHIND DIRECTIVE PRINCIPLES

Sir B N Rau, the Constitutional Advisor to the Constituent Assembly, recommended that the rights of an individual should be divided into two categories—justiciable and non-justiciable, which was accepted by the Drafting Committee. Consequently, the Fundamental Rights, which are justiciable in nature, are incorporated in Part III and the Directive Principles, which are non-justiciable in nature, are incorporated in Part IV of the Constitution.

Though the Directive Principles are non-justiciable, the Constitution (Article 37) make it clear that 'these principles are fundamental in the governance of the country and it shall be the duty of the state to apply these principles in making laws'. Thus, they impose a moral obligation on the state authorities for their application, but the real force behind them is political, that is, public opinion. As observed by Alladi Krishna Swamy Ayyar, 'no ministry responsible to the people can afford light-heartedly to ignore the provisions in Part IV of the Constitution'. Similarly, Dr B R Ambedkar said in the Constituent Assembly that 'a government which rests on popular vote can hardly ignore the Directive Principles while shaping its policy. If any government ignores them, it will certainly have to answer for that before the electorate at the election time.'[11]

The framers of the Constitution made the Directive Principles non-justiciable and legally non-enforceable because:

1. The country did not possess sufficient financial resources to implement them.
2. The presence of vast diversity and backwardness in the country would stand in the way of their implementation.
3. The newly born independent Indian State with its many preoccupations might be crushed under the burden unless it was free to decide the order, the time, the place and the mode of fulfilling them.

'The Constitution makers, therefore, taking a pragmatic view, refrained from giving teeth to these principles. They believed more in an awakened public opinion rather than in court procedures as the ultimate sanction for the fulfilment of these principles'[12].

CRITICISM OF THE DIRECTIVE PRINCIPLES

The Directive Principles of State Policy have been criticised by some members of the Constituent Assembly as well as other constitutional and political experts on the following grounds:

1. No Legal Force

The Directives have been criticised mainly because of their non-justiciable character. While K T Shah dubbed them as 'pious superfluities' and compared them with 'a cheque on a bank, payable only when the resources of the bank permit'[13], Nasiruddin contended that these principles are 'no better than the new year's resolutions, which are broken on the second of January'. Even as T T Krishnamachari described the Directives as 'a veritable dustbin of sentiments', K C Wheare called them as a 'manifesto of aims and aspirations' and opined that they serve as mere 'moral homily', and Sir Ivor Jennings thought they are only as 'pious aspirations'.

2. Illogically Arranged

Critics opine that the Directives are not arranged in a logical manner based on a consistent philosophy. According to N Srinivasan, 'the Directives are neither properly classified nor logically arranged. The declaration mixes up relatively unimportant issues with the most vital economic and social questions. It combines rather incongruously the modern with the old and provisions suggested by the reason and science with provisions based purely on sentiment and prejudice'[14]. Sir Ivor Jennings too pointed out that these principles have no consistent philosophy.

3. Conservative

According to Sir Ivor Jennings, the Directives are based on the political philosophy of the 19th century England. He remarked: 'The ghosts of Sydney Webb and Beatrice Webb stalk through the pages of the text. Part IV of the Constitution expresses Fabian Socialism without the socialism'. He opined that the Directives 'are deemed to be suitable in India in the middle of the twentieth century. The question whether they are suitable for the twenty-first century cannot be answered; but it is quite probable that they will be entirely out moded.'[15]

4. Constitutional Conflict

K Santhanam has pointed out that the Directives lead to a constitutional conflict **(a)** between the Centre and the states, **(b)** between the President and the Prime Minister, and **(c)** between the governor and the chief minister. According to him, the Centre can give directions to the states with regard to the implementation of these principles, and in case of non-compliance, can dismiss the state government. Similarly, when the Prime Minister gets a bill (which violates the Directive Principles) passed by the Parliament, the president may reject the bill on the ground that these principles are fundamental to the governance of the country and hence, the ministry has no right to ignore them. The same constitutional conflict may occur between the governor and the chief minister at the state level.

UTILITY OF DIRECTIVE PRINCIPLES

In spite of the above criticisms and shortcomings, the Directive Principles are not an unnecessary appendage to the Constitution. The Constitution itself declares that they are fundamental to the governance of the country. According to L M Singhvi, an eminent jurist and diplomat, 'the Directives are the life giving provisions of the Constitution. They constitute the stuff of the Constitution and its philosophy of social justice'[16]. M C Chagla, former Chief Justice of India, is of the opinion that, 'if all these principles are fully carried out, our country would indeed be a heaven on earth. India would then be not only democracy in the political sense, but also a welfare state looking after the welfare of its citizens'[17]. Dr B R Ambedkar had pointed out that the Directives have great value because they lay down that the goal of Indian polity is 'economic democracy' as distinguished from 'political democracy'. Granville Austin opined that the Directive Principles are 'aimed at furthering the goals of the social revolution or to foster this revolution by establishing the conditions necessary for its achivement'[18]. Sir B N Rau, the constitutional advisor to the Constituent Assembly, stated that the Directive Principles are intended as 'moral precepts for the authorities of the state. They have at least an educative value.'

According to M C Setalvad, the former Attorney General of India, the Directive Principles, although confer no legal rights and creates no legal remedies, are significant and useful in the following ways:

1. They are like an 'Instrument of Instructions' or general recommendations addressed to all authorities in the Indian Union. They remind them of the basic principles of the new social and economic order, which the Constitution aims at building.

2. They have served as useful beacon-lights to the courts. They have helped the courts in exercising their power of judicial review, that is, the power to determine the constitutional validity of a law.

3. They form the dominating background to all State action, legislative or executive and also a guide to the courts in some respects.

4. They amplify the Preamble, which solemnly resolves to secure to all citizens of India justice, liberty, equality and fraternity.

The Directives also play the following roles:

1. They facilitate stability and continuity in domestic and foreign policies in political, economic and social spheres in spite of the changes of the party in power.

2. They are supplementary to the fundamental rights of the citizens. They are intended to fill in the vacuum in Part III by providing for social and economic rights.

3. Their implementation creates a favourable atmosphere for the full and proper enjoyment of the fundamental rights by the citizens. Political democracy, without economic democracy, has no meaning.

4. They enable the opposition to exercise influence and control over the operations of the government. The Opposition can blame the ruling party on the ground that its activities are opposed to the Directives.

5. They serve as a crucial test for the performance of the government. The people can examine the policies and programmes of the government in the light of these constitutional declarations.

6. They serve as common political manifesto. 'A ruling party, irrespective of its political ideology, has to recognise the fact that these principles are intended to be its guide, philosopher and friend in its legislative and executive acts'[19].

CONFLICT BETWEEN FUNDAMENTAL RIGHTS AND DIRECTIVE PRINCIPLES

The justiciability of Fundamental Rights and non-justiciability of Directive Principles on the one hand and the moral obligation of State to implement Directive Principles (Article 37) on the other hand have led to a conflict between the two since the commencement of the Constitution. In the *Champakam Dorairajan* case[20] (1951), the Supreme Court ruled that in case of any conflict between the Fundamental Rights and the Directive Principles, the former would prevail. It declared that the Directive Principles have to conform to and run as subsidiary to the Fundamental Rights. But, it also held that the Fundamental Rights could be amended by the Parliament by enacting constitutional amendments acts. As a result, the Parliament made the First Amendment Act (1951), the Fourth Amendment Act (1955) and the Seventeenth Amendment Act (1964) to implement some of the Directives.

The above situation underwent a major change in 1967 following the Supreme Court's judgement in the *Golaknath* case[21] (1967). In that case, the Supreme Court ruled that the Parliament cannot take away or abridge any of the Fundamental Rights, which are 'sacrosanct' in nature. In other words, the Court held that the Fundamental Rights cannot be amended for the implementation of the Directive Principles.

The Parliament reacted to the Supreme Court's judgement in the *Golaknath Case* (1967) by enacting the 24th Amendment Act (1971) and the 25th Amendment Act (1971). The 24th Amendment Act declared that the Parliament has the power to abridge or take away any of the Fundamental Rights by enacting Constitutional Amendment Acts. The 25th Amendment Act inserted a new Article 31C which contained the following two provisions:

1. No law which seeks to implement the socialistic Directive Principles specified in Article 39 (b)[22] and (c)[23] shall be void on the ground of contravention of the Fundamental Rights conferred by Article 14 (equality before law

Table 8.1 *Distinction Between Fundamental Rights and Directive Principles*

Fundamental Rights	Directive Principles
1. These are negative as they prohibit the State from doing certain things.	1. These are positive as they require the State to do certain things.
2. These are justiciable, that is, they are legally enforceable by the courts in case of their violation.	2. These are non-justiciable, that is, they are not legally enforceable by the courts for their violation.
3. They aim at establishing political democracy in the country.	3. They aim at establishing social and economic democracy in the country.
4. These have legal sanctions.	4. These have moral and political sanctions.
5. They promote the welfare of the individual. Hence, they are personal and individualistic.	5. They promote the welfare of the community. Hence, they are societarian and socialistic.
6. They do not require any legislation for their implementation. They are automatically enforced.	6. They require legislation for their implementation. They are not automatically enforced.
7. The courts are bound to declare a law violative of any of the Fundamental Rights as unconstitutional and invalid.	7. The courts cannot declare a law violative of any of the Directive Principles as unconstitutional and invalid. However, they can uphold the validity of a law on the ground that it was enacted to give effect to a directive.

and equal protection of laws), Article 19 (protection of six rights in respect of speech, assembly, movement, etc) or Article 31 (right to property).

2. No law containing a declaration for giving effect to such policy shall be questioned in any court on the ground that it does not give effect to such a policy.

In the *Kesavananda Bharati* case[24] (1973), the Supreme Court declared the above second provision of Article 31C as unconstitutional and invalid on the ground that judicial review is a basic feature of the Constitution and hence, cannot be taken away. However, the above first provision of Article 31C was held to be constitutional and valid.

Later, the 42nd Amendment Act (1976) extended the scope of the above first provision of Article 31C by including within its protection any law to implement any of the Directive Principles and not merely those specified in Article 39 (b) and (c). In other words, the 42nd Amendment Act accorded the position of legal primacy and supremacy to the Directive Principles over the Fundamental Rights conferred by Articles 14, 19 and 31. However, this extension was declared as unconstitutional and invalid by the Supreme Court in the *Minerva Mills* case[25] (1980).

It means that the Directive Principles were once again made subordinate to the Fundamental Rights. But the Fundamental Rights conferred by Article 14 and Article 19 were accepted as subordinate to the Directive Principles specified in Article 39 (b) and (c). Further, Article 31 (right to property) was abolished by the 44th Amendment Act (1978).

In the *Minerva Mills* case (1980), the Supreme Court also held that 'the Indian Constitution is founded on the bedrock of the balance between the Fundamental Rights and the Directive Principles. They together constitute the core of commitment to social revolution. They are like two wheels of a chariot, one no less than the other. To give absolute primacy to one over the other is to disturb the harmony of the Constitution. This harmony and balance between the two is an essential feature of the basic structure of the Constitution. The goals set out by the Directive Principles have to be achieved without the abrogation of the means provided by the Fundamental Rights'.

Therefore, the present position is that the Fundamental Rights enjoy supremacy over the Directive Principles. Yet, this does not mean that the Directive Principles cannot be implemented. The Parliament can amend the Fundamental Rights for implementing the Directive Principles, so long as the amendment does not damage or destroy the basic structure of the Constitution.

IMPLEMENTATION OF DIRECTIVE PRINCIPLES

Since 1950, the successive governments at the Centre and in the states have made several laws and formulated various programmes for implementing the Directive Principles. These are mentioned below:

1. The Planning Commission was established in 1950 to take up the development of the country in a planned manner. The successive Five Year Plans aimed at securing socio-economic justice and reducing inequalities of income, status and opportunities.

2. Almost all the states have passed land reform laws to bring changes in the agrarian society and to improve the conditions of the rural masses. These measures include (a) abolition of intermediaries like zamindars, jagirdars, inamdars, etc; (b) tenancy reforms like security of tenure, fair rents, etc; (c) imposition of ceilings on land holdings; (d) distribution of surplus land among the landless labourers; and (e) cooperative farming.

3. The Minimum Wages Act (1948), the Payment of Wages Act (1936), the Payment of Bonus Act (1965), the Contract Labour Regulation and Abolition Act (1970), the Child Labour Prohibition and Regulation Act (1986), the Bonded Labour System Abolition Act (1976), the Trade Unions Act (1926), the Factories Act (1948), the Mines Act (1952), the Industrial Disputes Act (1947), the Workmen's Compensation Act (1923) and so on have been enacted to protect the interests of the labour sections. In 2006, the government banned the child labour.

4. The Maternity Benefit Act (1961) and the Equal Remuneration Act (1976) have been made to protect the interests of women workers.

5. Various measures have been taken to utilise the financial resources for promoting the common good. These include nationalisation of life insurance (1956), the nationalisation of fourteen leading commercial banks (1969), nationalisation of general insurance (1971), abolition of Privy Purses (1971) and so on.

6. The Legal Services Authorities Act (1987) has established a nation-wide network to provide free and competent legal aid to the poor and to organise lok adalats for promoting equal justice. Lok adalat is a statutory forum for conciliatory settlement of legal disputes. It has been given the status of a civil court. Its awards are enforceable, binding on the parties and final as no appeal lies before any court against them.

7. Khadi and Village Industries Board, Khadi and Village Industries Commission, Small-Scale Industries Board, National Small Industries Corporation, Handloom Board, Handicrafts Board, Coir Board, Silk Board and so on have been set up for the development of cottage industries in rural areas.

8. The Community Development Programme (1952), Hill Area Development Programme (1960), Drought-Prone Area Programme (1973), Minimum Needs Programme (1974), Integrated Rural Development Programme (1978), Jawahar Rozgar Yojana (1989), Swarnajayanti Gram Swarozgar Yojana (1999), Sampoorna Grameena Rozgar Yojana (2001), National Rural Employment Guarantee Programme (2006) and so on have been launched for raising the standard of living of people.

9. The Wildlife (Protection) Act, 1972 and the Forest (Conservation) Act, 1980, have been enacted to safeguard the wildlife and the forests respectively. Further, the Water and Air Acts have provided for the establishment of the Central and State Pollution Control Boards, which are engaged in the protection and improvement of environment. The National Forest Policy (1988) aims at the protection, conservation and development of forests.

10. Agriculture has been modernised by providing improved agricultural inputs, seeds, fertilisers and irrigation facilities. Various steps have also been taken to organise animal husbandry on modern and scientific lines.

11. Three-tier panchayati raj system (at village, taluka and zila levels) has been introduced to

translate into reality Gandhiji's dream of every village being a republic. The 73rd Amendment Act (1992) has been enacted to provide constitutional status and protection to these panchayati raj institutions.

12. Seats are reserved for SCs, STs and other weaker sections in educational institutions, government services and representative bodies. The Untouchability (Offences) Act, 1955, which was renamed as the Protection of Civil Rights Act in 1976 and the Scheduled Castes and Scheduled Tribes (Prevention of Atrocities) Act, 1989, have been enacted to protect the SCs and STs from social injustice and exploitation. The 65th Constitutional Amendment Act of 1990 established the National Commission for Scheduled Castes and Scheduled Tribes to protect the interests of SCs and STs. The 89th Constitutional Amendment Act of 2003 bifurcated this combined commission into two separate bodies, namely, National Commission for Schedule Castes and National Commission for Schedule Tribes.

13. The Criminal Procedure Code (1973) separated the judiciary from the executive in the public services of the state. Prior to this separation, the district authorities like the collector, the sub-divisional officer, the tehsildar and so on used to exercise judicial powers along with the traditional executive powers. After the separation, the judicial powers were taken away from these executive authorities and vested in the hands of district judicial magistrates who work under the direct control of the state high court.

14. The Ancient and Historical Monument and Archaeological Sites and Remains Act (1951) has been enacted to protect the monuments, places and objects of national importance.

15. Primary health centres and hospitals have been established throughout the country to improve the public health. Also, special programmes have been launched to eradicate widespread diseases like malaria, TB, leprosy, AIDS, cancer, filaria, kala-azar, guineaworm, yaws, Japanese encephalitis and so on.

16. Laws to prohibit the slaughter of cows, calves, and bullocks have been enacted in some states.

17. Some states have initiated the old age pension schemes for people above 65 years.

18. India has been following the policy of non-alignment and panchsheel to promote international peace and security.

In spite of the above steps by the Central and state governments, the Directive Principles have not been implemented fully and effectively due to several reasons like inadequate financial resources, unfavourable socio-economic conditions, population explosion, strained Centre-state relations and so on.

DIRECTIVES OUTSIDE PART IV

Apart from the Directives included in Part IV, there are some other Directives contained in other Parts of the Constitution. They are:

1. *Claims of SCs and STs to Services:* The claims of the members of the Scheduled Castes and the Scheduled Tribes shall be taken into consideration, consistently with the maintenance of efficiency of administration, in the making of appointments to services and posts in connection with the affairs of the Union or a State (Article 335 in Part XVI).

2. *Instruction in mother tongue:* It shall be the endeavour of every state and every local authority within the state to provide adequate facilities for instruction in the mother-tongue at the primary stage of education to children belonging to linguistic minority groups (Article 350-A in Part XVII).

3. *Development of the Hindi Language:* It shall be the duty of the Union to promote the spread of the Hindi language and to develop it so that it may serve as a medium of expression for all the elements of the composite culture of India (Article 351 in Part XVII).

The above Directives are also non-justiciable in nature. However, they are also given equal importance and attention by the judiciary on the ground that all parts of the constitution must be read together.

Table 8.2 *Articles Related to Directive Principles of State Policy at a Glance*

Article No.	Subject-matter
36.	Definition of State
37.	Application of the principles contained in this part
38.	State to secure a social order for the promotion of welfare of the people
39.	Certain principles of policy to be followed by the State
39A.	Equal justice and free legal aid
40.	Organisation of village panchayats
41.	Right to work, to education and to public assistance in certain cases
42.	Provision for just and humane conditions of work and maternity relief
43.	Living wage, etc., for workers
43A.	Participation of workers in management of industries
43B.	Promotion of co-operative societies
44.	Uniform civil code for the citizens
45.	Provision for early childhood care and education to children below the age of six years
46.	Promotion of educational and economic interests of Scheduled Castes, Scheduled Tribes and other weaker sections
47.	Duty of the State to raise the level of nutrition and the standard of living and to improve public health
48.	Organisation of agriculture and animal husbandry
48A.	Protection and improvement of environment and safeguarding of forests and wildlife
49.	Protection of monuments and places and objects of national importance
50.	Separation of judiciary from executive
51.	Promotion of international peace and security

NOTES AND REFERENCES

1. Actually, Directive Principles are mentioned in Articles 38 to 51. Article 36 deals with the definition of State while Article 37 deals with the nature and significance of Directive Principles.
2. Granville Austin, *The Indian Constitution— Cornerstone of a Nation*, Oxford, 1966, P. 75.
3. A 'Police State' is mainly concerned with the maintenance of law and order and defence of the country against external aggression. Such a restrictive concept of state is based on the nineteenth century theory of individualism or laissez-faire.
4. This second provision was added by the 44th Constitutional Amendment Act of 1978.

5. The last point (f) was modified by the 42nd Constitutional Amendment Act of 1976.
6. This Directive was added by the 42nd Constitutional Amendment Act of 1976.
7. 'Living wage' is different from 'minimum wage', which includes the bare needs of life like food, shelter and clothing. In addition to these bare needs, a 'living wage' includes education, health, insurance, etc. A 'fair wage' is a mean between 'living wage' and 'minimum wage'.
8. This Directive was added by the 42nd Constitutional Amendment Act of 1976.
8a. This Directive was added by the 97th Constitutional Amendment Act of 2011.

9. This Directive was changed by the 86th Constitutional Amendment Act of 2002. Originally, it made a provision for free and compulsory education for all children until they complete the age of 14 years.

10. This Directive was added by the 42nd Constitutional Amendment Act of 1976.

11. *Constituent Assembly Debates*, volume VII, P. 476.

12. M P Jain, *Indian Constitutional Law,* Wadhwa, Third Edition (1978), P. 595.

13. *Constituent Assembly Debates,* volume VII, P. 470.

14. N. Srinivasan, *Democratic Government in India,* P. 182.

15. Sir Ivor Jennings, *Some Characteristics of the Indian Constitution*, 1953, P. 31–33.

16. *Journal of Constitutional and Parliamentary Studies,* June 1975.

17. M.C. Chagla, *An Ambassador Speaks,* P. 35.

18. Granville Austin, *The Indian Constitution—Cornerstone of a Nation*, Oxford, 1966, P. 50–52.

19. P B Gajendragadker, *The Constitution of India (Its Philosophy and Postulates),* P. 11.

20. *State of Madras* v. *Champakam Dorairajan,* (1951).

21. *Golak Nath* v. *State of Punjab,* (1967).

22. Article 39 (b) says: The State shall direct its policy towards securing that the ownership and control of the material resources of the community are so distributed as best to subserve the common good.

23. Article 39 (c) says: The state shall direct its policy towards securing that the operation of the economic system does not result in the concentration of wealth and means of production to the common detriment.

24. *Kesavananda Bharati* v. *State of Kerala,* (1973).

25. *Minerva Mills* v. *Union of India,* (1980).

Fundamental Duties

Though the rights and duties of the citizens are correlative and inseparable, the original constitution contained only the fundamental rights and not the fundamental duties. In other words, the framers of the Constitution did not feel it necessary to incorporate the fundamental duties of the citizens in the Constitution. However, they incorporated the duties of the State in the Constitution in the form of Directive Principles of State Polity. Later in 1976, the fundamental duties of citizens were added in the Constitution. In 2002, one more Fundamental Duty was added.

The Fundamental Duties in the Indian Constitution are inspired by the Constitution of erstwhile USSR. Notably, none of the Constitutions of major democratic countries like USA, Canada, France, Germany, Australia and so on specifically contain a list of duties of citizens. Japanese Constitution is, perhaps, the only democratic Constitution in world which contains a list of duties of citizens. The socialist countries, on the contrary, gave equal importance to the fundamental rights and duties of their citizens. Hence, the Constitution of erstwhile USSR declared that the citizen's exercise of their rights and freedoms was inseparable from the performance of their duties and obligations.

SWARAN SINGH COMMITTEE RECOMMENDATIONS

In 1976, the Congress Party set up the Sardar Swaran Singh Committee to make recommendations about fundamental duties, the need and necessity of which was felt during the operation of the internal emergency (1975–1977). The committee recommended the inclusion of a separate chapter on fundamental duties in the Constitution. It stressed that the citizens should become conscious that in addition to the enjoyment of rights, they also have certain duties to perform as well. The Congress Government at Centre accepted these recommendations and enacted the 42nd Constitutional Amendment Act in 1976. This amendment added a new part, namely, Part IVA to the Constitution. This new part consists of only one Article, that is, Article 51A which for the first time specified a code of ten fundamental duties of the citizens. The ruling Congress party declared the non-inclusion of fundamental duties in the Constitution as a historical mistake and claimed that what the framers of the Constitution failed to do was being done now.

Though the Swaran Singh Committee suggested the incorporation of eight Fundamental Duties in the Constitution, the 42nd Constitutional Amendment Act (1976) included ten Fundamental Duties.

Interestingly, certain recommendations of the Committee were not accepted by the Congress Party and hence, not incorporated in the Constitution. These include:

1. The Parliament may provide for the imposition of such penalty or punishment as may be considered appropriate for any non-compliance with or refusal to observe any of the duties.

2. No law imposing such penalty or punishment shall be called in question in any court on the

ground of infringement of any of Fundamental Rights or on the ground of repugnancy to any other provision of the Constitution.

3. Duty to pay taxes should also be a Fundamental Duty of the citizens.

LIST OF FUNDAMENTAL DUTIES

According to Article 51 A, it shall be the duty of every citizen of India:

(a) to abide by the Constitution and respect its ideals and institutions, the National Flag and the National Anthem;

(b) to cherish and follow the noble ideals that inspired the national struggle for freedom;

(c) to uphold and protect the sovereignty, unity and integrity of India;

(d) to defend the country and render national service when called upon to do so;

(e) to promote harmony and the spirit of common brotherhood amongst all the people of India transcending religious, linguistic and regional or sectional diversities and to renounce practices derogatory to the dignity of women;

(f) to value and preserve the rich heritage of the country's composite culture;

(g) to protect and improve the natural environment including forests, lakes, rivers and wildlife and to have compassion for living creatures;

(h) to develop scientific temper, humanism and the spirit of inquiry and reform;

(i) to safeguard public property and to abjure violence;

(j) to strive towards excellence in all spheres of individual and collective activity so that the nation constantly rises to higher levels of endeavour and achievement; and

(k) to provide opportunities for education to his child or ward between the age of six and fourteen years. This duty was added by the 86th Constitutional Amendment Act, 2002.

FEATURES OF THE FUNDAMENTAL DUTIES

Following points can be noted with regard to the characteristics of the Fundamental Duties:

1. Some of them are moral duties while others are civic duties. For instance, cherishing noble ideals of freedom struggle is a moral precept and respecting the Constitution, National Flag and National Anthem is a civic duty.

2. They refer to such values which have been a part of the Indian tradition, mythology, religions and practices. In other words, they essentially contain just a codification of tasks integral to the Indian way of life.

3. Unlike some of the Fundamental Rights which extend to all persons whether citizens or foreigners[1], the Fundamental Duties are confined to citizens only and do not extend to foreigners.

4. Like the Directive Principles, the fundamental duties are also non-justiciable. The Constitution does not provide for their direct enforcement by the courts. Moreover, there is not legal sanction against their violation. However, the Parliament is free to enforce them by suitable legislation.

CRITICISM OF FUNDAMENTAL DUTIES

The Fundamental Duties mentioned in Part VIA of the Constitution have been criticised on the following grounds:

1. The list of duties is not exhaustive as it does not cover other important duties like casting vote, paying taxes, family planning and so on. In fact, duty to pay taxes was recommended by the Swaran Singh Committee.

2. Some of the duties are vague, ambiguous and difficult to be understood by the common man. For example, different interpretations can be given to the phrases like 'noble ideals', 'composite culture', 'scientific temper' and so on[2].

3. They have been described by the critics as a code of moral precepts due to their non-justiciable character. Interestingly, the Swaran Singh Committee had suggested for penalty or punishment for the non-performance of Fundamental Duties.

4. Their inclusion in the Constitution was described by the critics as superfluous. This is because the duties included in the Constitution

as fundamental would be performed by the people even though they were not incorporated in the Constitution[3].

5. The critics said that the inclusion of fundamental duties as an appendage to Part IV of the Constitution has reduced their value and significance. They should have been added after Part III so as to keep them on par with Fundamental Rights.

SIGNIFICANCE OF FUNDAMENTAL DUTIES

In spite of criticisms and opposition, the fundamental duties are considered significant from the following viewpoints:

1. They serve as a reminder to the citizens that while enjoying their rights, they should also be conscious of duties they owe to their country, their society and to their fellow citizens.
2. They serve as a warning against the anti-national and antisocial activities like burning the national flag, destroying public property and so on.
3. They serve as a source of inspiration for the citizens and promote a sense of discipline and commitment among them. They create a feeling that the citizens are not mere spectators but active participants in the realisation of national goals.
4. They help the courts in examining and determining the constitutional validity of a law. In 1992, the Supreme Court ruled that in determining the constitutionality of any law, if a court finds that the law in question seeks to give effect to a fundamental duty, it may consider such law to be 'reasonable' in relation to Article 14 (equality before law) or Article 19 (six freedoms) and thus save such law from unconstitutionality.
5. They are enforceable by law. Hence, the Parliament can provide for the imposition of appropriate penalty or punishment for failure to fulfil any of them.

H R Gokhale, the then Law Minister, gave the following reason for incorporating the fundamental duties in the Constitution after twenty-six years of its inauguration: 'In post-independent India, particularly on the eve of emergency in June 1975, a section of the people showed no anxiety to fulfil their fundamental obligations of respecting the established legal order ..... the provisions of chapter on fundamental duties would have a sobering effect on these restless spirits who have had a host of anti-national subversive and unconstitutional agitations in the past'.

Indira Gandhi, the then Prime Minister, justified the inclusion of fundamental duties in the Constitution and argued that their inclusion would help to strengthen democracy. She said, 'the moral value of fundamental duties would be not to smoother rights but to establish a democratic balance by making the people conscious of their duties equally as they are conscious of their rights'.

The Opposition in the Parliament strongly opposed the inclusion of fundamental duties in the Constitution by the Congress government. However, the new Janata Government headed by Morarji Desai in the post-emergency period did not annull the Fundamental Duties. Notably, the new government sought to undo many changes introduced in the Constitution by the 42nd Amendment Act (1976) through the 43rd Amendment Act (1977) and the 44th Amendment Act (1978). This shows that there was an eventual consensus on the necessity and desirability of including the Fundamental Duties in the Constitution. This is more clear with the addition of one more Fundamental Duty in 2002 by the 86th Amendment Act.

VERMA COMMITTEE OBSERVATIONS

The Verma Committee on Fundamental Duties of the Citizens (1999) identified the existence of legal provisions for the implementation of some of the Fundamental Duties. They are mentioned below:

1. The Prevention of Insults to National Honour Act (1971) prevents disrespect to the Constitution of India, the National Flag and the National Anthem.
2. The various criminal laws in force provide for punishments for encouraging enmity between different sections of people on grounds of language, race, place of birth, religion and so on.

3. The Protection of Civil Rights Act[4] (1955) provides for punishments for offences related to caste and religion.
4. The Indian Penal Code (IPC) declares the imputations and assertions prejudicial to national integration as punishable offences.
5. The Unlawful Activities (Prevention) Act of 1967 provides for the declaration of a communal organisation as an unlawful association.
6. The Representation of People Act (1951) provides for the disqualification of members of the Parliament or a state legislature for indulging in corrupt practice, that is, soliciting votes on the ground of religion or promoting enmity between different sections of people on grounds of caste, race, language, religion and so on.
7. The Wildlife (Protection) Act of 1972 prohibits trade in rare and endangered species.
8. The Forest (Conservation) Act of 1980 checks indiscriminate deforestation and diversion of forest land for non-forest purposes.

NOTES AND REFERENCES

1. The Fundamental Rights guaranteed by Articles 14, 20, 21, 21A, 22, 23, 24, 25, 26, 27 and 28 are available to all persons whether citizens or foreigners.
2. D D Chawla, the then president of the National Forum of Lawyers and Legal Aid, Delhi, observed: 'The duties may be spelt out in a more concrete form, one is left guessing the noble ideals. To some even the Bhagat Singh cult may be such an ideal as inspired our national struggle. Again what is the rich heritage of our composite culture and what is scientific temper, humanism and the spirit of inquiry and reform? The values are beyond the ken of the general run of the people and carry no meaning to them. Duties should be such and so worded as to catch the imagination of the common man.'
D D Chawla, 'The Concept of Fundamental Duties', *Socialist India* (New Delhi), October 23, 1976, P. 44–45.
3. C K Daphtary, former Attorney General of India, while opposing the inclusion of fundamental duties in the Constitution, said that more than 99.9 per cent of the citizens were law-abiding and there was no need to tell them about their duties. He argued that as long as the people are satisfied and contended, they willingly perform their duties. He said, 'To tell them what their duties are implies that they are not content. If that is the case after 26 years, it is not their fault'. A K Sen also opposed the inclusion of fundamental duties in the Constitution and remarked, 'A democratic set-up, instead of thriving on the willing cooperation and confidence of people, is reduced to the position of a harsh school master asking the student to stand up on the class room bench because he has not done the home work. To begin with, it were the people of India who created the Sovereign Democratic Republic of India in 1950, but the Republic is now claiming to be the master of the citizens enjoining habitual obedience to its command to do his duty. The state's confidence in the citizens is obviously shaken'.
4. This Act was known as the Untouchability (Offences) Act till 1976.

Amendment of the Constitution

Like any other written Constitution, the Constitution of India also provides for its amendment in order to adjust itself to the changing conditions and needs. However, the procedure laid down for its amendment is neither as easy as in Britain nor as difficult as in USA. In other words, the Indian Constitution is neither flexible nor rigid but a synthesis of both.

Article 368 in Part XX of the Constitution deals with the powers of Parliament to amend the Constitution and its procedure. It states that the Parliament may, in exercise of its constituent power, amend by way of addition, variation or repeal any provision of the Constitution in accordance with the procedure laid down for the purpose. However, the Parliament cannot amend those provisions which form the 'basic structure' of the Constitution. This was ruled by the Supreme Court in the *Kesavananda Bharati* case[1] (1973).

PROCEDURE FOR AMENDMENT

The procedure for the amendment of the Constitution as laid down in Article 368 is as follows:

1. An amendment of the Constitution can be initiated only by the introduction of a bill for the purpose in either House of Parliament and not in the state legislatures.
2. The bill can be introduced either by a minister or by a private member and does not require prior permission of the president.
3. The bill must be passed in each House by a special majority, that is, a majority (that is, more than 50 per cent) of the total membership of the House and a majority of two-thirds of the members of the House present and voting.
4. Each House must pass the bill separately. In case of a disagreement between the two Houses, there is no provision for holding a joint sitting of the two Houses for the purpose of deliberation and passage of the bill.
5. If the bill seeks to amend the federal provisions of the Constitution, it must also be ratified by the legislatures of half of the states by a simple majority, that is, a majority of the members of the House present and voting.
6. After duly passed by both the Houses of Parliament and ratified by the state legislatures, where necessary, the bill is presented to the president for assent.
7. The president must give his assent to the bill. He can neither withhold his assent to the bill nor return the bill for reconsideration of the Parliament.[2]
8. After the president's assent, the bill becomes an Act (i.e., a constitutional amendment act) and the Constitution stands amended in accordance with the terms of the Act.

TYPES OF AMENDMENTS

Article 368 provides for two types of amendments, that is, by a special majority of Parliament and also through the ratification of half of the states by a simple majority. But, some other articles provide for the amendment of certain provisions of the Constitution by a simple majority of Parliament, that is, a majority of the members of each House present and voting (similar to the ordinary legislative process). Notably, these amendments are not deemed to be amendments of the Constitution for the purposes of Article 368.

Therefore, the Constitution can be amended in three ways:

(a) Amendment by simple majority of the Parliament,

(b) Amendment by special majority of the Parliament, and

(c) Amendment by special majority of the Parliament and the ratification of half of the state legislatures.

By Simple Majority of Parliament

A number of provisions in the Constitution can be amended by a simple majority of the two Houses of Parliament outside the scope of Article 368. These provisions include:

1. Admission or establishment of new states.
2. Formation of new states and alteration of areas, boundaries or names of existing states.
3. Abolition or creation of legislative councils in states.
4. Second Schedule—emoluments, allowances, privileges and so on of the president, the governors, the Speakers, judges, etc.
5. Quorum in Parliament.
6. Salaries and allowances of the members of Parliament.
7. Rules of procedure in Parliament.
8. Privileges of the Parliament, its members and its committees.
9. Use of English language in Parliament.
10. Number of puisne judges in the Supreme Court.
11. Conferment of more jurisdiction on the Supreme Court.
12. Use of official language.
13. Citizenship—acquisition and termination.
14. Elections to Parliament and state legislatures.
15. Delimitation of constituencies.
16. Union territories.

17. Fifth Schedule—administration of scheduled areas and scheduled tribes.
18. Sixth Schedule—administration of tribal areas.

By Special Majority of Parliament

The majority of the provisions in the Constitution need to be amended by a special majority of the Parliament, that is, a majority (that is, more than 50 per cent) of the total membership of each House and a majority of two-thirds of the members of each House present and voting. The expression 'total membership' means the total number of members comprising the House irrespective of fact whether there are vacancies or absentees.

'Strictly speaking, the special majority is required only for voting at the third reading stage of the bill but by way of abundant caution the requirement for special majority has been provided for in the rules of the Houses in respect of all the effective stages of the bill'[3].

The provisions which can be amended by this way includes: (i) Fundamental Rights; (ii) Directive Principles of State Policy; and (iii) All other provisions which are not covered by the first and third categories.

By Special Majority of Parliament and Consent of States

Those provisions of the Constitution which are related to the federal structure of the polity can be amended by a special majority of the Parliament and also with the consent of half of the state legislatures by a simple majority. If one or some or all the remaining states take no action on the bill, it does not matter; the moment half of the states give their consent, the formality is completed. There is no time limit within which the states should give their consent to the bill.

The following provisions can be amended in this way:

1. Election of the President and its manner.
2. Extent of the executive power of the Union and the states.
3. Supreme Court and high courts.
4. Distribution of legislative powers between the Union and the states.

5. Any of the lists in the Seventh Schedule.
6. Representation of states in Parliament.
7. Power of Parliament to amend the Constitution and its procedure (Article 368 itself).

CRITICISM OF THE AMENDMENT PROCEDURE

Critics have criticised the amendment procedure of the Constitution on the following grounds:

1. There is no provision for a special body like Constitutional Convention (as in USA) or Constitutional Assembly for amending the Constitution. The constituent power is vested in the Parliament and only in few cases, in the state legislatures.
2. The power to initiate an amendment to the Constitution lies with the Parliament. Hence, unlike in USA[4], the state legislatures cannot initiate any bill or proposal for amending the Constitution except in one case, that is, passing a resolution requesting the Parliament for the creation or abolition of legislative councils in the states. Here also, the Parliament can either approve or disapprove such a resolution or may not take any action on it.
3. Major part of the Constitution can be amended by the Parliament alone either by a special majority or by a simple majority. Only in few cases, the consent of the state legislatures is required and that too, only half of them, while in USA, it is three-fourths of the states.
4. The Constitution does not prescribe the time frame within which the state legislatures should ratify or reject an amendment submitted to them. Also, it is silent on the issue whether the states can withdraw their approval after according the same.
5. There is no provision for holding a joint sitting of both the Houses of Parliament if there is a deadlock over the passage of a constitutional amendment bill. On the other hand, a provision for a joint sitting is made in the case of an ordinary bill.
6. The process of amendment is similar to that of a legislative process. Except for the special majority, the constitutional amendment bills are to be passed by the Parliament in the same way as ordinary bills.
7. The provisions relating to the amendment procedure are too sketchy. Hence, they leave a wide scope for taking the matters to the judiciary.

Despite these defects, it cannot be denied that the process has proved to be simple and easy and has succeeded in meeting the changed needs and conditions. The procedure is not so flexible as to allow the ruling parties to change it according to their whims. Nor is it so rigid as to be incapable of adopting itself to the changing needs. It, as rightly said by K C Wheare, 'strikes a good balance between flexibility and rigidity'[5]. In this context, Pandit Jawaharlal Nehru said in the Constituent Assembly, 'While we want this Constitution to be as solid and permanent as we can make it, there is no permanence in a Constitution. There should be a certain flexibility. If you make any Constitution rigid and permanent, you stop the nation's growth, the growth of a living, vital, organic people'[6].

Similarly, Dr B R Ambedkar observed in the Constituent Assembly that, 'The Assembly has not only refrained from putting a seal of finality and infallibility upon this Constitution by denying the people the right to amend the Constitution as in Canada or by making the amendment of the Constitution subject to the fulfilment of extraordinary terms and conditions as in America or Australia, but has provided for a facile procedure for amending the Constitution'[7].

K C Wheare has admired the variety of amendment procedures contained in the Constitution of India. He said, 'this variety in the amending process is wise but rarely found'. According to Granville Austin, 'the amending process has proved itself one of the most ably conceived aspects of the Constitution. Although it appears complicated, it is merely diverse'.[8]

NOTES AND REFERENCES

1. *Kesavananda Bharati* v. *State of Kerala*, (1973).
2. The 24th Constitutional Amendment Act of 1971 made it obligatory for the President to give his assent to a constitutional Amendment Bill.
3. Subhas C. Kashyap, *Our Parliament,* National Book Trust, 1999, P. 168.
4. In USA, an amendment can also be proposed by a constitutional convention called by the Congress (American Legislature) on the petition of two-thirds of the state legislatures.
5. K C Wheare, *Modern Constitutions,* 1966, P. 43.
6. *Constituent Assembly Debates,* Vol. VII, P. 322–23.
7. *Constituent Assembly Debates,* Vol. IX, P. 976.
8. Granville Austin, *The Indian Constitution: Cornerstone of a Nation,* Oxford, 1966, P. 25.

Basic Structure of the Constitution

EMERGENCE OF THE BASIC STRUCTURE

The question whether Fundamental Rights can be amended by the Parliament under Article 368 came for consideration of the Supreme Court within a year of the Constitution coming into force. In the Shankari Prasad case[1] (1951), the constitutional validity of the First Amendment Act (1951), which curtailed the right to property, was challenged. The Supreme Court ruled that the power of the Parliament to amend the Constitution under Article 368 also includes the power to amend Fundamental Rights. The word 'law' in Article 13 includes only ordinary laws and not the constitutional amendment acts (constituent laws). Therefore, the Parliament can abridge or take away any of the Fundamental Rights by enacting a constitutional amendment act and such a law will not be void under Article 13.

But in the Golak Nath case[2] (1967), the Supreme Court reversed its earlier stand. In that case, the constitutional validity of the Seventeenth Amendment Act (1964), which inserted certain state acts in the Ninth Schedule, was challenged. The Supreme Court ruled that the Fundamental Rights are given a 'transcendental and immutable' position and hence, the Parliament cannot abridge or take away any of these rights. A constitutional amendment act is also a law within the meaning of Article 13 and hence, would be void for violating any of the Fundamental Rights.

The Parliament reacted to the Supreme Court's judgement in the Golak Nath case (1967) by enacting the 24th Amendment Act (1971). This Act amended Articles 13 and 368. It declared that the Parliament has the power to abridge or take away any of the Fundamental Rights under Article 368 and such an act will not be a law under the meaning of Article 13.

However, in the Kesavananda Bharati case[3] (1973), the Supreme Court overruled its judgement in the Golak Nath case (1967). It upheld the validity of the 24th Amendment Act (1971) and stated that Parliament is empowered to abridge or take away any of the Fundamental Rights. At the same time, it laid down a new doctrine of the 'basic structure' (or 'basic features') of the Constitution. It ruled that the constituent power of Parliament under Article 368 does not enable it to alter the 'basic structure' of the Constitution. This means that the Parliament cannot abridge or take away a Fundamental Right that forms a part of the 'basic structure' of the Constitution.

Again, the Parliament reacted to this judicially innovated doctrine of 'basic structure' by enacting the 42nd Amendment Act (1976). This Act amended Article 368 and declared that there is no limitation on the constituent power of Parliament and no amendment can be questioned in any court on any ground including that of the contravention of any of the Fundamental Rights.

However, the Supreme Court in the Minerva Mills case[4] (1980) invalidated this provision as it excluded judicial review which is a 'basic feature' of the Constitution. Applying the doctrine of 'basic structure' with respect to Article 368, the court held that:

"Since the Constitution had conferred a limited amending power on the Parliament, the Parliament cannot under the exercise of that limited power enlarge that very power into an absolute power. Indeed, a limited amending power is one of the basic features of the Constitution and, therefore, the limitations on that power cannot be destroyed. In other words, Parliament cannot, under article 368, expand its amending power so as to acquire for itself the right to repeal or abrogate the Constitution or to destroy its basic features. The donee of a limited power cannot by the exercise of that power convert the limited power into an unlimited one".

Again in the Waman Rao case[5] (1981), the Supreme Court adhered to the doctrine of the 'basic structure' and further clarified that it would apply to constitutional amendments enacted after April 24, 1973 (i.e., the date of the judgement in the Kesavananda Bharati case).

Elements of the Basic Structure

The present position is that the Parliament under Article 368 can amend any part of the Constitution including the Fundamental Rights but without affecting the 'basic structure' of the Constitution.

However, the Supreme Court is yet to define or clarify as to what constitutes the 'basic structure' of the Constitution. From the various judgements, the following have emerged as 'basic features' of the Constitution or elements / components / ingredients of the 'basic structure' of the constitution:

1. Supremacy of the Constitution
2. Sovereign, democratic and republican nature of the Indian polity
3. Secular character of the Constitution
4. Separation of powers between the legislature, the executive and the judiciary
5. Federal character of the Constitution
6. Unity and integrity of the nation
7. Welfare state (socio-economic justice)
8. Judicial review
9. Freedom and dignity of the individual
10. Parliamentary system
11. Rule of law
12. Harmony and balance between Fundamental Rights and Directive Principles
13. Principle of equality
14. Free and fair elections
15. Independence of Judiciary
16. Limited power of Parliament to amend the Constitution
17. Effective access to justice
18. Principle of reasonableness
19. Powers of the Supreme Court under Articles 32, 136, 141 and 142[6]

Notes and References

1. Shankari Prasad v. Union of India, (1951)
2. Golak Nath v. State of Punjab, (1967)
3. Kesavananda Bharati v. State of Kerala, (1973)
4. Minerva Mills v. Union of India, (1980)
5. Waman Rao v. Union of India, (1981)
6. For the subject-matter of these Articles, see Appendix-1.

PART II

SYSTEM OF GOVERNMENT

Parliamentary System

The Constitution of India provides for a parliamentary form of government, both at the Centre and in the states. Articles 74 and 75 deal with the parliamentary system at the Centre and Articles 163 and 164 in the states.

Modern democratic governments are classified into parliamentary and presidential on the basis of nature of relations between the executive and the legislative organs of the government. The parliamentary system of government is the one in which the executive is responsible to the legislature for its policies and acts. The presidential system of government, on the other hand, is one in which the executive is not responsible to the legislature for its policies and acts, and is constitutionally independent of the legislature in respect of its term of office.

The parliamentary government is also known as cabinet government or responsible government or Westminster model of government and is prevalent in Britain, Japan, Canada, India among others. The presidential government, on the other hand, is also known as non-responsible or non-parliamentary or fixed executive system of government and is prevalent in USA, Brazil, Russia, Sri Lanka among others.

Ivor Jennings called the parliamentary system as 'cabinet system' because the cabinet is the nucleus of power in a parliamentary system. The parliamentary government is also known as 'responsible government' as the cabinet (the real executive) is accountable to the Parliament and stays in office so long as it enjoys the latter's confidence. It is described as 'Westminster model of government' after the location of the British Parliament, where the parliamentary system originated.

In the past, the British constitutional and political experts described the Prime Minister as '*primus inter pares*' (first among equals) in relation to the cabinet. In the recent period, the Prime Minister's power, influence and position have increased significantly vis-a-vis the cabinet. He has come to play a 'dominant' role in the British politico-administrative system. Hence, the later political analysts, like Cross-man, Mackintosh and others have described the British system of government as 'prime ministerial government'. The same description holds good in the Indian context too.

FEATURES OF PARLIAMENTARY GOVERNMENT

The features or principles of parliamentary government in India are:

1. Nominal and Real Executives The President is the nominal executive (*de jure* executive or titular executive) while the Prime Minister is the real executive (*de facto* executive). Thus, the President is head of the State, while the Prime Minister is head of the government. Article 74 provides for a council of ministers headed by the Prime Minister to aid and advise the President in the exercise of his functions. The advice so tendered is binding on the President[1].

2. Majority Party Rule The political party which secures majority seats in the Lok Sabha forms the government. The leader of that party is appointed as the Prime Minister by the President; other ministers are appointed by the President on the advice of the prime minister. However, when no single party gets the majority, a coalition of parties may be invited by the President to form the government.

3. Collective Responsibility   This is the bedrock principle of parliamentary government. The ministers are collectively responsible to the Parliament in general and to the Lok Sabha in particular (Article 75). They act as a team, and swim and sink together. The principle of collective responsibility implies that the Lok Sabha can remove the ministry (i.e., council of ministers headed by the prime minister) from office by passing a vote of no confidence.

4. Political Homogeneity   Usually members of the council of ministers belong to the same political party, and hence they share the same political ideology. In case of coalition government, the minister are bound by consensus.

5. Double Membership   The ministers are members of both the legislature and the executive. This means that a person cannot be a minister without being a member of the Parliament. The Constitution stipulates that a minister who is not a member of the Parliament for a period of six consecutive months ceases to be a minister.

6. Leadership of the Prime Minister   The Prime Minister plays the leadership role in this system of government. He is the leader of council of ministers, leader of the Parliament and leader of the party in power. In these capacities, he plays a significant and highly crucial role in the functioning of the government.

7. Dissolution of the Lower House   The lower house of the Parliament (Lok Sabha) can be dissolved by the President on recommendation of the Prime Minister. In other words, the prime minister can advise the President to dissolve the Lok Sabha before the expiry of its term and hold fresh elections. This means that the executive enjoys the right to get the legislature dissolved in a parliamentary system.

8. Secrecy   The ministers operate on the principle of secrecy of procedure and cannot divulge information about their proceedings, policies and decisions. They take the oath of secrecy before entering their

office. The oath of secrecy to the ministers is administered by the President.

FEATURES OF PRESIDENTIAL GOVERNMENT

Unlike the Indian Constitution, the American Constitution provides for the presidential form of government. The features of the American presidential system of government are as follows:

(a) The American President is both the head of the State and the head of government. As the head of State, he occupies a ceremonial position. As the head of government, he leads the executive organ of government.

(b) The President is elected by an electoral college for a fixed tenure of four years. He cannot be removed by the Congress except by impeachment for a grave unconstitutional act.

(c) The President governs with the help of a cabinet or a smaller body called 'Kitchen Cabinet'. It is only an advisory body and consists of non-elected departmental secretaries. They are selected and appointed by him, are responsible only to him, and can be removed by him any time.

(d) The President and his secretaries are not responsible to the Congress for their acts. They neither possess membership in the Congress nor attend its sessions.

(e) The President cannot dissolve the House of Representatives—the lower house of the Congress.

(f) The doctrine of separation of powers is the basis of the American presidential system. The legislative, executive and judicial powers of the government are separated and vested in the three independent organs of the government.

MERITS OF THE PARLIAMENTARY SYSTEM

The parliamentary system of government has the following merits:

1. Harmony Between Legislature and Executive   The greatest advantage of the parliamentary system is that it ensures harmonious relationship and cooperation between the legislative and executive organs of the government. The executive is a part of the legislature and both are interdependent at work. As a result, there is less scope for disputes and conflicts between the two organs.

2. Responsible Government By its very nature, the parliamentary system establishes a responsible government. The ministers are responsible to the Parliament for all their acts of omission and commission. The Parliament exercises control over the ministers through various devices like question hour, discussions, adjournment motion, no confidence motion, etc.

3. Prevents Despotism Under this system, the executive authority is vested in a group of individuals (council of ministers) and not in a single person. This dispersal of authority checks the dictatorial tendencies of the executive. Moreover, the executive is responsible to the Parliament and can be removed by a no-confidence motion.

4. Ready Alternative Government In case the ruling party loses its majority, the Head of the State can invite the opposition party to form the government. This means an alternative government can be formed without fresh elections. Hence, Dr Jennings says, 'the leader of the opposition is the alternative prime minister'.

5. Wide Representation In a parliamentary system, the executive consists of a group of individuals (i.e., ministers who are representatives of the people). Hence, it is possible to provide representation to all sections and regions in the government. The prime minister while selecting his ministers can take this factor into consideration.

DEMERITS OF THE PARLIAMENTARY SYSTEM

In spite of the above merits, the parliamentary system suffers from the following demerits:

1. Unstable Government The parliamentary system does not provide a stable government. There is no guarantee that a government can survive its tenure. The ministers depend on the mercy of the majority legislators for their continuity and survival in office. A no-confidence motion or political defection

or evils of multiparty coalition can make the government unstable. The Government headed by Morarji Desai, Charan Singh, V P Singh, Chandra Sekhar, Deva Gowda and I K Gujral are some such examples.

2. No Continuity of Policies The parliamentary system is not conductive for the formulation and implementation of long-term policies. This is due to the uncertainty of the tenure of the government. A change in the ruling party is usually followed by changes in the policies of the government. For example, the Janata Government headed by Morarji Desai in 1977 reversed a large number of policies of the previous Congress Government. The same was repeated by the Congress government after it came back to power in 1980.

3. Dictatorship of the Cabinet When the ruling party enjoys absolute majority in the Parliament, the cabinet becomes autocratic and exercises nearly unlimited powers. H J Laski says that the parliamentary system gives the executive an opportunity for tyranny. Ramsay Muir, the former British Prime Minister, also complained of the 'dictatorship of the cabinet'[2]. This phenomena was witnessed during the era of Indira Gandhi and Rajiv Gandhi.

4. Against Separation of Powers In the parliamentary system, the legislature and the executive are together and inseparable. The cabinet acts as the leader of legislature as well as the executive. As Bagehot point out, 'the cabinet is a hyphen that joins the buckle that binds the executive and legislative departments together.' Hence, the whole system of government goes against the letter and spirit of the theory of separation of powers[3]. In fact, there is a fusion of powers.

5. Government by Amateurs The parliamentary system is not conductive to administrative efficiency as the ministers are not experts in their fields. The Prime Minister has a limited choice in the selection of ministers; his choice is restricted to the members of Parliament alone and does not extend to external talent. Moreover, the ministers devote most of their time to parliamentary work, cabinet meetings and party activities.

Now, let us compare the parliamentary and presidential systems in terms of their features, merits and demerits.

Table 12.1   *Comparing Parliamentary and Presidential Systems*

Parliamentary System	Presidential System
Features:	*Features:*
1. Dual executive.	1. Single executive.
2. Majority party rule	2. President and legislators elected separately for a fixed term.
3. Collective responsibility.	3. Non-responsibility
4. Political homogeneity	4. Political homogeneity may not exist.
5. Double membership.	5. Single membership
6. Leadership of prime minister.	6. Domination of president.
7. Dissolution of Lower House.	7. No dissolution of Lower House.
8. Fusion of powers.	8. Separation of powers.
Merits:	*Demerits:*
1. Harmony between legislature and executive.	1. Conflict between legislature and executive.
2. Responsible government.	2. Non-responsible government.
3. Prevents despotism.	3. May lead to autocracy.
4. Wide representation.	4. Narrow representation.
Demerits:	*Merits:*
1. Unstable government.	1. Stable government.
2. No continuity of policies.	2. Definiteness in policies.
3. Against separation of powers	3. Based on separation of powers.
4. Government by amateurs.	4. Government by experts

REASONS FOR ADOPTING PARLIAMENTARY SYSTEM

A plea was made in favour of US presidential system of government in the Constituent Assembly[4]. But, the founding fathers preferred the British parliamentary system due to the following reasons:

1. Familiarity with the System   The Constitution-makers were somewhat familiar with the parliamentary system as it had been in operation in India during the British rule. K M Munshi argued that, 'For the last thirty or forty years, some kind of responsibility has been introduced in the governance of this country. Our constitutional traditions have become Parliamentary. After this experience, why should we go back and buy a novel experience.'[5]

2. Preference to More Responsibility   Dr B R Ambedkar pointed out in the Constituent Assembly that 'a democratic executive must satisfy two conditions: stability and responsibility. Unfortunately, it has not been possible so far to devise a system which can ensure both in equal degree. The American

system gives more stability but less responsibility. The British system, on the other hand, gives more responsibility but less stability. The Draft Constitution in recommending the parliamentary system of Executive has preferred more responsibility to more stability.'[6]

3. Need to Avoid Legislative—Executive Conflicts   The framers of the Constitution wanted to avoid the conflicts between the legislature and the executive which are bound to occur in the presidential system prevalent in USA. They thought that an infant democracy could not afford to take the risk of a perpetual cleavage, feud or conflict or threatened conflict between these two organs of the government. They wanted a form of government that would be conductive to the manifold development of the country.

4. Nature of Indian Society   India is one of the most heterogeneous States and most complex plural societies in the world. Hence, the Constitution-makers adopted the parliamentary system as it offers greater scope for giving representation to various section, interests and regions in the government. This promotes a national spirit among the people and builds a united India.

Whether the parliamentary system should be continued or should be replaced by the presidential system has been a point of discussion and debate in our country since the 1970s. This matter was considered in detail by the Swaran Singh Committee appointed by the Congress government in 1975. The committee opined that the parliamentary system has been doing well and hence, there is no need to replace it by the presidential system.

DISTINCTION BETWEEN INDIAN AND BRITISH MODELS

The parliamentary system of government in India is largely based on the British parliamentary system. However, it never became a replica of the British system and differs in the following respects:

1. India has a republican system in place of British monarchical system. In other words, the Head of the State in India (that is, President) is elected, while the Head of the State in Britain (that is, King or Queen) enjoys a hereditary position.

2. The British system is based on the doctrine of the sovereignty of Parliament, while the Parliament is not supreme in India and enjoys limited and restricted powers due to a written Constitution, federal system, judicial review and fundamental rights[7].

3. In Britain, the prime minister should be a member of the Lower House (House of Commons) of the Parliament. In India, the prime minister may be a member of any of the two Houses of Parliament.[8]

4. Usually, the members of Parliament alone are appointed as ministers in Britain. In India, a person who is not a member of Parliament can also be appointed as minister, but for a maximum period of six months.

5. Britain has the system of legal responsibility of the minister while India has no such system. Unlike in Britain, the ministers in India are not required to countersign the official acts of the Head of the State.

6. 'Shadow cabinet' is an unique institution of the British cabinet system. It is formed by the opposition party to balance the ruling cabinet and to prepare its members for future ministerial office. There is no such institution in India.

NOTES AND REFERENCES

1. The 42nd and 44th Amendment Acts of 1976 and 1978 respectively have made the ministerial advice binding on the president.

2. *How Britain is Governed* is a popular book written by him.

3. This theory was propounded by Montesquieu, a French political thinker, in his book *The Spirit of Laws* (1748) to promote individual liberty. He stated that concentration of powers in one person or a body of persons would result in despotism and negate individual liberty.

4. K T Shah favoured the adoption of the presidential system.

5. *Constituent Assembly Debates,* Volume VII, p. 284–5.

6. *Constituent Assembly Debates,* Volume VII, p. 32.

7. For details in this regard, see the section on the 'Sovereignty of Parliament' in Chapter 22.

8. For example, three prime ministers, Indira Gandhi (1966), Deve Gowda (1996), and Manmohan Singh (2004), were members of the Rajya Sabha.

Federal System

Political scientists have classified governments into unitary and federal on the basis of the nature of relations between the national government and the regional governments. By definition, a unitary government is one in which all the powers are vested in the national government and the regional governments, if at all exist, derive their authority from the national government. A federal government, on the other hand, is one in which powers are divided between the national government and the regional governments by the Constitution itself and both operate in their respective jurisdictions independently.

Britain, France, Japan, China, Italy, Belgium, Norway, Sweden, Spain and so on have the unitary model of government while the US, Switzerland, Australia, Canada, Russia, Brazil, Argentina and so on have the federal model of government. In a federal model, the national government is known as the Federal government or the Central government or the Union government and the regional government is known as the state government or the provincial government.

The specific features of the federal and unitary governments are mentioned below in a comparative manner:

Table 13.1 *Comparing Features of Federal and Unitary Governments*

Federal Government	Unitary Government
1. Dual Government (that is, national government and regional government)	1. Single government, that is, the national government which may create regional governments
2. Written Constitution	2. Constitution may be written (France) or unwritten (Britain)
3. Division of powers between the national and regional government	3. No division of powers. All powers are vested in the national government
4. Supremacy of the Constitution	4. Constitution may be supreme (Japan) or may not be supreme (Britain)
5. Rigid Constitution	5. Constitution may be rigid (France) or flexible (Britain)
6. Independent judiciary	6. Judiciary may be independent or may not be independent
7. Bicameral legislature	7. Legislature may be bicameral (Britain) or unicameral (China)

The term 'federation' is drived from a Latin word *foedus* which means 'treaty' or 'agreement'. Thus, a federation is a new state (political system) which is formed through a treaty or an agreement between the various units. The units of a federation are known by various names like states (as in US) or cantons (as in Switzerland) or provinces (as in Canada) or republics (as in Russia).

A federation can be formed in two ways, that is, by way of integration or by way of disintegration. In the first case, a number of militarily weak or economically backward states (independent) come together to form a big and a strong union, as for example, the US. In the second case, a big unitary state is converted into a federation by granting autonomy to the provinces to promote regional interest (for example, Canada). The US is the first and the oldest federation in the world. It was formed in 1787 following the American Revolution (1775–83). It comprises 50 states (originally 13 states) and is taken as the model of federation. The Canadian Federation, comprising 10 provinces (originally 4 provinces) is also quite old—formed in 1867.

The Constitution of India provides for a federal system of government in the country. The framers adopted the federal system due to two main reasons—the large size of the country and its socio-cultural diversity. They realised that the federal system not only ensures the efficient governance of the country but also reconciles national unity with regional autonomy.

However, the term 'federation' has no where been used in the Constitution. Instead, Article 1 of the Constitution describes India as a 'Union of States'. According to Dr B R Ambedkar, the phrase 'Union of States' has been preferred to 'Federation of States' to indicate two things: **(i)** the Indian federation is not the result of an agreement among the states like the American federation; and **(ii)** the states have no right to secede from the federation. The federation is union because it is indestructible.[1]

The Indian federal system is based on the 'Canadian model' and not on the 'American model'. The 'Canadian model' differs fundamentally from the 'American model' in so far as it establishes a very strong centre. The Indian federation resembles the Candian federation **(i)** in its formation (i.e., by way of disintegration); **(ii)** in its preference to the term

'Union' (the Canadian federation is also called a 'Union'); and **(iii)** in its centralising tendency (i.e., vesting more powers in the centre vis-a-vis the states).

FEDERAL FEATURES OF THE CONSTITUTION

The federal features of the Constitution of India are explained below:

1. Dual Polity

The Constitution establishes a dual polity consisting the Union at the Centre and the states at the periphery. Each is endowed with sovereign powers to be exercised in the field assigned to them respectively by the Constitution. The Union government deals with the matters of national importance like defence, foreign affairs, currency, communication and so on. The state governments, on the other hand, look after the matters of regional and local importance like public order, agriculture, health, local government and so on.

2. Written Constitution

The Constitution is not only a written document but also the lengthiest Constitution of the world. Originally, it contained a Preamble, 395 Articles (divided into 22 Parts) and 8 Schedules.[2] At present (2013), it consists of a Preamble, about 465 Articles (divided into 25 Parts) and 12 Schedules.[3] It specifies the structure, organisation, powers and functions of both the Central and state governments and prescribes the limits within which they must operate. Thus, it avoids the misunderstandings and disagreements between the two.

3. Division of Powers

The Constitution divided the powers between the Centre and the states in terms of the Union List, State List and Concurrent List in the Seventh Schedule. The Union List consists of 100 subjects (originally 97), the State List 61 subjects (originally 66) and the Concurrent List 52 subjects (originally 47). Both the Centre and the states can make laws on the subjects of the concurrent list, but in case of a conflict, the Central law prevails. The residuary subjects (ie, which are not mentioned in any of the three lists) are given to the Centre.

4. Supremacy of the Constitution

The Constitution is the supreme (or the highest) law of the land. The laws enacted by the Centre and the states must confirm to its provisions. Otherwise, they can be declared invalid by the Supreme Court or the high courts through their power of judicial review. Thus, the organs of the government (legislative, executive and judicial) at both the levels must operate within the jurisdiction prescribed by the Constitution.

5. Rigid Constitution

The division of powers established by the Constitution as well as the supremacy of the Constitution can be maintained only if the method of its amendment is rigid. Hence, the Constitution is rigid to the extent that those provisions which are concerned with the federal structure (i.e., Centre–state relations and judicial organisation) can be amended only by the joint action of the Central and state governments. Such provisions require for their amendment a special majority[4] of the Parliament and also an approval of half of the state legislatures.

6. Independent Judiciary

The Constitution establishes an independent judiciary headed by the Supreme Court for two purposes: one, to protect the supremacy of the Constitution by exercising the power of judicial review; and two, to settle the disputes between the Centre and the states or between the states. The Constitution contains various measures like security of tenure to judges, fixed service conditions and so on to make the judiciary independent of the government.

7. Bicameralism

The Constitution provides for a bicameral legislature consisting of an Upper House (Rajya Sabha) and a Lower House (Lok Sabha). The Rajya Sabha represents the states of Indian Federation, while the Lok Sabha represents the people of India as a whole. The Rajya Sabha (even though a less powerful chamber) is required to maintain the federal equilibrium by protecting the interests of the states against the undue interference of the Centre.

UNITARY FEATURES OF THE CONSTITUTION

Besides the above federal features, the Indian Constitution also possesses the following unitary or non-federal features:

1. Strong Centre

The division of powers is in favour of the Centre and highly inequitable from the federal angle. Firstly, the Union List contains more subjects than the State List. Secondly, the more important subjects have been included in the Union List. Thirdly, the Centre has overriding authority over the Concurrent List. Finally, the residuary powers have also been left with the Centre, while in the US, they are vested in the states. Thus, the Constitution has made the Centre very strong.

2. States Not Indestructible

Unlike in other federations, the states in India have no right to territorial integrity. The Parliament can by unilateral action change the area, boundaries or name of any state. Moreover, it requires only a simple majority and not a special majority. Hence, the Indian Federation is "an indestructible Union of destructible states". The American Federation, on the other hand, is described as "an indestructible Union of indestructible states".

3. Single Constitution

Usually, in a federation, the states have the right to frame their own Constitution separate from that of the Centre. In India, on the contrary, no such power is given to the states. The Constitution of India embodies not only the Constitution of the Centre but also those of the states. Both the Centre and the states must operate within this single-frame. The only exception in this regard is the case of Jammu and Kashmir which has its own (state) Constitution.[5]

4. Flexibility of the Constitution

The process of constitutional amendment is less rigid than what is found in other federations. The bulk of the Constitution can be amended by the unilateral action of the Parliament, either by simple majority or by special majority. Further, the power to initiate an amendment to the Constitution lies only with the Centre. In US, the states can also propose an amendment to the Constitution.

5. No Equality of State Representation

The states are given representation in the Rajya Sabha on the basis of population. Hence, the membership varies from 1 to 31. In US, on the other hand, the principle of equality of representation of states in the Upper House is fully recognised. Thus, the American Senate has 100 members, two from each state. This principle is regarded as a safeguard for smaller states.

6. Emergency Provisions

The Constitution stipulates three types of emergencies—national, state and financial. During an emergency, the Central government becomes all powerful and the states go into the total control of the Centre. It converts the federal structure into a unitary one without a formal amendment of the Constitution. This kind of transformation is not found in any other federation.

7. Single Citizenship

In spite of a dual polity, the Constitution of India, like that of Canada, adopted the system of single citizenship. There is only Indian Citizenship and no separate state citizenship. All citizens irrespective of the state in which they are born or reside enjoy the same rights all over the country. The other federal states like US, Switzerland and Australia have dual citizenship, that is, national citizenship as well as state citizenship.

8. Integrated Judiciary

The Indian Constitution has established an integrated judicial system with the Supreme Court at the top and the state high courts below it. This single system of courts enforces both the Central laws as well as the state laws. In US, on the other hand, there is a double system of courts whereby the federal laws are enforced by the federal judiciary and the state laws by the state judiciary.

9. All-India Services

In US, the Federal government and the state governments have their separate public services. In India also, the Centre and the states have their separate public services. But, in addition, there are all-India services (IAS, IPS, and IFS) which are common to both the Centre and the states. The members of these services are recruited and trained by the Centre which also possess ultimate control over them. Thus, these services violate the principle of federalism under the Constitution.

10. Integrated Audit Machinery

The Comptroller and Auditor-General of India audits the accounts of not only the Central government but also those of the states. But, his appointment and removal is done by the president without consulting the states. Hence, this office restricts the financial autonomy of the states. The American Comptroller-General, on the contrary, has no role with respect to the accounts of the states.

11. Parliament's Authority Over State List

Even in the limited sphere of authority allotted to them, the states do not have exclusive control. The Parliament is empowered to legislate on any subject of the State List if Rajya Sabha passes a resolution to that effect in the national interest. This means that the legislative competence of the Parliament can be extended without amending the Constitution. Notably, this can be done when there is no emergency of any kind.

12. Appointment of Governor

The governor, who is the head of the state, is appointed by the President. He holds office during the pleasure of the President. He also acts as an agent of the Centre. Through him, the Centre exercises control over the states. The American Constitution, on the contrary, provided for an elected head in the states. In this respect, India adopted the Canadian system.

13. Integrated Election Machinery

The Election Commission conducts elections not only to the Central legislature but also to the state legislatures. But, this body is constituted by the President and the states have no say in this matter. The position is same with regard to the removal of its members as well. On the other hand, US has separate machineries for the conduct of elections at the federal and state levels.

14. Veto Over State Bills

The governor is empowered to reserve certain types of bills passed by the state legislature for the consideration of the President. The President can withhold his assent to such bills not only in the first instance but also in the second instance. Thus, the President enjoys absolute veto (and not suspensive veto) over state bills. But in US and Australia, the states are autonomous within their fields and there is no provision for any such reservation.

CRITICAL EVALUATION OF THE FEDERAL SYSTEM

From the above, it is clear that the Constitution of India has deviated from the traditional federal systems like US, Switzerland and Australia and incorporated a large number of unitary or non-federal features, tilting the balance of power in favour of the Centre. This has promoted the Constitutional experts to challenge the federal character of the Indian Constitution. Thus, KC Wheare described the Constitution of India as "quasi-federal". He remarked that "Indian Union is a unitary state with subsidiary federal features rather than a federal state with subsidiary unitary features."[6]

According to K Santhanam, the two factors have been responsible for increasing the unitary bias (tendency of centralisation) of the Constitution. These are: **(i)** the dominance of the Centre in the financial sphere and the dependence of the states upon the Central grants; and **(ii)** the emergence of a powerful planning commission which controls the developmental process in the states. He observed: "India has practically functioned as a unitary state though the Union and the states have tried to function formally and legally as a federation."[7]

However, there are other political scientists who do not agree with the above descriptions. Thus, Paul Appleby[8] characterises the Indian system as "extremely federal". Morris Jones[9] termed it as a "bargaining federalism". Ivor Jennings[10] has described it as a "federation with a strong centralising tendency". He observed that "the Indian Constitution is mainly federal with unique safeguards for enforcing national unity and growth". Alexandrowicz[11] stated that "India is a case *sui generis* (i.e., unique in character). Granville Austin[12] called the Indian federalism as a "cooperative federalism". He said that though the Constitution of India has created a strong Central government, it has not made the state governments weak and has not reduced them to the level of administrative agencies for the execution of policies of the Central government. He described the Indian federation as "a new kind of federation to meet India's peculiar needs".

On the nature of Indian Constitution, Dr B R Ambedkar made the following observation in the Constituent Assembly: "The Constitution is a Federal Constitution in as much as it establishes a dual polity. The Union is not a league of states, united in a loose relationship, nor are the states the agencies of the Union, deriving powers from it. Both the Union and the states are created by the Constitution, both derive their respective authority from the Constitution."[13] He further observed: "Yet the Constitution avoids the tight mould of federalism and could be both unitary as well as federal according to the requirements of time and circumstances".[14] While replying to the criticism of over-centralisation in the Constitution, he stated: "A serious complaint is made on the ground that there is too much centralisation and the states have been reduced to municipalities. It is clear that this view is not only an exaggeration but is also founded on a misunderstanding of what exactly the Constitution contrives to do. As to the relations between the Centre and the states, it is necessary to bear in mind the fundamental principle on which it rests. The basic principle of federalism is that the legislative and executive authority is partitioned between the Centre and the states not by any law to be made by the Centre but by the Constitution itself. This is what the Constitution does. The states are in no way dependent upon the Centre for their legislative or executive authority. The states and the

Centre are co-equal in this matter. It is difficult to see how such a Constitution can be called centralism. It is, therefore, wrong to say that the states have been placed under the Centre. The Centre cannot by its own will alter the boundary of this partition. Nor can the judiciary".[15]

In *Bommai* case[16] (1994), the Supreme Court laid down that the Constitution is federal and characterised federalism as its 'basic feature'. It observed: "The fact that under the scheme of our Constitution, greater power is conferred upon the Centre *vis-a-vis* the states does not mean that the states are mere appendages of the Centre. The states have an independent constitutional existence. They are not satellites or agents of the Centre. Within the sphere allotted to them, the states are supreme. The fact that during emergency and in certain other eventualities their powers are overridden or invaded by the Centre is not destructive of the essential federal feature of the Constitution. They are exceptions and the exceptions are not a rule. Let it be said that the federalism in the Indian Constitution is not a matter of administrative convenience, but one of principle—the outcome of our own process and a recognition of the ground realities".

In fact, the federalism in India represents a compromise between the following two conflicting considerations[17]:

(i) normal division of powers under which states enjoy autonomy within their own spheres; and

(ii) need for national integrity and a strong Union government under exceptional circumstances.

The following trends in the working of Indian political system reflects its federal spirit: **(i)** Territorial disputes between states, for example, between Maharashtra and Karnataka over Belgaum; **(ii)** Disputes between states over sharing of river water, for example, between Karnataka and Tamil Nadu over Cauvery Water; **(iii)** The emergence of regional parties and their coming to power in states like Andhra Pradesh, Tamil Nadu, etc.; **(iv)** The creation of new states to fulfil the regional aspirations, for example, Mizoram or recently Jharkhand; **(v)** Demand of the states for more financial grants from the Centre to meet their developmental needs; **(vi)** Assertion of autonomy by the states and their resistance to the interference from the Centre; **(vii)** Supreme Court's imposition of several procedural limitations on the use of Article 356 (President's Rule in the States) by the Centre.[18]

NOTES AND REFERENCES

1. *Constituent Assembly Debates*, Volume VII, P. 43.
2. The American Constitution originally consisted only 7 Articles, the Australian 128 and the Canadian 147.
3. The various amendments carried out since 1951 have deleted about 20 Articles and one Part (VII) and added about 85 Articles, four Parts (IVA, IXA, IXB and XIVA) and four Schedules (9,10,11 and 12).
4. A majority of 2/3 of the members of each House present and voting and a majority of the total membership of each House.
5. Jammu and Kashmir enjoys a special status by virtue of Article 370 of the Constitution of India.
6. K C Wheare: *Federal Government*, 1951, P. 28.
7. K Santhanam: *Union-State Relations in India*, 1960, PP. 50–70.
8. Paul Appleby: *Public Administration in India*, 1953, P. 51.
9. Morris Jones: *The Government and Politics in India*, 1960, P. 14.
10. Ivor Jennings: *Some Characteristics of the Indian Constitution*, 1953, P. 1.
11. C H Alexandrowicz: *Constitutional Development in India*, 1957, PP. 157–70.
12. Granville Austin: *The Indian Constitution—Cornerstone of a Nation*, Oxford, 1966, PP. 186–88.
13. *Constituent Assembly Debates*, Vol. VIII, P. 33.
14. Ibid, Vol.VII, PP. 33–34.
15. Dr B R Ambedkar's speech in the Constituent Assembly on 25.11.1949 reproduced in *The Constitution and the Constituent Assembly*; Lok Sabha Secretariat, 1990, P. 176.
16. *S R Bommai* v. *Union of India* (1994).
17. Subash C Kashyap: *Our Parliament*, National Book Trust, 1999 Edition, P. 40.
18. *S R Bommai* v. *Union of India* (1994). For the details of the judgement, see "President's Rule" in Chapter 16.

Centre–State Relations

The Constitution of India, being federal in structure, divides all powers (legislative, executive and financial) between the Centre and the states. However, there is no division of judicial power as the Constitution has established an integrated judicial system to enforce both the Central laws as well as state laws.

Though the Centre and the states are supreme in their respective fields, the maximum harmony and coordination between them is essential for the effective operation of the federal system. Hence, the Constitution contains elaborate provisions to regulate the various dimensions of the relations between the Centre and the states.

The Centre-state relations can be studied under three heads:

- Legislative relations.
- Administrative relations.
- Financial relations.

LEGISLATIVE RELATIONS

Articles 245 to 255 in Part XI of the Constitution deal with the legislative relations between the Centre and the states. Besides these, there are some other articles dealing with the same subject.

Like any other Federal Constitution, the Indian Constitution also divides the legislative powers between the Centre and the states with respect to both the territory and the subjects of legislation. Further, the Constitution provides for the parliamentary legislation in the state field under five extraordinary situations as well as the centre's control over state legislation in certain cases. Thus, there are four aspects in the Centre–states legislative relations, viz.,

- Territorial extent of Central and state legislation;
- Distribution of legislative subjects;
- Parliamentary legislation in the state field; and
- Centre's control over state legislation.

1. Territorial Extent of Central and State Legislation

The Constitution defines the territorial limits of the legislative powers vested in the Centre and the states in the following way:

(i) The Parliament can make laws for the whole or any part of the territory of India. The territory of India includes the states, the union territories, and any other area for the time being included in the territory of India.

(ii) A state legislature can make laws for the whole or any part of the state. The laws made by a state legislature are not applicable outside the state, except when there is a sufficient nexus between the state and the object.

(iii) The Parliament alone can make 'extra-territorial legislation'. Thus, the laws of the Parliament are also applicable to the Indian citizens and their property in any part of the world.

However, the Constitution places certain restrictions on the plenary territorial jurisdiction of the Parliament. In other words, the laws of Parliament are not applicable in the following areas:

(i) The President can make regulations for the peace, progress and good government of the four Union Territories—the Andaman and Nicobar Islands, Lakshadweep, Dadra and Nagar Haveli and Daman and Diu. A regulation so made has the same force and effect as an act of Parliament. It may also repeal or amend any act of Parliament in relation to these union territories.

(ii) The governor is empowered to direct that an act of Parliament does not apply to a scheduled area in the state or apply with specified modifications and exceptions.

(iii) The Governor of Assam may likewise direct that an act of Parliament does not apply to a tribal area (autonomours district) in the state or apply with specified modifications and exceptions. The President enjoys the same power with respect to tribal areas (autonomous districts) in Meghalaya, Tripura and Mizoram.

2. Distribution of Legislative Subjects

The Constitution provides for a three-fold distribution of legislative subjects between the Centre and the states, viz., List-I (the Union List), List-II (the State List) and List-III (the Concurrent List) in the Seventh Schedule:

(i) The Parliament has exclusive powers to make laws with respect to any of the matters enumerated in the Union List. This list has at present 100 subjects (originally 97[1] subjects) like defence, banking, foreign affairs, currency, atomic energy, insurance, communication, inter-state trade and commerce, census, audit and so on.

(ii) The state legislature has "in normal circumstances" exclusive powers to make laws with respect to any of the matters enumerated in the State List. This has at present 61 subjects (originally 66[2] subjects) like public order, police, public health and sanitation, agriculture, prisons, local government, fisheries, markets, theaters, gambling and so on.

(iii) Both, the Parliament and state legislature can make laws with respect to any of the matters enumerated in the Concurrent List. This list has at present **52** subjects (originally 47[3] subjects) like criminal law and procedure, civil procedure, marriage and divorce, population control and family planning, electricity, labour welfare, economic and social planning, drugs, newspapers, books and printing press, and others. The 42nd Amendment Act of 1976 transferred five subjects to Concurrent List from State List, that is, **(a)** education, **(b)** forests, **(c)** weights and measures, **(d)** protection of wild animals and birds, and **(e)** administration of justice; constitution and organisation of all courts except the Supreme Court and the high courts.

The power to make laws with respect to residuary subjects (i.e., the matters which are not enumerated in any of the three lists) is vested in the Parliament. This residuary power of legislation includes the power to levy residuary taxes.

From the above scheme, it is clear that the matters of national importance and the matters which requires uniformity of legislation nationwide are included in the Union List. The matters of regional and local importance and the matters which permits diversity of interest are specified in the State List. The matters on which uniformity of legislation throughout the country is desirable but not essential are enumerated in the concurrent list. Thus, it permits diversity along with uniformity.

In US, only the powers of the Federal Government are enumerated in the Constitution and the residuary powers are left to the states. The Australian Constitution followed the American pattern of single enumeration of powers. In Canada, on the other hand, there is a double enumeration—Federal and Provincial, and the residuary powers are vested in the Centre.

The Government of India (GoI) Act of 1935 provided for a three-fold emumenration, viz., federal, provincial and concurrent. The present Constitution follows the scheme of this act but with one difference, that is, under this act, the residuary powers were given neither to the federal legislature nor to the provincial legislature but to the governor-general of India. In this respect, India follows the Canadian precedent.

The Constitution expressly secure the predominance of the Union List over the State List and the Concurrent List and that of the Concurrent List over the State List. Thus, in case of overlapping between the Union List and the State List, the former should prevail. In case of overlapping between the Union List and the Concurrent List, it is again the former which should prevail. Where there is a conflict between the Concurrent List and the State List, it is the former that should prevail.

In case of a conflict between the Central law and the state law on a subject enumerated in the Concurrent List, the Central law prevails over the state law. But, there is an exception. If the state law has been reserved for the consideration of the president and has received his assent, then the state law prevails in that state. But, it would still be competent for the Parliament to override such a law by subsequently making a law on the same matter.

3. Parliamentary Legislation in the State Field

The above scheme of distribution of legislative powers between the Centre and the states is to be maintained in normal times. But, in abnormal times, the scheme of distribution is either modified or suspended. In other words, the Constitution empowers the Parliament to make laws on any matter enumerated in the State List under the following five extraordinary circumstances:

When Rajya Sabha Passes a Resolution If the Rajya Sabha declares that it is necessary in the national interest that Parliament should make laws on a matter in the State List, then the Parliament becomes competent to make laws on that matter. Such a resolution must be supported by two-thirds of the members present and voting. The resolution remains in force for one year; it can be renewed any number of times but not exceeding one year at a time. The laws cease to have effect on the expiration of six months after the resolution has ceased to be in force.

This provision does not restrict the power of a state legislature to make laws on the same matter. But, in case of inconsistency between a state law and a parliamentary law, the latter is to prevail.

During a National Emergency The Parliament acquires the power to legislate with respect to matters in the State List, while a proclamation of national emergency is in operation. The laws become inoperative on the expiration of six months after the emergency has ceased to operate.

Here also, the power of a state legislature to make laws on the same matter is not restricted. But, in case of repugnancy between a state law and a parliamentary law, the latter is to prevail.

When States Make a Request When the legislatures of two or more states pass resolutions requesting the Parliament to enact laws on a matter in the State List, then the Parliament can make laws for regulating that matter. A law so enacted applies only to those states which have passed the resolutions. However, any other state may adopt it afterwards by passing a resolution to that effect in its legislature. Such a law can be amended or repealed only by the Parliament and not by the legislatures of the concerned states.

The effect of passing a resolution under the above provision is that the Parliament becomes entitled to legislate with respect to a matter for which it has no power to make a law. On the other hand, the state legislature ceases to have the power to make a law with respect to that matter. The resolution operates as abdication or surrender of the power of the state legislature with respect to that matter and it is placed entirely in the hands of Parliament which alone can then legislate with respect to it.

Some examples of laws passed under the above provision are Prize Competition Act, 1955; Wild Life (Protection) Act, 1972; Water (Prevention and Control of Pollution) Act, 1974; Urban Land (Ceiling and Regulation) Act, 1976; and Transplantation of Human Organs Act, 1994.

To Implement International Agreements The Parliament can make laws on any matter in the State List for implementing the international treaties, agreements or conventions. This provision enables the Central government to fulfil its international obligations and commitments.

Some examples of laws enacted under the above provision are United Nations (Privileges and Immunities) Act, 1947; Geneva Convention Act, 1960; Anti-Hijacking Act, 1982 and legislations relating to environment and TRIPS.

During President's Rule When the President's rule is imposed in a state, the Parliament becomes empowered to make laws with respect to any matter in the State List in relation to that state. A law made so by the Parliament continues to be operative even after the president's rule. This means that the period for which such a law remains in force is not co-terminus with the duration of the President's rule. But, such a law can be repealed or altered or re-enacted by the state legislature.

4. Centre's Control Over State Legislation

Besides the Parliament's power to legislate directly on the state subjects under the exceptional situations, the Constitution empowers the Centre to exercise control over the state's legislative matters in the following ways:

(i) The governor can reserve certain types of bills passed by the state legislature for the consideration of the President. The president enjoys absolute veto over them.

(ii) Bills on certain matters enumerated in the State List can be introduced in the state legislature only with the previous sanction of the president. (For example, the bills imposing restrictions on the freedom of trade and commerce).

(iii) The President can direct the states to reserve money bills and other financial bills passed by the state legislature for his consideration during a financial emergency.

From the above, it is clear that the Constitution has assigned a position of superiority to the Centre in the legislative sphere. In this context, the Sarkaria Commission on Centre–State Relations (1983–87) observed: "The rule of federal supremacy is a technique to avoid absurdity, resolve conflict and ensure harmony between the Union and state laws. If this principle of union supremacy is excluded, it is not difficult to imagine its deleterious results. There will be every possibility of our two-tier political system being stultified by interference, strife, legal chaos and confusion caused by a host of conflicting laws, much to the bewilderment of the common citizen. Integrated legislative policy and uniformity on basic issues of common Union–state concern will be stymied. The federal principle of unity in diversity will be very much a casualty. This rule of federal supremacy, therefore, is indispensable for the successful functioning of the federal system".[4]

ADMINISTRATIVE RELATIONS

Articles 256 to 263 in Part XI of the Constitution deal with the administrative relations between the Centre and the states. In addition, there are various other articles pertaining to the same matter.

Distribution of Executive Powers

The executive power has been divided between the Centre and the states on the lines of the distribution of legislative powers, except in few cases. Thus, the executive power of the Centre extends to the whole of India: **(i)** to the matters on which the Parliament has exclusive power of legislation (i.e., the subjects enumerated in the Union List); and **(ii)** to the exercise of rights, authority and jurisdiction conferred on it by any treaty or agreement. Similarly, the executive power of a state extends to its territory in respect of matters on which the state legislature has exclusive power of legislation (i.e., the subjects enumerated in the State List).

In respect of matters on which both the Parliament and the state legislatures have power of legislation (i.e., the subjects enumerated in the Concurrent List), the executive power rests with the states except when a Constitutional provision or a parliamentary law specifically confers it on the Centre. Therefore, a law on a concurrent subject, though enacted by the Parliament, is to be executed by the states except when the Constitution or the Parliament has directed otherwise.[5]

Obligation of States and the Centre

The Constitution has placed two restrictions on the executive power of the states in order to give ample scope to the Centre for exercising its executive power in an unrestricted manner. Thus, the executive power of every state is to be exercised in such a way **(a)** as to ensure compliance with the laws made by the Parliament and any existing law which apply in the state; and **(b)** as not to impede or prejudice the exercise of executive power of the Centre in the state. While the former lays down a general obligation upon the state, the latter imposes a specific obligation on the state not to hamper the executive power of the Centre.

In both the cases, the executive power of the Centre extends to giving of such directions to the state as are necessary for the purpose. The sanction behind these directions of the Centre is coercive in nature. Thus, Article 365 says that where any state has failed to comply with (or to give effect to) any directions given by the Centre, it will be lawful for the President to hold that a situation has arisen in which the government of the state cannot be carried on in accordance with the provisions of the Constitution. It means that, in such a situation, the President's rule can be imposed in the state under Article 356.

Centre's Directions to the States

In addition to the above two cases, the Centre is empowered to give directions to the states with regard to the exercise of their executive power in the following matters:
(i) the construction and maintenance of means of communication (declared to be of national or military importance) by the state;
(ii) the measures to be taken for the protection of the railways within the state;
(iii) the provision of adequate facilities for instruction in the mother-tongue at the primary stage of education to children belonging to linguistic minority groups in the state; and
(iv) the drawing up and execution of the specified schemes for the welfare of the Scheduled Tribes in the state.

The coercive sanction behind the Central directions under Article 365 (mentioned above) is also applicable in these cases.

Mutual Delegation of Functions

The distribution of legislative powers between the Centre and the states is rigid. Consequently, the Centre cannot delegate its legislative powers to the states and a single state cannot request the Parliament to make a law on a state subject. The distribution of executive power in general follows the distribution of legislative powers. But, such a rigid division in the executive sphere may lead to occasional conflicts between the two. Hence, the Constitution provides for inter-government delegation of executive functions in order to mitigate rigidity and avoid a situation of deadlock.

Accordingly, the President may, with the consent of the state government, entrust to that government any of the executive functions of the Centre. Conversely, the governor of a state may, with the consent of the Central government, entrust to that government any of the executive functions of the state.[6] This mutual delegation of administrative functions may be conditional or unconditional.

The Constitution also makes a provision for the entrustment of the executive functions of the Centre to a state without the consent of that state. But, in this case, the delegation is by the Parliament and not by the president. Thus, a law made by the Parliament on a subject of the Union List can confer powers and impose duties on a state, or authorise the conferring of powers and imposition of duties by the Centre upon a state (irrespective of the consent of the state concerned). Notably, the same thing cannot be done by the state legislature.

From the above, it is clear that the mutual delegation of functions between the Centre and the state can take place either under an agreement or by a legislation. While the Centre can use both the methods, a state can use only the first method.

Cooperation Between the Centre and States

The Constitution contains the following provisions to secure cooperation and coordination between the Centre and the states:
(i) The Parliament can provide for the adjudication of any dispute or complaint with respect to the use, distribution and control of waters of any inter-state river and river valley.
(ii) The President can establish (under Article 263) an Inter-State Council to investigate and discuss subject of common interest between the Centre and the states. Such a council was set up in 1990.[7]

(iii) Full faith and credit is to be given throughout the territory of India to public acts, records and judicial proceedings of the Centre and every state.

(iv) The Parliament can appoint an appropriate authority to carry out the purposes of the constitutional provisions relating to the interstate freedom of trade, commerce and intercourse. But, no such authority has been appointed so far.

All-India Services

Like in any other federation, the Centre and the states also have their separate public services called as the Central Services and the State Services respectively. In addition, there are all-India services—IAS, IPS and IFS. The members of these services occupy top positions (or key posts) under both the Centre and the states and serve them by turns. But, they are recruited and trained by the Centre.

These services are controlled jointly by the Centre and the states. The ultimate control lies with the Central government while the immediate control vests with the state governments.

In 1947, Indian Civil Service (ICS) was replaced by IAS and the Indian Police (IP) was replaced by IPS and were recognised by the Constitution as All-India Services. In 1966, the Indian Forest Service (IFS) was created as the third All-India Service. Article 312 of the Constitution authorises the Parliament to create new All-India Services on the basis of a Rajya Sabha resolution to that effect.

Each of these three all-India services, irrespective of their division among different states, form a single service with common rights and status and uniform scales of pay throughout the country.

Though the all-India services violate the principle of federalism under the Constitution by restricting the autonomy and patronage of the states, they are supported on the ground that **(i)** they help in maintaining high standard of administration in the Centre as well as in the states; **(ii)** they help to ensure uniformity of the administrative system throughout the country; and **(iii)** they facilitate liaison, cooperation, coordination and joint action on the issues of common interest between the Centre and the states.

While justifying the institution of all-India services in the Constituent Assembly, Dr B R Ambedkar observed that: "The dual polity which is inherent in a federal system is followed in all federations by a dual service. In all federations, there is a Federal Civil Service and a State Civil Service. The Indian federation, though a dual polity, will have a dual service, but with one exception. It is recognised that in every country there are certain posts in its administrative set up which might be called strategic from the point of view of maintaining the standard of administration. There can be no doubt that the standard of administration depends upon the calibre of the civil servants who are appointed to the strategic posts. The Constitution provides that without depriving the states of their rights to form their own civil services, there shall be an all-India service, recruited on an all-India basis with common qualifications, with uniform scale of pay and members of which alone could be appointed to those strategic posts throughout the Union".[8]

Public Service Commissions

In the field of public service commissions, the Centre–state relations are as follows:

(i) The Chairman and members of a state public service commission, though appointed by the governor of the state, can be removed only by the President.

(ii) The Parliament can establish a Joint State Public Service Commission (JSPSC) for two or more states on the request of the state legislatures concerned. The chairman and members of the JSPSC are appointed by the president.

(iii) The Union Public Service Commission (UPSC) can serve the needs of a state on the request of the state governor and with the approval of the President.

(iv) The UPSC assists the states (when requested by two or more states) in framing and operating schemes of joint recruitment for any services for which candidates possessing special qualifications are required.

Integrated Judicial System

Though India has a dual polity, there is no dual system of administration of justice. The Constitution, on the other hand, established an integrated judicial system with the Supreme Court at the top and the state high courts below it. This single system of courts enforces both the Central laws as well as the state laws. This is done to eliminate diversities in the remedial procedure.

The judges of a state high court are appointed by the president in consultation with the Chief Justice of India and the governor of the state. They can also be transferred and removed by the president.

The Parliament can establish a common high court for two or more states. For example, Maharashtra and Goa or Punjab and Haryana have a common high court.

Relations During Emergencies

(i) During the operation of a national emergency (under Article 352), the Centre becomes entitled to give executive directions to a state on 'any' matter. Thus, the state governments are brought under the complete control of the Centre, though they are not suspended.

(ii) When the President's Rule is imposed in a state (under Article 356), the President can assume to himself the functions of the state government and powers vested in the Governor or any other executive authority in the state.

(iii) During the operation of a financial emergency (under Article 360), the Centre can direct the states to observe canons of financial propriety and the President can give other necessary directions including the reduction of salaries of persons serving in the state and the high court judges.

Other Provisions

The Constitution contains the following other provisions which enable the Centre to exercise control over the state administration:

(i) Article 355 imposes two duties on the Centre: **(a)** to protect every state against external aggression and internal disturbance; and **(b)** to ensure that the government of every state is carried on in accordance with the provisions of the Constitution.

(ii) The governor of a state is appointed by the president. He holds office during the pleasure of the President. In addition to the Constitutional head of the state, the governor acts as

an agent of the Centre in the state. He submits periodical reports to the Centre about the administrative affairs of the state.

(iii) The state election commissioner, though appointed by the governor of the state, can be removed only by the President.

Extra-Constitutional Devices

In addition to the above-mentioned constitutional devices, there are extra-constitutional devices to promote cooperation and coordination between the Centre and the states. These include a number of advisory bodies and conferences held at the Central level.

The non-constitutional advisory bodies include the Planning Commission,[9] the National Development Council, the National Integration Council,[10] the Central Council of Health, the Central Council of Local Government and Urban Development, the Zonal Councils,[11] the North-Eastern Council, the Central Council of Indian Medicine, Central Council of Homoeopathy, the Central Family Welfare Council, the Transport Development Council, the University Grants Commission and so on.

The important conferences held either annually or otherwise to facilitate Centre–state consultation on a wide range of matters are as follows: **(i)** The governors' conference (presided over by the President). **(ii)** The chief ministers' conference (presided over by the prime minister). **(iii)** The chief secretaries' conference (presided over by the cabinet secretary). **(iv)** The conference of inspector-general of police. **(v)** The chief justices' conference (presided over by the chief justice of India). **(vi)** The conference of vice-cancellors. **(vii)** The home ministers' conference (presided over by the Central home minister). **(viii)** The law ministers' conference (presided over by the Central law minister).

FINANCIAL RELATIONS

Articles 268 to 293 in Part XII of the Constitution deal with Centre–state financial relations. Besides these, there are other provisions dealing with the same subject. These together can be studied under the following heads:

Allocation of Taxing Powers

The Constitution divides the taxing powers between the Centre and the states in the following way:

- The Parliament has exclusive power to levy taxes on subjects enumerated in the Union List (which are 15 in number[12]).
- The state legislature has exclusive power to levy taxes on subjects enumerated in the State List (which are 20 in number[13]).
- Both the Parliament and the state legislature can levy taxes on subjects enumerated in the Concurrent List (which are 3 in number[14]).
- The residuary power of taxation (that is, the power to impose taxes not enumerated in any of the three lists) is vested in the Parliament. Under this provision, the Parliament has imposed gift tax, wealth tax and expenditure tax.

The Constitution also draws a distinction between the power to levy and collect a tax and the power to appropriate the proceeds of the tax so levied and collected. For example, the income-tax is levied and collected by the Centre but its proceeds are distributed between the Centre and the states.

Further, the Constitution has placed the following restrictions on the taxing powers of the states:

(i) A state legislature can impose taxes on professions, trades, callings and employments. But, the total amount of such taxes payable by any person should not exceed Rs. 2,500 per annum.[15]

(ii) A state legislature can impose taxes on the sale or purchase of goods (other than newspapers). But, this power of the states to impose sales tax is subjected to the four restrictions: **(a)** no tax can be imposed on the sale or purchase taking place outside the states; **(b)** no tax can be imposed on the sale or purchase taking place in the course of import or export; **(c)** no tax can be imposed on the sale or purchase taking place in the course of inter-state trade and commerce; and **(d)** a tax imposed on the sale or purchase of goods declared by Parliament to be of special importance in inter-state trade and commerce is subject to the restrictions and conditions specified by the Parliament.[16]

(iii) A state legislature can impose tax on the consumption or sale of electricity. But, no tax can be imposed on the consumption or sale of electricity which is **(a)** consumed by the Centre or sold to the Centre; or **(b)** consumed in the construction, maintenance or operation of any railway by the Centre or by the concerned railway company or sold to the Centre or the railway company for the same purpose.

(iv) A state legislature can impose a tax in respect of any water or electricity stored, generated, consumed, distributed or sold by any authority established by Parliament for regulating or developing any inter-state river or river valley. But, such a law, to be effective, should be reserved for the president's consideration and receive his assent.

Distribution of Tax Revenues

The 80th Amendment of 2000 and the 88th Amendment of 2003 have introduced major changes in the scheme of the distribution of tax revenues between the centre and the states. The 80th Amendment was enacted to give effect to the recommendations of the 10th Finance Commission. The Commission recommended that out of the total income obtained from certain central taxes and duties, 29% should go to the states. This is known as the 'Alternative Scheme of Devolution' and came into effect retrospectively from April 1, 1996. This amendment has brought several central taxes and duties like Corporation Tax and Customs Duties at par with Income Tax (taxes on income other than agricultural income) as far as their constitutionally mandated sharing with the states is concerned.[17]

The 88th Amendment has added a new Article 268-A dealing with service tax. It also added a new subject in the Union List – entry 92-C (taxes on services). Service tax is levied by the centre but collected and appropriated by both the centre and the states.

After these two Amendments, the present position in this regard is as follows:

A. Taxes Levied by the Centre but Collected and Appropriated by the States (Article 268):
This category includes the following taxes and duties:

(i) Stamp duties on bills of exchange, cheques, promissory notes, policies of insurance, transfer of shares and others.

(ii) Excise duties on medicinal and toilet preparations containing alcohol and narcotics.

The proceeds of these duties levied within any state do not form a part of the Consolidated Fund of India, but are assigned to that state.

B. Service Tax Levied by the Centre but Collected and Appropriated by the Centre and the States (Article 268-A):

Taxes on services are levied by the Centre. But, their proceeds are collected as well as appropriated by both the Centre and the states. The principles of their collection and appropriation are formulated by the Parliament.

C. Taxes Levied and Collected by the Centre but Assigned to the States (Article 269):

The following taxes fall under this category:

(i) Taxes on the sale or purchase of goods (other than newspapers) in the course of inter-state trade or commerce.

(ii) Taxes on the consignment of goods in the course of inter-state trade or commerce.

The net proceeds of these taxes do not form a part of the Consolidated Fund of India. They are assigned to the concerned states in accordance with the principles laid down by the Parliament.

D. Taxes Levied and Collected by the Centre but Distributed between the Centre and the States (Article 270):

This category includes all taxes and duties referred to in the Union List except the following:

(i) Duties and taxes referred to in Articles 268, 268-A and 269 (mentioned above);

(ii) Surcharge on taxes and duties referred to in Article 271 (mentioned below); and

(iii) Any cess levied for specific purposes.

The manner of distribution of the net proceeds of these taxes and duties is prescribed by the President on the recommendation of the Finance Commission.

E. Surcharge on Certain Taxes and Duties for Purposes of the Centre (Article 271):

The Parliament can at any time levy the surcharges on taxes and duties referred to in Articles 269 and 270 (mentioned above). The proceeds of such surcharges go to the Centre exclusively. In other words, the states have no share in these surcharges.

F. Taxes Levied and Collected and Retained by the States

These are the taxes belonging to the states exclusively. They are enumerated in the state list and are 20 in number. These are[18]: **(i)** land revenue; **(ii)** taxes on agricultural income, succession and estate duties in respect of agricultural land; **(iii)** taxes on lands and buildings, on mineral rights, on animals and boats, on road vehicles, on luxuries, on entertainments, and on gambling; **(iv)** excise duties on alcoholic liquors for human consumption and narcotics; **(v)** taxes on the entry of goods into a local area, on advertisements (except newspapers), on consumption or sale of electricity, and on goods and passengers carried by road or on inland waterways; **(vi)** taxes on professions, trades, callings and employments not exceeding Rs. 2,500 per annum; **(vii)** capitation taxes; **(viii)** tolls; **(ix)** stamp duty on documents (except those specified in the Union List); **(x)** sales tax (other than newspaper); and **(xi)** fees on the matters enumerated in the State List (except court fees).

Distribution of Non-tax Revenues

A. The Centre The receipts from the following form the major sources of non-tax revenues of the Centre: **(i)** posts and telegraphs; **(ii)** railways; **(iii)** banking; **(iv)** broadcasting **(v)** coinage and currency; **(vi)** central public sector enterprises; and **(vii)** escheat and lapse.[19]

B. The States The receipts from the following form the major sources of non-tax revenues of the states: **(i)** irrigation; **(ii)** forests; **(iii)** fisheries; **(iv)** state public sector enterprise; and **(v)** escheat and lapse.[20]

Grants-in-Aid to the States

Besides sharing of taxes between the Centre and the states, the Constitution provides for grants-in-aid to the states from the Central resources. There are two types of grants-in-aid, viz, statutory grants and discretionary grants:

Statutory Grants Article 275 empowers the Parliament to make grants to the states which are in need of financial assistance and not to every state. Also, different sums may be fixed for different states. These sums are charged on the Consolidated Fund of India every year.

Apart from this general provision, the Constitution also provides for specific grants for promoting the welfare of the scheduled tribes in a state or for raising the level of administration of the scheduled areas in a state including the State of Assam.

The statutory grants under Article 275 (both general and specific) are given to the states on the recommendation of the Finance Commission.

Discretionary Grants Article 282 empowers both the Centre and the states to make any grants for any public purpose, even if it is not within their respective legislative competence. Under this provision, the Centre makes grants to the states on the recommendations of the Planning Commission—an extra-constitutional body.

"These grants are also known as discretionary grants, the reason being that the Centre is under no obligation to give these grants and the matter lies within its discretion. These grants have a two-fold purpose: to help the state financially to fulfil plan targets; and to give some leverage to the Centre to influence and coordinate state action to effectuate the national plan."[21]

Notably, the discretionary grants form the larger part of the Central grants to the states (when compared with that of the statutory grants). Hence, the Planning Commission has assumed greater significance than the Finance Commission in Centre state financial relations.[22]

Other Grants The Constitution also provided for a third type of grants-in-aid, but for a temporary period. Thus, a provision was made for grants in lieu of export duties on jute and jute products to the States of Assam, Bihar, Orissa and West Bengal. These grants were to be given for a period of ten years from the commencement of the Constitution. These sums were charged on the Consolidated Fund of India and were made to the states on the recommendation of the Finance Commission.

Finance Commission

Article 280 provides for a Finance Commission as a quasi-judicial body. It is constituted by the President every fifth year or even earlier. It is required to make recommendations to the President on the following matters:

- The distribution of the net proceeds of taxes to be shared between the Centre and the states,

and the allocation between the states, the respective shares of such proceeds.

- The principles which should govern the grants-in-aid to the states by the Centre (i.e., out of the Consolidated Fund of India).
- The measures needed to augment the Consolidated fund of a state to supplement the resources of the panchayats and the municipalities in the state on the basis of the recommendations made by the State Finance Commission.[23]
- Any other matter referred to it by the President in the interests of sound finance.

Till 1960, the Commission also suggested the amounts paid to the States of Assam, Bihar, Orissa and West Bengal in lieu of assignment of any share of the net proceeds in each year of export duty on jute and jute products.

The Constitution envisages the Finance Commission as the balancing wheel of fiscal federalism in India. However, its role in the Centre–state fiscal relations has been undermined by the emergence of the planning commission, a non-constitutional and non-statutory body.

Protection of the States' Interest

To protect the interest of states in the financial matters, the Constitution lays down that the following bills can be introduced in the Parliament only on the recommendation of the President:

- A bill which imposes or varies any tax or duty in which states are interested;
- A bill which varies the meaning of the expression 'agricultural income' as defined for the purposes of the enactments relating to Indian income tax;
- A bill which affects the principles on which moneys are or may be distributable to states; and
- A bill which imposes any surcharge on any specified tax or duty for the purpose of the Centre.

The expression "tax or duty in which states are interested" means: **(a)** a tax or duty the whole or part of the net proceeds whereof are assigned to any state; or **(b)** a tax or duty by reference to the net proceeds whereof sums are for the time being payable, out of the Consolidated Fund of India to any state.

The phrase 'net proceeds' means the proceeds of a tax or a duty minus the cost of collection. The net proceeds of a tax or a duty in any area is to be ascertained and certified by the Comptroller and Auditor-General of India. His certificate is final.

Borrowing by the Centre and the States

The Constitution makes the following provisions with regard to the borrowing powers of the Centre and the states:

- The Central government can borrow either within India or outside upon the security of the Consolidated Fund of India or can give guarantees, but both within the limits fixed by the Parliament. So far, no such law has been enacted by the Parliament.
- Similarly, a state government can borrow within India (and not abroad) upon the security of the Consolidated Fund of the State or can give guarantees, but both within the limits fixed by the legislature of that state.
- The Central government can make loans to any state or give guarantees in respect of loans raised by any state. Any sums required for the purpose of making such loans are to be charged on the Consolidated Fund of India.
- A state cannot raise any loan without the consent of the Centre, if there is still outstanding any part of a loan made to the state by the Centre or in respect of which a guarantee has been given by the Centre.

Inter-Governmental Tax Immunities

Like any other federal Constitution, the Indian Constitution also contain the rule of 'immunity from mutual taxation' and makes the following provisions in this regard:

Exemption of Central Property from State Taxation The property of Centre is exempted from all taxes imposed by a state or any authority within a state like municipalities, district boards, panchayats and so on. But, the Parliament is empowered to remove this ban. The word 'property' includes lands, buildings, chattels, shares, debts, everything that has a money value, and every kind of property—movable or immovable and tangible or intangible. Further,

the property may be used for sovereign (like armed forces) or commercial purposes.

The corporations or the companies created by the Central government are not immune from state taxation or local taxation. The reason is that a corporation or a company is a separate legal entity.

Exemption of State Property or Income from Central Taxation The property and income of a state is exempted from Central taxation. Such income may be derived from sovereign functions or commercial functions. But the Centre can tax the commercial operations of a state if Parliament so provides. However, the Parliament can declare any particular trade or business as incidental to the ordinary functions of the government and it would then not be taxable.

Notably, the property and income of local authorities situated within a state are not exempted from the Central taxation. Similarly, the property or income of corporations and companies owned by a state can be taxed by the Centre.

The Supreme Court, in an advisory opinion[24] (1963), held that the immunity granted to a state in respect of Central taxation does not extend to the duties of customs or duties of excise. In other words, the Centre can impose customs duty on goods imported or exported by a state, or an excise duty on goods produced or manufactured by a state.

Effects of Emergencies

The Centre–state financial relations in normal times (described above) undergo changes during emergencies. These are as follows:

National Emergency While the proclamation of national emergency (under Article 352) is in operation, the president can modify the constitutional distribution of revenues between the Centre and the states. This means that the president can either reduce or cancel the transfer of finances (both tax sharing and grants-in-aid) from the Centre to the states. Such modification continues till the end of the financial year in which the emergency ceases to operate.

Financial Emergency While the proclamation of financial emergency (under Article 360) is in operation, the Centre can give directions to the states: **(i)** to observe the specified canons of financial propriety; **(ii)** to reduce the salaries and allowances of all class of persons serving in the state (including the high court judges); and **(iii)** to reserve all money bills and other financial bills for the consideration of the President.

TRENDS IN CENTRE–STATE RELATIONS

Till 1967, the centre–state relations by and large were smooth due to one-party rule at the Centre and in most of the states. In 1967 elections, the Congress party was defeated in nine states and its position at the Centre became weak. This changed political scenario heralded a new era in the Centre–state relations. The non-Congress Governments in the states opposed the increasing centralisation and intervention of the Central government. They raised the issue of state autonomy and demanded more powers and financial resources to the states. This caused tensions and conflicts in Centre–state relations.

Tension Areas in Centre-State Relations

The issues which created tensions and conflicts between the Centre and states are: **(1)** Mode of appointment and dismissal of governor; **(2)** Discriminatory and partisan role of governors; **(3)** Imposition of President's Rule for partisan interests; **(4)** Deployment of Central forces in the states to maintain law and order; **(5)** Reservation of state bills for the consideration of the President; **(6)** Discrimination in financial allocations to the states; **(7)** Role of Planning Commission in approving state projects; **(8)** Management of All-India Services (IAS, IPS, and IFS); **(9)** Use of electronic media for political purposes; **(10)** Appointment of enquiry commissions against the chief ministers; **(11)** Sharing of finances (between Centre and states); and **(12)** Encroachment by the Centre on the State List.

The issues in Centre-State relations have been under consideration since the mid 1960s. In this direction, the following developments have taken place:

Administrative Reforms Commission

The Central government appointed a six-member Administrative Reforms Commission (ARC) in 1966 under the chairmanship of Morarji Desai (followed by K Hanumanthayya). Its terms of references included, among others, the examination of Centre–State relations. In order to examine thoroughly the various issues in Centre–state relations, the ARC constituted a study team under M C Setalvad. On the basis of the report of this study team, the ARC finalised its own report and submitted it to the Central government in 1969. It made 22 recommendations for improving the Centre–state relations. The important recommendations are:

- Establishment of an Inter-State Council under Article 263 of the Constitution.
- Appointment of persons having long experience in public life and administration and non-partisan attitude as governors.
- Delegation of powers to the maximum extent to the states.
- Transferring of more financial resources to the states to reduce their dependency upon the Centre.
- Deployment of Central armed forces in the states either on their request or otherwise.

No action was taken by the Central government on the recommendations of the ARC.

Rajamannar Committee

In 1969, the Tamil Nadu Government (DMK) appointed a three-member committee under the chairmanship of Dr P V Rajamannar to examine the entire question of Centre–state relations and to suggest amendments to the Constitution so as to secure utmost autonomy to the states.[25] The committee submitted its report to the Tamil Nadu Government in 1971.

The Committee identified the reasons for the prevailing unitary trends (tendencies of centralisation) in the country. They include: **(i)** certain provisions in the Constitution which confer special powers on the Centre; **(ii)** one-party rule both at the Centre and in the states; **(iii)** inadequacy of states' fiscal resources and consequent dependence on the Centre for financial assistance; and **(iv)** the institution of Central planning and the role of the Planning Commission.

The important recommendations of the committee are as follows: **(i)** An Inter-State Council should be set up immediately; **(ii)** Finance Commission should be made a permanent body; **(iii)** Planning Commission should be disbanded and its place should be taken by a statutory body; **(iv)** Articles 356, 357 and 365 (dealing with President's Rule) should be totally omitted; **(v)** The provision that the state ministry holds office during the pleasure of the governor should be omitted; **(vi)** Certain subjects of the Union List and the Concurrent List should be transferred to the State List; **(vii)** the residuary powers should be allocated to the states; and **(viii)** All-India services (IAS, IPS and IFS) should be abolished.

The Central government completely ignored the recommendations of the Rajamannar Committee.

Anandpur Sahib Resolution

In 1973, the Akali Dal adopted a resolution containing both political and religious demands in a meeting held at Anandpur Sahib in Punjab. The resolution, generally known as Anandpur Sahib Resolution, demanded that the Centre's jurisdiction should be restricted only to defence, foreign affairs, communications, and currency and the entire residuary powers should be vested in the states. It stated that the Constitution should be made federal in the real sense and should ensure equal authority and representation to all the states at the Centre.

West Bengal Memorandum

In 1977, the West Bengal Government (led by the Communists) published a memorandum on Centre–state relations and sent to the Central government. The memorandum *inter alia* suggested the following: **(i)** The word 'union' in the Constitution should be replaced by the word 'federal'; **(ii)** The jurisdiction of the Centre should be confined to defence, foreign affairs, currency, communications and economic co-ordination; **(iii)** All other subjects including the residuary should be vested in the states; **(iv)** Articles 356 and 357 (President's Rule) and 360 (financial emergency) should be repealed; **(v)** State's consent should be made obligatory for formation of new states or reorganisation of existing states; **(vi)** Of the total revenue raised by the Centre from all sources, 75 per cent should be allocated to the states; **(vii)** Rajya Sabha should have equal powers with that of the Lok Sabha; and **(viii)** There should be only Central and state services and the all-India services should be abolished.

The Central government did not accept the demands made in the memorandum.

Sarkaria Commission

In 1983, the Central government appointed a three-member Commission on Centre–state relations under the chairmanship of R S Sarkaria, a retired judge of the Supreme Court.[26] The commission was asked to examine and review the working of existing arrangements between the Centre and states in all spheres and recommend appropriate changes and measures. It was initially given one year to complete its work, but its term was extended four times. The final report was submitted in October 1987, and the summary was later officially released in January 1988.

The Commission did not favour structural changes and regarded the existing constitutional arrangements and principles relating to the institutions basically sound. But, it emphasised on the need for changes in the functional or operational aspects. It observed that federalism is more a functional arrangement for co-operative action than a static institutional concept. It outrightly rejected the demand for curtailing the powers of the Centre and stated that a strong Centre is essential to safeguard the national unity and integrity which is being threatened by the fissiparious tendencies in the body politic. However, it did not equate strong Centre with centralisation of powers. It observed that over-centralisation leads to blood pressure at the centre and anemia at the pheriphery.

The Commission made 247 recommendations to improve Centre–state relations. The important recommendations are mentioned below:

1. A permanent Inter-State Council called the Inter-Governmental Council should be set up under Article 263.
2. Article 356 (President's Rule) should be used very sparingly, in extreme cases as a last resort when all the available alternatives fail.
3. The institution of All-India Services should be further strengthened and some more such services should be created.
4. The residuary powers of taxation should continue to remain with the Parliament, while the other residuary powers should be placed in the Concurrent List.

5. When the president withholds his assent to the state bills, the reasons should be communicated to the state government.

6. The National Development Council (NDC) should be renamed and reconstituted as the National Economic and Development Council (NEDC).

7. The zonal councils should be constituted afresh and reactivated to promote the spirit of federalism.

8. The Centre should have powers to deploy its armed forces, even without the consent of states. However, it is desirable that the states should be consulted.

9. The Centre should consult the states before making a law on a subject of the Concurrent List.

10. The procedure of consulting the chief minister in the appointment of the state governor should be prescribed in the Constitution itself.

11. The net proceeds of the corporation tax may be made permissibly shareable with the states.

12. The governor cannot dismiss the council of ministers so long as it commands a majority in the assembly.

13. The governor's term of five years in a state should not be disturbed except for some extremely compelling reasons.

14. No commission of enquiry should be set up against a state minister unless a demand is made by the Parliament.

15. The surcharge on income tax should not be levied by the Centre except for a specific purpose and for a strictly limited period.

16. The present division of functions between the Finance Commission and the Planning Commission is reasonable and should continue.

17. Steps should be taken to uniformly implement the three language formula in its true spirit.

18. No autonomy for radio and television but decentralisation in their operations.

19. No change in the role of Rajya Sabha and Centre's power to reorganise the states.

20. The commissioner for linguistic minorities should be activated.

Till December 2011, the Central government has implemented 180 (out of 247) recommendations of the Sarkaria Commission.[27] The most important is the establishment of the Inter-State Council in 1990.

Punchhi Commission

The Second commission on Centre-State Relations was set-up by the Government of India in April 2007 under the Chairmanship of Madan Mohan Punchhi, former Chief Justice of India.[28] It was required to look into the issues of Centre-State relations keeping in view the sea-changes that have taken place in the polity and economy of India since the Sarkaria Commission had last looked at the issue of Centre-State relations over two decades ago.

The terms of reference of the Commission were as follows:

(i) The Commission was required to examine and review the working of the existing arrangements between the Union and States as per the Constitution of India, the healthy precedents being followed, various pronouncements of the Courts in regard to powers, functions and responsibilities in all spheres including legislative relations, administrative relations, role of governors, emergency provisions, financial relations, economic and social planning, Panchayati Raj institutions, sharing of resources including inter-state river water and recommend such changes or other measures as may be appropriate keeping in view the practical difficulties.

(ii) In examining and reviewing the working of the existing arrangements between the Union and States and making recommendations as to the changes and measures needed, the Commission was required to keep in view the social and economic developments that have taken place over the years, particularly over the last two decades and have due regard to the scheme and framework of the Constitution. Such recommendations were also needed to address the growing challenges of ensuring good governance for promoting the welfare of the people whilst strengthening the unity and integrity of the country, and of availing emerging opportunities for sustained and rapid economic growth for alleviating poverty and illiteracy in the early decades of the new millennium.

(iii) While examining and making its recommendations on the above, the Commission was required to have particular regard, but not limit its mandate to the following:-

(a) The role, responsibility and jurisdiction of the Centre vis-à-vis States during major and prolonged outbreaks of communal violence, caste violence or any other social conflict leading to prolonged and escalated violence.

(b) The role, responsibility and jurisdiction of the Centre vis-à-vis States in the planning and implementation of the mega projects like the inter-linking of rivers, that would normally take 15–20 years for completion and hinge vitally on the support of the States.

(c) The role, responsibility and jurisdiction of the Centre vis-à-vis States in promoting effective devolution of powers and autonomy to Panchayati Raj Institutions and Local Bodies including the Autonomous Bodies under the sixth Schedule of the Constitution within a specified period of time.

(d) The role, responsibility and jurisdiction of the Centre vis-à-vis States in promoting the concept and practice of independent planning and budgeting at the District level.

(e) The role, responsibility and jurisdiction of the Centre vis-à-vis States in linking Central assistance of various kinds with the performance of the States.

(f) The role, responsibility and jurisdiction of the Centre in adopting approaches and policies based on positive discrimination in favour of backward States.

(g) The impact of the recommendations made by the 8th to 12th Finance Commissions on the fiscal relations between the Centre and the States, especially the greater dependence of the States on devolution of funds from the Centre.

(h) The need and relevance of separate taxes on the production and on the sales of goods and services subsequent to the introduction of Value Added Tax regime.

(i) The need for freeing inter-State trade in order to establish a unified and integrated domestic market as also in the context of the reluctance of State Governments to adopt the relevant Sarkaria Commission's recommendation in chapter XVIII of its report.

(j) The need for setting up a Central Law Enforcement Agency empowered to take up suo moto investigation of crimes having inter-State and/or international ramifications with serious implications on national security.

(k) The feasibility of a supporting legislation under Article 355 for the purpose of suo moto deployment of Central forces in the States if and when the situation so demands.

The Commission submitted its report to the government in April 2010. In finalising the 1,456 page report, in seven volumes, the Commission took extensive help from the Sarkaria Commission report, the National Commission to Review the Working of the Constitution (NCRWC) report and the Second Administrative Reforms Commission report. However, in a number of areas, the Commission report differed from the Sarkaria Commission recommendations.

After examining at length the issues raised in its Terms of Reference and the related aspects in all their hues and shades, the Commission came to the conclusion that 'cooperative federalism' will be the key for sustaining India's unity, integrity and social and economic development in future. The principles of cooperative federalism thus may have to act as a practical guide for Indian polity and governance.

In all, the Commission made over 310 recommendations, touching upon several significant areas in the working of Centre-state relations. The important recommendations are mentioned below:

1. To facilitate effective implementation of the laws on List III subjects, it is necessary that some broad agreement is reached between the Union and states before introducing legislation in Parliament on matters in the Concurrent List.

2. The Union should be extremely restrained in asserting Parliamentary supremacy in matters assigned to the states. Greater flexibility to states in relation to subjects in the State List and "transferred items" in the Concurrent List is the key for better Centre-state relations.

3. The Union should occupy only that many of subjects in concurrent or overlapping jurisdiction which are absolutely necessary to achieve uniformity of policy in demonstrable national interest.

4. There should be a continuing auditing role for the Inter-state Council in the management of matters in concurrent or overlapping jurisdiction.

5. The period of six months prescribed in Article 201 for State Legislature to act when the bill is returned by the President can be made applicable for the President also to decide on assenting or withholding assent to a state bill reserved for consideration of the President.

6. Parliament should make a law on the subject of Entry 14 of List I (treaty making and implementing it through Parliamentary legislation) to streamline the procedures involved. The exercise of the power obviously cannot be absolute or unchartered in view of the federal structure of legislative and executive powers.

7. Financial obligations and its implications on state finances arising out of treaties and agreements should be a permanent term of reference to the Finance Commissions constituted from time to time.

8. While selecting Governors, the Central Government should adopt the following strict guidelines as recommended in the Sarkaria Commission report and follow its mandate in letter and spirit :
   (i) He should be eminent in some walk of life
   (ii) He should be a person from outside the state
   (iii) He should be a detached figure and not too intimately connected with the local politics of the states
   (iv) He should be a person who has not taken too great a part in politics generally and particularly in the recent past

9. Governors should be given a fixed tenure of five years and their removal should not be at the sweet will of the Government at the Centre.

10. The procedure laid down for impeachment of President, *mutatis mutandis* can be made applicable for impeachment of Governors as well.

11. Article 163 does not give the Governor a general discretionary power to act against or without the advice of his Council of Ministers. In fact, the area for the exercise of discretion is limited and even in this limited area, his choice of action should not be arbitrary or fanciful. It

must be a choice dictated by reason, activated by good faith and tempered by caution.

12. In respect of bills passed by the Legislative Assembly of a state, the Governor should take the decision within six months whether to grant assent or to reserve it for consideration of the President.

13. On the question of Governor's role in appointment of Chief Minister in the case of an hung assembly, it is necessary to lay down certain clear guidelines to be followed as Constitutional conventions. These guidelines may be as follows:
   (i) The party or combination of parties which commands the widest support in the Legislative Assembly should be called upon to form the Government.
   (ii) If there is a pre-poll alliance or coalition, it should be treated as one political party and if such coalition obtains a majority, the leader of such coalition shall be called by the Governor to form the Government.
   (iii) In case no party or pre-poll coalition has a clear majority, the Governor should select the Chief Minister in the order of preference indicated here.
      (a) The group of parties which had pre-poll alliance commanding the largest number
      (b) The largest single party staking a claim to form the government with the support of others
      (c) A post-electoral coalition with all partners joining the government
      (d) A post-electoral alliance with some parties joining the government and the remaining including independents supporting the government from outside

14. On the question of dismissal of a Chief Minister, the Governor should invariably insist on the Chief Minister proving his majority on the floor of the House for which he should prescribe a time limit.

15. The Governor should have the right to sanction for prosecution of a state minister against the advice of the Council of Ministers, if the Cabinet decision appears to the Governor to be

motivated by bias in the face of overwhelming material.

16. The convention of Governors acting as Chancellors of Universities and holding other statutory positions should be done away with. His role should be confined to the Constitutional provisions only.

17. When an external aggression or internal disturbance paralyses the state administration creating a situation of a potential break down of the Constitutional machinery of the state, all alternative courses available to the Union for discharging its paramount responsibility under Article 355 should be exhausted to contain the situation and the exercise of the power under Article 356 should be limited strictly to rectifying a "failure of the Constitutional machinery in the state".

18. On the question of invoking Article 356 in case of failure of Constitutional machinery in states, suitable amendments are required to incorporate the guidelines set forth in the landmark judgement of the Supreme Court in *S.R. Bommai V. Union of India (1994)*. This would remove possible misgivings in this regard on the part of states and help in smoothening Centre-state relations.

19. Given the strict parameters now set for invoking the emergency provisions under Articles 352 and 356 to be used only as a measure of "last resort", and the duty of the Union to protect states under Article 355, it is necessary to provide a Constitutional or legal framework to deal with situations which require Central intervention but do not warrant invoking the extreme steps under Articles 352 and 356. Providing the framework for "localised emergency" would ensure that the state government can continue to function and the Assembly would not have to be dissolved while providing a mechanism to let the Central Government respond to the issue specifically and locally. The imposition of local emergency is fully justified under the mandate of Article 355 read with Entry 2A of List I and Entry 1 of List II of the Seventh Schedule.

20. Suitable amendments to Article 263 are required to make the Inter-State Council a credible, powerful and fair mechanism for management of inter-state and Centre-state differences.

21. The Zonal Councils should meet at least twice a year with an agenda proposed by states concerned to maximise co-ordination and promote harmonisation of policies and action having inter-state ramification. The Secretariat of a strengthened Inter-State Council can function as the Secretariat of the Zonal Councils as well.

22. The Empowered Committee of Finance Ministers of States proved to be a successful experiment in inter-state co-ordination on fiscal matters. There is need to institutionalise similar models in other sectors as well. A forum of Chief Ministers, Chaired by one of the Chief Minister by rotation can be similarly thought about particularly to co-ordinate policies of sectors like energy, food, education, environment and health.

23. New all-India services in sectors like health, education, engineering and judiciary should be created.

24. Factors inhibiting the composition and functioning of the Second Chamber as a representative forum of states should be removed or modified even if it requires amendment of the Constitutional provisions. In fact, Rajya Sabha offers immense potential to negotiate acceptable solutions to the friction points which emerge between Centre and states in fiscal, legislative and administrative relations.

25. A balance of power between states *inter se* is desirable and this is possible by equality of representation in the Rajya Sabha. This requires amendment of the relevant provisions to give equality of seats to states in the Rajya Sabha, irrespective of their population size.

26. The scope of devolution of powers to local bodies to act as institutions of self-government should be constitutionally defined through appropriate amendments.

27. All future Central legislations involving states' involvement should provide for cost sharing as in the case of the RTE Act. Existing Central legislations where the states are entrusted with the responsibility of implementation should be suitably amended providing for sharing of costs by the Central Government.

28. The royalty rates on major minerals should be revised at least every three years without any delay. States should be properly compensated for any delay in the revision of royalty beyond three years.

29. The current ceiling on profession tax should be completely done away with by a Constitutional amendment.

30. The scope for raising more revenue from the taxes mentioned in article 268 should be examined afresh. This issue may be either referred to the next Finance Commission or an expert committee be appointed to look into the matter.

31. To bring greater accountability, all fiscal legislations should provide for an annual assessment by an independent body and the reports of these bodies should be laid in both Houses of Parliament/state legislature.

32. Considerations specified in the Terms of Reference (ToR) of the Finance Commission should be even handed as between the Centre and the states. There should be an effective mechanism to involve the states in the finalisation of the ToR of the Finance Commissions.

33. The Central Government should review all the existing cesses and surcharges with a view to bringing down their share in the gross tax revenue.

34. Because of the close linkages between the plan and non-plan expenditure, an expert committee may be appointed to look into the issue of distinction between the plan and non-plan expenditure.

35. There should be much better coordination between the Finance Commission and the Planning Commission. The synchronisation of the periods covered by the Finance Commission and the Five-Year Plan will considerably improve such coordination.

36. The Finance Commission division in the Ministry of Finance should be converted into a full-fledged department, serving as the permanent secretariat for the Finance Commissions.

37. The Planning Commission has a crucial role in the current situation. But its role should be that of coordination rather that of micro managing sectoral plans of the Central ministries and the states.

38. Steps should be taken for the setting up of an Inter-State Trade and Commerce Commission under Article 307 read with Entry 42 of List-I. This Commission should be vested with both advisory and executive roles with decision making powers. As a Constitutional body, the decisions of the Commission should be final and binding on all states as well as the Union of India. Any party aggrieved with the decision of the Commission may prefer an appeal to the Supreme Court.

Table 14.1 *Articles Related to Centre-State Legislative Relations at a Glance*

Article No.	Subject-matter
245.	Extent of laws made by Parliament and by the legislatures of states
246.	Subject-matter of laws made by Parliament and by the legislatures of states
247.	Power of Parliament to provide for the establishment of certain additional courts
248.	Residuary powers of legislation
249.	Power of Parliament to legislate with respect to a matter in the state list in the national interest
250.	Power of Parliament to legislate with respect to any matter in the state list if a Proclamation of Emergency is in operation
251.	Inconsistency between laws made by Parliament under articles 249 and 250 and laws made by the legislatures of states
252.	Power of Parliament to legislate for two or more states by consent and adoption of such legislation by any other state
253.	Legislation for giving effect to international agreements
254.	Inconsistency between laws made by Parliament and laws made by the legislatures of states
255.	Requirements as to recommendations and previous sanctions to be regarded as matters of procedure only

Table 14.2 *Articles Related to Centre-State Administrative Relations at a Glance*

Article No.	Subject-matter
256.	Obligation of states and the Union
257.	Control of the Union over states in certain cases
257A.	Assistance to states by deployment of armed forces or other forces of the Union (Repealed)
258.	Power of the Union to confer powers, etc., on states in certain cases
258A.	Power of the states to entrust functions to the Union
259.	Armed Forces in states in Part B of the First Schedule (Repealed)
260.	Jurisdiction of the Union in relation to territories outside India
261.	Public acts, records and judicial proceedings
262.	Adjudication of disputes relating to waters of inter-state rivers or river valleys
263.	Provisions with respect to an inter-state Council

Table 14.3 *Articles Related to Centre-State Financial Relations at a Glance*

Article No.	Subject-matter
	Distribution of Revenues between the Union and the States
268.	Duties levied by the Union but collected and appropriated by the states
268A.	Service tax levied by Union and collected and appropriated by the Union and the states
269.	Taxes levied and collected by the Union but assigned to the states
270.	Taxes levied and distributed between the Union and the states
271.	Surcharge on certain duties and taxes for purposes of the Union
272.	Taxes which are levied and collected by the Union and may be distributed between the Union and the states (Repealed)
273.	Grants in *lieu* of export duty on jute and jute products
274.	Prior recommendation of President required to bills affecting taxation in which states are interested
275.	Grants from the Union to certain states
276.	Taxes on professions, trades, callings and employments
277.	Savings
278.	Agreement with states in Part B of the First Schedule with regard to certain financial matters (Repealed)
279.	Calculation of "net proceeds", etc.
280.	Finance Commission
281.	Recommendations of the Finance Commission
	Miscellaneous Financial Provisions
282.	Expenditure defrayable by the Union or a state out of its revenues

(Contd.)

Article No.	Subject-matter
283.	Custody, etc., of Consolidated Funds, Contingency Funds and moneys credited to the public accounts
284.	Custody of suitors' deposits and other moneys received by public servants and courts
285.	Exemption of property of the Union from state taxation
286.	Restrictions as to imposition of tax on the sale or purchase of goods
287.	Exemption from taxes on electricity
288.	Exemption from taxation by states in respect of water or electricity in certain cases
289.	Exemption of property and income of a state from Union taxation
290.	Adjustment in respect of certain expenses and pensions
290A.	Annual payment to certain Devaswom Funds
291.	Privy purse sums of Rulers (Repealed)
Borrowing	
292.	Borrowing by the Government of India
293.	Borrowing by states

NOTES AND REFERENCES

1. Even now, the last entry is numbered as 97 but the total number of entries is 100. The entries numbered as 2A, 92A, 92B and 92C have been added and entry 33 has been omitted. See Appendix II.
2. Even now, the last entry is numbered as 66 but the total number of entries is 61. The entries numbered as 11, 19, 20, 29 and 36 have been omitted. See Appendix II.
3. Even now, the last entry is numbered as 47 but the total number of entries is 52. The entries numbered as 11A, 17A, 17B, 20A and 33A have been added. See Appendix II.
4. Report of the Commission on centre-state Relations, Part I (Government of India, 1988) PP. 28–29.
5. For example, under the Essential Commodities Act, made by the Parliament on a concurrent subject, the executive power is vested in the Centre.
6. This provision (the power of the states to entrust functions to the Centre) was added by the 7th Constitutional Amendment Act of 1956. Before that, only the Centre had the power.
7. For details in this regard, see Chapter 15.
8. *Constituent Assembly Debates*, Volume VII, PP. 41-42.
9. For details, see Chapters 48 and 49.
10. For details, see Chapter 69.
11. For details, see Chapter 15.
12. Entries—82, 83, 84, 85, 86, 87, 88, 89, 90, 91, 92, 92A, 92B, 92C and 96. See Appendix II.
13. Entries—45, 46, 47, 48, 49, 50, 51, 52, 53, 54, 55, 56, 57, 58, 59, 60, 61, 62, 63, and 66. See Appendix II.
14. Entries—35, 44 and 47. See Appendix II.
15. Originally, this limit was only Rs 250 per annum. The 60th Amendment Act of 1988 raised it to Rs. 2,500 per annum.
16. The Additional Duties of Excise (Goods of Special Importance) Act of 1957, enacted by the Parliament, has declared tobacco, sugar, silk, cotton and woolen fabrics to be goods of special importance in inter-state trade and commerce.
17. This amendment deleted Article 272 (Taxes which are levied and collected by the Centre and may be distributed between the Centre and the states).

18. Mentioned group-wise. Hence, reduced to 11 (from 20). See Appendix II.
19. See 'Property of the Union' in Chapter 61.
20. See 'Property of the States' in Chapter 61.
21. M P Jain: *Indian Constitutional Law*, Wadhwa, Fourth Edition, PP. 342–43.
22. See 'Impact of Planning Commission' in Chapter 41.
23. This function was added by the 73rd and 74th Amendment Acts of 1992 which have granted constitutional status on the panchayats and the municipalities respectively.
24. In Re. Sea Customs Act (1963).
25. The other two members of the committee were Dr. Lakshmanswamy Mudaliar and P C Chandra Reddy.
26. B. Sivaraman and S R Sen were two other members of the Commission.
27. Annual Report 2011-12, Ministry of Home Affairs, Government of India, P.79.
28. The other four Members of the Commission were Dhirendra Singh (Former Secretary to the Government of India), Vinod Kumar Duggal (Former Secretary to the Government of India), Prof. N.R. Madhava Menon (Former Director, National Judicial Academy, Bhopal and National Law School of India, Bangalore) and Dr. Amaresh Bagchi (Emeritus Professor, National Institute of Public Finance and Policy, New Delhi). With the passing away of Dr. Bagchi in February 2008, Vijay Shanker (Former Director, Central Bureau of Investigation, Government of India) was appointed in his place as a Member of the Commission in October 2008.

Inter-State Relations

The successful functioning of the Indian federal system depends not only on the harmonious relations and close cooperation between the Centre and the states but also between the states *inter se*. Hence, the Constitution makes the following provisions with regard to inter-state comity:

1. Adjudication of inter-state water disputes.
2. Coordination through inter-state councils.
3. Mutual recognition of public acts, records and judicial proceedings.
4. Freedom of inter-state trade, commerce and intercourse.

In addition, the zonal councils have been established by the Parliament to promote inter-state cooperation and coordination.

INTER-STATE WATER DISPUTES

Article 262 of the Constitution provides for the adjudication of inter-state water disputes. It makes two provisions:

(i) Parliament may by law provide for the adjudication of any dispute or complaint with respect to the use, distribution and control of waters of any inter-state river and river valley.

(ii) Parliament may also provide that neither the Supreme Court nor any other court is to exercise jurisdiction in respect of any such dispute or complaint.

Under this provision, the Parliament has enacted two laws [the River Boards Act (1956) and the Inter-State Water Disputes Act (1956)]. The River Boards Act provides for the establishment of river boards for the regulation and development of inter-state river and river valleys. A river board is established by the Central government on the request of the state governments concerned to advise them.

The Inter-State Water Disputes Act empowers the Central government to set up an ad hoc tribunal for the adjudication of a dispute between two or more states in relation to the waters of an inter-state river or river valley. The decision of the tribunal would be final and binding on the parties to the dispute. Neither the Supreme Court nor any other court is to have jurisdiction in respect of any water dispute which may be referred to such a tribunal under this Act.

The need for an extra judicial machinery to settle inter-state water disputes is as follows: "The Supreme Court would indeed have jurisdiction to decide any dispute between states in connection with water supplies, if legal rights or interests are concerned; but the experience of most countries has shown that rules of law based upon the analogy of private proprietary interests in water do not afford a satisfactory basis for settling disputes between the states where the interests of the public at large in the proper use of water supplies are involved."[1]

So far (2013), the Central government has set up eight inter-state water dispute tribunals. The name of the tribunals, the years in which they were constituted and the states involved in the dispute are mentioned below in Table 15.1:

Table 15.1 *Inter-State Water Dispute Tribunals Set-up So Far*

SI. No.	Name	Set-up in	State Involved
1.	Krishna Water Disputes Tribunal	1969	Maharashtra, Karnataka and Andhra Pradesh
2.	Godavari Water Disputes Tribunal	1969	Maharashtra, Karnataka, Andhra Pradesh, Madhya Pradesh and Orissa
3.	Narmada Water Disputes Tribunal	1969	Rajasthan, Gujarat, Madhya Pradesh and Maharashtra
4.	Ravi and Beas Water Disputes Tribunal	1986	Punjab and Haryana
5.	Cauvery Water Disputes Tribunal	1990	Karnataka, Kerala, Tamil Nadu and Puducherry
6.	Second Krishna Water Disputes Tribunal	2004	Maharashtra, Karnataka and Andhra Pradesh
7.	Vansadhara Water Disputes Tribunal	2010	Odisha and Andhra Pradesh
8.	Mahadayi Water Disputes Tribunal	2010	Goa, Karnataka and Maharashtra

INTER-STATE COUNCILS

Article 263 contemplates the establishment of an Inter-State Council to effect coordination between the states and between Centre and states. Thus, the President can establish such a council if at any time it appears to him that the public interest would be served by its establishment. He can define the nature of duties to be performed by such a council and its organisation and procedure.

Even though the president is empowered to define the duties of an inter-state council, Article 263 specifies the duties that can be assigned to it in the following manner:

(a) enquiring into and advising upon disputes which may arise between states;

(b) investigating and discussing subjects in which the states or the Centre and the states have a common interest; and

(c) making recommendations upon any such subject, and particularly for the better co-ordination of policy and action on it.

"The council's function to enquire and advice upon inter-state disputes is complementary to the Supreme Court's jurisdiction under Article 131 to decide a legal controversy between the governments. The Council can deal with any controversy whether legal or non-legal, but its function is advisory unlike that of the court which gives a binding decision."[2]

Under the above provisions of Article 263, the president has established the following councils to make recommendations for the better coordination of policy and action in the related subjects:

- Central Council of Health.
- Central Council of Local Government and Urban Development.[3]
- Four Regional Councils for Sales Tax for the Northern, Eastern, Western and Southern Zones.

The Central Council of Indian Medicine and the Central Council of Homoeopathy were set up under the Acts of Parliament.[4]

Establishment of Inter-State Council

The Sarkaria Commission on Centre-State Relations (1983–87) made a strong case for the establishment of a permanent Inter-State Council under Article 263 of the Constitution. It recommended that in order to differentiate the Inter-State Council from other bodies established under the same Article 263, it must be called as the Inter-Governmental Council. The Commission recommended that the Council should be charged with the duties laid down in clauses (b) and (c) of Article 263 (see above).

In pursuance of the above recommendations of the Sarkaria Commission, **the Janata Dal Government headed by V. P. Singh established the Inter-State Council in 1990.**[5] It consists of the following members:

(i) Prime minister as the Chairman

(ii) Chief ministers of all the states

(iii) Chief ministers of union territories having legislative assemblies

(iv) Administrators of union territories not having legislative assemblies

(v) Governors of States under President's rule

(vi) Six Central cabinet ministers, including the home minister, to be nominated by the Prime Minister.

Five Ministers of Cabinet rank / Minister of State (independent charge) nominated by the Chairman of the Council (i.e., Prime Minister) are permanent invitees to the Council.

The council is a recommendatory body on issues relating to inter-state, Centre–state and Centre–union territories relations. It aims at promoting coordination between them by examining, discussing and deliberating on such issues. Its duties, in detail, are as follows:

- investigating and discussing such subjects in which the states or the centre have a common interest;
- making recommendations upon any such subject for the better coordination of policy and action on it; and
- deliberating upon such other matters of general interest to the states as may be referred to it by the chairman.

The Council may meet at least thrice in a year. Its meetings are held in camera and all questions are decided by consensus.

There is also a Standing Committee of the Council. It was set up in 1996 for continuous consultation and processing of matters for the consideration of the Council. It consists of the following members:

(i) Union Home Minister as the Chairman

(ii) Five Union Cabinet Ministers

(iii) Nine Chief Ministers

The Council is assisted by a secretariat called the Inter-State Council Secretariat. This secretariat was set-up in 1991 and is headed by a secretary to the Government of India. Since 2011, it is also functioning as the secretariat of the Zonal Councils.

PUBLIC ACTS, RECORDS AND JUDICIAL PROCEEDINGS

Under the Constitution, the jurisdiction of each state is confined to its own territory. Hence, it is possible that the acts and records of one state may not be recognised in another state. To remove any such difficulty, the Constitution contains the "Full Faith and Credit" clause which lays down the following:

(i) Full faith and credit is to be given throughout the territory of India to public acts, records and judicial proceedings of the Centre and every state. The expression 'public acts' includes both legislative and executive acts of the government. The expression 'public record' includes any official book, register or record made by a public servant in the discharge of his official duties.

(ii) The manner in which and the conditions under which such acts, records and proceedings are to be proved and their effect determined would be as provided by the laws of Parliament. This means that the general rule mentioned above is subject to the power of Parliament to lay down the mode of proof as well as the effect of such acts, records and proceedings of one state in another state.

(iii) Final judgements and orders of civil courts in any part of India are capable of execution anywhere within India (without the necessity of a fresh suit upon the judgement). The rule applies only to civil judgements and not to criminal judgements. In other words, it does not require the courts of a state to enforce the penal laws of another state.

INTER-STATE TRADE AND COMMERCE

Articles 301 to 307 in Part XIII of the Constitution deal with the trade, commerce and intercourse within the territory of India.

Article 301 declares that trade, commerce and intercourse throughout the territory of India shall be free. The object of this provision is to break down the border barriers between the states and to create one unit with a view to encourage the free flow of trade, commerce and intercourse in the country. The freedom under this provision is not confined to inter-state trade, commerce and intercourse but also extends to intra-state trade, commerce and intercourse. Thus, Article 301 will be violated whether restrictions are imposed at the frontier of any state or at any prior or subsequent stage.

The freedom guaranteed by Article 301 is a freedom from all restrictions, except those which are provided for in the other provisions (Articles 302 to 305) of Part XIII of the Constitution itself. These are explained below:

(i) Parliament can impose restrictions on the freedom of trade, commerce and intercourse between the states or within a state in public interest.[6] But, the Parliament cannot give preference to one state over another or discriminate between the states except in the case of scarcity of goods in any part of India.

(ii) The legislature of a state can impose reasonable restrictions on the freedom of trade, commerce and intercourse with that state or within that state in public interest. But, a bill for this purpose can be introduced in the legislature only with the previous sanction of the president. Further, the state legislature cannot give preference to one state over another or discriminate between the states.

(iii) The legislature of a state can impose on goods imported from other states or the union territories any tax to which similar goods manufactured in that state are subject. This provision prohibits the imposition of discriminatory taxes by the state.

(iv) The freedom (under Article 301) is subject to the nationalisation laws (i.e., laws providing for monopolies in favour of the Centre or the states). Thus, the Parliament or the state legislature can make laws for the carrying on by the respective government of any trade, business, industry or service, whether to the exclusion, complete or partial, of citizens or otherwise.

The Parliament can appoint an appropriate authority for carrying out the purposes of the above provisions relating to the freedom of trade, commerce and intercourse and restricts on it. The Parliament can also confer on that authority the necessary powers and duties. But, no such authority has been appointed so far.[7]

ZONAL COUNCILS

The Zonal Councils are the statutory (and not the constitutional) bodies. They are established by an Act of the Parliament, that is, States Reorganisation Act of 1956. The act divided the country into five zones

(Northern, Central, Eastern, Western and Southern) and provided a zonal council for each zone.

While forming these zones, several factors have been taken into account which include: the natural divisions of the country, the river systems and means of communication, the cultural and linguistic affinity and the requirements of economic development, security and law and order.

Each zonal council consists of the following members: **(a)** home minister of Central government. **(b)** chief ministers of all the States in the zone. **(c)** Two other ministers from each state in the zone. **(d)** Administrator of each union territory in the zone.

Besides, the following persons can be associated with the zonal council as advisors (i.e., without the right to vote in the meetings):

(i) a person nominated by the Planning Commission; **(ii)** chief secretary of the government of each state in the zone; and **(iii)** development commissioner of each state in the zone.

The home minister of Central government is the common chairman of the five zonal councils. Each chief minister acts as a vice-chairman of the council by rotation, holding office for a period of one year at a time.

The zonal councils aim at promoting cooperation and coordination between states, union territories and the Centre. They discuss and make recommendations regarding matters like economic and social planning, linguistic minorities, border disputes, inter-state transport, and so on. They are only deliberative and advisory bodies.

The objectives (or the functions) of the zonal councils, in detail, are as follows:

- To achieve an emotional integration of the country.
- To help in arresting the growth of acute state-consciousness, regionalism, linguism and particularistic trends.
- To help in removing the after-effects of separation in some cases so that the process of reorganisation, integration and economic advancement may synchronise.
- To enable the Centre and states to cooperate with each other in social and economic matters and exchange ideas and experience in order to evolve uniform policies.

- To cooperate with each other in the successful and speedy execution of major development projects.
- To secure some kind of political equilibrium between different regions of the country.

North-Eastern Council In addition to the above Zonal Councils, a North-Eastern Council was created by a separate Act of Parliament—the North-Eastern Council Act of 1971.[8] Its members include Assam, Manipur, Mizoram, Arunchal Pradesh, Nagaland, Meghalaya, Tripura and Sikkim.[9] Its functions are similar to those of the zonal councils, but with few additions. It has to formulate a unified and coordinated regional plan covering matters of common importance. It has to review from time to time the measures taken by the member states for the maintenance of security and public order in the region.

Table 15.2 *Zonal Councils at a Glance*

Name	Members	Headquarters
1. Northern Zonal Council	Jammu and Kashmir, Himachal Pradesh, Haryana, Punjab, Rajasthan, Delhi, and Chandigarh	New Delhi
2. Central Zonal Council	Uttar Pradesh, Uttarakhand, Chhattisgarh, and Madhya Pradesh	Allahabad
3. Eastern Zonal Council	Bihar, Jharkhand, West Bengal and Orissa	Kolkata
4. Western Zonal Council	Gujarat, Maharastra, Goa, Dadra and Nagar Haveli and Daman and Diu	Mumbai
5. Southern Zonal Council	Andhra Pradesh, Karnataka, Tamil Nadu, Kerala and Puducherry	Chennai

Table 15.3 *Articles Related to Inter-State Relations at a Glance*

Article No.	Subject-matter
Mutual Recognition of Public Acts, etc.	
261.	Public acts, records and judicial proceedings
Disputes Relating to Waters	
262.	Adjudication of disputes relating to waters of inter-state rivers or river valleys
Co-ordination between States	
263.	Provisions with respect to an inter-state council
Inter-State Trade and Commerce	
301.	Freedom of trade, commerce and intercourse
302.	Power of Parliament to impose restrictions on trade, commerce and intercourse
303.	Restrictions on the legislative powers of the Union and of the states with regard to trade and commerce
304.	Restrictions on trade, commerce and intercourse among states
305.	Saving of existing laws and laws providing for state monopolies
306.	Power of certain states in Part B of the First Schedule to impose restrictions on trade and commerce (Repealed)
307.	Appointment of authority for carrying out the purposes of Articles 301 to 304

NOTES AND REFERENCES

1. Report of the Joint Parliamentary Committee. Select Committee of the House of Lords appointed to join with a Committee of the House of Commons to consider the future Government of India.
2. M P Jain: *Indian Constitutional Law*, Wadhwa, Fourth Edition, P. 382.
3. It was originally known as the Central Council of Local Self-Government (1954).
4. India 2003, P. 242.
5. The Inter-State Council Order dated May 28, 1990.
6. For example, the Parliament has made the Essential Commodities Act (1955). This Act enables the Central government to control the production, supply and distribution of certain essential commodities like petroleum, coal, iron and steel and so on.
7. In USA such authority is known as the Inter-State Commerce Commission.
8. It came into existence on August 8, 1972.
9. In 2002, Sikkim was added as the eighth member of the North-Eastern Council.

16

Emergency Provisions

The Emergency provisions are contained in Part XVIII of the Constitution, from Articles 352 to 360. These provisions enable the Central government to meet any abnormal situation effectively. The rationality behind the incorporation of these provisions in the Constitution is to safeguard the sovereignty, unity, integrity and security of the country, the democratic political system, and the Constitution.

During an Emergency, the Central government becomes all powerful and the states go into the total control of the Centre. It converts the federal structure into a unitary one without a formal amendment of the Constitution. This kind of transformation of the political system from federal during normal times to unitary during Emergency is a unique feature of the Indian Constitution. In this context, Dr B R Ambedkar observed in the Constituent Assembly that[1]:

> 'All federal systems including American are placed in a tight mould of federalism. No matter what the circumstances, it cannot change its form and shape. It can never be unitary. On the other hand, the Constitution of India can be both unitary as well as federal according to the requirements of time and circumstances. In normal times, it is framed to work as a federal system. But in times of Emergency, it is so designed as to make it work as though it was a unitary system.'

The Constitution stipulates three types of emergencies:

1. An emergency due to war, external aggression or armed rebellion[2] (Article 352). This is popularly known as 'National Emergency'.

However, the Constitution employs the expression 'proclamation of emergency' to denote an emergency of this type.

2. An Emergency due to the failure of the constitutional machinery in the states (Article 356). This is popularly known as 'President's Rule'. It is also known by two other names—'State Emergency' or 'constitutional Emergency'. However, the Constitution does not use the word 'emergency' for this situation.

3. Financial Emergency due to a threat to the financial stability or credit of India (Article 360).

NATIONAL EMERGENCY

Grounds of Declaration

Under Article 352, the President can declare a national emergency when the security of India or a part of it is threatened by war or external aggression or armed rebellion. It may be noted that the president can declare a national emergency even before the actual occurrence of war or external aggression or armed rebellion, if he is satisfied that there is an imminent danger.

The President can also issue different proclamations on grounds of war, external aggression, armed rebellion, or imminent danger thereof, whether or not there is a proclamation already issued by him and such proclamation is in operation. This provision was added by the 38th Amendment Act of 1975.

When a national emergency is declared on the ground of 'war' or 'external aggression', it is known as 'External Emergency'. On the other hand, when it is declared on the ground of 'armed rebellion', it is known as 'Internal Emergency'.

A proclamation of national emergency may be applicable to the entire country or only a part of it. The 42nd Amendment Act of 1976 enabled the president to limit the operation of a National Emergency to a specified part of India.

Originally, the Constitution mentioned 'internal disturbance' as the third ground for the proclamation of a National Emergency, but the expression was too vague and had a wider connotation. Hence, the 44th Amendment Act of 1978 substituted the words 'armed rebellion' for 'internal disturbance'. Thus, it is no longer possible to declare a National Emergency on the ground of 'internal disturbance' as was done in 1975 by the Congress government headed by Indira Gandhi.

The President, however, can proclaim a national emergency only after receiving a written recommendation from the cabinet[3]. This means that the emergency can be declared only on the concurrence of the cabinet and not merely on the advice of the prime minister. In 1975, the then Prime Minister, Indira Gandhi advised the president to proclaim emergency without consulting her cabinet. The cabinet was informed of the proclamation after it was made, as a *fait accompli*. The 44th Amendment Act of 1978 introduced this safeguard to eliminate any possibility of the prime minister alone taking a decision in this regard.

The 38th Amendment Act of 1975 made the declaration of a National Emergency immune from the judicial review. But, this provision was subsequently deleted by the 44th Amendment Act of 1978. Further, in the *Minerva Mills* case[4], (1980), the Supreme Court held that the proclamation of a national emergency can be challenged in a court on the ground of malafide or that the declaration was based on wholly extraneous and irrelevant facts or is absurd or perverse.

Parliamentry Approval and Duration

The proclamation of Emergency must be approved by both the Houses of Parliament within one month from the date of its issue. Originally, the period allowed for approval by the Parliament was two months, but was reduced by the 44th Amendment Act of 1978. However, if the proclamation of emergency is issued at a time when the Lok Sabha has been dissolved or the dissolution of the Lok Sabha takes place during the period of one month without approving the proclamation, then the proclamation survives until 30 days from the first sitting of the Lok Sabha after its reconstitution, provided the Rajya Sabha has in the meantime approved it.

If approved by both the Houses of Parliament, the emergency continues for six months, and can be extended to an indefinite period with an approval of the Parliament for every six months. This provision for periodical parliamentary approval was also added by the 44th Amendment Act of 1978. Before that, the emergency, once approved by the Parliament, could remain in operation as long as the Executive (cabinet) desired. However, if the dissolution of the Lok Sabha takes place during the period of six months without approving the further continuance of Emergency, then the proclamation survives until 30 days from the first sitting of the Lok Sabha after its reconstitution, provided the Rajya Sabha has in the mean-time approved its continuation.

Every resolution approving the proclamation of emergency or its continuance must be passed by either House of Parliament by a special majority, that is, (a) a majority of the total membership of that house, and (b) a majority of not less than two-thirds of the members of that house present and voting. This special majority provision was introduced by the 44th Amendment Act of 1978. Previously, such resolution could be passed by a simple majority of the Parliament.

Revocation of Proclamation

A proclamation of emergency may be revoked by the President at any time by a subsequent proclamation. Such a proclamation does not require the parliamentary approval.

Further, the President must revoke a proclamation if the Lok Sabha passes a resolution disapproving its continuation. Again, this safeguard was introduced by the 44th Amendment Act of 1978. Before the amendment, a proclamation could be revoked by the president on his own and the Lok Sabha had no control in this regard.

The 44th Amendment Act of 1978 also provided that, where one-tenth of the total number of members of the Lok Sabha give a written notice to the Speaker (or to the president if the House is not in session), a special sitting of the House should be held within 14 days for the purpose of considering a resolution disapproving the continuation of the proclamation.

A resolution of disapproval is different from a resolution approving the continuation of a proclamation in the following two respects:

1. The first one is required to be passed by the Lok Sabha only, while the second one needs to be passed by the both Houses of Parliament.
2. The first one is to be adopted by a simple majority only, while the second one needs to be adopted by a special majority.

Effects of National Emergency

A proclamation of Emergency has drastic and wide ranging effects on the political system. These consequences can be grouped into three categories:

1. Effect on the Centre–state relations,
2. Effect on the life of the Lok Sabha and State assembly, and
3. Effect on the Fundamental Rights.

Effect on the Centre–state Relations While a proclamation of Emergency is in force, the normal fabric of the Centre–state relations undergoes a basic change. This can be studied under three heads, namely, executive, legislative and financial.

(a) Executive During a national emergency, the executive power of the Centre extends to directing any state regarding the manner in which its executive power is to be exercised. In normal times, the Centre can give executive directions to a state only on certain specified matters. However, during a national emergency, the Centre becomes entitled to give executive directions to a state on 'any' matter. Thus, the state governments are brought under the complete control of the Centre, though they are not suspended.

(b) Legislative During a national emergency, the Parliament becomes empowered to make laws on any subject mentioned in the State List. Although the legislative power of a state legislature is not suspended, it becomes subject to the overriding power of the Parliament. Thus, the normal distribution of the legislative powers between the Centre and states is suspended, though the state Legislatures are not suspended. In brief, the Constitution becomes unitary rather than federal.

The laws made by Parliament on the state subjects during a National Emergency become inoperative six months after the emergency has ceased to operate.

Notably, while a proclamation of national emergency is in operation, the President can issue ordinances on the state subjects also, if the Parliament is not in session.

Further, the Parliament can confer powers and impose duties upon the Centre or its officers and authorities in respect of matters outside the Union List, in order to carry out the laws made by it under its extended jurisdiction as a result of the proclamation of a National Emergency.

The 42nd Amendment Act of 1976 provided that the two consequences mentioned above (executive and legislative) extends not only to a state where the Emergency is in operation but also to any other state.

(c) Financial While a proclamation of national emergency is in operation, the President can modify the constitutional distribution of revenues between the centre and the states. This means that the president can either reduce or cancel the transfer of finances from Centre to the states. Such modification continues till the end of the financial year in which the Emergency ceases to operate. Also, every such order of the President has to be laid before both the Houses of Parliament.

Effect on the Life of the Lok Sabha and State Assembly While a proclamation of National Emergency is in operation, the life of the Lok Sabha may be extended beyond its normal term (five years) by a law of Parliament for one year at a time (for any length of time). However, this extension cannot continue beyond a period of six months after the emergency has ceased to operate. For example, the term of the Fifth Lok Sabha (1971–1977) was extended two times by one year at a time[5].

Similarly, the Parliament may extend the normal tenure of a state legislative assembly (five years) by one year each time (for any length of time) during a national emergency, subject to a maximum period of six months after the Emergency has ceased to operate.

Effect on the Fundamental Rights Articles 358 and 359 describe the effect of a National Emergency on the Fundamental Rights. Article 358 deals with the suspension of the Fundamental Rights guaranteed by Article 19, while Article 359 deals with the suspension of other Fundamental Rights (except those guaranteed by Articles 20 and 21). These two provisions are explained below:

(a) Suspension of Fundamental Rights under Article 19 According to Article 358, when a proclamation of national emergency is made, the six Fundamental Rights under Article 19 are automatically suspended. No separate order for their suspension is required.

While a proclamation of national emergency is in operation, the state is freed from the restrictions imposed by Article 19. In other words, the state can make any law or can take any executive action abridging or taking away the six Fundamental Rights guaranteed by Article 19. Any such law or executive action cannot be challenged on the ground that they are inconsistent with the six Fundamental Rights guaranteed by Article 19. When the National Emergency ceases to operate, Article 19 automatically revives and comes into force. Any law made during Emergency, to the extent of inconsistency with Article 19, ceases to have effect. However, no remedy lies for anything done during the Emergency even after the Emergency expires. This means that the legislative and executive actions taken during the emergency cannot be challenged even after the Emergency ceases to operate.

The 44th Amendment Act of 1978 restricted the scope of Article 358 in two ways. Firstly, the six Fundamental Rights under Article 19 can be suspended only when the National Emergency is declared on the ground of war or external aggression and not on the ground of armed rebellion. Secondly, only those laws which are related with the Emergency are protected from being challenged and not other laws. Also, the executive action taken only under such a law is protected.

(b) Suspension of other Fundamental Rights Article 359 authorises the president to suspend the right to move any court for the enforcement of Fundamental Rights during a National Emergency. This means that under Article 359, the Fundamental Rights as such are not suspended, but only their enforcement. The said rights are theoretically alive but the right to seek remedy is suspended. The suspension of enforcement relates to only those Fundamental Rights that are specified in the Presidential Order. Further, the suspension could be for the period during the operation of emergency or for a shorter period as mentioned in the order, and the suspension order may extend to the whole or any part of the country. It should be laid before each House of Parliament for approval.

While a Presidential Order is in force, the State can make any law or can take any executive action abridging or taking away the specified Fundamental Rights. Any such law or executive action cannot be challenged on the ground that they are inconsistent with the specified Fundamental Rights. When the Order ceases to operate, any law so made, to the extent of inconsistency with the specified Fundamental Rights, ceases to have effect. But no remedy lies for anything done during the operation of the order even after the order ceases to operate. This means that the legislative and executive actions taken during the operation of the Order cannot be challenged even after the Order expires.

The 44th Amendment Act of 1978 restricted the scope of Article 359 in two ways. Firstly, the President cannot suspend the right to move the Court for the enforcement of fundamental rights guaranteed by Articles 20 to 21. In other words, the right to protection in respect of conviction for offences (Article 20) and the right to life and personal liberty (Article 21) remain enforceable even during emergency. Secondly, only those laws which are related with the emergency are protected from being challenged and not other laws and the executive action taken only under such a law, is protected.

Distinction Between Articles 358 and 359

The differences between Articles 358 and 359 can be summarised as follows:

1. Article 358 is confined to Fundamental Rights under Article 19 only whereas Article 359 extends to all those Fundamental Rights whose enforcement is suspended by the Presidential Order.

2. Article 358 automatically suspends the fundamental rights under Article 19 as soon as the emergency is declared. On the other hand, Article 359 does not automatically suspend any Fundamental Right. It only empowers the president to suspend the enforcement of the specified Fundamental Rights.

3. Article 358 operates only in case of External Emergency (that is, when the emergency is declared on the grounds of war or external aggression) and not in the case of Internal Emergency (ie, when the Emergency is declared on the ground of armed rebellion). Article 359, on the other hand, operates in case of both External Emergency as well as Internal Emergency.

4. Article 358 suspends Fundamental Rights under Article 19 for the entire duration of Emergency while Article 359 suspends the enforcement of Fundamental Rights for a period specified by the president which may either be the entire duration of Emergency or a shorter period.

5. Article 358 extends to the entire country whereas Article 359 may extend to the entire country or a part of it.

6. Article 358 suspends Article 19 completely while Article 359 does not empower the suspension of the enforcement of Articles 20 and 21.

7. Article 358 enables the State to make any law or take any executive action inconsistent with Fundamental Rights under Article 19 while Article 359 enables the State to make any law or take any executive action inconsistent with those Fundamental Rights whose enforcement is suspended by the Presidential Order.

There is also a similarity between Article 358 and Article 359. Both provide immunity from challenge to only those laws which are related with the Emergency and not other laws. Also, the executive action taken only under such a law is protected by both.

Declarations Made So Far

This type of Emergency has been proclaimed three times so far—in 1962, 1971 and 1975.

The first proclamation of National Emergency was issued in October 1962 on account of Chinese aggression in the NEFA (North-East Frontier Agen-

cy—now Arunachal Pradesh), and was in force till January 1968. Hence, a fresh proclamation was not needed at the time of war against Pakistan in 1965.

The second proclamation of national emergency was made in December 1971 in the wake of attack by Pakistan. Even when this Emergency was in operation, a third proclamation of National Emergency was made in June 1975. Both the second and third proclamations were revoked in March 1977.

The first two proclamations (1962 and 1971) were made on the ground of 'external aggression', while the third proclamation (1975) was made on the ground of 'internal disturbance', that is, certain persons have been inciting the police and the armed forces against the discharge of their duties and their normal functioning.

The Emergency declared in 1975 (internal emergency) proved to be the most controversial. There was widespread criticism of the misuse of Emergency powers. In the elections held to the Lok Sabha in 1977 after the Emergency, the Congress Party led by Indira Gandhi lost and the Janta Party came to power. This government appointed the Shah Commission to investigate the circumstances that warranted the declaration of an Emergency in 1975. The commission did not justify the declaration of the Emergency. Hence, the 44th Amendment Act was enacted in 1978 to introduce a number of safeguards against the misuse of Emergency provisions.

PRESIDENT'S RULE

Grounds of Imposition

Article 355 imposes a duty on the Centre to ensure that the government of every state is carried on in accordance with the provisions of the Constitution. It is this duty in the performance of which the Centre takes over the government of a state under Article 356 in case of failure of constitutional machinery in state. This is popularly known as 'President's Rule'. It is also known as 'State Emergency' or 'Constitutional Emergency'.

The President's Rule can be proclaimed under Article 356 on two grounds—one mentioned in Article 356 itself and another in Article 365:

1. Article 356 empowers the President to issue a proclamation, if he is satisfied that a situation has arisen in which the government of a

state cannot be carried on in accordance with the provisions of the Constitution. Notably, the president can act either on a report of the governor of the state or otherwise too (ie, even without the governor's report).

2. Article 365 says that whenever a state fails to comply with or to give effect to any direction from the Centre, it will be lawful for the president to hold that a situation has arisen in which the government of the state cannot be carried on in accordance with the provisions of the Constitution.

Parliamentary Approval and Duration

A proclamation imposing President's Rule must be approved by both the Houses of Parliament within two months from the date of its issue. However, if the proclamation of President's Rule is issued at a time when the Lok Sabha has been dissolved or the dissolution of the Lok Sabha takes place during the period of two months without approving the proclamation, then the proclamation survives until 30 days from the first sitting of the Lok Sabha after its reconstitution, provided the Rajya Sabha approves it in the mean time.

If approved by both the Houses of Parliament, the President's Rule continues for six months[6]. It can be extended for a maximum period of three years[7] with the approval of the Parliament, every six months. However, if the dissolution of the Lok Sabha takes place during the period of six months without approving the further continuation of the President's Rule, then the proclamation survives until 30 days from the first sitting of the Lok Sabha after its reconstitution, provided the Rajya Sabha has in the meantime approved its continuance.

Every resolution approving the proclamation of President's Rule or its continuation can be passed by either House of Parliament only by a simple majority, that is, a majority of the members of that House present and voting.

The 44th Amendment Act of 1978 introduced a new provision to put restraint on the power of Parliament to extend a proclamation of President's Rule beyond one year. Thus, it provided that, beyond one year, the President's Rule can be extended by six months at a time only when the following two conditions are fulfilled:

1. a proclamation of National Emergency should be in operation in the whole of India, or in the whole or any part of the state; and
2. the Election Commission must certify that the general elections to the legislative assembly of the concerned state cannot be held on account of difficulties.

A proclamation of President's Rule may be revoked by the President at any time by a subsequent proclamation. Such a proclamation does not require the parliamentary approval.

Consequences of President's Rule

The President acquires the following extraordinary powers when the President's Rule is imposed in a state:

1. He can take up the functions of the state government and powers vested in the governor or any other executive authority in the state.
2. He can declare that the powers of the state legislature are to be exercised by the Parliament.
3. He can take all other necessary steps including the suspension of the constitutional provisions relating to any body or authority in the state.

Therefore, when the President's Rule is imposed in a state, the President dismisses the state council of ministers headed by the chief minister. The state governor, on behalf of the President, carries on the state administration with the help of the chief secretary of the state or the advisors appointed by the President. This is the reason why a proclamation under Article 356 is popularly known as the imposition of 'President's Rule' in a state. Further, the President either suspends or dissolves the state legislative assembly[8]. The Parliament passes the state legislative bills and the state budget.

When the state legislature is thus suspended or dissolved:

1. the Parliament can delegate the power to make laws for the state to the President or to any other authority specified by him in this regard,
2. the Parliament or in case of delegation, the President or any other specified authority can make laws conferring powers and imposing duties on the Centre or its officers and authorities,
3. the President can authorise, when the Lok Sabha is not in session, expenditure from the state

Table 16.1 *Comparing National Emergency and President's Rule*

National Emergency (Article 352)	President's Rule (Article 356)
1. It can be proclaimed only when the security of India or a part of it is threatened by war, external aggression or armed rebellion.	1. It can be proclaimed when the government of a state cannot be carried on in accordance with the provisions of the Constitution due to reasons which may not have any connection with war, external aggression or armed rebellion.
2. During its operation, the state executive and legislature continue to function and exercise the powers assigned to them under the Constitution. Its effect is that the Centre gets concurrent powers of administration and legislation in the state.	2. During its operation, the state executive is dismissed and the state legislature is either suspended or dissolved. The president administers the state through the governor and the Parliament makes laws for the state. In brief, the executive and legislative powers of the state are assumed by the Centre.
3. Under this, the Parliament can make laws on the subjects enumerated in the State List only by itself, that is, it cannot delegate the same to any other body or authority.	3. Under this, the Parliament can delegate the power to make laws for the state to the President or to any other authority specified by him. So far, the practice has been for the president to make laws for the state in consultation with the members of Parliament from that state. Such laws are known as President's Acts.
4. There is no maximum period prescribed for its operation. It can be continued indefinitely with the approval of Parliament for every six months.	4. There is a maximum period prescribed for its operation, that is, three years. Thereafter, it must come to an end and the normal constitutional machinery must be restored in the state.
5. Under this, the relationship of the Centre with all the states undergoes a modification.	5. Under this, the relationship of only the state under emergency with the Centre undergoes a modification.
6. Every resolution of Parliament approving its proclamation or its continuance must be passed by a special majority.	6. Every resolution of Parliament approving its proclamation or its continuance can be passed only by a simple majority.
7. It affects fundamental rights of the citizens.	7. It has no effect on Fundamental Rights of the citizens.
8. Lok Sabha can pass a resolution for its revocation.	8. There is no such provision. It can be revoked by the President only on his own.

consolidated fund pending its sanction by the Parliament, and

4. the President can promulgate, when the Parliament is not in session, ordinances for the governance of the state.

A law made by the Parliament or president or any other specified authority continues to be operative even after the President's Rule. This means that the period for which such a law remains in force is not co-terminous with the duration of the proclamation. But it can be repealed or altered or re-enacted by the state legislature.

It should be noted here that the President cannot assume to himself the powers vested in the concerned state high court or suspend the provisions of the Constitution relating to it. In other words, the constitutional position, status, powers and functions of the concerned state high court remain same even during the President's Rule.

Use of Article 356

Since 1950, the President's Rule has been imposed on more than 100 occasions, that is, on an average twice a year. Further, on a number of occasions, the President's Rule has been imposed in an arbitrary manner for political or personal reasons. Hence, Article 356 has become one of the most controversial and most criticised provision of the Constitution.

For the first time, the President's Rule was imposed in Punjab in 1951. By now, all most all the states have been brought under the President's Rule, once or twice or more. The details in this regard are given in Table 16.2 at the end of this chapter.

When general elections were held to the Lok Sabha in 1977 after the internal emergency, the ruling Congress Party lost and the Janta Party came to power. The new government headed by Morarji Desai imposed President's Rule in nine states[9] (where the Congress Party was in power) on the ground that the assemblies in those states no longer represented the wishes of the electorate. When the Congress Party returned to power in 1980, it did the same in nine states[10] on the same ground.

In 1992, President's Rule was imposed in three BJP-ruled states (Madhya Pradesh, Himachal Pradesh and Rajasthan) by the Congress Party on the ground that they were not implementing sincerely the ban imposed by the Centre on religious organisations. In a landmark judgement in *Bommai* case[11] (1994), the Supreme Court upheld the validity of this proclamation on the ground that secularism is a 'basic feature' of the Constitution. But, the court did not uphold the validity of the imposition of the President's Rule in Nagaland in 1988, Karnataka in 1989 and Meghalaya in 1991.

Dr B R Ambedkar, while replying to the critics of this provision in the Constituent Assembly, hoped that the drastic power conferred by Article 356 would remain a 'dead-letter' and would be used only as a measure of last resort. He observed[12]:

"The intervention of the Centre must be deemed to be barred, because that would be an invasion on the sovereign authority of the province (state). That is a fundamental proposition which we must accept by reason of the fact that we have a Federal Constitution. That being so, if the Centre is to interfere in the administration of provincial affairs, it must be under some obligation which the Constitution imposes upon the Centre. The proper thing we ought to expect is that such Articles will never be called into operation and that they would remain a dead-letter. If at all they are brought into operation, I hope the President who is endowed with this power will take proper precautions before actually suspending the administration of the province."

However, the subsequent events shows that what was hoped to be a 'dead-letter' of the Constitution has turned to be a 'deadly-weapon' against a number of state governments and legislative assemblies. In this context, HV Kamath, a member of the Constituent Assembly commented a decade ago: 'Dr Ambedkar is dead and the Articles are very much alive'.

Scope of Judicial Review

The 38th Amendment Act of 1975 made the satisfaction of the President in invoking Article 356 final and conclusive which could not be challenged in any court on any ground. But, this provision was subsequently deleted by the 44th Amendment Act of 1978 implying that the satisfaction of the President is not beyond judicial review.

In *Bommai* case (1994), the following propositions have been laid down by the Supreme Court on imposition of President's Rule in a state under Article 356:

1. The presidential proclamation imposing President's Rule is subject to judicial review.

2. The satisfaction of the President must be based on relevant material. The action of the president can be struck down by the court if it is based on irrelevant or extraneous grounds or if it was found to be malafide or perverse.

3. Burden lies on the Centre to prove that relevant material exist to justify the imposition of the President's Rule.

4. The court cannot go into the correctness of the material or its adequacy but it can see whether it is relevant to the action.

5. If the court holds the presidential proclamation to be unconstitutional and invalid, it has power to restore the dismissed state government and revive the state legislative assembly if it was suspended or dissolved.

6. The state legislative assembly should be dissolved only after the Parliament has approved the presidential proclamation. Until such approval is given, the president can only suspend the assembly. In case the Parliament fails to approve the proclamation, the assembly would get reactivated.

7. Secularism is one of the 'basic features' of the Constitution. Hence, a state government pur-

suing anti-secular politics is liable to action under Article 356.

8. The question of the state government losing the confidence of the legislative assembly should be decided on the floor of the House and until that is done the ministry should not be unseated.

9. Where a new political party assumes power at the Centre, it will not have the authority to dismiss ministries formed by other parties in the states.

10. The power under Article 356 is an exceptional power and should be used only occassionally to meet the requirements of special situations.

Cases of Proper and Improper Use

Based on the report of the Sarkaria Commission on Centre–state Relations (1988), the Supreme Court in *Bommai* case (1994) enlisted the situations where the exercise of power under Article 356 could be proper or improper[13]. Imposition of President's Rule in a state would be proper in the following situations:

1. Where after general elections to the assembly, no party secures a majority, that is, 'Hung Assembly'.

2. Where the party having a majority in the assembly declines to form a ministry and the governor cannot find a coalition ministry commanding a majority in the assembly.

3. Where a ministry resigns after its defeat in the assembly and no other party is willing or able to form a ministry commanding a majority in the assembly.

4. Where a constitutional direction of the Central government is disregarded by the state government.

5. Internal subversion where, for example, a government is deliberately acting against the Constitution and the law or is fomenting a violent revolt.

6. Physical breakdown where the government wilfully refuses to discharge its constitutional obligations endangering the security of the state.

The imposition of President's Rule in a state would be improper under the following situations:

1. Where a ministry resigns or is dismissed on losing majority support in the assembly and the governor recommends imposition of President's Rule without probing the possibility of forming an alternative ministry.

2. Where the governor makes his own assessment of the support of a ministry in the assembly and recommends imposition of President's Rule without allowing the ministry to prove its majority on the floor of the Assembly.

3. Where the ruling party enjoying majority support in the assembly has suffered a massive defeat in the general elections to the Lok Sabha such as in 1977 and 1980.

4. Internal disturbances not amounting to internal subversion or physical breakdown.

5. Maladministration in the state or allegations of corruption against the ministry or stringent financial exigencies of the state.

6. Where the state government is not given prior warning to rectify itself except in case of extreme urgency leading to disastrous consequences.

7. Where the power is used to sort out intra-party problems of the ruling party, or for a purpose extraneous or irrelevant to the one for which it has been conferred by the Constitution.

FINANCIAL EMERGENCY

Grounds of Declaration

Article 360 empowers the president to proclaim a Financial Emergency if he is satisfied that a situation has arisen due to which the financial stability or credit of India or any part of its territory is threatened.

The 38th Amendment Act of 1975 made the satisfaction of the president in declaring a Financial Emergency final and conclusive and not questionable in any court on any ground. But, this provision was subsequently deleted by the 44th Amendment Act of 1978 implying that the satisfaction of the president is not beyond judicial review.

Parliamentary Approval and Duration

A proclamation declaring financial emergency must be approved by both the Houses of Parliament within two months from the date of its issue. However, if the proclamation of Financial Emergency is issued at a time when the Lok Sabha has been dissolved or the dissolution of the Lok Sabha takes place during the period of two months without approving the proclamation, then the proclamation survives until 30 days from the first sitting of the Lok Sabha after its reconstitution, provided the Rajya Sabha has in the meantime approved it.

Once approved by both the Houses of Parliament, the Financial Emergency continues indefinitely till it is revoked. This implies two things:

1. there is no maximum period prescribed for its operation; and
2. repeated parliamentary approval is not required for its continuation.

A resolution approving the proclamation of financial emergency can be passed by either House of Parliament only by a simple majority, that is, a majority of the members of that house present and voting.

A proclamation of Financial Emergency may be revoked by the president at anytime by a subsequent proclamation. Such a proclamation does not require the parliamentry approval.

Effects of Financial Emergency

The consequences of the proclamation of a Financial Emergency are as follows:

1. The executive authority of the Centre extends (a) to directing any state to observe such canons of financial propriety as are specified by it; and (b) to directions as the President may deem necessary and adequate for the purpose.
2. Any such direction may include a provision requiring (a) the reduction of salaries and allowances of all or any class of persons serving in the state; and (b) the reservation of all money bills or other financial bills for the consideration of the President after they are passed by the legislature of the state.
3. The President may issue directions for the reduction of salaries and allowances of (a) all or any class of persons serving the Union; and (b) the judges of the Supreme Court and the high court.

Thus, during the operation of a financial emergency, the Centre acquires full control over the states

in financial matters. H N Kunzru, a member of the Constituent Assembly, stated that the financial emergency provisions pose a serious threat to the financial autonomy of the states. Explaining the reasons for their inclusion in the Constitution, Dr BR Ambedkar observed in the Constituent Assembly[14]:

"This Article more or less follows the pattern of what is called the National Recovery Act of the United States passed in 1933, which gave the president power to make similar provisions in order to remove the difficulties, both economical and financial, that had overtaken the American people, as a result of the Great Depression."

No Financial Emergency has been declared so far, though there was a financial crisis in 1991.

CRITICISM OF THE EMERGENCY PROVISIONS

Some members of the Constituent Assembly criticised the incorporation of emergency provisions in the Constitution on the following grounds[15]:

1. 'The federal character of the Constitution will be destroyed and the Union will become all powerful.
2. The powers of the State—both the Union and the units—will entirely be concentrated in the hands of the Union executive.
3. The President will become a dictator.
4. The financial autonomy of the state will be nullified.
5. Fundamental rights will become meaningless and, as a result, the democratic foundations of the Constitution will be destroyed.'

Thus, H V Kamath observed: 'I fear that by this single chapter we are seeking to lay the foundation of a totalitarian state, a police state, a state completely opposed to all the ideals and principles that we have held aloft during the last few decades, a State where the rights and liberties of millions of innocent men and women will be in continuous jeopardy, a State where if there be peace, it will be the peace of the grave and the void of the desert(. . .) It will be a day of shame and sorrow when the President makes use of these Powers having no parallel in any Constitution of the democratic countries of the world'[16].

K T Shah described them as:

Table 16.2 *Imposition of President's Rule (1951-2000)*

Sl. No.	States / Union Territories	No. of Times Imposed	Years of Imposition
1.	Andhra Pradesh	2	1954, 1973
2.	Arunachal Pradesh	1	1979
3.	Assam	4	1979, 1981, 1982, 1990
4.	Bihar	7	1968, 1969, 1972, 1977, 1980, 1995, 1999
5.	Goa	4	1966, 1979, 1990, 1999
6.	Gujarat	5	1971, 1974, 1976, 1980, 1996
7.	Haryana	3	1967, 1977, 1991
8.	Himachal Pradesh	2	1977, 1992
9.	Jammu and Kashmir	2	1986, 1990
10.	Karnataka	4	1971, 1977, 1989, 1990
11.	Kerala	9	1956, 1956, 1959, 1964, 1965, 1970, 1979, 1981, 1982
12.	Madhya Pradesh	3	1977, 1980, 1992
13.	Maharashtra	1	1980
14.	Manipur	7	1972, 1973, 1977, 1979, 1981, 1992, 1994
15.	Mizoram	3	1977, 1978, 1988
16.	Meghalaya	1	1991
17.	Nagaland	3	1975, 1988, 1992
18.	Orissa	6	1961, 1971, 1973, 1976, 1977, 1980
19.	Patiala and East Punjab States Union (PEPSU)	1	1953
20.	Puducherry	6	1968, 1974, 1974, 1978, 1983, 1991
21.	Punjab	8	1951, 1966, 1968, 1971, 1977, 1980, 1983, 1987
22.	Rajasthan	4	1967, 1977, 1980, 1992
23.	Sikkim	2	1979, 1984
24.	Tamil Nadu	4	1976, 1980, 1988, 1991
25.	Tripura	3	1972, 1977, 1993
26.	Uttar Pradesh	9	1968, 1970, 1973, 1975, 1977, 1980, 1992, 1995, 1996
27.	West Bengal	4	1968, 1970, 1971, 1977

Table 16.3 *Articles Related to Emergency Provisions at a Glance*

Article No.	Subject-matter
352.	Proclamation of Emergency
353.	Effect of Proclamation of Emergency
354.	Application of provisions relating to distribution of revenues while a Proclamation of Emergency is in operation
355.	Duty of the Union to protect states against external aggression and internal disturbance
356.	Provisions in case of failure of constitutional machinery in states

(Contd.)

Article No.	Subject-matter
357.	Exercise of legislative powers under proclamation issued under Article 356
358.	Suspension of provisions of Article 19 during Emergencies
359.	Suspension of the enforcement of the rights conferred by Part III during Emergencies
359A.	Application of this part to the state of Punjab (Repealed)
360.	Provisions as to Financial Emergency

'A chapter of reaction and retrogression. (. . .) I find one cannot but notice two distinct currents of thought underlying and influencing throughout the provisions of this chapter: **(a)** to arm the Centre with special powers against the units and **(b)** to arm the government against the people . . . Looking at all the provisions of this chapter particularly and scrutinising the powers that have been given in almost every article, it seems to me, the name only of liberty or democracy will remain under the Constitution'.

T T Krishnamachari feared that 'by means of these provisions the President and the Executive would be exercising a form of constitutional dictatorship'[17].

H N Kunzru opined that 'the emergency financial provisions pose a serious threat to the financial autonomy of the States.'

However, there were also protagonists of the emergency provisions in the Constituent Assembly. Thus, Sir Alladi Krishnaswami Ayyar labelled them as 'the very life-breath of the Constitution'. Mahabir Tyagi opined that they would work as a 'safety-valve' and thereby help in the maintenance of the Constitution[18].

While defending the emergency provisions in the Constituent Assembly, Dr B R Ambedkar also accepted the possibility of their misuse. He observed, 'I do not altogether deny that there is a possibility of the Articles being abused or employed for political purposes'[19].

NOTES AND REFERENCES

1. *Constituent Assembly Debates,* Volume VII, p. 34.
2. The phrase 'armed rebellion' was inserted by the 44th Amendment Act of 1978, replacing the original phrase 'internal disturbance'.
3. Article 352 defines the term 'Cabinet' as the council consisting of the Prime Minister and other ministers of the Cabinet rank.
4. *Minerva Mills* v. *Union of India,* (1980).
5. The term of the Fifth Lok Sabha which was to expire on 18 March, 1976 was extended by one year upto 18 March, 1977 by the House of the People (Extension of Duration) Act, 1976. It was extend for a further period of one year upto 18 March, 1978 by the House of the People (Extension of Duration) Amendment Act, 1976. However, the House was dissolved on 18 January, 1977, after having been in existence for a period of five years, ten months and six days.
6. The 42nd Amendment Act of 1976 had raised the period of six months to one year. Thus, once approved by both the Houses of Parliament, the proclamation of President's Rule could continue for one year. But, the 44th Amendment Act of 1978 again reduced the period to six months.
7. The President's Rule imposed in May, 1987 in Punjab was allowed to continue for five years under the 68th Amendment Act of 1991.
8. In case of dissolution, fresh elections are held for constituting a new legislative assembly in the state.
9. Those nine States include Rajasthan, Uttar Pradesh, Madhya Pradesh, Punjab, Bihar, Himachal Pradesh, Orissa, West Bengal and Haryana.
10. Those nine states include Uttar Pradesh, Bihar, Rajasthan, Madhya Pradesh, Punjab, Orissa, Gujarat, Maharashtra and Tamil Nadu.

11. *S. R. Bommai v. Union of India* (1994).
12. *Constituent Assembly Debates*, Volume IX, p. 133 and 177.
13. *Report of the Commission on Centre– State Relations*, Part I, p. 165–180 (1988).
14. *Constituent Assembly Debates*, Volume X, p. 361–372.
15. Quoted from M V Pylee, *India's Constitution*, S Chand, Fifth Edition, 1994, p. 280.
16. *Constituent Assembly Debates*, Volume IX, p. 105.
17. Ibid, p. 123.
18. Ibid, p. 547.
19. Ibid, p. 177.

P ART III

CENTRAL GOVERNMENT

President

Articles 52 to 78 in Part V of the Constitution deal with the Union executive.

The Union executive consists of the President, the Vice-President, the Prime Minister, the council of ministers and the attorney general of India.

The President is the head of the Indian State. He is the first citizen of India and acts as the symbol of unity, integrity and solidarity of the nation.

ELECTION OF THE PRESIDENT

The President is elected not directly by the people but by members of electoral college consisting of:

1. the elected members of both the Houses of Parliament;
2. the elected members of the legislative assemblies of the states; and
3. the elected members of the legislative assemblies of the Union Territories of Delhi and Puducherry[1].

Thus, the nominated members of both of Houses of Parliament, the nominated members of the state legislative assemblies, the members (both elected and nominated) of the state legislative councils (in case of the bicameral legislature) and the nominated members of the Legislative Assemblies of Delhi and Puducherry do not participate in the election of the President. Where an assembly is dissolved, the members cease to be qualified to vote in presidential election, even if fresh elections to the dissolved assembly are not held before the presidential election.

The Constitution provides that there shall be uniformity in the scale of representation of different states as well as parity between the states as a whole and the Union at the election of the President. To achieve this, the number of votes which each elected member of the legislative assembly of each state and the Parliament is entitled to cast at such election shall be determined in the following manner:

1. Every elected member of the legislative assembly of a state shall have as many votes as there are multiples of one thousand in the quotient obtained by dividing the population of the state by the total number of the elected members of the assembly[2]. This can be expressed as:

$$\text{Value of the vote of an MLA} = \frac{\text{Total population of state}}{\text{Total number of elected members in the state legislative assembly}} \times \frac{1}{1000}$$

2. Every elected member of either House of Parliament shall have such number of votes as may be obtained by dividing the total number of votes assigned to members of the legislative assemblies of the states by the total number of the elected members of both the Houses of Parliament. This can be expressed as:

$$\text{Value of the vote of an MP} = \frac{\text{Total value of votes of all MLAs of all states}}{\text{Total number of elected members of Parliament}}$$

The President's election is held in accordance with the system of proportional representation by means of the single transferable vote and the voting is by secret ballot. This system ensures that the successful candidate is returned by the absolute majority of votes. A candidate, in order to be declared elected to the office of President, must secure a fixed quota of votes. The quota of votes is determined by dividing the total number of valid votes polled by the number of candidates to be elected (here only one candidate is to be elected as President) plus one and adding one to the quotient. The formula can be expressed as:

$$\text{Electoral quota} = \frac{\text{Total number of valid votes polled}}{1+1=(2)} + 1$$

Each member of the electoral college is given only one ballot paper. The voter, while casting his vote, is required to indicate his preferences by marking 1, 2, 3, 4, etc. against the names of candidates. This means that the voter can indicate as many preferences as there are candidates in the fray.

In the first phase, the first preference votes are counted. In case a candidate secures the required quota in this phase, he is declared elected. Otherwise, the process of transfer of votes is set in motion. The ballots of the candidate securing the least number of first preference votes are cancelled and his second preference votes are transferred to the first preference votes of other candidates. This process continues till a candidate secures the required quota.

All doubts and disputes in connection with election of the President are inquired into and decided by the Supreme Court whose decision is final. The election of a person as President cannot be challenged on the ground that the electoral college was incomplete (ie, existence of any vacancy among the members of electoral college). If the election of a person as President is declared void by the Supreme Court, acts done by him before the date of such declaration of the Supreme Court are not invalidated and continue to remain in force.

Some members of the Constituent Assembly criticised the system of indirect election for the President as undemocratic and proposed the idea of direct election. However, the Constitution makers chose the indirect election due to the following reasons[3]:

1. The indirect election of the President is in harmony with the parliamentary system of government envisaged in the Constitution. Under this system, the President is only a nominal executive and the real powers are vested in the council of ministers headed by the prime minister. It would have been anomalous to have the President elected directly by the people and not give him any real power.

2. The direct election of the President would have been very costly and time- and energy-consuming due to the vast size of the electorate. This is unwarranted keeping in view that he is only a symbolic head.

Some members of the Constituent Assembly suggested that the President should be elected by the members of the two Houses of Parliament alone. The makers of the Constitution did not prefer this as the Parliament, dominated by one political party, would have invariably chosen a candidate from that party and such a President could not represent the states of the Indian Union. The present system makes the President a representative of the Union and the states equally.

Further, it was pointed out in the Constituent Assembly that the expression 'proportional representation' in the case of presidential election is a misnomer. Proportional representation takes place where two or more seats are to be filled. In case of the President, the vacancy is only one. It could better be called a preferential or alternative vote system. Similarly, the expression 'single transferable vote' was also objected on the ground that no voter has a single vote; every voter has plural votes.

QUALIFICATIONS, OATH AND CONDITIONS

Qualifications for Election as President

A person to be eligible for election as President should fulfil the following qualifications:

1. He should be a citizen of India.
2. He should have completed 35 years of age.
3. He should be qualified for election as a member of the Lok Sabha.
4. He should not hold any office of profit under the Union government or any state government or any local authority or any other public

Table 17.1 *Elections of the Presidents (1952-2012)*

Sl. No.	Election Year	Victorious Candidate	No. of Votes secured (%)	Main Rival Candidate	No. of Votes secured (%)
1.	1952	Dr. Rajendra Prasad	507400 (83.81)	K.T. Shah	92827 (15.3)
2.	1957	Dr. Rajendra Prasad	459698 (99.35)	N.N. Das	2000 (0.4)
3.	1962	Dr. S. Radhakrishnan	553067 (98.24)	Ch.Hari Ram	6341 (1.1)
4.	1967	Dr. Zakir Hussain	471244 (56.23)	K. Subba Rao	363971 (43.4)
5.	1969	V.V. Giri	420077 (50.22)	N. Sanjeeva Reddy	405427 (48.5)
6.	1974	Fakhruddin Ali Ahmed	756587 (80.18)	Tridev Chaudhuri	189186 (19.8)
7.	1977	N. Sanjeeva Reddy	—	Unopposed	—
8.	1982	Giani Zail Singh	754113 (72.73)	H.R. Khanna	282685 (27.6)
9.	1987	R. Venkataraman	740148 (72.29)	V.Krishna Ayyer	281550 (27.1)
10.	1992	Dr. Shankar Dayal Sharma	675564 (65.86)	George Swell	346485 (33.21)
11.	1997	K.R. Narayanan	956290 (94.97)	T.N. Sheshan	50431 (5.07)
12.	2002	Dr. A.P.J. Abdul Kalam	922844 (89.58)	Laxmi Sehgal	107366 (10.42)
13.	2007	Ms. Pratibha Patil	638116 (65.82)	B.S. Shekhawat	331306 (34.17)
14.	2012	Pranab Mukherjee	713763 (68.12)	P.A. Sangma	315987 (30.15)

authority. A sitting President or Vice-President of the Union, the Governor of any state and a minister of the Union or any state is not deemed to hold any office of profit and hence qualified as a presidential candidate.

Further, the nomination of a candidate for election to the office of President must be subscribed by at least 50 electors as proposers and 50 electors as seconders. Every candidate has to make a security deposit of Rs 15,000 in the Reserve Bank of India. The security deposit is liable to be forefeited in case the candidate fails to secure one-sixth of the votes polled. Before 1997, number of proposers and seconders was ten each and the amount of security deposit was Rs 2,500. In 1997, they were increased to discourage the non-serious candidates[4].

Oath or Affirmation by the President

Before entering upon his office, the President has to make and subscribe to an oath or affirmation. In his oath, the President swears:

1. to faithfully execute the office;
2. to preserve, protect and defend the Constitution and the law; and
3. to devote himself to the service and well-being of the people of India.

The oath of office to the President is administered by the Chief Justice of India and in his absence, the seniormost judge of the Supreme Court available.

Any other person acting as President or discharging the functions of the President also undertakes the similar oath or affirmation.

Conditions of President's Office

The Constitution lays down the following conditions of the President's office:

1. He should not be a member of either House of Parliament or a House of the state legislature. If any such person is elected as President, he is deemed to have vacated his seat in that House on the date on which he enters upon his office as President.
2. He should not hold any other office of profit.
3. He is entitled, without payment of rent, to the use of his official residence (the Rastrapathi Bhavan).
4. He is entitled to such emoluments, allowances and privileges as may be determined by Parliament.
5. His emoluments and allowances cannot be diminished during his term of office.

In 2008, the Parliament increased the salary of the President from Rs.50,000 to Rs.1.50 lakh per month and the pension to 50% of his salary per month. In addition, the former Presidents are entitled to furnished residence, phone facilities, car, medical treatment, travel facility, secretarial staff and office expenses upto Rs. 60,000 per annum. The spouse of a deceased President is also entitled to a family pension at the rate of 50% of pension of a retired President, furnished residence, phone facility, car, medical treatment, travel facility, secretarial staff and office expenses upto Rs.12,000 per annum.[5]

The President is entitled to a number of privileges and immunities. He enjoys personal immunity from legal liability for his official acts. During his term of office, he is immune from any criminal proceedings, even in respect of his personal acts. He cannot be arrested or imprisoned. However, after giving two months' notice, civil proceedings can be instituted against him during his term of office in respect of his personal acts.

TERM, IMPEACHMENT AND VACANCY

Term of President's office

The President holds office for a term of five years from the date on which he enters upon his office. However, he can resign from his office at any time by addressing the resignation letter to the Vice-President. Further, he can also be removed from the office before completion of his term by the process of impeachment.

The President can hold office beyond his term of five years until his successor assumes charge. He is also eligible for re-election to that office. He may be elected for any number of terms[6]. However, in USA, a person cannot be elected to the office of the President more than twice.

Impeachment of President

The President can be removed from office by a process of impeachment for 'violation of the Constitution'. However, the Constitution does not define the meaning of the phrase 'violation of the Constitution'.

The impeachment charges can be initiated by either House of Parliament. These charges should be signed by one-fourth members of the House (that framed the charges), and a 14 days' notice should be given to the President. After the impeachment resolution is passed by a majority of two-thirds of the total membership of that House, it is sent to the other House, which should investigate the charges. The President has the right to appear and to be represented at such investigation. If the other House also sustains the charges and passes the impeachment resolution by a majority of two-thirds of the total membership, then the President stands removed from his office from the date on which the bill is so passed.

Thus, an impeachment is a quasi-judicial procedure in the Parliament. In this context, two things should be noted: **(a)** the nominated members of either House of Parliament can participate in the impeachment of the President though they do not participate in his election; **(b)** the elected members of the legislative assemblies of states and the Union Territories of Delhi and Puducherry do not participate in the impeachment of the President though they participate in his election.

No President has so far been impeached.

Vacancy in the President's Office

A vacancy in the President's office can occur in any of the following ways:
1. On the expiry of his tenure of five years.
2. By his resignation.
3. On his removal by the process of impeachment.
4. By his death[7].
5. Otherwise, for example, when he becomes disqualified to hold office or when his election is declared void.

When the vacancy is going to be caused by the expiration of the term of the sitting President, an election to fill the vacancy must be held before the expiration of the term. In case of any delay in conducting the election of new President by any reason, the outgoing President continues to hold office (beyond his term of five years) until his successor assumes charge. This is provided by the Constitution in order to prevent an 'interregnum'. In this situation, the Vice-President does not get the opportunity to act as President or to discharge the functions of the President.

If the office falls vacant by resignation, removal, death or otherwise, then election to fill the vacancy should be held within six months from the date of the occurrence of such a vacancy. The newly-elected President remains in office for a full term of five years from the date he assumes charge of his office.

When a vacancy occurs in the office of the President due to his resignation, removal, death or otherwise, the Vice-President acts as the President until a new President is elected. Further, when the sitting President is unable to discharge his functions due to absence, illness or any other cause, the Vice-President discharges his functions until the President resumes his office.

In case the office of Vice-President is vacant, the Chief Justice of India (or if his office is also vacant, the seniormost judge of the Supreme Court available) acts as the President or discharges the functions of the President[8].

When any person, ie, Vice-President, chief justice of India, or the seniormost judge of the Supreme Court is acting as the President or discharging the functions of the President, he enjoys all the powers and immunities of the President and is entitled to such emoluments, allowances and privileges as are determined by the Parliament.

POWERS AND FUNCTIONS OF THE PRESIDENT

The powers enjoyed and the functions performed by the President can be studied under the following heads.

1. Executive powers
2. Legislative powers
3. Financial powers
4. Judicial powers
5. Diplomatic powers
6. Military powers
7. Emergency powers

Executive Powers

The executive powers and functions of the President are:

(a) All executive actions of the Government of India are formally taken in his name.

(b) He can make rules specifying the manner in which the orders and other instruments made and executed in his name shall be authenticated.

(c) He can make rules for more convenient transaction of business of the Union government, and for allocation of the said business among the ministers.

(d) He appoints the prime minister and the other ministers. They hold office during his pleasure.

(e) He appoints the attorney general of India and determines his remuneration. The attorney general holds office during the pleasure of the President.

(f) He appoints the comptroller and auditor general of India, the chief election commissioner and other election commissioners, the chairman and members of the Union Public Service Commission, the governors of states, the chairman and members of finance commission, and so on.

(g) He can seek any information relating to the administration of affairs of the Union, and proposals for legislation from the prime minister.

(h) He can require the Prime Minister to submit, for consideration of the council of ministers, any matter on which a decision has been taken by a minister but, which has not been considered by the council.

(i) He can appoint a commission to investigate into the conditions of SCs, STs and other backward classes.

(j) He can appoint an inter-state council to promote Centre–state and inter-state cooperation.

(k) He directly administers the union territories through administrators appointed by him.

(l) He can declare any area as scheduled area and has powers with respect to the administration of scheduled areas and tribal areas.

Legislative Powers

The President is an integral part of the Parliament of India, and enjoys the following legislative powers.

(a) He can summon or prorogue the Parliament and dissolve the Lok Sabha. He can also summon a joint sitting of both the Houses of Parliament, which is presided over by the Speaker of the Lok Sabha.

(b) He can address the Parliament at the commencement of the first session after each general election and the first session of each year.

(c) He can send messages to the Houses of Parliament, whether with respect to a bill pending in the Parliament or otherwise.

(d) He can appoint any member of the Lok Sabha to preside over its proceedings when the offices of both the Speaker and the Deputy Speaker fall vacant. Similarly, he can also appoint any member of the Rajya Sabha to preside over its proceedings when the offices of both the Chairman and the Deputy Chairman fall vacant.

(e) He nominates 12 members of the Rajya Sabha from amongst persons having special knowledge or practical experience in literature, science, art and social service.

(f) He can nominate two members to the Lok Sabha from the Anglo-Indian Community.

(g) He decides on questions as to disqualifications of members of the Parliament, in consultation with the Election Commission.

(h) His prior recommendation or permission is needed to introduce certain types of bills in the Parliament. For example, a bill involving expenditure from the Consolidated Fund of India, or a bill for the alteration of boundaries of states or creation of a new state.

(i) When a bill is sent to the President after it has been passed by the Parliament, he can:
  (i) give his assent to the bill, or
  (ii) withhold his assent to the bill, or
  (iii) return the bill (if it is not a money bill) for reconsideration of the Parliament.
However, if the bill is passed again by the Parliament, with or without amendments, the President has to give his assent to the bill.

(j) When a bill passed by a state legislature is reserved by the governor for consideration of the President, the President can:

  (i) give his assent to the bill, or
  (ii) withhold his assent to the bill, or
  (iii) direct the governor to return the bill (if it is not a money bill) for reconsideration of the state legis lature. It should be noted here that it is not obligatory for the President to give his assent even if the bill is again passed by the state legislature and sent again to him for his consideration.

(k) He can promulgate ordinances when the Parliament is not in session. These ordinances must be approved by the Parliament within six weeks from its reassembly. He can also withdraw an ordinance at any time.

(l) He lays the reports of the Comptroller and Auditor General, Union Public Service Commission, Finance Commission, and others, before the Parliament.

(m) He can make regulations for the peace, progress and good government of the Andaman and Nicobar Islands, Lakshadweep, Dadra and Nagar Haveli and Daman and Diu. In the case of Puducherry also, the President can legislate by making regulations but only when the assembly is suspended or dissolved.

Financial Powers

The financial powers and functions of the President are:

(a) Money bills can be introduced in the Parliament only with his prior recommendation.

(b) He causes to be laid before the Parliament the annual financial statement (ie, the Union Budget).

(c) No demand for a grant can be made except on his recommendation.

(d) He can make advances out of the contingency fund of India to meet any unforeseen expenditure.

(e) He constitutes a finance commission after every five years to recommend the distribution of revenues between the Centre and the states.

Judicial Powers

The judicial powers and functions of the President are:

(a) He appoints the Chief Justice and the judges of Supreme Court and high courts.

(b) He can seek advice from the Supreme Court on any question of law or fact. However, the advice tendered by the Supreme Court is not binding on the President.

(c) He can grant pardon, reprieve, respite and remission of punishment, or suspend, remit or commute the sentence of any person convicted of any offence:

  (i) In all cases where the punishment or sentence is by a court martial;

  (ii) In all cases where the punishment or sentence is for an offence against a Union law; and

  (iii) In all cases where the sentence is a sentence of death.

Diplomatic Powers

The international treaties and agreements are negotiated and concluded on behalf of the President. However, they are subject to the approval of the Parliament. He represents India in international forums and affairs and sends and receives diplomats like ambassadors, high commissioners, and so on.

Military Powers

He is the supreme commander of the defence forces of India. In that capacity, he appoints the chiefs of the Army, the Navy and the Air Force. He can declare war or conclude peace, subject to the approval of the Parliament.

Emergency Powers

In addition to the normal powers mentioned above, the Constitution confers extraordinary powers on the President to deal with the following three types of emergencies[9]:

(a) National Emergency (Article 352);

(b) President's Rule (Article 356 & 365); and

(c) Financial Emergency (Article 360)

VETO POWER OF THE PRESIDENT

A bill passed by the Parliament can become an act only if it receives the assent of the President. When such a bill is presented to the President for his assent, he has three alternatives (under Article 111 of the Constitution):

1. He may give his assent to the bill, or

2. He may withhold his assent to the bill, or

3. He may return the bill (if it is not a Money bill) for reconsideration of the Parliament. However, if the bill is passed again by the Parliament with or without amendments and again presented to the President, the President must give his assent to the bill.

Thus, the President has the veto power over the bills passed by the Parliament[10], that is, he can withhold his assent to the bills. The object of conferring this power on the President is two-fold—(a) to prevent hasty and ill-considered legislation by the Parliament; and (b) to prevent a legislation which may be unconstitutional.

The veto power enjoyed by the executive in modern states can be classified into the following four types:

1. Absolute veto, that is, withholding of assent to the bill passed by the legislature.

2. Qualified veto, which can be overridden by the legislature with a higher majority.

3. Suspensive veto, which can be over ridden by the legislature with an ordinary majority.

4. Pocket veto, that is, taking no action on the bill passed by the legislature.

Of the above four, the President of India is vested with three—absolute veto, suspensive veto and pocket veto. There is no qualified veto in the case of Indian President; it is possessed by the American President. The three vetos of the President of India are explained below:

Absolute Veto

It refers to the power of the President to withhold his assent to a bill passed by the Parliament. The bill then ends and does not become an act. Usually, this veto is exercised in the following two cases:

(a) With respect to private members' bills (ie, bills introduced by any member of Parliament who is not a minister); and

(b) With respect to the government bills when the cabinet resigns (after the passage of the bills but before the assent by the President) and the new cabinet advises the President not to give his assent to such bills.

In 1954, President Dr Rajendra Prasad withheld his assent to the PEPSU Appropriation Bill. The bill was passed by the Parliament when the President's Rule was in operation in the state of PEPSU. But, when the bill was presented to the President for his assent, the President's Rule was revoked.

Again in 1991, President R Venkataraman withheld his assent to the Salary, Allowances and Pension of Members of Parliament (Amendment) Bill. The bill was passed by the Parliament (on the last day before dissolution of Lok Sabha) without obtaining the previous recommendation of the President.

Suspensive Veto

The President exercises this veto when he returns a bill for reconsideration of the Parliament. However, if the bill is passed again by the Parliament with or without amendments and again presented to the President, it is obligatory for the President to give his assent to the bill. This means that the presidential veto is overridden by a re-passage of the bill by the same ordinary majority (and not a higher majority as required in USA).

As mentioned earlier, the President does not possess this veto in the case of money bills. The President can either give his assent to a money bill or withhold his assent to a money bill but cannot return it for the reconsideration of the Parliament. Normally, the President gives his assent to money bill as it is introduced in the Parliament with his previous permission.

Pocket Veto

In this case, the President neither ratifies nor rejects nor returns the bill, but simply keeps the bill pending for an indefinite period. This power of the President not to take any action (either positive or negative) on the bill is known as the pocket veto. The President can exercise this veto power as the Constitution does not prescribe any time-limit within which he has to take the decision with respect to a bill presented to

him for his assent. In USA, on the other hand, the President has to return the bill for reconsideration within 10 days. Hence, it is remarked that the pocket of the Indian President is bigger than that of the American President.

In 1986, President Zail Singh exercised the pocket veto with respect to the Indian Post Office (Amendment) Bill. The bill, passed by the Rajiv Gandhi Government, imposed restrictions on the freedom of press and hence, was widely criticised. After three years, in 1989, the next President R Venkataraman sent the bill back for reconsideration, but the new National Front Government decided to drop the bill.

It should be noted here that the President has no veto power in respect of a constitutional amendment bill. The 24th Constitutional Amendment Act of 1971 made it obligatory for the President to give his assent to a constitutional amendment bill.

Presidential Veto over State Legislation

The President has veto power with respect to state legislation also. A bill passed by a state legislature can become an act only if it receives the assent of the governor or the President (in case the bill is reserved for the consideration of the President).

When a bill, passed by a state legislature, is presented to the governor for his assent, he has four alternatives (under Article 200 of the Constitution):

1. He may give his assent to the bill, or
2. He may withhold his assent to the bill, or
3. He may return the bill (if it is not a money bill) for reconsideration of the state legislature, or
4. He may reserve the bill for the consideration of the President.

When a bill is reserved by the governor for the consideration of the President, the President has three alternatives (Under Article 201 of the Constitution):

1. He may give his assent to the bill, or
2. He may withhold his assent to the bill, or
3. He may direct the governor to return the bill (if it is not a money bill) for the reconsideration of the state legislature. If the bill is passed again by the state legislature with or without amendments and presented again to the President for his assent, the President is not bound to give his assent to the bill. This means that the state legislature cannot over-

Table 17.2 *Veto Power of the President At a Glance*

Central Legislation	State Legislation
With Regard to Ordinary Bills	
1. Can be ratified	1. Can be ratified
2. Can be rejected	2. Can be rejected
3. Can be returned	3. Can be returned
With Regard to Money Bills	
1. Can be ratified	1. Can be ratified
2. Can be rejected (but cannot be returned)	2. Can be rejected (but cannot be returned)
With Regard to Constitutional Amendment Bills	
Can only be ratified (that is, cannot be rejected or returned)	Constitutional amendment bills cannot be introduced in the state legislature.

ride the veto power of the President. Further, the Constitution has not prescribed any time limit within which the President has to take decision with regard to a bill reserved by the governor for his consideration. Hence, the President can exercise pocket veto in respect of state legislation also.

Table 17.2 summarises the discussion on the veto power of the President with regard to Central as well as state legislation.

ORDINANCE-MAKING POWER OF THE PRESIDENT

Article 123 of the Constitution empowers the President to promulgate ordinances during the recess of Parliament. These ordinances have the same force and effect as an act of Parliament, but are in the nature of temporary laws.

The ordinance-making power is the most important legislative power of the President. It has been vested in him to deal with unforeseen or urgent matters. But, the exercises of this power is subject to the following four limitations:

1. He can promulgate an ordinance only when both the Houses of Parliament are not in session or when either of the two Houses of Parliament is not in session. An ordinance can also be issued when only one House is in session because a law can be passed by both the Houses and not by one House alone. An ordinance made when both the Houses are in session

is void. Thus, the power of the President to legislate by ordinance is not a parallel power of legislation.

2. He can make an ordinance only when he is satisfied that the circumstances exist that render it necessary for him to take immediate action. In *Cooper* case[11], (1970), the Supreme Court held that the President's satisfaction can be questioned in a court on the ground of malafide. This means that the decision of the President to issue an ordinance can be questioned in a court on the ground that the President has prorogued one House or both Houses of Parliament deliberately with a view to promulgate an ordinance on a controversial subject, so as to bypass the parliamentary decision and thereby circumventing the authority of the Parliament. The 38th Constitutional Amendment Act of 1975 made the President's satisfaction final and conclusive and beyond judicial review. But, this provision was deleted by the 44th Constitutional Amendment Act of 1978. Thus, the President's satisfaction is justiciable on the ground of malafide.

3. His ordinance-making power is coextensive as regards all matters except duration, with the law-making powers of the Parliament. This has two implications:

(a) An ordinance can be issued only on those subjects on which the Parliament can make laws.

(b) An ordinance is subject to the same constitutional limitation as an act of Parliament. Hence, an ordinance cannot abridge or take away any of the fundamental rights[12].

4. Every ordinance issued by the President during the recess of Parliament must be laid before both the Houses of Parliament when it reassembles. If the ordinance is approved by both the Houses, it becomes an act. If Parliament takes no action at all, the ordinance ceases to operate on the expiry of six weeks from the reassembly of Parliament. The ordinance may also cease to operate even earlier than the prescribed six weeks, if both the Houses of Parliament pass resolutions disapproving it. If the Houses of Parliament are summoned to reassemble on different dates, the period of six weeks is calculated from the later of those dates. This means that the maximum life of an ordinance can be six months and six weeks, in case of non-approval by the Parliament (six months being the maximum gap between the two sessions of Parliament). If an ordinance is allowed to lapse without being placed before Parliament, then the acts done and completed under it, before it ceases to operate, remain fully valid and effective.

The President can also withdraw an ordinance at any time. However, his power of ordinance-making is not a discretionary power, and he can promulgate or withdraw an ordinance only on the advice of the council of ministers headed by the prime minister.

An ordinance like any other legislation, can be retrospective, that is, it may come into force from a back date. It may modify or repeal any act of Parliament or another ordinance. It can alter or amend a tax law also. However, it cannot be issued to amend the Constitution.

The ordinance-making power of the President in India is rather unusual and not found in most of the democratic Constitutions of the world including that of USA, and UK. In justification of the ordinance-making power of the President, Dr BR Ambedkar said in the Constituent Assembly that the mechanism of issuing an ordinance has been devised in order to enable the Executive to deal with a situation that may suddenly and immediately arise when the Parliament is not in session[13]. It must be clarified here that the ordinance-making power of the President has no necessary connection with the national emergency envisaged in Article 352. The President can issue an ordinance even when there is no war or external aggression or armed rebellion.

The rules of Lok Sabha require that whenever a bill seeking to replace an ordinance is introduced in the House, a statement explaining the circumstances that had necessitated immediate legislation by ordinance should also be placed before the House.

So far, no case has gone to the Supreme Court regarding repromulgation of ordinance by the President.

But, the judgement of the Supreme Court in the *D C Wadhwa* case[14] (1987) is highly relevant here. In that case, the court pointed out that between 1967–1981 the Governor of Bihar promulgated 256 ordinances and all these were kept in force for periods ranging from one to fourteen years by repromulgation from time to time. The court ruled that successive repromulgation of ordinances with the same text without any attempt to get the bills passed by the assembly would amount to violation of the Constitution and the ordinance so repromulgated is liable to be struck down. It held that the exceptional power of law-making through ordinance cannot be used as a substitute for the legislative power of the state legislature.

PARDONING POWER OF THE PRESIDENT

Article 72 of the Constitution empowers the President to grant pardons to persons who have been tried and convicted of any offence in all cases where the:

1. Punishment or sentence is for an offence against a Union Law;
2. Punishment or sentence is by a court martial (military court); and
3. Sentence is a sentence of death.

The pardoning power of the President is independent of the Judiciary; it is an executive power. But, the President while exercising this power, does not sit as a court of appeal. The object of conferring this power on the President is two-fold: (a) to keep the door open for correcting any judicial errors in the operation of law; and, (b) to afford relief from a sentence, which the President regards as unduly harsh.

The pardoning power of the President includes the following:

1. Pardon It removes both the sentence and the conviction and completely absolves the convict from all sentences, punishments and disqualifications.

2. Commutation It denotes the substitution of one form of punishment for a lighter form. For example, a death sentence may be commuted to rigorous imprisonment, which in turn may be commuted to a simple imprisonment.

3. Remission It implies reducing the period of sentence without changing its character. For example, a sentence of rigorous imprisonment for two years may be remitted to rigorous imprisonment for one year.

4. Respite It denotes awarding a lesser sentence in place of one originally awarded due to some special fact, such as the physical disability of a convict or the pregnancy of a woman offender.

5. Reprieve It implies a stay of the execution of a sentence (especially that of death) for a temporary period. Its purpose is to enable the convict to have time to seek pardon or commutation from the President.

Under Article 161 of the Constitution, the governor of a state also possesses the pardoning power. Hence, the governor can also grant pardons, reprieves, respites and remissions of punishment or suspend, remit and commute the sentence of any person convicted of any offence against a state law. But, the pardoning power of the governor differs from that of the President in following two respects:

1. The President can pardon sentences inflicted by court martial (military courts) while the governor cannot.
2. The President can pardon death sentence while governor cannot. Even if a state law prescribes death sentence, the power to grant pardon lies with the President and not the governor. However, the governor can suspend, remit or commute a death sentence. In other words, both the governor and the President have concurrent power in respect of suspension, remission and commutation of death sentence.

The Supreme Court examined the pardoning power of the President under different cases and laid down the following principles:

1. The petitioner for mercy has no right to an oral hearing by the President.
2. The President can examine the evidence afresh and take a view different from the view taken by the court.
3. The power is to be exercised by the President on the advice of the union cabinet.
4. The President is not bound to give reasons for his order.
5. The President can afford relief not only from a sentence that he regards as unduly harsh but also from an evident mistake.
6. There is no need for the Supreme Court to lay down specific guidelines for the exercise of power by the President.
7. The exercise of power by the President is not subject to judicial review except where the presidential decision is arbitrary, irrational, *mala fide* or discriminatory.
8. Where the earlier petition for mercy has been rejected by the President, stay cannot be obtained by filing another petition.

CONSTITUTIONAL POSITION OF THE PRESIDENT

The Constitution of India has provided for a parliamentary form of government. Consequently, the President has been made only a nominal executive; the real executive being the council of ministers headed by the prime minister. In other words, the President has to exercise his powers and functions with the aid and advise of the council of ministers headed by the prime minister.

Dr B R Ambedkar summed up the true position of the President in the following way[15]:

"In the Indian Constitution, there is placed at the head of the Indian Union a functionary who is called the President of the Union. The title of the functionary reminds of the President of the United States. But beyond the identity of names, there is nothing in common between the form of government prevalent in America and the form of government adopted under the Indian Constitution. The American form of government is called the presidential system of government and what the Indian Constitution adopted is the Parliamentary system. Under the presidential system of America, the President is the Chief head of the Executive and administration is vested in him. Under the Indian Constitution, the President occupies the same position as the King under the English Constitution. He is the head of the State but not of the Executive. He represents the nation but does not rule the nation. He is the symbol of the nation. His place in administration is that of a ceremonial device or a seal by which the nation's decisions are made known. He is generally bound by the advice of his ministers. He can do nothing contrary to their advice nor can he do anything without their advice. The President of the United States can dismiss any secretary at any time. The President of the Indian Union has no power to do so, so long as his ministers command a majority in Parliament".

In estimating the constitutional position of the President, particular reference has to be made to the provisions of Articles 53, 74 and 75. These are:

1. The executive power of the Union shall be vested in President and shall be exercised by him either directly or through officers subordinate to him in accordance with this Constitution (Article 53).

2. There shall be a council of ministers with the Prime Minister at the head to aid and advise the President who 'shall', in the exercise of his functions, act in accordance with such advice (Article 74).

3. The council of ministers shall be collectively responsible to the Lok Sabha (Article 75). This provision is the foundation of the parliamentary system of government.

The 42nd Constitutional Amendment Act of 1976 (enacted by the Indira Gandhi Government) made the President bound by the advice of the council of ministers headed by the prime minister[16]. The 44th Constitutional Amendment Act of 1978 (enacted by the Janata Party Government headed by Morarji Desai) authorised the President to require the council of ministers to reconsider such advice either generally or otherwise. However, he 'shall' act in accordance with the advice tendered after such reconsideration. In other words, the President may return a matter once for reconsideration of his ministers, but the reconsidered advice shall be binding.

In October 1997, the cabinet recommended President K R Narayanan to impose President's Rule (under Article 356) in Uttar Pradesh. The President returned the matter for the reconsideration of the cabinet, which then decided not to move ahead in the matter. Hence, the BJP-led government under Kalyan Singh was saved. Again in September 1998, the President KR Narayanan returned a recommendation of the cabinet that sought the imposition of the President's Rule in Bihar. After a couple of months, the cabinet re-advised the same. It was only then that the President's Rule was imposed in Bihar, in February 1999.

Though the President has no constitutional discretion, he has some situational discretion. In other words, the President can act on his discretion (that is, without the advice of the ministers) under the following situations:

(i) Appointment of Prime Minister when no party has a clear majority in the Lok Sabha or when the Prime Minister in office dies suddenly and there is no obvious successor.

(ii) Dismissal of the council of ministers when it cannot prove the confidence of the Lok Sabha.

(iii) Dissolution of the Lok Sabha if the council of ministers has lost its majority.

Table 17.3 *Articles Related to President at a Glance*

Article No.	Subject-matter
52.	The President of India
53	Executive power of the Union
54.	Election of President
55.	Manner of election of President

(Contd.)

Article No.	Subject-matter
56.	Term of office of President
57.	Eligibility for re-election
58.	Qualifications for election as President
59.	Conditions of President's office
60.	Oath or affirmation by the President
61.	Procedure for impeachment of the President
62.	Time of holding election to fill vacancy in the office of President
65.	Vice-President to act as President or to discharge his functions
71.	Matters relating to the election of President
72.	Power of President to grant pardons etc., and to suspend, remit or commute sentences in certain cases
74.	Council of ministers to aid and advise the President
75.	Other provisions as to ministers like appointment, term, salaries, etc.
76.	Attorney-General of India
77.	Conduct of business of the Government of India
78.	Duties of Prime Minister in respect to furnishing of information to the President, etc.
85.	Sessions of Parliament, prorogation and dissolution
111.	Assent to bills passed by the Parliament
112.	Union Budget (annual financial statement)
123.	Power of President to promulagate ordinances
143.	Power of President to consult Supreme Court

NOTES AND REFERENCES

1. This provision was added by the 70th Constitutional Amendment Act of 1992 with effect from June 1, 1995.
2. According to the 84th Constitutional Amendment Act of 2001, the expression 'population' means the population as ascertained at the 1971 census, until the relevant figures for the first census taken after 2026 have been published.
3. *Constituent Assembly Debates*, Volume-IV, p. 733–736.
4. The presidential and vice-presidential Elections Act of 1952, as amended in 1997.
5. The President's Emoluments and Pension Amendment Act of 2008.
6. No person except Dr Rajendra Prasad has occupied the office for two terms.
7. So far two Presidents, Dr Zakir Hussain and Fakhruddin Ali Ahmed, have died during their term of office.
8. For example, when President Dr Zakir Hussain died in May, 1969, the then Vice-President, VV Giri was acting as the President. Soon after VV Giri resigned to contest the election of the President. Then the Chief Justice of India, M Hidayatullah worked as the officiating President from 20 July, 1969 to 24 August, 1969.
9. For details in this regard, see Chapter 16.
10. 'Veto' is a Latin word that connotes 'forbid'.
11. *Cooper* v. *Union of India*, (1970).
12. The definition of 'law' contained in Article 13 expressly includes ordinances. See, Chapter 7.
13. *Constituent Assembly Debates*, Volume VIII, p. 213.
14. *D.C. Wadhwa* v. *State of Bihar*, (1987).
15. *Constituent Assembly Debates*, Volume VII, p. 32–34.
16. In the original Constitution, there was no such specific provision in Article 74.

Vice-President

The Vice-President occupies the second highest office in the country. He is accorded a rank next to the President in the official warrant of precedence. This office is modelled on the lines of the American Vice-President.

ELECTION

The Vice-President, like the president, is elected not directly by the people but by the method of indirect election. He is elected by the members of an electoral college consisting of the members of both Houses of Parliament.[1] Thus, this electoral college is different from the electoral college for the election of the President in the following two respects:

1. It consists of both elected and nominated members of the Parliament (in the case of president, only elected members).
2. It does not include the members of the state legislative assemblies (in the case of President, the elected members of the state legislative assemblies are included). Explaining the reason for this difference, Dr B R Ambedkar observed:[2]

"The President is the head of the State and his power extends both to the administration by the Centre as well as to the states. Consequently, it is necessary that in his election, not only members of Parliament should play their part, but the members of the state legislatures should have a voice. But, when we come to the Vice-President, his normal functions are to preside over the council of states. It is only on a rare occasion, and that too for a temporary period, that he may be called upon to assume the duties of the president. That being so, it does not seem necessary that the members of the state legislatures should also be invited to take part in the election of the Vice-President".

But, the manner of election is same in both the cases. Thus, the Vice-President's election, like that of the President's election, is held in accordance with the system of proportional representation by means of the single transferable vote and the voting is by secret ballot.[3]

QUALIFICATIONS

To be eligible for election as Vice-President, a person should fulfil the following qualifications:

1. He should be a citizen of India.
2. He should have completed 35 years of age.
3. He should be qualified for election as a member of the Rajya Sabha.
4. He should not hold any office of profit under the Union government or any state government or any local authority or any other public authority.

Table 18.1 *Elections of the Vice-Presidents (1952–2012)*

Sl. No.	Election Year	Victorious Candidate	No. of Votes secured	Runner-up Candidate	No. of Votes secured
1.	1952	Dr. S. Radhakrishnan	—	Unopposed	—
2.	1957	Dr. S. Radhakrishnan	—	Unopposed	—
3.	1962	Dr. Zakir Hussain	568	N. Samant Singh	14
4.	1967	V.V. Giri	486	Prof. Habib	192
5.	1969	G.S. Pathak	400	H.V. Kamath	156
6.	1974	B.D. Jatti	521	N.E. Horo	141
7.	1979	M. Hidaytullah	—	unopposed	—
8.	1984	R. Venkataraman	508	B.C. Kambley	207
9.	1987	Dr. Shankar Dayal Sharma	—	unopposed	—
10.	1992	K.R. Narayanan	700	Kaka Joginder Singh	01
11.	1997	Krishna Kant	441	Surjeet Singh Barnala	273
12.	2002	B.S. Shekhawat	454	Shushil Kumar Shinde	305
13.	2007	Mohd. Hamid Ansari	455	Najma Heptullah	222
14.	2012	Mohd. Hamid Ansari	490	Jaswant Singh	238

But, a sitting President or Vice-President of the Union, the governor of any state and a minister for the Union or any state is not deemed to hold any office of profit and hence qualified for being a candidate for Vice-President.

Further, the nomination of a candidate for election to the office of Vice-President must be subscribed by at least 20 electors as proposers and 20 electors as seconders. Every candidate has to make a security deposit of ₹15,000 in the Reserve Bank of India.[4]

OATH OR AFFIRMATION

Before entering upon his office, the Vice-President has to make and subscribe to an oath or affirmation. In his oath, the Vice-President swears:

1. to bear true faith and allegiance to the Constitution of India; and
2. to faithfully discharge the duties of his office.

The oath of office to the Vice-President is administered by the President or some person appointed in that behalf by him.

CONDITIONS OF OFFICE

The Constitution lays down the following two conditions of the Vice-President's office:

1. He should not be a member of either House of Parliament or a House of the state legislature. If any such person is elected Vice-President, he is deemed to have vacated his seat in that House on the date on which he enters upon his office as Vice-President.
2. He should not hold any other office of profit.

TERM OF OFFICE

The Vice-President holds office for a term of five years from the date on which he enters upon his office. However, he can resign from his office at any time by addressing the resignation letter to the President. He can also be removed from the office before completion of his term. A formal impeachment is not required for his removal. He can be removed by a resolution of the Rajya Sabha passed by an absolute majority (ie, a majority of the total members of the House) and agreed to by the Lok Sabha. But, no such resolution can be moved unless at least 14 days' advance notice has been given. Notably, no ground has been mentioned in the Constitution for his removal.

The Vice-President can hold office beyond his term of five years until his successor assumes charge. He is also eligible for re-election to that office. He may be elected for any number of terms.[5]

VACANCY IN OFFICE

A vacancy in the Vice-President's office can occur in any of the following ways:

1. On the expiry of his tenure of five years.
2. By his resignation.
3. On his removal.
4. By his death.[6]
5. Otherwise, for example, when he becomes disqualified to hold office or when his election is declared void.

When the vacancy is going to be caused by the expiration of the term of the sitting vice-president, an election to fill the vacancy must be held before the expiration of the term.

If the office falls vacant by resignation, removal, death or otherwise, then election to fill the vacancy should be held as soon as possible after the occurrence of the vacancy. The newly-elected vice-president remains in office for a full term of five years from the date he assumes charge of his office.

ELECTION DISPUTES

All doubts and disputes in connection with election of the Vice-President are inquired into and decided by the Supreme Court whose decision is final. The election of a person as Vice-President cannot be challenged on the ground that the electoral college was incomplete (i.e., existence of any vacancy among the members of electoral college). If the election of a person as Vice-President is declared void by the Supreme Court, acts done by him before the date of such declaration of the Supreme Court are not invalidated (i.e., they continue to remain in force).

POWERS AND FUNCTIONS

The functions of Vice-President are two-fold:

1. He acts as the *ex-officio* Chairman of Rajya Sabha. In this capacity, his powers and functions are similar to those of the Speaker of Lok Sabha. In this respect, he resembles the American vice-president who also acts as the Chairman of the Senate—the Upper House of the American legislature.

2. He acts as President when a vacancy occurs in the office of the President due to his resignation, removal, death or otherwise.[7] He can act as President only for a maximum period of six months within which a new President has to be elected. Further, when the sitting President is unable to discharge his functions due to absence, illness or any other cause, the Vice-President discharges his functions until the President resumes his office.[8]

While acting as President or discharging the functions of President, the Vice-President does not perform the duties of the office of the chairman of Rajya Sabha. During this period, those duties are performed by the Deputy Chairman of Rajya Sabha.

INDIAN AND AMERICAN VICE-PRESIDENTS COMPARED

Though the office of the Indian Vice-President is modelled on the lines of the American Vice-President, there is a difference. The American Vice-President succeeds to the presidency when it falls vacant, and remains President for the unexpired term of his predecessor. The Indian Vice-President, on the other hand, does not assume the office of the President when it falls vacant for the unexpired term. He merely serves as an acting President until the new President assumes charge.

From the above it is clear that the Constitution has not assigned any significant function to the Vice-President in that capacity. Hence, some scholars call him 'His Superfluous Highness'. This office was created with a view to maintain the political continuity of the Indian State.

EMOLUMENTS

The Constitution has not fixed any emoluments for the Vice-President in that capacity. He draws his regular salary in his capacity as the *ex-officio* Chairman of the Rajya Sabha. In 2008, the Parliament increased the salary of the Chairman of the Rajya Sabha from ₹ 40,000 to ₹ 1.25 lakh per month[9]. In addition, he is entitled to daily allowance, free furnished residence, medical, travel and other facilities.

During any period when the Vice-President acts as President or discharges the functions of the President, he is not entitled to the salary or allowance payable to the Chairman of Rajya Sabha, but the salary and allowance of the President.

Table 18.2 Articles Related to Vice-President at a Glance

Article No.	Subject-matter
63.	The Vice-President of India
64.	The Vice-President to be ex-officio Chairman of the Council of States
65.	The Vice-President to act as President or to discharge his functions during casual vacancies in the office, or during the absence, of President
66.	Election of Vice-President
67.	Term of office of Vice-President
68.	Time of holding election to fill vacancy in the office of Vice-President and the term of office of person elected to fill casual vacancy
69.	Oath or affirmation by the Vice-President
70.	Discharge of President's functions in other contingencies
71.	Matters relating to, or connected with, the election of Vice-President

NOTES AND REFERENCES

1. The original Constitution provided that the Vice-President would be elected by the two Houses of Parliament assembled at a joint meeting. This cumbersome procedure was done away by the 11th Constitutional Amendment Act of 1961.
2. *Constituent Assembly Debates,* Volume VII, p. 1001.
3. This method is discussed in Chapter 17.
4. Presidential and Vice-Presidential Elections Act, 1952 as amended in 1997.
5. Dr S Radhakrishnan was elected for a second term.
6. Krishna Kant was the first Vice-President to die in office.
7. When two Presidents, Dr Zakir Hussain and Fakruddin Ali Ahmed, died in office, the then respective Vice-Presidents, V V Giri and B D Jatti acted as President.
8. The Vice-President Dr S Radhakrishnan discharged the functions of the President in June 1960 when the then President Dr Rajendra Prasad was on a 15-day tour to the USSR and again in July 1961 when he (Dr Rajendra Prasad) was very ill.
9. The Salaries and Allowances of Officers of Parliament (Amendment) Act, 2008.

Prime Minister

In the scheme of parliamentary system of government provided by the constitution, the President is the nominal executive authority (*de jure* executive) and Prime Minister is the real executive authority (*de facto* executive). In other words, president is the head of the State while Prime Minister is the head of the government.

APPOINTMENT OF THE PRIME MINISTER

The Constitution does not contain any specific procedure for the selection and appointment of the Prime Minister. Article 75 says only that the Prime Minister shall be appointed by the president. However, this does not imply that the president is free to appoint any one as the Prime Minister. In accordance with the conventions of the parliamentary system of government, the President has to appoint the leader of the majority party in the Lok Sabha as the Prime Minister. But, when no party has a clear majority in the Lok Sabha, then the President may exercise his personal discretion in the selection and appointment of the Prime Minister. In such a situation, the President usually appoints the leader of the largest party or coalition in the Lok Sabha as the Prime Minister and asks him to seek a vote of confidence in the House within a month. This discretion was exercised by the President, for the first time in 1979, when Neelam Sanjiva Reddy (the then President) appointed Charan Singh (the coalition leader) as the Prime Minister after the fall of the Janata Party government headed by Morarji Desai.

There is also one more situation when the president may have to exercise his individual judgement in the selection and appointment of the Prime Minister, that is, when the Prime Minister in office dies suddenly and there is no obvious successor. This is what happened when Indira Gandhi was assassinated in 1984. The then President Zail Singh appointed Rajiv Gandhi as the Prime Minister by ignoring the precedent of appointing a caretaker Prime Minister.[1] Later on, the Congress parliamentary party unanimously elected him as its leader. However, if, on the death of an incumbent Prime Minister, the ruling party elects a new leader, the President has no choice but to appoint him as Prime Minister.

In 1980, the Delhi High Court held that the Constitution does not require that a person must prove his majority in the Lok Sabha before he is appointed as the Prime Minister. The President may first appoint him the Prime Minister and then ask him to prove his majority in the Lok Sabha within a reasonable period. For example, Charan Singh (1979), VP Singh (1989), Chandrasekhar (1990), PV Narasimha Rao (1991), AB Vajyapee (1996), Deve Gowda (1996), IK Gujral (1997) and again AB Vajpayee (1998) were appointed as Prime Ministers in this way.

In 1997, the Supreme Court held that a person who is not a member of either House of Parliament can be appointed as Prime Minister for six months, within which, he should become a member of either House of Parliament; otherwise, he ceases to be the Prime Minister.

Constitutionally, the Prime Minister may be a member of any of the two Houses of parliament. For example, three Prime Ministers, Indira Gandhi (1966), Deve Gowda (1996) and Manmohan Singh (2004), were members of the Rajya Sabha. In Britain, on the other hand, the Prime Minister should definitely be a member of the Lower House (House of Commons).

OATH, TERM AND SALARY

Before the Prime Minister enters upon his office, the president administers to him the oaths of office and secrecy.[2] In his oath of office, the Prime Minister swears:

1. to bear true faith and allegiance to the Constitution of India,
2. to uphold the sovereignty and integrity of India,
3. to faithfully and conscientiously discharge the duties of his office, and
4. to do right to all manner of people in accordance with the Constitution and the law, without fear or favour, affection or ill will.

In his oath of secrecy, the Prime Minister swears that he will not directly or indirectly communicate or reveal to any person(s) any matter that is brought under his consideration or becomes known to him as a Union Minister except as may be required for the due discharge of his duties as such minister.

The term of the Prime Minister is not fixed and he holds office during the pleasure of the president. However, this does not mean that the president can dismiss the Prime Minister at any time. So long as the Prime Minister enjoys the majority support in the Lok Sabha, he cannot be dismissed by the President. However, if he loses the confidence of the Lok Sabha, he must resign or the President can dismiss him.[3]

The salary and allowances of the Prime Minister are determined by the Parliament from time to time. He gets the salary and allowances that are payable to a member of Parliament. Additionally, he gets a sumptuary allowance, free accommodation, travelling allowance, medical facilities, etc. In 2001, the Parliament increased his sumptuary allowance from ₹1,500 to ₹3,000 per month.

POWERS AND FUNCTIONS OF THE PRIME MINISTER

The powers and functions of Prime Minister can be studied under the following heads:

In Relation to Council of Ministers

The Prime Minister enjoys the following powers as head of the Union council of ministers:

1. He recommends persons who can be appointed as ministers by the president. The President can appoint only those persons as ministers who are recommended by the Prime Minister.
2. He allocates and reshuffles various portfolios among the ministers.
3. He can ask a minister to resign or advise the President to dismiss him in case of difference of opinion.
4. He presides over the meeting of council of ministers and influences its decisions.
5. He guides, directs, controls, and coordinates the activities of all the ministers.
6. He can bring about the collapse of the council of ministers by resigning from office.

Since the Prime Minister stands at the head of the council of ministers, the other ministers cannot function when the Prime Minister resigns or dies. In other words, the resignation or death of an incumbent Prime Minister automatically dissolves the council of ministers and thereby generates a vacuum. The resignation or death of any other minister, on the other hand, merely creates a vacancy which the Prime Minister may or may not like to fill.

In Relation to the President

The Prime Minister enjoys the following powers in relation to the President:

1. He is the principal channel of communication between the President and the council of ministers.[4] It is the duty of the prime minister :
   (a) to communicate to the President all decisions of the council of ministers relating to the administration of the affairs of the Union and proposals for legislation;

(b) to furnish such information relating to the administration of the affairs of the Union and proposals for legislation as the President may call for; and

(c) if the President so requires, to submit for the consideration of the council of ministers any matter on which a decision has been taken by a minister but which has not been considered by the council.

2. He advises the president with regard to the appointment of important officials like attorney general of India, Comptroller and Auditor General of India, chairman and members of the UPSC, election commissioners, chairman and members of the finance commission and so on.

In Relation to Parliament

The Prime Minister is the leader of the Lower House. In this capacity, he enjoys the following powers:

1. He advises the President with regard to summoning and proroguing of the sessions of the Parliament.
2. He can recommend dissolution of the Lok Sabha to President at any time.
3. He announces government policies on the floor of the House.

Other Powers & Functions

In addition to the above-mentioned three major roles, the Prime Minister has various other roles. These are:

1. He is the chairman of the Planning Commission, National Development Council, National Integration Council, Inter-State Council and National Water Resources Council.
2. He plays a significant role in shaping the foreign policy of the country.
3. He is the chief spokesman of the Union government.
4. He is the crisis manager-in-chief at the political level during emergencies.
5. As a leader of the nation, he meets various sections of people in different states and receives memoranda from them regarding their problems, and so on.
6. He is leader of the party in power.
7. He is political head of the services.

Thus, the Prime Minister plays a very significant and highly crucial role in the politico-administrative system of the country. Dr B R Ambedkar stated, 'If any functionary under our constitution is to be compared with the US president, he is the Prime Minister and not the president of the Union'.

Role Descriptions

The various comments made by the eminent political scientists and constitutional experts on the role of Prime Minister in Britain holds good in the Indian context also. These are mentioned below:

Lord Morely He described Prime Minister as 'primus inter pares' (first among equals) and 'key stone of the cabinet arch'. He said, "The head of the cabinet is 'primus inter pares', and occupied a position which so long as it lasts, is one of exceptional and peculiar authority".

Herbert Marrison "As the head of the Government, he (prime minister) is 'primus inter pares'. But, it is today for too modest an appreciation of the Prime Minister's position".

Sir William Vernor Harcourt He described Prime Minister as 'inter stellas luna minores' (a moon among lesser stars).

Jennings "He is, rather, a sun around which planets revolve. He is the key-stone of the constitution. All roads in the constitution lead to the Prime Minister."

H.J. Laski On the relationship between the Prime Minister and the cabinet, he said that the Prime Minister "is central to its formation, central to its life, and central to its death". He described him as "the pivot around which the entire governmental machinery revolves."

H.R.G. Greaves "The Government is the master of the country and he (Prime Minister) is the master of the Government."

Munro He called Prime Minister as "the captain of the ship of the state".

Ramsay Muir He described Prime Minister as "the steersman of steering wheel of the ship of the state."

The role of the Prime Minister in the British parliamentary government is so significant and crucial that observers like to call it a 'Prime Ministerial government.' Thus, R H Crossman says, 'The post-war epoch has been the final transformation of cabinet government into Prime Ministerial government.' Similarly, Humphrey Berkely points out, 'Parliament is not, in practice, sovereign. The parliamentary democracy has now collapsed at Westminster. The basic defect in the British system of governing is the super-ministerial powers of the Prime Minister.' The same description holds good to the Indian context too.

RELATIONSHIP WITH THE PRESIDENT

The following provisions of the Constitution deal with the relationship between the President and the Prime Minister:

1. Article 74 There shall be a council of ministers with the Prime Minister at the head to aid and advise the President who shall, in the exercise of his functions, act in accordance with such advice. However, the President may require the council of ministers to reconsider such advice and the President shall act in accordance with the advice tendered after such reconsideration.

2. Article 75 (a) The Prime Minister shall be appointed by the President and the other ministers shall be appointed by the president on the advice of the Prime Minister; (b) The ministers shall hold office during the pleasure of the president; and (c) The council of ministers shall be collectively responsible to the House of the People.

3. Article 78 It shall be the duty of the Prime Minister:

  (a) to communicate to the President all decisions of the council of ministers relating to the administration of the affairs of the Union and proposals for legislation;

  (b) to furnish such information relating to the administration of the affairs of the Union and proposals for legislation as the President may call for; and

  (c) if the President so requires, to submit for the consideration of the council of ministers any matter on which a decision has been taken by a minister but which has not been considered by the council.

CHIEF MINISTERS WHO BECAME PRIME MINISTERS

Five people—Morarji Desai, Charan Singh, V.P. Singh, P.V. Narasimha Rao and H.D. Deve Gowda—became Prime Ministers after being Chief Ministers of their respective States. Morarji Desai, Chief Minister of the erstwhile Bombay State during 1952–56, became the first non-Congress Prime Minister in March 1977. Charan Singh, who succeeded him, was the Chief Minister of the undivided Uttar Pradesh in 1967–1968 and again in 1970. V.P. Singh, also from U.P., became Prime Minister in the short lived National Front government (December 1989-November 1990). P.V. Narasimha Rao, the first Prime Minister from South India, who held the post from 1991–1996, was Chief Minister of Andhra Pradesh between 1971–1973. H.D. Deve Gowda was Chief Minister of Karnataka when he was chosen to lead the United Front government in June 1996[5].

Table 19.1 *Articles Related to Prime Minister at a Glance*

Article No.	Subject-matter
74.	Council of Ministers to aid and advise President
75.	Other provisions as to Ministers
77.	Conduct of business of the Government of India
78.	Duties of Prime Minister as respects the furnishing of information to the President, etc.

NOTES AND REFERENCES

1. On the death of Jawaharlal Nehru and Lal Bahadur Shastri when the leadership was contested, the president made temporary arrangements by appointing the seniormost minister as the Prime Minister, until the formal election of the leader by the party. Both the times, it was Gulzari Lal Nanda who acted as the Prime Minister.

2. The form of oath of office and secrecy for the Prime Minister is similar to that for any Union minister. See Chapter 20.

3. For example, VP Singh in 1990 and Deve Gowda in 1997 resigned after defeat in the Lok Sabha.

4. Article 78 specifically deals with this function of the Prime Minister.

5. The Hindu, April 6, 2009.

Central Council of Ministers

As the Constitution of India provides for a parliamentary system of government modelled on the British pattern, the council of ministers headed by the prime minister is the real executive authority is our politico-administrative system.

The principles of parliamentary system of government are not detailed in the Constitution, but two Articles (74 and 75) deal with them in a broad, sketchy and general manner. Article 74 deals with the status of the council of ministers while Article 75 deals with the appointment, tenure, responsibility, qualification, oath and salaries and allowances of the ministers.

CONSTITUTIONAL PROVISIONS

Article 74—Council of Ministers to aid and advise President

1. There shall be a Council of Ministers with the Prime Minister at the head to aid and advise the President who shall, in the exercise of his functions, act in accordance with such advice. However, the President may require the Council of Ministers to reconsider such advice and the President shall act in accordance with the advice tendered after such reconsideration.

2. The advice tendered by Ministers to the President shall not be inquired into in any court.

Article 75—Other Provisions as to Ministers

1. The Prime Minister shall be appointed by the President and the other Ministers shall be appointed by the President on the advice of the Prime Minister.

2. The total number of ministers, including the Prime Minister, in the Council of Ministers shall not exceed 15% of the total strength of the Lok Sabha. The provision was added by the 91st Amendment Act of 2003.

3. A member of either house of Parliament belonging to any political party who is disqualified on the ground of defection shall also be disqualified to be appointed as a minister. This provision was also added by the 91st Amendment Act of 2003.

4. The ministers shall hold office during the pleasure of the President.

5. The council of ministers shall be collectively responsible to the Lok Sabha.

6. The President shall administer the oaths of office and secrecy to a minister.

7. A minister who is not a member of the Parliament (either house) for any period of six consecutive months shall cease to be a minister.

8. The salaries and allowances of ministers shall be determined by the Parliament.

Article 77—Conduct of Business of the Government of India

1. All executive action of the Government of India shall be expressed to be taken in the name of the President.
2. Orders and other instruments made and executed in the name of the President shall be authenticated in such manner as may be specified in rules to be made by the President. Further, the validity of an order or instrument which is so authenticated shall not be called in question on the ground that it is not an order or instrument made or executed by the President.
3. The President shall make rules for the more convenient transaction of the business of the Government of India, and for the allocation among Ministers of the said business.

Article 78—Duties of Prime Minister

It shall be the duty of the Prime Minister
1. To communicate to the President all decisions of the Council of Ministers relating to the administration of the affairs of the Union and proposals for legislation
2. To furnish such information relating to the administration of the affairs of the Union and proposals for legislation as the President may call for
3. If the President so requires, to submit for the consideration of the Council of Ministers any matter on which a decision has been taken by a Minister but which has not been considered by the Council

NATURE OF ADVICE BY MINISTERS

Article 74 provides for a council of ministers with the Prime Minister at the head to aid and advise the President in the exercise of his functions. The 42nd and 44th Constitutional Amendment Acts have made the advice binding on the President.[1] Further, the nature of advice tendered by ministers to the President cannot be enquired by any court. This pro-

vision emphasises the intimate and the confidential relationship between the President and the ministers.

In 1971, the Supreme Court held that 'even after the dissolution of the Lok Sabha, the council of ministers does not cease to hold office. Article 74 is mandatory and, therefore, the president cannot exercise the executive power without the aid and advise of the council of ministers. Any exercise of executive power without the aid and advice will be unconstitutional as being violative of Article 74'. Again in 1974, the court held that 'wherever the Constitution requires the satisfaction of the President, the satisfaction is not the personal satisfaction of the President but it is the satisfaction of the council of ministers with whose aid and on whose advice the President exercises his powers and functions'.

APPOINTMENT OF MINISTERS

The Prime Minister is appointed by the President, while the other ministers are appointed by the President on the advice of the Prime Minister. This means that the President can appoint only those persons as ministers who are recommended by the Prime minister.

Usually, the members of Parliament, either Lok Sabha or Rajya Sabha, are appointed as ministers. A person who is not a member of either House of Parliament can also be appointed as a minister. But, within six months, he must become a member (either by election or by nomination) of either House of Parliament, otherwise, he ceases to be a minister.

A minister who is a member of one House of Parliament has the right to speak and to take part in the proceedings of the other House also, but he can vote only in the House of which he is a member.

Oath and Salary of Ministers

Before a minister enters upon his office, the president administers to him the oaths of office and secrecy. In his oath of office, the minister swears:
1. to bear true faith and allegiance to the Constitution of India,
2. to uphold the sovereignty and integrity of India,
3. to faithfully and conscientiously discharge the duties of his office, and

4. to do right to all manner of people in accordance with the Constitution and the law, without fear or favour, affection or ill will.

In his oath of secrecy, the minister swears that he will not directly or indirectly communicate or reveal to any person(s) any matter that is brought under his consideration or becomes known to him as a Union minister except as may be required for the due discharge of his duties as such minister.

In 1990, the oath by Devi Lal as deputy prime minister was challenged as being unconstitutional as the Constitution provides only for the Prime Minister and ministers. The Supreme Court upheld the oath as valid and stated that describing a person as Deputy Prime Minister is descriptive only and such description does not confer on him any powers of Prime Minister. It ruled that the description of a minister as Deputy Prime Minister or any other type of minister such as minister of state or deputy minister of which there is no mention in the Constitution does not vitiate the oath taken by him so long as the substantive part of the oath is correct.

The salaries and allowances of ministers are determined by Parliament from time to time.[2] A minister gets the salary and allowances that are payable to a member of Parliament. Additionally, he gets a sumptuary allowance (according to his rank), free accommodation, travelling allowance, medical facilities, etc. In 2001, the sumptuary allowance for the prime minister was raised from ₹1,500 to ₹3,000 per month, for a cabinet minister from ₹1,000 to ₹2,000 per month, for a minister of state from ₹500 to ₹1,000 per month and for a deputy minister from ₹300 to ₹600 per month.

RESPONSIBILITY OF MINISTERS

Collective Responsibility

The fundamental principle underlying the working of parliamentary system of government is the principle of collective responsibility. Article 75 clearly states that the council of ministers is collectively responsible to the Lok Sabha. This means that all the ministers own joint responsibility to the Lok Sabha for all their acts of ommission and commission. They work as a team and swim or sink together. When the Lok Sabha passes a no-confidence motion against the council of ministers, all the ministers have to resign including those ministers who are from the Rajya Sabha.[3] Alternatively, the council of ministers can advise the president to dissolve the Lok Sabha on the ground that the House does not represent the views of the electorate faithfully and call for fresh elections. The President may not oblige the council of ministers that has lost the confidence of the Lok Sabha.

The principle of collective responsibility also means that the Cabinet decisions bind all cabinet ministers (and other ministers) even if they differed in the cabinet meeting. It is the duty of every minister to stand by cabinet decisions and support them both within and outside the Parliament. If any minister disagrees with a cabinet decision and is not prepared to defend it, he must resign. Several ministers have resigned in the past owing to their differences with the cabinet. For example, Dr BR Ambedkar resigned because of his differences with his colleagues on the Hindu Code Bill in 1953. CD Deshmukh resigned due to his differences on the policy of reorganisation of states. Arif Mohammed resigned due to his opposition to the Muslim Women (Protection of Rights on Divorce) Act, 1986.

Individual Responsibility

Article 75 also contains the principle of individual responsibility. It states that the ministers hold office during the pleasure of the president, which means that the President can remove a minister even at a time when the council of ministers enjoys the confidence of the Lok Sabha. However, the President removes a minister only on the advice of the Prime Minister. In case of a difference of opinion or dissatisfaction with the performance of a minister, the Prime Minister can ask him to resign or advice the President to dismiss him. By exercising this power, the Prime Minister can ensure the realisation of the rule of collective responsibility. In this context, Dr B R Ambedkar observed:

"Collective responsibility can be achieved only through the instrumentality of the Prime Minister. Therefore, unless and until we create that office and endow that office with statutory authority to nominate and dismiss ministers, there can be no collective responsibility."[4]

No Legal Responsibility

In Britain, every order of the King for any public act is countersigned by a minister. If the order is in violation of any law, the minister would be held responsible and would be liable in the court. The legally accepted phrase in Britain is, "The king can do no wrong." Hence, he cannot be sued in any court.

In India, on the other hand, there is no provision in the Constitution for the system of legal responsibility of a minister. It is not required that an order of the President for a public act should be countersigned by a minister. Moreover, the courts are barred from enquiring into the nature of advice rendered by the ministers to the president.

COMPOSITION OF THE COUNCIL OF MINISTERS

The council of ministers consists of three categories of ministers, namely, cabinet ministers, ministers of state,[5] and deputy ministers. The difference between them lies in their respective ranks, emoluments, and political importance. At the top of all these ministers stands the Prime Minister—the supreme governing authority of the country.

The cabinet ministers head the important ministries of the Central government like home, defence, finance, external affairs and so forth. They are members of the cabinet, attend its meetings and play an important role in deciding policies. Thus, their responsibilities extend over the entire gamut of Central government.

The ministers of state can either be given independent charge of ministries/departments or can be attached to cabinet ministers. In case of attachment, they may either be given the charge of departments of the ministries headed by the cabinet ministers or allotted specific items of work related to the ministries headed by cabinet ministers. In both the cases, they work under the supervision and guidance as well as under the overall charge and responsibility of the cabinet ministers. In case of independent charge, they perform the same functions and exercise the same powers in relation to their ministries/departments as cabinet ministers do. However, they are not members of the cabinet and do not attend the cabinet meetings unless specially invited when something related to their ministries/departments are considered by the cabinet.

Next in rank are the deputy ministers. They are not given independent charge of ministries/departments. They are attached to the cabinet ministers or ministers of state and assist them in their administrative, political, and parliamentary duties. They are not members of the cabinet and do not attend cabinet meetings.

It must also be mentioned here that there is one more category of ministers, called parliamentary secretaries. They are the members of the last category of the council of ministers (which is also known as the 'ministry'). They have no department under their control. They are attached to the senior ministers and assist them in the discharge of their parliamentary duties. However, since 1967, no parliamentary secretaries have been appointed except during the first phase of Rajiv Gandhi Government.

At times, the council of ministers may also include a deputy prime minister. Thus Sardar Patel in Pandit Nehru's ministry, Morarji Desai in the Indira Gandhi's Ministry, Charan Singh in the Morarji Desai's ministry, Jagjivan Ram in the Charan Singh's ministry, Devi Lal in the VP Singh's ministry and L.K. Advani in the AB Vajpayee's ministry served as deputy prime ministers. The deputy prime ministers are appointed mostly for political reasons.

COUNCIL OF MINISTERS VS CABINET

The words 'council of ministers' and 'cabinet' are often used interchangeably though there is a definite distinction between them. They differ from each other in respects of composition, functions, and role. These differences are shown in Table 20.1.

ROLE OF CABINET

1. It is the highest decision-making authority in our politico-administrative system.
2. It is the chief policy formulating body of the Central government.
3. It is the supreme executive authority of the Central government.
4. It is chief coordinator of Central administration.
5. It is an advisory body to the president and its advice is binding on him.

Table 20.1 *Distinction Between Council of Ministers and Cabinet*

Council of ministers	Cabinet
1. It is a wider body consisting of 60 to 70 ministers.	1. It is a smaller body consisting of 15 to 20 ministers.
2. It includes all the three categories of ministers, that is, cabinet ministers, ministers of state, and deputy ministers.	2. It includes the cabinet ministers only. Thus, it is a part of the council of ministers.
3. It does not meet, as a body, to transact government business. It has no collective functions.	3. It meets, as a body, frequently and usually once in a week to deliberate and take decisions regarding the transaction of government business. Thus, it has collective functions.
4. It is vested with all powers but in theory.	4. It exercises, in practice, the powers of the council of ministers and thus, acts for the latter.
5. Its functions are determined by the cabinet.	5. It directs the council of ministers by taking policy decisions which are binding on all ministers.
6. It implements the decisions taken by the cabinet.	6. It supervises the implementation of its decisions by the council of ministers.
7. It is a constitutional body, dealt in detail by the Articles 74 and 75 of the Constitution. Its size and classification are, however, not mentioned in the Constitution. Its size is determined by the prime minister according to the exigencies of the time and requirements of the situation. Its classification into a three-tier body is based on the conventions of parliamentary government as developed in Britain. It has, however, got a legislative sanction. Thus, the Salaries and Allowances Act of 1952 defines a 'minister' as a 'member of the council of ministers, by whatever name called, and includes a deputy minister'.	7. It was inserted in Article 352 of the Constitution in 1978 by the 44th Constitutional Amendment Act. Thus, it did not find a place in the original text of the Constitution. Now also, Article 352 only defines the cabinet saying that it is 'the council consisting of the prime minister and other ministers of cabinet rank appointed under Article 75' and does not describe its powers and functions. In other words, its role in our politico-administrative system is based on the conventions of parliamentary government as developed in Britain.
8. It is collectively responsible to the Lower House of the Parliament.	8. It enforces the collective responsibility of the council of ministers to the Lower House of Parliament.

6. It is the chief crisis manager and thus deals with all emergency situations.

7. It deals with all major legislative and financial matters.

8. It exercises control over higher appointments like constitutional authorities and senior secretariat administrators.

9. It deals with all foreign policies and foreign affairs.

ROLE DESCRIPTIONS

The various comments made by the eminent political scientists and constitutional experts on the role of cabinet in Britain holds good in the Indian context also. These are mentioned below.

Ramsay Muir "The Cabinet is the steering wheel of the ship of the state."

Lowell "The Cabinet is the keystone of the political arch".

Sir John Marriott "The Cabinet is the pivot around which the whole political machinery revolves".

Gladstone "The Cabinet is the solar orb around which the other bodies revolve".

Barker "The Cabinet is the magnet of policy".

Bagehot "The Cabinet is a hyphen that joins, the buckle that binds the executive and legislative departments together".

Sir Ivor Jennings "The Cabinet is the core of the British Constitutional System. It provides unity to the British system of Government".

L.S. Amery "The Cabinet is the central directing instrument of Government".

The position of the Cabinet in the British Government has become so strong that Ramsay Muir referred to it as the 'Dictatorship of the Cabinet'. In his book *'How Britain is Governed'*, he writes "A body which wields such powers as these may fairly be described as 'omnipotent' in theory, however, incapable it may be of using its omnipotence. Its position, whenever it commands a majority, is a dictatorship only qualified by publicity. This dictatorship is far more absolute that it was two generations ago". The same description holds good in the Indian context too.

KITCHEN CABINET

The cabinet, a small body consisting of the prime minister as its head and some 15 to 20 most important ministers, is the highest decision-making body in the formal sense. However, a still smaller body called the 'inner Cabinet' or 'Kitchen Cabinet' has become the real centre of power. This informal body consists of the Prime Minister and two to four influential colleagues in whom he has faith and with whom he can discuss every problem. It advises the prime minister on important political and administrative issues and assists him in making crucial decisions. It is composed of not only cabinet ministers but also outsiders like friends and family members of the prime minister.

Every prime minister in India has had his 'Inner Cabinet'—a circle within a circle. Prime Minister Jawaharlal Nehru's 'Inner Cabinet' consisted of Sardar Patel, Maulana Azad, Gopalaswamy Ayyangar, and Kidwai. Lal Bahadur Shastri relied upon YB Chavan, Swaran Singh, and GL Nanda. During the era of Indira Gandhi, the 'Inner Cabinet' which came to be called the 'Kitchen Cabinet' was particularly powerful and consisted of persons like YB Chavan, Uma Shanker Dixit, Fakhruddin Ali Ahmed, Dr Karan Singh and others. AB Vajpayee's 'inner cabinet' consisted of LK Advani, George Fernandes, MM Joshi, Pramod Mahajan, and so on.

The prime ministers have resorted to the device of 'inner cabinet' (extra-constitutional body) due to its merits, namely:

1. It being a small unit, is much more efficient decision-making body than a large cabinet.
2. It can meet more often and deal with business much more expeditiously than the large cabinet.
3. It helps the Prime Minister in maintaining secrecy in making decisions on important political issues.

However, it has many demerits also. Thus,[6]

1. It reduces the authority and status of the cabinet as the highest decision-making body.
2. It circumvents the legal process by allowing outside persons to play an influential role in the government functioning.

The phenomenon of 'kitchen cabinet' (where decisions are cooked and placed before the cabinet for formal approval) is not unique to India. It also exists in USA and Britain and is quite powerful in influencing government decisions there.

Table 20.2 *Articles Related to Central Council of Ministers at a Glance*

Article No.	Subject-matter
74.	Council of Ministers to aid and advise President
75.	Other provisions as to Ministers
77.	Conduct of business of the Government of India
78.	Duties of Prime Minister as respects the furnishing of information to the President, etc.

NOTES AND REFERENCES

1. This Article was amended by the 42nd Constitutional Amendment Act of 1976 to the effect that the president shall, in the exercise of his functions, act in accordance with the advice rendered by the council of ministers. The 44th Constitutional Amendment Act of 1978 further added a proviso to this article to the effect that the president may require the council of ministers to reconsider such advice and the president shall act in accordance with the advice tendered after such reconsideration.

2. The Salaries and Allowances of Ministers Act, 1952, has been passed for this purpose.

3. Each minister need not resign separately; the resignation of the prime minister amounts to the resignation of the entire council of ministers.

4. *Constituent Assembly Debates*, Volume VIII, p. 1160

5. In 1952, the minister of state was given the new designation of 'Minister of Cabinet Rank'. But in 1957, the earlier designation was restored.

6. Avasthi and Avasthi, *Indian Administration*, Laksmi Narain Agarwal, First Edition, 1993, p. 79.

Cabinet Committees

FEATURES OF CABINET COMMITTEES

The following are the features of Cabinet Committees:

1. They are extra-constitutional in emergence. In other words, they are not mentioned in the Constitution. However, the Rules of Business provide for their establishment.
2. They are of two types—standing and *ad hoc*. The former are of a permanent nature while the latter are of a temporary nature. The *ad hoc* committees are constituted from time to time to deal with special problems. They are disbanded after their task is completed.[1]
3. They are set up by the Prime Minister according to the exigencies of the time and requirements of the situation. Hence, their number, nomenclature, and composition varies from time to time.
4. Their membership varies from three to eight. They usually include only Cabinet Ministers. However, the non-cabinet Ministers are not debarred from their membership.
5. They not only include the Ministers in charge of subjects covered by them but also include other senior Ministers.
6. They are mostly headed by the Prime Minister. Some times other Cabinet Ministers, particularly the Home Minister or the Finance Minister, also acts as their Chairman. But, in case the Prime Minister is a member of a committee, he invariably presides over it.
7. They not only sort out issues and formulate proposals for the consideration of the Cabinet, but also take decisions. However, the Cabinet can review their decisions.
8. They are an organisational device to reduce the enormous workload of the Cabinet. They also facilitate in-depth examination of policy issues and effective coordination. They are based on the principles of division of labour and effective delegation.

LIST OF CABINET COMMITTEES

In 1994, there were the following 13 Cabinet Committees:

1. Cabinet Committee on Political Affairs
2. Cabinet Committee on Natural Calamities
3. Cabinet Committee on Parliamentary Affairs
4. Appointments Committee of the Cabinet
5. Cabinet Committee on Accommodation
6. Cabinet Committee on Foreign Investment
7. Cabinet Committee on Drug Abuse Control
8. Cabinet Committee on Prices
9. Cabinet Committee on Minority Welfare
10. Cabinet Committee on Economic Affairs
11. Cabinet Committee on Trade and Investment
12. Cabinet Committee on Expenditure
13. Cabinet Committee on Infrastructure

At present (2013), the following 10 Cabinet Committees are functional:

1. Cabinet Committee on Economic Affairs
2. Cabinet Committee on Prices
3. Cabinet Committee on Political Affairs

4. Appointments Committee of the Cabinet
5. Cabinet Committee on Security
6. Cabinet Committee on World Trade Organisation (WTO) Matters
7. Cabinet Committee on Investment
8. Cabinet Committee on Unique Identification Authority of India (UIDAI) related issues
9. Cabinet Committee on Parliamentary Affairs
10. Cabinet Committee on Accommodation

FUNCTIONS OF CABINET COMMITTEES

The following four are the more important cabinet committees:

1. The Political Affairs Committee deals with all policy matters pertaining to domestic and foreign affairs.
2. The Economic Affairs Committee directs and coordinates the governmental activities in the economic sphere.
3. Appointments Committee decides all higher level appointments in the Central Secretariat, Public Enterprises, Banks and Financial Institutions.
4. Parliamentary Affairs Committee looks after the progress of government business in the Parliament.

The first three committees are chaired by the Prime Minister and the last one by the Home Minister. Of all the Cabinet Committees, the most powerful is the Political Affairs Committee, often described as a "Super-Cabinet".

GROUPS OF MINISTERS

In addition to cabinet committees, several Groups of Ministers (GoMs) have been constituted to look into different issues / subjects. Some of these GoMs have been empowered to take decisions on behalf of the Cabinet whereas the others make recommendations to the Cabinet.[2]

In the past two decades, the institution of GoMs has become a viable and effective instrument of co-ordination among the ministries. These are *ad hoc* bodies formed to give recommendations to the cabinet on certain emergent issues and critical problem areas. Ministers heading the concerned ministries

are inducted into the relevant GoMs and when the advice is crystallised they are disbanded.[3]

As of now (in 2013), the following 21 Groups of Ministers (GoMs) are in existence:

1. Group of Ministers (GoM) for evolving an **integrated strategy for water management**
2. Group of Ministers (GoM) to consider the **reports of the Administrative Reforms Commission**
3. Group of Ministers (GoM) for the **civil aviation sector**
4. Group of Ministers (GoM) on **National Pharmaceuticals Policy**, 2006
5. Group of Ministers (GoM) on **power sector** issues
6. Group of Ministers (GoM) to examine various issues pertaining to the **functioning of the Prasar Bharati**
7. Group of Ministers (GoM) regarding **Bhopal Gas Leak Disaster**
8. Group of Ministers (GoM) to consider measures that can be taken by the Government to **tackle corruption**
9. Group of Ministers (GoM) to consider **environmental and developmental issues** relating to coal mining and other developmental projects
10. Group of Ministers (GoM) on **media**
11. Group of Ministers (GoM) to consider, and make recommendations with regard to reports of the high level committee on **Commonwealth Games**, 2010
12. Group of Ministers (GoM) to look into the constitution of an independent **regulatory authority for the coal sector** – approval for introducing the Coal Regulatory Authority Bill, 2012 in the Parliament
13. Group of Ministers (GoM) to look into the issue of inclusion of **erosion as an eligible calamity for relief** under National Disaster Response Fund (NDRF)/State Disaster Response Fund (SDRF)
14. Group of Ministers (GoM) to consider the **official amendments to the Land Acquisition, Rehabilitation and Resettlement Bill, 2011**
15. Group of Ministers (GoM) to formulate **policy for existing urea units** beyond Stage-III of New Pricing Scheme (NPS)

16. Group of Ministers (GoM) on **setting up of the National Skill Development Authority**
17. Group of Ministers (GoM) regarding **issue of Resident Identity Cards** to all usual residents of the country of age 18 years and above under the scheme of National Population Register (NPR)
18. Group of Ministers (GoM) to **consider the recommendations of the panel of experts on reforms in central public sector enterprises**
19. Group of Ministers (GoM) to consider **prescribing uniform terms and conditions of service** of chairpersons and members of quasi-judicial tribunals / commissions / regulatory bodies, etc
20. Group of Ministers (GoM) to consider and **suggest an appropriate cadre structure** for the Indian Revenue Service (Income Tax) and other support systems
21. Group of Ministers (GoM) to look into the matter of **reviving and revitalising** Bharat Sanchar Nigam Limited (BSNL) and Mahanagar Telephone Nigam Limited (MTNL)

Presently (2013), there are the following six Empowered Groups of Ministers (EGoMs):

1. Empowered Group of Ministers (EGoM) to decide the price band and final price of sale of shares held by Government of India in all central public sector enterprises
2. Empowered Group of Ministers (EGoM) on gas pricing and commercial utilisation of gas
3. Empowered Group of Ministers (EGoM) on ultra mega power projects
4. Empowered Group of Ministers (EGoM) on Mass Rapid Transit System (MRTS)
5. Empowered Group of Ministers (EGoM) on vacation of spectrum and auction of 3G spectrum, and to look into the grant of license and allocation of spectrum in 2G band in 22 service areas
6. Empowered Group of Ministers (EGoM) on drought

The Second Administrative Reforms Commission (2005-2009) made the following observations and recommendations with respect to the working of the GoMs[4]:

1. The Commission observed that the constitution of a large number of GoMs has resulted in many GoMs not being able to meet regularly to complete their work thus leading to significant delays on many major issues.
2. The Commission felt that more selective use of the institution of GoMs would perhaps lead to more effective coordination particularly if they are empowered to arrive at a decision on behalf of the Cabinet with time limits that are prescribed for completing the work entrusted to them.
3. The Commission recommended that there is need to ensure that the existing coordination mechanism of GoMs function effectively and helps in early resolution of issues. Selective, but effective use of GoMs with clear mandate and prescribed time limits would be helpful.

NOTES AND REFERENCES

1. For example, the Emergency Committee was set-up in 1962 after the Chinese invasion.
2. Second Administrative Reforms Commission, Government of India, Report on Organizational Structure of Government of India, 2009, P.136. This commission was headed by Veerappa Moily, a senior Congress leader and former Karnataka Chief Minister.
3. Ramesh K. Arora and Rajni Goyal, *Indian Public Administration*, New Age International Publishers, Third Edition, 2013, pp. 238-239.
4. Second Administrative Reforms Commission, Government of India, Report on Organisational Structure of Government of India, 2009, pp. 136-137 and 140.

Parliament

The Parliament is the legislative organ of the Union government. It occupies a pre-eminent and central position in the Indian democratic political system due to adoption of the parliamentary form of government, also known as 'Westminster' model of government[1].

Articles 79 to 122 in Part V of the Constitution deal with the organisation, composition, duration, officers, procedures, privileges, powers and so on of the Parliament.

ORGANISATION OF PARLIAMENT

Under the Constitution, the Parliament of India consists of three parts viz, the President, the Council of States and the House of the People. In 1954, the Hindi names 'Rajya Sabha' and 'Lok Sabha' were adopted by the Council of States and the House of People respectively. The Rajya Sabha is the Upper House (Second Chamber or House of Elders) and the Lok Sabha is the Lower House (First Chamber or Popular House). The former represents the states and union territories of the Indian Union, while the latter represents the people of India as a whole.

Though the President of India is not a member of either House of Parliament and does not sit in the Parliament to attend its meetings, he is an integral part of the Parliament. This is because a bill passed by both the Houses of Parliament cannot become law without the President's assent. He also performs certain functions relating to the proceedings of the Parliament, for example, he summons and pro-rogues both the Houses, dissolves the Lok Sabha, addresses both the Houses, issues ordinances when they are not in session, and so on.

In this respect, the framers of the Indian Constitution relied on the British pattern rather than the American pattern. In Britain, the Parliament consists of the Crown (King or Queen), the House of Lords (Upper House) and the House of Commons (Lower House). By contrast, the American president is not an integral part of the legislature. In USA, the legislature, which is known as Congress, consists of the Senate (Upper House) and the House of Representatives (Lower House).

The parliamentary form of government emphasises on the interdependence between the legislative and executive organs. Hence, we have the 'President-in-Parliament' like the 'Crown-in-Parliament' in Britain. The presidential form of government, on the other hand, lays stress on the separation of legislative and executive organs. Hence, *the American president is not regarded as a constituent part of the Congress.*

COMPOSITION OF THE TWO HOUSES

Composition of Rajya Sabha

The maximum strength of the Rajya Sabha is fixed at 250, out of which, 238 are to be the representatives of the states and union territories (elected indirectly) and 12 are nominated by the president.

At present, the Rajya Sabha has **245** members. Of these, 229 members represent the states, 4 members represent the union territories and 12 members are nominated by the president.

The Fourth Schedule of the Constitution deals with the allocation of seats in the Rajya Sabha to the states and union territories[2].

1. Representation of States The representatives of states in the Rajya Sabha are elected by the elected members of state legislative assemblies. The election is held in accordance with the system of proportional representation by means of the single transferable vote. The seats are allotted to the states in the Rajya Sabha on the basis of population. Hence, the number of representatives varies from state to state. For example, Uttar Pradesh has 31 members while Tripura has 1 member only. However, in USA, all states are given equal representation in the Senate irrespective of their population. USA has 50 states and the Senate has 100 members—2 from each state.

2. Representation of Union Territories The representatives of each union territory in the Rajya Sabha are indirectly elected by members of an electroral college specially constituted for the purpose. This election is also held in accordance with the system of proportional representation by means of the single transferable vote. Out of the seven union territories, only two (Delhi and Puducherry) have representation in Rajya Sabha. The populations of other five union territories are too small to have any representative in the Rajya Sabha.

3. Nominated Members The president nominates 12 members to the Rajya Sabha from people who have special knowledge or practical experience in art, literature, science and social service. The rationale behind this principle of nomination is to provide eminent persons a place in the Rajya Sabha without going through the process of election. It should be noted here that the American Senate has no nominated members.

Composition of Lok Sabha

The maximum strength of the Lok Sabha is fixed at 552. Out of this, 530 members are to be the representatives of the states, 20 members are to be the representatives of the union territories and 2 members are to be nominated by the president from the Anglo-Indian community[3].

At present, the Lok Sabha has 545 members. Of these, 530 members represent the states, 13 members represent the union territories and 2 Anglo-Indian members are nominated by the President[4].

1. Representation of States The representatives of states in the Lok Sabha are directly elected by the people from the territorial constituencies in the states. The election is based on the principle of universal adult franchise. Every Indian citizen who is above 18 years of age and who is not disqualified under the provisions of the Constitution or any law is eligible to vote at such election. The voting age was reduced from 21 to 18 years by the 61st Constitutional Amendment Act, 1988.

2. Representation of Union Territories The Constitution has empowered the Parliament to prescribe the manner of choosing the representatives of the union territories in the Lok Sabha. Accordingly, the Parliament has enacted the Union Territories (Direct Election to the House of the People) Act, 1965, by which the members of Lok Sabha from the union territories are also chosen by direct election.

3. Nominated Members The president can nominate two members from the Anglo-Indian community if the community is not adequately represented in the Lok Sabha. Originally, this provision was to operate till 1960 but has been extended till 2020 by the 95th Amendment Act, 2009.

SYSTEM OF ELECTIONS TO LOK SABHA

The various aspects related to the system of elections to the Lok Sabha are as follows:

Territorial Constituencies

For the purpose of holding direct elections to the Lok Sabha, each state is divided into territorial constituencies. In this respect, the Constitution makes the following two provisions:

1. Each state is allotted a number of seats in the Lok Sabha in such a manner that the ratio between that number and its population is the same for all states. This provision does not apply to a state having a population of less than six millions.

2. Each state is divided into territorial constituencies in such a manner that the ratio between

the population of each constituency and the number of seats allotted to it is the same throughout the state.

In brief, the Constitution ensures that there is uniformity of representation in two respects: (a) between the different states, and (b) between the different constituencies in the same state.

The expression 'population' means the population as ascertained at the preceding census of which the relevant figures have been published.

Readjustment after each Census

After every census, a readjustment is to be made in (a) allocation of seats in the Lok Sabha to the states, and (b) division of each state into territorial constituencies. Parliament is empowered to determine the authority and the manner in which it is to be made. Accordingly, the Parliament has enacted the Delimitation Commission Acts in 1952, 1962, 1972 and 2002 for this purpose.

The 42nd Amendment Act of 1976 froze the allocation of seats in the Lok Sabha to the states and the division of each state into territorial constituencies till the year 2000 at the 1971 level. This ban on readjustment was extended for another 25 years (ie, upto year 2026) by the 84th Amendment Act of 2001, with the same objective of encouraging population limiting measures.

The 84th Amendment Act of 2001 also empowered the government to undertake readjustment and rationalisation of territorial constituencies in the states on the basis of the population figures of 1991 census. Later, the 87th Amendment Act of 2003 provided for the delimitation of constituencies on the basis of 2001 census and not 1991 census. However, this can be done without altering the number of seats allotted to each state in the Lok Sabha.

Reservation of Seats for SCs and STs

Though the Constitution has abandoned the system of communal representation, it provides for the reservation of seats for scheduled castes and scheduled tribes in the Lok Sabha on the basis of population ratios[5].

Originally, this reservation was to operate for ten years (ie, up to 1960), but it has been extended continuously since then by 10 years each time. Now, under the 95th Amendment Act of 2009, this reservation is to last until 2020.

Though seats are reserved for scheduled castes and scheduled tribes, they are elected by all the voters in a constituency, without any separate electorate. A member of scheduled castes and scheduled tribes is also not debarred from contesting a general (non-reserved) seat.

The 84th Amendment Act of 2001 provided for refixing of the reserved seats on the basis of the population figures of 1991 census as applied to rationalisation of the general seats. Later, the 87th Amendment Act of 2003 provided for the refixing of the reserved seats on the basis of 2001 census and not 1991 census.

Proportional Representation not Adopted

Though the Constitution has adopted the system of proportional representation in the case of Rajya Sabha, it has not preferred the same system in the case of Lok Sabha. Instead, it has adopted the system of territorial representation for the election of members to the Lok Sabha.

Under territorial representation, every member of the legislature represents a geographical area known as a constituency. From each constituency, only one representative is elected. Hence such a constituency is known as single-member constituency. In this system, a candidate who secures majority of votes is declared elected. This simple majority system of representation does not represent the whole electorate. In other words, it does not secure due representation to minorities (small groups).

The system of proportional representation aims at removing the defects of territorial representation. Under this system, all sections of the people get representation in proportion to their number. Even the smallest section of the population gets its due share of representation in the legislature.

There are two kinds of proportional representation, namely, single transferable vote system and list system. In India, the first kind is adopted for the election of members to the Rajya Sabha and state legislative council and for electing the President and the Vice-President.

Though some members of the Constituent Assembly had advocated the system of proportional representation for the election of members to the Lok Sabha, the Constitution has not adopted the system due to two reasons.

1. Difficulty for the voters to understand the system (which is complicated) due to low literacy scale in the country.

2. Unsuitability to the parliamentary government due to the tendency of the system to multiply political parties leading to instability in government.

Additionally, the system of proportional representation has the following demerits:

1. It is highly expensive.
2. It does not give any scope for organising by-elections.
3. It eliminates intimate contacts between voters and representatives.
4. It promotes minority thinking and group interests.
5. It increases the significance of party system and decreases that of voter.

DURATION OF TWO HOUSES

Duration of Rajya Sabha

The Rajya Sabha (first constituted in 1952) is a continuing chamber, that is, it is a permanent body and not subject to dissolution. However, one-third of its members retire every second year. Their seats are filled up by fresh elections and presidential nominations at the beginning of every third year. The retiring members are eligible for re-election and renomination any number of times.

The Constitution has not fixed the term of office of members of the Rajya Sabha and left it to the Parliament. Accordingly, the Parliament in the Representation of the People Act (1951) provided that the term of office of a member of the Rajya Sabha shall be six years. The act also empowered the president of India to curtail the term of members chosen in the first Rajya Sabha. In the first batch, it was decided by lottery as to who should retire. Further, the act also authorised the President to make provisions to govern the order of retirement of the members of the Rajya Sabha[6].

Duration of Lok Sabha

Unlike the Rajya Sabha, the Lok Sabha is not a continuing chamber. Its normal term is five years from the date of its first meeting after the general elections, after which it automatically dissolves. However, the President is authorised to dissolve the Lok Sabha at any time even before the completion of five years and this cannot be challenged in a court of law.

Further, the term of the Lok Sabha can be extended during the period of national emergency be a law of Parliament for one year at a time[7] for any length of time. However, this extension cannot continue beyond a period of six months after the emergency has ceased to operate.

MEMBERSHIP OF PARLIAMENT

Qualifications

The Constitution lays down the following qualifications for a person to be chosen a member of the Parliament:

1. He must be a citizen of India.
2. He must make and subscribe to an oath or affirmation before the person authorised by the election commission for this purpose. In his oath or affirmation, he swears
   (a) To bear true faith and allegiance to the Constitution of India
   (b) To uphold the sovereignty and integrity of India
3. He must be not less than 30 years of age in the case of the Rajya Sabha and not less than 25 years of age in the case of the Lok Sabha.
4. He must posses other qualifications prescribed by Parliament.

The Parliament has laid down the following additional qualifications in the Representation of People Act (1951).

1. He must be registered as an elector for a parliamentary constituency. This is same in the case of both, the Rajya Sabha and the Lok Sabha. The requirement that a candidate contesting an election to the Rajya Sabha from a particular state should be an elector in that particular state was dispensed with in 2003. In 2006,

the Supreme Court upheld the constitutional validity of this change.

2. He must be a member of a scheduled caste or scheduled tribe in any state or union territory, if he wants to contest a seat reserved for them. However, a member of scheduled castes or scheduled tribes can also contest a seat not reserved for them.

Disqualifications

Under the Constitution, a person shall be disqualified for being elected as a member of Parliament:

1. if he holds any office of profit under the Union or state government (except that of a minister or any other office exempted by Parliament).[8]
2. if he is of unsound mind and stands so declared by a court.
3. if he is an undischarged insolvent.
4. if he is not a citizen of India or has voluntarily acquired the citizenship of a foreign state or is under any acknowledgement of allegiance to a foreign state; and
5. if he is so disqualified under any law made by Parliament.

The Parliament has laid down the following additional disqualifications in the Representation of People Act (1951):

1. He must not have been found guilty of certain election offences or corrupt practices in the elections.
2. He must not have been convicted for any offence resulting in imprisonment for two or more years. But, the detention of a person under a preventive detention law is not a disqualification.
3. He must not have failed to lodge an account of his election expenses within the time.
4. He must not have any interest in government contracts, works or services.
5. He must not be a director or managing agent nor hold an office of profit in a corporation in which the government has at least 25 per cent share.
6. He must not have been dismissed from government service for corruption or disloyalty to the State.
7. He must not have been convicted for promoting enmity between different groups or for the offence of bribery.

8. He must not have been punished for preaching and practising social crimes such as untouchability, dowry and sati.

On the question whether a member is subject to any of the above disqualifications, the president's decision is final. However, he should obtain the opinion of the election commission and act accordingly.

Disqualification on Ground of Defection The Constitution also lays down that a person shall be disqualified from being a member of Parliament if he is so disqualified on the ground of defection under the provisions of the Tenth Schedule. A member incurs disqualification under the defection law:

1. if he voluntary gives up the membership of the political party on whose ticket he is elected to the House;
2. if he votes or abstains from voting in the House contrary to any direction given by his political party;
3. if any independently elected member joins any political party; and
4. if any nominated member joins any political party after the expiry of six months.

The question of disqualification under the Tenth Schedule is decided by the Chairman in the case of Rajya Sabha and Speaker in the case of Lok Sabha (and not by the president of India). In 1992, the Supreme Court ruled that the decision of the Chairman/Speaker in this regard is subject to judicial review.

Vacating of Seats

In the following cases, a member of Parliament vacates his seat.

1. Double Membership A person cannot be a member of both Houses of Parliament at the same time. Thus, the Representation of People Act (1951) provides for the following:

(a) If a person is elected to both the Houses of Parliament, he must intimate within 10 days in which House he desires to serve. In default of such intimation, his seat in the Rajya Sabha becomes vacant.

(b) If a sitting member of one House is also elected to the other House, his seat in the first House becomes vacant.

(c) If a person is elected to two seats in a House, he should exercise his option for one. Otherwise, both seats become vacant.

Similarly, a person cannot be a member of both the Parliament and the state legislature at the same time. If a person is so elected, his seat in Parliament becomes vacant if he does not resign his seat in the state legislature within 14 days[9].

2. Disqualification If a member of Parliament becomes subject to any of the disqualifications specified in the Constitution, his seat becomes vacant. Here, the list of disqualifications also include the disqualification on the grounds of defection under the provisions of the Tenth Schedule of the Constitution.

3. Resignation A member may resign his seat by writing to the Chairman of Rajya Sabha or Speaker of Lok Sabha, as the case may be. The seat falls vacant when the resignation is accepted. However, the Chairman/Speaker may not accept the resignation if he is satisfied that it is not voluntary or genuine.

4. Absence A House can declare the seat of a member vacant if he is absent from all its meetings for a period of sixty days without its permission. In computing the period of sixty days, no account shall be taken of any period during which the House is prorogued or adjourned for more than four consecutive days.

5. Other cases A member has to vacate his seat in the Parliament:

(a) if his election is declared void by the court;
(b) if he is expelled by the House;
(c) if he is elected to the office of President or Vice-President; and
(d) if he is appointed to the office of governor of a state.

If a disqualified person is elected to the Parliament, the Constitution lays down no procedure to declare the election void. This matter is dealt by the Representation of the People Act (1951), which enables the high court to declare an election void if a disqualified candidate is elected. The aggrieved party can appeal to the Supreme Court against the order of the high court in this regard.

Oath or Affirmation

Every member of either House of Parliament, before taking his seat in the House, has to make and subscribe to an oath or affirmation before the President or some person appointed by him for this purpose. In his oath or affirmation, a member of Parliament swears:

1. to bear true faith and allegiance to the Constitution of India;
2. to uphold the sovereignty and integrity of India; and
3. to faithfully discharge the duty upon which he is about to enter.

Unless a member takes the oath, he cannot vote and participate in the proceedings of the House and does not become eligible to parliamentary privileges and immunities.

A person is liable to a penalty of Rs 500 for each day he sits or votes as a member in a House in the following conditions:

1. Before taking and subscribing to the prescribed oath or affirmation; or
2. When he knows that he is not qualified or that he is disqualified for its membership; or
3. When he knows that he is prohibited from sitting or voting in the House by virtue of any parliamentary law.

Salaries and Allowances

Members of either House of Parliament are entitled to receive such salaries and allowances as may be determined by Parliament, and there is no provision of pension in the Constitution. However, Parliament has provided pension to the members.

In 1954, the Parliament enacted the Salaries, Allowances and Pension of Members of Parliament Act. In 2010, the Parliament increased the salary of members from ₹ 16,000 to ₹ 50,000 per month, the constituency allowance from ₹ 20,000 to ₹ 45,000 per month, the daily allowance from ₹ 1,000 to ₹ 2,000 for five years and office expenses allowance from ₹ 20,000 to ₹ 45,000 per month.

From 1976, the members are also entitled to a pension on a graduated scale for each five-year-term as members of either House of Parliament. Besides, they are provided with travelling facilities, free accommodation, telephone, vehicle advance, medical facilities and so on.

The salaries and allowances of the Speaker of Lok Sabha and the Chairman of Rajya Sabha are also determined by Parliament. They are charged on the Consolidated Fund of India and thus are not subject to the annual vote of Parliament.

In 1953, the Parliament enacted the Salaries and Allowances of Officers of Parliament Act. Under this Act, the Parliament has fixed the salaries as well as allowances of both the Speaker and the Chairman.

PRESIDING OFFICERS OF PARLIAMENT

Each House of Parliament has its own presiding officer. There is a Speaker and a Deputy Speaker for the Lok Sabha and a Chairman and a Deputy Chairman for the Rajya Sabha. A panel of chairpersons for the Lok Sabha and a panel of vice-chairpersons for the Rajya Sabha is also appointed.

Speaker of Lok Sabha

Election and Tenure The Speaker is elected by the Lok Sabha from amongst its members (as soon as may be, after its first sitting). Whenever the office of the Speaker falls vacant, the Lok Sabha elects another member to fill the vacancy. The date of election of the Speaker is fixed by the President.

Usually, the Speaker remains in office during the life of the Lok Sabha. However, he has to vacate his office earlier in any of the following three cases:

1. if he ceases to be a member of the Lok Sabha;
2. if he resigns by writing to the Deputy Speaker; and
3. if he is removed by a resolution passed by a majority of all the members of the Lok Sabha. Such a resolution can be moved only after giving 14 days' advance notice.

When a resolution for the removal of the Speaker is under consideration of the House, he cannot preside at the sitting of the House, though he may be present. However, he can speak and take part in the proceedings of the House at such a time and vote in the first instance, though not in the case of an equality of votes.

It should be noted here that, whenever the Lok Sabha is dissolved, the Speaker does not vacate his office and continues till the newly-elected Lok Sabha meets.

Role, Powers and Functions The Speaker is the head of the Lok Sabha, and its representative.

He is the guardian of powers and privileges of the members, the House as a whole and its committees. He is the principal spokesman of the House, and his decision in all Parliamentary matters is final. He is thus much more than merely the presiding officer of the Lok Sabha. In these capacities, he is vested with vast, varied and vital responsibilities and enjoys great honour, high dignity and supreme authority within the House.

The Speaker of the Lok Sabha derives his powers and duties from three sources, that is, the Constitution of India, the Rules of Procedure and Conduct of Business of Lok Sabha, and Parliamentary Conventions (residuary powers that are unwritten or unspecified in the Rules). Altogether, he has the following powers and duties:

1. He maintains order and decorum in the House for conducting its business and regulating its proceedings. This is his primary responsibility and he has final power in this regard.
2. He is the final interpreter of the provisions of (a) the Constitution of India, (b) the Rules of Procedure and Conduct of Business of Lok Sabha, and (c) the parliamentary precedents, within the House.
3. He adjourns the House or suspends the meeting in absence of a quorum. The quorum to constitute a meeting of the House is one-tenth of the total strength of the House.
4. He does not vote in the first instance. But he can exercise a casting vote in the case of a tie. In other words, only when the House is divided equally on any question, the Speaker is entitled to vote. Such vote is called casting vote, and its purpose is to resolve a deadlock.
5. He presides over a joint setting of the two Houses of Parliament. Such a sitting is summoned by the President to settle a deadlock between the two Houses on a bill.
6. He can allow a 'secret' sitting of the House at the request of the Leader of the House. When the House sits in secret, no stranger can be present in the chamber, lobby or galleries except with the permission of the Speaker.
7. He decides whether a bill is a money bill or not and his decision on this question is final. When a money bill is transmitted to the Rajya

Sabha for recommendation and presented to the President for assent, the Speaker endorses on the bill his certificate that it is a money bill.

8. He decides the questions of disqualification of a member of the Lok Sabha, arising on the ground of defection under the provisions of the Tenth Schedule. In 1992, the Supreme Court ruled that the decision of the Speaker in this regard is subject to judicial review[10].

9. He acts as the *ex-officio* chairman of the Indian Parliamentary Group of the Inter-Parliamentary Union. He also acts as the *ex-officio* chairman of the conference of presiding officers of legislative bodies in the country.

10. He appoints the chairman of all the parliamentary committees of the Lok Sabha and supervises their functioning. He himself is the chairman of the Business Advisory Committee, the Rules Committee and the General Purpose Committee.

Independence and Impartiality

As the office of the Speaker is vested with great prestige, position and authority, independence and impartiality becomes its *sine qua non*[11].

The following provisions ensure the independence and impartiality of the office of the Speaker:

1. He is provided with a security of tenure. He can be removed only by a resolution passed by the Lok Sabha by an absolute majority (ie, a majority of the total members of the House) and not by an ordinary majority (ie, a majority of the members present and voting in the House). This motion of removal can be considered and discussed only when it has the support of at least 50 members.

2. His salaries and allowances are fixed by Parliament. They are charged on the Consolidated Fund of India and thus are not subject to the annual vote of Parliament.

3. His work and conduct cannot be discussed and criticised in the Lok Sabha except on a substantive motion.

4. His powers of regulating procedure or conducting business or maintaining order in the House are not subject to the jurisdiction of any Court.

5. He cannot vote in the first instance. He can only exercise a casting vote in the event of a tie. This makes the position of Speaker impartial.

6. He is given a very high position in the order of precedence. He is placed at seventh rank, along with the Chief Justice of India. This means, he has a higher rank than all cabinet ministers, except the Prime Minister or Deputy Prime Minister.

In Britain, the Speaker is strictly a non-party man. There is a convention that the Speaker has to resign from his party and remain politically neutral. This healthy convention is not fully established in India where the Speaker does not resign from the membership of his party on his election to the exalted office.

Deputy Speaker of Lok Sabha

Like the Speaker, the Deputy Speaker is also elected by the Lok Sabha itself from amongst its members. He is elected after the election of the Speaker has taken place. The date of election of the Deputy Speaker is fixed by the Speaker. Whenever the office of the Deputy Speaker falls vacant, the Lok Sabha elects another member to fill the vacancy.

Like the Speaker, the Deputy Speaker remains in office usually during the life of the Lok Sabha. However, he may vacate his office earlier in any of the following three cases:

1. if he ceases to be a member of the Lok Sabha;
2. if he resigns by writing to the Speaker; and
3. if he is removed by a resolution passed by a majority of all the members of the Lok Sabha. Such a resolution can be moved only after giving 14 days' advance notice.

The Deputy Speaker performs the duties of the Speaker's office when it is vacant. He also acts as the Speaker when the latter is absent from the sitting of the House. In both the cases, he assumes all the powers of the Speaker. He also presides over the joint sitting of both the Houses of Parliament, in case the Speaker is absent from such a sitting.

It should be noted here that the Deputy Speaker is not subordinate to the Speaker. He is directly responsible to the House.

The Deputy Speaker has one special privilege, that is, whenever he is appointed as a member of a parliamentary committee, he automatically becomes its chairman.

Like the Speaker, the Deputy Speaker, while presiding over the House, cannot vote in the first instance; he can only exercise a casting vote in the case of a tie. Further, when a resolution for the removal of the Deputy Speaker is under consideration of the House, he cannot preside at the sitting of the House, though he may be present.

When the Speaker presides over the House, the Deputy Speaker is like any other ordinary member of the House. He can speak in the House, participate in its proceedings and vote on any question before the House.

The Deputy Speaker is entitled to a regular salary and allowance fixed by Parliament, and charged on the Consolidated Fund of India.

Upto the 10th Lok Sabha, both the Speaker and the Deputy Speaker were usually from the ruling party. Since the 11th Lok Sabha, there has been a consensus that the Speaker comes from the ruling party (or ruling alliance) and the post of Deputy Speaker goes to the main opposition party.

The Speaker and the Deputy Speaker, while assuming their offices, do not make and subscribe any separate oath or affirmation.

The institutions of Speaker and Deputy Speaker originated in India in 1921 under the provisions of the Government of India Act of 1919 (Montague–Chelmsford Reforms). At that time, the Speaker and the Deputy Speaker were called the President and Deputy President respectively and the same nomenclature continued till 1947. Before 1921, the Governor-General of India used to preside over the meetings of the Central Legislative Council. In 1921, the Frederick Whyte and Sachidanand Sinha were appointed by the Governor-General of India as the first Speaker and the first Deputy Speaker (respectively) of the central legislative assembly. In 1925, Vithalbhai J. Patel became the first Indian and the first elected Speaker of the central legislative assembly. The Government of India Act of 1935 changed the nomenclatures of President and Deputy President of the Central Legislative Assembly to the Speaker and Deputy Speaker respectively. However, the old nomenclature continued till 1947 as the federal part of the 1935 Act was not implemented. G V Mavalankar and Ananthasayanam Ayyangar had the distinction of being the first Speaker and the first Deputy Speaker (respectively) of the Lok Sabha. G V Mavalankar also held the post of Speaker in the Constituent Assembly (Legislative) as well as the provisional Parliament. He held the post of Speaker

of Lok Sabha continuously for one decade from 1946 to 1956.

Panel of Chairpersons of Lok Sabha

Under the Rules of Lok Sabha, the Speaker nominates from amongst the members a panel of not more than ten chairpersons. Any of them can preside over the House in the absence of the Speaker or the Deputy Speaker. He has the same powers as the Speaker when so presiding. He holds office until a new panel of chairpersons is nominated. When a member of the panel of chairpersons is also not present, any other person as determined by House acts as the Speaker.

It must be emphasised here that a member of the panel of chairpersons cannot preside over the House, when the office of the Speaker or the Deputy Speaker is vacant. During such time, the Speaker's duties are to be performed by such member of the House as the President may appoint for the purpose. The elections are held, as soon as possible, to fill the vacant posts.

Speaker *Pro Tem*

As provided by the Constitution, the Speaker of the last Lok Sabha vacates his office immediately before the first meeting of the newly-elected Lok Sabha. Therefore, the President appoints a member of the Lok Sabha as the Speaker *Pro Tem*. Usually, the seniormost member is selected for this. The President himself administers oath to the Speaker *Pro Tem*.

The Speaker *Pro Tem* has all the powers of the Speaker. He presides over the first sitting of the newly-elected Lok Sabha. His main duty is to administer oath to the new members. He also enables the House to elect the new Speaker.

When the new Speaker is elected by the House, the office of the Speaker *Pro Tem* ceases to exist. Hence, this office is a temporary office, existing for a few days[12].

Chairman of Rajya Sabha

The presiding officer of the Rajya Sabha is known as the Chairman. The vice-president of India is the *ex-officio* Chairman of the Rajya Sabha. During any period when the Vice-President acts as President or discharges the functions of the President, he does not perform the duties of the office of the Chairman of Rajya Sabha.

The Chairman of the Rajya Sabha can be removed from his office only if he is removed from the office of the Vice-President. As a presiding officer, the powers and functions of the Chairman in the Rajya Sabha are similar to those of the Speaker in the Lok Sabha. However, the Speaker has two special powers which are not enjoyed by the Chairman:

1. The Speaker decides whether a bill is a money bill or not and his decision on this question is final.
2. The Speaker presides over a joint sitting of two Houses of Parliament.

Unlike the Speaker (who is a member of the House), the Chairman is not a member of the House. But like the Speaker, the Chairman also cannot vote in the first instance. He too can cast a vote in the case of an equality of votes.

The Vice-President cannot preside over a sitting of the Rajya Sabha as its Chairman when a resolution for his removal is under consideration. However, he can be present and speak in the House and can take part in its proceedings, without voting, even at such a time (while the Speaker can vote in the first instance when a resolution for his removal is under consideration of the Lok Sabha).

As in case of the Speaker, the salaries and allowances of the Chairman are also fixed by the Parliament. They are charged on the Consolidated Fund of India and thus are not subject to the annual vote of Parliament.

During any period when the Vice-President acts as President or discharges the functions of the President, he is not entitled to any salary or allowance payable to the Chairman of the Rajya Sabha. But he is paid the salary and allowance of the President during such a time.

Deputy Chairman of Rajya Sabha

The Deputy Chairman is elected by the Rajya Sabha itself from amongst its members. Whenever the office of the Deputy Chairman falls vacant, the Rajya Sabha elects another member to fill the vacancy.

The Deputy Chairman vacates his office in any of the following three cases:

1. if he ceases to be a member of the Rajya Sabha;
2. if he resigns by writing to the Chairman; and
3. if he is removed by a resolution passed by a majority of all the members of the Rajya

Sabha. Such a resolution can be moved only after giving 14 days' advance notice.

The Deputy Chairman performs the duties of the Chairman's office when it is vacant or when the Vice-President acts as President or discharges the functions of the President. He also acts as the Chairman when the latter is absent from the sitting of the House. In both the cases, he has all the powers of the Chairman.

It should be emphasised here that the Deputy Chairman is not subordinate to the Chairman. He is directly responsible to the Rajya Sabha.

Like the Chairman, the Deputy Chairman, while presiding over the House, cannot vote in the first instance; he can only exercise a casting vote in the case of a tie. Further, when a resolution for the removal of the Deputy Chairman is under consideration of the House, he cannot preside over a sitting of the House, though he may be present.

When the Chairman presides over the House, the Deputy Chairman is like any other ordinary member of the House. He can speak in the House, participate in its proceedings and vote on any question before the House.

Like the Chairman, the Deputy Chairman is also entitled to a regular salary and allowance. They are fixed by Parliament and are charged on the Consolidated Fund of India.

Panel of Vice-Chairpersons of Rajya Sabha

Under the Rules of Rajya Sabha, the Chairman nominates from amongst the members a panel of vice-chairpersons. Any one of them can preside over the House in the absence of the Chairman or the Deputy Chairman. He has the same powers as the Chairman when so presiding. He holds office until a new panel of vice-chairpersons is nominated.

When a member of the panel of vice-chairpersons is also not present, any other person as determined by the House acts as the Chairman.

It must be emphasised here that a member of the panel of vice-chairpersons cannot preside over the House, when the office of the Chairman or the Deputy Chairman is vacant. During such time, the Chairman's duties are to be performed by such member of the House as the president may appoint for the purpose. The elections are held, as soon as possible, to fill the vacant posts.

Secretariat of Parliament

Each House of Parliament has separate secretarial staff of its own, though there can be some posts common to both the Houses. Their recruitment and service conditions are regulated by Parliament. The secretariat of each House is headed by a secretary-general. He is a permanent officer and is appointed by the presiding officer of the House.

LEADERS IN PARLIAMENT

Leader of the House

Under the Rules of Lok Sabha, the 'Leader of the House' means the prime minister, if he is a member of the Lok Sabha, or a minister who is a member of the Lok Sabha and is nominated by the prime minister to function as the Leader of the House. There is also a 'Leader of the House' in the Rajya Sabha. He is a minister and a member of the Rajya Sabha and is nominated by the prime minister to function as such. The leader of the house in either House is an important functionary and exercises direct influence on the conduct of business. He can also nominate a deputy leader of the House. The same functionary in USA is known as the 'majority leader'.

Leader of the Opposition

In each House of Parliament, there is the 'Leader of the Opposition'. The leader of the largest Opposition party having not less than one-tenth seats of the total strength of the House is recognised as the leader of the Opposition in that House. In a parliamentary system of government, the leader of the opposition has a significant role to play. His main functions are to provide a constructive criticism of the policies of the government and to provide an alternative government. Therefore, the leader of Opposition in the Lok Sabha and the Rajya Sabha were accorded statutory recognition in 1977. They are also entitled to the salary, allowances and other facilities equivalent to that of a cabinet minister. It was in 1969 that an official leader of the opposition was recognised for the first time. The same functionary in USA is known as the 'minority leader'.

The British political system has an unique institution called the 'Shadow Cabinet'. It is formed by the Opposition party to balance the ruling cabinet and to prepare its members for future ministerial offices. In this shadow cabinet, almost every member in the ruling cabinet is 'shadowed' by a corresponding member in the opposition cabinet. This shadow cabinet serves as the 'alternate cabinet' if there is change of government. That is why Ivor Jennings described the leader of Opposition as the 'alternative Prime Minister'. He enjoys the status of a minister and is paid by the government.

Whip

Though the offices of the leader of the House and the leader of the Opposition are not mentioned in the Constitution of India, they are mentioned in the Rules of the House and Parliamentary Statute respectively. The office of 'whip', on the other hand, is mentioned neither in the Constitution of India nor in the Rules of the House nor in a Parliamentary Statute. It is based on the conventions of the parliamentary government.

Every political party, whether ruling or Opposition has its own whip in the Parliament. He is appointed by the political party to serve as an assistant floor leader. He is charged with the responsibility of ensuring the attendance of his party members in large numbers and securing their support in favour of or against a particular issue. He regulates and monitors their behaviour in the Parliament. The members are supposed to follow the directives given by the whip. Otherwise, disciplinary action can be taken.

SESSIONS OF PARLIAMENT
Summoning

The president from time to time sumons each House of Parliament to meet. But, the maximum gap between two sessions of Parliament cannot be more than six months. In other words, the Parliament should meet at least twice a year. There are usually three sessions in a year, viz,

1. the Budget Session (February to May);
2. the Monsoon Session (July to September); and
3. the Winter Session (November to December).

A 'session' of Parliament is the period spanning between the first sitting of a House and its prorogation (or dissolution in the case of the Lok Sabha).

Table 22.1 *Adjournment vs Prorogation*

	Adjournment		Prorogation
1.	It only terminates a sitting and not a session of the House.	1.	It not only terminates a sitting but also a session of the House.
2.	It is done by presiding officer of the House.	2.	It is done by the president of India.
3.	It does not affect the bills or any other business pending before the House and the same can be resumed when the House meets again.	3.	It also does not affect the bills or any other business pending before the House.[13] However, all pending notices (other than those for introducing bills) lapse on prorogation and fresh notices have to be given for the next session. In Britain, prorogation brings to an end all bills or any other business pending before the House.

During a session, the House meets everyday to transact business. The period spanning between the prorogation of a House and its reassembly in a new session is called 'recess'.

Adjournment

A session of Parliament consists of many meetings. Each meeting of a day consists of two sittings, that is, a morning sitting from 11 am to 1 pm and post-lunch sitting from 2 pm to 6 pm. A sitting of Parliament can be terminated by adjournment or adjournment *sine die* or prorogation or dissolution (in the case of the Lok Sabha). An adjournment suspends the work in a sitting for a specified time, which may be hours, days or weeks.

Adjournment *Sine Die*

Adjournment *sine die* means terminating a sitting of Parliament for an indefinite period. In other words, when the House is adjourned without naming a day for reassembly, it is called adjournment *sine die*. The power of adjournment as well as adjournment *sine die* lies with the presiding officer of the House. He can also call a sitting of the House before the date or time to which it has been adjourned or at any time after the House has been adjourned *sine die*.

Prorogation

The presiding officer (Speaker or Chairman) declares the House adjourned *sine die*, when the business of a session is completed. Within the next few days, the President issues a notification for prorogation of the session. However, the President can also prorogue the House while in session.

The specific differences between adjournment and prorogation are summarised in Table 22.1.

Dissolution

Rajya Sabha, being a permanent House, is not subject to dissolution. Only the Lok Sabha is subject to dissolution. Unlike a prorogation, a dissolution ends the very life of the existing House, and a new House is constituted after general elections are held. The dissolution of the Lok Sabha may take place in either of two ways:

1. Automatic dissolution, that is, on the expiry of its tenure of five years or the terms as extended during a national emergency; or
2. Whenever the President decides to dissolve the House, which he is authorised to do. Once the Lok Sabha is dissolved before the completion of its normal tenure, the dissolution is irrevocable.

When the Lok Sabha is dissolved, all business including bills, motions, resolutions, notices, petitions and so on pending before it or its committees lapse. They (to be pursued further) must be reintroduced in the newly-constituted Lok Sabha. However, some pending bills and all pending assurances that are to be examined by the Committee on Government Assurances do not lapse on the dissolution of the Lok Sabha. The position with respect to lapsing of bills is as follows:

1. A bill pending in the Lok Sabha lapses (whether originating in the Lok Sabha or transmitted to it by the Rajya Sabha).

2. A bill passed by the Lok Sabha but pending in the Rajya Sabha lapses.

3. A bill not passed by the two Houses due to disagreement and if the president has notified the holding of a joint sitting before the dissolution of Lok Sabha, does not lapse.

4. A bill pending in the Rajya Sabha but not passed by the Lok Sabha does not lapse.

5. A bill passed by both Houses but pending assent of the president does not lapse.

6. A bill passed by both Houses but returned by the president for reconsideration of Houses does not lapse.

Quorum

Quorum is the minimum number of members required to be present in the House before it can transact any business. It is one-tenth of the total number of members in each House including the presiding officer. It means that there must be at least 55 members present in the Lok Sabha and 25 members present in the Rajya Sabha, if any business is to be conducted. If there is no quorum during a meeting of the House, it is the duty of the presiding officer either to adjourn the House or to suspend the meeting until there is a quorum.

Voting in House

All matters at any sitting of either House or joint sitting of both the Houses are decided by a majority of votes of the members present and voting, excluding the presiding officer. Only a few matters, which are specifically mentioned in the Constitution like impeachment of the President, amendment of the Constitution, removal of the presiding officers of the Parliament and so on, require special majority, not ordinary majority.

The presiding officer of a House does not vote in the first instance, but exercises a casting vote in the case of an equality of votes. The proceedings of a House are to be valid irrespective of any unauthorised voting or participation or any vacancy in its membership.

Language in Parliament

The Constitution has declared Hindi and English to be the languages for transacting business in the Parliament. However, the presiding officer can permit a member to address the House in his mother-tongue. In both the Houses, arrangements are made for simultaneous translation. Though English was to be discontinued as a floor language after the expiration of fifteen years from the commencement of the Constitution (that is, in 1965), the Official Languages Act (1963) allowed English to be continued along with Hindi.

Rights of Ministers and Attorney General

In addition to the members of a House, every minister and the attorney general of India have the right to speak and take part in the proceedings of either House, any joint sitting of both the Houses and any committee of Parliament of which he is a member, without being entitled to vote. There are two reasons underlying this constitutional provision:

1. A minister can participate in the proceedings of a House, of which he is not a member. In other words, a minister belonging to the Lok Sabha can participate in the proceedings of the Rajya Sabha and vice-versa.

2. A minister, who is not a member of either House, can participate in the proceedings of both the Houses. It should be noted here that a person can remain a minister for six months, without being a member of either House of Parliament.

Lame-duck Session

It refers to the last session of the existing Lok Sabha, after a new Lok Sabha has been elected. Those members of the existing Lok Sabha who could not get re-elected to the new Lok Sabha are called lame-ducks.

DEVICES OF PARLIAMENTARY PROCEEDINGS

Question Hour

The first hour of every parliamentary sitting is slotted for this. During this time, the members ask questions and the ministers usually give answers. The questions are of three kinds, namely, starred, unstarred and short notice.

A **starred question** (distinguished by an asterisk) requires an oral answer and hence supplementary questions can follow.

An **unstarred question**, on the other hand, requires a written answer and hence, supplementary questions cannot follow.

A **short notice question** is one that is asked by giving a notice of less than ten days. It is answered orally.

Zero Hour

Unlike the question hour, the zero hour is not mentioned in the Rules of Procedure. Thus it is an informal device available to the members of the Parliament to raise matters without any prior notice. The zero hour starts immediately after the question hour and lasts until the agenda for the day (ie, regular business of the House) is taken up. In other words, the time gap between the question hour and the agenda is known as zero hour. It is an Indian innovation in the field of parliamentary procedures and has been in existence since 1962.

Motions

No discussion on a matter of general public importance can take place except on a motion made with the consent of the presiding officer. The House expresses its decisions or opinions on various issues through the adoption or rejection of motions moved by either ministers or private members.

The motions moved by the members to raise discussions on various matters fall into three principal categories:[14]

1. *Substantive Motion:* It is a self-contained independent proposal dealing with a very important matter like impeachment of the President or removal of Chief Election Commissioner.
2. *Substitute Motion:* It is a motion that is moved in substitution of an original motion and proposes an alternative to it. If adopted by the House, it supersedes the original motion.
3. *Subsidiary Motion:* It is a motion that, by itself, has no meaning and cannot state the decision of the House without reference to the original motion or proceedings of the House. It is divided into three sub-categories:

(a) *Ancillary Motion:* It is used as the regular way of proceeding with various kinds of business.
(b) *Superseding Motion:* It is moved in the course of debate on another issue and seeks to supersede that issue.
(c) *Amendment:* It seeks to modify or substitute only a part of the original motion.

Closure Motion   It is a motion moved by a member to cut short the debate on a matter before the House. If the motion is approved by the House, debate is stopped forthwith and the matter is put to vote. There are four kinds of closure motions[15]:

(a) *Simple Closure:* It is one when a member moves that the 'matter having been sufficiently discussed be now put to vote'.
(b) *Closure by Compartments:* In this case, the clauses of a bill or a lengthy resolution are grouped into parts before the commencement of the debate. The debate covers the part as a whole and the entire part is put to vote.
(c) *Kangaroo Closure:* Under this type, only important clauses are taken up for debate and voting and the intervening clauses are skipped over and taken as passed.
(d) *Guillotine Closure:* It is one when the undiscussed clauses of a bill or a resolution are also put to vote along with the discussed ones due to want of time (as the time allotted for the discussion is over).

Privilege Motion   It is concerned with the breach of parliamentary privileges by a minister. It is moved by a member when he feels that a minister has committed a breach of privilege of the House or one or more of its members by withholding facts of a case or by giving wrong or distorted facts. Its purpose is to censure the concerned minister.

Calling Attention Motion   It is introduced in the Parliament by a member to call the attention of a minister to a matter of urgent public importance, and to seek an authoritative statement from him on that matter. Like the zero hour, it is also an Indian innovation in the parliamentary procedure and has been in existence since 1954. However, unlike the zero hour, it is mentioned in the Rules of Procedure.

Table 22.2 *Censure Motion vs No Confidence Motion*

	Censure Motion		No-Confidence Motion
1.	It should state the reasons for its adoption in the Lok Sabha.	1.	It need not state the reasons for its adoption in the Lok Sabha.
2.	It can be moved against an individual minister or a group of ministers or the entire council of ministers.	2.	It can be moved against the entire council of ministers only.
3.	It is moved for censuring the council of ministers for specific policies and actions.	3.	It is moved for ascertaining the confidence of Lok Sabha in the council of ministers.
4.	If it is passed in the Lok Sabha, the council of ministers need not resign from the office.	4.	If it is passed in the Lok Sabha, the council of ministers must resign from office.

Adjournment Motion It is introduced in the Parliament to draw attention of the House to a definite matter of urgent public importance, and needs the support of 50 members to be admitted. As it interrupts the normal business of the House, it is regarded as an extraordinary device. It involves an element of censure against the government and hence Rajya Sabha is not permitted to make use of this device. The discussion on an adjournment motion should last for not less than two hours and thirty minutes.

The right to move a motion for an adjournment of the business of the House is subject to the following restrictions:

1. It should raise a matter which is definite, factual, urgent and of public importance;
2. It should not cover more than one matter;
3. It should be restricted to a specific matter of recent occurrence and should not be framed in general terms;
4. It should not raise a question of privilege;
5. It should not revive discussion on a matter that has been discussed in the same session;
6. It should not deal with any matter that is under adjudication by court; and
7. It should not raise any question that can be raised on a distinct motion.

No-Confidence Motion Article 75 of the Constitution says that the council of ministers shall be collectively responsible to the Lok Sabha. It means that the ministry stays in office so long as it enjoys confidence of the majority of the members of the Lok Sabha. In other words, the Lok Sabha can remove the ministry from office by passing a no-confidence motion. The motion needs the support of 50 members to be admitted.

Censure Motion A censure motion is different from a no-confidence motion as shown in Table 22.2.

Motion of Thanks The first session after each general election and the first session of every fiscal year is addressed by the president. In this address, the president outlines the policies and programmes of the government in the preceding year and ensuing year. This address of the president, which corresponds to the 'speech from the Throne in Britain', is discussed in both the Houses of Parliament on a motion called the 'Motion of Thanks'. At the end of the discussion, the motion is put to vote. This motion must be passed in the House. Otherwise, it amounts to the defeat of the government. This inaugural speech of the president is an occasion available to the members of Parliament to raise discussions and debates to examine and criticise the government and administration for its lapses and failures.

No-Day-Yet-Named Motion It is a motion that has been admitted by the Speaker but no date has been fixed for its discussion. The Speaker, after considering the state of business in the House and in consultation with the leader of the House or on the recommendation of the Business Advisory Committee, allots a day or days or part of a day for the discussion of such a motion.

Point of Order

A member can raise a point of order when the proceedings of the House do not follow the normal rules of procedure. A point of order should relate to the interpretation or enforcement of the Rules of the House or such articles of the Constitution that regulate the business of the House and should raise a question that is within the cognizance of the Speaker. It is usually raised by an opposition member in order to control the government. It is an extraordinary device as it suspends the proceedings before the House. No debate is allowed on a point of order.

Half-an-Hour Discussion

It is meant for discussing a matter of sufficient public importance, which has been subjected to a lot of debate and the answer to which needs elucidation on a matter of fact. The Speaker can allot three days in a week for such discussions. There is no formal motion or voting before the House.

Short Duration Discussion

It is also known as two-hour discussion as the time allotted for such a discussion should not exceed two hours. The members of the Parliament can raise such discussions on a matter of urgent public importance. The Speaker can allot two days in a week for such discussions. There is neither a formal motion before the house nor voting. This device has been in existence since 1953.

Special Mention

A matter which is not a point of order or which cannot be raised during question hour, half-an hour discussion, short duration discussion or under adjournment motion, calling attention notice or under any rule of the House can be raised under the special mention in the Rajya Sabha. Its equivalent procedural device in the Lok Sabha is known as 'Notice (Mention) Under Rule 377'.

Resolutions

The members can move resolutions to draw the attention of the House or the government to matters of general public interest. The discussion on a resolution is strictly relevant to and within the scope of the resolution. A member who has moved a resolution or amendment to a resolution cannot withdraw the same except by leave of the House.

Resolutions are classified into three categories:[16]

1. *Private Member's Resolution:* It is one that is moved by a private member (other than a min-

ister). It is discussed only on alternate Fridays and in the afternoon sitting.

2. *Government Resolution:* It is one that is moved by a minister. It can be taken up any day from Monday to Thursday.

3. *Statutory Resolution:* It can be moved either by a private member or a minister. It is so called because it is always tabled in pursuance of a provision in the Constitution or an Act of Parliament.

Resolutions are different from motions in the following respects:

"All resolutions come in the category of substantive motions, that is to say, every resolution is a particular type of motion. All motions need not necessarily be substantive. Further, all motions are not necessarily put to vote of the House, whereas all the resolutions are required to be voted upon."[17]

Youth Parliament

The scheme of Youth Parliament was started on the recommendation of the Fourth All India Whips Conference. Its objectives are:

1. to acquaint the younger generations with practices and procedures of Parliament;

2. to imbibe the spirit of discipline and tolerance cultivating character in the minds of youth; and

3. to inculcate in the student community the basic values of democracy and to enable them to acquire a proper perspective on the functioning of democratic institutions.

The ministry of parliamentary affairs provides necessary training and encouragement to the states in introducing the scheme.

LEGISLATIVE PROCEDURE IN PARLIAMENT

The legislative procedure is identical in both the Houses of Parliament. Every bill has to pass through the same stages in each House. A bill is a proposal for legislation and it becomes an act or law when duly enacted.

Bills introduced in the Parliament are of two kinds: public bills and private bills (also known

Table 22.3 *Public Bill vs Private Bill*

	Public Bill		*Private Bill*
1.	It is introduced in the Parliament by a minister.	1.	It is introduced by any member of Parliament other than a minister.
2.	It reflects of the policies of the government (ruling party).	2.	It reflects the stand of opposition party on public matter.
3.	It has greater chance to be approved by the Parliament.	3.	It has lesser chance to be approved by the Parliament.
4.	Its rejection by the House amounts to the expression of want of parliamentary confidence in the government and may lead to its resignation.	4.	Its rejection by the House has no implication on the parliamentary confidence in the government or its resignation.
5.	Its introduction in the House requires seven days' notice.	5.	Its introduction in the House requires one month's notice.
6.	It is drafted by the concerned department in consultation with the law department.	6.	Its drafting is the responsibility of the member concerned.

as government bills and private members' bills respectively). Though both are governed by the same general procedure and pass through the same stages in the House, they differ in various respects as shown in Table 22.3.

The bills introduced in the Parliament can also be classified into four categories:

1. Ordinary bills, which are concerned with any matter other than financial subjects.
2. Money bills, which are concerned with the financial matters like taxation, public expenditure, etc.
3. Financial bills, which are also concerned with financial matters (but are different from money bills).
4. Constitution amendment bills, which are concerned with the amendment of the provisions of the Constitution.

The Constitution has laid down separate procedures for the enactment of all the four types of bills. The procedures with regard to ordinary bills, money bills and financial bills are explained here. The procedure with regard to Constitution amendment bills is explained in detail in Chapter 10.

Ordinary Bills

Every ordinary bill has to pass through the following five stages in the Parliament before it finds a place on the Statute Book:

1. First Reading An ordinary bill can be introduced in either House of Parliament. Such a bill can be introduced either by a minister or by any other member. The member who wants to introduce the bill has to ask for the leave of the House. When the House grants leave to introduce the bill, the mover of the bill introduces it by reading its title and objectives. No discussion on the bill takes place at this stage. Later, the bill is published in the Gazette of India. If a bill is published in the Gazette before its introduction, leave of the House to introduce the bill is not necessary.[18] The introduction of the bill and its publication in the Gazette constitute the first reading of the bill.

2. Second Reading During this stage, the bill receives not only the general but also the detailed scrutiny and assumes its final shape. Hence, it forms the most important stage in the enactment of a bill. In fact, this stage involves three more sub-stages, namely, stage of general discussion, committee stage and consideration stage.

(a) Stage of General Discussion The printed copies of the bill are distributed to all the members. The principles of the bill and its provisions are discussed generally, but the details of the bill are not discussed.

At this stage, the House can take any one of the following four actions:

(i) It may take the bill into consideration immediately or on some other fixed date;

(ii) It may refer the bill to a select committee of the House;

(iii) It may refer the bill to a joint committee of the two Houses; and

(iv) It may circulate the bill to elicit public opinion.

A Select Committee consists of members of the House where the bill has originated and a joint committee consists of members of both the Houses of Parliament.

(b) Committee Stage The usual practice is to refer the bill to a select committee of the House. This committee examines the bill thoroughly and in detail, clause by clause. It can also amend its provisions, but without altering the principles underlying it. After completing the scrutiny and discussion, the committee reports the bill back to the House.

(c) Consideration Stage The House, after receiving the bill from the select committee, considers the provisions of the bill clause by clause. Each clause is discussed and voted upon separately. The members can also move amendments and if accepted, they become part of the bill.

3. Third Reading At this stage, the debate is confined to the acceptance or rejection of the bill as a whole and no amendments are allowed, as the general principles underlying the bill have already been scrutinised during the stage of second reading. If the majority of members present and voting accept the bill, the bill is regarded as passed by the House. Thereafter, the bill is authenticated by the presiding officer of the House and transmitted to the second House for consideration and approval. A bill is deemed to have been passed by the Parliament only when both the Houses have agreed to it, either with or without amendments.

4. Bill in the Second House In the second House also, the bill passes through all the three stages, that is, first reading, second reading and third reading. There are four alternatives before this House:

(a) it may pass the bill as sent by the first house (ie, without amendments);

(b) it may pass the bill with amendments and return it to the first House for reconsideration;

(c) it may reject the bill altogether; and

(d) it may not take any action and thus keep the bill pending.

If the second House passes the bill without any amendments or the first House accepts the amendments suggested by the second House, the bill is deemed to have been passed by both the Houses and the same is sent to the president for his assent. On the other hand, if the first House rejects the amendments suggested by the second House or the second House rejects the bill altogether or the second House does not take any action for six months, a deadlock is deemed to have taken place. To resolve such a deadlock, the president can summon a joint sitting of the two Houses. If the majority of members present and voting in the joint sitting approves the bill, the bill is deemed to have been passed by both the Houses.

5. Assent of the President Every bill after being passed by both Houses of Parliament either singly or at a joint sitting, is presented to the president for his assent. There are three alternatives before the president:

(a) he may give his assent to the bill; or

(b) he may withhold his assent to the bill; or

(c) he may return the bill for reconsideration of the Houses.

If the president gives his assent to the bill, the bill becomes an act and is placed on the Statute Book. If the President withholds his assent to the bill, it ends and does not become an act. If the President returns the bill for reconsideration and if it is passed by both the Houses again with or without amendments and presented to the President for his assent, the president must give his assent to the bill. Thus, the President enjoys only a "suspensive veto."[19]

Money Bills

Article 110 of the Constitution deals with the definition of money bills. It states that a bill is deemed to be a money bill if it contains 'only' provisions dealing with all or any of the following matters:

1. The imposition, abolition, remission, alteration or regulation of any tax;

2. The regulation of the borrowing of money by the Union government;

3. The custody of the Consolidated Fund of India or the contingency fund of India, the payment of moneys into or the withdrawal of money from any such fund;

4. The appropriation of money out of the Consolidated Fund of India;

5. Declaration of any expenditure charged on the Consolidated Fund of India or increasing the amount of any such expenditure;

6. The receipt of money on account of the Consolidated Fund of India or the public account of India or the custody or issue of such money, or the audit of the accounts of the Union or of a state; or

7. Any matter incidental to any of the matters specified above.

However, a bill is not to be deemed to be a money bill by reason only that it provides for:

1. the imposition of fines or other pecuniary penalties, or

2. the demand or payment of fees for licenses or fees for services rendered; or

3. the imposition, abolition, remission, alteration or regulation of any tax by any local authority or body for local purposes.

If any question arises whether a bill is a money bill or not, the decision of the Speaker of the Lok Sabha is final. His decision in this regard cannot be questioned in any court of law or in the either House of Parliament or even the president. When a money bill is transmitted to the Rajya Sabha for recommendation and presented to the president for assent, the Speaker endorses it as a money bill.

The Constitution lays down a special procedure for the passing of money bills in the Parliament. A money bill can only be introduced in the Lok Sabha and that too on the recommendation of the president. Every such bill is considered to be a government bill and can be introduced only by a minister.

After a money bill is passed by the Lok Sabha, it is transmitted to the Rajya Sabha for its consideration. The Rajya Sabha has restricted powers with regard to a money bill. It cannot reject or amend a money bill. It can only make the recommendations. It must return the bill to the Lok Sabha within 14 days, wither with or without recommendations. The Lok Sabha can either accept or reject all or any of the recommendations of the Rajya Sabha.

If the Lok Sabha accepts any recommendation, the bill is then deemed to have been passed by both the Houses in the modified form. If the Lok Sabha does not accept any recommendation, the bill is then deemed to have passed by both the Houses in the form originally passed by the Lok Sabha without any change.

If the Rajya Sabha does not return the bill to the Lok Sabha within 14 days, the bill is deemed to have been passed by both the Houses in the form originally passed by the Lok Sabha. Thus, the Lok Sabha has more powers than Rajya Sabha with regard to a money bill. On the other hand, both the Houses have equal powers with regard to an ordinary bill.

Finally, when a money bill is presented to the president, he may either give his assent to the bill or withhold his assent to the bill but cannot return the bill for reconsideration of the Houses. Normally, the president gives his assent to a money bill as it is introduced in the Parliament with his prior permission.

Table 22.4 shows the differences between the procedures for the enactment of ordinary bills and money bills.

Financial Bills

Financial bills are those bills that deal with fiscal matters, that is, revenue or expenditure. However, the Constitution uses the term 'financial bill' in a technical sense. Financial bills are of three kinds:

1. Money bills—Article 110
2. Financial bills (I)—Article 117 (1)
3. Financial bills (II)—Article 117 (3)

This classification implies that money bills are simply a species of financial bills. Hence, all money bills are financial bills but all financial bills are not money bills. Only those financial bills are money bills which contain exclusively those matters which are mentioned in Article 110 of the Constitution. These are also certified by the Speaker of Lok Sabha as money bills. The financial bills (I) and (II), on the other hand, have been dealt with in Article 117 of the Constitution.

Financial Bills (I) A financial bill (I) is a bill that contains not only any or all the matters mentioned in Article 110, but also other matters of general legislation. For instance, a bill that contains a borrowing clause, but does not exclusively deal

Table 22.4 *Ordinary Bill Vs Money Bill*

	Ordinary Bill		Money Bill
1.	It can be introduced either in the Lok Sabha or the Rajya Sabha.	1.	It can be introduced only in the Lok Sabha and not in the Rajya Sabha.
2.	It can be introduced either by a minister or by a private member.	2.	It can be introduced only by a minister.
3.	It is introduced without the recommendation of the president.	3.	It can be introduced only on the recommendation of the President.
4.	It can be amended or rejected by the Rajya Sabha.	4.	It cannot be amended or rejected by the Rajya Sabha. The Rajya Sabha should return the bill with or without recommendations, which may be accepted or rejected by the Lok Sabha.
5.	It can be detained by the Rajya Sabha for a maximum period of six months.	5.	It can be detained by the Rajya Sabha for a maximum period of 14 days only.
6.	It does not require the certification of the Speaker when transmitted to the Rajya Sabha (if it has originated in the Lok Sabha).	6.	It requires the certification of the Speaker when transmitted to the Rajya Sabha.
7.	It is sent for the President's assent only after being approved by both the Houses. In case of a deadlock due to disagreement between the two Houses, a joint sitting of both the houses can be summoned by the president to resolve the deadlock.	7.	It is sent for the President's assent even if it is approved by only Lok Sabha. There is no chance of any disagreement between the two Houses and hence, there is no provision of joint sitting of both the Houses in this regard.
8.	Its defeat in the Lok Sabha may lead to the resignation of the government (if it is introduced by a minister).	8.	Its defeat in the Lok Sabha leads to the resignation of the government.
9.	It can be rejected, approved, or returned for reconsideration by the President.	9.	It can be rejected or approved but cannot be returned for reconsideration by the President.

with borrowing. In two respects, a financial bill (I) is similar to a money bill—(a) both of them can be introduced only in the Lok Sabha and not in the Rajya Sabha, and (b) both of them can be introduced only on the recommendation of the president. In all other respects, a financial bill (I) is governed by the same legislative procedure applicable to an ordinary bill. Hence, it can be either rejected or amended by the Rajya Sabha (except that an amendment other than for reduction or abolition of a tax cannot be moved in either House without the recommendation of the president). In case of a disagreement between the two Houses over such a bill, the president can summon a joint sitting of the two Houses to resolve the deadlock. When the bill is presented to the President, he can either give his assent to the bill or withhold his assent to the bill or return the bill for reconsideration of the Houses.

Financial Bills (II) A financial bill (II) contains provisions involving expenditure from the Consolidated Fund of India, but does not include any of the matters mentioned in Article 110. It is treated as an ordinary bill and in all respects, it is governed by the same legislative procedure which is applicable to an ordinary bill. The only special feature of this bill is that it cannot be passed by either House of Parliament unless the President has recommended to that House the consideration of the bill. Hence, financial bill (II) can be introduced in either House of Parliament and recommendation of the President is not necessary for its introduction. It can be either rejected or amended by either House of Parliament. In case of a disagreement between the two Houses over such a bill, the President can summon a joint sitting of the two Houses to resolve the deadlock. When the bill is presented to the President, he can either give his assent to the bill or withhold his assent to the bill or return the bill for reconsideration of the Houses.

JOINT SITTING OF TWO HOUSES

Joint sitting is an extraordinary machinery provided by the Constitution to resolve a deadlock between the two Houses over the passage of a bill. A deadlock is deemed to have taken place under any one of the following three situations after a bill has been passed by one House and transmitted to the other House:

1. if the bill is rejected by the other House;
2. if the Houses have finally disagreed as to the amendments to be made in the bill; or
3. if more than six months have elapsed from the date of the receipt of the bill by the other House without the bill being passed by it.

In the above three situations, the president can summon both the Houses to meet in a joint sitting for the purpose of deliberating and voting on the bill. It must be noted here that the provision of joint sitting is applicable to ordinary bills or financial bills only and not to money bills or Constitutional amendment bills. In the case of a money bill, the Lok Sabha has overriding powers, while a Constitutional amendment bill must be passed by each House separately.

In reckoning the period of six months, no account can be taken of any period during which the other House (to which the bill has been sent) is prorogued or adjourned for more than four consecutive days.

If the bill (under dispute) has already lapsed due to the dissolution of the Lok Sabha, no joint sitting can be summoned. But, the joint sitting can be held if the Lok Sabha is dissolved after the President has notified his intention to summon such a sitting (as the bill does not lapse in this case). After the President notifies his intention to summon a joint sitting of the two Houses, none of the Houses can proceed further with the bill.

The Speaker of Lok Sabha presides over a joint sitting of the two Houses and the Deputy Speaker, in his absence. If the Deputy Speaker is also absent from a joint sitting, the Deputy Chairman of Rajya Sabha presides. If he is also absent, such other person as may be determined by the members present at the joint sitting, presides over the meeting. It is clear that the Chairman of Rajya Sabha does not preside over a joint sitting as he is not a member of either House of Parliament.

The quorum to constitute a joint sitting is one-tenth of the total number of members of the two Houses. The joint sitting is governed by the Rules of Procedure of Lok Sabha and not of Rajya Sabha.

If the bill in dispute is passed by a majority of the total number of members of both the Houses present and voting in the joint sitting, the bill is deemed to have been passed by both the Houses. Normally, the Lok Sabha with greater number wins the battle in a joint sitting.

The Constitution has specified that at a joint sitting, new amendments to the bill cannot be proposed except in two cases:

1. those amendments that have caused final disagreement between the Houses; and
2. those amendments that might have become necessary due to the delay in the passage of the bill.

Since 1950, the provision regarding the joint sitting of the two Houses has been invoked only thrice. The bills that have been passed at joint sittings are:

1. Dowry Prohibition Bill, 1960.[20]
2. Banking Service Commission (Repeal) Bill, 1977.[21]
3. Prevention of Terrorism Bill, 2002.[22]

BUDGET IN PARLIAMENT

The Constitution refers to the budget as the 'annual financial statement'. In other words, the term 'budget' has nowhere been used in the Constitution. It is the popular name for the 'annual financial statement' that has been dealt with in Article 112 of the Constitution.

The budget is a statement of the estimated receipts and expenditure of the Government of India in a financial year, which begins on 1 April and ends on 31 March of the following year.

In addition to the estimates of receipts and expenditure, the budget contains certain other elements. Overall, the budget contains the following:

1. Estimates of revenue and capital receipts;
2. Ways and means to raise the revenue;

3. Estimates of expenditure;
4. Details of the actual receipts and expenditure of the closing financial year and the reasons for any deficit or surplus in that year; and
5. Economic and financial policy of the coming year, that is, taxation proposals, prospects of revenue, spending programme and introduction of new schemes/projects.

The Government of India has two budgets, namely, the Railway Budget and the General Budget. While the former consists of the estimates of receipts and expenditures of only the Ministry of Railways, the latter consists of the estimates of receipts and expenditure of all the ministries of the Government of India (except the railways).

The Railway Budget was separated from the General Budget in 1921 on the recommendations of the Acworth Committee. The reasons or objectives of this separation are as follows:

1. To introduce flexibility in railway finance.
2. To facilitate a business approach to the railway policy.
3. To secure stability of the general revenues by providing an assured annual contribution from railway revenues.
4. To enable the railways to keep their profits for their own development (after paying a fixed annual contribution to the general revenues).

Constitutional Provisions

The Constitution of India contains the following provisions with regard to the enactment of budget:

1. The President shall in respect of every financial year cause to be laid before both the Houses of Parliament a statement of estimated receipts and expenditure of the Government of India for that year.
2. No demand for a grant shall be made except on the recommendation of the President.
3. No money shall be withdrawn from the Consolidated Fund of India except under appropriation made by law.
4. No money bill imposing tax shall be introduced in the Parliament except on the recommendation of the President, and such a bill shall not be introduced in the Rajya Sabha.
5. No tax shall be levied or collected except by authority of law.

6. Parliament can reduce or abolish a tax but cannot increase it.
7. The Constitution has also defined the relative roles or position of both the Houses of Parliament with regard to the enactment of the budget in the following way:
   (a) A money bill or finance bill dealing with taxation cannot be introduced in the Rajya Sabha—it must be introduced only in the Lok Sabha.
   (b) The Rajya Sabha has no power to vote on the demand for grants; it is the exclusive privilege of the Lok Sabha.
   (c) The Rajya Sabha should return the Money bill (or Finance bill) to the Lok Sabha within fourteen days. The Lok Sabha can either accept or reject the recommendations made by Rajya Sabha in this regard.
8. The estimates of expenditure embodied in the budget shall show separately the expenditure charged on the Consolidated Fund of India and the expenditure made from the Consolidated Fund of India.
9. The budget shall distinguish expenditure on revenue account from other expenditure.

Charged Expenditure

The budget consists of two types of expenditure—the expenditure 'charged' upon the Consolidated Fund of India and the expenditure 'made' from the Consolidated Fund of India. The charged expenditure is non-votable by the Parliament, that is, it can only be discussed by the Parliament, while the other type has to be voted by the Parliament. The list of the charged expenditure is as follows:

1. Emoluments and allowances of the President and other expenditure relating to his office.
2. Salaries and allowances of the Chairman and the Deputy Chairman of the Rajya Sabha and the Speaker and the Deputy Speaker of the Lok Sabha.
3. Salaries, allowances and pensions of the judges of the Supreme Court.
4. Pensions of the judges of high courts.
5. Salary, allowances and pension of the Comptroller and Auditor General of India.
6. Salaries, allowances and pension of the chairman and members of the Union Public Service Commission.

7. Administrative expenses of the Supreme Court, the office of the Comptroller and Auditor General of India and the Union Public Service Commission including the salaries, allowances and pensions of the persons serving in these offices.
8. The debt charges for which the Government of India is liable, including interest, sinking fund charges and redemption charges and other expenditure relating to the raising of loans and the service and redemption of debt.
9. Any sum required to satisfy any judgement, decree or award of any court or arbitral tribunal.
10. Any other expenditure declared by the Parliament to be so charged. .

Stages in Enactment

The budget goes through the following six stages in the Parliament:
1. Presentation of budget.
2. General discussion.
3. Scrutiny by departmental committees.
4. Voting on demands for grants.
5. Passing of appropriation bill.
6. Passing of finance bill.

1. Presentation of Budget   The budget is presented in two parts—Railway Budget and General Budget. Both are governed by the same procedure.

The introduction of Railway Budget precedes that of the General Budget. While the former is presented to the Lok Sabha by the railway minister in the third week of February, the latter is presented to the Lok Sabha by the finance minister on the last working day of February.

The Finance Minister presents the General Budget with a speech known as the 'budget speech'. At the end of the speech in the Lok Sabha, the budget is laid before the Rajya Sabha, which can only discuss it and has no power to vote on the demands for grants.

2. General Discussion   The general discussion on budget begins a few days after its presentation. It takes place in both the Houses of Parliament and lasts usually for three to four days.

During this stage, the Lok Sabha can discuss the budget as a whole or on any question of principle involved therein but no cut motion can be moved nor can the budget be submitted to the vote of the House. The finance minister has a general right of reply at the end of the discussion.

3. Scrutiny by Departmental Committees
After the general discussion on the budget is over, the Houses are adjourned for about three to four weeks. During this gap period, the 24 departmental standing committees of Parliament examine and discuss in detail the demands for grants of the concerned ministers and prepare reports on them. These reports are submitted to both the Houses of Parliament for consideration.

The standing committee system established is 1993 (and expanded in 2004) makes parliamentary financial control over ministries much more detailed, close, in-depth and comprehensive.

4. Voting on Demands for Grants   In the light of the reports of the departmental standing committees, the Lok Sabha takes up voting of demands for grants. The demands are presented ministrywise. A demand becomes a grant after it has been duly voted.

Two points should be noted in this context. One, the voting of demands for grants is the exclusive privilege of the Lok Sabha, that is, the Rajya Sabha has no power of voting the demands. Second, the voting is confined to the votable part of the budget— the expenditure charged on the Consolidated Fund of India is not submitted to the vote (it can only be discussed).

While the General Budget has a total of 109 demands (103 for civil expenditure and 6 for defence expenditure), the Railway Budget has 32 demands. Each demand is voted separately by the Lok Sabha. During this stage, the members of Parliament can discuss the details of the budget. They can also move motions to reduce any demand for grant. Such motions are called as 'cut motion', which are of three kinds:

(a) Policy Cut Motion   It represents the disapproval of the policy underlying the demand. It states that the amount of the demand be reduced to Re 1. The members can also advocate an alternative policy.

(b) Economy Cut Motion   It represents the economy that can be affected in the proposed expenditure. It states that the amount of the demand be reduced by a specified amount (which may be either a lumpsum reduction in the demand or ommission or reduction of an item in the demand).

(c) Token Cut Motion It ventilates a specific grievance that is within the sphere of responsibility of the Government of India. It states that the amount of the demand be reduced by Rs 100.

A cut motion, to be admissible, must satisfy the following conditions:

(i) It should relate to one demand only.

(ii) It should be clearly expressed and should not contain arguments or defamatory statements.

(iii) It should be confined to one specific matter.

(iv) It should not make suggestions for the amendment or repeal of existing laws.

(v) It should not refer to a matter that is not primarily the concern of Union government.

(vi) It should not relate to the expenditure charged on the Consolidated Fund of India.

(vii) It should not relate to a matter that is under adjudication by a court.

(viii) It should not raise a question of privilege.

(ix) It should not revive discussion on a matter on which a decision has been taken in the same session.

(x) It should not relate to a trivial matter.

The significance of a cut motion lies in: (a) facilitating the initiation of concentrated discussion on a specific demand for grant; and (b) upholding the principle of responsible government by probing the activities of the government. However, the cut motion do not have much utility in practice. They are only moved and discussed in the House but not passed as the government enjoys majority support. Their passage by the Lok Sabha amounts to the expressions of want of parliamentary confidence in the government and may lead to its resignation.

In total, 26 days are allotted for the voting of demands. On the last day the Speaker puts all the remaining demands to vote and disposes them whether they have been discussed by the members or not. This is known as 'guillotine'.

5. Passing of Appropriation Bill The Constitution states that 'no money shall be withdrawn from the Consolidated Fund of India except under appropriation made by law'. Accordingly, an appropriation bill is introduced to provide for the appropriation, out of the Consolidated Fund of India, all money required to meet:

(a) The grants voted by the Lok Sabha.

(b) The expenditure charged on the Consolidated Fund of India.

No such amendment can be proposed to the appropriation bill in either house of the Parliament that will have the effect of varying the amount or altering the destination of any grant voted, or of varying the amount of any expenditure charged on the Consolidated Fund of India.

The Appropriation Bill becomes the Appropriation Act after it is assented to by the President. This act authorises (or legalises) the payments from the Consolidated Fund of India. This means that the government cannot withdraw money from the Consolidated Fund of India till the enactment of the appropriation bill. This takes time and usually goes on till the end of April. But the government needs money to carry on its normal activities after 31 March (the end of the financial year). To overcome this functional difficulty, the Constitution has authorised the Lok Sabha to make any grant in advance in respect to the estimated expenditure for a part of the financial year, pending the completion of the voting of the demands for grants and the enactment of the appropriation bill. This provision is known as the 'vote on account'. It is passed (or granted) after the general discussion on budget is over. It is generally granted for two months for an amount equivalent to one-sixth of the total estimation.

6. Passing of Finance Bill The Finance Bill is introduced to give effect to the financial proposals of the Government of India for the following year. It is subjected to all the conditions applicable to a Money Bill. Unlike the Appropriation Bill, the amendments (seeking to reject or reduce a tax) can be moved in the case of finance bill.

According to the Provisional Collection of Taxes Act of 1931, the Finance Bill must be enacted (i.e., passed by the Parliament and assented to by the president) within 75 days.

The Finance Act legalises the income side of the budget and completes the process of the enactment of the budget.

Other Grants

In addition to the budget that contains the ordinary estimates of income and expenditure for one financial year, various other grants are made by the Parliament under extraordinary or special circumstances:

Supplementary Grant It is granted when the amount authorised by the Parliament through the appropriation act for a particular service for the current financial year is found to be insufficient for that year.

Additional Grant It is granted when a need has arisen during the current financial year for additional expenditure upon some new service not contempleted in the budget for that year.

Excess Grant It is granted when money has been spent on any service during a financial year in excess of the amount granted for that service in the budget for that year. It is voted by the Lok Sabha after the financial year. Before the demands for excess grants are submitted to the Lok Sabha for voting, they must be approved by the Public Accounts Committee of Parliament.

Vote of Credit It is granted for meeting an unexpected demand upon the resources of India, when on account of the magnitude or the indefinite character of the service, the demand cannot be stated with the details ordinarily given in a budget. Hence, it is like a blank cheque given to the Executive by the Lok Sabha.

Exceptional Grant It is granted for a special purpose and forms no part of the current service of any financial year.

Token Grant It is granted when funds to meet the proposed expenditure on a new service can be made available by reappropriation. A demand for the grant of a token sum (of Re 1) is submitted to the vote of the Lok Sabha and if assented, funds are made available. Reappropriation involves transfer of funds from one head to another. It does not involve any additional expenditure.

Supplementary, additional, excess and exceptional grants and vote of credit are regulated by the same procedure which is applicable in the case of a regular budget.

Funds

The Constitution of India provides for the following three kinds of funds for the Central government:

1. Consolidated Fund of India (Article 266)
2. Public Account of India (Article 266)
3. Contingency Fund of India (Article 267)

Consolidated Fund of India It is a fund to which all receipts are credited and all payments are debited. In other words, (a) all revenues received by the Government of India; (b) all loans raised by the Government by the issue of treasury bills, loans or ways and means of advances; and (c) all money received by the government in repayment of loans forms the Consolidated Fund of India. All the legally authorised payments on behalf of the Government of India are made out of this fund. No money out of this fund can be appropriated (issued or drawn) except in accordance with a parliamentary law.

Public Account of India All other public money (other than those which are credited to the Consolidated Fund of India) received by or on behalf of the Government of India shall be credited to the Public Account of India. This includes provident fund deposits, judicial deposits, savings bank deposits, departmental deposits, remittances and so on. This account is operated by executive action, that is, the payments from this account can by made without parliamentary appropriation. Such payments are mostly in the nature of banking transactions.

Contingency Fund of India The Constitution authorised the Parliament to establish a 'Contingency Fund of India', into which amounts determined by law are paid from time to time. Accordingly, the Parliament enacted the contingency fund of India Act in 1950. This fund is placed at the disposal of the president, and he can make advances out of it to meet unforeseen expenditure pending its authorisation by the Parliament. The fund is held by the finance secretary on behalf of the president. Like the public account of India, it is also operated by executive action.

MULTIFUNCTIONAL ROLE OF PARLIAMENT

In the 'Indian politico-administrative system', the Parliament occupies a central position and has a multifunctional role. It enjoys extensive powers and performs a variety of functions towards the fulfilment of its constitutionally expected role. Its powers and functions can be classified under the following heads:

1. Legislative Powers and Functions

2. Executive Powers and Functions
3. Financial Powers and Functions
4. Constituent Powers and Functions
5. Judicial Powers and Functions
6. Electoral Powers and Functions
7. Other powers and functions.

1. Legislative Powers and Functions

The primary function of Parliament is to make laws for the governance of the country. It has exclusive power to make laws on the subjects enumerated in the Union List (which at present has 100 subjects, originally 97 subjects) and on the residuary subjects (that is, subjects not enumerated in any of the three lists). With regard to Concurrent List (which has at present 52 subjects, originally 47 subjects), the Parliament has overriding powers, that is, the law of Parliament prevails over the law of the state legislature in case of a conflict between the two.

The Constitution also empowers the Parliament to make laws on the subjects enumerated in the State List (which at present has 61 subjects, originally 66 subjects) under the following five abnormal circumstances:

(a) when Rajya Sabha passes a resolution to that effect.
(b) when a proclamation of National Emergency is in operation.
(c) when two or more states make a joint request to the Parliament.
(d) when necessary to give effect to international agreements, treaties and conventions.
(e) when President's Rule is in operation in the state.

All the ordinances issued by the president (during the recess of the Parliament) must be approved by the Parliament within six weeks after its reassembly. An ordinance becomes inoperative if it is not approved by the parliament within that period.

The Parliament makes laws in a skeleton form and authorises the Executive to make detailed rules and regulations within the framework of the parent law. This is known as **delegated legislation** or executive legislation or subordinate legislation. Such rules and regulations are placed before the Parliament for its examination.

2. Executive Powers and Functions

The Constitution of India established a parliamentary form of government in which the Executive is responsible to the Parliament for its policies and acts. Hence, the Parliament exercises control over the Executive through question-hour, zero hour, half-an-hour discussion, short duration discussion, calling attention motion, adjournment motion, no-confidence motion, censure motion and other discussions. It also supervises the activities of the Executive with the help of its committees like committee on government assurance, committee on subordinate legislation, committee on petitions, etc.

The ministers are collectively responsible to the Parliament in general and to the Lok Sabha in particular. As a part of collective responsibility, there is individual responsibility, that is, each minister is individually responsible for the efficient administration of the ministry under his charge. This means that they continue in office so long as they enjoy the confidence of the majority members in the Lok Sabha. In other words, the council of ministers can be removed from office by the Lok Sabha by passing a no-confidence motion. The Lok Sabha can also express lack of confidence in the government in the following ways:

(a) By not passing a motion of thanks on the President's inaugural address.
(b) By rejecting a money bill.
(c) By passing a censure motion or an adjournment motion.
(d) By defeating the government on a vital issue.
(e) By passing a cut motion.

Therefore, "the first function of Parliament can be said to be to select the group which is to form the government, support and sustain it in power so long as it enjoys its confidence, and to expel it when it ceases to do so, and leave it to the people to decide at the next general election."[23]

3. Financial Powers and Functions

No tax can be levied or collected and no expenditure can be incurred by the Executive except under the authority and with the approval of Parliament. Hence, the budget is placed before the Parliament for its approval. The enactment of the budget by the

Parliament legalises the receipts and expenditure of the government for the ensuing financial year.

The Parliament also scrutinises government spending and financial performance with the help of its financial committees. These include public accounts committee, estimates committee and committee on public undertakings. They bring out the cases of illegal, irregular, unauthorised, improper usage and wastage and extravagance in public expenditure.

Therefore, the parliamentary control over the Executive in financial matters operates in two stages:

(a) budgetary control, that is, control before the appropriation of grants through the enactment of the budget; and

(b) post-budgetary control, that is, control after the appropriation of grants through the three financial committees.

The budget is based on the principle of annuality, that is, the Parliament grants money to the government for one financial year. If the granted money is not spent by the end of the financial year, then the balance expires and returns to the Consolidated Fund of India. This practice is known as the 'rule of lapse'. It facilitates effective financial control by the Parliament as no reserve funds can be built without its authorisation. However, the observance of this rule leads to heavy rush of expenditure towards the close of the financial year. This is popularly called as 'March Rush'.

4. Constituent Powers and Functions

The Parliament is vested with the powers to amend the Constitution by way of addition, variation or repeal of any provision. The major part of the Constitution can be amended by the Parliament with special majority, that is, a majority (that is, more than 50 per cent) of the total membership of each House and a majority of not less than two-thirds of the members present and voting in each House. Some other provisions of the Constitution can be amended by the Parliament with simple majority, that is, a majority of the members present and voting in each House of Parliament. Only a few provisions of the Constitution can be amended by the Parliament (by special majority) and with the consent of at least half of the state Legislatures (by simple majority). However, the power to initiate the process of the amendment of the Constitution (in all the three cases) lies exclusively in the hands of the Parliament and not the state legislature. There is only one exception, that is, the state legislature can pass a resolution requesting the Parliament for the creation or abolition of the legislative council in the state. Based on the resolution, the Parliament makes an act for amending the Constitution to that effect. To sum up, the Parliament can amend the Constitution in three ways:

(a) By simple majority;

(b) By special majority; and

(c) By special majority but with the consent of half of all the state legislatures.

The constituent power of the Parliament is not unlimited; it is subject to the 'basic structure' of the Constitution. In others words, the Parliament can amend any provision of the Constitution except the 'basic features' of the Constitution. This was ruled by the Supreme Court in the *Kesavananda Bharati* case (1973) and reaffirmed in the *Minerva Mills* case (1980)[24].

5. Judicial Powers and Functions

The judicial powers and functions of the Parliament include the following:

(a) It can impeach the President for the violation of the Constitution.

(b) It can remove the Vice-President from his office.

(c) It can recommend the removal of judges (including chief justice) of the Supreme Court and the high courts, chief election commissioner, comptroller and auditor general to the president.

(d) It can punish its members or outsiders for the breach of its privileges or its contempt.

6. Electoral Powers and Functions

The Parliament participates in the election of the President (along with the state legislative assemblies) and elects the Vice-President. The Lok Sabha elects its Speaker and Deputy Speaker, while the Rajya Sabha elects its Deputy Chairman.

The Parliament is also authorised to make laws to regulate the elections to the offices of President and Vice-President, to both the Houses of Parliament and to both the Houses of state legislature. Accordingly, Parliament enacted the Presidential and Vice-Presidential Election Act (1952), the Representation of People Act (1950), the Representation of People Act (1951), etc.

7. Other Powers and Functions

The various other powers and functions of the Parliament include:

(a) It serves as the highest deliberative body in the country. It discusses various issues of national and international significance.

(b) It approves all the three types of emergencies (national, state and financial) proclaimed by the President.

(c) It can create or abolish the state legislative councils on the recommendation of the concerned state legislative assemblies.

(d) It can increase or decrease the area, alter the boundaries and change the names of states of the Indian Union.

(e) It can regulate the organisation and jurisdiction of the Supreme Court and high courts and can establish a common high court for two or more states.

INEFFECTIVENESS OF PARLIAMENTARY CONTROL

The parliamentary control over government and administration in India is more theoretical than practical. In reality, the control is not as effective as it ought to be. The following factors are responsible for this:

(a) The Parliament has neither time nor expertise to control the administration which has grown in volume as well as complexity.

(b) Parliament's financial control is hindered by the technical nature of the demands for grants. The parliamentarians being laymen cannot understand them properly and fully.

(c) The legislative leadership lies with the Executive and it plays a significant role in formulating policies.

(d) The very size of the Parliament is too large and unmanagable to be effective.

(e) The majority support enjoyed by the Executive in the Parliament reduces the possibility of effective criticism.

(f) The financial committees like Public Accounts Committee examines the public expenditure after it has been incurred by the Executive. Thus, they do post mortem work.

(g) The increased recourse to 'guillotine' reduced the scope of financial control.

(h) The growth of 'delegated legislation' has reduced the role of Parliament in making detailed laws and has increased the powers of bureaucracy.

(i) The frequent promulgation of ordinances by the president dilutes the Parliament's power of legislation.

(j) The Parliament's control is sporadic, general and mostly political in nature.

(k) Lack of strong and steady opposition in the Parliament, and a setback in the parliamentary behaviour and ethics, have also contributed to the ineffectiveness of legislative control over administration in India.

POSITION OF RAJYA SABHA

The Constitutional position of the Rajya Sabha (as compared with the Lok Sabha) can be studied from three angles:

1. Where Rajya Sabha is equal to Lok Sabha.
2. Where Rajya Sabha is unequal to Lok Sabha.
3. Where Rajya Sabha has special powers that are not at all shared with the Lok Sabha.

Equal Status with Lok Sabha

In the following matters, the powers and status of the Rajya Sabha are equal to that of the Lok Sabha:

1. Introduction and passage of ordinary bills.
2. Introduction and passage of Constitutional amendment bills.
3. Introduction and passage of financial bills involving expenditure from the Consolidated Fund of India.

4. Election and impeachment of the president.
5. Election and removal of the Vice-President. However, Rajya Sabha alone can initiate the removal of the vice-president. He is removed by a resolution passed by the Rajya Sabha by a special majority and agreed to by the Lok Sabha by a simple majority.
6. Making recommendation to the President for the removal of Chief Justice and judges of Supreme Court and high courts, chief election commissioner and comptroller and auditor general.
7. Approval of ordinances issued by the President.
8. Approval of proclamation of all three types of emergencies by the President.
9. Selection of ministers including the Prime Minister. Under the Constitution, the ministers including the Prime Minister can be members of either House. However, irrespective of their membership, they are responsible only to the Lok Sabha.
10. Consideration of the reports of the constitutional bodies like Finance Commission, Union Public Service Commission, comptroller and auditor general, etc.
11. Enlargement of the jurisdiction of the Supreme Court and the Union Public Service Commission.

Unequal Status with Lok Sabha

In the following matters, the powers and status of the Rajya Sabha are unequal to that of the Lok Sabha:

1. A Money Bill can be introduced only in the Lok Sabha and not in the Rajya Sabha.
2. Rajya Sabha cannot amend or reject a Money Bill. It should return the bill to the Lok Sabha within 14 days, either with recommendations or without recommendations.
3. The Lok Sabha can either accept or reject all or any of the recommendations of the Rajya Sabha. In both the cases, the money bill is deemed to have been passed by the two Houses.
4. A financial bill, not containing solely the matters of Article 110, also can be introduced only in the Lok Sabha and not in the Rajya Sabha. But, with regard to its passage, both the Houses have equal powers.

5. The final power to decide whether a particular bill is a Money Bill or not is vested in the Speaker of the Lok Sabha.
6. The Speaker of Lok Sabha presides over the joint sitting of both the Houses.
7. The Lok Sabha with greater number wins the battle in a joint sitting except when the combined strength of the ruling party in both the Houses is less than that of the opposition parties.
8. Rajya Sabha can only discuss the budget but cannot vote on the demands for grants (which is the exclusive privilege of the Lok Sabha).
9. A resolution for the discontinuance of the national emergency can be passed only by the Lok Sabha and not by the Rajya Sabha.
10. The Rajya Sabha cannot remove the council of ministers by passing a no-confidence motion. This is because the Council of ministers is collectively responsible only to the Lok Sabha. But, the Rajya Sabha can discuss and criticise the policies and activities of the government.

Special Powers of Rajya Sabha

Due to its federal character, the Rajya Sabha has been given two exclusive or special powers that are not enjoyed by the Lok Sabha:

1. It can authorise the Parliament to make a law on a subject enumerated in the State List (Article 249).
2. It can authorise the Parliament to create new All-India Services common to both the Centre and states (Article 312).

An analysis of the above points makes it clear that the position of the Rajya Sabha in our constitutional system is not as weak as that of the House of Lords in the British constitutional system nor as strong as that of the Senate in the American constitutional system. Except in financial matters and control over the council of ministers, the powers and status of the Rajya Sabha in all other spheres are broadly equal and coordinate with that of the Lok Sabha.

Even though the Rajya Sabha has been given less powers as compared with the Lok Sabha, its utility is supported on the following grounds:

1. It checks hasty, defective, careless and ill-considered legislation made by the Lok Sabha by making provision of revision and thought.

2. It facilitates giving representation to eminent professionals and experts who cannot face the direct election. The President nominates 12 such persons to the Rajya Sabha.
3. It maintains the federal equilibrium by protecting the interests of the states against the undue interference of the Centre.

Public Accounts Committee

This committee was setup first in 1921 under the provisions of the Government of India Act of 1919 and has since been in existence. At present, it consists of 22 members (15 from the Lok Sabha and 7 from the Rajya Sabha). The members are elected by the Parliament every year from amongst its members according to the principle of proportional representation by means of the single transferable vote. Thus, all parties get due representation in it. The term of office of the members is one year. A minister cannot be elected as a member of the committee. The chairman of the committee is appointed by the Speaker from amongst its members. Until 1966–67, the chairman of the committee belonged to the ruling party. However, since 1967 a convention has developed whereby the chairman of the committee is selected invariably from the Opposition.

The function of the committee is to examine the annual audit reports of the comptroller and auditor general of India (CAG), which are laid before the Parliament by the president. The CAG submits three audit reports to the president, namely, audit report on appropriation accounts, audit report on finance accounts and audit report on public undertakings.

The committee examines public expenditure not only from legal and formal point of view to discover technical irregularities but also from the point of view of economy, prudence, wisdom and propriety to bring out the cases of waste, loss, corruption, extravagance, inefficiency and nugatory expenses.

In more detail, the functions of the Committee are:
1. To examine the appropriation accounts and the finance accounts of the Union government and any other accounts laid before the Lok Sabha. The appropriation accounts compare the actual expenditure with the expenditure sanctioned by the Parliament through the appropriation act, while the finance accounts shows the annual receipts and disbursements of the Union government.
2. In scrutinising the appropriation accounts and the audit report of CAG on it, the Committee has to satisfy itself that:
   (a) the money that has been disbursed was legally available for the applied service or purpose;
   (b) the expenditure conforms to the authority that governs it; and
   (c) every reappropriation has been made in accordance with the related rules.
3. To examine the accounts of state corporations, trading concerns and manufacturing projects and the audit report of CAG on them (except those public undertakings which are allotted to the committee on public undertakings).
4. To examine the accounts of autonomous and semi-autonomous bodies, the audit of which is conducted by the CAG.
5. To consider the report of the CAG relating to an audit of any receipts or to examine the accounts of stores and stocks.
6. To examine money spent on any service during a financial year in excess of the amount granted by the Lok Sabha for that purpose.

In the fulfilment of the above functions, the committee is assisted by the CAG.

Estimates Committee

The origin of this committee can be traced to the standing financial committee set up in 1921. The first Estimates Committee in the post-independence era was constituted in 1950 on the recommendation of John Mathai, the then finance minister. Originally, it had 25 members but in 1956 its membership was raised to 30. All the thirty members are from Lok Sabha only. The Rajya Sabha has no representation in this committee. These members are elected by the Lok Sabha every year from amongst its members, according to the principles of proportional representation by means of a single transferable vote. Thus, all parties get due representation in it. The term of office is one year. A minister cannot be elected as a member of the committee. The chairman of the committee is appointed by the Speaker from amongst its members and he is invariably from the ruling party.

The function of the committee is to examine

the estimates included in the budget and suggest 'economies' in public expenditure. Hence, it has been described as a 'continuous economy committee'. In more detail, the functions of the committee are:

1. To report what economies, improvements in organisation, efficiency and administrative reform consistent with the policy underlying the estimates, can be affected.
2. To suggest alternative policies in order to bring about efficiency and economy in administration.
3. To examine whether the money is well laid out within the limits of the policy implied in the estimates.
4. To suggest the form in which the estimates are to be presented to Parliament.

The committee continues the examination of the estimates from time to time, throughout the financial year and report to the House as its examination proceeds. It is not incumbent on the committee to examine the entire estimates of any one year. The demands for grants are finally voted despite the fact that the committee has made no report.

Committee on Public Undertakings

This committee was created in 1964 on the recommendation of the Krishna Menon Committee. Originally, it had 15 members (10 from the Lok Sabha and 5 from the Rajya Sabha). However, in 1974, its membership was raised to 22 (15 from the Lok Sabha and 7 from the Rajya Sabha). The members are elected by the Parliament every year from amongst its members according to the principle of proportional representation by means of a single transferable vote. Thus, all parties get due representation in it. The term of office of the members is one year. A minister cannot be elected as a member of the committee. The chairman of the committee is appointed by the Speaker from amongst its members who are drawn from the Lok Sabha only. Thus, the members of the committee who are from the Rajya Sabha cannot be appointed as the chairman.

The functions of the committee are:

1. To examine the reports and accounts of public undertakings.
2. To examine the reports of the comptroller and auditor general on public undertakings.

3. To examine whether the affairs of the public undertakings are being managed in accordance with sound business principles and prudent commercial practices.
4. To exercise such other functions vested in the public accounts committee and the estimates committee in relation to public undertakings which are allotted to it by the Speaker from time to time.

The committee is not to examine and investigate any of the following:

1. Matters of major government policy as distinct from business or commercial functions of the public undertakings.
2. Matters of day-to-day administration.
3. Matters for the consideration of which machinery is established by any special statute under which a particular public undertaking is established.

Departmental Standing Committees

On the recommendation of the Rules Committee of the Lok Sabha, 17 departmentally related standing committees were set-up in 1993. In 2004, seven more such committees were set-up, thus increasing their number from 17 to 24.

The standing committees assist the Parliament in debating the budget more effectively. The main objective is to secure more accountability of the Executive to the Parliament, particularly financial accountability.

The 24 standing committees cover under their jurisdiction all the ministries / departments of the Central Government.

Each standing committee consists of 31 members (21 from Lok Sabha and 10 from Rajya Sabha). The members of the Lok Sabha are nominated by the Speaker from amongst its members, while the members of the Rajya Sabha are nominated by the Chairman from amongst its members.

A minister is not eligible to be nominated as a member of any of the standing committee. In case a member, after his nomination to any of the standing committee, is appointed as a minister, he then ceases to be a member of the committee.

The term of office of each standing committee is one year from the date of its constitution.

Out of the 24 standing committees, 8 committees work under the Rajya Sabha and 16 committees work under the Lok Sabha.

The functions of each of the standing committees are:

1. To consider the demands for grants of the concerned ministries/departments before they are discussed and voted in the Lok Sabha. Its report should not suggest anything of the nature of cut motions.
2. To examine bills pertaining to the concerned ministries/departments.
3. To consider annual reports of ministries/departments.
4. To consider national basic long-term policy documents presented to the Houses.

The limitations that are imposed on the functioning of these standing committees are:

1. They should not consider the matters of day-to-day administration of the concerned ministries/departments.
2. They should not generally consider the matters which are considered by other parliamentary committees.

It should be noted here that the recommendations of these committees are advisory in nature and hence not binding on Parliament.

The merits of the standing committee system in the Parliament are:

1. Their proceedings are devoid of any party bias.
2. The procedure adopted by them is more flexible than in the Lok Sabha.
3. The system makes parliamentary control over Executive much more detailed, close, continuous, indepth and comprehensive.
4. The system ensures economy and efficiency in public expenditure as the ministries/departments would now be more careful in formulating their demands.
5. They facilitate opportunities to all the members of Parliament to participate and understand the functioning of the government and contribute to it.
6. They can avail of expert opinion or public opinion to make the reports. They are authorised to invite experts and eminent persons to testify before them and incorporate their opinions in their reports.

7. The opposition parties and the Rajya Sabha can now play a greater role in exercising financial control over the Executive.

Business Advisory Committee

It regulates the programme and time table of the House. It allocates time for the transaction of legislative and other business brought before the House by the government. The Lok Sabha committee consists of 15 members including the Speaker as its chairman. In the Rajya Sabha, it has 11 members including the Chairman as its *ex-officio* chairman.

Committee on Private Members' Bills and Resolutions

It classifies the bills and allocates time for the discussion of bills and resolutions introduced by private members (other than ministers). This is a special committee of the Lok Sabha and consists of 15 members including the Deputy Speaker as its chairman. The Rajya Sabha does not have such a committee. The same function in the Rajya Sabha is performed by the business advisory committee of that House.

Committee on Government Assurances

It examines the assurances, promises and undertakings given by ministers from time to time on the floor of the House and reports on the extent to which they have been implemented. In the Lok Sabha, it consists of 15 members and in the Rajya Sabha, it consists of 10 members. It was constituted in 1953.

Committee on Subordinate Legislation

It examines and reports to the House whether the powers to make regulations, rules, sub-rules and bye-laws delegated by the Parliament or conferred by the Constitution to the Executive are being properly exercised by it. In both the Houses, the committee consists of 15 members. It was constituted in 1953.

Committee on Welfare of SCs and STs

It consists of 30 members (20 from Lok Sabha and

10 from Rajya Sabha). Its functions are: (i) to consider the reports of the National Commission for the SCs and the National Commission for the STs; (ii) to examine all matters relating to the welfare of SCs and STs like implementation of constitutional and statutory safeguards, working of welfare programmes, etc.

Committee on Absence of Members

It considers all applications from members for leave of absence from the sittings of the House; and examines the cases of members who had been absent for a period of 60 days or more without permission. It is a special committee of the Lok Sabha and consists of 15 members. There is no such committee in the Rajya Sabha and all such matters are dealt by the House itself.

Rules Committee

It considers the matters of procedure and conduct of business in the House and recommends necessary amendments, or additions to the Rules of the House. The Lok Sabha committee consists of 15 members including the Speaker as its *ex-officio* chairman. In Rajya Sabha, it consists of 16 members including the Chairman as its *ex-officio* chairman.

General Purposes Committee

It considers and advises on matters concerning affairs of the House, which do not fall within the jurisdiction of any other parliamentary committee. In each House, the committee consists of the presiding officer (Speaker/Chairman) as its *ex-officio* chairman, Deputy Speaker (Deputy Chairman in the case of Rajya Sabha), members of panel of chairpersons (panel of vice-chairpersons in the case of Rajya Sabha), chairpersons of all the departmental standing committees of the House, leaders of recognised parties and groups in the House and such other members as nominated by the presiding officer.

Committee of Privileges

Its functions are semi-judicial in nature. It examines the cases of breach of privileges of the House and its members and recommends appropriate action. The Lok Sabha committee has 15 members, while the Rajya Sabha committee has 10 members.

Joint Committee on Salaries and Allowances of Members

It was constituted under the Salary, Allowances and Pension of Members of Parliament Act, 1954. It consists of 15 members (10 from Lok Sabha and 5 from Rajya Sabha). It frames rules for regulating payment of salary, allowances and pension to members of Parliament.

House Committee

It deals with residential accommodation of members and other amenities like food, medical aid, etc. accorded to them in their houses and hostels in Delhi. Both the Houses have their respective House committee. In the Lok Sabha, it consists of 12 members.

Committee on Petitions

It examines petitions on bills and on matters of general public importance. It also entertains representations from individuals and associations on matters pertaining to Union subjects. The Lok Sabha committee consists of 15 members, while the Rajya Sabha committee consists of 10 members.

Library Committee

It considers all matters relating to library of Parliament and assist the members in utilising the library services. It consists of nine members (six from Lok Sabha and three from Rajya Sabha).

Ethics Committee

It was constituted in Rajya Sabha in 1997 and in Lok Sabha in 2000. It enforces the code of conduct of members of Parliament. It examines the cases of misconduct and recommends appropriate action. Thus, it is engaged in maintaining discipline and decorum in Parliament.

Committee on Empowerment of Women

It was constituted in 1997 and consists of 30 members (20 from Lok Sabha and 10 from Rajya Sabha). It considers the reports of the National Commission for Women and examines the measures taken by the Union government to secure status, dignity and equality for women in all fields.

Committee on Papers Laid on the Table

It was constituted in 1975. The Lok Sabha Committee has 15 members, while the Rajya Sabha Committee has 10 members. It examines all papers laid on the table of the House by ministers to see whether they comply with provisions of the Constitution, Act or Rule. It does not examine statutory notifications and orders that fall under the jurisdiction of the Committee on Subordinate Legislation.

Joint Committee on Offices of Profit

It examines the composition and character of committees and other bodies appointed by the Central, state and union territory governments and recommends whether persons holding these offices should be disqualified from being elected as members of Parliament or not. It consists of 15 members (10 from Lok Sabha and 5 from Rajya Sabha).

Consultative Committees

The consultative committees are attached to various ministries / departments of the Central Government. They consists of members of both the Houses of Parliament. The Minister/Minister of State in-charge of the Ministry concerned acts as the chairman of the consultative committee of that ministry.

These committees provide a forum for informal discussions between the ministers and the members of Parliament on policies and programmes of the government and the manner of their implementation.

These committees are constituted by the Ministry of Parliamentary Affairs. The guidelines regarding the composition, functions and procedures of these committees are formulated by this Ministry. The Ministry also makes arrangements for holding their meetings both during the session and the inter-session period of Parliament.

These committees are normally constituted after the new Lok Sabha is constituted, after general elections for the Lok Sabha. After the constitution of the 14th Lok Sabha, 29 consultative committees were constituted in October 2004. Subsequently, three more consultative committees were constituted, thus raising their number to 32.

In addition, the separate Informal Consultative Committees of the members of Parliament are also constituted for all the Railway Zones. The members of Parliament belonging to the area falling under a particular Railway Zone are nominated on the Informal Consultative Committee of that Railway Zone. After the constitution of 14th Lok Sabha, 16 Informal Consultative Committees for the 16 Railway Zones have been constituted.

Unlike the Consultative Committees attached to various ministries/departments, the meetings of the Informal Consultative Committees are to be arranged during the session periods only.

PARLIAMENTARY PRIVILEGES

Meaning

Parliamentary privileges are special rights, immunities and exemptions enjoyed by the two Houses of Parliament, their committees and their members. They are necessary in order to secure the independence and effectiveness of their actions. Without these privileges, the Houses can neither maintain their authority, dignity and honour nor can protect their members from any obstruction in the discharge of their parliamentary responsibilities.

The Constitution has also extended the parliamentary privileges to those persons who are entitled to speak and take part in the proceedings of a House of Parliament or any of its committees. These include the attorney general of India and Union ministers.

It must be clarified here that the parliamentary privileges do not extend to the president who is also an integral part of the Parliament.

Classification

Parliamentary privileges can be classified into two broad categories:

1. those that are enjoyed by each House of Parliament collectively, and
2. those that are enjoyed by the members individually.

Collective Privileges   The privileges belonging to each House of Parliament collectively are:

1. In has the right to publish its reports, debates and proceedings and also the right to prohibit others from publishing the same. The 44th Amendment Act of 1978 restored the freedom

of the press to publish true reports of parliamentary proceedings without prior permission of the House. But this is not applicable in the case of a secret sitting of the House.

2. It can exclude strangers from its proceedings and hold secret sittings to discuss some important matters.

3. It can make rules to regulate its own procedure and the conduct of its business and to adjudicate upon such matters.

4. It can punish members as well as outsiders for breach of its privileges or its contempt by reprimand, admonition or imprisonment (also suspension or expulsion, in case of members).[25]

5. It has the right to receive immediate information of the arrest, detention, conviction, imprisonment and release of a member.

6. It can institute inquiries and order the attendance of witnesses and send for relevant papers and records.

7. The courts are prohibited to inquire into the proceedings of a House or its committees.

8. No person (either a member or outsider) can be arrested, and no legal process (civil or criminal) can be served within the precincts of the House without the permission of the presiding officer.

Individual Privileges The privileges belonging to the members individually are:

1. They cannot be arrested during the session of Parliament and 40 days before the beginning and 40 days after the end of a session. This privilege is available only in civil cases and not in criminal cases or preventive detention cases.

2. They have freedom of speech in Parliament. No member is liable to any proceedings in any court for anything said or any vote given by him in Parliament or its committees. This freedom is subject to the provisions of the Constitution and to the rules and standing orders regulating the procedure of Parliament.[26]

3. They are exempted from jury service. They can refuse to give evidence and appear as a witness in a case pending in a court when Parliament is in session.

Breach of Privilege and Contempt of the House

"When any individual or authority disregards or attacks any of the privileges, rights and immunities, either of the member individually or of the House in its collective capacity, the offence is termed as breach of privilege and is punishable by the House."[27]

Any act or omission which obstructs a House of Parliament, its member or its officer in the performance of their functions or which has a tendency, directly or indirectly to produce results against the dignity, authority and honour of the House is treated as a contempt of the House.[28]

Though the two phrases, 'breach of privilege' and 'contempt of the House' are used interchangeably, they have different implications. 'Normally, a breach of privilege may amount to contempt of the House. Likewise, contempt of the House may include a breach of privilege also. Contempt of the House, however, has wider implications. There may be a contempt of the House without specifically committing a breach of privilege'.[29] Similarly, 'actions which are not breaches of any specific privilege but are offences against the dignity and authority of the House amount to contempt of the House'.[30] For example, disobedience to a legitimate order of the House is not a breach of privilege, but can be punished as contempt of the House.

Sources of Privileges

Originally, the Constitution (Article 105) expressedly mentioned two privileges, that is, freedom of speech in Parliament and right of publication of its proceedings. With regard to other privileges, it provided that they were to be the same as those of the British House of Commons, its committees and its members on the date of its commencement (ie, 26 January, 1950), until defined by Parliament. The 44th Amendment Act of 1978 provided that the other privileges of each House of Parliament, its committees and its members are to be those which they had on the date of its commencement (ie, 20 June, 1979), until defined by Parliament. This means that the position with regard to other privileges remains same. In other words, the amendment has made only verbal changes by dropping a direct reference to the British House of Commons, without making any change in the implication of the provision.[31]

It should be noted here that the Parliament, till now, has not made any special law to exhaustively codify all the privileges. They are based on five sources, namely,

1. Constitutional provisions,
2. Various laws made by Parliament,
3. Rules of both the Houses,
4. Parliamentary conventions, and
5. Judicial interpretations.

SOVEREIGNTY OF PARLIAMENT

The doctrine of 'sovereignty of Parliament' is associated with the British Parliament. Sovereignty means the supreme power within the State. That supreme power in Great Britain lies with the Parliament. There are no 'legal' restrictions on its authority and jurisdiction.

Therefore, the sovereignty of Parliament (parliamentary supremacy) is a cardinal feature of the British constitutional system. According to AV Dicey, the British jurist, this principle has three implications:[32]

1. The Parliament can make, amend, substitute or repeal any law. De Lolme, a British political analyst, said, 'The British Parliament can do every thing except make a woman a man and a man a woman'.
2. The Parliament can make constitutional laws by the same procedure as ordinary laws. In other words, there is no legal distinction between the constituent authority and the legislative authority of the British Parliament.
3. The Parliamentary laws cannot be declared invalid by the Judiciary as being unconstitutional. In other words, there is no system of judicial review in Britain.

The Indian Parliament, on the other hand, cannot be regarded as a sovereign body in the similar sense as there are 'legal' restrictions on its authority and jurisdiction. The factors that limit the sovereignty of Indian Parliament are:

1. Written Nature of the Constitution

The Constitution is the fundamental law of the land in our country. It has defined the authority and

jurisdiction of all the three organs of the Union government and the nature of interrelationship between them. Hence, the Parliament has to operate within the limits prescribed by the Constitution. There is also a legal distinction between the legislative authority and the constituent authority of the Parliament. Moreover, to effect certain amendments to the Constitution, the ratification of half of the states is also required. In Britain, on the other hand, the Constitution is neither written nor there is anything like a fundamental law of the land.

2. Federal System of Government

India has a federal system of government with a constitutional division of powers between the Union and the states. Both have to operate within the spheres allotted to them. Hence, the law-making authority of the Parliament gets confined to the subjects enumerated in the Union List and Concurrent List and does not extend to the subjects enumerated in the State List (except in five abnormal circumstances and that too for a short period). Britain, on the other hand, has a unitary system of government and hence, all the powers are vested in the Centre.

3. System of Judicial Review

The adoption of an independent Judiciary with the power of judicial review also restricts the supremacy of our Parliament. Both the Supreme Court and high courts can declare the laws enacted by the Parliament as void and *ultra vires* (unconstitutional), if they contravene any provision of the Constitution. On the other hand, there is no system of judicial review in Britain. The British Courts have to apply the Parliamentary laws to specific cases, without examining their constitutionality, legality or reasonableness.

4. Fundamental Rights

The authority of the Parliament is also restricted by the incorporation of a code of justiciable fundamental rights under Part III of the Constitution. Article 13 prohibits the State from making a law that either takes away totally or abrogates in part a fundamental right. Hence, a Parliamentary law that contravenes the fundamental rights shall be void. In Britain, on the other hand, there is no codification of justiciable fundamental rights in the Constitution. The British

Table 22.5 *Allocation of Seats in Parliament*

S.No.	States/UTs	No. of Seats in Rajya Sabha	No. of Seats in Lok Sabha
I. States			
1.	Andhra Pradesh	18	42
2.	Arunachal Pradesh	1	2
3.	Assam	7	14
4.	Bihar	16	40
5.	Chhattisgarh	5	11
6.	Goa	1	2
7.	Gujarat	11	26
8.	Haryana	5	10
9.	Himachal Pradesh	3	4
10.	Jammu and Kashmir	4	6
11.	Jharkhand	6	14
12.	Karnataka	12	28
13.	Kerala	9	20
14.	Madhya Pradesh	11	29
15.	Maharashtra	19	48
16.	Manipur	1	2
17.	Meghalaya	1	2
18.	Mizoram	1	1
19.	Nagaland	1	1
20.	Orissa	10	21
21.	Punjab	7	13
22.	Rajasthan	10	25
23.	Sikkim	1	1
24.	Tamil Nadu	18	39
25.	Tripura	1	2
26.	Uttarakhand	3	5
27.	Uttar Pradesh	31	80
28.	West Bengal	16	42
II. Union Territories			
1.	Andaman and Nicobar Islands	—	1
2.	Chandigarh	—	1
3.	Dadra and Nagar Haveli	—	1
4.	Daman and Diu	—	1
5.	Delhi (The National Capital Territory of Delhi)	3	7
6.	Lakshadweep	—	1
7.	Puducherry	1	1
III. Nominated members		12	2
	Total	245	545

Table 22.6 *Seats Reserved for SCs and STs in the Lok Sabha*

Name of the State/Union Territory	Number of Seats in the House before the Delimitation in 2008			Number of Seats in the House after the Delimitation in 2008		
	Total	Reserved for the Scheduled	Reserved for the Scheduled Castes Tribes	Total	Reserved for the Scheduled Castes	Reserved for the Scheduled Tribes
I. STATES:						
1. Andhra Pradesh	42	6	2	42	7	3
2. Arunachal Pradesh*	2	—	—	2	—	—
3. Assam*	14	1	2	14	1	2
4. Bihar	40	7	—	40	6	—
5. Chhattisgarh	11	2	4	11	1	4
6. Goa	2	—	—	2	—	—
7. Gujarat	26	2	4	26	2	4
8. Haryana	10	2	—	10	2	—
9. Himachal Pradesh	4	1	—	4	1	—
10. Jammu and Kashmir*	6	—	—	6	—	—
11. Jharkhand@	14	1	5	14	1	5
12. Karnataka	28	4	—	28	5	2
13. Kerala	20	2	—	20	2	—
14. Madhya Pradesh	29	4	5	29	4	6
15. Maharashtra	48	3	4	48	5	4
16. Manipur*	2	—	1	2	—	1
17. Meghalaya	2	—	—	2	—	2
18. Mizoram	1	—	1	1	—	1
19. Nagaland*	1	—	—	1	—	—
20. Orissa	21	3	5	21	3	5
21. Punjab	13	3	—	13	4	—
22. Rajasthan	25	4	3	25	4	3
23. Sikkim	1	—	—	1	—	—
24. Tamil Nadu	39	7	—	39	7	—
25. Tripura	2	—	1	2	—	1
26. Uttarakhand	5	—	—	5	1	—
27. Uttar Pradesh	80	18	—	80	17	—
28. West Bengal	42	8	2	42	10	2

(Contd.)

Table 22.6 (*Contd.*)

II. UNION TERRITORIES:

1.	Andaman and Nicobar Islands	1	—	—	1	—	—
2.	Chandigarh	1	—	—	1	—	—
3.	Dadra and Nagar Haveli	1	—	1	1	—	1
4.	Daman and Diu	1	—	—	1	—	—
5.	Delhi (The National Capital Territory of Delhi)	7	1	—	7	1	—
6.	Lakshadweep	1	—	1	1	—	1
7.	Puducherry	1	—	—	1	—	—
	Total	**543**	**79**	**41**	**543**	**84**	**47**

*States excluded from Delimitation Exercise
@Order issued by the Delimitation Commission was nullified by the Sec 10 B of the Delimitation Amendment Act, 2008

Table 22.7 *Durations of the Lok Sabha*

Lok Sabha	Duration	Remarks
First	1952–1957	Dissolved 38 days before expiry of its term.
Second	1957–1962	Dissolved 40 days before expiry of its term.
Third	1962–1967	Dissolved 44 days before expiry of its term.
Fourth	1967–1970	Dissolved one year and 79 days before expiry of its term.
Fifth	1971–1977	Term of the Lok Sabha was extended two times by one year at a time. However, the House was dissolved after having been in existence for a period of five years, 10 months and six days.
Sixth	1977–1979	Dissolved after having been in existence for a period of two years, four months and 28 days.
Seventh	1980–1984	Dissolved 20 days before expiry of its term.
Eighth	1985–1989	Dissolved 48 days before expiry of its term.
Ninth	1989–1991	Dissolved after having been in existence for a period of one year, two months and 25 days.
Tenth	1991–1996	—
Eleventh	1996–1997	Dissolved after having been in existence for a period of one year, six months and 13 days.
Twelfth	1998–1999	Dissolved after having been in existence for a period of one year, one month and four days.
Thirteenth	1999–2004	Dissolved 253 days before expiry of its term.
Fourteenth	2004–2009	—
Fifteenth	2009–continuing	—

Table 22.8 *Speakers of the Lok Sabha*

Lok Sabha	Name	Tenure (Remarks)
First	1. Ganesh Vasudev Mavalanker	1952 to 1956 (Died)
	2. Ananthasayanam Ayyangar	1956 to 1957
Second	Ananthasayanam Ayyangar	1957 to 1962
Third	Hukum Singh	1962 to 1967
Fourth	1. Neelam Sanjiva Reddy	1967 to 1969 (Resigned)
	2. Gurdial Singh Dhillan	1969 to 1971
Fifth	1. Gurdial Singh Dhillan	1971 to 1975 (Resigned)
	2. Bali Ram Bhagat	1976 to 1977
Sixth	1. Neelam Sanjiva Reddy	1977 to 1977 (Resigned)
	2. K.S. Hegde	1977 to 1980
Seventh	Balram Jakhar	1980 to 1985
Eighth	Balram Jakhar	1985 to 1989
Ninth	Rabi Ray	1989 to 1991
Tenth	Shivraj Patil	1991 to 1996
Eleventh	P.A. Sangma	1996 to 1998
Twelfth	G.M.C. Balayogi	1998 to 1999
Thirteenth	1. G.M.C. Balayogi	1999 to 2002 (Died)
	2. Manohar Joshi	2002 to 2004
Fourteenth	Somnath Chatterjee	2004 to 2009
Fifteenth	Ms. Meira Kumar	2009 – till date

Table 22.9 *Articles Related to Parliament at a Glance*

Article No.	Subject-matter
General	
79.	Constitution of Parliament
80.	Composition of the Council of States
81.	Composition of the House of the People
82.	Readjustment after each census
83.	Duration of Houses of Parliament
84.	Qualification for membership of Parliament
85.	Sessions of Parliament, prorogation and dissolution
86.	Right of President to address and send messages to Houses
87.	Special address by the President
88.	Rights of Ministers and Attorney-General as respects Houses

(Contd.)

Table 22.9 *(Contd.)*

Article No.	Subject-matter
Officers of Parliament	
89.	The Chairman and Deputy Chairman of the Council of States
90.	Vacation and resignation of, and removal from, the office of Deputy Chairman
91.	Power of the Deputy Chairman or other person to perform the duties of the office of, or to act as, Chairman
92.	The Chairman or the Deputy Chairman not to preside while a resolution for his removal from office is under consideration
93.	The Speaker and Deputy Speaker of the House of the People
94.	Vacation and resignation of, and removal from, the offices of Speaker and Deputy Speaker
95.	Power of the Deputy Speaker or other person to perform the duties of the office of, or to act as, Speaker
96.	The Speaker or the Deputy Speaker not to preside while a resolution for his removal from office is under consideration
97.	Salaries and allowances of the Chairman and Deputy Chairman and the Speaker and Deputy Speaker
98.	Secretariat of Parliament
Conduct of Business	
99.	Oath or affirmation by members
100.	Voting in Houses, power of Houses to act notwithstanding vacancies and quorum
Disqualifications of Members	
101.	Vacation of seats
102.	Disqualifications for membership
103.	Decision on questions as to disqualifications of members
104.	Penalty for sitting and voting before making oath or affirmation under article 99 or when not qualified or when disqualified
Powers, Privileges and Immunities of Parliament and its Members	
105.	Powers, privileges, etc., of the Houses of Parliament and of the members and committees thereof
106.	Salaries and allowances of members
Legislative Procedure	
107.	Provisions as to introduction and passing of Bills
108.	Joint sitting of both Houses in certain cases
109.	Special procedure in respect of Money Bills
110.	Definition of "Money Bills"
111.	Assent to Bills
Procedures in Financial Matters	
112.	Annual financial statement
113.	Procedure in Parliament with respect to estimates

(Contd.)

Article No.	Subject-matter
114.	Appropriation Bills
115.	Supplementary, additional or excess grants
116.	Votes on account, votes of credit and exceptional grants
117.	Special provisions as to financial Bills
Procedure Generally	
118.	Rules of procedure
119.	Regulation by law of procedure in Parliament in relation to financial business
120.	Language to be used in Parliament
121.	Restriction on discussion in Parliament
122.	Courts not to inquire into proceedings of Parliament
Legislative Powers of the President	
123.	Power of President to promulgate Ordinances during recess of Parliament

Parliament has also not made any law that lays down the fundamental rights of the citizens. However, it does not mean that the British citizens do not have rights. Though there is no charter guaranteeing rights, there is maximum liberty in Britain due to the existence of the Rule of Law.

Therefore, even though the nomenclature and organisational pattern of our Parliament is similar to that of the British Parliament, there is a substantial difference between the two. The Indian Parliament is not a sovereign body in the sense in which the British Parliament is a sovereign body. Unlike the British Parliament, the authority and jurisdiction of the Indian Parliament are defined, limited and restrained.

In this regard, the Indian Parliament is similar to the American Legislature (known as Congress). In USA also, the sovereignty of Congress is legally restricted by the written character of the Constitution, the federal system of government, the system of judicial review and the Bill of Rights.

NOTES AND REFERENCES

1. Westminster is a place in London where the British Parliament is located. It is often used as a symbol of the British Parliament.
2. See Table 22.5 at the end of this chapter.
3. An Anglo-Indian is a person whose father or any of whose other male progenitors in the male line is or was of European descent but who is domiciled within the territory of India and is or was born within such territory of parents habitually resident therein and not merely established there for temporary purposes.
4. See Table 22.5 at the end of this chapter.
5. This means that the number of Lok Sabha seats reserved in a state or union territory for such castes and tribes is to bear the same proportion to the total number of seats allotted to that state or union territory in the Lok Sabha as the population of such castes and tribes in the concerned state or union territory bears to the total population of state or union territory.
6. Under this, the president has made the Rajya Sabha (Term of Office of Members) Order, 1952.
7. The term of the fifth Lok Sabha that was to expire on 18 March, 1976, was extended by one year upto 18 March, 1977 by the House of the People (Extension of Duration) Act, 1976. It was extended for a further period of one year up to 18 March, 1978 by the House of the People (Extension of Duration) Amendment Act, 1976. However, the House was dissolved on 18 January 1977, after having been in existence for a period of five years, 10 months and six days.
8. A minister in the Union or state government is not considered as holding the office

of profit. Also, the Parliament can declare that a particular office of profit will not disqualify its holder from parliamentary membership.

9. According to the Prohibition of Simultaneous Membership Rules (1950) made by the President.

10. *Kihota Hollohan* Vs. *Zachilhu* (1992).

11. In this context, V V Giri observed: "The holder of an office provided with such extensive authority and power must discharge the duties of his office impartially. So impartiality is regarded as an indispensable condition of the office of the Speaker, who is the guardian of the powers and privileges of the House and not of the political party with whose support he might have been elected to the office. It is not possible for him to maintain order in the House unless he enjoys the confidence of the minority parties by safeguarding their rights and privileges". ('Powers of the Presiding Officers in Indian Legislature' in *Journal of Consitutional and Parliamentary Studies*, New Delhi, Vol II, No. 4, Oct-Dec. 1968, p. 22)

12. For example, in the 13th Lok Sabha, Mr Indrajit Gupta was appointed as Speaker *Pro Tem* on 20 October 1999 and remained in that office till 22 October 1999 when the new Speaker, Mr G M C Balayogi was elected.

13. Under Article 107 (3) of the Constitution, a bill pending in Parliament shall not lapse by reason of the prorogation of the Houses.
Under Rule 336 of the Lok Sabha, a motion, resolution or an amendment, which has been moved and is pending in the House, shall not lapse by reason only of the prorogation of the House.

14. Subhash C Kashyap: *Our Parliament,* National Book Trust, 1999 Edition, P. 135–136.

15. J C Johari: *Indian Government and Politics*, Vishal, Volume II, Thirteenth Edition, 2001, P. 360.

16. Subhash C Kashyap: *Our Parliament*, National Book Trust, 1999 Edition, P. 139–141.

17. Ibid, P. 139.

18. Under Rule 64 of Lok Sabha, the Speaker may, on request being made to him, order the publication of any bill in the Gazette, although no

motion has been made for leave to introduce the bill. In that case, it shall not be necessary to move for leave to introduce the bill and if the bill is afterwards introduced, it shall not be necessary to publish it again.

19. For different kinds of veto, see 'Veto Power of the President' under Chapter 17.

20. The Lok Sabha did not agree to the amendments made by the Rajya Sabha. A joint siting was held on 6 May 1961.

21. The bill was passed by the Lok Sabha but rejected by the Rajya Sabha. A joint sitting was held on 16 May 1978.

22. The bill was passed by the Lok Sabha but rejected by the Rajya Sabha. A joint sitting was held on 26 March 2002. The bill was passed when 425 members voted for it and 296 against.

23. N N Mallya: *Indian Parliament*, P. 39.

24. *Kesavananda Bharati* V. *State of Kerala* (1973); *Minerva Mills* V. *Union of India* (1980).

25. In 1977, the sixth Lok Sabha expelled Mrs. Indira Gandhi from its membership and sentenced her to jail for a week for committing a contempt of House while she was Prime Minister. But, the seventh Lok Sabha rescinded the resolution expelling her by describing it as politically motivated. In 1990, a former Minister, K K Tiwari, was reprimanded by the Rajya Sabha.

26. Article 121 of the Constitution says that no discussion shall take place in Parliament with respect to the conduct of any judge of the Supreme Court or of a high court in the discharge of his duties except upon a motion for presenting an address to the president praying for the removal of the judge. Under Rules 349 to 350 of the Lok Sabha, use of unparliamentary language or unparliamentary conduct of a member is prohibited.

27. Kaul and Shakdher: *Practice and Procedure of Parliament*, First Edition, P. 157.

28. Thomas Erskine May: *Parliamentary Practice*, 15th Edition, P. 109.

29. Subhash C. Kashyap: *Our Parliament*, National Book Trust, 1999 Edition, P. 241.

30. Thomas Erskine May: *Parliamentary Practice*, 16th Edition, P. 43.

31. The then law minister gave the following reason for dropping reference to the British House of Commons: "That the original provision—there was no escape from it—had referred to the British House of Commons. Now a proud country like India would like to avoid making any reference to a foreign insitution in its own solemn consitutional document. Therefore, this verbal change is being introduced so that there may not be any reference to a foreign institution."

32. A V Dicey: Introduction to the Study of the Law of the Constitution, Macmillan, 1965 Edition, P. 39–40.

Parliamentary Committees

MEANING AND CLASSIFICATION

The Parliament is too unwieldy a body to deliberate effectively the issues that come up before it. The functions of the Parliament are varied, complex and voluminous. Moreover, it has neither the adequate time nor necessary expertise to make a detailed scrutiny of all legislative measures and other matters. Therefore, it is assisted by a number of committees in the discharge of its duties.

The Constitution of India makes a mention of these committees at different places, but without making any specific provisions regarding their composition, tenure, functions, etc. All these matters are dealt by the rules of two Houses. Accordingly, a parliamentary committee means a committee that:

1. Is appointed or elected by the House or nominated by the Speaker / Chairman[1]
2. Works under the direction of the Speaker / Chairman
3. Presents its report to the House or to the Speaker / Chairman
4. Has a secretariat provided by the Lok Sabha / Rajya Sabha

The consultative committees, which also consist of members of Parliament, are not parliamentary committees as they do not fulfill above four conditions.[2]

Broadly, parliamentary committees are of two kinds—Standing Committees and *Ad Hoc* Committees. The former are permanent (constituted every year or periodically) and work on a continuous basis, while the latter are temporary and cease to exist on completion of the task assigned to them.

Standing Committees

On the basis of the nature of functions performed by them, standing committees can be classified into the following six categories:

1. Financial Committees

(a) Public Accounts Committee
(b) Estimates Committee
(c) Committee on Public Undertakings

2. Departmental Standing Committees (24)

3. Committees to Inquire

(a) Committee on Petitions
(b) Committee of Privileges
(c) Ethics Committee

4. Committees to Scrutinise and Control

(a) Committee on Government Assurances
(b) Committee on Subordinate Legislation
(c) Committee on Papers Laid on the Table
(d) Committee on Welfare of SCs and STs
(e) Committee on Empowerment of Women
(f) Joint Committee[3] on Offices of Profit

5. Committees Relating to the Day-to-Day Business of the House

(a) Business Advisory Committee
(b) Committee on Private Members' Bills and Resolutions
(c) Rules Committee
(d) Committee on Absence of Members from Sittings of the House

6. House-Keeping Committees or Service Committees (i.e., Committees concerned with the Provision of Facilities and Services to Members):

(a) General Purposes Committee
(b) House Committee
(c) Library Committee
(d) Joint Committee on Salaries and Allowances of Members

Ad Hoc Committees

Ad hoc committees can be divided into two categories, that is, Inquiry Committees and Advisory Committees.

1. Inquiry Committees are constituted from time to time, either by the two Houses on a motion adopted in that behalf, or by the Speaker / Chairman, to inquire into and report on specific subjects. For example:
   (a) Committee on the Conduct of Certain Members during President's Address
   (b) Committee on Draft Five-Year Plan
   (c) Railway Convention Committee[4]
   (d) Committee on Members of Parliament Local Area Development Scheme (MPLADS)
   (e) Joint Committee on Bofors Contract
   (f) Joint Committee on Fertilizer Pricing
   (g) Joint Committee to Enquire into Irregularities in Securities and Banking Transactions
   (h) Joint Committee on Stock Market Scam
   (i) Joint Committee on Security in Parliament Complex
   (j) Committee on Provision of Computers to Members of Parliament, Offices of Political Parties and Officers of the Lok Sabha Secretariat
   (k) Committee on Food Management in Parliament House Complex
   (l) Committee on Installation of Portraits / Statues of National Leaders and Parliamentarians in Parliament House Complex
   (m) Joint Committee on Maintenance of Heritage Character and Development of Parliament House Complex
   (n) Committee on Violation of Protocol Norms and Contemptuous Behaviour of Government Officers with Members of Lok Sabha
   (o) Joint Committee to Examine Matters Relating to Allocation and Pricing of Telecom Licences and Spectrum

2. Advisory Committees include select or joint committees on bills, which are appointed to consider and report on particular bills. These committees are distinguishable from the other *ad hoc* committees in as much as they are concerned with bills and the procedure to be followed by them is laid down in the Rules of Procedure and the Directions by the Speaker / Chairman.

When a Bill comes up before a House for general discussion, it is open to that House to refer it to a Select Committee of the House or a Joint Committee of the two Houses. A motion to this effect has to be moved and adopted in the House in which the Bill comes up for consideration. In case the motion adopted is for reference of the Bill to a Joint Committee, the decision is conveyed to the other House, requesting the members to nominate members of the other House to serve on the Committee.

The Select or Joint Committee considers the Bill clause by clause just as the two Houses do. Amendments to various clauses can be moved by members of the Committee. The Committee can also take evidence of associations, public bodies or experts who are interested in the Bill. After the Bill has thus been considered, the Committee submits its report to the House. Members who do not agree with the majority report may append their minutes of dissent to the report.

Financial Committees

Public Accounts Committee

This committee was set up first in 1921 under the provisions of the Government of India Act of 1919 and has since been in existence. At present, it consists of 22 members (15 from the Lok Sabha and 7 from the Rajya Sabha). The members are elected by the Parliament every year from amongst its members according to the principle of proportional representation by means of the single transferable vote. Thus, all parties get due representation in it. The term of office of the members is one year. A minister cannot be elected as a member of the committee. The chairman of the committee is appointed from amongst its members by the Speaker. Until 1966 – '67, the chairman of the committee belonged to the ruling party. However, since 1967 a convention has developed whereby the chairman of the committee is selected invariably from the Opposition.

The function of the committee is to examine the annual audit reports of the Comptroller and Auditor General of India (CAG), which are laid before the Parliament by the President. The CAG submits three audit reports to the President, namely, audit report on appropriation accounts, audit report on finance accounts and audit report on public undertakings.

The committee examines public expenditure not only from legal and formal point of view to discover technical irregularities but also from the point of view of economy, prudence, wisdom and propriety to bring out the cases of waste, loss, corruption, extravagance, inefficiency and nugatory expenses.

In more detail, the functions of the committee are:

1. To examine the appropriation accounts and the finance accounts of the Union government and any other accounts laid before the Lok Sabha. The appropriation accounts compare the actual expenditure with the expenditure sanctioned by the Parliament through the *Appropriation Act*, while the finance accounts shows the annual receipts and disbursements of the Union Government.

2. In scrutinising the appropriation accounts and the audit report of CAG on it, the committee has to satisfy itself that
   (a) The money that has been disbursed was legally available for the applied service or purpose
   (b) The expenditure conforms to the authority that governs it
   (c) Every re-appropriation has been made in accordance with the related rules

3. To examine the accounts of state corporations, trading concerns and manufacturing projects and the audit report of CAG on them (except those public undertakings which are allotted to the Committee on Public Undertakings)

4. To examine the accounts of autonomous and semi-autonomous bodies, the audit of which is conducted by the CAG

5. To consider the report of the CAG relating to the audit of any receipt or to examine the accounts of stores and stocks

6. To examine the money spent on any service during a financial year in excess of the amount granted by the Lok Sabha for that purpose

In the fulfillment of the above functions, the committee is assisted by the CAG. In fact, the CAG acts as a guide, friend and philosopher of the committee.

On the role played by the committee, Ashok Chanda (who himself has been a CAG of India) observed: "Over a period of years, the committee has entirely fulfilled the expectation that it should develop into a powerful force in the control of public expenditure. It may be claimed that the traditions established and conventions developed by the Public Accounts Committee conform to the highest traditions of a parliamentary democracy."[5]

However, the effectiveness of the role of the committee is limited by the following:

(a) It is not concerned with the questions of policy in broader sense.

(b) It conducts a post-mortem examination of accounts (showing the expenditure already incurred).

(c) It cannot intervene in the matters of day-to-day administration.

(d) Its recommendations are advisory and not binding on the ministries.

(e) It is not vested with the power of disallowance of expenditures by the departments.

(f) It is not an executive body and hence, cannot issue an order. Only the Parliament can take a final decision on its findings.

Estimates Committee

The origin of this committee can be traced to the standing financial committee set up in 1921. The first Estimates Committee in the post-independence era was constituted in 1950 on the recommendation of John Mathai, the then finance minister. Originally, it had 25 members but in 1956 its membership was raised to 30. All the thirty members are from Lok Sabha only. The Rajya Sabha has no representation in this committee. These members are elected by the Lok Sabha every year from amongst its own members, according to the principles of proportional representation by means of a single transferable vote. Thus, all parties get due representation in it. The term of office is one year. A minister cannot be elected as a member of the committee. The chairman of the committee is appointed by the Speaker from amongst its members and he is invariably from the ruling party.

The function of the committee is to examine the estimates included in the budget and suggest 'economies' in public expenditure. Hence, it has been described as a 'continuous economy committee'.

In more detail, the functions of the committee are:

1. To report what economies, improvements in organisation, efficiency and administrative reform consistent with the policy underlying the estimates, can be affected

2. To suggest alternative policies in order to bring about efficiency and economy in administration

3. To examine whether the money is well laid out within the limits of the policy implied in the estimates

4. To suggest the forth in which the estimates are to be presented to Parliament

The Committee shall not exercise its functions in relation to such public undertakings as are allotted to the Committee on Public Undertakings. The Committee may continue the examination of the estimates from time to time, throughout the financial year and report to the House as its examination proceeds. It shall not be incumbent on the Committee to examine the entire estimates of any one year. The demands for grants may be finally voted despite the fact that the Committee has made no report.

However, the effectiveness of the role of the committee is limited by the following:

(a) It examines the budget estimates only after they have been voted by the Parliament, and not before that.

(b) It cannot question the policy laid down by the Parliament.

(c) Its recommendations are advisory and not binding on the ministries.

(d) It examines every year only certain selected ministries and departments. Thus, by rotation, it would cover all of them over a number of years.

(e) It lacks the expert assistance of the CAG which is available to the Public Accounts Committee.

(f) Its work is in the nature of a post-mortem.

Committee on Public Undertakings

This committee was created in 1964 on the recommendation of the Krishna Menon Committee. Originally, it had 15 members (10 from the Lok Sabha and 5 from the Rajya Sabha). However, in 1974, its membership was raised to 22 (15 from the Lok Sabha and 7 from the Rajya Sabha). The members of this committee are elected by the Parliament every year from amongst its own members according to the principle of proportional representation by means of a single transferable vote. Thus, all parties get due representation in it. The term of office of the members is one year. A minister cannot be elected as a member of the committee. The chairman of the committee is appointed by the Speaker from amongst its members who are drawn from the Lok Sabha only. Thus, the members of the committee who are from the Rajya Sabha cannot be appointed as the chairman.

The functions of the committee are:

1. To examine the reports and accounts of public undertakings

2. To examine the reports of the Comptroller and Auditor General on public undertakings

3. To examine (in the context of autonomy and efficiency of public undertakings) whether the affairs of the public undertakings are being managed in accordance with sound business principles and prudent commercial practices

4. To exercise such other functions vested in the public accounts committee and the estimates committee in relation to public undertakings which are allotted to it by the Speaker from time to time

The committee is not to examine and investigate any of the following:

(i) Matters of major government policy as distinct from business or commercial functions of the public undertakings

(ii) Matters of day-to-day administration

(iii) Matters for the consideration of which machinery is established by any special statute under which a particular public undertaking is established

Further, the effectiveness of the role of the committee is limited by the following:

(a) It cannot take up the examination of more than ten to twelve public undertakings in a year.

(b) Its work is in the nature of a post-mortem.

(c) It does not look into technical matters as its members are not technical experts.

(d) Its recommendations are advisory and not binding on the ministries.

Departmental Standing Committees

On the recommendation of the Rules Committee of the Lok Sabha, 17 Departmentally-Related Standing Committees (DRSCs) were set up in the Parliament in 1993.[6] In 2004, seven more such committees were setup, thus increasing their number from 17 to 24.

The main objective of the standing committees is to secure more accountability of the Executive (i.e., the Council of Ministers) to the Parliament, particularly financial accountability. They also assist the Parliament in debating the budget more effectively.[7]

The 24 standing committees cover under their jurisdiction all the ministries / departments of the Central Government.

Each standing committee consists of 31 members (21 from Lok Sabha and 10 from Rajya Sabha). The members of the Lok Sabha are nominated by the Speaker from amongst its own members, just as the members of the Rajya Sabha are nominated by the Chairman from amongst its members.[8]

A minister is not eligible to be nominated as a member of any of the standing committees. In case a member, after his nomination to any of the standing committees, is appointed a minister, he then ceases to be a member of the committee.

The term of office of each standing committee is one year from the date of its constitution.

Out of the 24 standing committees, 8 work under the Rajya Sabha and 16 under the Lok Sabha.[9]

The 24 standing committees and the ministries / departments placed under their jurisdiction are shown below in Table 23.1.

Table 23.1 *Departmental Standing Committees*

Sl. No.	Name of the Committees	Ministries / Departments Covered
I. Committees under Rajya Sabha		
1.	Committee on Commerce	Commerce and Industry
2.	Committee on Home Affairs	(1) Home Affairs
		(2) Development of North-Eastern Region
3.	Committee on Human Resource Development	(1) Human Resource Development
		(2) Youth Affairs and Sports
4.	Committee on Industry	(1) Heavy Industries and Public Enterprises
		(2) Small Scale Industries
		(3) Agro and Rural Industries
5.	Committee on Science & Technology, Environment & Forests	(1) Science and Technology
		(2) Space
		(3) Earth Sciences
		(4) Atomic Energy
		(5) Environment & Forests

(Contd.)

Sl. No.	Name of the Committees	Ministries / Departments Covered
6.	Committee on Transport, Tourism and Culture	(1) Civil Aviation
		(2) Shipping, Road Transport and Highways
		(3) Culture
		(4) Tourism
7.	Committee on Health and Family Welfare	Health and Family Welfare
8.	Committee on Personnel, Public Grievances, Law and Justice	(1) Law and Justice
		(2) Personnel, Public Grievances and Pensions
II. Committees under Lok Sabha		
9.	Committee on Agriculture	(1) Agriculture
		(2) Food Processing Industries
10.	Committee on Information Technology	(1) Communications and Information Technology
		(2) Information & Broadcasting
11.	Committee on Defence	Defence
12.	Committee on Energy	(1) New and Renewable Energy
		(2) Power
13.	Committee on External Affairs	(1) External Affairs
		(2) Non Resident Indians Affairs
14.	Committee on Finance	(1) Finance
		(2) Company Affairs
		(3) Planning
		(4) Statistics and Programme Implementation
15.	Committee on Food, Consumer Affairs and Public Distribution	Consumer Affairs, Food and Public Distribution
16.	Committee on Labour	(1) Labour and Employment
		(2) Textiles
17.	Committee on Petroleum & Natural Gas	Petroleum and Natural Gas
18.	Committee on Railways	Railways
19.	Committee on Urban Development	(1) Urban Development
		(2) Housing and Urban Poverty Alleviation
20.	Committee on Water Resources	Water Resources
21.	Committee on Chemicals and Fertilizers	Chemicals and Fertilizers
22.	Committee on Rural Development	(1) Rural Development
		(2) Panchayati Raj
23.	Committee on Coal and Steel	(1) Coal and Mines
		(2) Steel
24.	Committee on Social Justice and Empowerment	(1) Social Justice and Empowerment
		(2) Tribal Affairs

The functions of each of the standing committees are:

1. To consider the demands for grants of the concerned ministries / departments before they are discussed and voted in the Lok Sabha. Its report should not suggest anything of the nature of cut motions

2. To examine bills pertaining to the concerned ministries / departments

3. To consider annual reports of ministries / departments

4. To consider national basic long-term policy documents presented to the Houses

The following limitations are imposed on the functioning of these standing committees:

(i) They should not consider the matters of day-to-day administration of the concerned ministries / departments.

(ii) They should not generally consider the matters which are considered by other parliamentary committees.

It should be noted here that the recommendations of these committees are advisory in nature and hence not binding on the Parliament.

The following procedure shall be followed by each of the standing committees in their consideration of the demands for grants, and making a report thereon to the Houses.

(a) After general discussion on the budget in the Houses is over, the Houses shall be adjourned for a fixed period.

(b) The committees shall consider the demands for grants of the concerned ministries during the aforesaid period.

(c) The committees shall make their report within the period and shall not ask for more time.

(d) The demands for grants shall be considered by the House in the light of the reports of the committees.

(e) There shall be a separate report on the demands for grants of each ministry.

The following procedure shall be followed by each of the standing committees in examining the bills and making report thereon.

(a) The committee shall consider the general principles and clauses of bills referred to it.

(b) The Committee shall consider only such bills as introduced in either of the Houses and referred to it.

(c) The Committee shall make report on bills in a given time.

The merits of the standing committee system in the Parliament are:

(1) Their proceedings are devoid of any party bias.

(2) The procedure adopted by them is more flexible than in the Lok Sabha.

(3) The system makes parliamentary control over executive much more detailed, close, continuous, in-depth and comprehensive.

(4) The system ensures economy and efficiency in public expenditure as the ministries / departments would now be more careful in formulating their demands.

(5) They facilitate opportunities to all the members of Parliament to participate and understand the functioning of the government and contribute to it.

(6) They can avail of expert opinion or public opinion to make the reports. They are authorised to invite experts and eminent persons to testify before them and incorporate their opinions in their reports.

(7) The opposition parties and the Rajya Sabha can now play a greater role in exercising financial control over the executive.

Committees to Inquire

Committee on Petitions

This committee examines petitions on bills and on matters of general public importance. It also entertains representations from individuals and associations on matters pertaining to Union subjects. The Lok Sabha committee consists of 15 members, while the Rajya Sabha committee consists of 10 members.

Committee of Privileges

The functions of this committee are semi-judicial in nature. It examines the cases of breach of privileges of the House and its members and recommends appropriate action. The Lok Sabha committee has 15 members, while the Rajya Sabha committee has 10 members.

Ethics Committee

This committee was constituted in Rajya Sabha in 1997 and in Lok Sabha in 2000. It enforces the code of conduct of members of Parliament. It examines the cases of misconduct and recommends appropriate action. Thus, it is engaged in maintaining discipline and decorum in Parliament.

Committees to Scrutinise and Control

Committee on Government Assurances

This committee examines the assurances, promises and undertakings given by ministers from time to time on the floor of the House and reports on the extent to which they have been carried through. In the Lok Sabha, it consists of 15 members and in the Rajya Sabha, it consists of 10 members. It was constituted in 1953.

Committee on Subordinate Legislation

This committee examines and reports to the House whether the powers to make regulations, rules, sub-rules and bye-laws delegated by the Parliament or conferred by the Constitution to the Executive are being properly exercised by it. In both the Houses, the committee consists of 15 members. It was constituted in 1953.

Committee on Papers Laid on the Table

This committee was constituted in 1975. The Lok Sabha Committee has 15 members, while the Rajya Sabha Committee has 10 members. It examines all papers laid on the table of the House by ministers to see whether they comply with provisions of the Constitution, or the related Act or Rule. It does not examine statutory notifications and orders that fall under the jurisdiction of the Committee on Subordinate Legislation.

Committee on Welfare of SCs and STs

This committee consists of 30 members (20 from Lok Sabha and 10 from Rajya Sabha). Its functions are: (i) to consider the reports of the National Commission for the SCs and the National Commission for the STs; (ii) to examine all matters relating to the welfare of SCs and STs, like implementation of constitutional and statutory safeguards, working of welfare programmes, etc.

Committee on Empowerment of Women

This committee was constituted in 1997 and consists of 30 members (20 from Lok Sabha and 10 from Rajya Sabha). It considers the reports of the National Commission for Women and examines the measures taken by the Union Government to secure status, dignity and equality for women in all fields.

Joint Committee on Offices of Profit

This committee examines the composition and character of committees and other bodies appointed by the Central, state and union territory governments and recommends whether persons holding these offices should be disqualified from being elected as members of Parliament or not. It consists of 15 members (10 from Lok Sabha and 5 from Rajya Sabha).

Committees Relating to the Day-to-Day Business of the House

Business Advisory Committee

This committee regulates the programme and time table of the House. It allocates time for the transaction of legislative and other business brought before the House by the government. The Lok Sabha committee consists of 15 members including the Speaker as its chairman. In the Rajya Sabha, it has 11 members including the Chairman as its ex-officio chairman.

Committee on Private Members' Bills and Resolutions

This committee classifies bills and allocates time for the discussion on bills and resolutions introduced by private members (other than ministers). This is a special committee of the Lok Sabha and consists of 15 members including the Deputy Speaker as its chairman. The Rajya Sabha does not have any such committee. The same function in the Rajya Sabha is performed by the Business Advisory Committee of that House.

Rules Committee

This committee considers the matters of procedure and conduct of business in the House and recommends necessary amendments or additions to the rules of the House. The Lok Sabha committee consists of 15 members including the Speaker as its ex-officio chairman. In the Rajya Sabha, it consists of 16 members including the Chairman as its ex-officio chairman.

Committee on Absence of Members

This committee considers all applications from members for leave of absence from the sittings of the House, and examines the cases of members who have been absent for a period of 60 days or more without permission. It is a special committee of the Lok Sabha and consists of 15 members. There is no such committee in the Rajya Sabha and all such matters are dealt by the House itself.

House-Keeping Committees

General Purposes Committee

This committee considers and advises on matters concerning affairs of the House, which do not fall within the jurisdiction of any other parliamentary committee. In each House, this committee consists of the presiding officer (Speaker / Chairman) as its ex-officio chairman, Deputy Speaker (Deputy Chairman in the case of Rajya Sabha), members of panel of chairpersons (panel of vice-chairpersons in the case of Rajya Sabha), chairpersons of all the departmental standing committees of the House, leaders of recognised parties and groups in the House and such other members as nominated by the presiding officer.

House Committee

This committee deals with residential accommodation of members and other amenities like food, medical aid, etc., accorded to them in their houses and hostels in Delhi. Both the Houses have their respective House Committees. In the Lok Sabha, it consists of 12 members.

Library Committee

This committee considers all matters relating to library of the Parliament and assists the members in utilising the library's services. It consists of nine members (six from Lok Sabha and three from Rajya Sabha).

Joint Committee on Salaries and Allowances of Members

This committee was constituted under the Salary, Allowances and Pension of Members of Parliament Act, 1954. It consists of 15 members (10 from Lok Sabha and 5 from Rajya Sabha). It frames rules for regulating payment of salary, allowances and pension to members of Parliament.

Consultative Committees

Consultative committees are attached to various ministries / departments of the Central Government. They consist of members of both the Houses of Parliament. The Minister / Minister of State in charge of the Ministry concerned acts as the chairman of the consultative committee of that ministry.

These committees provide a forum for informal discussions between the ministers and the members of Parliament on policies and programmes of the government and the manner of their implementation.

These committees are constituted by the Ministry of Parliamentary Affairs. The guidelines regarding the composition, functions and procedures of these committees are formulated by this Ministry. The Ministry also makes arrangements for holding their meetings both during the session and the inter-session period of Parliament.

The membership of these committees is voluntary and is left to the choice of the members and the leaders of their parties. The maximum membership of a committee is 30 and the minimum is 10.

These committees are normally constituted after the new Lok Sabha is constituted, after General Elections for the Lok Sabha. In other words, these committees shall stand dissolved upon dissolution of every Lok Sabha and shall be reconstituted upon constitution of each Lok Sabha[10].

In addition, separate Informal Consultative Committees of the members of Parliament are also constituted for all the Railway Zones. Members of Parliament belonging to the area falling under a particular Railway Zone are nominated on the Informal Consultative Committee of that Railway Zone.

Unlike the Consultative Committees attached to various ministries / departments, the meetings of the Informal Consultative Committees are to be arranged during the session periods only.

NOTES AND REFERENCES

1. A Minister is not eligible for election or nomination to the Financial Committees, Departmental Standing Committees, and Committees on Empowerment of Women, Government Assurances, Petitions, Subordinate Legislation and Welfare of Scheduled Castes and Scheduled Tribes.

2. Consultative Committees are explained at the end of this Chapter.

3. A joint committee consists of members of both the Houses of Parliament.

4. The Railway Convention Committee, 1949 was the first Committee after independence. This Committee and subsequent Committees confined themselves to determining the Rate of Dividend payable by the Railways to General Revenues. Since 1971, the Railway Convention Committees have been taking up subjects which have a bearing on the working of the Railways and Railway Finances.

5. Ashok Chanda: *Indian Administration*, George Allen & Unwin Ltd, London, 1967, P. 180.

6. In 1989, three Standing Committees were constituted which dealt with Agriculture, Science & Technology and Environment & Forests. In 1993, they were superseded by the Departmentally-Related Standing Committees (DRSCs).

7. While inaugurating the Standing Committee system in the Central Hall of Parliament on 31st March 1993, the then Vice-President of India and the Chairman of Rajya Sabha, K.R. Narayanan observed that the main purpose of these Committees is: "to ensure the accountability of Government to Parliament through more detailed consideration of measures in these Committees. The intention is not to weaken or criticise the administration but to strengthen it by investing it with more meaningful Parliamentary support".

8. Till 13th Lok Sabha, each Standing Committee consisted of not more than 45 members – 30 to be nominated by the Speaker from amongst the members of Lok Sabha and 15 to be nominated by the Chairman from amongst the members of Rajya Sabha. However, with restructuring of DRSCs in July 2004, each DRSC consists of 31 members – 21 from Lok Sabha and 10 from Rajya Sabha.

9. The procedure regarding constitution and functioning of DRSCs, serviced by Lok Sabha, has been enumerated in Rules 331C to 331Q of the Rules of Procedure and Conduct of Business in the Lok Sabha. Rules 268 to 277 of the Rules of Procedure and Conduct of Business in the Rajya Sabha govern DRSCs serviced by Rajya Sabha.

10. After the constitution of the 15th Lok Sabha, 35 consultative committees were constituted in September 2009.

Parliamentary Forums

ESTABLISHMENT OF FORUMS

The first Parliamentary Forum on Water Conservation and Management was constituted in the year 2005.[1] Subsequently, five more Parliamentary forums were constituted. At present, there are six Parliamentary forums.[2]

1. Parliamentary Forum on Water Conservation and Management (2005)
2. Parliamentary Forum on Youth (2006)
3. Parliamentary Forum on Children (2006)
4. Parliamentary Forum on Population and Public Health (2006)
5. Parliamentary Forum on Global Warming and Climate Change (2008)
6. Parliamentary Forum on Disaster Management (2011)

OBJECTIVES OF THE FORUMS

The objectives behind the constitution of the Parliamentary forums are:

(i) To provide a platform to the members to have interactions with the ministers concerned, experts and key officials from the nodal ministries with a view to have a focused and meaningful discussion on critical issues with a result-oriented approach for speeding up the implementation process;

(ii) To sensitise members about the key areas of concern and also about the ground level situation and equip them with the latest information, knowledge, technical know-how and valuable inputs from experts both from the country and abroad for enabling them to raise these issues effectively on the Floor of the House and in the meetings of the Departmentally-Related Standing Committees (DRSCs); and

(iii) To prepare a data-base through collection of data on critical issues from ministries concerned, reliable NGOs, newspapers, United Nations, Internet, etc. and circulation thereof to the members so that they can meaningfully participate in the discussions of the forums and seek clarifications from experts or officials from the Ministry present in the meetings.

It has been mandated that the Parliamentary Fora will not interfere with or encroach upon the jurisdiction of the Departmentally-Related Standing Committees of the Ministry/Department concerned.

COMPOSITION OF THE FORUMS

The Speaker of Lok Sabha is the President of all the Forums except the Parliamentary Forum on Population and Public Health wherein the Chairman of Rajya Sabha is the President and the Speaker is the Co-President. The Deputy Chairman of Rajya Sabha, the Deputy Speaker of Lok Sabha, the concerned Ministers and the Chairmen of Departmentally-Related Standing Committees are the ex-officio Vice-Presidents of the respective Forums.

Each Forum consists of not more than 31 members (excluding the President and ex-officio Vice-Presidents) out of whom not more than 21 are from the Lok Sabha and not more than 10 are from the Rajya Sabha.

Members (other than the President and Vice-Presidents) of these forums are nominated by the Speaker/Chairman from amongst the leaders of various political parties/groups or their nominees, who have special knowledge/keen interest in the subject.[3]

The duration of the office of members of the forum is co-terminus with their membership in the respective Houses. A member may also resign from the forum by writing to the Speaker/Chairman.

The President of the forum appoints a member-convener for each forum to conduct regular, approved programmes/meetings of the forum in consultation with the President. The meetings of the forums are held from time to time, as may be necessary, during Parliament sessions.

FUNCTIONS OF THE FORUMS

Parliamentary Forum on Water Conservation and Management

The functions of the forum are:

1. To identify problems relating to water and make suggestions/recommendations for consideration and appropriate action by Government/organisations concerned
2. To identify the ways of involving members of Parliament in conservation and augmentation of water resources in their respective states/constituencies
3. To organise seminars/workshops to create awareness for conservation and efficient management of water
4. To undertake such other related task as it may deem fit

Parliamentary Forum on Youth

The functions of this forum are:

1. To have focused deliberations on strategies to leverage human capital in the youth for accelerating development initiatives

2. To build greater awareness amongst public leaders and at the grass-roots level of the potential of youth for effecting socio-economic change
3. To interact on a regular basis with youth representatives and leaders, in order to better appreciate their hopes, aspirations, concerns and problems
4. To consider ways for improving Parliament's out-reach to different sections of youth, in order to reinforce their faith and commitment in democratic institutions and encourage their active participation therein
5. To hold consultations with experts, national and international academicians and government agencies concerned on redesigning of public policy in the matter of youth empowerment.[4]

Parliamentary Forum on Children

The functions of the forum are:

1. To further enhance awareness and attention of Parliamentarians towards critical issues affecting children's well being so that they may provide due leadership to ensure their rightful place in the development process
2. To provide a platform to Parliamentarians to exchange ideas, views, experiences, expert practices in relation to children, in a structured manner, through workshops, seminars, orientation programmes, etc.
3. To provide Parliamentarians an interface with civil society for highlighting children's issues, including, *inter-alia*, the voluntary sector, media and corporate sector, and thereby to foster effective strategic partnerships in this regard
4. To enable Parliamentarians to interact, in an institutionalised manner with specialised UN agencies like the UNICEF and other comparable multilateral agencies on expert reports, studies, news and trend-analyses, etc., worldwide, which are germane to developments in the sector
5. To undertake any other tasks, projects, assignments, etc., as the Forum may deem fit.

Parliamentary Forum on Population and Public Health

The functions of the forum are:

1. To have focused deliberations on strategies relating to population stabilisation and matters connected therewith
2. To discuss and prepare strategies on issues concerning public health
3. To build greater awareness in all sections of the society, particularly at the grass-root level, regarding population control and public health
4. To hold comprehensive dialogue and discussion in the matter of population and public health with experts at the national and international levels and to have interactions with multilateral organisations like WHO, United Nations Population Fund, and academicians and government agencies concerned.

Parliamentary Forum on Global Warming and Climate Change

The functions of the forum are:

1. To identify problems relating to global warming and climate change and make suggestions/ recommendations for consideration and appropriate action by the government/organisations concerned to reduce the extent of global warming

2. To identify the ways of involving members of Parliament to interact with specialists of national and international bodies working on global warming and climate change with increased effort to develop new technologies to mitigate global warming
3. To organise seminars/workshops to create awareness about the causes and effects of global warming and climate change among the members of Parliament
4. To identify the ways of involving members of Parliament to spread awareness to prevent global warming and climate change
5. To undertake such other related task as it may deem fit

Parliamentary Forum on Disaster Management

The functions of the forum are:

1. To identify and discuss the problems relating to disaster management
2. To equip the members of Parliament with the information and knowledge on disaster management, for making them aware of the seriousness of the issues involved and enabling them to adopt a result-oriented approach towards this critical issue

NOTES AND REFERENCES

1. On 12th May 2005, the then Speaker of Lok Sabha, Somnath Chatterjee informed the House of his decision to constitute a Parliamentary forum on water conservation and management so that the members of Parliament may discuss the critical issue of water in a structured manner and also to raise the issue more effectively on the floor of the House. Accordingly, the forum was constituted on 12th August, 2005.

2. The years mentioned in the brackets indicate the years of their establishment.
3. The Secretary-General of Lok Sabha is the Secretary to the forums.
4. The Speaker also constituted four sub-forums of the Parliamentary Forum on Youth, *viz.* (i) Sub-Forum on Sports and Youth Development (ii) Sub-Forum on Health (iii) Sub-Forum on Education (iv) Sub-Forum on Employment. Each Sub-Forum has its own convener.

Supreme Court

Unlike the American Constitution, the Indian Constitution has established an integrated judicial system with the Supreme Court at the top and the high courts below it. Under a high court (and below the state level), there is a hierarchy of subordinate courts, that is, district courts and other lower courts. This single system of courts, adopted from the Government of India Act of 1935, enforces both Central laws as well as the state laws. In USA, on the other hand, the federal laws are enforced by the federal judiciary and the state laws are enforced by the state judiciary. There is thus a double system of courts in USA—one for the centre and the other for the states. To sum up, India, although a federal country like the USA, has a unified judiciary and one system of fundamental law and justice.

The Supreme Court of India was inaugurated on January 28, 1950. It succeeded the Federal Court of India, established under the Government of India Act of 1935. However, the jurisdiction of the Supreme Court is greater than that of its prodecessor. This is because, the Supreme Court has replaced the British Privy Council as the highest court of appeal.[1]

Articles 124 to 147 in Part V of the Constitution deal with the organisation, independence, jurisdiction, powers, procedures and so on of the Supreme Court. The Parliament is also authorised to regulate them.

ORGANISATION OF SUPREME COURT

At present, the Supreme Court consists of thirty-one judges (one chief justice and thirty other judges). In February 2009, the centre notified an increase in the number of Supreme Court judges from twenty-six to thirty-one, including the Chief Justice of India. This followed the enactment of the Supreme Court (Number of Judges) Amendment Act, 2008. Originally, the strength of the Supreme Court was fixed at eight (one chief justice and seven other judges). The Parliament has increased this number of other judges progressively to ten in 1956, to thirteen in 1960, to seventeen in 1977 and to twenty-five in 1986.

Judges

Appointment of Judges The judges of the Supreme Court are appointed by the president. The chief justice is appointed by the president after consultation with such judges of the Supreme Court and high courts as he deems necessary. The other judges are appointed by president after consultation with the chief justice and such other judges of the Supreme Court and the high courts as he deems necessary. The consultation with the chief justice is obligatory in the case of appointment of a judge other than Chief justice.

Controversy over Consultation The Supreme Court has given different interpretation of the word 'consultation' in the above provision. In the *First*

Judges case (1982), the Court held that consultation does not mean concurrence and it only implies exchange of views. But, in the *Second Judges* case (1993), the Court reversed its earlier ruling and changed the meaning of the word consultation to concurrence. Hence, it ruled that the advice tendered by the Chief Justice of India is binding on the President in the matters of appointment of the judges of the Supreme Court. But, the Chief Justice would tender his advice on the matter after consulting two of his seniormost colleagues. Similarly, in the *third judges* case[2] (1998), the Court opined that the consultation process to be adopted by the Chief justice of India requires 'consultation of plurality judges'. The sole opinion of the chief justice of India does not constitute the consultation process. He should consult a collegium of four seniormost judges of the Supreme Court and even if two judges give an adverse opinion, he should not send the recommendation to the government. The court held that the recommendation made by the chief justice of India without complying with the norms and requirements of the consultation process are not binding on the government.

Appointment of Chief Justice   From 1950 to 1973, the practice has been to appoint the seniormost judge of the Supreme Court as the chief justice of India. This established convention was violated in 1973 when A N Ray was appointed as the Chief Justice of India by superseding three senior judges.[3] Again in 1977, M U Beg was appointed as the chief justice of India by superseding the then senior-most judge.[4] This discretion of the government was curtailed by the Supreme Court in the Second Judges Case (1993), in which the Supreme Court ruled that the senior-most judge of the Supreme Court should alone be appointed to the office of the chief justice of India.

Qualifications of Judges   A person to be appointed as a judge of the Supreme Court should have the following qualifications:

1. He should be a citizen of India.
2. (a) He should have been a judge of a High Court (or high courts in succession) for five years; or (b) He should have been an advocate of a High Court (or High Courts in succession) for ten years; or (c) He should be a distinguished jurist in the opinion of the president.

From the above, it is clear that the Constitution has not prescribed a minimum age for appointment as a judge of the Supreme Court.

Oath or Affirmation   A person appointed as a judge of the Supreme Court, before entering upon his Office, has to make and subscribe an oath or affirmation before the President, or some person appointed by him for this purpose. In his oath, a judge of the Supreme Court swears:

1. to bear true faith and allegiance to the Constitution of India;
2. to uphold the sovereignty and integrity of India;
3. to duly and faithfully and to the best of his ability, knowledge and judgement perform the duties of the Office without fear or favour, affection or ill-will; and
4. to uphold the Constitution and the laws.

Tenure of Judges   The Constitution has not fixed the tenure of a judge of the Supreme Court. However, it makes the following three provisions in this regard:

1. He holds office until he attains the age of 65 years. Any question regarding his age is to be determined by such authority and in such manner as provided by Parliament.
2. He can resign his office by writing to the president.
3. He can be removed from his office by the President on the recommendation of the Parliament.

Removal of Judges   A judge of the Supreme Court can be removed from his Office by an order of the president. The President can issue the removal order only after an address by Parliament has been presented to him in the same session for such removal.[5] The address must be supported by a special majority of each House of Parliament (ie, a majority of the total membership of that House and a majority of not less than two-thirds of the members of that House present and voting). The grounds of removal are two—proved misbehaviour or incapacity.

The Judges Enquiry Act (1968) regulates the procedure relating to the removal of a judge of the Supreme Court by the process of impeachment:

1. A removal motion signed by 100 members (in the case of Lok Sabha) or 50 members (in the case of Rajya Sabha) is to be given to the Speaker/Chairman.

2. The Speaker/Chairman may admit the motion or refuse to admit it.
3. If it is admitted, then the Speaker/Chairman is to constitute a three-member committee to investigate into the charges.
4. The committee should consist of (a) the chief justice or a judge of the Supreme Court, (b) a chief justice of a high court, and (c) a distinguished jurist.
5. If the committee finds the judge to be guilty of misbehaviour or suffering from an incapacity, the House can take up the consideration of the motion.
6. After the motion is passed by each House of Parliament by special majority, an address is presented to the president for removal of the judge.
7. Finally, the president passes an order removing the judge.

It is interesting to know that no judge of the Supreme Court has been impeached so far. The first and the only case of impeachment is that of Justice V Ramaswami of the Supreme Court (1991–1993). Though the enquiry Committee found him guilty of misbehaviour, he could not be removed as the impeachment motion was defeated in the Lok Sabha. The Congress Party abstained from voting.

Salaries and Allowances The salaries, allowances, privileges, leave and pension of the judges of the Supreme Court are determined from time to time by the Parliament. They cannot be varied to their disadvantage after their appointment except during a financial emergency. In 2009, the salary of the chief justice was increased from ₹33,000 to ₹1 lakh per month and that of a judge from ₹30,000 to ₹90,000 per month[6]. They are also paid sumptuary allowance and provided with free accommodation and other facilities like medical, car, telephone, etc.

The retired chief justice and judges are entitled to 50 per cent of their last drawn salary as monthly pension.

Acting Chief Justice

The President can appoint a judge of the Supreme Court as an acting Chief Justice of India when:
1. the office of Chief Justice of India is vacant; or

2. the Chief Justice of India is temporarily absent; or
3. the Chief Justice of India is unable to perform the duties of his office.

Ad hoc Judge

When there is a lack of quorum of the permanent judges to hold or continue any session of the Supreme Court, the Chief Justice of India can appoint a judge of a High Court as an ad hoc judge of the Supreme Court for a temporary period. He can do so only after consultation with the chief justice of the High Court concerned and with the previous consent of the president. The judge so appointed should be qualified for appointment as a judge of the Supreme Court. It is the duty of the judge so appointed to attend the sittings of the Supreme Court, in priority to other duties of his office. While so attending, he enjoys all the jurisdiction, powers and privileges (and discharges the duties) of a judge of the Supreme Court.

Retired Judges

At any time, the chief justice of India can request a retired judge of the Supreme Court or a retired judge of a high court (who is duly qualified for appointment as a judge of the Supreme Court) to act as a judge of the Supreme Court for a temporary period. He can do so only with the previous consent of the president and also of the person to be so appointed. Such a judge is entitled to such allowances as the president may determine. He will also enjoy all the jurisdiction, powers and privileges of a judge of Supreme Court. But, he will not otherwise be deemed to be a judge of the Supreme Court.

SEAT OF SUPREME COURT

The Constitution declares Delhi as the seat of the Supreme Court. But, it also authorises the chief justice of India to appoint other place or places as seat of the Supreme Court. He can take decision in this regard only with the approval of the President. This provision is only optional and not compulsory. This means that no court can give any direction either to the President or to the Chief Justice to appoint any other place as a seat of the Supreme Court.

PROCEDURE OF THE COURT

The Supreme Court can, with the approval of the president, make rules for regulating generally the practice and procedure of the Court. The Constitutional cases or references made by the President under Article 143 are decided by a Bench consisting of at least five judges. All other cases are usually decided by a bench consisting of not less than three judges. The judgements are delivered by the open court. All judgements are by majority vote but if differing, then judges can give dissenting judgements or opinions.

INDEPENDENCE OF SUPREME COURT

The Supreme Court has been assigned a very significant role in the Indian democratic political system. It is a federal court, the highest court of appeal, the guarantor of the fundamental rights of the citizens and guardian of the Constitution. Therefore, its independence becomes very essential for the effective discharge of the duties assigned to it. It should be free from the encroachments, pressures and interferences of the executive (council of ministers) and the Legislature (Parliament). It should be allowed to do justice without fear or favour.

The Constitution has made the following provisions to safeguard and ensure the independent and impartial functioning of the Supreme Court:

1. Mode of Appointment The judges of the Supreme Court are appointed by the President (which means the cabinet) in consultation with the members of the judiciary itself (ie, judges of the Supreme Court and the high courts). This provision curtails the absolute discretion of the executive as well as ensures that the judicial appointments are not based on any political or practical considerations.

2. Security of Tenure The judges of the Supreme Court are provided with the Security of Tenure. They can be removed from office by the President only in the manner and on the grounds mentioned in the Constitution. This means that they do not hold their office during the pleasure of the President, though they are appointed by him. This is obvious from the fact that no judge of the Supreme Court has been removed (or impeached) so far.

3. Fixed Service Conditions The salaries, allowances, privileges, leave and pension of the judges of the Supreme Court are determined from time to time by the Parliament. They cannot be changed to their disadvantage after their appointment except during a financial emergency. Thus, the conditions of service of the judges of the Supreme Court remain same during their term of Office.

4. Expenses Charged on Consolidated Fund The salaries, allowances and pensions of the judges and the staff as well as all the administrative expenses of the Supreme Court are charged on the Consolidated Fund of India. Thus, they are non-votable by the Parliament (though they can be discussed by it).

5. Conduct of Judges cannot be Discussed The Constitution prohibits any discussion in Parliament or in a State Legislature with respect to the conduct of the judges of the Supreme Court in the discharge of their duties, except when an impeachment motion is under consideration of the Parliament.

6. Ban on Practice after Retirement The retired judges of the Supreme Court are prohibited from pleading or acting in any Court or before any authority within the territory of India. This ensures that they do not favour any one in the hope of future favour.

7. Power to Punish for its Contempt The Supreme Court can punish any person for its contempt. Thus, its actions and decisions cannot be criticised and opposed by any body. This power is vested in the Supreme Court to maintain its authority, dignity and honour.

8. Freedom to Appoint its Staff The Chief Justice of India can appoint officers and servants of the Supreme Court without any interference from the executive. He can also prescribe their conditions of service.

9. Its Jurisdiction cannot be Curtailed The Parliament is not authorised to curtail the jurisdiction and powers of the Supreme Court. The Constitution has guaranteed to the Supreme Court, jurisdiction of various kinds. However, the Parliament can extend the same.

10. Separation from Executive The Constitution directs the State to take steps to separate the Judiciary from the Executive in the public services. This means that the executive authorities should not possess the judicial powers. Consequently, upon its implementation, the role of executive authorities in judicial administration came to an end.[7]

JURISDICTION AND POWERS OF SUPREME COURT

The Constitution has conferred a very extensive jurisdiction and vast powers on the Supreme Court. It is not only a Federal Court like the American Supreme Court but also a final court of appeal like the British House of Lords (the Upper House of the British Parliament). It is also the final interpreter and guardian of the Constitution and guarantor of the fundamental rights of the citizens. Further, it has advisory and supervisory powers. Therefore, Alladi Krishnaswamy Ayyar, a member of the Drafting Committee of the Constitution, rightly remarked: "The Supreme Court of India has more powers than any other Supreme Court in any part of the world." The jurisdiction and powers of the Supreme Court can be classified into the following:

1. Original Jurisdiction.
2. Writ Jurisdiction.
3. Appellate Jurisdiction.
4. Advisory Jurisdiction.
5. A Court of Record.
6. Power of Judicial Review.
7. Other Powers.

1. Original Jurisdiction

As a federal court, the Supreme Court decides the disputes between different units of the Indian Federation. More elaborately, any dispute between:

(a) the Centre and one or more states; or

(b) the Centre and any state or states on one side and one or more states on the other; or

(c) between two or more states.

In the above federal disputes, the Supreme Court has exclusive original jurisdiction. Exclusive means, no other court can decide such disputes and original means, the power to hear such disputes in the first instance, not by way of appeal.

With regard to the exclusive original jurisdiction of the Supreme Court, two points should be noted. One, the dispute must involve a question (whether of law or fact) on which the existence or extent of a legal right depends. Thus, the questions of political nature are excluded from it. Two, any suit brought before the Supreme Court by a private citizen against the Centre or a state cannot be entertained under this.

Further, this jurisdiction of the Supreme Court does not extend to the following:

(a) A dispute arising out of any pre-Constitution treaty, agreement, covenant, engagement, sanad or other similar instrument.[8]

(b) A dispute arising out of any treaty, agreement, etc., which specifically provides that the said jurisdiction does not extent to such a dispute.[9]

(c) Inter-state water disputes.[10]

(d) Matters referred to the Finance Commission.

(e) Adjustment of certain expenses and pensions between the Centre and the states.

(f) Ordinary dispute of Commercial nature between the Centre and the states.

(g) Recovery of damages by a state against the Centre.

In 1961, the first suit, under the original jurisdiction of the Supreme Court, was brought by West Bengal against the Centre. The State Government challenged the Constitutional validity of the Coal Bearing Areas (Acquisition and Development) Act, 1957, passed by the Parliament. However, the Supreme Court dismissed the suit by upholding the validity of the Act.

2. Writ Jurisdiction

The Constitution has constituted the Supreme Court as the guarantor and defender of the fundamental rights of the citizens. The Supreme Court is empowered to issue writs including *habeas corpus*, *mandamus*, prohibition, *quo-warrento* and *certiorari* for the enforcement of the fundamental rights of an aggrieved citizen. In this regard, the Supreme Court has original jurisdiction in the sense that an aggrieved citizen can directly go to the Supreme Court, not necessarily by way of appeal. However, the writ jurisdiction of the Supreme Court is not exclusive. The high courts are also empowered to issue writs for the enforcement of the Fundamental Rights. It means, when the Fundamental Rights of a citizen are violated, the aggrieved party has the option of moving either the high court or the Supreme Court directly.

Therefore, the original jurisdiction of the Supreme Court with regard to federal disputes is different from its original jurisdiction with regard to disputes relating to fundamental rights. In the first case, it is exclusive and in the second case, it is concurrent with high courts jurisdiction. Moreover, the parties involved in the first case are units of the federation (Centre and states) while the dispute in the second case is between a citizen and the Government (Central or state).

There is also a difference between the writ jurisdiction of the Supreme Court and that of the high court. The Supreme Court can issue writs only for the enforcement of the Fundamental Rights and not for other purposes. The high court, on the other hand, can issue writs not only for the enforcement of the fundamental rights but also for other purposes. It means that the writ jurisdiction of the high court is wider than that of the Supreme Court. But, the Parliament can confer on the Supreme Court, the power to issue writs for other purposes also.

3. Appellate Jurisdiction

As mentioned earlier, the Supreme Court has not only succeeded the Federal Court of India but also replaced the British Privy Council as the highest court of appeal. The Supreme Court is primarily a court of appeal and hears appeals against the judgements of the lower courts. It enjoys a wide appellate jurisdiction which can be classified under four heads:

(a) Appeals in constitutional matters.
(b) Appeals in civil matters.
(c) Appeals in criminal matters.
(d) Appeals by special leave.

(a) Constitutional Matters In the constitutional cases, an appeal can be made to the Supreme Court against the judgement of a high court if the high court certifies that the case involves a substantial question of law that requires the interpretation of the Constitution. Based on the certificate, the party in the case can appeal to the Supreme Court on the ground that the question has been wrongly decided.

(b) Civil Matters In civil cases, an appeal lies to the Supreme Court from any judgement of a high court if the high court certifies—

(i) that the case involves a substantial question of law of general importance; and
(ii) that the question needs to be decided by the Supreme Court.

Originally, only those civil cases that involved a sum of ₹20,000 could be appealed before the Supreme Court. But this monetary limit was removed by the 30th Constitutional Amendment Act of 1972.

(c) Criminal Matters The Supreme Court hears appeals against the judgement in a criminal proceeding of a high court if the high court—

(i) has on appeal reversed an order of acquittal of an accused person and sentenced him to death; or
(ii) has taken before itself any case from any subordinate court and convicted the accused person and sentenced him to death; or
(iii) certifies that the case is a fit one for appeal to the Supreme Court.

In the first two cases, an appeal lies to the Supreme Court as a matter of right (ie, without any certificate of the high court). But if the high court has reversed the order of conviction and has ordered the acquittal of the accused, there is no right to appeal to the Supreme Court.

In 1970, the Parliament had enlarged the Criminal Appellate Jurisdiction of the Supreme Court. Accordingly, an appeal lies to the Supreme Court from the judgement of a high court if the high court:

(i) has on appeal, reversed an order of acquittal of an accused person and sentenced him to imprisonment for life or for ten years; or
(ii) has taken before itself any case from any subordinate court and convicted the accused person and sentenced him to imprisonment for life or for ten years.

Further, the appellate jurisdiction of the Supreme Court extends to all civil and criminal cases in which the Federal Court of India had jurisdiction to hear appeals from the high court but which are not covered under the civil and criminal appellate jurisdiction of the Supreme Court mentioned above.

(d) Appeal by Special Leave The Supreme Court is authorised to grant in its discretion special leave to appeal from any judgement in any matter passed by any court or tribunal in the country (except military tribunal and court martial). This provision contains the four aspects as under:

(i) It is a discretionary power and hence, cannot be claimed as a matter of right.

(ii) It can be granted in any judgement whether final or interlocutory.

(iii) It may be related to any matter—constitutional, civil, criminal, income-tax, labour, revenue, advocates, etc.

(iv) It can be granted against any court or tribunal and not necessarily against a high court (of course, except a military court).

Thus, the scope of this provision is very wide and it vests the Supreme Court with a plenary jurisdiction to hear appeals. On the exercise of this power, the Supreme Court itself held that 'being an exceptional and overriding power, it has to be exercised sparingly and with caution and only in special extraordinary situations. Beyond that it is not possible to fetter the exercise of this power by any set formula or rule'.

4. Advisory Jurisdiction

The Constitution (Article 143) authorises the president to seek the opinion of the Supreme Court in the two categories of matters:

(a) On any question of law or fact of public importance which has arisen or which is likely to arise.

(b) On any dispute arising out of any pre-constitution treaty, agreement, covenant, engagement, sanad or other similar instruments.[11]

In the first case, the Supreme Court may tender or may refuse to tender its opinion to the president. But, in the second case, the Supreme Court 'must' tender its opinion to the president. In both the cases, the opinion expressed by the Supreme Court is only advisory and not a judicial pronouncement. Hence, it is not binding on the president; he may follow or may not follow the opinion. However, it facilitates the government to have an authoritative legal opinion on a matter to be decided by it.

So far (2013), the President has made fifteen references to the Supreme Court under its advisory jurisdiction (also known as consultative jurisdiction). These are mentioned below in the chronological order.

1. Delhi Laws Act in 1951
2. Kerala Education Bill in 1958
3. Berubari Union in 1960
4. Sea Customs Act in 1963
5. Keshav Singh's case relating to the privileges of the Legislature in 1964

6. Presidential Election in 1974
7. Special Courts Bill in 1978
8. Jammu and Kashmir Resettlement Act in 1982
9. Cauvery Water Disputes Tribunal in 1992
10. Rama Janma Bhumi case in 1993
11. Consultation process to be adopted by the chief justice of India in 1998
12. Legislative competence of the Centre and States on the subject of natural gas and liquefied natural gas in 2001
13. The constitutional validity of the Election Commission's decision on deferring the Gujarat Assembly Elections in 2002
14. Punjab Termination of Agreements Act in 2004
15. 2G spectrum case verdict and the mandatory auctioning of natural resources across all sectors in 2012

5. A Court of Record

As a Court of Record, the Supreme Court has two powers:

(a) The judgements, proceedings and acts of the Supreme Court are recorded for perpetual memory and testimony. These records are admitted to be of evidentiary value and cannot be questioned when produced before any court. They are recognised as legal precedents and legal references.

(b) It has power to punish for contempt of court, either with simple imprisonment for a term up to six months or with fine up to ₹2,000 or with both. In 1991, the Supreme Court has ruled that it has power to punish for contempt not only of itself but also of high courts, subordinate courts and tribunals functioning in the entire country.

Contempt of court may be civil or criminal. Civil contempt means wilful disobedience to any judgement, order, writ or other process of a court or wilful breach of an undertaking given to a court. Criminal contempt means the publication of any matter or doing an act which—(i) scandalises or lowers the authority of a court; or (ii) prejudices or interferes with the due course of a judicial proceeding; or (iii) interferes or obstructs the administration of justice in any other manner.

However, innocent publication and distribution of some matter, fair and accurate report of judicial proceedings, fair and reasonable criticism of judicial acts and comment on the administrative side of the judiciary do not amount to contempt of court.

6. Power of Judicial Review

Judicial review is the power of the Supreme Court to examine the constitutionality of legislative enactments and executive orders of both the Central and state governments. On examination, if they are found to be violative of the Constitution (*ultra-vires*), they can be declared as illegal, unconstitutional and invalid (null and void) by the Supreme Court. Consequently, they cannot be enforced by the Government.

Judicial review is needed for the following reasons:

  (a) To uphold the principle of the supremacy of the Constitution.

  (b) To maintain federal equilibrium (balance between Centre and states).

  (c) To protect the fundamental rights of the citizens.

The Supreme Court used the power of judicial review in various cases, as for example, the *Golaknath* case (1967), the *Bank Nationalisation* case (1970), the *Privy Purses Abolition* case (1971), the *Kesavananda Bharati* case (1973), the *Minerva Mills* case (1980) and so on.

Though the phrase 'Judicial Review' has nowhere been used in the Constitution, the provisions of several articles[12] explicitly confer the power of judicial review on the Supreme Court. The constitutional validity of a legislative enactment or an executive order can be challenged in the Supreme Court on the following three grounds:

  (a) it infringes the Fundamental Rights (Part III),

  (b) it is outside the competence of the authority which has framed it, and

  (c) it is repugnant to the constitutional provisions.

From the above, it is clear that the scope of judicial review in India is narrower than that of what exists in USA, though the American Constitution does not explicitly mention the concept of judicial review in any of its provisions. This is because, the American Constitution provides for 'due process of law' against that of 'procedure established by law' which is contained in the Indian Constitution. The difference between the two is : 'The due process

of law gives wide scope to the Supreme Court to grant protection to the rights of its citizens. It can declare laws violative of these rights void not only on substantive grounds of being unlawful, but also on procedural grounds of being unreasonable. Our Supreme Court, while determining the constitutionality of a law, however examines only the substantive question i.e., whether the law is within the powers of the authority concerned or not. It is not expected to go into the question of its reasonableness, suitability or policy implications.'[13]

The exercise of wide power of judicial review by the American Supreme Court in the name of 'due process of law' clause has made the critics to describe it as a 'third chamber' of the Legislature, a super-legislature, the arbiter of social policy and so on. This American principle of judicial supremacy is also recognised in our constitutional system, but to a limited extent. Nor do we fully follow the British Principle of parliamentary supremacy. There are many limitations on the sovereignty of Parliament in our country, like the written character of the Constitution, the federalism with division of powers, the Fundamental Rights and the judicial review. In effect, what exists in India is a synthesis of both, that is, the American principle of judicial supremacy and the British principle of parliamentary supremacy.

7. Other Powers

Besides the above, the Supreme Court has numerous other powers:

  (a) It decides the disputes regarding the election of the president and the vice-president. In this regard, it has the original, exclusive and final authority.

  (b) It enquires into the conduct and behaviour of the chairman and members of the Union Public Service Commission on a reference made by the president. If it finds them guilty of misbehaviour, it can recommend to the president for their removal. The advice tendered by the Supreme Court in this regard is binding on the President.

  (c) It has power to review its own judgement or order. Thus, it is not bound by its previous decision and can depart from it in the interest of justice or community welfare. In brief, the

Supreme Court is a self-correcting agency. For example, in the *Kesavananda Bharati* case (1973), the Supreme Court departed from its previous judgement in the *Golak Nath* case (1967).

(d) It is authorised to withdraw the cases pending before the high courts and dispose them by itself. It can also transfer a case or appeal pending before one high court to another high court.

(e) Its law is binding on all courts in India. Its decree or order is enforceable throughout the country. All authorities (civil and judicial) in the country should act in aid of the Supreme Court.

(f) It is the ultimate interpreter of the Constitution. It can give final version to the spirit and content of the provisions of the Constitution and the verbiage used in the Constitution.

(g) It has power of judicial superintendence and control over all the courts and tribunals functioning in the entire territory of the country.

The Supreme Court's jurisdiction and powers with respect to matters in the Union list can be enlarged by the Parliament. Further, its jurisdiction and powers with respect to other matters can be enlarged by a special agreement of the Centre and the states.

SUPREME COURT ADVOCATES

Three categories of Advocates are entitled to practice law before the Supreme Court. They are :

1. Senior Advocates These are Advocates who are designated as Senior Advocates by the Supreme Court of India or by any High Court. The Court can designate any Advocate, with his consent, as Senior Advocate if in its opinion by virtue of his ability, standing at the Bar or special knowledge or experience in law the said Advocate is deserving of such distinction. A Senior Advocate is not entitled to appear without an Advocate-on-Record in the Supreme Court or without a junior in any other court or tribunal in India. He is also not entitled to accept instructions to draw pleadings or affidavits, advise on evidence or do any drafting work of an analogous kind in any court or tribunal in India or undertake conveyancing work of any kind whatsoever but this prohibition shall not extend to settling any such matter as aforesaid in consultation with a junior.

2. Advocates-on-Record Only these advocates are entitled to file any matter or document before the Supreme Court. They can also file an appearance or act for a party in the Supreme Court.

Table 25.1 *Comparing Indian and American Supreme Courts*

Indian Supreme Court	*American Supreme Court*
1. Its original jurisdiction is confined to federal cases.	1. Its original jurisdiction covers not only federal cases but also cases relating to naval forces, maritime activities, ambassadors, etc.
2. Its appellate jurisdiction covers constitutional, civil and criminal cases.	2. Its appellate jurisdiction is confined to constitutional cases only.
3. It has a very wide discretion to grant special leave to appeal in any matter against the judgement of any court or tribunal (except military).	3. It has no such plenary power.
4. It has advisory jurisdiction.	4. It has no advisory jurisdiction.
5. Its scope of judicial review is limited.	5. Its scope of judicial review is very wide.
6. It defends rights of the citizen according to the 'procedure established by law'.	6. It defends rights of the citizen according to the 'due process of law'.
7. Its jurisdiction and powers can be enlarged by Parliament.	7. Its jurisdiction and powers are limited to that conferred by the Constitution.
8. It has power of judicial superintendence and control over state high courts due to integrated judicial system.	8. It has no such power due to double (or separated) judicial system.

Table 25.2 *Articles Related to Supreme Court at a Glance*

Article No.	Subject-matter
124.	Establishment and Constitution of Supreme Court
125.	Salaries, etc., of Judges
126.	Appointment of acting Chief Justice
127.	Appointment of *ad hoc* Judges
128.	Attendance of retired Judges at sittings of the Supreme Court
129.	Supreme Court to be a court of record
130.	Seat of Supreme Court
131.	Original jurisdiction of the Supreme Court
131A.	Exclusive jurisdiction of the Supreme Court in regard to questions as to constitutional validity of Central Laws (Repealed)
132.	Appellate jurisdiction of Supreme Court in appeals from High Courts in certain cases
133.	Appellate jurisdiction of Supreme Court in appeals from High Courts in regard to civil matters
134.	Appellate jurisdiction of Supreme Court in regard to criminal matters
134A.	Certificate for appeal to the Supreme Court
135.	Jurisdiction and powers of the Federal Court under existing law to be exercisable by the Supreme Court
136.	Special leave to appeal by the Supreme Court
137.	Review of judgments or orders by the Supreme Court
138.	Enlargement of the jurisdiction of the Supreme Court
139.	Conferment on the Supreme Court of powers to issue certain writs
139A.	Transfer of certain cases
140.	Ancillary powers of Supreme Court
141.	Law declared by Supreme Court to be binding on all courts
142.	Enforcement of decrees and orders of Supreme Court and orders as to discovery, etc.
143.	Power of President to consult Supreme Court
144.	Civil and judicial authorities to act in aid of the Supreme Court
144A.	Special provisions as to disposal of questions relating to constitutional validity of laws (Repealed)
145.	Rules of court, etc.
146.	Officers and servants and the expenses of the Supreme Court
147.	Interpretation

3. Other Advocates These are advocates whose names are entered on the roll of any State Bar Council maintained under the Advocates Act, 1961 and they can appear and argue any matter on behalf of a party in the Supreme Court but they are not entitled to file any document or matter before the Court.

NOTES AND REFERENCES

1. Before 1950, the British Privy Council had the jurisdiction to hear appeals from India.
2. In Re-Presidential Reference (1998). The president sought the Supreme Court's opinion (under Article 143) on certain doubts over the Consultation process to be adopted by the chief justice of India as stipulated in the 1993 case.
3. A N Ray was fourth in seniority. The three superseded judges were J M Shelat, K S Hegde and A N Grover. All the three judges resigned from the Supreme Court. They were superseded due to their judgement in *Kesavananda Bharati* case (1973), which was not favourable to the Government.
4. He was H R Khanna and he too resigned. His dissenting judgement upholding the right to life even during emergency in the *ADM Jabalpur v Shivkant Shukla* case (1976) was not appreciated by the Government.
5. An impeachment motion for the removal of a judge does not lapse on the dissolution of the Lok Sabha.
6. In 1950, their salaries were fixed at ₹5,000 per month and ₹4,000 per month respectively. In 1986, their salaries were raised to ₹10,000 per month and ₹9,000 per month respectively. In 1998, their salaries were raised to ₹33,000 per month and ₹30,000 per month respectively.
7. The Criminal Procedure Code (1973) has effected the separation of Judiciary from the Executive (Article 50 under the Directive Principles of State Policy).
8. Pre-Constitution means that, which have been entered into or executed before the commencement of the Constitution and which continues to be in operation after such commencement.
9. This means that the inter-government agreements (i.e., the agreements between states or between Centre and states) can exclude the original jurisdiction of the Supreme Court in so far as the disputes arising out of them are concerned.
10. The Inter-State Water Disputes Act of 1956 has excluded the original jurisdiction of the Supreme Court in disputes between states with respect to the use, distribution or control of the water of inter-state river or river valley.
11. These include treaties, covenants, etc. between the Central Government and the formerly princely states during 1947 to 1950.
12. These include 13, 32, 131, 132, 133, 134, 135, 136, 143, 145, 226, 246, 256, etc.
13. Subhash C Kashyap, *Our Constitution*, National Book Trust, Third Edition, 2001, p. 232.

PART IV

STATE GOVERNMENT

Governor

The Constitution of India envisages the same pattern of government in the states as that for the Centre, that is, a parliamentary system. Part VI of the Constitution, which deals with the government in the states, is not applicable to the State of Jammu and Kashmir, which enjoys a special status and has a separate Constitution of its own.

Articles 153 to 167 in Part VI of the Constitution deal with the state executive. The state executive consists of the governor, the chief minister, the council of ministers and the advocate general of the state. Thus, there is no office of vice-governor (in the state) like that of Vice-President at the Centre.

The governor is the chief executive head of the state. But, like the president, he is a nominal executive head (titular or constitutional head). The governor also acts as an agent of the central government. Therefore, the office of governor has a dual role.

Usually, there is a governor for each state, but the 7th Constitutional Amendment Act of 1956 facilitated the appointment of the same person as a governor for two or more states.

APPOINTMENT OF GOVERNOR

The governor is neither directly elected by the people nor indirectly elected by a specially constituted electoral college as is the case with the president. He is appointed by the president by warrant under his hand and seal. In a way, he is a nominee of the Central government. But, as held by the Supreme Court in 1979, the office of governor of a state is not an employment under the Central government. It is an independent constitutional office and is not under the control of or subordinate to the Central government.

The Draft Constitution provided for the direct election of the governor on the basis of universal adult suffrage. But the Constituent Assembly opted for the present system of appointment of governor by the president because of the following reasons[1]:

1. The direct election of the governor is incompatible with the parliamentary system established in the states.
2. The mode of direct election is more likely to create conflicts between the governor and the chief minister.
3. The governor being only a constitutional (nominal) head, there is no point in making elaborate arrangements for his election and spending huge amount of money.
4. The election of a governor would be entirely on personal issues. Hence, it is not in the national interest to involve a large number of voters in such an election.
5. An elected governor would naturally belong to a party and would not be a neutral person and an impartial head.
6. The election of governor would create separatist tendencies and thus affect the political stability and unity of the country.
7. The system of presidential nomination enables the Centre to maintain its control over the states.
8. The direct election of the governor creates a serious problem of leadership at the time of a general election in the state.

9. The chief minister would like his nominee to contest for governorship. Hence, a second rate man of the ruling party is elected as governor.

Therefore, the American model, where the Governor of a state is directly elected, was dropped and the Canadian model, where the governor of a province (state) is appointed by the Governor-General (Centre), was accepted in the Constituent Assembly.

The Constitution lays down only two qualifications for the appointment of a person as a governor. These are:

1. He should be a citizen of India.
2. He should have completed the age of 35 years.

Additionally, two conventions have also developed in this regard over the years. First, he should be an outsider, that is, he should not belong to the state where he is appointed, so that he is free from the local politics. Second, while appointing the governor, the president is required to consult the chief minister of the state concerned, so that the smooth functioning of the constitutional machinery in the state is ensured. However, both the conventions have been violated in some of the cases.

Conditions of Governor's Office

The Constitution lays down the following conditions for the the governor's office:

1. He should not be a member of either House of Parliament or a House of the state legislature. If any such person is appointed as governor, he is deemed to have vacated his seat in that House on the date on which he enters upon his office as the governor.
2. He should not hold any other office of profit.
3. He is entitled without payment of rent to the use of his official residence (the *Raj Bhavan*).
4. He is entitled to such emoluments, allowances and privileges as may be determined by Parliament.
5. When the same person is appointed as the governor of two or more states, the emoluments and allowances payable to him are shared by the states in such proportion as determined by the president.
6. His emoluments and allowances cannot be diminished during his term of office.

In 2008, the Parliament has increased the salary of the governor from ₹36,000 to ₹1.10 lakh per month.[2]

Like the President, the governor is also entitled to a number of privileges and immunities. He enjoys personal immunity from legal liability for his official acts. During his term of office, he is immune from any criminal proceedings, even in respect of his personal acts. He cannot be arrested or imprisoned. However, after giving two months' notice, civil proceedings can be instituted against him during his term of office in respect of his personal acts.

Before entering upon his office, the governor has to make and subscribe to an oath or affirmation. In his oath, the governor swears:

(a) to faithfully execute the office;
(b) to preserve, protect and defend the Constitution and the law; and
(c) to devote himself to the service and well-being of the people of the state.

The oath of office to the governor is administered by the chief justice of the concerned state high court and in his absence, the senior-most judge of that court available.

Every person discharging the functions of the governor also undertakes the similar oath or affirmation.

Term of Governor's Office

A governor holds office for a term of five years from the date on which he enters upon his office. However, this term of five years is subject to the pleasure of the President. Further, he can resign at any time by addressing a resignation letter to the President.

The Supreme Court held that the pleasure of the President is not justifiable. The governor has no security of tenure and no fixed term of office. He may be removed by the President at any time.[3]

The Constitution does not lay down any grounds upon which a governor may be removed by the President. Hence, the National Front Government headed by V P Singh (1989) asked all the governors to resign as they were appointed by the Congress government. Eventually, some of the governors were replaced and some were allowed to continue. The same thing was repeated in 1991, when the Congress Government headed by P V Narasimha Rao changed fourteen governors appointed by the V P Singh and Chandra Sekhar governments.

The President may transfer a Governor appointed to one state to another state for the rest of the term. Further, a Governor whose term has expired may be reappointed in the same state or any other state.

A governor can hold office beyond his term of five years until his successor assumes charge. The underlying idea is that there must be a governor in the state and there cannot be an interregnum.

The President can make such provision as he thinks fit for the discharge of the functions of the governor in any contingency not provided for in the Constitution, for example, the death of a sitting governor. Thus, the chief justice of the concerned state high court may be appointed temporarily to discharge the functions of the governor of that state.

POWERS AND FUNCTIONS OF GOVERNOR

A governor possesses executive, legislative, financial and judicial powers more or less analogous to the President of India. However, he has no diplomatic, military or emergency powers like the president.

The powers and functions of the governor can be studied under the following heads:

1. Executive powers.
2. Legislative powers.
3. Financial powers.
4. Judicial powers.

Executive Powers

The executive powers and functions of the Governor are:

1. All executive actions of the government of a state are formally taken in his name.
2. He can make rules specifying the manner in which the Orders and other instruments made and executed in his name shall be authenticated.
3. He can make rules for more convenient transaction of the business of a state government and for the allocation among the ministers of the said business.
4. He appoints the chief minister and other ministers. They also hold office during his pleasure. There should be a Tribal Welfare minister in

the states of Chattisgarh, Jharkhand, Madhya Pradesh and Odisha appointed by him.

5. He appoints the advocate general of a state and determines his remuneration. The advocate general holds office during the pleasure of the governor.
6. He appoints the state election commissioner and determines his conditions of service and tenure of office. However, the state election commissioner can be removed only in like manner and on the like grounds as a judge of a high court.
7. He appoints the chairman and members of the state public service commission. However, they can be removed only by the president and not by a governor.
8. He can seek any information relating to the administration of the affairs of the state and proposals for legislation from the chief minister.
9. He can require the chief minister to submit for the consideration of the council of ministers any matter on which a decision has been taken by a minister but which has not been considered by the council.
10. He can recommend the imposition of constitutional emergency in a state to the president. During the period of President's rule in a state, the governor enjoys extensive executive powers as an agent of the President.
11. He acts as the chancellor of universities in the state. He also appoints the vice-chancellors of universities in the state.

Legislative Powers

A governor is an integral part of the state legislature. In that capacity, he has the following legislative powers and functions:

1. He can summon or prorogue the state legislature and dissolve the state legislative assembly.
2. He can address the state legislature at the commencement of the first session after each general election and the first session of each year.
3. He can send messages to the house or houses of the state legislature, with respect to a bill pending in the legislature or otherwise.
4. He can appoint any member of the State legislative assembly to preside over its proceedings when the offices of both the Speaker and the Deputy Speaker fall vacant. Similarly, he can

appoint any member of the state legislature council to preside over its proceedings when the offices of both Chairman and Deputy Chairman fall vacant.

5. He nominates one-sixth of the members of the state legislative council from amongst persons having special knowledge or practical experience in literature, science, art, cooperative movement and social service.

6. He can nominate one member to the state legislature assembly from the Anglo-Indian Community.

7. He decides on the question of disqualification of members of the state legislature in consultation with the Election Commission.

8. When a bill is sent to the governor after it is passed by state legislature, he can:
   (a) Give his assent to the bill, or
   (b) Withhold his assent to the bill, or
   (c) Return the bill (if it is not a money bill) for reconsideration of the state legislature. However, if the bill is passed again by the state legislature with or without amendments, the governor has to give his assent to the bill, or
   (d) Reserve the bill for the consideration of the president. In one case such reservation is obligatory, that is, where the bill passed by the state legislature endangers the position of the state high court. In addition, the governor can also reserve the bill if it is of the following nature:[4]
      (i) *Ultra-vires,* that is, against the provisions of the Constitution.
      (ii) Opposed to the Directive Principles of State Policy.
      (iii) Against the larger interest of the country.
      (iv) Of grave national importance.
      (v) Dealing with compulsory acquisition of property under Article 31A of the Constitution.

9. He can promulgate ordinances when the state legislature is not in session. These ordinances must be approved by the state legislature within six weeks from its reassembly. He can also withdraw an ordinance anytime. This is the most important legislative power of the governor.

10. He lays the reports of the State Finance Commission, the State Public Service Commission and the Comptroller and Auditor-General relating to the accounts of the state, before the state legislature.

Financial Powers

The financial powers and functions of the governor are:

1. He sees that the Annual Financial Statement (state budget) is laid before the state legislature.

2. Money bills can be introduced in the state legislature only with his prior recommendation.

3. No demand for a grant can be made except on his recommendation.

4. He can make advances out of the Contingency Fund of the state to meet any unforeseen expenditure.

5. He constitutes a finance commission after every five years to review the financial position of the panchayats and the municipalities.

Judicial Powers

The judicial powers and functions of the governor are:

1. He can grant pardons, reprives, respites and remissions of punishment or suspend, remit and commute the sentence of any person convicted of any offence against any law relating to a matter to which the executive power of the state extends.[5]

2. He is consulted by the president while appointing the judges of the concerned state high court.

3. He makes appointments, postings and promotions of the district judges in consultation with the state high court.

4. He also appoints persons to the judicial service of the state (other than district judges) in consultation with the state high court and the State Public Service Commission.

Now, we will study in detail the three important powers of the governor (veto power, ordinance-making power and pardoning power) by comparing them with that of the President.

Table 26.1 *Comparing Veto Powers of President and Governor*

President	Governor
With Regard to Ordinary Bills	**With Regard to Ordinary Bills**
Every ordinary bill, after it is passed by both the Houses of the Parliament either singly or at a joint sitting, is presented to the President for his assent. He has three alternatives: 1. He may give his assent to the bill, the bill then becomes an act. 2. He may withhold his assent to the bill, the bill then ends and does not become an act. 3. He may return the bill for reconsideration of the Houses. If the bill is passed by both the Houses again with or without amendments and presented to the President for his assent, the president must give his assent to the bill. Thus the president enjoys only a 'suspensive veto'.	Every ordinary bill, after it is passed by the legislative assembly in case of a unicameral legislature or by both the Houses in case of a bicameral legislature either in the first instance or in the second instance, is presented to the governor for his assent. He has four alternatives: 1. He may give his assent to the bill, the bill then becomes an act. 2. He may withhold his assent to the bill, the bill then ends and does not become an act. 3. He may return the bill for reconsideration of the House or Houses. If the bill is passed by the House or Houses again with or without amendments and presented to the governor for his assent, the governor must give his assent to the bill. Thus, the governor enjoys only a 'suspensive veto'. 4. He may reserve the bill for the consideration of the President.
When a state bill is reserved by the governor for the consideration of the President, the President has three alternatives: (a) He may give his assent to the bill, the bill then becomes an act. (b) He may withhold his assent to the bill, the bill then ends and does not become an Act. (c) He may return the bill for reconsideration of the House or Houses of the state legislature. When a bill is so returned, the House or Houses have to reconsider it within six months. If the bill is passed by the House or Houses again with or without amendments and presented to the president for his assent, the president is not bound to give his assent to the bill. He may give his assent to such a bill or withhold his assent.	When the governor reserves a bill for the consideration of the President, he will not have any further role in the enactment of the bill. If the bill is returned by the President for the reconsideration of the House or Houses and is passed again, the bill must be presented again for the presidential assent only. If the President gives his assent to the bill, it becomes an act. This means that the assent of the Governor is no longer required.
With Regard to Money Bills Every money bill after it is passed by the Parliament, is presented to the President for his assent. He has two alternatives: 1. He may give his assent to the bill, the bill then becomes an act. 2. He may withhold his assent to the bill, the bill then ends and does not become an act.	Every money bill, after it is passed by the state legislature (unicameral or bicameral), is presented to the governor for his assent. He has three alternatives: 1. He may give his assent to the bill, the bill then becomes an act. 2. He may withhold his assent to the bill, the bill then ends and does not become an act. 3. He may reserve the bill for the consideration of the president.

(Contd.)

President	Governor
Thus, the President cannot return a money bill for the reconsideration of the Parliament. Normally, the president gives his assent to a money bill as it is introduced in the Parliament with his previous permission. When a Money Bill is reserved by the Governor for the consideration of the President, the President has two alternatives: (a) He may give his assent to the bill, the bill then becomes an Act. (b) He may withhold his assent to the bill, the bill then ends and does not become an act. Thus, the President cannot return a money bill for the reconsideration of the state legislature (as in the case of the Parliament).	Thus, the governor cannot return a money bill for the reconsideration of the state legislature. Normally, the governor gives his assent to a money bill as it is introduced in the state legislature with his previous permission. When the governor reserves a money bill for the consideration of the President, he will not have any further role in the enactment of the bill. If the President gives his assent to the bill, it becomes an Act. This means that the assent of the governor is no longer required.

Table 26.2 *Comparing Ordinance-Making Power of President and Governor*

President	Governor
1. He can promulgate an ordinance only when both the Houses of Parliament are not in session or when either of the two Houses of Parliament is not in session. The second provision implies that an ordinance can also be promulgated by the president when only one House is in session because a law can be passed by both the Houses and not by one House alone.	1. He can promulgate an ordinance only when the legislative assembly (in case of a unicameral legislature) is not in session or (in case of a bi-cameral legislature) when both the Houses of the state legislature are not in session or when either of the two Houses of the state legislature is not in session. The last provision implies that an ordinance can be promulgated by the governor when only one House (in case of a bicameral legislature) is in session because a law can be passed by both the Houses and not by one House alone.
2. He can promulgate an ordinance only when he is satisfied that circumstances exist which render it necessary for him to take immediate action.	2. He can promulgate an ordinance only when he is satisfied that circumstances exist which render it necessary for him to take immediate action.
3. His ordinance-making power is co-extensive with the legislative power of the Parliament. This means that he can issue ordinances only on those subjects on which the Parliament can make laws.	3. His ordinance-making power is co-extensive with the legislative power of the state legislature. This means that he can issue ordinances only on those subjects on which the state legislature can make laws.
4. An ordinance issued by him has the same force and effect as an act of the Parliament.	4. An ordinance issued by him has the same force and effect as an act of the state legislature.
5. An ordinance issued by him is subject to the same limitations as an act of Parliament. This means that an ordinance issued by him will be invalid to the extent it makes any provision which the Parliament cannot make.	5. An ordinance issued by him is subject to the same limitations as an act of the state legislature. This means that an ordinance issued by him will be invalid to the extent it makes any provision which the state legislature cannot make.
6. He can withdraw an ordinance at any time.	6. He can withdraw an ordinance at any time.

(Contd.)

President	Governor
7. His ordinance-making power is not a discretionary power. This means that he can promulgate or withdraw an ordinance only on the advice of the council of ministers headed by the prime minister.	7. His ordinance-making power is not a discretionary power. This means that he can promulgate or withdraw an ordinance only on the advice of the council of ministers headed by the chief minister.
8. An ordinance issued by him should be laid before both the Houses of Parliament when it reassembles.	8. An ordinance issued by him should be laid before the legislative assembly or both the Houses of the state legislature (in case of a bicameral legislature) when it reassembles.
9. An ordinance issued by him ceases to operate on the expiry of six weeks from the reassembly of Parliament. It may cease to operate even earlier than the prescribed six weeks, if both the Houses of Parliament passes resolutions disapproving it.	9. An ordinance issued by him ceases to operate on the expiry of six weeks from the reassembly of the state legislature. It may cease to operate even earlier than the prescribed six weeks, if a resolution disapproving it is passed by the legislative assembly and is agreed to by the legislative council (in case of a bicameral legislature).
10. He needs no instruction for making an ordinance.	10. He cannot make an ordinance without the instructions from the President in three cases: (a) If a bill containing the same provisions would have required the previous sanction of the President for its introduction into the state legislature. (b) If he would have deemed it necessary to reserve a bill containing the same provisions for the consideration of the President. (c) If an act of the state legislature containing the same provisions would have been invalid without receiving the President's assent.

Table 26.3 *Comparing Pardoning Powers of President and Governor*

President	Governor
1. He can pardon, reprive, respite, remit, suspend or commute the punishment or sentence of any person convicted of any offence against a Central law.	1. He can pardon, reprieve, respite, remit, suspend or commute the punishment or sentence of any person convicted of any offence against a state law.
2. He can pardon, reprieve, respite, remit, suspend or commute a death sentence. He is the only authority to pardon a death sentence.	2. He cannot pardon a death sentence. Even if a state law prescribes for death sentence, the power to grant pardon lies with the President and not the governor. But, the governor can suspend, remit or commute a death sentence.
3. He can grant pardon, reprieve, respite, suspension, remission or commutation in respect to punishment or sentence by a court-martial (military court).	3. He does not possess any such power.

CONSTITUTIONAL POSITION OF GOVERNOR

The Constitution of India provides for a parliamentary form of government in the states as in the Centre. Consequently, the governor has been made only a nominal executive, the real executive constitutes the council of ministers headed by the chief minister. In other words, the governor has to exercise his powers and functions with the aid and advise of the council of ministers headed by the chief minister, except in matters in which he is required to act in his discretion (i.e., without the advice of ministers).

In estimating the constitutional position of the governor, particular reference has to be made to the provisions of Articles 154, 163 and 164. These are:

(a) The executive power of the state shall be vested in the governor and shall be exercised by him either directly or through officers subordinate to him in accordance with this Constitution (Article 154).

(b) There shall be a council of ministers with the chief minister as the head to aid and advise the governor in the exercise of his functions, except in so far as he is required to exercise his functions in his discretion (Article 163).

(c) The council of ministers shall be collectively responsible to the legislative assembly of the state (Article 164). This provision is the foundation of the parliamentary system of government in the state.

From the above, it is clear that constitutional position of the governor differs from that of the president in the following two respects:[6]

1. While the Constitution envisages the possibility of the governor acting at times in his discretion, no such possibility has been envisaged for the President.

2. After the 42nd Constitutional Amendment (1976), ministerial advice has been made binding on the President, but no such provision has been made with respect to the governor.

The Constitution makes it clear that if any question arises whether a matter falls within the governor's discretion or not, the decision of the governor is final and the validity of anything done by him cannot be called in question on the ground that he ought or ought not to have acted in his discretion. The governor has constitutional discretion in the following cases:

1. Reservation of a bill for the consideration of the President.

2. Recommendation for the imposition of the President's Rule in the state.

3. While exercising his functions as the administrator of an adjoining union territory (in case of additional charge).

4. Determining the amount payable by the Government of Assam, Meghalaya, Tripura and Mizoram to an autonomous Tribal District Council as royalty accruing from licenses for mineral exploration[7].

5. Seeking information from the chief minister with regard to the administrative and legislative matters of the state.

In addition to the above constitutional discretion (i.e., the express discretion mentioned in the Constitution), the governor, like the president, also has situational discretion (i.e., the hidden discretion derived from the exigencies of a prevailing political situation) in the following cases:

1. Appointment of chief minister when no party has a clear-cut majority in the state legislative assembly or when the chief minister in office dies suddenly and there is no obvious successor.

2. Dismissal of the council of ministers when it cannot prove the confidence of the state legislative assembly.

3. Dissolution of the state legislative assembly if the council of ministers has lost its majority.

Moreover, the governor has certain special responsibilities to discharge according to the directions issued by the President. In this regard, the governor, though has to consult the council of ministers led by the chief minister, acts finally on his discretion. They are as follows:

1. Maharashtra—Establishment of separate development boards for Vidarbha and Marathwada.

2. Gujarat—Establishment of separate development boards for Saurashtra and Kutch.

3. Nagaland—With respect to law and order in the state for so long as the internal disturbance in the Naga Hills–Tuensang Area continues.

4. Assam—With respect to the administration of tribal areas.

5. Manipur—Regarding the administration of the hill areas in the state.
6. Sikkim—For peace and for ensuring social and economic advancement of the different sections of the population.
7. Arunachal Pradesh—With respect to law and order in the state.

8. Karnataka – Establishment of a separate development board for Hyderabad-Karnataka region[8].

Thus, the Constitution has assigned a dual role to the office of a governor in the Indian federal system. He is the constitutional head of the state as well as the representative of the Centre (i.e., President).

Table 26.4 *Articles Related to Governor at a Glance*

Article No.	Subject-matter
153.	Governors of states
154	Executive power of state
155.	Appointment of Governor
156.	Term of office of Governor
157.	Qualifications for appointment as Governor
158.	Conditions of Governor's office
159.	Oath or affirmation by the Governor
160.	Discharge of the functions of the Governor in certain contingencies
161.	Power of the Governor to grant pardons and others
162.	Extent of executive power of state
163.	Council of ministers to aid and advise the Governor
164.	Other provisions as to ministers like appointments, term, salaries, and others
165.	Advocate-General for the state
166.	Conduct of business of the government of a state
167.	Duties of the Chief Minister regarding furnishing of information to the Governor, and so on
174.	Sessions of the state legislature, prorogation and dissolution
175.	Right of the Governor to address and send messages to the house or houses of state legislature
176.	Special address by the Governor
200.	Assent to bills (i.e. assent of the Governor to the bills passed by the state legislature)
201.	Bills reserved by the Governor for consideration of the President
213.	Power of Governor to promulgate ordinances
217.	Governor being consulted by the President in the matter of the appointments of the judges of the High Courts
233.	Appointment of district judges by the Governor
234.	Appointments of persons (other than district judges) to the judicial service of the state by the Governor.

Notes and References

1. *Constituent Assembly Debates,* Volume IV, pp. 588–607.
2. Governor's (Emoluments, Allowances and Privileges) Act, 1982, as amended in 2008 (by Act 1 of 2009) with effect from 1 January 2006.
3. *Surya Narain* v *Union of India,* (1982).
4. Soli Sorabji, *The Governor: Sage or Saboteur,* Roli Books (New Delhi), 1985, p. 25.
5. For the meanings of these legal terms, see 'Pardoning Power of the President' under Chapter 17.
6. MP Jain, *Indian Constitutional Law,* Wadhwa, Fourth Ed, p. 186.
7. Paragraph 9(2) of the Sixth Schedule says: 'If any dispute arises as to the share of such royalties to be made over to a district council, it shall be referred to the governor for determination and the amount determined by the governor in his discretion shall be deemed to be the amount payable to the district council and the decision of the governor shall be final'. The Sixth Schedule contains the provisions as to the administration of tribal areas in the States of Assam, Meghalaya, Tripura and Mizoram.
8. This provision was added by the 98th Constitutional Amendment Act of 2012.

Chief Minister

In the scheme of parliamentary system of government provided by the Constitution, the governor is the nominal executive authority (*de jure* executive) and the Chief Minister is the real executive authority (*de facto* executive). In other words, the governor is the head of the state while the Chief Minister is the head of the government. Thus the position of the Chief Minister at the state level is analogous to the position of prime minister at the Centre.

APPOINTMENT OF CHIEF MINISTER

The Constitution does not contain any specific procedure for the selection and appointment of the Chief Minister. Article 164 only says that the Chief Minister shall be appointed by the governor. However, this does not imply that the governor is free to appoint any one as the Chief Minister. In accordance with the convections of the parliamentary system of government, the governor has to appoint the leader of the majority party in the state legislative assembly as the Chief Minister. But, when no party has a clear majority in the assembly, then the governor may exercise his personal discretion in the selection and appointment of the Chief Minister. In such a situation, the governor usually appoints the leader of the largest party or coalition in the assembly as the Chief Minister and ask him to seek a vote of confidence in the House within a month.[1]

The governor may have to exercise his individual judgement in the selection and appointed of the Chief Minister when the Chief Minister in office dies suddenly and there is no obvious successor. However, on the death of a Chief Minister, the ruling party usually elects a new leader and the governor has no choice but to appoint him as Chief Minister.

The Constitution does not require that a person must prove his majority in the legislative assembly before he is appointed as the Chief Minister. The governor may first appoint him as the Chief Minister and then ask him to prove his majority in the legislative assembly within a reasonable period. This is what has been done in a number of cases[2].

A person who is not a member of the state legislature can be appointed as Chief Minister for six months, within which time, he should be elected to the state legislature, failing which he ceases to be the Chief Minister.[3]

According to the Constitution, the Chief Minister may be a member of any of the two Houses of a state legislature. Usually Chief Ministers have been selected from the Lower House (legislative assembly), but, on a number of occasions, a member of the Upper House (legislative council) has also been appointed as Chief Minister.[4]

OATH, TERM AND SALARY

Before the Chief Minister enters his office, the governor administers to him the oaths of office and secrecy.[5] In his oath of office, the Chief Minister swears:

1. to bear true faith and allegiance to the Constitution of India,

2. to uphold the sovereignty and integrity of India,
3. to faithfully and conscientiously discharge the duties of his office, and
4. to do right to all manner of people in accordance with the Constitution and the law, without fear or favour, affection or ill-will.

In his oath of secrecy, the Chief Minister swears that he will not directly or indirectly communicate or reveal to any person(s) any matter that is brought under his consideration or becomes known to him as a state minister except as may be required for the due discharge of his duties as such minister.

The term of the Chief Minister is not fixed and he holds office during the pleasure of the governor. However, this does not mean that the governor can dismiss him at any time. He cannot be dismissed by the governor as long as he enjoys the majority support in the legislative assembly.[6] But, if he loses the confidence of the assembly, he must resign or the governor can dismiss him.

The salary and allowances of the Chief Minister are determined by the state legislature. In addition to the salary and allowances, which are payable to a member of the state legislature, he gets a sumptuary allowance, free accommodation, travelling allowance, medical facilities, etc.

POWERS AND FUNCTIONS OF CHIEF MINISTER

The powers and functions of the Chief Minister can be studied under the following heads:

In Relation to Council of Ministers

The Chief Minister enjoys the following powers as head of the state council of ministers:

(a) The governor appoints only those persons as ministers who are recommended by the Chief Minister.
(b) He allocates and reshuffles the portfolios among ministers.
(c) He can ask a minister to resign or advise the governor to dismiss him in case of difference of opinion.
(d) He presides over the meetings of the council of ministers and influences its decisions.
(e) He guides, directs, controls and coordinates the activities of all the ministers.

(f) He can bring about the collapse of the council of ministers by resigning from office. Since the Chief Minister is the head of the council of ministers, his resignation or death automatically dissolves the council of ministers. The resignation or death of any other minister, on the other hand, merely creates a vacancy, which the Chief Minister may or may not like to fill.

In Relation to the Governor

The Chief Minister enjoys the following powers in relation to the governor:

(a) He is the principal channel of communication between the governor and the council of ministers.[7] It is the duty of the Chief Minister:
   (i) to communicate to the Governor of the state all decisions of the council of ministers relating to the administration of the affairs of the state and proposals for legislation;
   (ii) to furnish such information relating to the administration of the affairs of the state and proposals for legislation as the governor may call for; and
   (iii) if the governor so requires, to submit for the consideration of the council of ministers any matter on which a decision has been taken by a minister but which has not been considered by the council.

(b) He advises the governor with regard to the appointment of important officials like advocate general, chairman and members of the state public service commission, state election commissioner, and so on.

In Relation to State Legislature

The Chief Minister enjoys the following powers as the leader of the house:

(a) He advises the governor with regard to the summoning and proroguing of the sessions of the state legislature.
(b) He can recommend the dissolution of the legislative assembly to the governor at any time.
(c) He announces the government policies on the floor of the house.

Other Powers and Functions

In addition, the Chief Minister also performs the following functions:

(a) He is the chairman of the State Planning Board.

(b) He acts as a vice-chairman of the concerned zonal council by rotation, holding office for a period of one year at a time.[8]

(c) He is a member of the Inter-State Council and the National Development Council, both headed by the prime minister.

(d) He is the chief spokesman of the state government.

(e) He is the crisis manager-in-chief at the political level during emergencies.

(f) As a leader of the state, he meets various sections of the people and receives memoranda from them regarding their problems, and so on.

(g) He is the political head of the services.

Thus, he plays a very significant and highly crucial role in the state administration. However, the discretionary powers enjoyed by the governor reduces to some extent the power, authority, influence, prestige and role of the Chief Minister in the state administration.

RELATIONSHIP WITH THE GOVERNOR

The following provisions of the Constitution deal with the relationship between the governor and the Chief Minister:

1. *Article 163:* There shall be a council of ministers with the Chief Minister as the head to aid and advise the governor on the exercise of his functions, except in so far as he is required to exercise his functions or any of them in his discretion.

2. *Article 164:*

 (a) The Chief Minister shall be appointed by the governor and other ministers shall be appointed by the governor on the advise of the Chief Minister;

 (b) The ministers shall hold office during the pleasure of the governor; and

 (c) The council of ministers shall be collectively responsible to the legislative assembly of the state.

3. *Article 167:* It shall be the duty of the Chief Minister:

 (a) to communicate to the governor of the state all decisions of the council of ministers relating to the administration of the affairs of the state and proposals for legislation;

 (b) to furnish such information relating to the administration of the affairs of the state and proposals for legislation as the governor may call for ; and

 (c) if the governor so requires, to submit for the consideration of the council of ministers any matter on which a decision has been taken by a minister but which has not been considered by the council.

Table 27.1 *Articles Related to Chief Minister at a Glance*

Article No.	Subject-matter
163.	Council of Ministers to aid and advise Governor
164.	Other provisions as to Ministers
166.	Conduct of business of the Government of a State
167.	Duties of Chief Minister as respects the furnishing of information to Governor, etc.

NOTES AND REFERENCES

1. For example, the governors of Tamil Nadu (1951), Rajasthan (1967), and Haryana (1982) invited the leader of the largest party to form the ministry. The governors of Punjab (1967), West Bengal (1970), and Maharashtra (1978), on the other hand, invited the leader of the coalition to form the ministry.

2. For example, the governor of J & K (Jagmohan) appointed G M Shah as the Chief Minister and asked him to prove his majority on the floor of the House within a month. He proved his majority. Similarly, the Governor of Andhra Pradesh (Ram Lal) appointed Bhasker Rao as the Chief Minister and gave him one month to prove his majority on the floor of the House. However, he could not prove his majority.

3. For example, Bansilal and S B Chavan were appointed as Chief Ministers of Haryana and Maharashtra respectively, even though they were not members of the state legislature. Subsequently, they were elected to the state legislature.

4. For example, C Rajagopalachari in Madras (now Tamil Nadu) in 1952, Morarji Desai in Bombay (now Maharashtra) in 1952, CB Gupta in UP in 1960 and BP Mandal in Bihar in 1968 were appointed as Chief Ministers, while they were members of the state legislative council.

5. The form of oath of office and secrecy for the Chief Minister is similar to that for any state minister. See Chapter 28.

6. This was ruled by the Supreme Court in *S R Bommai* v. *Union of India,* (1994). However, there have been many violations of this rule, whereby the governors have dismissed the Chief Ministers without giving them an opportunity to prove their majority in the legislative assembly.

7. Article 167 specifically deals with this function of the Chief Minister.

8. Union home minister is the chairman of all the zonal councils.

State Council of Ministers

As the Constitution of India provides for a parliamentary system of government in the states on the Union pattern, the council of ministers headed by the chief minister is the real executive authority in the politico-administrative system of a state. The council of ministers in the states is constituted and function in the same way as the council of ministers at the Centre.

The principles of parliamentary system of government are not detailed in the Constitution; but two Articles (163 and 164) deal with them in a broad, sketchy and general manner. Article 163 deals with the status of the council of ministers while Article 164 deals with the appointment, tenure, responsibility, qualifications, oath and salaries and allowances of the ministers.

CONSTITUTIONAL PROVISIONS

Article 163—Council of Ministers to aid and advise Governor

1. There shall be a Council of Ministers with the Chief Minister as the head to aid and advise the Governor in the exercise of his functions, except in so far as he is required to exercise his functions in his discretion.
2. If any question arises whether a matter falls within the Governor's discretion or not, decision of the Governor shall be final, and the validity of anything done by the Governor shall not be called in question on the ground

that he ought or ought not to have acted in his discretion.
3. The advice tendered by Ministers to the Governor shall not be inquired into in any court.

Article 164—Other Provisions as to Ministers

1. The Chief Minister shall be appointed by the Governor and the other Ministers shall be appointed by the Governor on the advice of the Chief Minister. However, in the states of Chhattisgarh, Jharkhand, Madhya Pradesh and Odisha, there shall be a Minister in charge of tribal welfare who may in addition be in charge of the welfare of the scheduled castes and backward classes or any other work. The state of Bihar was excluded from this provision by the 94th Amendment Act of 2006.
2. The total number of ministers, including the chief minister, in the council of ministers in a state shall not exceed 15 per cent of the total strength of the legislative assembly of that state. But, the number of ministers, including the chief minister, in a state shall not be less than 12. This provision was added by the 91st Amendment Act of 2003.
3. A member of either House of state legislature belonging to any political party who is disqualified on the ground of defection shall also be disqualified to be appointed as a minister. The provision was also added by the 91st Amendment Act of 2003.

4. The ministers shall hold office during the pleasure of the Governor.
5. The council of ministers shall be collectively responsible to the state Legislative Assembly.
6. The Governor shall administer the oaths of office and secrecy to a minister.
7. A minister who is not a member of the state legislature for any period of six consecutive months shall cease to be a minister.
8. The salaries and allowances of ministers shall be determined by the state legislature.

Article 166—Conduct of Business of the Government of a State

1. All executive action of the Government of a State shall be expressed to be taken in the name of the Governor.
2. Orders and other instruments made and executed in the name of the Governor shall be authenticated in such manner as may be specified in rules to be made by the Governor. Further, the validity of an order or instrument which is so authenticated shall not be called in question on the ground that it is not an order or instrument made or executed by the Governor.
3. The Governor shall make rules for the more convenient transaction of the business of the government of the state, and for the allocation among ministers of the said business in so far as it is not business with respect to which the Governor is required to act in his discretion.

Article 167—Duties of Chief Minister

It shall be the duty of the Chief Minister of each state
1. To communicate to the governor of the state all decisions of the council of ministers relating to the administration of the affairs of the state and proposals for legislation
2. To furnish such information relating to the administration of the affairs of the state and proposals for legislation as the governor may call for
3. If the governor so requires, to submit for the consideration of the council of ministers any matter on which a decision has been taken by a minister but which has not been considered by the council

NATURE OF ADVICE BY MINISTERS

Article 163 provides for a council of ministers with the chief minister at the head to aid and advise the governor in the exercise of his functions except the discretionary ones. If any question arises whether a matter falls within the governor's discretion or not, the decision of the governor is final and the validity of anything done by him cannot be called in question on the ground that he ought or ought not to have acted in his discretion. Further, the nature of advice tendered by ministers to the governor cannot be enquired by any court. This provision emphasises the intimate and the confidential relationship between the governor and the ministers.

In 1971, the Supreme Court ruled that a council of ministers must always exist to advise the governor, even after the dissolution of the state legislative assembly or resignation of a council of ministers. Hence, the existing ministry may continue in the office until its successor assumes charge. Again in 1974, the Court clarified that except in spheres where the governor is to act in his discretion, the governor has to act on the aid and advice of the council of ministers in the exercise of his powers and functions. He is not required to act personally without the aid and advice of the council of ministers or against the aid and advice of the council of ministers. Wherever the Constitution requires the satisfaction of the governor, the satisfaction is not the personal satisfaction of the governor but it is the satisfaction of the council of ministers.

APPOINTMENT OF MINISTERS

The chief minister is appointed by the governor. The other ministers are appointed by the governor on the advice of the chief minister. This means that the governor can appoint only those persons as ministers who are recommended by the chief minister.

But, there should be a tribal welfare minister in Chhattisgarh, Jharkhand, Madhya Pradesh and Odisha[1]. Originally, this provision was applicable to Bihar, Madhya Pradesh and Odisha. The 94th Amendment Act of 2006 freed Bihar from the obligation of having a tribal welfare minister as there are no Scheduled Areas in Bihar now and the fraction of population of the Scheduled Tribes is very small. The same Amendment also extended the above provision to the newly formed states of Chhattisgarh and Jharkhand.

Usually, the members of the state legislature, either the legislative assembly or the legislative council, are appointed as ministers. A person who is not a member of either House of the state legislature can also be appointed as a minister. But, within six months, he must become a member (either by election or by nomination) of either House of the state legislature, otherwise, he ceases to be a minister.

A minister who is a member of one House of the state legislature has the right to speak and to take part in the proceedings of the other House. But, he can vote only in the House of which he is a member.

OATH AND SALARY OF MINISTERS

Before a minister enters upon his office, the governor administers to him the oaths of office and secrecy. In his oath of office, the minister swears:

1. to bear true faith and allegiance to the Constitution of India,
2. to uphold the sovereignty and integrity of India,
3. to faithfully and conscientiously discharge the duties of his office, and
4. to do right to all manner of people in accordance with the Constitution and the law, without fear or favour, affection or ill-will.

In his oath of secrecy, the minister swears that he will not directly or indirectly communicate or reveal to any person(s) any matter that is brought under his consideration or becomes known to him as a state minister except as may be required for the due discharge of his duties as such minister.

The salaries and allowances of ministers are determined by the state legislature from time to time. A minister gets the salary and allowances which are payable to a member of the state legislature. Additionally, he gets a sumptuary allowance (according to his rank), free accommodation, travelling allowance, medical facilities, etc.

RESPONSIBILITY OF MINISTERS

Collective Responsibility

The fundamental principle underlying the working of parliamentary system of government is the principle of collective responsibility. Article 164 clearly states that the council of ministers is collectively responsible to the legislative assembly of the state. This means that all the ministers own joint responsibility to the legislative assembly for all their acts of omission and commission. They work as a team and swim or sink together. When the legislative assembly passes a no-confidence motion against the council of ministers, all the ministers have to resign including those ministers who are from the legislative council[2]. Alternatively, the council of ministers can advice the governor to dissolve the legislative assembly on the ground that the House does not represent the views of the electorate faithfully and call for fresh elections. The governor may not oblige the council of ministers which has lost the confidence of the legislative assembly.

The principle of collective responsibility also mean that the cabinet decisions bind all cabinet ministers (and other ministers) even if they deferred in the cabinet meeting. It is the duty of every minister to stand by the cabinet decisions and support them both within and outside the state legislature. If any minister disagrees with a cabinet decision and is not prepared to defend it, he must resign. Several ministers have resigned in the past owing to their differences with the cabinet.

Individual Responsibility

Article 164 also contains the principle of individual responsibility. It states that the ministers hold office during the pleasure of the governor. This means that the governor can remove a minister at a time when the council of ministers enjoys the confidence of the legislative assembly. But, the governor can remove a minister only on the advice of the chief minister. In case of difference of opinion or dissatisfaction with the performance of a minister, the chief minister can ask him to resign or advice the governor to dismiss him. By exercising this power, the chief minister can ensure the realisation of the rule of collective responsibility.

No Legal Responsibility

As at the Centre, there is no provision in the Constitution for the system of legal responsibility of the minister in the states. It is not required that an order of the governor for a public act should be countersigned by a minister. Moreover, the courts are barred from enquiring into the nature of advice rendered by the ministers to the governor.

COMPOSITION OF THE COUNCIL OF MINISTERS

The Constitution does not specify the size of the state council of ministers or the ranking of ministers. They are determined by the chief minister according to the exigencies of the time and requirements of the situation.

Like at the Centre, in the states too, the council of ministers consists of three categories of ministers, namely, cabinet ministers, ministers of state, and deputy ministers. The difference between them lies in their respective ranks, emoluments, and political importance. At the top of all these ministers stands the chief minister—supreme governing authority in the state.

The cabinet ministers head the important departments of the state government like home, education, finance, agriculture and so forth[3]. They are members of the cabinet, attend its meetings and play an important role in deciding policies. Thus, their responsibilities extend over the entire gamut of state government.

The ministers of state can either be given independent charge of departments or can be attached to cabinet ministers. However, they are not members of the cabinet and do not attend the cabinet meetings unless specially invited when something related to their departments are considered by the cabinet.

Next in rank are the deputy ministers. They are not given independent charge of departments. They are attached to the cabinet ministers and assist them in their administrative, political and parliamentary duties. They are not members of the cabinet and do not attend cabinet meetings.

At times, the council of ministers may also include a deputy chief minister. Thus, Andhra Pradesh had the office of deputy chief minister till 1956. This post was created in West Bengal in 1967. More recently, Rajasthan, Madhya Pradesh and Karnataka have created this office. The deputy chief ministers are appointed mostly for local political reasons.

CABINET

A smaller body called *cabinet* is the nucleus of the council of ministers. It consists of only the cabinet ministers. It is the real centre of authority in the state government. It performs the following role:

1. It is the highest decisionmaking authority in the politico-administrative system of a state.
2. It is the chief policy formulating body of the state government.
3. It is the supreme executive authority of the state government.
4. It is the chief coordinator of state administration.
5. It is an advisory body to the governor.
6. It is the chief crisis manager and thus deals with all emergency situations.
7. It deals with all major legislative and financial matters.
8. It exercises control over higher appointments like constitutional authorities and senior secretariat administrators.

Cabinet Committees

The cabinet works through various committees called cabinet committees. They are of two types—standing and ad hoc. The former are of a permanent nature while the latter are of a temporary nature.

They are set up by the chief minister according to the exigencies of the time and requirements of the situation. Hence, their number, nomenclature and composition varies from time to time.

They not only sort out issues and formulate proposals for the consideration of the cabinet but also take decisions. However, the cabinet can review their decisions.

Table 28.1 *Articles Related to State Council of Ministers at a Glance*

Article No.	Subject-matter
163.	Council of Ministers to aid and advise Governor
164.	Other provisions as to Ministers
166.	Conduct of business of the Government of a State
167.	Duties of Chief Minister as respects the furnishing of information to Governor, etc.

NOTES AND REFERENCES

1. They may, in addition, be in charge of the welfare of the SCs and BCs or any other work.
2. Each minister need not resign separately; the resignation of the chief minister amounts to the resignation of the entire council of ministers.
3. The term 'ministry' or 'ministries' is used only in the centre and not in the states. In other words, the state government is divided into departments and not ministries.

State Legislature

The state legislature occupies a pre-eminent and central position in the political system of a state.

Articles 168 to 212 in Part VI of the Constitution deal with the organisation, composition, duration, officers, procedures, privileges, powers and so on of the state legislature. Though these are similar to that of Parliament, there are some differences as well.

ORGANISATION OF STATE LEGISLATURE

There is no uniformity in the organisation of state legislatures. Most of the states have an unicameral system, while others have a bicameral system. At present (2013), only six states have two Houses (bicameral). These are Andhra Pradesh, Uttar Pradesh, Bihar, Maharashtra, Karnataka and Jammu and Kashmir[1]. The Tamil Nadu Legislative Council Act, 2010 has not come into force. The Legislative Council in Andhra Pradesh was revived by the Andhra Pradesh Legislative Council Act, 2005. The 7th Amendment Act of 1956 provided for a Legislative Council in Madhya Pradesh. However, a notification to this effect has to be made by the President. So far, no such notification has been made. Hence, Madhya Pradesh continues to have one House only.

The twenty-two states have unicameral system. Here, the state legislature consists of the governor and the legislative assembly. In the states having bicameral system, the state legislature consists of the governor, the legislative council and the legislative assembly. The legislative council (Vidhan Parishad) is the upper house (second chamber or house of elders), while the legislative assembly (Vidhan Sabha) is the lower house (first chamber or popular house).

The Constitution provides for the abolition or creation of legislative councils in states. Accordingly, the Parliament can abolish a legislative council (where it already exists) or create it (where it does not exist), if the legislative assembly of the concerned state passes a resolution to that effect. Such a specific resolution must be passed by the state assembly by a special majority, that is, a majority of the total membership of the assembly and a majority of not less than two-thirds of the members of the assembly present and voting. This Act of Parliament is not to be deemed as an amendment of the Constitution for the purposes of Article 368 and is passed like an ordinary piece of legislation (ie, by simple majority).

"The idea of having a second chamber in the states was criticised in the Constituent Assembly on the ground that it was not representative of the people, that it delayed legislative process and that it was an expensive institution[2]." Consequently the provision was made for the abolition or creation of a legislative council to enable a state to have a second chamber or not according to its own willingness and financial strength. For example, Andhra Pradesh got the legislative council created in 1957 and got the same abolished in 1985. The Legislative Council in Andhra Pradesh was again revived in 2007, after the enactment of the Andhra Pradesh Legislative Council Act, 2005. The legislative council of Tamil Nadu had been abolished in 1986 and that of Punjab and West Bengal in 1969.

In 2010, the Legislative Assembly of Tamil Nadu passed a resolution for the revival of the Legislative Council in the state. Accordingly, the Parliament enacted the Tamil Nadu Legislative Council Act, 2010 which provided for the creation of Legislative Council in the state. However, before this Act was enforced, the Legislative Assembly of Tamil Nadu passed another resolution in 2011 seeking the abolition of the proposed Legislative Council.

COMPOSITION OF TWO HOUSES

Composition of Assembly

Strength The legislative assembly consists of representatives directly elected by the people on the basis of universal adult franchise. Its maximum strength is fixed at 500 and minimum strength at 60. It means that its strength varies from 60 to 500 depending on the population size of the state[3]. However, in case of Arunachal Pradesh, Sikkim and Goa, the minimum number is fixed at 30 and in case of Mizoram and Nagaland, it is 40 and 46 respectively. Further, some members of the legislative assemblies in Sikkim and Nagaland are also elected indirectly.

Nominated Member The governor can nominate one member from the Anglo-Indian community, if the community is not adequately represented in the assembly.[4] Originally, this provision was to operate for ten years (ie, upto 1960). But this duration has been extended continuously since then by 10 years each time. Now, under the 95th Amendment Act of 2009, this is to last until 2020.

Territorial Constituencies For the purpose of holding direct elections to the assembly, each state is divided into territorial constituencies. The demarcation of these constituencies is done in such a manner that the ratio between the population of each constituency and the number of seats allotted to it is the same throughout the state. In other words, the Constitution ensures that there is uniformity of representation between different constituencies in the state. The expression 'population' means, the

population as ascertained at the last preceding census of which the relevant figures have been published.

Readjustment after each census After each census, a readjustment is to be made in the **(a)** total number of seats in the assembly of each state and **(b)** the division of each state into territorial constituencies. The Parliament is empowered to determine the authority and the manner in which it is to be made. Accordingly, Parliament has enacted the Delimitation Commission Acts in 1952, 1962, 1972 and 2002 for this purpose.

The 42nd Amendment Act of 1976 had frozen total number of seats in the assembly of each state and the division of such state into territorial constituencies till the year 2000 at the 1971 level. This ban on readjustment has been extended for another years (i.e., upto year 2026) by the 84th Amendment Act of 2001 with the same objective of encouraging population limiting measures.

The 84th Amendment Act of 2001 also empowered the government to undertake readjustment and rationalisation of territorial constituencies in a state on the basis of the population figures of 1991 census. Later, the 87th Amendment Act of 2003 provided for the delimitation of constituencies on the basis of 2001 census and not 1991 census. However, this can be done without altering the total number of seats in the assembly of each state.

Reservation of seats for SCs and STs The Constitution provided for the reservation of seats for scheduled castes and scheduled tribes in the assembly of each state on the basis of population ratios.[5]

Originally, this reservation was to operate for ten years (i.e., up to 1960). But this duration has been extended continuously since then by 10 years each time. Now, under the 95th Amendment Act of 2009, this reservation is to last until 2020.

Composition of Council

Strength Unlike the members of the legislative assembly, the members of the legislative council are indirectly elected. The maximum strength of the council is fixed at one-third of the total strength of the assembly and the minimum strength is fixed at 40[6]. It means that the size of the council depends on the size of the assembly of the concerned state. This is done to ensure the predominance of the directly elected House (assembly) in the legislative affairs of the state. Though the Constitution has fixed the maximum and the minimum limits, the actual strength of a Council is fixed by Parliament[7].

Manner of Election Of the total number of members of a legislative council:

1. 1/3 are elected by the members of local bodies in the state like municipalities, district boards, etc.,
2. 1/12 are elected by graduates of three years standing and residing within the state,
3. 1/12 are elected by teachers of three years standing in the state, not lower in standard than secondary school,
4. 1/3 are elected by the members of the legislative assembly of the state from amongst persons who are not members of the assembly, and
5. the remainder are nominated by the governor from amongst persons who have a special knowledge or practical experience of literature, science, art, cooperative movement and social service.

Thus, 5/6 of the total number of members of a legislative council are indirectly elected and 1/6 are nominated by the governor. The members are elected in accordance with the system of proportional representation by means of a single transferable vote. The bonafides or propriety of the governor's nomination in any case cannot be challenged in the courts.

This scheme of composition of a legislative council as laid down in the Constitution is tentative and not final. The Parliament is authorised to modify or replace the same. However, it has not enacted any such law so far.

DURATION OF TWO HOUSES

Duration of Assembly

Like the Lok Sabha, the legislative assembly is not a continuing chamber. Its normal term is five years from the date of its first meeting after the general elections[8]. The expiration of the period of five years operates as automatic dissolution of the assembly. However, the governor is authorised to dissolve the assembly at any time (i.e., even before the completion of five years) to pave the way for fresh elections.

Further, the term of the assembly can be extended during the period of national emergency by a law of Parliament for one year at a time (for any length of time). However, this extension cannot continue beyond a period of six months after the emergency has ceased to operate. This means that the assembly should be re-elected within six months after the revocation of emergency.

Duration of Council

Like the Rajya Sabha, the legislative council is a continuing chamber, that is, it is a permanent body and is not subject to dissolution. But, one-third of its members retire on the expiration of every second year. So, a member continues as such for six years. The vacant seats are filled up by fresh elections and nominations (by governor) at the beginning of every third year. The retiring members are also eligible for re-election and re-nomination any number of times.

MEMBERSHIP OF STATE LEGISLATURE

1. Qualifications

The Constitution lays down the following qualifications for a person to be chosen a member of the state legislature.

(a) He must be a citizen of India.
(b) He must make and subscribe to an oath or affirmation before the person authorised by the Election Commission for this purpose. In his oath or affirmation, he swears
    (i) To bear true faith and allegiance to the Constitution of India
    (ii) To uphold the sovereignty and integrity of India
(c) He must be not less than 30 years of age in the case of the legislative council and not less than 25 years of age in the case of the legislative assembly.
(d) He must posses other qualifications prescribed by Parliament.

Accordingly, the Parliament has laid down the following additional qualifications in the Representation of People Act (1951):

(a) A person to be elected to the legislative council must be an elector for an assembly constituency in the concerned state and to be qualified for the governor's nomination, he must be a resident in the concerned state.

(b) A person to be elected to the legislative assembly must be an elector for an assembly constituency in the concerned state.

(c) He must be a member of a scheduled caste or scheduled tribe if he wants to contest a seat reserved for them. However, a member of scheduled castes or scheduled tribes can also contest a seat not reserved for them.

2. Disqualifications

Under the Constitution, a person shall be disqualified for being chosen as and for being a member of the legislative assembly or legislative council of a state:

(a) if he holds any office of profit under the Union or state government (except that of a minister or any other office exempted by state legislature[9]),

(b) if he is of unsound mind and stands so declared by a court,

(c) if he is an undischarged insolvent,

(d) if he is not a citizen of India or has voluntarily acquired the citizenship of a foreign state or is under any acknowledgement of allegiance to a foreign state, and

(e) if he is so disqualified under any law made by Parliament.

Accordingly, the Parliament has prescribed a number of additional disqualifications in the Representation of People Act (1951). These are similar to those for Parliament. *These are mentioned here:*

1. He must not have been found guilty of certain election offences or corrupt practices in the elections.

2. He must not have been convicted for any offence resulting in imprisonment for two or more years. But, the detention of a person under a preventive detention law is not a disqualification.

3. He must not have failed to lodge an account of his election expenses within the time.

4. He must not have any interest in government contracts, works or services.

5. He must not be a director or managing agent nor hold an office of profit in a corporation in which the government has at least 25 per cent share.

6. He must not have been dismissed from government service for corruption or disloyalty to the state.

7. He must not have been convicted for promoting enmity between different groups or for the offence of bribery.

8. He must not have been punished for preaching and practicing social crimes such as untouchability, dowry and *sati*.

On the question whether a member has become subject to any of the above disqualifications, the governor's decision is final. However, he should obtain the opinion of the Election Commission and act accordingly.

Disqualification on Ground of Defection The Constitution also lays down that a person shall be disqualified for being a member of either House of state legislature if he is so disqualified on the ground of defection under the provisions of the Tenth Schedule.

The question of disqualification under the Tenth Schedule is decided by the Chairman, in the case of legislative council and, Speaker, in the case of legislative assembly (and not by the governor). In 1992, the Supreme Court ruled that the decision of Chairman/Speaker in this regard is subject to judicial review[10].

3. Oath or Affirmation

Every member of either House of state legislature, before taking his seat in the House, has to make and subscribe an oath or affirmation before the governor or some person appointed by him for this purpose.

In this oath, a member of the state legislature swears:

(a) to bear true faith and allegiance to the Constitution of India;

(b) to uphold the sovereignty and integrity of India; and

(c) to faithfully discharge the duty of his office.

Unless a member takes the oath, he cannot vote and participate in the proceedings of the House and does not become eligible to the privileges and immunities of the state legislature.

A person is liable to a penalty of ₹500 for each day he sits or votes as a member in a House:

(a) before taking and subscribing the prescribed oath or affirmation; or

(b) when he knows that he is not qualified or that he is disqualified for its membership; or

(c) when he knows that he is prohibited from sitting or voting in the House by virtue of any law made by Parliament or the state legislature.

Members of a state legislature are entitled to receive such salaries and allowances as may from time to time be determined by the state legislature.

4. Vacation of Seats

In the following cases, a member of the state legislature vacates his seat:

(a) *Double Membership:* A person cannot be a member of both Houses of state legislature at one and the same time. If a person is elected to both the Houses, his seat in one of the Houses falls vacant as per the provisions of a law made by the state legislature.

(b) *Disqualification:* If a member of the state legislature becomes subject to any of the disqualifications, his seat becomes vacant.

(c) *Resignation:* A member may resign his seat by writing to the Chairman of legislative council or Speaker of legislative assembly, as the case may be. The seat falls vacant when the resignation is accepted[11].

(d) *Absence:* A House of the state legislature can declare the seat of a member vacant if he absents himself from all its meeting for a period of sixty days without its permission.

(e) *Other Cases:* A member has to vacate his seat in the either House of state legislature,

(i) if his election is declared void by the court,

(ii) if he is expelled by the House,

(iii) if he is elected to the office of president or office of vice-president, and

(iv) if he is appointed to the office of governor of a state.

PRESIDING OFFICERS OF STATE LEGISLATURE

Each House of state legislature has its own presiding officer. There is a Speaker and a Deputy Speaker for the legislative assembly and Chairman and a Deputy Chairman for the legislative council. A panel of chairmen for the assembly and a panel of vice-chairmen for the council is also appointed.

Speaker of Assembly

The Speaker is elected by the assembly itself from amongst its members.

Usually, the Speaker remains in office during the life of the assembly. However, he vacates his office earlier in any of the following three cases:

1. if he ceases to be a member of the assembly;

2. if he resigns by writing to the deputy speaker; and

3. if he is removed by a resolution passed by a majority of all the then members of the assembly. Such a resolution can be moved only after giving 14 days advance notice.

The Speaker has the following powers and duties:

1. He maintains order and decorum in the assembly for conducting its business and regulating its proceedings. This is his primary responsibility and he has final power in this regard.

2. He is the final interpreter of the provisions of (a) the Constitution of India, (b) the rules of procedure and conduct of business of assembly, and (c) the legislative precedents, within the assembly.

3. He adjourns the assembly or suspends the meeting in the absence of a quorum.

4. He does not vote in the first instance. But, he can exercise a casting vote in the case of a tie.

5. He can allow a 'secret' sitting of the House at the request of the leader of the House.

6. He decides whether a bill is a Money Bill or not and his decision on this question is final.

7. He decides the questions of disqualification of a member of the assembly, arising on the ground of defection under the provisions of the Tenth Schedule.

8. He appoints the chairmen of all the committees of the assembly and supervises their functioning. He himself is the chairman of the Business Advisory Committee, the Rules Committee and the General Purpose Committee.

Deputy Speaker of Assembly

Like the Speaker, the Deputy Speaker is also elected by the assembly itself from amongst its members. He is elected after the election of the Speaker has taken place.

Like the Speaker, the Deputy Speaker remains in office usually during the life of the assembly. However, he also vacates his office earlier in any of the following three cases:

1. if he ceases to be a member of the assembly;
2. if he resigns by writing to the speaker; and
3. if he is removed by a resolution passed by a majority of all the then members of the assembly. Such a resolution can be moved only after giving 14 days' advance notice.

The Deputy Speaker performs the duties of the Speaker's office when it is vacant. He also acts as the Speaker when the latter is absent from the sitting of assembly. In both the cases, he has all the powers of the Speaker.

The Speaker nominates from amongst the members a panel of chairmen. Any one of them can preside over the assembly in the absence of the Speaker or the Deputy Speaker. He has the same powers as the speaker when so presiding. He holds office until a new panel of chairmen is nominated.

Chairman of Council

The Chairman is elected by the council itself from amongst its members.

The Chairman vacates his office in any of the following three cases:

1. if he ceases to be a member of the council;
2. if he resigns by writing to the deputy chairman; and
3. if he is removed by a resolution passed by a majority of all the then members of the council. Such a resolution can be moved only after giving 14 days advance notice.

As a presiding officer, the powers and functions of the Chairman in the council are similar to those of the Speaker in the assembly. However, the Speaker has one special power which is not enjoyed by the Chairman. The Speaker decides whether a bill is a Money Bill or not and his decision on this question is final.

As in the case of the Speaker, the salaries and allowances of the Chairman are also fixed by the state legislature. They are charged on the Consolidated Fund of the State and thus are not subject to the annual vote of the state legislature.

Deputy Chairman of Council

Like the Chairman, the Deputy Chairman is also elected by the council itself from amongst its members.

The deputy chairman vacates his office in any of the following three cases:

1. if he ceases to be a member of the council;
2. if he resigns by writing to the Chairman; and
3. if he is removed by a resolution passed by a majority of all the then members of the council. Such a resolution can be moved only after giving 14 days advance notice.

The Deputy Chairman performs the duties of the Chairman's office when it is vacant. He also acts as the Chairman when the latter is absent from the sitting of the council. In both the cases, he has all the powers of the Chairman.

The Chairman nominates from amongst the members a panel of vice-chairmen. Any one of them can preside over the council in the absence of the Chairman or the Deputy Chairman. He has the same powers as the chairman when so presiding. He holds office until a new panel of vice-chairmen is nominated.

SESSIONS OF STATE LEGISLATURE

Summoning

The governor from time to time summons each House of state legislature to meet. The maximum gap between the two sessions of state legislature cannot be more than six months, ie, the state legislature should meet at least twice a year. A session of the state legislature consists of many sittings.

Adjournment

An adjournment suspends the work in a sitting for a specified time which may be hours, days or weeks.

Adjournment *sine die* means terminating a sitting of the state legislature for an indefinte period. The power of the adjournment as well as adjournment *sine die* lies with the presiding officer of the House.

Prorogation

The presiding officer (Speaker or Chairman) declares the House adjourned *sine die*, when the business of the session is completed. Within the next few days, the governor issues a notification for prorogation of the session.

However, the governor can also prorogue the House which is in session. Unlike an adjournment, a prorogation terminates a session of the House.

Dissolution

The legislative council, being a permanent house, is not subject to dissolution. Only the legislative assembly is subject to dissolution. Unlike a prorogation, a dissolution ends the very life of the existing House, and a new House is constituted after the general elections are held.

The position with respect to lapsing of bills on the dissolution of the assembly is mentioned below:

1. A Bill pending in the assembly lapses (whether originating in the assembly or transmitted to it by the council).
2. A Bill passed by the assembly but pending in the council lapses.
3. A Bill pending in the council but not passed by the assembly does not lapse.
4. A Bill passed by the assembly (in a unicameral state) or passed by both the houses (in a bicameral state) but pending assent of the governor or the President does not lapse.
5. A Bill passed by the assembly (in a unicameral state) or passed by both the Houses (in a bicameral state) but returned by the president for reconsideration of House (s) does not lapse.

Quorum

Quorum is the minimum number of members required to be present in the House before it can transact any business. It is ten members or one-tenth of the total number of members of the House (including the presiding officer), whichever is greater. If there is no quorum during a meeting of the House, it is the duty of the presiding officer either to adjourn the House or to suspend the meeting until there is a quorum.

Voting in House

All matters at any sitting of either House are decided by a majority of votes of the members present and voting excluding the presiding officer. Only a few matters which are specifically mentioned in the Constitution like removal of the speaker of the assembly, removal of the Chairman of the council and so on require special majority, not ordinary majority. The presiding officer (i.e., Speaker in the case of assembly or chairman in the case of council or the person acting as such) does not vote in the first instance, but exercises a casting vote in the case of an equality of votes.

Language in State Legislature

The Constitution has declared the official language(s) of the state or Hindi or English, to be the languages for transacting business in the state legislature. However, the presiding officer can permit a member to address the House in his mother-tongue. The state legislature is authorised to decide whether to continue or discontinue English as a floor language after the completion of fifteen years from the commencement of the Constitution (i.e., from 1965). In case of Himachal Pradesh, Manipur, Meghalaya and Tripura, this time limit is twenty-five years and that of Arunachal Pradesh, Goa and Mizoram, it is forty years.

Rights of Ministers and Advocate General

In addition to the members of a House, every minister and the advocate general of the state have the right to speak and take part in the proceedings of either House or any of its committees of which he is named a member, without being entitled to vote. There are two reasons underlying this constitutional provision:

1. A minister can participate in the proceedings of a House, of which he is not a member.
2. A minsiter, who is not a member of either House, can participate in the proceedings of both the Houses[12].

LEGISLATIVE PROCEDURE IN STATE LEGISLATURE

Ordinary Bills

Bill in the Originating House   An ordinary bill can originate in either House of the state legislature (in case of a bicameral legislature). Such a bill can be introduced either by a minister or by anyother member. The bill passes through three stages in the originating House, viz,

1. First reading,
2. Second reading, and
3. Third reading.

After the bill is passed by the originating House, it is transmitted to the second House for consideration and passage. A bill is deemed to have been passed by the state legislature only when both the Houses have agreed to it, either with or without amendments. In case of a unicameral legislature, a bill passed by the legislative assembly is sent directly to the governor for his assent.

Bill in the Second House   In the second House also, the bill passes through all the three stages, that is, first reading, second reading and third reading.

When a bill is passed by the legislative assembly and transmitted to the legislative council, the latter has four alternatives before it:

1. it may pass the bill as sent by the assembly (i.e., without amendments);
2. it may pass the bill with amendments and return it to the assembly for reconsideration;
3. it may reject the bill altogether; and
4. it may not take any action and thus keep the bill pending.

If the council passes the bill without amendments or the assembly accepts the amendments suggested by the council, the bill is deemed to have been passed by both the Houses and the same is sent to the the governor for his assent. On the other hand, if the assembly rejects the amendments suggested by the council or the council rejects the bill altogether or the council does not take any action for three months, then the assembly may pass the bill again and transmit the same to the council. If the council rejects the bill again or passes the bill with amendments not acceptable to the assembly or does not pass the bill within one month, then the bill is deemed to have been passed by both the Houses in the form in which it was passed by the assembly for the second time.

Therefore, the ultimate power of passing an ordinary bill is vested in the assembly. At the most, the council can detain or delay the bill for a period of four months—three months in the first instance and one month in the second instance. The Constitution does not provide for the mechanism of joint sitting of both the Houses to resolve the disagreement between the two Houses over a bill. On the other hand, there is a provision for joint sitting of the Lok Sabha and the Rajya Sabha to resolve a disagreement between the two over an ordinary bill. Moreover, when a bill, which has originated in the council and was sent to the assembly, is rejected by the assembly, the bill ends and becomes dead.

Thus, the council has been given much lesser significance, position and authority than that of the Rajya Sabha at the Centre.

Assent of the Governor   Every bill, after it is passed by the assembly or by both the Houses in case of a bicameral legislature, is presented to the governor for his assent. There are four alternatives before the governor:

1. he may give his assent to the bill;
2. he may withhold his assent to the bill;
3. he may return the bill for reconsideration of the House or Houses; and
4. he may reserve the bill for the consideration of the President.

If the governor gives his assent to the bill, the bill becomes an Act and is placed on the Statute Book. If the governor withholds his assent to the bill, the bill ends and does not become an Act. If the governor returns the bill for reconsideration and if the bill is passed by the House or both the Houses again, with or without amendments, and presented to the governor for his assent, the governor must give his assent to the bill. Thus, the governor enjoys only a *suspensive veto*. The position is same at the Central level also[13].

Assent of the President   When a bill is reserved by the governor for the consideration of the President, the President may either give his assent to the bill or withhold his assent to the bill or return the bill for reconsideration of the House or Houses of the state legislature. When a bill is so returned, the House or Houses have to reconsider it within a period of six months. The bill is presented again to the presidential assent after it is passed by the House or Houses with or without amendments. It is not mentioned in the Constitution whether it is obligatory on the part of the president to give his assent to such a bill or not.

Money Bills

The Constitution lays down a special procedure for the passing of Money Bills in the state legislature. This is as follows:

A Money Bill cannot be introduced in the legislative council. It can be introduced in the legislative assembly only and that too on the recommendation of the governor. Every such bill is considered to be a government bill and can be introduced only by a minister.

After a Money Bill is passed by the legislative assembly, it is transmitted to the legislative council for its consideration. The legislative council has restricted powers with regard to a Money Bill. It cannot reject or amend a Money Bill. It can only make recommendations and must return the bill to the legislative assembly within 14 days. The legislative assembly can either accept or reject all or any of the recommendations of the legislative council.

If the legislative assembly accepts any recommendation, the bill is then deemed to have been passed by both the Houses in the modified form. If the legislative assembly does not accept any recommendation, the bill is then deemed to have been passed by both the Houses in the form originally passed by the legislative assembly without any change.

If the legislative council does not return the bill to the legislative assembly within 14 days, the bill is deemed to have been passed by both Houses at the expiry of the said period in the form originally passed by the legislative assembly. Thus, the legislative assembly has more powers than legislative council with regard to a money bill. At the most, the legislative council can detain or delay a money bill for a period of 14 days.

Finally, when a Money Bill is presented to the governor, he may either give his assent, withhold his assent or reserve the bill for presidential assent but cannot return the bill for reconsideration of the state legislature. Normally, the governor gives his assent to a money bill as it is introduced in the state legislature with his prior permission.

When a money bill is reserved for consideration of the President, the president may either give his assent to the bill or withhold his assent to the bill but cannot return the bill for reconsideration of the state legislature.

Table 29.1 *Comparing Legislative Procedure in the Parliament and State Legislature*

Parliament	State Legislature
A. With Regard to Ordinary Bills	
1. It can be introduced in either House of the Parliament.	1. It can be introduced in either House of the state legislature.
2. It can be introduced either by a minister or by a private member.	2. It can be introduced either by a minister or by private member.
3. It passes through first reading, second reading and third reading in the originating House.	3. It passes through first reading, second reading and third reading in the orginating House.
4. It is deemed to have been passed by the Parliament only when both the Houses have agreed to it, either with or without amendments.	4. It is deemed to have been passed by the state legislature only when both the Houses have agreed to it, either with or without amendments.
5. A deadlock between the two Houses takes place when the second House, after receiving a bill passed by the first House, rejects the bill or proposes amendments that are not acceptable to the first House or does not pass the bill within six months.	5. A deadlock between the two Houses takes place when the legislative council, after receiving a bill passed by the legislative assembly, rejects the bill or proposes amendments that are not acceptable to the legislative assembly or does not pass the bill within three months.

(Contd.)

Parliament	*State Legislature*
6. The Constitution provides for the mechanism of joint sitting of two Houses of the Parliament to resolve a deadlock between them over the passage of a bill.	6. The Constitution does not provide for the mechanism of joint sitting of two Houses of the state legislature to resolve a deadlock between them over the passage of a bill.
7. The Lok Sabha cannot override the Rajya Sabha by passing the bill for the second time and vice versa. A joint sitting is the only way to resolve a deadlock between the two Houses.	7. The legislative assembly can override the legislative council by passing the bill for the second time and not *vice versa*. When a bill is passed by the assembly for the second time and transmitted to the legislative council, if the legislative council rejects the bill again, or porposes amendments that are not acceptable to the legislative assembly, or does not pass the bill within one month, then the bill is deemed to have been passed by both the Houses in the form in which it was passed by the legislative assembly for the second time.
8. The mechanism of joint sitting for resolving a deadlock applies to a bill whether originating in the Lok Sabha or the Rajya Sabha. If a joint sitting is not summoned by the president, the bill ends and becomes dead.	8. The mechanism of passing the bill for the second time to resolve a deadlock applies to a bill originating in the legislative assembly only. When a bill, which has originated in the legislative council and sent to the legislative assembly, is rejected by the latter, the bill ends and becomes dead.
B. With Regard to Money Bills	
1. It can be introduced only in the Lok Sabha and not in the Rajya Sabha.	1. It can be introduced only in the legislative assembly and not in the legislative council.
2. It can be introduced only on the recommendation of the president.	2. It can be introduced only on the recommendation of the governor.
3. It can be introduced only by a minister and not by a private member.	3. It can be introduced only by a minister and not by a private member.
4. It cannot be rejected or amended by the Rajya Sabha. It should be returned to the Lok Sabha within 14 days, either with or without recommendations.	4. It cannot be rejected or amended by the legislative council. It should be returned to the legislative assembly within 14 days, either with or without amendments.
5. The Lok Sabha can either accept or reject all or any of the recommendations of the Rajya Sabha.	5. The legislative assembly can either accept or reject all or any of the recommendations of the legislative council.
6. If the Lok Sabha accepts any recommendation, the bill is then deemed to have been passed by both the Houses in the modified form.	6. If the legislative assembly accepts any recommendation, the bill is then deemed to have been passed by both the Houses in the modified form.
7. If the Lok Sabha does not accept any recommendation, the bill is then deemed to have been passed by both the Houses in the form originally passed by the Lok Sabha without any change.	7. If the legislative assembly does not accept any recommendation, the bill is then deemed to have been passed by both the Houses in the form originally passed by the legislative assembly without any change.

(Contd.)

Parliament	State Legislature
8. If the Rajya Sabha does not return the bill to the Lok Sabha within 14 days, the bill is deemed to have been passed by both the Houses at the expiration of the said period in the form originally passed by the Lok Sabha.	8. If the legislative council does not return the bill to the legislative assembly within 14 days, the bill is deemed to have been passed by both the Houses at the expiration of the said period in the form originally passed by the legislative assembly.
9. The Constitution does not provide for the resolution of any deadlock between the two Houses. This is because, the will of the Lok Sabha is made to prevail over that of the Rajya Sabha, if the latter does not agree to the bill passed by the former.	9. The Constitution does not provide for the resolution of any deadlock between the two Houses. This is because, the will of the legislative assembly is made to prevail over that of legislative council, if the latter does not agree to the bill passed by the former.

POSITION OF LEGISLATIVE COUNCIL

The constitutional position of the council (as compared with the assembly) can be studied from two angles:

   A. Spheres where council is equal to assembly.

   B. Spheres where council is unequal to assembly.

Equal with Assembly

In the following matters, the powers and status of the council are broadly equal to that of the assembly:

1. Introduction and passage of ordinary bills. However, in case of disagreement between the two Houses, the will of the assembly prevails over that of the council.
2. Approval of ordinances issued by the governor[14].
3. Selection of ministers including the chief minister. Under the Constitution the, ministers including the chief minister can be members of either House of the state legislature. However, irrespective of their membership, they are responsible only to the assembly.
4. Consideration of the reports of the constitutional bodies like State Finance Commission, state public service commission and Comptroller and Auditor General of India.
5. Enlargement of the jurisdiction of the state public service commission.

Unequal with Assembly

In the following matters, the powers and status of the council are unequal to that of the assembly:

1. A Money Bill can be introduced only in the assembly and not in the council.
2. The council cannot amend or reject a money bill. It should return the bill to the assembly within 14 days, either with recommendations or without recommendations.
3. The assembly can either accept or reject all or any of the recommendation of the council. In both the cases, the money bill is deemed to have been passed by the two Houses.
4. The final power to decide whether a particular bill is a money bill or not is vested in the Speaker of the assembly.
5. The final power of passing an ordinary bill also lies with the assembly. At the most, the council can detain or delay the bill for the period of four months—three months in the first instance and one month in the second instance. In other words, the council is not even a revising body like the Rajya Sabha; it is only a dilatory chamber or an advisory body.
6. The council can only discuss the budget but cannot vote on the demands for grants (which is the exclusive privilege of the assembly).
7. The council cannot remove the council of ministers by passing a no-confidence motion. This is because, the council of ministers is collectively responsible only to the assembly. But, the council can discus and criticise the policies and activities of the Government.
8. When an ordinary bill, which has originated in the council and was sent to the assembly, is rejected by the assembly, the bill ends and becomes dead.

9. The council does not participate in the election of the president of India and representatives of the state in the Rajya Sabha.

10. The council has no effective say in the ratification of a constitutional amendment bill. In this respect also, the will of the assembly prevails over that of the council[15].

11. Finally, the very existence of the council depends on the will of the assembly. The council can be abolished by the Parliament on the recommendation of the assembly.

From the above, it is clear that the position of the czouncil *vis-a-vis* the assembly is much weaker than the position of the Rajya Sabha *vis-a-vis* the Lok Sabha. The Rajya Sabha has equal powers with the Lok Sabha in all spheres except financial matters and with regard to the control over the Government. On the other hand, the council is subordinate to the assembly in all respects. Thus, the predominance of the assembly over the council is fully established.

Even though both the council and the Rajya Sabha are second chambers, the Constitution has given the council much lesser importance than the Rajya Sabha due to the following reasons:

1. The Rajya Sabha consists of the representatives of the states and thus reflect the federal element of the polity. It maintains the federal equilibrium by protecting the interests of the states against the undue interference of the Centre. Therefore, it

   has to be an effective revising body and not just an advisory body or dilatory body like that of the council. On the other hand, the issue of federal significance does not arise in the case of a council.

2. The council is heterogeneously constituted. It represents different interests and consists of differently elected members and also include some nominated members. Its very composition makes its position weak and reduces its utility as an effective revising body. On the other hand, the Rajya Sabha is homogeneously constituted. It represents only the states and consists of mainly elected members (only 12 out of 250 are nominated).

3. The position accorded to the council is in accordance with the principles of democracy. The council should yield to the assembly,

which is a popular house. This pattern of relationship between the two Houses of the state legislature is adopted from the British model. In Britain, the House of Lords (Upper House) cannot oppose and obstruct the House of Commons (Lower House). The House of Lords is only a dilatory chamber—it can delay an ordinary bill for a maximum period of one year and a money bill for one month.[16]

Keeping in view its weak, powerless and insignificant position and role, the critics have described the council as a 'secondary chamber', 'costly ornamental luxury', 'white elephant', etc. The critics have opined that the council has served as a refuge for those who are defeated in the assembly elections. It enabled the unpopular, rejected and ambitious politicians to occupy the post of a chief minister or a minister or a member of the state legislature.

Even though the council has been given less powers as compared with the assembly, its utility is supported on the following grounds:

1. It checks the hasty, defective, careless and ill-considered legislation made by the assembly by making provision for revision and thought.

2. It facilitates representation of eminent professionals and experts who cannot face direct elections. The governor nominates one-sixth members of the council to provide representation to such people.

PRIVILEGES OF STATE LEGISLATURE

Privileges of a state legislature are a sum of special rights, immunities and exemptions enjoyed by the Houses of state legislature, their committees and their members. They are necessary in order to secure the independence and effectiveness of their actions. Without these previleges, the Houses can neither maintain their authority, dignity and honour nor can protect their members from any obstruction in the discharge of their legislative responsibilities.

The Constitution has also extended the privileges of the state legislature to those persons who are entitled to speak and take part in the proceedings of a House of the state legislature or any of its committees. These include advocate-general of the state and state ministers.

It must be clarified here that the privileges of the state legislature do not extend to the governor who is also an integral part of the state legislature.

The privileges of a state legislature can be classified into two broad categories—those that are enjoyed by each House of the state legislature collectively, and those that are enjoyed by the members individually.

Collective Privileges

The privileges belonging to each House of the state legislature collectively are:

1. It has the right to publish its reports, debates and proceedings and also the right to prohibit others from publishing the same[17].
2. It can exclude strangers from its proceedings and hold secret sittings to discuss some important matters.
3. It can make rules to regulate its own procedure and the conduct of its business and to adjudicate upon such matters.
4. It can punish members as well as outsiders for breach of its privileges or its contempt by reprimand, admonition or imprisonment (also suspension or expulsion, in case of members).
5. It has the right to receive immediate information of the arrest, detention, conviction, imprisonment and release of a member.
6. It can institute inquiries and order the attendence of witnesses and send for relevant papers and records.

7. The courts are prohibited to inquire into the proceedings of a House or its Committes.
8. No person (either a member or outsider) can be arrested, and no legal process (civil or criminal) can be served within the precincts of the House without the permission of the presiding officer.

Individual Privileges

The privileges belonging to the members individually are:

1. They cannot be arrested during the session of the state legislature and 40 days before the beginning and 40 days after the end of such session. This privilege is available only in civil cases and not in criminal cases or preventive detention cases.
2. They have freedom of speech in the state legislature. No member is liable to any proceedings in any court for anything said or any vote given by him in the state legislature or its committees. This freedom is subject to the provisions of the Constitution and to the rules and standing orders regulating the procedure of the state legislature[18].
3. They are exempted from jury service. They can refuse to give evidence and appear as a witness in a case pending in a court when the state legislature is in session.

Table 29.2 *Strength of State Legislatures*

S. No.	Name of the State/Union Territory	Number of Seats in Legislative Assembly	Number of Seats in Legislative Council
	I. STATES		
1.	Andhra Pradesh	294	90
2.	Arunachal Pradesh	60	—
3.	Assam	126	—
4.	Bihar	243	75
5.	Chhattisgarh	90	—
6.	Goa	40	—
7.	Gujarat	182	—
8.	Haryana	90	—

(Contd.)

S. No.	Name of the State/Union Territory	Number of Seats in Legislative Assembly	Number of Seats in Legislative Council
9.	Himachal Pradesh	68	—
10.	Jammu and Kashmir	87[19]	36
11.	Jharkhand	81	—
12.	Karnataka	224	75
13.	Kerala	140	—
14.	Madhya Pradesh	230	—
15.	Maharashtra	288	78
16.	Manipur	60	—
17.	Meghalaya	60	—
18.	Mizoram	40	—
19.	Nagaland	60	—
20.	Odisha	147	—
21.	Punjab	117	—
22.	Rajasthan	200	—
23.	Sikkim	32	—
24.	Tamil Nadu	234	—
25.	Tripura	60	—
26.	Uttarakhand	70	—
27.	Uttar Pradesh	403	100
28.	West Bengal	294	—
II. UNION TERRITORIES			
1.	Delhi	70	—
2.	Puducherry	30	—

Table 29.3 *Seats Reserved for SCs and STs in the Legislative Assemblies*

Name of the State/ Union Territory		Number of seats in the House before the Delimitation in 2008			Number of seats in the House after the Delimitation in 2008		
		Total	Reserved for the Scheduled Castes	Reserved for the Scheduled Tribes	Total	Reserved for the Scheduled Castes	Reserved for the Scheduled Tribes
I. STATES							
1.	Andhra Pradesh	294	39	15	294	48	19
2.	Arunachal Pradesh	60	—	59	60	—	59
3.	Assam	126	8	16	126	8	16
4.	Bihar	243	39	—	243	38	2

(Contd.)

Name of the State/ Union Territory		Number of seats in the House before the Delimitation in 2008			Number of seats in the House after the Delimitation in 2008		
		Total	Reserved for the Scheduled Castes	Reserved for the Scheduled Tribes	Total	Reserved for the Scheduled Castes	Reserved for the Scheduled Tribes
5.	Chhattisgarh	90	10	34	90	10	29
6.	Goa	40	1	—	40	1	—
7.	Gujarat	182	13	26	182	13	27
8.	Haryana	90	17	—	90	17	—
9.	Himachal Pradesh	68	16	3	68	17	3
10.	Jammu & Kashmir[20]	—	—	—	—	—	—
11.	Jharkhand	81	9	28	81	9	28
12.	Karnataka	224	33	2	224	36	15
13.	Kerala	140	13	1	140	14	2
14.	Madhya Pradesh	230	34	41	230	35	47
15.	Maharashtra	288	18	22	288	29	25
16.	Manipur	60	1	19	60	1	19
17.	Meghalaya	60	—	55	60	—	55
18.	Mizoram	40	—	39	40	—	38
19.	Nagaland	60	—	59	60	—	59
20.	Odisha	147	22	34	147	24	33
21.	Punjab	117	29	—	117	34	—
22.	Rajasthan	200	33	24	200	34	25
23.	Sikkim	32	2	12	32	2	12
24.	Tamil Nadu	234	42	3	234	44	2
25.	Tripura	60	7	20	60	10	20
26.	Uttarakhand	70	12	3	70	13	2
27.	Uttar Pradesh	403	89	—	403	85	—
28.	West Bengal	294	59	17	294	68	16
II. UNION TERRITORIES:							
1.	Delhi	70	13	—	70	12	—
2.	Puducherry	30	5	—	30	5	—

Table 29.4 *Articles Related to State Legislature at a Glance*

Article No.	Subject-matter
General	
168.	Constitution of Legislatures in states
169	Abolition or creation of Legislative Councils in states

(Contd.)

Article No.	Subject-matter
170.	Composition of the Legislative Assemblies
171.	Composition of the Legislative Councils
172.	Duration of State Legislatures
173.	Qualification for membership of the State Legislature
174.	Sessions of the State Legislature, prorogation and dissolution
175.	Right of Governor to address and send messages to the House or Houses
176.	Special address by the Governor
177.	Rights of Ministers and Advocate-General as respects the Houses

Officers of the State Legislature

178.	The Speaker and Deputy Speaker of the Legislative Assembly
179.	Vacation and resignation of, and removal from, the offices of Speaker and Deputy Speaker
180.	Power of the Deputy Speaker or other person to perform the duties of the office of, or to act as, Speaker
181.	The Speaker or the Deputy Speaker not to preside while a resolution for his removal from office is under consideration
182.	The Chairman and Deputy Chairman of the Legislative Council
183.	Vacation and resignation of, and removal from, the offices of Chairman and Deputy Chairman
184.	Power of the Deputy Chairman or other person to perform the duties of the office of, or to act as, Chairman
185.	The Chairman or the Deputy Chairman not to preside while a resolution for his removal from office is under consideration
186.	Salaries and allowances of the Speaker and Deputy Speaker and the Chairman and Deputy Chairman
187.	Secretariat of State Legislature

Conduct of Business

188.	Oath or affirmation by members
189.	Voting in Houses, power of Houses to act notwithstanding vacancies and quorum

Disqualifications of Members

190.	Vacation of seats
191.	Disqualifications for membership
192.	Decision on questions as to disqualifications of members
193.	Penalty for sitting and voting before making oath or affirmation under Article 188 or when not qualified or when disqualified

Powers, Privileges and Immunities of State Legislatures and their Members

194.	Powers, privileges, etc., of the House of Legislatures and of the members and committees thereof
195.	Salaries and allowances of members

Legislative Procedure

196.	Provisions as to introduction and passing of Bills

(Contd.)

Article No.	Subject-matter
197.	Restriction on powers of Legislative Council as to Bills other than Money Bills
198.	Special procedure in respect of Money Bills
199.	Definition of "Money Bills"
200.	Assent to Bills
201.	Bills reserved for consideration
Procedure in Financial Matters	
202.	Annual financial statement
203.	Procedure in Legislature with respect to estimates
204.	Appropriation Bills
205.	Supplementary, additional or excess grants
206.	Votes on account, votes of credit and exceptional grants
207.	Special provisions as to financial Bills
Procedure Generally	
208.	Rules of procedure
209.	Regulation by law of procedure in the Legislature of the state in relation to financial business
210.	Language to be used in the Legislature
211.	Restriction on discussion in the Legislature
212.	Courts not to inquire into proceedings of the Legislature
Legislative Powers of the Governor	
213.	Power of Governor to promulgate Ordinances during recess of Legislature

Notes and References

1. Jammu and Kashmir has adopted a bicameral legislature by its own state Constitution, which is separate from the Indian Constitution.
2. M P Jain, *Indian Constitutional Law,* Wadhwa Fourth edition, P. 159
3. See Table 29.2 at the end of this chapter.
4. An Anglo-Indian means a person whose father or any other male progenitor in the male line is or was of European descent, but who is domiciled within the territory of India and is or was born within such territory of parents habitually resident therein and not established there for temporary purposes only.
5. This means that the number of assembly seats reserved in a state for such castes and tribes is to bear the same proportion to the total number of seats in the assembly as the population of such castes and tribes in the concerned state

bears to the total population of the state.
6. The minimum strength fixed at 40 by the Constitution of India is not applicable to Jammu and Kashmir. Its council has 36 members under the provisions of its own state Constitution.
7. See Table 29.2 at the end of this Chapter.
8. The term of the legislative assembly of Jammu and Kashmir is six years under its own state Constitution.
9. A minister in the union or state government is not considered as holding an office of profit. Also, the state legislature can declare that a particular office of profit will not disqualify its holder from its membership.
10. *Kihota Hollohan* v. *Zachilhu,* (1992).
11. However, the Chairman/Speaker need not accept the resignation if he is satisfied that it is not voluntary or genuine.

12. A person can remain a minister for six months, without being a member of either house of the state legislature.

13. For a comparative study of the veto power of the president and the governor, see Chapter 26.

14. For a comparative study of the ordinance-making power of the president and the governor, see Chapter 26.

15. The position, in this regard, is very well analysed by J C Johari in the following way: 'The Constitution is not clear on this point whether a bill of consitutional amendment referred to the states for ratification by their legislatures shall include the Vidhan Parishad or not. In practice, it may be understood that the will of the Vidhan Sabha has to prevail. In case the Vidhan Parishad concurs with the view of the Vidhan Sabha, it is all right; in case it differs, the Vidhan Sabha may pass it again and thereby ignore the will of the Vidhan Parishad as it can do in case of a non-money bill'. (*Indian Government and Politics*, Vishal, Thirteenth Edition, 2001, P. 441).

16. The Parliament Act of 1911, and the Amending Act of 1949, have curtailed the powers of the House of Lords and established the supremacy of the House of Commons.

17. The 44th Amendment Act of 1978 restored the freedom of the press to publish true reports of state legislature without its prior permission. But, this is not applicable in the case of a secret sitting of the House.

18. Article 211 of the Constitution says that no discussion shall take place in the legislature of a state with respect to the conduct of any judge of the Supreme Court or of a high court in the discharge of his duties. Under the rules of a House(s) of the state legislature, use of unparliamentary language or unparliamentary conduct of a member is prohibited.

19. Under the Constitution of Jammu and Kashmir, the total number of seats fixed for the Legislative Assembly is 111. But, 24 seats fall in the Pakistan-occupied-Kashmir (PoK). These seats are vacant and are not to be taken into account for reckoning the total membership of the Assembly. Originally, the strength of J & K Assembly was 100 and this was increased to 111 in 1987.

20. Under the Constitution of Jammu and Kashmir, the number of seats in the Legislative Assembly of that State excluding the 24 seats earmarked for Pakistan occupied territory is 87 out of which 7 seats have been reserved for the Scheduled Castes in pursuance of the Jammu and Kashmir Representation of the People Act, 1957.

High Court

In the Indian single integrated judicial system, the high court operates below the Supreme Court but above the subordinate courts. The judiciary in a state consists of a high court and a hierarchy of subordinate courts. The high court occupies the top position in the judicial administration of a state.

The institution of high court originated in India in 1862 when the high courts were set up at Calcutta, Bombay and Madras[1]. In 1866, a fourth high court was established at Allahabad. In the course of time, each province in British India came to have its own high court. After 1950, a high court existing in a province became the high court for the corresponding state.

The Constitution of India provides for a high court for each state, but the Seventh Amendment Act of 1956 authorised the Parliament to establish a common high court for two or more states or for two or more states and a union territory. The territorial jurisdiction of a high court is co-terminus with the territory of a state. Similarly, the territorial jurisdiction of a common high court is co-terminus with the territories of the concerned states and union territory.

At present, there are 24 high courts in the country[2]. Out of them, three are common high courts. Delhi is the only union territory that has a high court of its own (since 1966). The other union territories fall under the jurisdiction of different state high courts. The Parilament can extend the jurisdiction of a high court to any union territory or exclude the jurisdiction of a high court from any union territory.

The name, year of establishment, territorial jurisdiction and seat (with bench or benches) of all the 24 high courts are mentioned in Table 30.1 at the end of this chapter.

Articles 214 to 231 in Part VI of the Constitution deal with the organisation, independence, jurisdiction, powers, procedures and so on of the high courts.

ORGANISATION OF HIGH COURT

Every high court (whether exclusive or common) consists of a chief justice and such other judges as the president may from time to time deem necessary to appoint. Thus, the Constitution does not specify the strength of a high court and leaves it to the discretion of the president. Accordingly, the President determines the strength of a high court from time to time depending upon its workload.

Judges

Appointment of Judges   The judges of a high court are appointed by the President. The chief justice is appointed by the President after consultation with the chief justice of India and the governor of the state concerned. For appointment of other judges, the chief justice of the concerned high court is also consulted. In case of a common high court for two or more states, the governors of all the states concerned are consulted by the president.

In the *Second Judges* case[3] (1993), the Supreme Court ruled that no appointment of a judge of the high court can be made, unless it is in conformity with the opinion of the chief justice of India. In the *Third Judges* case[4] (1998), the Supreme Court opined that in case of the appointment of high court judges, the chief justice of India should consult a collegium of two senior-most judges of the Supreme Court. Thus, the sole opinion of the chief justice of India alone does not constitute the 'consultation' process.

Qualifications of Judges

A person to be appointed as a judge of a high court, should have the following qualifications:

1. He should be a citizen of India.
2. (a) He should have held a judicial office in the territory of India for ten years; or
   (b) He should have been an advocate of a high court (or high courts in succession) for ten years.

From the above, it is clear that the Constitution has not prescribed a minimum age for appointment as a judge of a high court. Moreover, unlike in the case of the Supreme Court, the Consitution makes no provision for appointment of a distinguished jurist as a judge of a high court.

Oath or Affirmation

A person appointed as a judge of a high court, before entering upon his office, has to make and subscribe an oath or affirmation before the governor of the state or some person appointed by him for this purpose. In his oath, a judge of a high court swears:

1. to bear true faith and allegiance to the Constitution of India;
2. to uphold the sovereignty and integrity of India;
3. to duly and faithfully and to the best of his ability, knowledge and judgement perform the duties of the office without fear or favour, affection or ill-will; and
4. to uphold the Constitution and the laws.

Tenure of Judges

The Constitution has not fixed the tenure of a judge of a high court. However, it makes the following four provisions in this regard:

1. He holds office until he attains the age of 62 years[5]. Any questions regarding his age is to be decided by the president after consultation with the chief justice of India and the decision of the president is final.
2. He can resign his office by writing to the president.
3. He can be removed from his office by the President on the recommendation of the Parliament.

4. He vacates his office when he is appointed as a judge of the Supreme Court or when he is transferred to another high court.

Removal of Judges

A judge of a high court can be removed from his office by an order of the President. The President can issue the removal order only after an address by the Parliament has been presented to him in the same session for such removal. The address must be supported by a special majority of each House of Parliament (i.e., a majority of the total membership of that House and majority of not less than two-thirds of the members of that House present and voting). The grounds of removal are two—proved misbehaviour or incapacity. Thus, a judge of a high court can be removed in the same manner and on the same grounds as a judge of the Supreme Court.

The Judges Enquiry Act (1968) regulates the procedure relating to the removal of a judge of a high court by the process of impeachment:

1. A removal motion signed by 100 members (in the case of Lok Sabha) or 50 members (in the case of Rajya Sabha) is to be given to the Speaker/Chairman.
2. The Speaker/Chairman may admit the motion or refuse to admit it.
3. If it is admitted, then the Speaker/Chairman is to constitute a three-member committee to investigate into the charges.
4. The committee should consist of (a) the chief justice or a judge of the Supreme Court, (b) a chief justice of a high court, and (c) a distinguished jurist.
5. If the committee finds the judge to be guilty of misbehaviour or suffering from an incapacity, the House can take up the consideration of the motion.
6. After the motion is passed by each House of Parliament by special majority, an address is presented to the president for removal of the judge.
7. Finally, the president passes an order removing the judge.

From the above, it is clear that the procedure for the impeachment of a judge of a high court is the same as that for a judge of the Supreme Court.

It is interesting to know that no judge of a high court has been impeached so far.

Salaries and Allowances The salaries, allowances, privileges, leave and pension of the judges of a high court are determined from time to time by the Parliament. They cannot be varied to their disadvantage after their appointment except during a financial emergency. In 2009, the salary of the chief justice was increased from ₹30,000 to ₹90,000 per month and that of a judge from ₹26,000 to ₹80,000 per month[6]. They are also paid sumptuary allowance and provided with free accommodation and other facilities like medical, car, telephone, etc.

The retired chief justice and judges are entitled to 50% of their last drawn salary as monthly pension.

Transfer of Judges The President can transfer a judge from one high court to another after consulting the Chief Justice of India. On transfer, he is entitled to receive in addition to his salary such compensatory allowance as may be determined by Parliament.

In 1977, the Supreme Court ruled that the transfer of high court judges could be resorted to only as an exceptional measure and only in public interest and not by way of punishment. Again in 1994, the Supreme Court held that judicial review is necessary to check arbitrariness in transfer of judges. But, only the judge who is transferred can challenge it.

In the *Third Judges* case (1998), the Supreme Court opined that in case of the transfer of high court judges, the Chief Justice of India should consult, in addition to the collegium of four seniormost judges of the Supreme Court, the chief justice of the two high courts (one from which the judge is being transferred and the other receiving him). Thus, the sole opinion of the chief justice of India does not constitute the 'consultation' process.

Acting Chief Justice

The President can appoint a judge of a high court as an acting chief justice of the high court when:

1. the office of chief justice of the high court is vacant; or
2. the chief justice of the high court is temporarily absent; or
3. the chief justice of the high court is unable to perform the duties of his office.

Additional and Acting Judges

The President can appoint duly qualified persons as additional judges of a high court for a temporary period not exceeding two years when:

1. there is a temporary increase in the business of the high court; or
2. there are arrears of work in the high court.

The President can also appoint a duly qualified person as an acting judge of a high court when a judge of that high court (other than the chief justice) is:

1. unable to perform the duties of his office due to absence or any other reason; or
2. appointed to act temporarily as chief justice of that high court.

An acting judge holds office until the permanent judge resumes his office. However, both the additional or acting judge cannot hold office after attaining the age of 62 years.

Retired Judges

At any time, the chief justice of a high court of a state can request a retired judge of that high court or any other high court to act as a judge of the high court of that state for a temporary period. He can do so only with the previous consent of the President and also of the person to be so appointed. Such a judge is entitled to such allowances as the President may determine. He will also enjoy all the jurisdiction, powers and privileges of a judge of that high court. But, he will not otherwise be deemed to be a judge of that high court.

INDEPENDENCE OF HIGH COURT

The independence of a high court is very essential for the effective discharge of the duties assigned to it. It should be free from the encroachments, pressures and interferences of the executive (council of ministers) and the legislature. It should be allowed to do justice without fear or favour.

The Constitution has made the following provisions to safeguard and ensure the independent and impartial functioning of a high court.

1. Mode of Appointment The judges of a high court are appointed by the president (which means the cabinet) in consultation with the members of the judiciary itself (i.e., chief justice of India and the chief justice of the high court). This provision curtails the absolute discretion of the executive as well as ensures that the judicial appointments are not based on any political or practical considerations.

2. Security of Tenure The judges of a high court are provided with the security of tenure. They can be removed from office by the president only in the manner and on the grounds mentioned in the Constitution. This means that they do not hold their office during the pleasure of the president, though they are appointed by him. This is obvious from the fact that no judge of a high court has been removed (or impeached) so far.

3. Fixed Service Conditions The salaries, allowances, privileges, leave and pension of the judges of a high court are determined from time to time by the Parliament. But, they cannot be changed to their disadvantage after their appointment except during a financial emergency. Thus, the conditions of service of the judges of a high court remain same during their term of office.

4. Expenses Charged on Consolidated Fund The salaries and allowances of the judges, the salaries, allowances and pensions of the staff as well as the administrative expenses of a high court are charged on the consolidated fund of the state. Thus, they are non-votable by the state legislature (though they can be discussed by it). It should be noted here that the pension of a high court judge is charged on the Consolidated Fund of India and not the state.

5. Conduct of Judges cannot be Discussed The Constitution prohibits any discussion in Parliament or in a state legislature with respect to the conduct of the judges of a high court in the discharge of their duties, except when an impeachment motion is under consideration of the Parliament.

6. Ban on Practice after Retirement The retired permanent judges of a high court are prohibited from pleading or acting in any court or before any authority in India except the Supreme Court and the other high courts. This ensures that they do not favour any one in the hope of future favour.

7. Power to Punish for its Contempt A high court can punish any person for its contempt. Thus, its actions and decisions cannot be ciriticised and opposed by anybody. This power is vested in a high court to maintain its authority, dignity and honour.

8. Freedom to Appoint its Staff The chief justice of a high court can appoint officers and servants of the high court without any inteference from the executive. He can also prescribe their conditions of service.

9. Its Jurisdiction cannot be Curtailed The jurisdiction and powers of a high court in so far as they are specified in the Constitution cannot be curtailed both by the Parliament and the state legislature. But, in other respects, the jurisdiction and powers of a high court can be changed both by the parliament and the state legislature.

10. Separation from Executive The Constitution directs the state to take steps to separate the judiciary from the executive in public services. This means that the executive authorities should not possess the judicial powers. Consequent upon its implementation, the role of executive authorities in judicial administration came to an end[7].

Jurisdiction and Powers of High Court

Like the Supreme Court, the high court has been vested with quite extensive and effective powers. It is the highest court of appeal in the state. It is the protector of the Fundamental Rights of the citizens. It is vested with the power to interpret the Constitution. Besides, it has supervisory and consultative roles.

However, the Constitution does not contain detailed provisions with regard to the jurisdiction and powers of a high court. It only lays down that the jurisdiction and powers of a high court are to be the same as immediately before the commencement of the Constitution. But, there is one addition, that is, the Constitution gives a high court jurisdiction over revenue matters (which it did not enjoy in the pre-constitution era). The Constitution also confers (by other provisions) some more additional powers on a high court like writ jurisdiction, power of superintendence, consultative power, etc. Moreover, it empowers the Parliament and the state legislature to change the jurisdiction and powers of a high court.

At present, a high court enjoys the following jurisdiction and powers:

1. Original jurisdiction.
2. Writ jurisdiction.
3. Appellate jurisdiction.
4. Supervisory jurisdiction.
5. Control over subordinate courts.
6. A court of record.
7. Power of judicial review.

The present jurisdiction and powers of a high court are governed by (a) the constitutional provisions, (b) the Letters Patent, (c) the Acts of Parliament, (d) the Acts of State Legislature, (e) Indian Penal Code, 1860, (f) Cirminal Procedure Code, 1973, and (g) Civil Procedure Code, 1908.

1. Original Jurisdiction

It means the power of a high court to hear disputes in the first instance, not by way of appeal. It extends to the following:

(a) Matters of admirality, will, marriage, divorce, company laws and contempt of court.
(b) Disputes relating to the election of members of Parliament and state legislatures.
(c) Regarding revenue matter or an act ordered or done in revenue collection.
(d) Enforcement of fundamental rights of citizens.
(e) Cases ordered to be transferred from a subordinate court involving the interpretation of the Constitution to its own file.
(f) The four high courts (i.e., Calcutta, Bombay, Madras and Delhi High Courts) have original civil jurisdiction in cases of higher value.

Before 1973, the Calcutta, Bombay and Madras High Courts also had original criminal jurisdiction. This was fully abolished by the Criminal Procedure Code, 1973.

2. Writ Jurisdiction

Article 226 of the Constitution empowers a high court to issue writs including *habeas corpus, mandamus, certiorari*, prohibition and *quo-warrento* for the enforcement of the fundamental rights of the citizens and for any other purpose. The phrase 'for any other purpose' refers to the enforcement of an ordinary legal right. The high court can issue writs to any person, authority and government not only within its territorial jurisdiction but also outside its territorial jurisdiction if the cause of action arises within its territorial jurisdiction[8].

The writ jurisdiction of the high court (under Article 226) is not exclusive but concurrent with the writ jurisdiction of the Supreme Court (under Article 32). It means, when the fundamental rights of a citizen are violated, the aggrieved party has the option of moving either the high court or the Supreme Court directly. However, the writ jurisdiction of the high court is wider than that of the Supreme Court. This is because, the Supreme Court can issue writs only for the enforcement of fundamental rights and not for any other purpose, that is, it does not extend to a case where the breach of an ordinary legal right is alleged.

In the *Chandra Kumar* case[9] (1997), the Supreme Court ruled that the writ jurisdiction of both the high court and the Supreme Court constitute a part of the basic structure of the Constitution. Hence, it cannot be ousted or excluded even by way of an amendment to the Constitution.

3. Appellate Jurisdiction

A high court is primarily a court of appeal. It hears appeals against the judgements of subordinate courts functioning in its territorial jurisdiction. It has appellate jurisdiction in both civil and criminal matters. Hence, the appellate jurisdiction of a high court is wider than its original jurisdiction.

(a) Civil Matters The civil appellate jurisdiction of a high court is as follows:

(i) First appeals from the orders and judgements of the district courts, additional district courts and other subordinate courts lie directly to the high court, on both questions of law and fact, if the amount exceeds the stipulated limit.
(ii) Second appeals from the orders and judgements of the district court or other subordinate courts lie to the high court in the cases involving questions of law only (and not questions of fact).
(iii) The Calcutta, Bombay and Madras High Courts have provision for intra-court appeals. When a single judge of the high court has decided a case (either under the original or appellate jurisdiction of the high court), an

appeal from such a decision lies to the division bench of the same high court.

(iv) Appeals from the decisions of the administrative and other tribunals lie to the division bench of the state high court. In 1997, the Supreme Court ruled that the tribunals are subject to the writ jurisdiction of the high courts. Consequently, it is not possible for an aggrieved person to approach the Supreme Court directly against the decisions of the tribunals, without first going to the high courts.

(b) Criminal Matters The criminal appellate jurisdiction of a high court is as follows:

(i) Appeals from the judgements of sessions court and additional sessions court lie to the high court if the sentence is one of imprisonment for more than seven years. It should also be noted here that a death sentence (popularly known as capital punishment) awarded by a sessions court or an additional sessions court should be confirmed by the high court before it can be executed, whether there is an appeal by the convicted person or not.

(ii) In some cases specified in various provisions of the Criminal Procedure Code (1973), the appeals from the judgements of the assistant sessions judge, metropolitan magistrate or other magistrates (judicial) lie to the high court.

4. Supervisory Jurisdiction

A high court has the power of superintendence over all courts and tribunals functioning in its territorial jurisdiction (except military courts or tribunals). Thus, it may—

(a) call for returns from them;

(b) make and issue, general rules and prescribe forms for regulating the practice and proceedings of them;

(c) prescribe forms in which books, entries and accounts are to be kept by them; and

(d) settle the fees payable to the sheriff, clerks, officers and legal practitioners of them.

This power of superintendence of a high court is very broad because, (i) it extends to all courts and tribunals whether they are subject to the appellate jurisdiction of the high court or not; (ii) it covers not

only administrative superintendence but also judicial superintendence; (iii) it is a revisional jurisdiction; and (iv) it can be *suo-motu* (on its own) and not necessarily on the application of a party.

However, this power does not vest the high court with any unlimited authority over the subordinate courts and tribunals. It is an extraordinary power and hence has to be used most sparingly and only in appropriate cases. Usually, it is limited to, (i) excess of jurisdiction, (ii) gross violation of natural justice, (iii) error of law, (iv) disregard to the law of superior courts, (v) perverse findings, and (vi) manifest injustice.

5. Control over Subordinate Courts

In addition to its appellate jurisdiction and supervisory jurisdiction over the subordinate courts as mentioned above, a high court has an administrative control and other powers over them. These include the following:

(a) It is consulted by the governor in the matters of appointment, posting and promotion of district judges and in the appointments of persons to the judicial service of the state (other than district judges).

(b) It deals with the matters of posting, promotion, grant of leave, transfers and discipline of the members of the judicial service of the state (other than district judges).

(c) It can withdraw a case pending in a subordinate court if it involves a substantial question of law that require the interpretation of the Constitution. It can then either dispose of the case itself or determine the question of law and return the case to the subordinate court with its judgement.

(d) Its law is binding on all subordinate courts functioning within its territorial jurisdiction in the same sense as the law declared by the Supreme Court is binding on all courts in India.

6. A Court of Record

As a court of record, a high court has two powers:

(a) The judgements, proceedings and acts of the high courts are recorded for perpetual memory and testimony. These records are admitted to be of evidentiary value and cannot be questioned when produced before any subordinate court. They are recognised as legal precedents and legal references.

(b) It has power to punish for contempt of court, either with simple imprisonment or with fine or with both.

The expression 'contempt of court' has not been defined by the Constitution. However, the expression has been defined by the Contempt of Court Act of 1971. Under this, contempt of court may be civil or criminal. Civil contempt means wilful disobedience to any judgement, order, writ or other process of a court or wilful breach of an undertaking given to a court. Criminal contempt means the publication of any matter or doing an act which—(i) scandalises or lowers the authority of a court; or (ii) prejudices or interferes with the due course of a judicial proceeding; or (iii) interferes or obstructs the administration of justice in any other manner.

However, innocent publication and distribution of some matter, fair and accurate report of judicial proceedings, fair and reasonable criticism of judicial acts and comment on the administrative side of the judiciary do not amount to contempt of court.

As a court of record, a high court also has the power to review and correct its own judgement or order or decision, even though no specific power of review is conferred on it by the Constitution. The Supreme Court, on the other hand, has been spe-cifically conferred with the power of review by the constitution.

7. Power of Judicial Review

Judicial review is the power of a high court to examine the constitutionality of legislative enactments and executive orders of both the Central and state governments. On examination, if they are found to be violative of the Constitution (*ultra-vires*), they can be declared as illegal, unconstitutional and invalid (null and viod) by the high court. Consequently, they cannot be enforced by the government.

Though the phrase 'judicial review' has no where been used in the Constitution, the provisions of Articles 13 and 226 explicitly confer the power of judicial review on a high court. The constitutional validity of a legislative enactment or an executive order can be challenged in a high court on the following three grounds:

(a) it infringes the fundamental rights (Part III),

(b) it is outside the competence of the authority which has framed it, and

(c) it is repugant to the constitutional provisions.

The 42nd Amendment Act of 1976 curtailed the judicial review power of high court. It debarred the high courts from considering the constitutional validity of any central law. However, the 43rd Amendment Act of 1977 restored the original position.

Table 30.1 *Name and Jurisdiction of High Courts*

	Name	Year of establishment	Territorial Jurisdiction	Seat
1.	Allahabad	1866	Uttar Pradesh	Allahabad (Bench at Lucknow)
2.	Andhra Pradesh	1954	Andra Pradesh	Hyderabad
3.	Bombay[13]	1862	Maharashta, Goa, Dadra and Nagar Haveli and Daman and Diu	Mumbai (Benches at Nagpur, Panaji and Aurangabad)
4.	Calcutta[13]	1862	West Bengal and Andaman and Nicobar Islands	Kolkata (Circuit Bench at Port Blair)
5.	Chhattisgarh	2000	Chhattisgarh	Bilaspur
6.	Delhi	1966	Delhi	Delhi
7.	Guwahati	1948[10]	Assam, Nagaland, Mizoram and Arunachal Pradesh[14]	Guwahati (Benches at Kohima, Aizawl and Itanagar)

(Contd.)

	Name	Year of establishment	Territorial Jurisdiction	Seat
8.	Gujarat	1960	Gujarat	Ahmedabad
9.	Himachal Pradesh	1971	Himachal Pradesh	Simla
10.	Jammu and Kashmir	1928	Jammu and Kashmir	Srinagar and Jammu
11.	Jharkhand	2000	Jharkhand	Ranchi
12.	Karnataka	1884[11]	Karnataka	Bengaluru
13.	Kerala	1958	Kerala and Lakshadweep	Ernakulam
14.	Madhya Pradesh	1956	Madhya Pradesh	Jabalpur (Benches at Gwalior and Indore)
15.	Madras[13]	1862	Tamil Nadu and Puducherry	Chennai
16.	Manipur[15]	2013	Manipur	Imphal
17.	Meghalaya[15]	2013	Meghalaya	Shillong
18.	Orissa[16]	1948	Odisha	Cuttack
19.	Patna	1916	Bihar	Patna
20.	Punjab and Haryana	1875[12]	Punjab, Haryana and Chandigarh	Chandigarh
21.	Rajasthan	1949	Rajasthan	Jodhpur (Bench at Jaipur)
22.	Sikkim	1975	Sikkim	Gangtok
23.	Tripura[15]	2013	Tripura	Agartala
24.	Uttarakhand	2000	Uttarakhand	Nainital

Table 30.2 *Articles Related to High Courts at a Glance*

Article No.	Subject-matter
214.	High Courts for states
215.	High Courts to be courts of record
216.	Constitution of High Courts
217.	Appointment and conditions of the office of a Judge of a High Court
218.	Application of certain provisions relating to Supreme Court to High Courts
219.	Oath or affirmation by judges of High Courts
220.	Restriction on practice after being a permanent judge
221.	Salaries etc., of judges
222.	Transfer of a judge from one High Court to another
223.	Appointment of acting Chief Justice
224.	Appointment of additional and acting judges
224A.	Appointment of retired judges at sittings of High Courts
225.	Jurisdiction of existing High Courts
226.	Power of High Courts to issue certain writs

(Contd.)

Article No.	Subject-matter
226A.	Constitutional validity of Central laws not to be considered in proceedings under Article 226 (Repealed)
227.	Power of superintendence over all courts by the High Court
228.	Transfer of certain cases to High Court
228A.	Special provisions as to disposal of questions relating to constitutional validity of state laws (Repealed)
229.	Officers and servants and the expenses of High Courts
230.	Extension of jurisdiction of High Courts to union territories
231.	Establishment of a common High Court for two or more states
232.	Interpretation (Repealed)

NOTES AND REFERENCES

1. These three high courts were set up under the provisions of the Indian High Courts Act, 1861.
2. With the creation of three more new states in 2000, the number of high courts increased from 18 to 21. Again, with the creation of separate high courts for the three north-eastern states of Manipur, Meghalaya and Tripura in 2013, the number of high courts increased from 21 to 24.
3. *Supreme Court Advocates* v. *Union of India* (1993).
4. *In re* Presidential Reference (1998). The president sought the Supreme Court's opinion (under Article 143) on certain doubts over the consultation process to be adopted by the chief justice of India as stipulated in the 1993 case.
5. The retirement age has been raised from 60 to 62 years by the 15th Amendment Act of 1963.
6. In 1950, their salaries were fixed at ₹4,000 per month and ₹3,500 per month respectively. In 1986, their salaries were raised to ₹9,000 per month and ₹8,000 per month respectively. In 1998, their salaries were raised to ₹30,000 per month and ₹26,000 per month respectively.
7. The Criminal Procedure Code (1973) has effected the separation of judiciary from the executive (Article 50 under the Directive Principles of State Policy).
8. The second provision was added by the 15th Constitutional Amendment Act of 1963.
9. *L. Chandra Kumar* v. *Union of India* (1997).
10. Originally known as Assam High Court and renamed Guwahati High Court in 1971.
11. Originally known as Mysore High Court and renamed Karnataka High Court in 1973.
12. Originally known as Punjab High Court and renamed Punjab and Haryana High Court in 1966.
13. Though the names of Bombay, Calcutta and Madras are changed to Mumbai, Kolkata and Chennai respectively, the names of respective high courts are not changed.
14. In 2013, separate high courts were created for the three north-eastern states of Manipur, Meghalaya and Tripura.
15. Established by the North-Eastern Areas (Reorganisation) and other Related Laws (Amendment) Act, 2012.
16. Though the name of Orissa is changed to Odisha, the name of Orissa High Court is not changed.

Subordinate Courts

The state judiciary consists of a high court and a hierarchy of subordinate courts, also known as lower courts. The subordinate courts are so called because of their subordination to the state high court. They function below and under the high court at district and lower levels.

CONSTITUTIONAL PROVISIONS

Articles 233 to 237 in Part VI of the Constitution make the following provisions to regulate the organization of subordinate courts and to ensure their independence from the executive[1].

1. Appointment of District Judges

The appointment, posting and promotion of district judges in a state are made by the governor of the state in consultation with the high court.

A person to be appointed as district judge should have the following qualifications:

(a) He should not already be in the service of the Central or the state government.

(b) He should have been an advocate or a pleader for seven years.

(c) He should be recommended by the high court for appointment.

2. Appointment of other Judges

Appointment of persons (other than district judges) to the judicial service of a state are made by the governor of the state after consultation with the State Public Service Commission and the high court[2].

3. Control over Subordinate Courts

The control over district courts and other subordinate courts including the posting, promotion and leave of persons belonging to the judicial service of a state and holding any post inferior to the post of district judge is vested in the high court.

4. Interpretation

The expression 'district judge' includes judge of a city civil court, additional district judge, joint district judge, assistant district judge, chief judge of a small cause court, chief presidency magistrate, additional chief presidency magistrate, sessions judge, additional sessions judge and assistant sessions judge.

The expression 'judicial service' means a service consisting exclusively of persons intended to fill the post of district judge and other civil judicial posts inferior to the post of district judge.

5. Application of the above Provisions to Certain Magistrates

The Governor may direct that the above mentioned provisions relating to persons in the state judicial service would apply to any class or classes of magistrates in the state.

STRUCTURE AND JURISDICTION

The organisational structure, jurisdiction and nomenclature of the subordinate judiciary are laid down by the states. Hence, they differ slightly from state to state. Broadly speaking, there are three tiers of civil and criminal courts below the High Court. This is shown below :

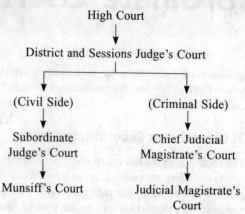

The district judge is the highest judicial authority in the district. He possesses original and appellate jurisdiction in both civil as well as criminal matters. In other words, the district judge is also the sessions judge. When he deals with civil cases, he is known as the district judge and when he hears the criminal cases, he is called as the sessions judge. The district judge exercises both judicial and administrative powers. He also has supervisory powers over all the subordinate courts in the district. Appeals against his orders and judgements lie to the High Court. The sessions judge has the power to impose any sentence including life imprisonment and capital punishment (death sentence). However, a capital punishment passed by him is subject to confirmation by the High Court, whether there is an appeal or not.

Below the District and Sessions Court stands the Court of Subordinate Judge on the civil side and the Court of Chief Judicial Magistrate on the criminal side. The subordinate judge exercises unlimited pecuniary jurisdiction over civil suits[3]. The chief judicial magistrate decides criminal cases which are punishable with imprisonment for a term up to seven years.

At the lowest level, on the civil side, is the Court of Munsiff and on the criminal side, is the Court of Judicial Magistrate. The munsiff possesses limited jurisdiction and decides civil cases of small pecuniary stake[4]. The judicial magistrate tries criminal cases which are punishable with imprisonment for a term up to three years.

In some metropolitan cities, there are city civil courts (chief judges) on the civil side and the courts of metropolitan magistrates on the criminal side.

Some of the States and Presidency towns have established small causes courts[5]. These courts decide the civil cases of small value in a summary manner. Their decisions are final, but the High Court possesses a power of revision.

In some states, Panchayat Courts try petty civil and criminal cases. They are variously known as Nyaya Panchayat, Gram Kutchery, Adalati Panchayat, Panchayat Adalat and so on.

NOTES AND REFERENCES

1. The 20th Constitutional Amendment Act of 1966 added a new Article 233-A which retrospectively validated the appointment of certain district judges as well as the judgements delivered by them.

2. In practice, the State Public Service Commission conducts a competitive examination for recruitment to the judicial service of the state.

3. A subordinate judge is also known as civil judge (senior division), civil judge (class I) and so on. He may also be given the powers of an assistant sessions judge. In such a case, he combines in himself both civil as well as criminal powers like that of a District Judge.

4. A munsiff is also known as civil judge (junior division), civil judge (class-II) and so on.

5. Delhi, Bombay, Calcutta and Madras were formerly called presidency towns.

Special Status of Jammu & Kashmir

Under Article 1 of the Indian Constitution, the State of Jammu and Kashmir (J&K) is a constituent state of Indian Union and its territory forms a part of the territory of India. On the other hand, Article 370 in Part XXI of the Constitution grants a special status to it. Accordingly, all the provisions of the Constitution of India do not apply to it. It is also the only state in the Indian Union which has its own separate state Constitution—the Constitution of Jammu and Kashmir.

Under the same Part (XXI) of the Constitution, eleven other states[1] of the Indian Union also enjoy special status but only in certain minor matters. On the other hand, the special status enjoyed by the State of J&K (as mentioned above) is unparalleled.

ACCESSION OF J&K TO INDIA

With the end of the British paramountcy, the State of Jammu and Kashmir (J&K) became independent on 15 August 1947. Initially its ruler, Maharaja Hari Singh, decided not to join India or Pakistan and thereby remain independent. On 20 October 1947, the Azad Kashmir Forces supported by the Pakistan army attacked the frontiers of the state. Under this unusual and extraordinary political circumstance, the ruler of the state decided to accede the state to India. Accordingly, the 'Instrument of Accession of Jammu and Kashmir to India' was signed by Pandit Jawaharlal Nehru and Maharaja Hari Singh on 26

October 1947.[2] Under this, the state surrendered only three subjects (defence, external affairs and communications) to the Dominion of India. At that time, the Government of India made a commitment that 'the people of this state, through their own Constituent Assembly, would determine the internal Constitution of this state and the nature and extent of the jurisdiction of the Union of India over the state, and until the decision of the Constituent Assembly of the State, the Constitution of India could only provide an interim arrangement regarding the state.'[3] In pursuance of this commitment, Article 370 was incorporated in the Constitution of India. It clearly states that the provisions with respect to the State of J&K are only temporary and not permanent. It became operative on 17 November 1952, with the following provisions:

1. The provisions of Article 238 (dealing with the administration of Part B states) is not applicable to the state of J&K. The state of J&K was specified in the category of Part B states in the original Constitution (1950). This Article in Part VII was subsequently omitted from the Constitution by the 7th Constitutional Amendment Act (1956) in the wake of the reorganisation of states.

2. The power of Parliament to make laws for the state is limited to: **(a)** Those matters in the Union List and the Concurrent List which correspond to matters specified in the state's Instrument of Accession. These matters are to

be declared by the president in consultation with the state government. The Instrument of Accession contained matters classified under four heads, namely, external affairs, defence, communications and ancilliary matters. **(b)** Such other matters in the Union List and the Concurrent List which are specified by the president with the concurrence of the state government. This means that laws can be made on these matters only with the consent of the State of J&K.

3. The provisions of Article 1 (declaring India as a Union of states and its territory) and this Article (that is, Article 370) are applicable to the State of J&K.

4. Besides above, the other provisions of the Constitution can be applied to the state with such exceptions and modifications as specified by the President in consultation with the state government or with the concurrence of the state government.

5. The President can declare that Article 370 ceases to be operative or operates with exceptions and modifications. However, this can be done by the President only on the recommendation of Constituent Assembly of the state.

Therefore, Article 370 makes Article 1 and Article 370 itself applicable to the State of J&K at once and authorises the president to extend other Articles to the state.

Present Relationship Between J&K and India

In pursuance of the provisions of Article 370, the President issued an order called the Constitution (Application to Jammu and Kashmir) Order, 1950, to specify the Union's jurisdiction over the state. In 1952, the Government of India and the State of J&K entered into an agreement at Delhi regarding their future relationship. In 1954, the Constituent Assembly of J&K approved the state's accession to India as well as the Delhi Agreement. Then, the President issued another order with the same title, that is, the Constitution (Application to Jammu and Kashmir), Order, 1954. This order superseded the earlier order of 1950 and extended the Union's jurisdiction over

the state. This is the basic order that, as amended and modified from time to time, regulates the constitutional position of the state and its relationship with the Union.[4] At present, this is as follows:

1. Jammu and Kashmir is a constituent state of the Indian Union and has its place in Part I and Schedule I of the Constitution of India (dealing with the Union and its Territory). But its name, area or boundary cannot be changed by the Union without the consent of its legislature.

2. The State of J & K has its own Constitution and is administered according to that Constitution. Hence, Part VI of the Constitution of India (dealing with state governments) is not applicable to this state. The very definition of 'state' under this part does not include the State of J&K.

3. Parliament can make laws in relation to the state on most of the subjects enumerated in the Union List and on a good number of subjects enumerated in the Concurrent List.[5] But, the residuary power belongs to the state legislature except in few matters like prevention of activities involving terrorist acts, questioning or disrupting the sovereignty and territorial integrity of India and causing insult to the National Flag, National Anthem and the Constitution of India. Further, the power to make laws of preventive detention in the state belongs to the state legislature. This means that the preventive detention laws made by the Parliament are not applicable to the state.

4. Part III (dealing with Fundamental Rights) is applicable to the state with some exceptions and conditions. The Fundamental Right to Property is still guaranteed in the state. Also, certain special rights are granted to the permanent residents of the state with regard to public employment, acquisition of immovable property, settlement and government scholarships.

5. Part IV (dealing with Directive Principles of State Policy) and Part IVA (dealing with Fundamental Duties) are not applicable to the state.

6. A National Emergency declared on the ground of internal disturbance will not have effect in the state except with the concurrence of the state government.[6]

7. The President has no power to declare a financial emergency in relation to the state.
8. The President has no power to suspend the Constitution of the state on the ground of failure to comply with the directions given by him.
9. The State Emergency (President's Rule) is applicable to the state. However, this emergency can be imposed in the state on the ground of failure of the constitutional machinery under the provisions of state Constitution and not Indian Constitution. In fact, two types of Emergencies can be declared in the state, namely, President's Rule under the Indian Constitution and Governor's Rule under the state Constitution. In 1986, the President's Rule was imposed in the state for the first time.
10. International treaty or agreement affecting the disposition of any part of the territory of the state can be made by the Centre only with the consent of the state legislature.
11. An amendment made to the Constitution of India does not apply to the state unless it is extended by a presidential order.
12. Official language provisions are applicable to the state only in so far as they relate to the official language of the Union, the official language of inter-state and Centre–state communications and the language of the Supreme Court proceedings.
13. The Fifth Schedule (dealing with administration and control of schedule areas and scheduled tribes) and the Sixth Schedule (dealing with administration of tribal areas) do not apply to the state.
14. The special leave jurisdiction of the Supreme Court and the jurisdictions of the Election Commission and the comptroller and auditor general are applicable to the state.
15. The High Court of J&K can issue writs only for the enforcement of the fundamental rights and not for any other purpose.
16. The provisions of Part II regarding the denial of citizenship rights of migrants to Pakistan are not applicable to the permanent residents of J&K, who after having so migrated to Pakistan return to the state for resettlement. Every such person is deemed to be a citizen of India.

Therefore, the two characteristic features of the special relationship between the State of J&K and the Union of India are: (a) the state has a much greater measure of autonomy and power than enjoyed by the other states; and (b) Centre's jurisdiction within the state is more limited than what it has with respect to other states.[7]

FEATURES OF J&K CONSTITUTION

In September–October 1951, the Constituent Assembly of J&K was elected by the people of the state on the basis of adult franchise to prepare the future Constitution of the state and to determine its relationship with the Union of India. This sovereign body met for the first time on 31 October 1951, and took about five years to complete its task.

The Constitution of J&K was adopted on 17 November 1957, and came into force on 26 January 1957. Its salient features (as amended from time to time) are as follows:

1. It declares the State of J&K to be an integral part of India.
2. It secures justice, liberty, equality and fraternity to the people of the state.
3. It says that the State of J&K comprises all the territory that was under the ruler of the state on 15 August 1947. This means that the territory of the state also includes the area which is under the occupation of Pakistan.
4. It lays down that a citizen of India is treated as a 'permanent resident' of the state if on 14 May 1954 (a) he was a state subject of Class I or Class II, or (b) having lawfully acquired immovable property in the state, he has been ordinarily resident in the state for 10 years prior to that date, or (c) any person who before 14 May, 1954 was a state subject of Class I or Class II and who, having migrated to Pakistan after 1 March 1947, returns to the state for resettlement.
5. It clarifies that the permanent residents of the state are entitled to all rights guaranteed under the Constitution of India. But, any change in the definition of 'permanent' can be made by the state legislature only.

6. It contains a list of directive principles that are to be treated as fundamental in the governance of the state. However, they are not judicially enforceable.

7. It provides for a bicameral legislature consisting of the legislative assembly and the legislative council. The assembly consists of 111 members directly elected by the people.[8] Out of this, 24 seats are to remain vacant as they are allotted for the area that is under the occupation of Pakistan. Hence, as an interim measure, the total strength of the Assembly is to be taken as 87 for all practical purposes. The council consists of 36 members, most of them are elected in an indirect manner and some of them are nominated by the Governor, who is also an integral part of state legislature.

8. It vests the executive powers of the state in the governor appointed by the president for a term of five years. It provides for a council of ministers headed by the chief minister to aid and advise the governor in the exercise of his functions. The council of ministers is collectively responsible to the assembly. Under the original Constitution of J&K (1957), the head of the state and head of the government were designated as *Sadar-i-Riyasat* (President) and *Wazir-i-Azam* (Prime Minister) respectively. In 1965, they were redesignated as governor and chief Minister respectively. Also, the head of the state was to be elected by the state assembly.

9. It establishes a high court consisting of a chief justice and two or more other judges. They are appointed by the president in consultation with the Chief Justice of India and the Governor of the state. The High Court of J&K is a court of record and enjoys original, appelate and writ jurisdictions. However, it can issue writs only for the enforcement of fundamental rights and not for any other purpose.

10. It provides for Governor's Rule. Hence, the governor, with the concurrence of the President of India, can assume to himself all the powers of the state government, except those of the high court. He can dissolve the assembly and dismiss the council of ministers. The Governor's Rule can be imposed when the state adminis-

tration cannot be carried on in accordance with the provisions of the J&K Constitution. It was imposed for the first time in 1977. Notably, in 1964, Article 356 of the Indian Constitution (dealing with the imposition of President's Rule in a state) was extended to the state of J&K.

11. It declares **Urdu** as the official language of the state. It also permits the use of English for official purposes unless the state legislature provides otherwise.

12. It lays down the procedure for its amendment. It can be amended by a bill passed in each house of the state legislature by a majority of two-thirds of the total membership of that house. Such a bill must be introduced in the assembly only. However, no bill of constitutional amendment can be moved in either House if it seeks to change the relationship of the state with the Union of India.

J&K Autonomy Resolution Rejected

On June 26, 2000, in a historic move, the Jammu and Kashmir Legislative Assembly adopted by voice vote a resolution accepting the report of the State Autonomy Committee, recommending greater autonomy to the State. The Assembly sought the following:

1. The word 'temporary' in Article 370 to be substituted with 'special'.
2. Only defence, foreign affairs, communications and ancillary subjects to be with the Centre.
3. Article 356 not to apply to J&K.
4. Election Commission of India to have no role.
5. J&K Assembly to have final say on Central role in case of external aggression / internal emergency.
6. No room for All-India Services (IAS, IPS and IFS) in J&K.
7. Governor and Chief Minister to be called Sadar-e-Riyasat and Wazir-e-Azam.
8. Separate charter of fundamental rights for J&K.
9. Parliament's and President's role over J&K to be sharply curtailed.
10. No special leave to appeal by the Supreme Court.

11. No special provisions for scheduled castes/tribes and backward classes.
12. Centre to lose adjudication rights relating to inter-state rivers or river valleys.
13. No jurisdiction of the Supreme Court in appeals from the High Court in civil and criminal matters.
14. Parliament not to be empowered to amend the Constitution and procedure with respect to J&K.

On July 14, 2000, the Union Cabinet rejected as unacceptable the June 26 autonomy resolution of the Jammu and Kashmir Assembly, though at the same time committing itself to a greater devolution of powers to all states. The Cabinet found the June 26 resolution unacceptable because essentially it was a plea for restoration of the pre-1953 status to the state.

The Cabinet was unanimous in its judgement that the June 26 resolution could not be accepted, fully or even partially, because it would set the clock back and reverse the natural process of harmonizing the aspirations of the people of Jammu and Kashmir with the integrity of the nation.

Specifically about Jammu and Kashmir, the Cabinet wanted the people and the state government to join hands in the endeavour to address the real problems facing the state: to root out insurgency and cross-border terrorism, and to ensure accelerated development.

GROUP OF INTERLOCUTORS FOR J & K

The Group of Interlocutors for Jammu and Kashmir was appointed by the Central Government in October 2010 under the Chairmanship of the eminent journalist Dileep Padgaonkar[9]. It was tasked to hold-wide – ranging discussions with all sections of opinion in Jammu and Kashmir in order to identify the political contours of a solution to the problems of the state.

The Group submitted its report to the Union Home Minister in October 2011. The report is entitled *"A New Compact with the People of Jammu and Kashmir"*.

The Group did not recommend a pure and simple return to the pre-1953 situation. This would create a dangerous constitutional vacuum in the Centre-state relationship. The clock cannot be set back.

Instead, the Group recommended the establishment of a Constitutional Committee to review all Central Acts and Articles of the Constitution of India extended to the state of Jammu and Kashmir after signing of the Delhi Agreement of 1952[10].

The Constitutional Committee should be headed by a distinguished jurist who enjoys esteem and respect in the state and in the rest of the country. Its members should be constitutional / legal experts from the state and the rest of India. Their choice should be acceptable to all stake-holders.

In the exercise of its mandate, the Constitutional Committee should bear in mind the dual character of Jammu and Kashmir, *viz.*, that it is a constituent unit of the Indian Union and that it enjoys a special status in the said Union, enshrined in Article 370 of the Constitution of India. It should also bear in mind the dual character of the people of the state, *viz* that they are both state subjects and Indian citizens. The review should, therefore, have to determine whether – and to what extent – the Central Acts and Articles of the Constitution of India, extended with or without amendment to the state, have dented Jammu and Kashmir's special status and abridged the state government's powers to cater to the welfare of its people.

The Constitutional Committee should be future-oriented in that it should conduct its review solely on the basis of the powers that the state needs to address the political, economic, social and cultural interests, concerns, grievances and aspirations of the people in all the three regions of the state – Jammu, Kashmir and Ladakh – and all its sub-regions and communities. In this connection, the Committee should also need to reflect on the quantum of legislative, financial and administrative powers that the state government should delegate to the three regions at all levels of governance – the regional, district and panchayat / municipality.

The Constitutional Committee should be requested to complete its work within six months. Its recommendations must be reached through consensus so that they are acceptable to all stake-holders represented in the State Assembly and in Parliament. The next step would be for the President, in exercise of the powers conferred by Clauses (1) and (3) of Article 370 of the Constitution, to issue an order incorporating the recommendations of the Constitutional Committee. The order would need to be ratified by a bill in both Houses of Parliament and by each House in the State Legislature by a margin of not less than two-thirds majority of the total membership present and voting in each House. It would then be presented to the President for assent. Once this process is over, Clauses (1) and (3) of Article 370 shall cease to be operative and no orders shall be made by the President hereafter under the said clauses as from the date of the final order.

The recommendations of the Group on certain issues of contention are as follows:

1. Delete the word 'temporary' from the heading of Article 370 and from the title of Part XXI of the Constitution. Replace it with the word 'special' as it has been used for other States under article 371 (Maharashtra and Gujarat); Article 371A (Nagaland); 371B (Assam); 371C (Manipur); 371D and E (Andhra Pradesh); 371F (Sikkim); 371G (Mizoram); 371H (Arunachal Pradesh); 371I (Goa).

2. On the Governor: The state government, after consultations with opposition parties, should submit a list of three names to the President. The President can ask for more suggestions if required. The Governor should be appointed by the President and hold office at the pleasure of the President.

3. Article 356: The action of the Governor is now justiciable in the Supreme Court. The present arrangement should continue with the proviso that the Governor should keep the State Legislature under suspended animation and hold fresh elections within three months.

4. Article 312: The proportion of officers from the all-India services should be gradually reduced in favour of officers from the state civil service without curbing administrative efficiency.

5. The nomenclatures in English of the Governor and the Chief Minister should continue as at present. Equivalent nomenclatures in Urdu may be used while referring to the two offices in Urdu.

6. Create three Regional Councils, one each for Jammu, Kashmir and Ladakh. (The latter would no longer be a division of Kashmir). Devolve certain legislative, executive and financial powers to them. A further devolution of executive and financial powers to Panchayati Raj institutions – at the level of a district, a village panchayat, a municipality or a corporation – would be part of the overall package. All these bodies should be elected. Provisions should be made for representation of women, SC/ST, backward clans and minorities. MLAs should be *ex-officio* members with voting rights.

7. Parliament should make no laws applicable to the state unless it relates to the country's internal and external security and its vital economic interest, especially in the areas of energy and access to water resources.

8. Extend the writ of autonomous and statutory institutions to the state and ensure that their functioning conforms to the provisions of the Constitution of Jammu and Kashmir.

9. These changes should be harmonised in all parts of the former princely state. All opportunities for cross-LOC cooperation should be promoted. This would require substantial constitutional changes in Pakistan-administered Jammu and Kashmir.

10. Take all appropriate measures to regard Jammu and Kashmir as a bridge between South and Central Asia.

Notes and References

1. These include Maharashtra, Gujarat, Nagaland, Assam, Manipur, Andhra Pradesh, Sikkim, Mizoram, Arunachal Pradesh, Goa and Karnataka.

2. It was accepted by the Governor General of India, Lord Mountbatten, on 27 October, 1947.

3. D D Basu, *Commentary on the Constitution of India*, Prentice-Hall, Vol. V, 5th edition, 1970, p. 512.

4. This order was amended in 1963, 1964, 1965, 1966, 1972, 1974 and 1986.

5. The Concurrent List was not applicable to the state till 1963. The State List is not applicable to the state even today.

6. Unlike in other states, a proclamation of emergency can be made in J&K on the ground of internal disturbance also. An emergency declared on the ground of war or external aggression is directly (i.e., without the concurrence of the state government, as in the case of other states) applicable to J&K.

7. M P Jain, *Indian Constitutional Law,* Wadhwa, Fourth Edition, 1987, p. 435.

8. Originally, the strength of J&K Assembly was 100 and this was increased to 111 in 1987.

9. The other two members of the Group were academician Radha Kumar and former Information Commissioner M.M. Ansari.

10. This Agreement, along with the Instrument of Accession and Article 370 of the Constitution, has been adopted by the Indian Parliament and the Constituent Assembly of Jammu and Kashmir.

Special Provisions for Some States

Articles 371 to 371-J in Part XXI of the constitution contain special provisions for eleven states[1] viz., Maharashtra, Gujarat, Nagaland, Assam, Manipur, Andhra Pradesh, Sikkim, Mizoram, Arunachal Pradesh, Goa and Karnataka. The intention behind them is to meet the aspirations of the people of backward regions of the states or to protect the cultural and economic interests of the tribal people of the states or to deal with the disturbed law and order condition in some parts of the states or to protect the interests of the local people of the states.

Originally, the constitution did not make any special provisions for these states. They have been incorporated by the various subsequent amendments made in the context of reorganisation of the states or conferment of statehood on the Union Territories.

PROVISIONS FOR MAHARASHTRA AND GUJARAT

Under Article 371, the President is authorised to provide that the Governor of Maharashtra and that of Gujarat would have special responsibility for[2]:

1. the establishment of separate development boards for (i) Vidarbha, Marathwada and the rest of Maharashtra, (ii) Saurashtra, Kutch and the rest of Gujarat;
2. making a provision that a report on the working of these boards would be placed every year before the State Legislative Assembly;
3. the equitable allocation of funds for developmental expenditure over the above-mentioned areas; and
4. an equitable arrangement providing adequate facilities for technical education and vocational training, and adequate employment opportunities in the state services in respect of the above-mentioned areas.

PROVISIONS FOR NAGALAND

Article 371-A makes the following special provisions for Nagaland[3]:

1. The Acts of Parliament relating to the following matters would not apply to Nagaland unless the State Legislative Assembly so decides:
   (i) religious or social practices of the Nagas;
   (ii) Naga customary law and procedure;
   (iii) administration of civil and criminal justice involving decisions according to Naga customary law; and
   (iv) ownership and transfer of land and its resources.
2. The Governor of Nagaland shall have special responsibility for law and order in the state so long as internal disturbances caused by the hostile Nagas continue. In the discharge of this responsibility, the Governor, after consulting the Council of Ministers, exercises his individual judgement and his decision is final[4]. This special responsibility of the Governor shall cease when the President so directs.
3. The Governor has to ensure that the money provided by the Central Government for any

specific purpose is included in the demand for a grant relating to that purpose and not in any other demand moved in the State Legislative Assembly.

4. A regional council consisting of 35 members should be established for the Tuensang district of the state. The Governor should make rules for the composition of the council, manner of choosing its members[5], their qualifications, term, salaries and allowances; the procedure and conduct of business of the council; the appointment of officers and staff of the council and their service conditions; and any other matter relating to the constitution and proper functioning of the council.

5. For a period of ten years from the formation of Nagaland or for such further period as the Governor may specify on the recommendation of the regional council, the following provisions would be operative for the Tuensang district:

   (i) The administration of the Tuensang district shall be carried on by the Governor.

   (ii) The Governor shall in his discretion arrange for equitable distribution of money provided by the Centre between Tuensang district and the rest of Nagaland.

   (iii) Any Act of Nagaland Legislature shall not apply to Tuensang district unless the Governor so directs on the recommendation of the regional council.

   (iv) The Governor can make Regulations for the peace, progress and good government of the Tuensang district. Any such Regulation may repeal or amend an Act of Parliament or any other law applicable to that district.

   (v) There shall be a Minister for Tuensang affairs in the State Council of Ministers. He is to be appointed from amongst the members representing Tuensang district in the Nagaland Legislative Assembly.

   (vi) The final decision on all matters relating to Tuensang district shall be made by the Governor in his discretion.

   (vii) Members in the Nagaland Legislative Assembly from the Tuensang district are not elected directly by the people but by the regional council.

PROVISIONS FOR ASSAM AND MANIPUR

Assam

Under Article 371-B[6], the President is empowered to provide for the creation of a committee of the Assam Legislative Assembly consisting of the members elected from the Tribal Areas of the state and such other members as he may specify[7].

Manipur

Article 371-C makes the following special provisions for Manipur[8]:

1. The President is authorized to provide for the creation of a committee of the Manipur Legislative Assembly consisting of the members elected from the Hill Areas of the state[9].

2. The President can also direct that the Governor shall have special responsibility to secure the proper functioning of that committee.

3. The Governor should submit an annual report to the President regarding the administration of the Hill Areas.

4. The Central Government can give directions to the State Government as to the administration of the Hill Areas.

PROVISIONS FOR ANDHRA PRADESH

Articles 371-D and 371-E contain the special provisions for Andhra Pradesh[10]. Under Article 371-D, the following are mentioned:

1. The President is empowered to provide for equitable opportunities and facilities for the people belonging to different parts of the state in the matter of public employment and education and different provisions can be made for various parts of the state.

2. For the above purpose, the President may require the State Government to organise civil posts in local cadres for different parts of the state and provide for direct recruitment to posts in any local cadre. He may specify parts of the state which shall be regarded as the local area for admission to any educational institution. He may also specify the extent and manner of

preference or reservation given in the matter of direct recruitment to posts in any such cadre or admission to any such educational institution.

3. The President may provide for the establishment of an Administrative Tribunal in the state to deal with certain disputes and grievances relating to appointment, allotment or promotion to civil posts in the state[11]. The tribunal is to function outside the purview of the state High Court. No court (other than the Supreme Court) is to exercise any jurisdiction in respect of any matter subject to the jurisdiction of the tribunal. The President may abolish the tribunal when he is satisfied that its continued existence is not necessary.

Article 371-E empowers the Parliament to provide for the establishment of a Central University in the state.

PROVISIONS FOR SIKKIM

The 36th Constitutional Amendment Act of 1975 made Sikkim a full-fledged state of the Indian Union. It included a new Article 371-F containing special provisions with respect to Sikkim. These are as follows:

1. The Sikkim Legislative Assembly is to consist of not less than 30 members.
2. One seat is allotted to Sikkim in the Lok Sabha and Sikkim forms one Parliamentary constituency.
3. For the purpose of protecting the rights and interests of the different sections of the Sikkim population, the Parliament is empowered to provide for the:
   (i) number of seats in the Sikkim Legislative Assembly which may be filled by candidates belonging to such sections; and
   (ii) delimitation of the Assembly constituencies from which candidates belonging to such sections alone may stand for election to the Assembly.
4. The Governor shall have special responsibility for peace and for an equitable arrangement for ensuring the social and economic advancement of the different sections of the Sikkim popula-

tion. In the discharge of this responsibility, the Governor shall act in his discretion, subject to the directions issued by the President.

5. The President can extend (with restrictions or modifications) to Sikkim any law which is in force in a state of the Indian Union.

PROVISIONS FOR MIZORAM

Article 371-G specifies the following special provisions for Mizoram[12] :

1. The Acts of Parliament relating to the following matters would not apply to Mizoram unless the State Legislative Assembly so decides :
   (i) religious or social practices of the Mizos;
   (ii) Mizo customary law and procedure;
   (iii) administration of civil and criminal justice involving decisions according to Mizo customary law; and
   (iv) ownership and transfer of land.
2. The Mizoram Legislative Assembly is to consist of not less than 40 members.

PROVISIONS FOR ARUNACHAL PRADESH AND GOA

Arunachal Pradesh

Under Article 371-H, the following special provisions are made for Arunachal Pradesh[13]:

1. The Governor of Arunachal Pradesh shall have special responsibility for law and order in the state. In the discharge of this responsibility, the Governor, after consulting the Council of Ministers, exercises his individual judgement and his decision is final. This special responsibility of the Governor shall cease when the President so directs.
2. The Arunachal Pradesh Legislative Assembly is to consist of not less than 30 members.

Goa

Article 371-I provides that the Goa Legislative Assembly is to consist of not less than 30 members[14].

PROVISIONS FOR KARNATAKA

Under Article 371-J, the President is empowered to provide that the Governor of Karnataka would have special responsibility for

1. The establishment of a separate development board for Hyderabad-Karnataka region[15]
2. Making a provision that a report on the working of the board would be placed every year before the State Legislative Assembly
3. The equitable allocation of funds for developmental expenditure over the region
4. The reservation of seats in educational and vocational training institutions in the region for students who belong to the region
5. The reservation in state government posts in the region for persons who belong to the region

Article 371-J (which provided for special provisions for the Hyderabad-Karnataka region of the state of Karnataka) was inserted in the Constitution by the *98th Constitutional Amendment Act* of 2012. The special provisions aim to establish an institutional mechanism for equitable allocation of funds to meet the development needs over the region, as well as to enhance human resources and promote employment from the region by providing for local cadres in service and reservation in educational and vocational training institutions.

In 2010, the Legislative Assembly as well as the Legislative Council of Karnataka passed separate resolutions seeking special provisions for the Hyderabad-Karnataka region of the state of Karnataka. The government of Karnataka also endorsed the need for special provisions for the region. The resolutions sought to accelerate development of the most backward region of the state and promote inclusive growth with a view to reducing inter-district and inter-regional disparities in the state.

Table 33.1 *Articles Related to Special Provisions for some States at a Glance*

Article No.	Subject-matter
371.	Special provision with respect to the states of Maharashtra and Gujarat
371A.	Special provision with respect to the state of Nagaland
371B.	Special provision with respect to the state of Assam
371C.	Special provision with respect to the state of Manipur
371D.	Special provisions with respect to the state of Andhra Pradesh
371E.	Establishment of Central University in Andhra Pradesh
371F.	Special provisions with respect to the state of Sikkim
371G.	Special provision with respect to the state of Mizoram
371H.	Special provision with respect to the state of Arunachal Pradesh
371-I.	Special provision with respect to the state of Goa
371J.	Special provisions with respect to the state of Karnataka

NOTES AND REFERENCES

1. Part XXI is entitled as 'Temporary, Transitional and Special Provisions'.
2. This Article was amended by the 7th Constitutional Amendment Act of 1956 and the Bombay Reorganisation Act of 1960. Andhra Pradesh was taken out of this Article by the 32nd Constitutional Amendment Act of 1973 and provided for separately in two new Articles 371-D and 371-E.

3. This Article was added by the 13th Constitutional Amendment Act of 1962.

4. The validity of anything done by the Governor shall not be called in question on the ground that he ought or ought not to have acted in the exercise of his individual judgement.

5. The Deputy Commissioner of the Tuensang district shall be the ex-officio Chairman of the regional council and the Vice-Chairman shall be elected by the members of the council from amongst themselves.

6. This Article was added by the 22nd Constitutional Amendment Act of 1969.

7. The Tribal Areas of Assam are specified in the Sixth Schedule of the Constitution. They are North Cachar Hills District, Karbi Anglong District and Bodoland Territorial Areas District.

8. This Article was added by the 27th Constitutional Amendment Act of 1971.

9. In this Article, the expression 'Hill Areas' means such areas as the President may, by order, declare to be Hill Areas.

10. Both the Articles were added by the 32nd Constitutional Amendment Act of 1973.

11. The tribunal has been set up by the Andhra Pradesh Administrative Tribunal Order, 1975.

12. This Article was added by the 53rd Constitutional Amendment Act of 1986.

13. This Article was added by the 55th Constitutional Amendment Act of 1986.

14. This Article was added by the 56th Constitutional Amendment Act of 1987.

15. The Hyderabad – Karnataka region includes the six backward districts of Northern Karnataka, viz., Gulbarga, Bidar, Raichur, Koppal, Yadgir and Bellary.

PART V

LOCAL GOVERNMENT

Panchayati Raj

The term *Panchayati Raj* in India signifies the system of rural local self-government. It has been established in all the states of India by the Acts of the state legislatures to build democracy at the grass root level[1]. It is entrusted with rural development. It was constitutionalised through the 73rd Constitutional Amendment Act of 1992.

EVOLUTION OF PANCHAYATI RAJ

Balwant Rai Mehta Committee

In January 1957, the Government of India appointed a committee to examine the working of the Community Development Programme (1952) and the National Extension Service (1953) and to suggest measures for their better working. The chairman of this committee was Balwant Rai G Mehta. The committee submitted its report in November 1957 and recommended the establishment of the scheme of 'democratic decentralisation', which ultimately came to be known as Panchayati Raj. The specific recommendations made by it are:

1. Establishment of a three-tier panchayati raj system—gram panchayat at the village level, panchayat samiti at the block level and zila parishad at the district level. These tiers should be organically linked through a device of indirect elections.

2. The village panchayat should be constituted with directly elected representatives, whereas the panchayat samiti and zila parishad should be constituted with indirectly elected members.

3. All planning and development activities should be entrusted to these bodies.

4. The panchayat samiti should be the executive body while the zila parishad should be the advisory, coordinating and supervisory body.

5. The district collector should be the chairman of the zila parishad.

6. There should be a genuine transfer of power and responsibility to these democratice bodies.

7. Adequate resources should be transferred to these bodies to enable them to discharge their functions and fulfil their responsibilities.

8. A system should be evolved to effect further devolution of authority in future.

These recommendations of the committee were accepted by the National Development Council in January 1958. The council did not insist on a single rigid pattern and left it to the states to evolve their own patterns suitable to local conditions. But the basic principles and broad fundamentals should be identical throughout the country.

Rajasthan was the first state to establish Panchayati Raj. The scheme was inaugurated by the prime minister on October 2, 1959, in Nagaur district. Rajasthan was followed by Andhra Pradesh, which also adopted the system in 1959. Thereafter, most of the states adopted the system.

Though most of the states created panchayati raj institutions by mid 1960s, there were differences from one state to another with regard to the number of tiers, relative position of samiti and parishad, their tenure, composition, functions, finances and so on. For example, Rajasthan adopted the three-tier system while Tamil Nadu adopted the two-tier system. West Bengal, on the other hand, adopted the four-tier system. Further, in the Rajasthan–Andhra Pradesh pattern, panchayat samiti was powerful as the block was the unit of planning and development, while in Maharashtra–Gujarat pattern, zila parishad was powerful as the district was the unit of planning and development. Some states also established nyaya panchayats, that is, judicial panchayats to try petty civil and criminal cases.

Study Teams and Committees

Since 1960, many study teams, committees and working groups have been appointed to examine the various aspects of functioning of Panchayati Raj system. They are mentioned below in Table 34.1.

Table 34.1   *Study Teams and Committees on Panchayati Raj*

Sl. No.	Year	Name of the study Team / Committee	Chairman
1.	1960	Committee on Rationalisation of Panchayat Statistics	V.R. Rao
2.	1961	Working Group on Panchayats and Cooperatives	S.D. Mishra
3.	1961	Study Team on Panchayati Raj Administration	V. Iswaran
4.	1962	Study Team on Nyaya Panchayats	G.R. Rajgopal
5.	1963	Study Team on the Position of Gram Sabha in Panchayati Raj Movement	R.R. Diwakar
6.	1963	Study Group on Budgeting and Accounting Procedure of Panchayati Raj Institutions	M. Rama Krishnayya
7.	1963	Study Team on Panchayati Raj Finances	K. Santhanam
8.	1965	Committee on Panchayati Raj Elections	K. Santhanam
9.	1965	Study Team on the Audit and Accounts of Panchayati Raj Bodies	R.K. Khanna
10.	1966	Committee on Panchayati Raj Training Centres	G. Ramachandran
11.	1969	Study Team on Involvement of Community Development Agency and Panchayati Raj Institutions in the Implementation of Basic Land Reform Measures	V. Ramanathan
12.	1972	Working Group for Formulation of Fifth Five Year Plan on Community Development and Panchayati Raj	N. Ramakrishnayya
13.	1976	Committee on Community Development and Panchayati Raj	Smt. Daya Choubey

Ashok Mehta Committee

In December 1977, the Janata Government appointed a committee on panchayati raj institutions under the chairmanship of Ashok Mehta. It submitted its report in August 1978 and made 132 recommendations to revive and strengthen the declining panchayati raj system in the country. Its main recommendations were:

1. The three-tier system of panchayati raj should be replaced by the two-tier system, that is, zila parishad at the district level, and below it, the mandal panchayat consisting of a group of villages with a total population of 15,000 to 20,000.

2. A district should be the first point for decentralisation under popular supervision below the state level.

3. Zila parishad should be the executive body and made responsible for planning at the district level.

4. There should be an official participation of political parties at all levels of panchayat elections.

5. The panchayati raj institutions should have compulsory powers of taxation to mobilise their own financial resourses.

6. There should be a regular social audit by a district level agency and by a committee of legislators to check whether the funds allotted for the vulnerable social and economic groups are actually spent on them.

7. The state government should not supersede the panchayati raj institutions. In case of an imperative supersession, elections should be held within six months from the date of supersession.

8. The nyaya panchayats should be kept as separate bodies from that of development panchayats. They should be presided over by a qualified judge.

9. The chief electoral officer of a state in consultation with the chief election commissioner should organise and conduct the panchayati raj elections.

10. Development functions should be transferred to the zila parishad and all development staff should work under its control and supervision.

11. The voluntary agencies should play an important role in mobilising the support of the people for panchayati raj.

12. A minister for panchayati raj should be appointed in the state council of ministers to look after the affairs of the panchayati raj institutions.

13. Seats for SCs and STs should be reserved on the basis of their population.

14. A constitutional recognition should be accorded to the Panchayati Raj institutions. This would give them the requisite status (sanctity and stature) and an assurance of continuous functioning.

Due to the collapse of the Janata Government before the completion of its term, no action could be taken on the recommendations of the Ashok Mehta Committee at the central level. However, the three states of Karnataka, West Bengal and Andhra Pradesh took steps to revitalise the panchayati raj, keeping in view some of the recommendations of the Ashok Mehta Committee.

G V K Rao Committee

The Committee on Administrative Arrangement for Rural Development and Poverty Alleviation Programmes under the chairmanship of G.V.K. Rao was appointed by the Planning Commission in 1985. The Committee came to conclusion that the developmental process was gradually bureaucratised and divorced from the Panchayati Raj. This phenomena of bureaucratisation of development administration as against the democratisation weakened the Panchayati Raj institutions resulting in what is aptly called as 'grass without roots'. Hence, the Committee made the following recommendations to strengthen and revitalise the Panchayati Raj system:

(i) The district level body, that is, the Zila Parishad should be of pivotal importance in the scheme of democratic decentralisation. It stated that "the district is the proper unit for planning and development and the Zila Parishad should become the principal body for management of all development programmes which can be handled at that level."

(ii) The Panchayati Raj institutions at the district and lower levels should be assigned an important role with respect to planning, implementation and monitoring of rural development programmes.

(iii) Some of the planning functions at the state level should be transferred to the district level planning units for effective decentralized district planning.

(iv) A post of District Development Commissioner should be created. He should act as the chief executive officer of the Zila Parishad and should be in charge of all the development departments at the district level.

(v) Elections to the Panchayati Raj institutions should be held regularly. It found that elections became overdue for one or more tiers in 11 states.

Thus the committee, in its scheme of decentralised system of field administration, assigned a leading role to the Panchayati Raj in local planning and development. It is in this respect that the recommendation of the G.V.K. Rao Committee Report (1986) differed from those of the Dantwala Committee Report on Block-Level Planning (1978) and the Hanumantha Rao Committee Report on District Planning (1984). Both the committees have suggested that the basic decentralised planning function should be done at the district level. The Hanumantha Rao Committee advocated separate district planning bodies under either the District Collector or a minister. In both the models, the Collector should play a significant role in the decentralised planning though the Committee stated that Panchayati Raj institutions would also be associated with this process (of decentralised planning). The committee recommended that the Collector should be the coordinator, at the district level, of all developmental and planning activities. Thus the, Hanumantha Rao Committee differed in this respect from those of Balwantray Mehta Committee, the Administrative Reforms Commission of India, the Ashok Mehta Committee and finally the G.V.K. Rao Committee which recommended reduction in the developmental role of the District Collector and which assigned a major role to the Panchayati Raj in development administration.

L M Singhvi Committee

In 1986, Rajiv Gandhi government appointed a committee on 'Revitalisation of Panchayati Raj Institutions for Democracy and Development' under the chairmanship of L M Singhvi. It made the following recommendations.

  (i) The Panchayati Raj institutions should be constitutionally recognised, protected and preserved. For this purpose, a new chapter should be added in the Constitution of India. This will make their identity and integrity reasonably and substantially inviolate. It also suggested constitutional provisions to ensure regular, free and fair elections to the Panchayati Raj bodies.

  (ii) Nyaya Panchayats should be established for a cluster of villages.

  (iii) The villages should be reorganised to make Gram Panchayats more viable. It also emphasised the importance of the Gram Sabha and called it as the embodiment of direct democracy.

  (iv) The Village Panchayats should have more financial resources.

  (v) The judicial tribunals should be established in each state to adjudicate controversies about election to the Panchayati Raj institutions,

their dissolution and other matters related to their functioning.

Constitutionalisation

Rajiv Gandhi Government The Rajiv Gandhi Government introduced the 64th Constitutional Amendment Bill in the Lok Sabha in July 1989 to constitutionalise panchayati raj institutions and make them more powerful and broad based. Although, the Lok Sabha passed the bill in August 1989, it was not approved by the Rajya Sabha. The bill was vehemently opposed by the Opposition on the ground that it sought to strengthen centralisation in the federal system.

V P Singh Government The National Front Government, soon after assuming office in November 1989 under the Prime Ministership of V P Singh, announced that it would take steps to strengthen the panchayati raj institutions. In June 1990, a two-day conference of the state chief ministers under the chairmanship of V P Singh was held to discuss the issues relating to the strengthening of the panchayati raj bodies. The conference approved the proposals for the introduction of a fresh constitutional amendment bill. Consequently, a constitutional amendment bill was introduced in the Lok Sabha in September 1990. However, the fall of the government resulted in the lapse of the bill.

Narasimha Rao Government The Congress Government under the prime ministership of P V Narasimha Rao once again considered the matter of the constitutionalisation of panchayati raj bodies. It drastically modified the proposals in this regard to delete the controversial aspects and introduced a constitutional amendment bill in the Lok Sabha in September, 1991. This bill finally emerged as the 73rd Constitutional Amendment Act, 1992 and came into force on 24 April, 1993[2].

73RD AMENDMENT ACT OF 1992

Significance of the Act

This act has added a new Part-IX to the Constitution of India. It is entitled as 'The Panchayats' and consists of provisions from Articles 243 to 243 O. In addition, the act has also added a new Eleventh

Schedule to the Constitution. This schedule contains 29 functional items of the panchayats. It deals with Article 243-G.

The act has given a practical shape to Article 40 of the Constitution which says that, "The State shall take steps to organise village panchayats and endow them with such powers and authority as may be necessary to enable them to function as units of self-government." This article forms a part of the Directive Principles of State Policy.

The act gives a constitutional status to the panchayati raj institutions. It has brought them under the purview of the justiciable part of the Constitution. In other words, the state governments are under constitutional obligation to adopt the new panchayati raj system in accordance with the provisions of the act. Consequently, neither the formation of panchayats nor the holding of elections at regular intervals depend on the will of the state government any more.

The provisions of the act can be grouped into two categories—compulsory and voluntary. The compulsory (mandatory or obligatory) provisions of the act have to be included in the state laws creating the new panchayati raj system. The voluntary provisions, on the other hand, may be included at the discretion of the states. Thus the voluntary provisions of the act ensures the right of the states to take local factors like geographical, politico–administrative and others, into consideration while adopting the new panchayati raj system.

The act is a significant landmark in the evolution of grassroot democratic institutions in the country. It transfers the representative democracy into participatory democracy. It is a revolutionary concept to build democracy at the grassroot level in the country.

Salient Features

The salient features of the act are:

Gram Sabha   The act provides for a Gram Sabha as the foundation of the panchayati raj system. It is a body consisting of persons registered in the electoral rolls of a village comprised within the area of Panchayat at the village level. Thus, it is a village assembly consisting of all the registered voters in the area of a panchayat. It may exercise such powers and perform such functions at the village level as the legislature of a state determines.

Three-Tier System   The act provides for a three-tier system of panchayati raj in every state, that is, panchayats at the village, intermediate, and district levels[3]. Thus, the act brings about uniformity in the structure of panchayati raj throughout the country. However, a state having a population not exceeding 20 lakh may not constitute panchayats at the intermediate level.

Election of Members and Chairpersons   All the members of panchayats at the village, intermediate and district levels shall be elected directly by the people. Further, the chairperson of panchayats at the intermediate and district levels shall be elected indirectly—by and from amongst the elected members thereof. However, the chairperson of a panchayat at the village level shall be elected in such manner as the state legislature determines.

Reservation of Seats   The act provides for the reservation of seats for scheduled castes and scheduled tribes in every panchayat (i.e., at all the three levels) in proportion of their population to the total population in the panchayat area. Further, the state legislature shall provide for the reservation of offices of chairperson in the panchayat at the village or any other level for the SCs and STs.

The act provides for the reservation of not less than one-third of the total number of seats for women (including the number of seats reserved for women belonging the SCs and STs). Further, not less than one-third of the total number of offices of chairpersons in the panchayats at each level shall be reserved for women.

The act also authorises the legislature of a state to make any provision for reservation of seats in any panchayat or offices of chairperson in the panchayat at any level in favour of backward classes.

Duration of Panchayats   The act provides for a five-year term of office to the panchayat at every level. However, it can be dissolved before the completion of its term. Further, fresh elections to constitute a panchayat shall be completed (a) before the expiry of its duration of five years; or (b) in case of dissolution, before the expiry of a period of six months from the date of its dissolution.

Disqualifications   A person shall be disqualified for being chosen as or for being a member of panchayat if he is so disqualified, (a) under any law for the time being in force for the purpose of elections to the legislature of the state concerned, or (b) under any law made by the state legislature. However, no person shall be disqualified on the ground that he is less than 25 years of age if he has attained the age of 21 years. Further, all questions of disqualifications shall be referred to such authority as the state legislature determines.

State Election Commission   The superintendence, direction and control of the preparation of electoral rolls and the conduct of all elections to the panchayats shall be vested in the state election commission. It consists of a state election commissioner to be appointed by the governor. His conditions of service and tenure of office shall also be determined by the governor. He shall not be removed from the office except in the manner and on the grounds prescribed for the removal of a judge of the state high court[4]. His conditions of service shall not be varied to his disadvantage after his appointment.

The state legislature may make provision with respect to all matters relating to elections to the panchayats.

Powers and Functions   The state legislature may endow the Panchayats with such powers and authority as may be necessary to enable them to function as institutions of self-government. Such a scheme may contain provisions for the devolution of powers and responsibilities upon Panchayats at the appropriate level with respect to (a) the preparation of plans for economic development and social justice; (b) the implementation of schemes for economic development and social justice as may be entrusted to them, including those in relation to the 29 matters listed in the Eleventh Schedule.

Finances   The state legislature may (a) authorise a panchayat to levy, collect and appropriate taxes, duties, tolls and fees; (b) assign to a panchayat taxes, duties, tolls and fees levied and collected by the state government; (c) provide for making grants-in-aid to the panchayats from the consolidated fund of the state; and (d) provide for constitution of funds for crediting all moneys of the panchayats.

Finance Commission   The governor of a state shall, after every five years, constitute a finance commission to review the financial position of the panachayats. It shall make the following recommendations to the Governor:

1. The principles that should govern:
    (a) The distribution between the state and the panchayats of the net proceeds of the taxes, duties, tolls and fees levied by the state.
    (b) The determination of taxes, duties, tolls and fees that may be assigned to the panchayats.
    (c) The grants-in-aid to the panchayats from the consolidated fund of the state.
2. The measures needed to improve the financial position of the panchayats.
3. Any other matter referred to it by the governor in the interests of sound finance of the panchayats.

The state legislature may provide for the composition of the commission, the required qualifications of its members and the manner of their selection.

The governor shall place the recommendations of the commission along with the action taken report before the state legislature.

The Central Finance Commission shall also suggest the measures needed to augment the consolidated fund of a state to supplement the resources of the panchayats in the states (on the basis of the recommendations made by the finance commission of the state).

Audit of Accounts   The state legislature may make provisions with respect to the maintenance of accounts by the panchayats and the auditing of such accounts.

Application to Union Territories   The president of India may direct that the provisions of this act shall apply to any union territory subject to such exceptions and modifications as he may specify.

Exempted States and Areas   The act does not apply to the states of Jammu and Kashmir, Nagaland, Meghalaya and Mizoram and certain other areas. These areas include, (a) the scheduled areas and the tribal areas in the states[5]; (b) the hill area of Manipur for which a district council exists; and (c) Darjeeling district of West Bengal for which Darjeeling Gorkha Hill Council exists.

However, the Parliament may extend the provisions of this Part to the scheduled areas subject to such exceptions and modifications as it may specify. Under this provision, the Parliament has enacted the 'Provisions of the Panchayats (Extension to the Scheduled Areas) Act', 1996 (PESA).

Continuance of Existing Laws and Panchayats All the state laws relating to panchayats shall continue to be in force until the expiry of one year from the commencement of this act. In other words, the states have to adopt the new panchayati raj system based on this act within the maximum period of one year from 24 April, 1993, which was the date of the commencement of this act. However, all the panchayats existing immediately before the commencement of act shall continue till the expiry of their term, unless dissolved by the state legislature sooner.

Consequently, majority of states passed the panchayati raj acts in 1993 and 1994 to adopt the new system in accordance with the 73rd Constitutional Amendment Act of 1992.

Bar to Interference by Courts in Electoral Matters The act bars the interference by courts in the electoral matters of panchayats. It declares that the validity of any law relating to the delimitation of constituencies or the allotment of seats to such constituencies cannot be questioned in any court. It further lays down that no election to any panchayat is to be questioned except by an election petition presented to such authority and in such manner as provided by the state legislature.

Eleventh Schedule It contains the following 29 functional items placed within the purview of panchayats:

1. Agriculture, including agricultural extension
2. Land improvement, implementation of land reforms, land consolidation and soil conservation
3. Minor irrigation, water management and watershed development
4. Animal husbandry, dairying and poultry
5. Fisheries
6. Social forestry and farm forestry
7. Minor forest produce

8. Small-scale industries, including food processing industries
9. Khadi, village and cottage industries
10. Rural housing
11. Drinking water
12. Fuel and fodder
13. Roads, culverts, bridges, ferries, waterways and other means of communication
14. Rural electrification, including distribution of electricity
15. Non-conventional energy sources
16. Poverty alleviation programme
17. Education, including primary and secondary schools
18. Technical training and vocational education
19. Adult and non-formal education
20. Libraries
21. Cultural activities
22. Markets and fairs
23. Health and sanitation including hospitals, primary health centres and dispensaries
24. Family welfare
25. Women and child development
26. Social welfare, including welfare of the handicapped and mentally retarded
27. Welfare of the weaker sections, and in particular, of the scheduled castes and the scheduled tribes
28. Public distribution system
29. Maintenance of community assets.

COMPULSORY AND VOLUNTARY PROVISIONS

Now, we will identify separately the compulsory (obligatory or mandatory) and voluntary (discretionary or optional) provisions (features) of the 73rd Constitutional Amendment Act (1992) or the Part IX of the Constitution:

A. Compulsory Provisions

1. Organisation of Gram Sabha in a village or group of villages.
2. Establishment of panchayats at the village, intermediate and district levels.
3. Direct elections to all seats in panchayats at the village, intermediate and district levels.

4. Indirect elections to the post of chairperson of panchayats at the intermediate and district levels.

5. 21 years to be the minimum age for contesting elections to panchayats.

6. Reservation of seats (both members and chairpersons) for SCs and STs in panchayats at all the three levels.

7. Reservation of one-third seats (both members and chairpersons) for women in panchayats at all the three levels.

8. Fixing tenure of five years for panchayats at all levels and holding fresh elections within six months in the event of supersession of any panchayat.

9. Establishment of a State Election Commission for conducting elections to the panchayats.

10. Constitution of a State Finance Commission after every five years to review the financial position of the panchayats.

B. Voluntary Provisions

1. Giving representation to members of the Parliament (both the Houses) and the state legislature (both the Houses) in the panchayats at different levels falling within their constituencies.

2. Providing reservation of seats (both members and chairpersons) for backward classes in panchayats at any level.

3. Granting powers and authority to the panchayats to enable them to function as institutions of self-government (in brief, making them autonomous bodies).

4. Devolution of powers and responsibilities upon panchayats to prepare plans for economic development and social justice; and to perform some or all of the 29 functions listed in the Eleventh Schedule of the Constitution.

5. Granting financial powers to the pachayats, that is, authorizing them to levy, collect and appropriate taxes, duties, tolls and fees.

PESA ACT OF 1996 (EXTENSION ACT)

The provisions of Part IX of the constitution relating to the Panchayats are not applicable to the Fifth Schedule areas. However, the Parliament may extend

these provisions to such areas, subject to such exceptions and modifications as it may specify. Under this provision, the Parliament has enacted the "Provisions of the Panchayats (Extension to the Scheduled Areas) Act", 1996, popularly known as the PESA Act or the Extension Act.

At present (2013), nine states have Fifth Schedule Areas. These are: Andhra Pradesh, Chhatisgarh, Gujarat, Himachal Pradesh, Jharkhand, Madhya Pradesh, Maharashtra, Odisha and Rajasthan. All the nine states have enacted requisite compliance legislations by amending the respective Panchayati Raj Acts.

Objectives of the Act

The objectives of the PESA Act are as follows[6]:

1. To extend the provisions of Part IX of the Constitution relating to the panchayats to the scheduled areas with certain modifications

2. To provide self-rule for the bulk of the tribal population

3. To have village governance with participatory democracy and to make the gram sabha a nucleus of all activities

4. To evolve a suitable administrative framework consistent with traditional practices

5. To safeguard and to preserve the traditions and customs of tribal communities

6. To empower panchayats at the appropriate levels with specific powers conducive to tribal requirements

7. To prevent panchayats at the higher level from assuming the powers and authority of panchayats at the lower level of the gram sabha

Features of the Act

The features (or the provisions) of the PESA Act are as follows:

1. A state legislation on the Panchayats in the Scheduled Areas shall be in consonance with the customary law, social and religious practices and traditional management practices of community resources.

2. A village shall ordinarily consist of a habitation or a group of habitations or a hamlet or a group of hamlets comprising a community

and managing its affairs in accordance with traditions and customs.

3. Every village shall have a Gram Sabha consisting of persons whose names are included in the electoral rolls for the Panchayat at the village level.

4. Every Gram Sabha shall be competent to safeguard and preserve the traditions and customs of the people, their cultural identity, community resources and the customary mode of dispute resolution.

5. Every Gram Sabha shall—
   (i) approve of the plans, programmes and projects for social and economic development before they are taken up for implementation by the Panchayat at the village level; and
   (ii) be responsible for the identification of beneficiaries under the poverty alleviation and other programmes.

6. Every Panchayat at the village level shall be required to obtain from the Gram Sabha a certification of utilisation of funds for the above plans, programmes and projects.

7. The reservation of seats in the Scheduled Areas in every Panchayat shall be in proportion to the population of the communities for whom reservation is sought to be given under Part IX of the Constitution. However, the reservation for the Scheduled Tribes shall not be less than one-half of the total number of seats. Further, all seats of Chairpersons of Panchayats at all levels shall be reserved for the Scheduled Tribes.

8. The state government may nominate such Scheduled Tribes which have no representation in the Panchayat at the intermediate level or the Panchayat at the district level. But such nomination shall not exceed one-tenth of the total members to be elected in that Panchayat.

9. The Gram Sabha or the Panchayats at the appropriate level shall be consulted before making the acquisition of land in the Scheduled Areas for development projects and before resettling or rehabilitating persons affected by such projects in the Scheduled Areas. However, the actual planning and implementation of the projects in the Scheduled Areas shall be coordinated at the state level.

10. Planning and management of minor water bodies in the Scheduled Areas shall be entrusted to Panchayats at the appropriate level.

11. The recommendations of the Gram Sabha the Panchayats at the appropriate level shall be mandatory for grant of prospecting licence or mining lease for minor minerals in the Scheduled Areas.

12. The prior recommendation of the Gram Sabha or the Panchayats at the appropriate level shall be mandatory for grant of concession for the exploitation of minor minerals by auction.

13. While endowing Panchayats in the Scheduled Areas with such powers and authority as may be necessary to enable them to function as institutions of self-government, a State Legislature shall ensure that the Panchayats at the appropriate level and the Gram Sabha are endowed specifically with –
   (i) the power to enforce prohibition or to regulate or restrict the sale and consumption of any intoxicant
   (ii) the ownership of minor forest produce
   (iii) the power to prevent alienation of land in the Scheduled Areas and to take appropriate action to restore any unlawfully alienated land of a Scheduled Tribe
   (iv) the power to manage village markets
   (v) the power to exercise control over money lending to the Scheduled Tribes
   (vi) the power to exercise control over institutions and functionaries in all social sectors
   (vii) the power to control local plans and resources for such plans including tribal sub-plans

14. The State Legislations shall contain safeguards to ensure that Panchayats at the higher level do not assume the powers and authority of any Panchayat at the lower level or of the Gram Sabha.

15. The State Legislature shall endeavour to follow the pattern of the Sixth Schedule to the Constitution while designing the administrative arrangements in the Panchayats at district levels in the Scheduled Areas.

16. Any provision of any law (relating to Panchayats in the Scheduled Areas) which is inconsistent with the provisions of this Act

shall cease to be in force at the expiry of one year from the date on which this Act receives the assent of the President[7]. However, all the

Panchayats existing immediately before such date shall continue till the expiry of their term, unless dissolved by the State Legislature sooner.

Table 34.2 *Articles Related to Panchayats at a Glance*

Article No.	Subject-matter
243.	Definitions
243A.	Gram Sabha
243B.	Constitution of panchayats
243C.	Composition of panchayats
243D.	Reservation of seats
243E.	Duration of panchayats, and so on
243F.	Disqualifications for membership
243G.	Powers, authority and responsibilities of panchayats
243H.	Powers to impose taxes by, and funds of, the panchayats
243-I.	Constitution of finance commission to review financial position
243J.	Audit of accounts of panchayats
243K.	Elections to the panchayats
243L.	Application to union territories
243M.	Part not to apply to certain areas
243N.	Continuance of existing laws and panchayats
243-O.	Bar to interference by courts in electoral matters

Table 34.3 *Name and Number of Panchayats (2010)[8]*

Sl. No.	State	Panchayati Raj Institutions (including ADCs)	Number
1.	Andhra Pradesh	1. Gram Panchayats 2. Mandal Parishads 3. Zilla Parishads	21809 1097 22
2.	Arunachal Pradesh	1. Gram Panchayats 2. Anchal Samities 3. Zilla Parishads	1751 150 16
3.	Assam	1. Goan Panchayats 2. Anchalic Panchayats 3. Zilla Parishads 4. Autonomous District Councils	2202 185 20 4
4.	Bihar	1. Village Panchayats 2. Panchayat Samities 3. Zilla Parishads	8463 531 38

(Contd.)

Sl. No.	State	Panchayati Raj Institutions (including ADCs)	Number
5.	Chattisgarh	1. Gram Panchayats	9820
		2. Janpad Panchayats	146
		3. Zilla Panchayats	16
6.	Goa	1. Village Panchayats	189
		2. Zilla Panchayats	2
7.	Gujarat	1. Village Panchayats	13738
		2. Taluka Panchayats	224
		3. District Panchayats	26
8.	Haryana	1. Gram Panchayats	6187
		2. Panchayat Samities	119
		3. Zilla Parishads	19
9.	Himachal Pradesh	1. Gram Panchayats	3243
		2. Panchayat Samities	75
		3. Zilla Panchayats	12
10.	Jammu & Kashmir	1. Halqa Panchayats	4139
11.	Jharkhand	1. Gram Panchayats	4562
		2. Panchayat Samities	212
		3. Zilla Panchayats	24
12.	Karnataka	1. Gram Panchayats	5652
		2. Taluka Panchayats	176
		3. Zilla Panchayats	29
13.	Kerala	1. Village Panchayats	999
		2. Block Panchayats	152
		3. District Panchayats	14
14.	Madhya Pradesh	1. Village Panchayats	23040
		2. Block Panchayats	313
		3. District Panchayats	48
15.	Maharashtra	1. Village Panchayats	27916
		2. Panchayat Samities	351
		3. Zilla Parishads	33
16.	Manipur	1. Gram Panchayats	165
		2. Zilla Panchayats	4
		3. Autonomous District Councils	6
17.	Meghalaya	1. Autonomous District Councils	3
18.	Mizoram	1. Village Councils	707
19.	Nagaland	1. Village Councils	1110
20.	Odisha	1. Gram Panchayats	6234
		2. Panchayat Samities	314
		3. Zilla Parishads	30
21.	Punjab	1. Gram Panchayats	12447
		2. Panchayat Samities	141
		3. Zilla Parishads	20

(Contd.)

Sl. No.	State	Panchayati Raj Institutions (including ADCs)	Number
22.	Rajasthan	1. Gram Panchayats 2. Panchayat Samities 3. Zilla Parishads	9184 237 32
23.	Sikkim	1. Gram Panchayats 2. Zilla Panchayats	163 4
24.	Tamil Nadu	1. Village Panchayats 2. Panchayat Unions 3. District Panchayats	12618 385 29
25.	Tripura	1. Gram Panchayats 2. Panchayat Samities 3. Zilla Panchayats 4. Autonomous District Councils	513 23 4 1
26.	Uttar Pradesh	1. Gram Panchayats 2. Kshetra Panchayats 3. Zilla Panchayats	52000 820 70
27.	Uttarakhand	1. Gram Panchayats 2. Intermediate Panchayats 3. District Panchayats	7227 95 13
28.	West Bengal	1. Gram Panchayats 2. Panchayat Samities 3. Zilla Parishads	3354 341 18
	All India	1. Gram / Village Panchayats (including Village Councils) 2. Panchayat Samities 3. Zilla Panchayats 4. Autonomous District Councils	239432 6087 543 14

Table 34.4 *Milestones in the Evolution of Panchayati Raj*[9]

I. Towards First Generation Panchayats	
1948-49	Constituent Assembly debates on the role of Panchayati Raj in Indian polity
1950	The Constitution of India comes into force on 26 January; Directive Principles of State Policy mention village panchayats as 'units of self-government' (Art 40)
1952	Community Development Programme starts on 2nd October
1957	Balvantrai Mehta Committee, appointed in January, submits its report on 24 November
1958-60	Several state governments enact new Panchayat Acts bringing in three-tier panchayat system
1959	Jawaharlal Nehru inaugurates the first generation panchayat at Nagaur in Rajasthan on 2nd October Kerala District Council Bill is introduced in Kerala Assembly; lapses after Assembly is dissolved
1964-77	Decline of first generation Panchayati Raj Institutions

(Contd.)

II. Growth and Decline of Second Generation Panchayats

1978	Panchayat elections are held in West Bengal on party basis on 4th June—marking the beginning of second generation of Panchayati Raj. Ashok Mehta Committee on working of panchayats, appointed on 12 December 1977, submits its report on 21 August
1983	Karnataka government enacts new PR Act
1984	Hanumantha Rao Committee on district level planning, appointed by Planning Commission in September 1982, submits its report in May
1985	Karnataka PR Act receives President's assent in July; comes into force on 14th August
1985	G.V.K. Rao Committee on administrative aspects of rural development, appointed by Planning Commission on 25 March, submits its report in December
1986	Andhra Pradesh follows West Bengal and Karnataka Panchayati Raj Model
1987	Karnataka holds panchayat elections in January
1990-92	Panchayats are dissolved and brought under administrators in Karnataka

III. Constitutionalisation of Panchayati Raj

1986	L.M. Singhvi Committee submits its report on 27 November; recommends constitutional status for panchayats
1988	Consultative Committee of Parliament appoints a sub-committee under chairpersonship of P.K. Thungon to consider Constitutional Amendment
1989	64th Constitutional Amendment Bill is introduced in Parliament on 15 May; is defeated in Rajya Sabha on 15 October
1990	74th Constitutional Amendment Bill is introduced in Parliament on 7 September; lapses on dissolution of Lok Sabha
1991	72nd (Panchayats) and 73rd (Municipalities) Amendment Bills are introduced in Parliament; referred to the Parliament's Joint Select Committee in September
1992	Lok Sabha passes both the Bills on 22 December; Rajya Sabha passes them on 23 December
1993	73rd Amendment Act, 1992 comes into force on 24 April 74th Amendment Act, 1992 comes into force on 1 June
1993-94	All state governments pass Conformity Acts between 30 May, 1993 and 23 April, 1994
1994	Madhya Pradesh holds panchayat elections under the 73rd Amendment dispensation on 30 May
1996	Provisions of the Panchayats (Extension to the Scheduled Areas) Act, 1996, extending 73rd Amendment Act to Scheduled Areas, comes into force on 24 December. Kerala launches People's Plan Campaign on 16 August
2001	Bihar holds panchayat elections after 23 years (11-30 April)
2001	83rd Constitutional Amendment Act, 2000 amends Art. 243-M to dispense with reservations for Scheduled Castes in Arunachal Pradesh—paving way for panchayat elections in the only state yet to hold them under the new dispensation

NOTES AND REFERENCES

1. The subject of 'Local Government' is mentioned in the State List under the Seventh Schedule of the Constitution.

2. This bill was passed by the Lok Sabha on 22 December, 1992, and by the Rajya Sabha on 23 December, 1992. Later, it was approved by the 17 state assemblies and received the assent of the president on 20 April, 1993.

3. The Act defines all these terms in the following manner:

   (a) Panchayat means an institution (by whatever name called) of self-government for rural areas.

   (b) Village means a village specified by the governor by public notification to be a village for this purpose, and includes a group of villages so specified.

   (c) Intermediate level means a level between the village and district levels specified by the governor by public notification for this purpose.

   (d) District means a district in a state.

4. A judge of a high court can be removed from his office by the president on the recommendation of the Parliament. This means that a state election commissioner cannot be removed by the governor, though appointed by him.

5. At present (2013), nine states of India have scheduled areas. These are: Andhra Pradesh, Jharkhand, Chhatisgarh, Gujarat, Himachal Pradesh, Madhya Pradesh, Maharashtra, Odisha and Rajasthan. Presently (2013), there are a total of ten tribal areas (autonomous districts) in the four states of Assam (3), Meghalaya (3), Tripura (1) and Mizoram (3).

6. S.K. Singh, Panchayats in Scheduled Areas, Kurukshetra, May 2001, P.26.

7. This Act received the assent of the President on 24 December, 1996.

8. Report of the Thirteenth Finance Commission (2010-2015), Volume II, December 2009, P.424–426.

9. Panchayati Raj Update, October, 2002, Institute of Social Sciences, New Delhi.

Municipalities

The term 'Urban Local Government' in India signifies the governance of an urban area by the people through their elected representatives. The jurisdiction of an urban local government is limited to a specific urban area which is demarcated for this purpose by the state government[1].

There are eight types of urban local governments in India—municipal corporation, municipality, notified area committee, town area committee, cantonment board, township, port trust and special purpose agency.

The system of urban government was constitutionalised through the 74th Constitutional Amendment Act of 1992. At the Central level, the subject of 'urban local government' is dealt with by the following three ministries:

(i) Ministry of Urban Development, created as a separate ministry in 1985

(ii) Ministry of Defence in the case of cantonment boards

(iii) Ministry of Home Affairs in the case of Union Territories

EVOLUTION OF URBAN BODIES

Historical Perspective

The institutions of urban local government originated and developed in modern India during the period of British rule. The major events in this context are as follows:

(i) In 1687-88, the first municipal corporation in India was set up at Madras.

(ii) In 1726, the municipal corporations were set up in Bombay and Calcutta.

(iii) Lord Mayo's Resolution of 1870 on financial decentralisation visualised the development of local self-government institutions.

(iv) Lord Ripon's Resolution of 1882 has been hailed as the 'Magna Carta' of local self-government. He is called as the father of local-self government in India.

(v) The Royal Commission on decentralisation was appointed in 1907 and it submitted its report in 1909. Its chairman was Hobhouse.

(vi) Under the dyarchical scheme introduced in Provinces by the Government of India Act of 1919, local self-government became a transferred subject under the charge of a responsible Indian minister.

(vii) In 1924, the Cantonments Act was passed by the Central legislature.

(viii) Under the provincial autonomy scheme introduced by the Government of India Act of 1935, local self-government was declared a provincial subject.

Committees and Commissions

The committees and commissions appointed by the Central Government to improve the functioning of urban local governments are mentioned below in Table 35.1.

Table 35.1   *Committees and Commissions on Urban Local Governments*

Sl. No.	Year	Name of the Committee / Commission	Chairman
1.	1949–51	Local Finance Enquiry Committee	P.K. Wattal
2.	1953–54	Taxation Enquiry Commission	John Matthai
3.	1963–65	Committee on the Training of Municipal Employees	Nur-Ud-din Ahmed
4.	1963–66	Rural-Urban Relationship Committee	A.P. Jain
5.	1963	Committee of Ministers on Augmentation of Financial Resources of Urban Local Bodies	Rafiq Zakaria
6.	1965–68	Committee on Service Conditions of Municipal Employees	—
7.	1974	Committee on Budgetary Reform in Municipal Administration	Girijapati Mukharji
8.	1982	Study Group on Constitution, Powers and Laws of Urban Local Bodies and Municipal Corporations	K.N. Sahaya
9.	1985–88	National Commission on Urbanisation	C.M. Correa

In August 1989, the Rajiv Gandhi government introduced the 65th Constitutional Amendment Bill (i.e., Nagarpalika Bill) in the Lok Sabha. The bill aimed at strengthening and revamping the municipal bodies by conferring a constitutional status on them. Although the bill was passed in the Lok Sabha, it was defeated in the Rajya Sabha in October 1989 and hence, lapsed.

The National Front Government under V P Singh introduced the revised Nagarpalika Bill in the Lok Sabha again in September 1990. However, the bill was not passed and finally lapsed due to the dissolution of the Lok Sabha.

P V Narasimha Rao's Government also introduced the modified Municipalities Bill in the Lok Sabha in September 1991. It finally emerged as the 74th Constitutional Amendment Act of 1992 and came into force on 1 June 1993[2].

74TH AMENDMENT ACT OF 1992

This Act has added a new Part IX-A to the Constitution of India. It is entitled 'The Municipalities' and consists of provisions from Articles 243-P to 243-ZG. In addition, the act has also added a new Twelfth Schedule to the Constitution. This schedule contains eighteen functional items of municipalities. It deals with Article 243-W.

The act gave constitutional status to the municipalities. It has brought them under the purview of justiciable part of the Constitution. In other words, state governments are under constitutional obliga-

tion to adopt the new system of municipalities in accordance with the provisions of the act.

The act aims at revitalising and strengthening the urban governments so that they function effectively as units of local government.

Salient Features

The salient features of the act are:

Three Types of Municipalities   The act provides for the constitution of the following three types of municipalities in every state.

1. A *nagar panchayat* (by whatever name called) for a transitional area, that is, an area in transition from a rural area to an urban area.
2. A *municipal council* for a smaller urban area.
3. A *municipal corporation* for a larger urban area[3].

Composition   All the members of a municipality shall be elected directly by the people of the municipal area. For this purpose, each municipal area shall be divided into territorial constituencies to be known as wards. The state legislature may provide the manner of election of the chairperson of a municipality. It may also provide for the representation of the following persons in a municipality.

1. Persons having special knowledge or experience in municipal administration without the right to vote in the meetings of municipality.
2. The members of the Lok Sabha and the state legislative assembly representing constituen-

cies that comprise wholly or partly the municipal area.

3. The members of the Rajya Sabha and the state legislative council registered as electors within the municipal area.
4. The chairpersons of committees (other than wards committees).

Wards Committees There shall be constituted a wards committee, consisting of one or more wards, within the territorial area of a municipality having population of three lakh or more. The state legislature may make provision with respect to the composition and the territorial area of a wards committee and the manner in which the seats in a wards committee shall be filled. It may also make any provision for the constitution of committees in addition to the wards committees.

Reservation of Seats The act provides for the reservation of seats for the scheduled castes and the scheduled tribes in every municipality in proportion of their population to the total population in the municipal area. Further, it provides for the reservation of not less than one-third of the total number of seats for women (including the number of seats reserved for woman belonging to the SCs and the STs).

The state legislature may provide for the manner of reservation of offices of chairpersons in the municipalities for SCs, STs and women. It may also make any provision for the reservation of seats in any municipality or offices of chairpersons in municipalities in favour of backward classes.

Duration of Municipalities The act provides for a five-year term of office for every municipality. However, it can be dissolved before the completion of its term. Further, the fresh elections to constitute a municipality shall be completed (a) before the expiry of its duration of five years; or (b) in case of dissolution, before the expiry of a period of six months from the date of its dissolution.

Disqualifications A person shall be disqualified for being chosen as or for being a member of a municipality if he is so disqualified (a) under any law for the time being in force for the purposes of elections to the legislature of the state concerned; or (b) under any law made by the state legislature. However, no person shall be disqualified on the ground that he is less than 25 years of age if he has attained the age of 21 years. Further, all questions of disqualifications shall be referred to such authority as the state legislature determines.

State Election Commission The superintendence, direction and control of the preparation of electoral rolls and the conduct of all elections to the municipalities shall be vested in the state election commission.

The state legislature may make provision with respect to all matters relating to elections to the municipalities.

Powers and Functions The state legislature may endow the municipalities with such powers and authority as may be necessary to enable them to function as institutions of self-government. Such a scheme may contain provisions for the devolution of powers and responsibilities upon municipalities at the appropriate level with respect to (a) the preparation of plans for economic development and social justice; (b) the implementation of schemes for economic development and social justice as may be entrusted to them, including those in relation to the eighteen matters listed in the Twelfth Schedule.

Finances The state legislature may (a) authorise a municipality to levy, collect and appropriate taxes, duties, tolls and fees; (b) assign to a municipality taxes, duties, tolls and fees levied and collected by state government; (c) provide for making grants-in-aid to the municipalities from the consolidated fund of the state; and (d) provide for constitution of funds for crediting all moneys of the municipalities.

Finance Commission The finance commission (which is constituted for the panchayats) shall also, for every five years, review the financial position of municipalities and make recommendation to the governor as to:

1. The principles that should govern:
   (a) The distribution between the state and the municipalities, the net proceeds of the taxes, duties, tolls and fees levied by the state.
   (b) The determination of the taxes, duties, tolls and fees that may be assigned to the municipalities.

(c) The grants-in-aid to the municipalities from the consolidated fund of the state.

2. The measures needed to improve the financial position of the municipalities.

3. Any other matter referred to it by the governor in the interests of sound finance of municipalities.

The governor shall place the recommendations of the commission along with the action taken report before the state legislature.

The central finance commission shall also suggest the measures needed to augment the consolidated fund of a state to supplement the resources of the municipalities in the state (on the basis of the recommendations made by the finance commission of the state).

Audit of Accounts The state legislature may make provisions with respect to the maintenance of accounts by municipalities and the auditing of such accounts.

Application to Union Territories The president of India may direct that the provisions of this act shall apply to any union territory subject to such exceptions and modifications as he may specify.

Exempted Areas The act does not apply to the scheduled areas and tribal areas in the states[4]. It shall also not affect the functions and powers of the Darjeeling Gorkha Hill Council of the West Bengal.

District Planning Committee Every state shall constitute at the district level, a district planning committee to consolidate the plans prepared by panchayats and municipalities in the district, and to prepare a draft development plan for the district as a whole. The state legislature may make provisions with respect to the following:

1. The composition of such committees;

2. The manner of election of members of such committees;

3. The functions of such committees in relation to district planning; and

4. The manner of the election of the chairpersons of such committees.

The act lays down that four-fifths of the members of a district planning committee should be elected by the elected members of the district panchayat and municipalities in the district from amongst themselves. The representation of these members in the committee should be in proportion to the ratio between the rural and urban populations in the district.

The chairperson of such committee shall forward the development plan to the state government.

In preparing the draft development plan, a district planning committee shall

(a) Have regard to—

  (i) matters of common interest between the Panchayats and the Municipalities including spatial planning, sharing of water and other physical and natural resources, the integrated development of infrastructure and environmental conservation;

  (ii) the extent and type of available resources whether financial or otherwise; and

(b) Consult such institutions and organisations as the Governor may specify.

Metropolitan Planning Committee Every metropolitan area shall have a metropolitan planning committee to prepare a draft development plan[5]. The state legislature may make provisions with respect to the following:

1. The composition of such committees;

2. The manner of election of members of such committees;

3. The representation in such committes of the Central government, state government and other organisations;

4. The functions of such committees in relation to planning and coordination for the metropolitan area; and

5. The manner of election of chairpersons of such committees.

The act lays down that two-thirds of the members of a metropolitan planning committee should be elected by the elected members of the municipalities and chairpersons of the panchayats in the metropolitan area from amongst themselves. The representation of these members in the committee should be in proportion to the ratio between the population of the municipalities and the panchayats in that metropolitan area.

The chairpersons of such committees shall forward the development plan to the state government.

In preparing the draft development plan, a metropolitan planning committee shall

(a) Have regard to—

(i) the plans prepared by the Municipalities and the Panchayats in the Metropolitan area;

(ii) matters of common interest between the Municipalities and the Panchayats, including co-ordinated spatial planning of the area, sharing of water and other physical and natural resources, the integrated development of infrastructure and environmental conservation;

(iii) the overall objectives and priorities set by the Government of India and the government of the state;

(iv) the extent and nature of investments likely to be made in the Metropolitan area by agencies of the Government of India and of the Government of the State and other available resources whether financial or otherwise; and

(b) consult such institutions and organisations as the Governor may specify.

Continuance of Existing Laws and Municipalities

All the state laws relating to municipalities shall continue to be in force until the expiry of one year from the commencement of this act. In other words, the states have to adopt the new system of municipalities based on this act within the maximum period of one year from 1 June, 1993, which is the date of commencement of this act. However, all municipalities existing immediately before the commencement of this act shall continue till the expiry of their term, unless dissolved by the state legislature sooner.

Bar to Interference by Courts in Electoral Matters

The act bars the interference by courts in the electoral matters of municipalities. It declares that the validity of any law relating to the delimitation of constituencies or the allotment of seats to such constituencies cannot be questioned in any court. It further lays down that no election to any municipality is to be questioned except by an election petition presented to such authority and in such manner as provided by the state legislature.

Twelfth Schedule

It contains the following 18 functional items placed within the purview of municipalities:

1. Urban planning including town planning;
2. Regulation of land use and construction of buildings;
3. Planning for economic and social development;
4. Roads and bridges;
5. Water supply for domestic, industrial and commercial purposes;
6. Public health, sanitation, conservancy and solid waste management;
7. Fire services;
8. Urban forestry, protection of the environment and promotion of ecological aspects;
9. Safeguarding the interests of weaker sections of society, including the handicapped and mentally retarded;
10. Slum improvement and upgradation;
11. Urban poverty alleviation;
12. Provision of urban amenities and facilities such as parks, gardens, playgrounds;
13. Promotion of cultural, educational and aesthetic aspects;
14. Burials and burial grounds, cremations and cremation grounds and electric crematoriums;
15. Cattle ponds, prevention of cruelty to animals;
16. Vital statistics including registration of births and deaths;
17. Public amenities including street lighting, parking lots, bus stops and public conveniences; and
18. Regulation of slaughter houses and tanneries.

TYPES OF URBAN GOVERNMENTS

The following eight types of urban local bodies are created in India for the administration of urban areas:

- Municipal Corporation
- Municipality
- Notified Area Committee
- Town Area Committee
- Cantonment Board
- Township
- Port Trust
- Special Purpose Agency

1. Municipal Corporation

Municipal corporations are created for the administration of big cities like Delhi, Mumbai, Kolkata,

Hyderabad, Bangalore and others. They are established in the states by the acts of the concerned state legislatures, and in the union territories by the acts of the Parliament of India. There may be one common act for all the municipal corporations in a state or a separate act for each municipal corporation.

A municipal corporation has three authorities, namely, the council, the standing committees and the commissioner.

The Council is the deliberative and legislative wing of the corporation. It consists of the Councillors directly elected by the people, as well as a few nominated persons having knowledge or experience of municipal administration. In brief, the composition of the Council including the reservation of seats for SCs, STs and women is governed by the 74th Constitutional Amendment Act.

The Council is headed by a Mayor. He is assisted by a Deputy Mayor. He is elected in a majority of the states for a one-year renewable term. He is basically an ornamental figure and a formal head of the corporation. His main function is to preside over the meetings of the Council.

The standing committees are created to facilitate the working of the council, which is too large in size. They deal with public works, education, health, taxation, finance and so on. They take decisions in their fields.

The municipal commissioner is responsible for the implementation of the decisions taken by the council and its standing committees. Thus, he is the chief executive authority of the corporation. He is appointed by the state government and is generally a member of the IAS.

2. Municipality

The municipalities are established for the administration of towns and smaller cities. Like the corporations, they are also set up in the states by the acts of the concerned state legislatures and in the union territory by the acts of the Parliament of India. They are also known by various other names like municipal council, municipal committee, municipal board, borough municipality, city municipality and others.

Like a municipal corporation, a municipality also has three authorities, namely, the council, the standing committees and the chief executive officer.

The council is the deliberative and legislative wing of the municipality. It consists of the councillors directly elected by the people.

The council is headed by a president/chairman. He is assisted by a vice-president/vice-chairman. He presides over the meetings of the council.

Unlike the Mayor of a municipal corporation, he plays a significant role and is the pivot of the municipal administration. Apart from presiding over the meetings of the Council, he enjoys executive powers.

The standing committees are created to facilitate the working of the council. They deal with public works, taxation, health, finance and so on.

The chief executive officer/chief municipal officer is responsible for day-to-day general administration of the municipality. He is appointed by the state government.

3. Notified Area Committee

A notified area committee is created for the administration of two types of areas—a fast developing town due to industrialisation, and a town which does not yet fulfil all the conditions necessary for the constitution of a municipality, but which otherwise is considered important by the state government. Since it is established by a notification in the government gazette, it is called as notified area committee. Though it functions within the framework of the State Municipal Act, only those provisions of the act apply to it which are notified in the government gazette by which it is created. It may also be entrusted to exercise powers under any other act. Its powers are almost equivalent to those of a municipality. But unlike the municipality, it is an entirely nominated body, that is, all the members of a notified area committee including the chairman are nominated by the state government. Thus, it is neither an elected body nor a statutory body.

4. Town Area Committee

A town area committee is set up for the administration of a small town. It is a semi-municipal authority and is entrusted with a limited number of civic functions like drainage, roads, street lighting, and conservancy. It is created by a separate act of a state legislature. Its composition, functions and other matters are governed by the act. It may be wholly elected or wholly nominated by the state government or partly elected and partly nominated[6].

5. Cantonment Board

A cantonment board is established for municipal administration for civilian population in the cantonment area[7]. It is set up under the provisions of the Cantonments Act of 2006—a legislation enacted by the Central government. It works under the administrative control of the defence ministry of the Central government. Thus, unlike the above four types of urban local bodies, which are created and administered by the state government, a cantonment board is created as well as administered by the Central government.

The Cantonments Act of 2006 was enacted to consolidate and amend the law relating to the administration of cantonments with a view to impart greater democratisation, improvement of their financial base to make provisions for developmental activities and for matters connected with them. This Act has repealed the Cantonments Act of 1924.

At present (2013), there are 62 cantonment boards in the country. They are grouped into four categories on the basis of the civil population. This is shown below in Table 35.2.

Table 35.2 *Classification of Cantonment Boards*

Category	Civil Population
I	above 50,000
II	10,000 to 50,000
III	2,500 to 10,000
IV	Below 2,500

A cantonment board consists of partly elected and partly nominated members. The elected members hold office for a term of five years while the nominated members (i.e., ex-officio members) continue so long as they hold the office in that station. The military officer commanding the station is the ex-officio president of the board and presides over its meetings. The vice-president of the board is elected by the elected members from amongst themselves for a term of five years.

The Category I cantonment board consists of the following members:

  (i) A military officer commanding the station
 (ii) An executive engineer in the cantonment
 (iii) A health officer in the cantonment

 (iv) A first class magistrate nominated by the district magistrate
  (v) Three military officers nominated by the officer commanding the station
 (vi) Eight members elected by the people of the cantonment area
(vii) Chief Executive Officer of the cantonment board

The functions performed by a cantonment board are similar to those of a municipality. These are statutorily categorised into obligatory functions and discretionary functions. The sources of income includes both, tax revenue and non-tax revenue.

The executive officer of the cantonment board is appointed by the president of India. He implements all the resolutions and decisions of the board and its committees. He belongs to the central cadre established for the purpose.

6. Township

This type of urban government is established by the large public enterprises to provide civic amenities to its staff and workers who live in the housing colonies built near the plant. The enterprise appoints a town administrator to look after the administration of the township. He is assisted by some engineers and other technical and non-technical staff. Thus, the township form of urban government has no elected members. In fact, it is an extension of the bureaucratic structure of the enterprises.

7. Port Trust

The port trusts are established in the port areas like Mumbai, Kolkata, Chennai and so on for two purposes: (a) to manage and protect the ports; and (b) to provide civic amenities. A port trust is created by an Act of Parliament. It consists of both elected and nominated members. Its chairman is an official. Its civic functions are more or less similar to those of a municipality.

8. Special Purpose Agency

In addition to these seven area-based urban bodies (or multipurpose agencies), the states have set up certain agencies to undertake designated activities or specific functions that 'legitimately' belong to the domain of municipal corporations or municipalities or other local urban governments. In other words, these are function-based and not area-based. They are known as 'single purpose', 'uni-purpose' or 'special purpose' agencies or 'functional local bodies'. Some such bodies are:

1. Town improvement trusts.
2. Urban development authorities.
3. Water supply and sewerage boards.
4. Housing boards.
5. Pollution control boards.
6. Electricity supply boards.
7. City transport boards.

These functional local bodies are established as statutory bodies by an act of state legislature or as departments by an executive resolution. They function as autonomous bodies and deal with the functions allotted to them independently of the local urban governments, that is, municipal corporations or municipalities and so forth. Thus, they are not subordinate agencies of the local municipal bodies.

Municipal Personnel

There are three types of municipal personnel systems in India. The personnel working in the urban governments may belong to any one or all the three types. These are

1. Separate Personnel System: Under this system, each local body appoints, administers, and controls its own personnel. They are not transferable to other local bodies. It is the most widely prevalent system. This system upholds the principle of local autonomy and promotes undivided loyalty.

2. Unified Personnel System: In this system, the state government appoints, administers, and controls the municipal personnel. In other words, state-wide services (cadres) are created for all the urban bodies in the state. They are transferable between the local bodies in the state. This system is prevalent in Andhra Pradesh, Tamil Nadu, Uttar Pradesh, Rajasthan, Madhya Pradesh and so on.

3. Integrated Personnel System: Under this system, the personnel of the state government and those of the local bodies form part of the same service. In other words, the municipal personnel are the members of the state services. They are transferable

not only between the local bodies in the state but also between local bodies and departments of state government. Thus, there is no distinction between local civil service and state civil service. This system is prevalent in Odisha, Bihar, Karnataka, Punjab, Haryana and others.

The various national level institutions providing training to the municipal personnel are

1. All-India Institute of Local Self-Government (Mumbai) constituted in 1927; it is a private registered society
2. Centre for Urban and Environmental Studies (New Delhi) set up in 1967 on the recommendation of Nur-ud-din Ahmed Committee on Training of Municipal Employees (1963-1965)
3. Regional Centres for Urban and Environmental Studies (Kolkata, Lucknow, Hyderabad and Mumbai) set up in 1968 on the recommendation of Nur-ud-din Ahmed Committee on Training of Municipal Employees (1963-1965)
4. National Institute of Urban Affairs, established in 1976
5. Human Settlement Management Institute, established in 1985

Central Council of Local Government

The Central Council of Local Government was set up in 1954. It was constituted under Article 263 of the Constitution of India by an order of the President of India. Originally, it was known as the Central Council of Local Self-Government. However, the term 'self-government' was found to be superfluous and hence was replaced by the term 'government' in the 1980s. Till 1958, it dealt with both urban as well as rural local governments, but after 1958 it has been dealing with matters of urban local government only.

The Council is an advisory body. It consists of the Minister for Urban Development in the Government of India and the ministers for local self government in states. The Union minister acts as the Chairman of the Council.

The Council performs the following functions with regard to local government:

(i) Considering and recommending the policy matters
(ii) Making proposals for legislation

(iii) Examining the possibility of cooperation between the Centre and the states

(iv) Drawing up a common programme of action

(v) Recommending Central financial assistance

(vi) Reviewing the work done by the local bodies with the Central financial assistance

Table 35.3 *Articles Related to Municipalities at a Glance*

Article No.	Subject-matter
243P	Definitions
243Q	Constitution of municipalities
243R	Composition of municipalities
243S	Constitution and composition of wards committees, and so on
243T	Reservation of seats
243U	Duration of municipalities, and so on
243V	Disqualifications for membership
243W	Powers, authority and responsibilities of municipalities, and so on
243X	Powers to impose taxes by, and funds of, the municipalities
243Y	Finance commission
243Z	Audit of accounts of municipalities
243ZA	Elections to the municipalities
243ZB	Application to union territories
243ZC	Part not to apply to certain areas
243ZD	Committee for district planning
243ZE	Committee for metropolitan planning
243ZF	Continuance of existing laws and municipalities
243ZG	Bar to interference by courts in electoral matters

Table 35.4 *Name and Number of Municipalities (2010)*[8]

Sl. No.	State	Urban Local Bodies	Number
1.	Andhra Pradesh	1. Municipal Corporations 2. Municipalities 3. Nagar Panchayats	15 103 6
2.	Arunachal Pradesh	(ULBs do not exist)	
3.	Assam	1. Municipal Corporations 2. Municipalities 3. Town Panchayats	1 29 59
4.	Bihar	1. Municipal Corporations 2. Municipal Councils 3. Nagar Panchayats	11 43 84
5.	Chattisgarh	1. Municipal Corporations 2. Municipalities 3. Town Panchayats	10 28 124

(Contd.)

Sl. No.	State	Urban Local Bodies	Number
6.	Goa	1. Municipal Corporations 2. Municipal Councils	1 13
7.	Gujarat	1. Municipal Corporations 2. Municipalities 3. Notified Area Councils	7 159 2
8.	Haryana	1. Municipal Corporations 2. Municipal Councils 3. Municipal Committees	1 24 51
9.	Himachal Pradesh	1. Municipal Corporations 2. Municipal Councils 3. Nagar Panchayats	1 20 28
10.	Jammu & Kashmir	1. Municipal Corporations 2. Municipal Committees	2 80
11.	Jharkhand	1. Municipal Corporations 2. Municipalities / MC 3. Town Panchayats / NAC	2 15 22
12.	Karnataka	1. Municipal / City Corporations 2. Municipal / City Councils 3. Town Panchayats	8 138 73
13.	Kerala	1. Municipal Corporations 2. Municipalities	5 53
14.	Madhya Pradesh	1. Municipal Corporations 2. Municipalities 3. Nagar Panchayats	14 88 236
15.	Maharashtra	1. Municipal Corporations 2. Municipal Councils 3. Nagar Panchayats	22 222 5
16.	Manipur	1. Municipal Councils 2. Nagar Panchayats	10 18
17.	Meghalaya	1. Municipalities	6
18.	Mizoram	1. Municipalities	1
19.	Nagaland	1. Municipal Councils 2. Town Councils	3 16
20.	Odisha	1. Municipal Corporations 2. Municipalities 3. Notified Area Councils	3 36 64
21.	Punjab	1. Municipal Corporations 2. Municipalities 3. Nagar Panchayats	5 97 33
22.	Rajasthan	1. Municipal Corporations 2. Municipal Councils 3. Municipal Boards	3 11 169

(Contd.)

Sl. No.	State	Urban Local Bodies	Number
23.	Sikkim	1. Municipal Corporations 2. Municipal Councils 3. Nagar Panchayats	1 2 9
24.	Tamil Nadu	1. Municipal Corporations 2. Municipalities 3. Town Panchayats	8 150 561
25.	Tripura	1. Municipal Councils 2. Nagar Panchayats	1 12
26.	Uttar Pradesh	1. Nagar Nigam 2. Nagar Palika Parishads 3. Nagar Panchayats	12 194 422
27.	Uttarakhand	1. Nagar Nigam 2. Nagar Palika Parishads 3. Nagar Panchayats	1 31 31
28.	West Bengal	1. Municipal Corporations 2. Municipalities 3. Notified Area Authorities	6 118 3
	All India	1. Municipal Corporations 2. Municipalities 3. Nagar Panchayats	139 1595 2108

NOTES AND REFERENCES

1. 'Local Government' is a subject mentioned in the State List under the 7th Schedule of the Constitution.
2. The bill was passed in both the Lok Sabha and the Rajya Sabha in December 1992. After that, the bill was approved by the required number of state legislatures. It was assented by the president in April 1993.
3. A transitional area, a smaller urban area or a larger urban area means such area as the governor may specify by public notification for this purpose with regard to the following factors: (a) Population of the area; (b) Density of Population; (c) Revenue generated for local administration; (d) Percentage of employment in non-agricultural activities; and (e) Economic importance or such other factors as the governor may deem fit.
4. At present (2009), nine states of India have scheduled areas. These are: Andhra Pradesh, Jharkhand, Chhattisgarh, Gujarat, Himachal Pradesh, Madhya Pradesh, Maharashtra, Orissa and Rajasthan. Presently (2009), there are a total of ten tribal areas (autonomous districts) in the four states of Assam (3), Meghalaya (3), Tripura (1) and Mizoram (3).
5. Metropolitan area means an area having a population of 10 lakh or more, in one or more districts and consisting of two or more municipalities or panchayats or other contiguous areas.
6. The Rural–Urban Relationship Committee (1963–66) headed by A P Jain recommended that small town area committees should be merged with the panchayati raj institutions to avoid multiplicity in the pattern of local bodies.
7. A cantonment area is a delimited area where the military forces and troops are permanently stationed.
8. Report of the Thirteenth Finance Commission (2010-2015), Volume II, December 2009, P. 424-426.

PART VI

UNION TERRITORIES AND SPECIAL AREAS

36

Union Territories

Under Article 1 of the Constitution, the territory of India comprises three categories of territories: (a) territories of the states; (b) union territories; and (c) territories that may be acquired by the Government of India at any time. At present, there are twenty-eight states, seven union territories and no acquired territories.

The states are the members of the federal system in India and share a distribution of power with the Centre. The union territories, on the other hand, are those areas which are under the direct control and administration of the Central government. Hence, they are also known as 'centrally administered territories'. 'In this way, existence of these territories constitutes a conspicuous departure from federalism in India; the Government of India is plainly unitary in so far as the relationship between New Delhi and these Central enclaves is concerned'[1].

CREATION OF UNION TERRITORIES

During the British Rule, certain areas were constituted as 'scheduled districts' in 1874. Later, they came to be known as 'chief commissioners provinces'. After independence, they were placed in the category of Part 'C' and Part 'D' states[2]. In 1956, they were constituted as the 'union territories' by the 7th Constitutional Amendment Act (1956) and the States Reorganisation Act (1956). Gradually, some of these union territories have been elevated to statehood. Thus, Himachal Pradesh, Manipur, Tripura, Mizoram, Arunachal Pradesh and Goa, which are states today were formerly

union territories. On the other hand, the territories that were acquired from the Portuguese (Goa, Daman and Diu, and Dadra and Nagar Haveli) and the French (Puducherry) were constituted as the union territories.

At present, there are seven Union Territories. They are (along with the year of creation): (1) Andaman and Nicobar Islands—1956, (2) Delhi—1956, (3) Lakshadweep—1956, (4) Dadra and Nagar Haveli—1961, (5) Daman and Diu—1962, (6) Puducherry—1962, and (7) Chandigarh—1966. Till 1973, Lakshadweep was known by the name of Laccadive, Minicoy and Amindivi Islands. In 1992, Delhi was redesignated as the National Capital Territory of Delhi. Till 2006, Puducherry was known as Pondicherry.

The union territories have been created for a variety of reasons. These are mentioned below[3]:

1. Political and administrative consideration—Delhi and Chandigarh.
2. Cultural distinctiveness—Puducherry, Dadra and Nagar Haveli, and Daman and Diu.
3. Strategic importance—Andaman and Nicobar Islands and Lakshadweep.
4. Special treatment and care of the backward and tribal people—Mizoram, Manipur, Tripura and Arunachal Pradesh which later became states.

ADMINISTRATION OF UNION TERRITORIES

Articles 239 to 241 in Part VIII of the Constitution deal with the union territories. Even though all the union territories belong to one category, there is no uniformity in their administrative system.

Every union territory is administered by the President acting through an administrator appointed by him. An administrator of a union territory is an agent of the President and not head of state like a governor. The President can specify the designation of an administrator; it may be Lieutenant Governor or Chief Commissioner or Administrator. At present, it is Lieutenant Governor in the case of Delhi, Puducherry and Andaman and Nicobar Islands and Administrator in the case of Chandigarh, Dadra and Nagar Haveli, Daman and Diu and Lakshadweep. The President can also appoint the governor of a state as the administrator of an adjoining union territory. In that capacity, the governor is to act independently of his council of ministers.

The Union Territories of Puducherry (in 1963) and Delhi (in 1992) are provided with a legislative assembly[4] and a council of ministers headed by a chief minister. The remaining five union territories do not have such popular political institutions. But, the establishment of such institutions in the union territories does not diminish the supreme control of the president and Parliament over them.

The Parliament can make laws on any subject of the three lists (including the State List) for the union territories. This power of Parliament also extends to Puducherry and Delhi, which have their own local legislatures. This means that, the legislative power of Parliament for the union territories on subjects of the State List remain unaffected even after establishing a local legislature for them. But, the legislative assembly of Puducherry can also make laws on any subject of the State List and the Concurrent List. Similarly, the legislative assembly of Delhi can make laws on any subject of the State List (except public order, police and land) and the Concurrent List.

The President can make regulations for the peace, progress and good government of the Andaman and Nicobar Islands, Lakshadweep, Dadra and Nagar Haveli, and Daman and Diu. In the case of Puducherry also, the President can legislate by making regulations but only when the assembly is suspended or dissolved. A regulation made by the President has the same force and effect as an act of Parliament and can also repeal or amend any act of Parliament in relation to these union territories.

The Parliament can establish a high court for a union territory or put it under the jurisdiction of the high court of adjacent state. Delhi is the only union territory that has a high court of its own (since 1966). The Bombay High Court has got jurisdiction over two union territories—Dadra and Nagar Haveli, and Daman and Diu. Andaman and Nocobar Islands, Chandigarh, Lakshadweep and Puducherry are placed under the Calcutta, Punjab and Haryana, Kerala, and Madras High Courts respectively.

The Constitution does not contain any separate provisions for the administration of acquired territories. But, the constitutional provisions for the administration of union territories also apply to the acquired territories.

SPECIAL PROVISIONS FOR DELHI

The 69th Constitutional Amendment Act of 1991[5] provided a special status to the Union Territory of Delhi, and redesignated it the National Capital Territory of Delhi and designated the administrator of Delhi as the lieutenant (lt.) governor. It created a legislative assembly and a council of ministers for Delhi. Previously, Delhi had a metropolitan council and an executive council.

The strength of the assembly is fixed at 70 members, directly elected by the people. The elections are conducted by the election commission of India. The assembly can make laws on all the matters of the State List and the Concurrent List except the three matters of the State List, that is, public order, police and land. But, the laws of Parliament prevail over those made by the Assembly.

The strength of the council of ministers is fixed at ten per cent of the total strength of the assembly, that is, seven—one chief minister and six other ministers. The chief minister is appointed by the President (not by the lt. governor). The other ministers are appointed by the president on the advice of the chief minister. The ministers hold office during the pleasure of the president. The council of ministers is collectively responsible to the assembly.

The council of ministers headed by the chief minister aid and advise the lt. governor in the exercise of his functions except in so far as he is required to act in his discretion. In the case of difference of opinion between the lt. governor and his ministers, the lt. governor is to refer the matter to the president for decision and act accordingly.

When a situation arises in which the administration of the territory cannot be carried on in accordance with the above provisions, the president can suspend their (above provisions) operation and make the necessary incidental or consequential provisions for administering the territory. In brief, in case of failure of constitutional machinery, the president can impose his rule in the territory. This can be done on the report of the lt. governor or otherwise. This provision resembles Article 356 which deals with the imposition of President's Rule in the states.

The Lt. governor is empowered to promulgate ordinances during recess of the assembly. An ordinance has the same force as an act of the assembly. Every such ordinance must be approved by the assembly within six weeks from its reassembly. He can also withdraw an ordinance at any time. But, he cannot promulgate an ordinance when the assembly is dissolved or suspended. Further, no such ordinance can be promulgated or withdrawn without the prior permission of the President.

Table 36.1 *Administrative System of Union Territories at a Glance*

	Union Territories	Executive	Legislature	Judiciary
1.	Andaman and Nicobar Islands	Lt. Governor	—	Under Calcutta High Court
2.	Chandigarh	Administrator	—	Under Punjab and Haryana High Court
3.	Dadra and Nagar Haveli	Administrator	—	Under Bombay High Court
4.	Daman and Diu	Administrator	—	Under Bombay High Court
5.	Delhi	(a) Lt. Governor (b) Chief minister (c) Council of ministers	Legislative Assembly	Separate High Court
6.	Lakshadweep	Administrator	—	Under Kerala High Court
7.	Puducherry	(a) Lt. Governor (b) Chief minister (c) Council of ministers	Legislative Assembly	Under Madras High Court

Note: The Governor of Punjab is concurrently the Administrator of Chandigarh. The Administrator of Dadra and Nagar Haveli is concurrently the Administrator of Daman and Diu. Lakshadweep has a separate Administrator[6].

ADVISORY COMMITTEES OF UNION TERRITORIES

Under the Government of India (Allocation of Business) Rules 1961, Ministry of Home Affairs is the nodal ministry for all matters of Union Territories relating to legislation, finance and budget, services and appointment of Lt. Governors and Administrators.

All the five UTs without a legislature (Andaman and Nicobar Islands, Chandigarh, Daman and Diu, Dadra and Nagar Haveli, and Lakshadweep) have the forum of Home Minister's Advisory Committee (HMAC), on which, besides the Administrator and Member of Parliament from the respective Union Territory, members from the local elected bodies, e.g., District Panchayats and Municipal Council / Committees are nominated as members. Meetings of the HMAC are chaired by the Union Home Minister, or, in his absence, by the Minister of State in the Ministry of Home Affairs. The Committee discusses the general issues relating to social and economic development of the Union territories[7].

Table 36.2 *Comparing States and Union Territories*

	States		Union Territories
1.	Their relationship with Centre is federal.	1.	Their relationship with Centre is unitary.
2.	They share a distribution of power with the Centre.	2.	They are under the direct control and administration of the Centre.
3.	They have autonomy.	3.	They do not have any autonomy.
4.	There is uniformity in their administrative set-up.	4.	There is no uniformity in their administrative set-up.
5.	Their executive head is known as governor.	5.	Their executive head is known by various designations—administrator or lieutenant governor or chief commissioner.
6.	A governor is a constitutional head of the state.	6.	An administrator is an agent of the president.
7.	Parliament cannot make laws on the subjects of the state list in relation to the states except under extraordinary circumstances.	7.	Parliament can make laws on any subject of the three lists in relation to the union territories.

Table 36.3 *Articles Related to Union Territories at a Glance*

Article No.	Subject-matter
239.	Administration of Union territories
239A.	Creation of local Legislatures or Council of Ministers or both for certain Union territories
239AA.	Special provisions with respect to Delhi
239AB.	Provision in case of failure of constitutional machinery
239B.	Power of administrator to promulgate Ordinances during recess of Legislature
240.	Power of President to make regulations for certain Union territories
241.	High Courts for Union territories
242.	Coorg (Repealed)

Notes and References

1. S R Maheshwari, *State Governments in India*, Macmillan, 2000 Edition, p. 131.
2. Under the original Constitution of India (1950), the states were classified into four categories, namely, Part A, B, C and D States.
3. J C Johari : *Indian Government and Politics*, Vishal, volume II, 13th Edition, 2001, p. 499.
4. The Assembly of Puducherry consists of 30 members while that of Delhi 70 members.
5. With effect from 1 February 1992.
6. India 2013: A Reference Annual, Publications Division, Government of India, p.49.
7. Annual Report 2011-12, Ministry of Home Affairs, Government of India, P. 117-118.

Scheduled and Tribal Areas

Article 244 in Part X of the Constitution envisages a special system of administration for certain areas designated as 'scheduled areas' and 'tribal areas'. The Fifth Schedule of the Constitution deals with the administration and control of scheduled areas and scheduled tribes in any state except the four states of Assam, Meghalaya, Tripura and Mizoram[1]. The Sixth Schedule of the Constitution, on the other hand, deals with the administration of the tribal areas in the four northeastern states of Assam, Meghalaya, Tripura and Mizoram.

ADMINISTRATION OF SCHEDULED AREAS

'The scheduled areas are treated differently from the other areas in the country because they are inhabited by 'aboriginals' who are socially and economically rather backward, and special efforts need to be made to improve their condition. Therefore, the whole of the normal administrative machinery operating in a state is not extended to the scheduled areas and the Central government has somewhat greater responsibility for these areas'[2].

The various features of administration contained in the Fifth Schedule are as follows:

1. *Declaration of Scheduled Areas:* The president is empowered to declare an area to be a scheduled area. He can also increase or decrease its area, alter its boundary lines, rescind such designation or make fresh orders for such redesignation on an area in consultation with the governor of the state concerned.

2. *Executive Power of State and Centre:* The executive power of a state extends to the scheduled areas therein. But the governor has a special responsibility regarding such areas. He has to submit a report to the president regarding the administration of such areas, annually or whenever so required by the president. The executive power of the Centre extends to giving directions to the states regarding the administration of such areas.

3. *Tribes Advisory Council:* Each state having scheduled areas has to establish a tribes advisory council to advise on welfare and advancement of the scheduled tribes. It is to consist of 20 members, three-fourths of whom are to be the representatives of the scheduled tribes in the state legislative assembly. A similar council can also be established in a state having scheduled tribes but not scheduled areas therein, if the president so directs.

4. *Law applicable to Scheduled Areas:* The governor is empowered to direct that any particular act of Parliament or the state legislature does not apply to a scheduled area or apply with specified modifications and exceptions. He can also make regulations for the peace and good government of a scheduled area after consulting the tribes advisory council. Such regulations may prohibit or restrict the transfer of land by or among members of the scheduled tribes, regulate the allotment of land to members of the scheduled tribes and regulate the business of money-lending in relation to the

scheduled tribes. Also, a regulation may repeal or amend any act of Parliament or the state legislature, which is applicable to a scheduled area. But, all such regulations require the assent of the president.

The Constitution requires the president to appoint a commission to report on the administration of the scheduled areas and the welfare of the scheduled tribes in the states. He can appoint such a commission at any time but compulsorily after ten years of the commencement of the Constitution. Hence, a commission was appointed in 1960. It was headed by U N Dhebar and submitted its report in 1961. After four decades, the second commission was appointed in 2002 under the chairmanship of Dilip Singh Bhuria.

ADMINISTRATION OF TRIBAL AREAS

The Constitution, under Sixth Schedule, contains special provisions for the administration of tribal areas in the four north-eastern states of Assam, Meghalaya, Tripura and Mizoram. The rationality behind the special arrangements in respect of only these four states lies in the following:

"The tribes in Assam, Meghalaya, Tripura and Mizoram have not assimilated much the life and ways of the other people in these states. These areas have hitherto been anthropological specimens. The tribal people in other parts of India have more or less adopted the culture of the majority of the people in whose midst they live. The tribes in Assam, Meghalaya, Tripura and Mizoram, on the other hand, still have their roots in their own culture, customs and civilization. These areas are, therefore, treated differently by the Constitution and sizeable amount of autonomy has been given to these people for self-government.[3]"

The various features of administration contained in the Sixth Schedule are as follows:

1. The tribal areas in the four states of Assam, Meghalaya, Tripura and Mizoram have been constituted as autonomous districts[4]. But, they do not fall outside the executive authority of the state concerned.

2. The governor is empowered to organise and re-organise the autonomous districts. Thus, he can increase or decrease their areas or change their names or define their boundaries and so on.

3. If there are different tribes in an autonomous district, the governor can divide the district into several autonomous regions.

4. Each autonomous district has a district council consisting of 30 members, of whom four are nominated by the governor and the remaining 26 are elected on the basis of adult franchise. The elected members hold office for a term of five years (unless the council is dissolved earlier) and nominated members hold office during the pleasure of the governor. Each autonomous region also has a separate regional council.

5. The district and regional councils administer the areas under their jurisdiction. They can make laws on certain specified matters like land, forests, canal water, shifting cultivation, village administration, inheritance of property, marriage and divorce, social customs and so on. But all such laws require the assent of the governnor.

6. The district and regional councils within their territorial jurisdictions can constitute village councils or courts for trial of suits and cases between the tribes. They hear appeals from them. The jurisdiction of high court over these suits and cases is specified by the governor.

7. The district council can establish, construct or manage primary schools, dispensaries, markets, ferries, fisheries, roads and so on in the district. It can also make regulations for the control of money lending and trading by non-tribals. But, such regulations require the assent of the governor.

8. The district and regional councils are empowered to assess and collect land revenue and to impose certain specified taxes.

9. The acts of Parliament or the state legislature do not apply to autonomous districts and autonomous regions or apply with specified modifications and exceptions[5].

10. The governor can appoint a commission to examine and report on any matter relating to the administration of the autonomous districts or regions. He may dissolve a district or regional council on the recommendation of the commission.

Table 37.1 *Tribal Areas at a Glance (2013)*

	States		Tribal Areas
1.	Assam	1.	The North Cachar Hills District.
		2.	The Karbi Anglong District.
		3.	The Bodoland Territorial Areas District.
2.	Meghalaya	1.	Khasi Hills District.
		2.	Jaintia Hills District.
		3.	The Garo Hills District.
3.	Tripura		Tripura Tribal Areas District
4.	Mizoram	1.	The Chakma District.
		2.	The Mara District.
		3.	The Lai District.

Table 37.2 *Articles Related to Scheduled and Tribal Areas at a Glance*

Article No.	Subject-matter
244.	Administration of Scheduled Areas and Tribal Areas
244A.	Formation of an autonomous state comprising certain tribal areas in Assam and creation of local legislature or Council of Ministers or both therefore
339.	Control of the Union over the administration of Scheduled Areas and the welfare of Scheduled Tribes

Notes and References

1. At present (2013), nine states of India have scheduled areas. These are: Andhra Pradesh, Jharkhand, Chhattisgarh, Gujarat, Himachal Pradesh, Madhya Pradesh, Maharashtra, Odisha and Rajasthan.
2. M P Jain, *Indian Constitutional Law*, Wadhwa, Fourth Edition, 1987, p. 236.
3. *Ibid,* p. 237.
4. Presently (2013), there are a total of ten tribal areas. See Table 37.1.
5. The power of direction, in this regard, lies either with the president or governor. Thus, in the case of Assam, it lies with the Governor, both in respect of acts of Parliament or state legislature. In the case of Meghalaya, Tripura and Mizoram, it lies with the president in respect of acts of Parliament and governor in respect of acts of state legislature.

PART VII

CONSTITUTIONAL BODIES

Election Commission

The Election Commission is a permanent and an independent body established by the Constitution of India directly to ensure free and fair elections in the country. Article 324 of the Constitution provides that the power of superintendence, direction and control of elections to parliament, state legislatures, the office of president of India and the office of vice-president of India shall be vested in the election commission. Thus, the Election Commission is an all-India body in the sense that it is common to both the Central government and the state governments.

It must be noted here that the election commission is not concerned with the elections to panchayats and muncipalities in the states. For this, the Constitution of India provides for a separate State Election Commission[1].

COMPOSITION

Article 324 of the Constitution has made the following provisions with regard to the composition of election commission:

1. The Election Commission shall consist of the chief election commissioner and such number of other election commissioners, if any, as the president may from time to time fix.
2. The appointment of the chief election commissioner and other election commissioners shall be made by the president.
3. When any other election commissioner is so appointed, the chief election commis-

sioner shall act as the chairman of the election commission.
4. The president may also appoint after consultation with the election commission such regional commissioners as he may consider necessary to assist the election commission.
5. The conditions of service and tenure of office of the election commissioners and the regional commissioners shall be determined by the president.

Since its inception in 1950 and till 15 October 1989, the election commission functioned as a single member body consisting of the Chief Election Commissioner. On 16 October 1989, the president appointed two more election commissioners to cope with the increased work of the election commission on account of lowering of the voting age from 21 to 18 years.[2] Thereafter, the Election Commission functioned as a multimember body consisting of three election commissioners. However, the two posts of election commissioners were abolished in January 1990 and the Election Commission was reverted to the earlier position. Again in October 1993, the president appointed two more election commissioners. Since then and till today, the Election Commission has been functioning as a multi-member body consisting of three election commissioners.

The chief election commissioner and the two other election commissioners have equal powers and receive equal salary, allowances and other perquisites, which are similar to those of a judge of the Supreme Court.[3] In case of difference of opinion amongst the Chief Election Commissioner and/

or two other election commissioners, the matter is decided by the Commission by majority.

They hold office for a term of six years or until they attain the age of 65 years, whichever is earlier. They can resign at any time or can also be removed before the expiry of their term.

INDEPENDENCE

Article 324 of the Constitution has made the following provisions to safeguard and ensure the independent and impartial functioning of the Election Commission:

1. The chief election commissioner is provided with the security of tenure. He cannot be removed from his office except in same manner and on the same grounds as a judge of the Supreme Court. In other words, he can be removed by the president on the basis of a resolution passed to that effect by both the Houses of Parliament with special majority, either on the ground of proved misbehaviour or incapacity. Thus, he does not hold his office till the pleasure of the president, though he is appointed by him.
2. The service conditions of the chief election commissioner cannot be varied to his disadvantage after his appointment.
3. Any other election commissioner or a regional commissioner cannot be removed from office except on the recommendation of the chief election commissioner.

Though the constitution has sought to safeguard and ensure the independence and impartiality of the Election Commission, some flaws can be noted, viz.,

1. The Constitution has not prescribed the qualifications (legal, educational, administrative or judicial) of the members of the Election Commission.
2. The Constitution has not specified the term of the members of the Election Commission.
3. The Constitution has not debarred the retiring election commissioners from any further appointment by the government.

POWERS AND FUNCTIONS

The powers and functions of the Election Commission with regard to elections to the Parliament, state legislatures and offices of President and Vice-President can be classified into three categories, viz,
1. Administrative
2. Advisory
3. Quasi-Judicial
In details, these powers and functions are:
1. To determine the territorial areas of the electoral constituencies throughout the country on the basis of the Delimitation Commission Act of Parliament.[4]
2. To prepare and periodically revise electoral rolls and to register all eligible voters.
3. To notify the dates and schedules of elections and to scrutinise nomination papers.
4. To grant recognition to political parties and allot election symbols to them.
5. To act as a court for settling disputes related to granting of recognition to political parties and allotment of election symbols to them.
6. To appoint officers for inquiring into disputes relating to electoral arrangements.
7. To determine the code of conduct to be observed by the parties and the candidates at the time of elections.
8. To prepare a roster for publicity of the policies of the political parties on radio and TV in times of elections.
9. To advise the president on matters relating to the disqualifications of the members of Parliament.
10. To advise the governor on matters relating to the disqualifications of the members of state legislature.
11. To cancel polls in the event of rigging, booth capturing, violence and other irregularities.
12. To request the president or the governor for requisitioning the staff necessary for conducting elections.
13. To supervise the machinery of elections throughout the country to ensure free and fair elections.

14. To advise the president whether elections can be held in a state under president's rule in order to extend the period of emergency after one year.
15. To register political parties for the purpose of elections and grant them the status of national or state parties on the basis of their poll performance[5].

The Election Commission is assisted by deputy election commissioners. They are drawn from the civil service and appointed by the commission with tenure system. They are assisted, in turn, by the secretaries, joint secretaries, deputy secretaries and under secretaries posted in the secretariat of the commission.

At the state level, the Election Commission is assisted by the chief electoral officer who is appointed by the chief election commissioner in consultation with the state government. Below this, at the district level, the collector acts as the district returning officer. He appoints a returning officer for every constituency in the district and presiding officer for every polling booth in the constituency.

NOTES AND REFERENCES

1. Vide 73rd and 74th Constitutional Amendment Acts of 1992.
2. By the 61st Constitutional Amendment Act of 1988, which came into force in 1989.
3. In 2009, the salary of a judge of the Supreme Court had been fixed at ₹90,000 per month.
4. The Parliament has made the Delimitation Commission Acts in 1952, 1962, 1972 and 2002.
5. For details in this regard, see Chapter 64 (Political Parties).

Union Public Service Commission

The Union Public Service Commission (UPSC) is the central recruiting agency in India. It is an independent constitutional body in the sense that it has been directly created by the Constitution. Articles 315 to 323 in Part XIV of the Constitution contain elaborate provisions regarding the composition, appointment and removal of members along with the independence, powers and functions of the UPSC.

COMPOSITION

The UPSC consists of a chairman and other members appointed by the president of India. The Constitution, without specifying the strength of the Commission has left the matter to the discretion of the president, who determines its composition. Usually, the Commission consists of nine to eleven members including the chairman. Further, no qualifications are prescribed for the Commission's membership except that one-half of the members of the Commission should be such persons who have held office for at least ten years either under the Government of India or under the government of a state. The Constitution also authorises the president to determine the conditions of service of the chairman and other members of the Commission.

The chairman and members of the Commission hold office for a term of six years or until they attain the age of 65 years, whichever is earlier. However, they can relinquish their offices at any time by addressing their resignation to the president. They can also be removed before the expiry of their term by the president in the manner as provided in the Constitution.

The President can appoint one of the members of the UPSC as an acting chairman in the following two circumstances[1] :
(a) When the office of the chairman falls vacant; or
(b) When the chairman is unable to perform his functions due to absence or some other reason.

The acting chairman functions till a person appointed as chairman enters on the duties of the office or till the chairman is able to resume his duties.

REMOVAL

The President can remove the chairman or any other member of UPSC from the office under the following circumstances:
(a) If he is adjudged an insolvent (that is, has gone bankrupt);
(b) If he engages, during his term of office, in any paid employment outside the duties of his office; or
(c) If he is, in the opinion of the president, unfit to continue in office by reason of infirmity of mind or body.

In addition to these, the president can also remove the chairman or any other member of UPSC for misbehaviour. However, in this case, the president has to refer the matter to the Supreme Court for an enquiry. If the Supreme Court, after the enquiry, upholds the cause of removal and advises so, the president can remove the chairman or a member. Under the provisions of the Constitution, the advise tendered by the Supreme Court in this regard is binding on the president. During the course of enquiry by the Supreme Court, the president can suspend the chairman or the member of UPSC.

Defining the term 'misbehaviour' in this context, the Constitution states that the chairman or any other member of the UPSC is deemed to be guilty of misbehaviour if he (a) is concerned or interested in any contract or agreement made by the Government of India or the government of a state, or (b) participates in any way in the profit of such contract or agreement or in any benefit therefrom otherwise than as a member and in common with other members of an incorporated company.

INDEPENDENCE

The Constitution has made the following provisions to safeguard and ensure the independent and impartial functioning of the UPSC:

(a) The chairman or a member of the UPSC can be removed from office by the president only in the manner and on the grounds mentioned in the Constitution. Therefore, they enjoy security of tenure.

(b) The conditions of service of the chairman or a member, though determined by the president, cannot be varied to his disadvantage after his appointment.

(c) The entire expenses including the salaries, allowances and pensions of the chairman and members of the UPSC are charg ed on the Consolidated Fund of India. Thus, they are not subject to vote of Parliament.

(d) The chairman of UPSC (on ceasing to hold office) is not eligible for further employment in the Government of India or a state[2].

(e) A member of UPSC (on ceasing to hold office) is eligible for appointment as the chairman of UPSC or a State Public Service Commission (SPSC), but not for any other employment in the Government of India or a state[3].

(f) The chairman or a member or UPSC is (after having completed his first term) not eligible for reappointment to that office (i.e., not eligible for second term).

FUNCTIONS

The UPSC performs the following functions:

(a) It conducts examinations for appointments to the all-India services, Central services and public services of the centrally administered territories.

(b) It assists the states (if requested by two or more states to do so) in framing and operating schemes of joint recruitment for any services for which candidates possessing special qualifications are required.

(c) It serves all or any of the needs of a state on the request of the state governor and with the approval of the president of India.

(d) It is consulted on the following matters related to personnel management:

(i) All matters relating to methods of recruitment to civil services and for civil posts.

(ii) The principles to be followed in making appointments to civil services and posts and in making promotions and transfers from one service to another.

(iii) The suitability of candidates for appointments to civil services and posts; for promotions and transfers from one service to another; and appointments by transfer or deputation. The concerned departments make recommendations for promotions and request the UPSC to ratify them.

(iv) All disciplinary matters affecting a person serving under the Government of India in a civil capacity including memorials or petitions relating to such matters. These include:

— Censure (Severe disapproval)
— Withholding of increments
— Withholding of promotions
— Recovery of pecuniary loss
— Reduction to lower service or rank (Demotion)
— Compulsory retirement
— Removal from service
— Dismissal from service[4]

(v) Any claim for reimbursement of legal expenses incurred by a civil servant in defending legal proceedings instituted against him in respect of acts done in the execution of his official duties.

(vi) Any claim for the award of a pension in respect of injuries sustained by a person while serving under the Government of India and any question as to the amount of any such award.

(vii) Matters of temporary appointments for period exceeding one year and on regularisation of appointments.

(viii) Matters related to grant of extension of service and re-employment of certain retired civil servants.

(ix) Any other matter related to personnel management.

The Supreme Court has held that if the government fails to consult UPSC in the matters (mentioned above), the aggrieved public servant has no remedy in a court. In other words, the court held that any irregularity in consultation with the UPSC or acting without consultation does not invalidate the decision of the government. Thus, the provision is directory and not mandatory. Similarly, the court held that a selection by the UPSC does not confer any right to the post upon the candidate. However, the government is to act fairly and without arbitrariness or malafides.

The additional functions relating to the services of the Union can be conferred on UPSC by the Parliament. It can also place the personnel system of any authority, corporate body or public institution within the jurisdiction of the UPSC. Hence the jurisdiction of UPSC can be extended by an act made by the Parliament.

The UPSC presents, annually, to the president a report on its performance. The President places this report before both the Houses of Parliament, along with a memorandum explaining the cases where the advice of the Commission was not accepted and the reasons for such non-acceptance. All such cases of non-acceptance must be approved by the Appointments Committee of the Union cabinet. An individual ministry or department has no power to reject the advice of the UPSC.

LIMITATIONS

The following matters are kept outside the functional jurisdiction of the UPSC. In other words, the UPSC is not consulted on the following matters:

(a) While making reservations of appointments or posts in favour of any backward class of citizens.

(b) While taking into consideration the claims of scheduled castes and scheduled tribes in making appointments to services and posts.

(c) With regard to the selections for chairmanship or membership of commissions or tribunals, posts of the highest diplomatic nature and a bulk of group C and group D services.

(d) With regard to the selection for temporary or officiating appointment to a post if the person appointed is not likely to hold the post for more than a year.

The president can exclude posts, services and matters from the purview of the UPSC. The Constitution states that the president, in respect to the all-India services and Central services and posts may make regulations specifying the matters in which, it shall not be necessary for UPSC to be consulted. But all such regulations made by the president shall be laid before each House of Parliament for at least 14 days. The Parliament can amend or repeal them.

ROLE

The Constitution visualises the UPSC to be the 'watch-dog of merit system' in India. It is concerned with the recruitment to the all-India services and Central services—group A and group B and advises the government, when consulted, on promotion and disciplinary matters. It is not concerned with the classification of services, pay and service conditions, cadre management, training, and so on. These matters are handled by the Department of Personnel and Training—one of the three departments of the Ministry of Personnel, Public Grievances and Pensions[5]. Therefore, UPSC is only a central recruiting agency while the Department of Personnel and Training is the central personnel agency in India.

The role of UPSC is not only limited, but also recommendations made by it are only of advisory nature and hence, not binding on the government. It is upto the Union government to accept or reject that advise. The only safeguard is the answerability of the government to the Parliament for departing from the recommendation of the Commission. Further, the government can also make rules which regulate the scope of the advisory functions of UPSC[6].

The emergence of Central Vigilance Commission (CVC) in 1964 affected the role of UPSC in disciplinary matters. This is because both are consulted by the government while taking disciplinary action against a civil servant. The problem arises when the two bodies tender conflicting advise. However, the UPSC, being an independent constitutional body, has an edge over the CVC, which is created by an executive resolution of the Government of India and conferred a statutory status in October 2003.

Table 39.1 *Articles Related to UPSC at a Glance*

Article No.	Subject-matter
315	Public Service Commissions for the Union and for the states
316	Appointment and term of office of members
317	Removal and suspension of a member of a Public Service Commission
318	Power to make regulations as to conditions of service of members and staff of the Commission
319	Prohibition as to the holding of office by members of commission on ceasing to be such members
320	Functions of Public Service Commissions
321	Power to extend functions of Public Service Commissions
322	Expenses of Public Service Commissions
323	Reports of Public Service Commissions

Notes and References

1. Added by the 15th Amendment Act of 1963.
2. In 1979, the Supreme Court upheld the validity of appointment of A R Kidwai, a former Chairman of UPSC, as the governor of Bihar. It ruled that the office of the governor is a 'constitutional office' and not an employment under the government.
3. When a member of UPSC is appointed as its chairman, he holds the new office for six years or until the age of superannuation, whichever is earlier.
4. The difference between removal and dismissal is that the former does not disqualify for future employment under the government while the latter disqualifies for future employment under the government.
5. In 1985, a new full-fledged Ministry of Personnel, Public Grievances and Pensions was created with three separate departments. These are Department of Personnel and Training, Department of Administrative Reforms and Public Grievances, and Department of Pensions and Pensioners' Welfare.
6. Such Rules are known as the UPSC (Exemption From Consultation) Regulations.

State Public Service Commission

Parallel to the Union Public Service Commission (UPSC) at the Centre, there is a State Public Service Commission (SPSC) in a state. The same set of Articles (i.e., 315 to 323 in Part XIV) of the Constitution also deal with the composition, appointment and removal of members, power and functions and independence of a SPSC.

COMPOSITION

A State Public Service Commission consists of a chairman and other members appointed by the governor of the state. The Constitution does not specify the strength of the Commission but has left the matter to the discretion of the Governor. Further, no qualifications are prescribed for the commission's membership except that one-half of the members of the commission should be such persons who have held office for at least ten years either under the government of India or under the Government of a state. The Constitution also authorises the governor to determine the conditions of service of the chairman and members of the Commission.

The chairman and members of the Commission hold office for a term of six years or until they attain the age of 62 years[1], whichever is earlier (in the case of UPSC, the age limit is 65 years). However, they can relinquish their offices at any time by addressing their resignation to the governor.

The governor can appoint one of the members of the SPSC as an acting chairman in the following two circumstances[2]:

(a) When the office of the chairman falls vacant; or

(b) When the chairman is unable to perform his functions due to absence or some other reason.

The acting chairman functions till the person appointed as chairman enters on the duties of the office or till the chairman is able to resume his duties.

REMOVAL

Although the chairman and members of a SPSC are appointed by the governor, they can be removed only by the president (and not by the governor). The president can remove them on the same grounds and in the same manner as he can remove a chairman or a member of the UPSC. Thus, he can remove him under the following circumstances:

(a) If he is adjudged an insolvent (i.e., has gone bankrupt); or

(b) If he engages, during his term of office, in any paid employment outside the duties of his office; or

(c) If he is, in the opinion of the president, unfit to continue in office by reason of infirmity of mind or body[3].

In addition to these, the president can also remove the chairman or any other member of SPSC for misbehaviour. However, in this case, the president has to refer the matter to the Supreme Court for an enquiry. If the Supreme Court, after the enquiry, upholds the cause of removal and advises so, the president can remove the chairman or a member. Under the provisions of the Constitution, the advise tendered by the Supreme Court in this regard is binding on the president. However, during the course of enquiry by the Supreme Court, the governor can suspend the concerned chairman or member, pending the final removal order of the president on receipt of the report of the Supreme Court.

Further, the Constitution has also defined the term 'misbehaviour' in this context. The Constitution states that the chairman or any other member of a SPSC is deemed to be guilty of misbehaviour, if he (a) is concerned or interested in any contract or agreement made by the Government of India or the government of a state, or (b) participates in any way in the profit of such contract or agreement or in any benefit therefrom otherwise than as a member and in common with other members of an incorporated company.

INDEPENDENCE

As in the case of UPSC, the Constitution has made the following provisions to safeguard and ensure the independent and impartial functioning of a SPSC:

(a) The chairman or a member of a SPSC can be removed from office by the president only in the manner and on the grounds mentioned in the Constitution. Therefore, they enjoy the security of tenure.

(b) The conditions of service of the chairman or a member, though determined by the governor, cannot be varied to his disadvantage after his appointment.

(c) The entire expense including the salaries, allowances and pensions of the chairman and members of a SPSC are charged on the consolidated fund of the state. Thus, they are not subject to vote of the state legislature.

(d) The chairman of a SPSC (on ceasing to hold office) is eligible for appointment as the chairman or a member of the UPSC or as the chairman of any other SPSC, but not for any other employment under the Government of India or a state.

(e) A member of a SPSC (on ceasing to hold office) is eligible for appointment as the chairman or a member of the UPSC, or as the chairman of that SPSC or any other SPSC, but not for any other employment under the Government of India or a state.

(f) The chairman or a member of a SPSC is (after having completed his first term) not eligible for reappointment to that office (that is, not eligible for second term).

FUNCTIONS

A SPSC performs all those functions in respect of the state services as the UPSC does in relation to the Central services:

(a) It conducts examinations for appointments to the services of the state.

(b) It is consulted on the following matters related to personnel management:

   (i) All matters relating to methods of recruitment to civil services and for civil posts.

   (ii) The principles to be followed in making appointments to civil services and posts and in making promotions and transfers from one service to another.

   (iii) The suitability of candidates for appointments to civil services and posts; for promotions and transfers from one service to another; and appointments by transfer or deputation. The concerned departments make recommendations for promotions and request the SPSC to ratify them.

   (iv) All disciplinary matters affecting a person serving under the government of the state in a civil capacity including memorials or petitions relating to such matters. These include:

    — Censure (severe disapproval)
    — Withholding of increments
    — Withholding of promotions
    — Recovery of pecuniary loss
    — Reduction to lower service or rank (demotion)
    — Compulsory retirement
    — Removal from service
    — Dismissal from service[4]

   (v) Any claim for reimbursement of legal expenses incurred by a civil servant in defending legal proceedings instituted against him in respect of acts done in the execution of his official duties.

(vi) Any claim for the award of a pension in respect of injuries sustained by a person while serving under the government of the state and any question as to the amount of any such award.

(vii) Any other matter related to the personnel management.

The Supreme Court has held that if the government fails to consult the SPSC in these matters, the aggrieved public servant has no remedy in a court. In other words, the court held that any irregularity in consultation with the SPSC or acting without consultation does not invalidate the decision of the government. Thus, the provision is directory and not mandatory. Similarly, the court held that a selection by the SPSC does not confer any right to the post upon the candidate. However, the government is to act fairly and without arbitrariness or malafides.

The additional functions relating to the services of the state can be conferred on SPSC by the state legislature. It can also place the personnel system of any local authority, corporate body or public institution within the jurisdiction of the SPSC. Hence the jurisdiction of SPSC can be extended by an Act made by the state legislature.

The SPSC presents, annually, to the governor a report on its performance. The governor places this report before both the Houses of the state legislature, along with a memorandum explaining the cases where the advice of the Commission was not accepted and the reasons for such non-acceptance.

LIMITATIONS

The following matters are kept outside the functional jurisdiction of the SPSC. In other words, the SPSC is not consulted on the following matters:

(a) While making reservations of appointments or posts in favour of any backward class of citizens.

(b) While taking into consideration the claims of scheduled castes and scheduled tribes in making appointments to services and posts.

The governor can exclude posts, services and matters from the purview of the SPSC. The Constitution states that the governor, in respect to the state services and posts may make regulations specifying the matters in which, it shall not be necessary for

SPSC to be consulted. But all such regulations made by the governor shall be laid before each House of the state legislature for at least 14 days. The state legislature can amend or repeal them.

ROLE

The Constitution visualises the SPSC to be the 'watchdog of merit system' in the state. It is concerned with the recruitment to the state services and advises the government, when consulted, on promotion and disciplinary matters. It is not concerned with the classification of services, pay and service conditions, cadre management, training and so on. These matters are handled by the Department of Personnel or the General Administration Department. Therefore, the SPSC is only a central recruiting agency in the state while the Department of Personnel or the General Administration Department is the central personnel agency in the state.

The role of SPSC is not only limited, but also recommendations made by it are only of advisory nature and hence, not binding on the government. It is up to the state government to accept or reject that advice. The only safeguard is the answerability of the government to the state legislature for departing from the recommendation of the Commission. Further, the government can also make rules which regulate the scope of the advisory functions of SPSC[5].

Also, the emergence of State Vigilance Commission (SVC) in 1964 affected the role of SPSC in disciplinary matters. This is because both are consulted by the government while taking disciplinary action against a civil servant. The problem arises when the two bodies tender conflicting advice. However, the SPSC, being an independent constitutional body, has an edge over the SVC.

Finally, the SPSC is consulted by the governor while framing rules for appointment to judicial service of the state other than the posts of district judges. In this regard, the concerned state high court is also consulted.

JOINT STATE PUBLIC SERVICE COMMISSION

The Constitution makes a provision for the establishment of a Joint State Public Service Commission

(JSPSC) for two or more states. While the UPSC and the SPSC are created directly by the Constitution, a JSPSC can be created by an act of Parliament on the request of the state legislatures concerned. Thus, a JSPSC is a statutory and not a constitutional body. The two states of Punjab and Haryana had a JSPSC for a short period, after the creation of Haryana out of Punjab in 1966.

The chairman and members of a JSPSC are appointed by the president. They hold office for a term of six years or until they attain the age of 62 years, whichever is earlier. They can be suspended or removed by the president. They can also resign from their offices at any time by submitting their resignation letters to the president.

The number of members of a JSPSC and their conditions of service are determined by the president.

A JSPSC presents its annual performance report to each of the concerned state governors. Each governor places the report before the state legislature.

The UPSC can also serve the needs of a state on the request of the state governor and with the approval of the president.

As provided by the Government of India Act of 1919, a Central Public Service Commission was set up in 1926 and entrusted with the task of recruiting civil servants. The Government of India Act of 1935 provided for the establishment of not only a Federal Public Service Commission but also a Provincial Public Service Commission and Joint Public Service Commission for two or more provinces.

Table 40.1 *Articles Related to SPSC at a Glance*

Article No.	Subject-matter
315	Public Service Commissions for the Union and for the states
316	Appointment and term of office of members
317	Removal and suspension of a member of a Public Service Commission
318	Power to make regulations as to conditions of service of members and staff of the Commission
319	Prohibition as to the holding of office by members of commission on ceasing to be such members
320	Functions of Public Service Commissions
321	Power to extend functions of Public Service Commissions
322	Expenses of Public Service Commissions
323	Reports of Public Service Commissions

NOTES AND REFERENCES

1. Originally, it was 60 years. The 41st Amendment Act of 1976 raised it to 62 years.
2. Added by the 15th Amendment Act of 1963.
3. In 1993, the Supreme Court ruled that appointment of a university professor (known to be blind) as a member of a SPSC cannot be set aside on the ground of infirmity of body or mind.
4. The difference between removal and dismissal is that the former does not disqualify for future employment under the government while the latter disqualifies for future employment under the government.
5. Such Rules are known as the SPSC (Exemption from consultation) Regulations.

Finance Commission

Article 280 of the Constitution of India provides for a Finance Commission as a quasi judicial body. It is constituted by the president of India every fifth year or at such earlier time as he considers necessary.

COMPOSITION

The Finance Commission consists of a chairman and four other members to be appointed by the president. They hold office for such period as specified by the president in his order. They are eligible for reappointment.

The Constitution authorises the Parliament to determine the qualifications of members of the commission and the manner in which they should be selected. Accordingly, the Parliament has specified the qualifications of the chairman and members of the commission[1]. The chairman should be a person having experience in public affairs and the four other members should be selected from amongst the following:

1. A judge of high court or one qualified to be appointed as one.
2. A person who has specialised knowledge of finance and accounts of the government.
3. A person who has wide experience in financial matters and in administration.
4. A person who has special knowledge of economics.

FUNCTIONS

The Finance Commission is required to make recommendations to the president of India on the following matters:

1. The distribution of the net proceeds of taxes to be shared between the Centre and the states, and the allocation between the states of the respective shares of such proceeds.
2. The principles that should govern the grants-in-aid to the states by the Centre (i.e., out of the consolidated fund of India).
3. The measures needed to augment the consolidated fund of a state to supplement the resources of the panchayats and the municipalities in the state on the basis of the recommendations made by the state finance commission[2].
4. Any other matter referred to it by the president in the interests of sound finance.

Till 1960, the commission also suggested the grants given to the States of Assam, Bihar, Odisha and West Bengal in lieu of assignment of any share of the net proceeds in each year of export duty on jute and jute products. These grants were to be given for a temporary period of ten years from the commencement of the Constitution.

The commission submits its report to the president. He lays it before both the Houses of Parliament along with an explanatory memorandum as to the action taken on its recommendations.

ADVISORY ROLE

It must be clarified here that the recommendations made by the Finance Commission are only of advisory nature and hence, not binding on the government. It is up to the Union government to implement its recommendations on granting money to the states.

To put it in other words, 'It is nowhere laid down in the Constitution that the recommendations of the commission shall be binding upon the Government of India or that it would give rise to a legal right in favour of the beneficiary states to receive the money recommended to be offered to them by the Commission'[3].

As rightly observed by Dr. P.V. Rajamannar, the Chairman of the Fourth Finance Commission, "Since the Finance Commission is a constitutional body expected to be quasi-judicial, its recommendations should not be turned down by the Government of India unless there are very compelling reasons".

IMPACT OF PLANNING COMMISSION

The Constitution of India envisages the Finance commission as the balancing wheel of fiscal federalism in India. However, its role in the Centre–state fiscal relations has been undermined by the emergence of the Planning Commission, a non-constitutional and a non-statutory body. Dr P V Rajamannar, the Chairman of the Fourth Finance commission, highlighted the overlapping of functions and responsibilities between the Finance Commission and the Planning Commission in federal fiscal transfers in the following way[4]:

It is the setting up of the Planning Commission that has in practice restricted the scope and functions of the Finance Commission. I say 'in practice' because there has been no amendment of the Constitution to confine the functions of the Finance Commission to merely ascertain and cover the revenue gap of each state, on a review of the forecast of revenue and expenditure furnished by the state.

The reference in Article 275 to grants-in-aid to the revenues of states is not confined to revenue expenditure only. There is no legal warrant for excluding from the scope of the Finance Commission all capital grants; even the capital requirements of a state may be properly met by grants-in-aid under Article 275, made on the recommendations of the Finance Commission.

The legal position, therefore, is that there is nothing in the Constitution to prevent the finance commission from taking into consideration both capital and revenue requirements of the states in formulating a scheme of devolution and in recommending grants under Article 275 of the Constitution. But the setting up of Planning Commission inevitably has led to a duplication and overlapping of functions, to avoid which a practice has grown which has resulted in the curtailment of the functions of the finance commission.

As the entire plan, with regard to both policy and programme, comes within the purview of the Planning Commission and as the assistance to be given by the Centre for plan projects either by way of grants or loans is practically dependent on the recommendations of the Planning Commission, it is obvious that a body like the Finance Commission cannot operate in the same field. The main functions of the Finance Commission now consist in determining the revenue gap of each state and providing for filling up the gap by a scheme of devolution, partly by a distribution of taxes and duties and partly by grants-in-aid.

We, therefore, recommend that in future the Finance Commission may be asked to make recommendations on the principles which should govern the distribution of plan grants to the states. In order that the Finance Commission may be able to make such recommendations, it will be necessary that it should have before it an outline of the Five Year Plan as prepared by the Planning Commission. The appointment of the Finance Commission will, therefore, have to be so timed that it will have before it this outline before it finalises its recommendations. While the principles governing the distribution of the plan grants will be set out by the Finance Commission, the application of these principles from year to year will be left to the Planning Commission and the Government.

COMMISSIONS APPOINTED

Till now, fourteen finance commissions have been constituted. The name of the commission, the years in which they were constituted and submitted their reports, and the name of the chairman are given in Table 41.1.

Table 41.1 *Finance Commissions Appointed so far*

Finance Commission	Chairman	Appointed in	Submitted Report in	Period of implementation of Report
First	K.C. Neogy	1951	1952	1952–57
Second	K. Santhanam	1956	1957	1957–62
Third	A.K. Chanda	1960	1961	1962–66
Fourth	Dr. P.V. Rajamannar	1964	1965	1966–69
Fifth	Mahavir Tyagi	1968	1969	1969–74
Sixth	Brahamananda Reddy	1972	1973	1974–79
Seventh	J.M. Shelat	1977	1978	1979–84
Eighth	Y.B. Chavan	1982	1984	1984–89
Ninth	N.K.P. Salve	1987	1989	1989–95
Tenth	K.C. Pant	1992	1994	1995–2000
Eleventh	A.M. Khusro	1998	2000	2000–2005
Twelfth	Dr. C. Rangarajan	2002	2004	2005–2010
Thirteenth	Dr. Vijay Kelkar	2007	2009	2010–2015
Fourteenth	Y.V. Reddy	2013	2014 (expected)	2015–2020

Table 41.2 *Articles Related to Finance Commission at a Glance*

Article No.	Subject-matter
280.	Finance Commission
281.	Recommendations of the Finance Commission

NOTES AND REFERENCES

1. Vide the Finance Commission Act, 1951.
2. This function was added by the 73rd and 74th Constitutional Amendment Acts of 1992, which have granted constitutional status and protection on the panchayats and the municipalities respectively.
3. D D Basu, *Introduction to the Constitution of India*, Wadhwa 19th Edition, 2001, p. 331.
4. Report of the Fourth Finance Commission, New Delhi, Government of India, 1965, p. 88–90.

National Commission for SCs

The National Commission for Scheduled Castes (SCs) is a constitutional body in the sense that it is directly established by Article 338 of the Constitution[1]. On the other hand, the other national commissions like the National Commission for Women (1992), the National Commission for Minorities (1993), the National Commission for Backward Classes (1993), the National Human Rights Commission (1993) and the National Commission for Protection of Child Rights (2007) are statutory bodies in the sense that they are established by acts of the Parliament[2].

EVOLUTION OF THE COMMISSION

Originally, Article 338 of the Constitution provided for the appointment of a Special Officer for Scheduled Castes (SCs) and Scheduled Tribes (STs) to investigate all matters relating to the constitutional safeguards for the SCs and STs and to report to the President on their working[3]. He was designated as the Commissioner for SCs and STs and assigned the said duty.

In 1978, the Government (through a Resolution) set up a non-statutory multi-member Commission for SCs and STs; the Office of Commissioner for SCs and STs also continued to exist.

In 1987, the Government (through another Resolution) modified the functions of the Commission and renamed it as the National Commission for SCs and STs[4].

Later, the 65th Constitutional Amendment Act of 1990[5] provided for the establishment of a high level multi-member National Commission for SCs and STs in the place of a single Special Officer for SCs and STs. This constitutional body replaced the Commissioner for SCs and STs as well as the Commission set up under the Resolution of 1987.

Again, the 89th Constitutional Amendment Act of 2003[6] bifurcated the combined National Commission for SCs and STs into two separate bodies, namely, National Commission for Scheduled Castes (under Article 338) and National Commission for Scheduled Tribes (under Article 338-A).

The separate National Commission for SCs came into existence in 2004. It consists of a chairperson, a vice-chairperson and three other members. They are appointed by the President by warrant under his hand and seal. Their conditions of service and tenure of office are also determined by the President[7].

FUNCTIONS OF THE COMMISSION

The functions of the Commission are:
    (a) To investigate and monitor all matters relating to the constitutional and other legal safeguards for the SCs and to evaluate their working;
    (b) To inquire into specific complaints with respect to the deprivation of rights and safeguards of the SCs;
    (c) To participate and advise on the planning process of socio-economic development of the SCs and to evaluate the progress of their development under the Union or a state;

(d) To present to the President, annually and at such other times as it may deem fit, reports upon the working of those safeguards;

(e) To make recommendations as to the measures that should be taken by the Union or a state for the effective implementation of those safeguards and other measures for the protection, welfare and socio-economic development of the SCs; and

(f) To discharge such other functions in relation to the protection, welfare and development and advancement of the SCs as the president may specify.

REPORT OF THE COMMISSION

The commission presents an annual report to the president. It can also submit a report as and when it thinks necessary.

The President places all such reports before the Parliament, along with a memorandum explaining the action taken on the recommendations made by the Commission. The memorandum should also contain the reasons for the non-acceptance of any of such recommendations.

The President also forwards any report of the Commission pertaining to a state government to the state governor. The governor places it before the state legislature, along with a memorandum explaining the action taken on the recommendations of the Commission. The memorandum should also contain the reasons for the non-acceptance of any of such recommendations.

POWERS OF THE COMMISSION

The Commission is vested with the power to regulate its own procedure.

The Commission, while investigating any matter or inquiring into any complaint, has all the powers of a civil court trying a suit and in particular in respect of the following matters:

(a) summoning and enforcing the attendance of any person from any part of India and examining him on oath;

(b) requiring the discovery and production of any document;

(c) receiving evidence on affidavits;

(d) requisitioning any public record from any court or office;

(e) issuing summons for the examination of witnesses and documents; and

(f) any other matter which the President may determine.

The Central government and the state governments are required to consult the Commission on all major policy matters affecting the SCs.

The Commission is also required to discharge similar functions with regard to the other backward classes (OBCs) and the Anglo-Indian Community as it does with respect to the SCs. In other words, the Commission has to investigate all matters relating to the constitutional and other legal safeguards for the OBCs and the Anglo-Indian Community and report to the President upon their working[8].

NOTES AND REFERENCES

1. Article 338 is contained in Part XVI entitled as 'Special Provisions Relating to Certain Classes'.
2. The years in the bracket indicate the years of their establishment.
3. The constitutional safeguards for the SCs and STs are explained in Chapter 63.
4. It was made as a National Level Advisory Body to advise the Government on broad policy issues and levels of development of SCs and STs.
5. The Act came into force on 12-03-1992.

6. The Act came into force on 19-02-2004.
7. Under the Rules, they hold office for a term of three years.
8. Clause 10 of Article 338 reads as follows: "In this article, references to the Scheduled Castes shall be construed as including references to such other backward classes as the President may, on receipt of the report of a Commission appointed under clause (1) of article 340 by order specify and also to the Anglo-Indian Community".

National Commission for STs

Like the National Commission for Schedules Castes (SCs), the National Commission for Scheduled Tribes (STs) is also a constitutional body in the sense that it is directly established by Article 338-A of the Constitution[1].

SEPARATE COMMISSION FOR STS

The National Commission for SCs and STs came into being consequent upon passing of the 65th Constitutional Amendment Act of 1990[2]. The Commission was established under Article 338 of the Constitution with the objective of monitoring all the safeguards provided for the SCs and STs under the Constitution or other laws[3].

Geographically and culturally, the STs are different from the SCs and their problems are also different from those of SCs. In 1999, a new Ministry of Tribal Affairs was created to provide a sharp focus to the welfare and development of the STs. It was felt necessary that the Ministry of Tribal Affairs should co-ordinate all activities relating to the STs as it would not be administratively feasible for the Ministry of Social Justice and Empowerment to perform this role[4].

Hence, in order to safeguard the interests of the STs more effectively, it was proposed to set up a separate National Commission for STs by bifurcating the existing combined National Commission for SCs and STs. This was done by passing the 89th Constitutional Amendment Act of 2003[5]. This Act further amended Article 338 and inserted a new Article 338-A in the Constitution.

The separate National Commission for STs came into existence in 2004. It consists of a chairperson, a vice-chairperson and three other members. They are appointed by the President by warrant under his hand and seal. Their conditions of service and tenure of office are also determined by the President[6].

FUNCTIONS OF THE COMMISSION

The functions of the Commission are:
(a) To investigate and monitor all matters relating to the constitutional and other legal safeguards for the STs and to evaluate their working;
(b) To inquire into specific complaints with respect to the deprivation of rights and safeguards of the STs;
(c) To participate and advise on the planning process of socio-economic development of the STs and to evaluate the progress of their development under the Union or a state;
(d) To present to the President, annually and at such other times as it may deem fit, reports upon the working of those safeguards;
(e) To make recommendations as to the measures that should be taken by the Union or a state for the effective implementation of those safeguards and other measures for the protection, welfare and socio-economic development of the STs; and
(f) To discharge such other functions in relation to the protection, welfare and development and

advancement of the STs as the President may specify.

OTHER FUNCTIONS OF THE COMMISSION

In 2005, the President specified the following other functions of the Commission in relation to the protection, welfare and development and advancement of the STs[7]:

(i) Measures to be taken over conferring ownership rights in respect of minor forest produce to STs living in forest areas

(ii) Measures to be taken to safeguard rights of the tribal communities over mineral resources, water resources etc., as per law

(iii) Measures to be taken for the development of tribals and to work for more viable livelihood strategies

(iv) Measures to be taken to improve the efficacy of relief and rehabilitation measures for tribal groups displaced by development projects

(v) Measures to be taken to prevent alienation of tribal people from land and to effectively rehabilitate such people in whose case alienation has already taken place

(vi) Measures to be taken to elicit maximum cooperation and involvement of tribal communities for protecting forests and undertaking social afforestation

(vii) Measures to be taken to ensure full implementation of the Provisions of Panchayats (Extension to the Scheduled Areas) Act, 1996

(viii) Measures to be taken to reduce and ultimately eliminate the practice of shifting cultivation by tribals that lead to their continuous disempowerment and degradation of land and the environment

REPORT OF THE COMMISSION

The Commission presents an annual report to the President. It can also submit a report as and when it thinks necessary.

The President places all such reports before the Parliament, along with a memorandum explaining the action taken on the recommendations made by the Commission. The memorandum should also contain the reasons for the non-acceptance of any of such recommendations.

The President also forwards any report of the Commission pertaining to a state government to the state governor. The governor places it before the state legislature, along with a memorandum explaining the action taken on the recommendations of the Commission. The memorandum should also contain the reasons for the non-acceptance of any of such recommendations.

POWERS OF THE COMMISSION

The Commission is vested with the power to regulate its own procedure.

The Commission, while investigating any matter or inquiring into any complaint, has all the powers of a civil court trying a suit and in particular in respect of the following matters:

(a) summoning and enforcing the attendance of any person from any part of India and examining him on oath;

(b) requiring the discovery and production of any document;

(c) receiving evidence on affidavits;

(d) requisitioning any public record from any court or office;

(e) issuing summons for the examination of witnesses and documents; and

(f) any other matter which the President may determine.

The Central government and the state governments are required to consult the Commission on all major policy matters affecting the STs.

NOTES AND REFERENCES

1. Article 338-A is contained in Part XVI entitled as 'Special Provisions Relating to Certain Classes'. This Article was inserted by the 89th Constitutional Amendment Act of 2003.
2. The Act came into force on 12-03-1992.
3. The constitutional safeguards for the SCs and STs are explained in Chapter 63.
4. The Ministry of Social Justice and Empowerment co-ordinates all activities relating to the SCs.
5. The Act came into force on 19-02-2004.
6. Under the Rules, they hold office for a term of three years.
7. The National Commission for the Scheduled Tribes (Specification of Other Functions) Rules, 2005.

Special Officer for Linguistic Minorities

CONSTITUTIONAL PROVISIONS

Originally, the Constitution of India did not make any provision with respect to the Special Officer for Linguistic Minorities[1]. Later, the States Reorganisation Commission (1953-55) made a recommendation in this regard. Accordingly, the Seventh Constitutional Amendment Act of 1956 inserted a new Article 350-B in Part XVII of the Constitution[2]. This article contains the following provisions:

1. There should be a Special Officer for Linguistic Minorities. He is to be appointed by the President of India.

2. It would be the duty of the Special Officer to investigate all matters relating to the safeguards provided for linguistic minorities under the Constitution[3]. He would report to the President upon those matters at such intervals as the President may direct. The President should place all such reports before each House of Parliament and send to the governments of the states concerned.

It must be noted here that the Constitution does not specify the qualifications, tenure, salaries and allowances, service conditions and procedure for removal of the Special Officer for Linguistic Minorities.

COMMISSIONER FOR LINGUISTIC MINORITIES

In pursuance of the provision of Article 350-B of the Constitution, the office of the Special Officer for Linguistic Minorities was created in 1957. He is designated as the Commissioner for Linguistic Minorities.

The Commissioner has his headquarters at Allahabad (Uttar Pradesh). He has three regional offices at Belgaum (Karnataka), Chennai (Tamil Nadu) and Kolkata (West Bengal). Each is headed by an Assistant Commissioner.

The Commissioner is assisted at headquarters by Deputy Commissioner and an Assistant Commissioner. He maintains liaison with the State Governments and Union Territories through nodal officers appointed by them.

At the Central level, the Commissioner falls under the Ministry of Minority Affairs. Hence, he submits the annual reports or other reports to the President through the Union Minority Affairs Minister[4].

ROLE

The Commissioner takes up all the matters pertaining to the grievances arising out of the non-implementation of the Constitutional and Nationally Agreed Scheme of Safeguards provided to linguistic minorities that come to its notice or are brought to its knowledge by the linguistic minority individuals, groups, associations or organisations at the highest political and administrative levels of the state governments and UT administrations and recommends remedial actions to be taken[5].

To promote and preserve linguistic minority groups, the Ministry of Minority Affairs has requested the State Governments / Union Territories to give wide publicity to the constitutional safeguards provided to linguistic minorities and to take necessary administrative measures. The state governments and UT Administrations were urged to accord priority to the implementation of the scheme of safeguards for linguistic minorities. The Commissioner launched a 10 point programme to lend fresh impetus to Governmental efforts towards the preservation of the language and culture of linguistic minorities[6].

Vision and Mission

The vision and mission of the Commissioner are mentioned here.[7]

Vision

Streamlining and strengthening implementation machinery and mechanism for effective implementation of the Constitutional safeguards for the Linguistic Minorities, thereby ensuring protection of the rights of speakers of the minority languages so as to provide them equal opportunities for inclusive and integrated development.

Mission

To ensure that all the states / U.T.s effectively implement the Constitutional safeguards and the nationally agreed scheme of safeguards for the linguistic minorities for providing them equal opportunities for inclusive development.

Functions and Objectives

In more detail, the functions and objectives of the Commissioner are as follows[8]:

Functions

1. To investigate all matters related to safeguards provided to the linguistic minorities
2. To submit to the President of India, the reports on the status of implementation of the Constitutional and the nationally agreed safeguards for the linguistic minorities
3. To monitor the implementation of safeguards through questionnaires, visits, conferences, seminars, meetings, review mechanism, etc

Objectives

1. To provide equal opportunities to the linguistic minorities for inclusive development and national integration
2. To spread awareness amongst the linguistic minorities about the safeguards available to them
3. To ensure effective implementation of the safeguards provided for the linguistic minorities in the Constitution and other safeguards, which are agreed to by the states/U.T.s
4. To handle the representations for redress of grievances related to the safeguards for linguistic minorities

Notes and References

1. A linguistic minority is a group of people whose mother tongue is different from that of the majority in the state or part of a state. Thus, the linguistic minorities are determined on a state-wise basis.
2. Part XVII is entitled as 'Official Language' and consists of four chapters. Article 350-B is contained in the fourth chapter entitled as 'Special Directives'.
3. The constitutional safeguards for linguistic minorities are explained in Chapter 58.
4. So far, 47 reports have been presented.
5. India 2013, Publications Division, Government of India, P. 1012.
6. Annual Report 2011-2012, Ministry of Minority Affairs, Government of India, P. 38.
7. 47th Report of the Commissioner for Linguistic Minorities, July 2008 to June 2010, P. 222.
8. Ibid.

Comptroller and Auditor General of India

The Constitution of India (Article 148) provides for an independent office of the Comptroller and Auditor General of India (CAG). He is the head of the Indian Audit and Accounts Department[1]. He is the guardian of the public purse and controls the entire financial system of the country at both the levels—the Centre and the state. His duty is to uphold the Constitution of India and laws of Parliament in the field of financial administration. This is the reason why Dr B R Ambedkar said that the CAG shall be the most important Officer under the Constitution of India[2]. He is one of the bulwarks of the democratic system of government in India; the others being the Supreme Court, the Election Commission and the Union Public Service Commission.

APPOINTMENT AND TERM

The CAG is appointed by the president of India by a warrant under his hand and seal. The CAG, before taking over his office, makes and subscribes before the president an oath or affirmation:

1. to bear true faith and allegiance to the Constitution of India;
2. to uphold the sovereignty and integrity of India;
3. to duly and faithfully and to the best of his ability, knowledge and judgement perform the duties of his office without fear or favour, affection or ill-will; and
4. to uphold the Constitution and the laws.

He holds office for a period of six years or upto the age of 65 years, whichever is earlier. He can resign any time from his office by addressing the resignation letter to the president. He can also be removed by the president on same grounds and in the same manner as a judge of the Supreme Court. In other words, he can be removed by the president on the basis of a resolution passed to that effect by both the Houses of Parliament with special majority, either on the ground of proved misbehaviour or incapacity.

INDEPENDENCE

The Constitution has made the following provisions to safeguard and ensure the independence of CAG:

1. He is provided with the security of tenure. He can be removed by the president only in accordance with the procedure mentioned in the Constitution. Thus, he does not hold his office till the pleasure of the president, though he is appointed by him.
2. He is not eligible for further office, either under the Government of India or of any state, after he ceases to hold his office.
3. His salary and other service conditions are determined by the Parliament. His salary is equal to that of a judge of the Supreme Court[3].
4. Neither his salary nor his rights in respect of leave of absence, pension or age of retirement can be altered to his disadvantage after his appointment.

5. The conditions of service of persons serving in the Indian Audit and Accounts Department and the administrative powers of the CAG are prescribed by the president after consultation with the CAG.
6. The administrative expenses of the office of the CAG, including all salaries, allowances and pensions of persons serving in that office are charged upon the Consolidated Fund of India. Thus, they are not subject to the vote of Parliament.

Further, no minister can represent the CAG in Parliament (both Houses) and no minister can be called upon to take any responsibility for any actions done by him.

DUTIES AND POWERS

The Constitution (Article 149) authorises the Parliament to prescribe the duties and powers of the CAG in relation to the accounts of the Union and of the states and of any other authority or body. Accordingly, the Parliament enacted the CAG's (Duties, Powers and Conditions of Service) act, 1971. This Act was amended in 1976 to separate accounts from audit in the Central government.

The duties and functions of the CAG as laid down by the Parliament and the Constitution are:
1. He audits the accounts related to all expenditure from the Consolidated Fund of India, consolidated fund of each state and consolidated fund of each union territory having a Legislative Assembly.
2. He audits all expenditure from the Contingency Fund of India and the Public Account of India as well as the contingency fund of each state and the public account of each state.
3. He audits all trading, manufacturing, profit and loss accounts, balance sheets and other subsidiary accounts kept by any department of the Central Government and state governments.
4. He audits the receipts and expenditure of the Centre and each state to satisfy himself that the rules and procedures in that behalf are designed to secure an effective check on the assessment, collection and proper allocation of revenue.

5. He audits the receipts and expenditure of the following:
   (a) All bodies and authorities substantially financed from the Central or state revenues;
   (b) Government companies; and
   (c) Other corporations and bodies, when so required by related laws.
6. He audits all transactions of the Central and state governments related to debt, sinking funds, deposits, advances, suspense accounts and remittance business. He also audits receipts, stock accounts and others, with approval of the President, or when required by the President.
7. He audits the accounts of any other authority when requested by the President or Governor. For example, the audit of local bodies.
8. He advises the President with regard to prescription of the form in which the accounts of the Centre and the states shall be kept (Article 150).
9. He submits his audit reports relating to the accounts of the Centre to President, who shall, in turn, place them before both the Houses of Parliament (Article 151).
10. He submits his audit reports relating to the accounts of a state to governor, who shall, in turn, place them before the state legislature (Article 151).
11. He ascertains and certifies the net proceeds of any tax or duty (Article 279). His certificate is final. The 'net proceeds' means the proceeds of a tax or a duty minus the cost of collection.
12. He acts as a guide, friend and philosopher of the Public Accounts Committee of the Parliament.
13. He compiles and maintains the accounts of state governments. In 1976, he was relieved of his responsibilities with regard to the compilation and maintenance of accounts of the Central Government due to the separation of accounts from audit, that is, departmentalisation of accounts.

The CAG submits three audit reports to the President—audit report on appropriation accounts, audit report on finance accounts, and audit report on public undertakings. The President lays these reports before both the Houses of Parliament. After this, the Public Accounts Committee examines them and reports its findings to the Parliament.

The appropriation accounts compare the actual expenditure with the expenditure sanctioned by the Parliament through the Appropriation Act, while the finance accounts show the annual receipts and disbursements of the Union government.

ROLE

The role of CAG is to uphold the Constitution of India and the laws of Parliament in the field of financial administration. The accountability of the executive (i.e., council of ministers) to the Parliament in the sphere of financial administration is secured through audit reports of the CAG. The CAG is an agent of the Parliament and conducts audit of expenditure on behalf of the Parliament. Therefore, he is responsible only to the Parliament.

The CAG has more freedom with regard to audit of expenditure than with regard to audit of receipts, stores and stock. "Whereas in relation to expenditure he decides the scope of audit and frames his own audit codes and manuals, he has to proceed with the approval of the executive government in relation to rules for the conduct of the other audits."[3a]

The CAG has 'to ascertain whether money shown in the accounts as having been disbursed was legally available for and applicable to the service or the purpose to which they have been applied or charged and whether the expenditure conforms to the authority that governs it'. In addition to this legal and regulatory audit, the CAG can also conduct the propriety audit, that is, he can look into the 'wisdom, faithfulness and economy' of government expenditure and comment on the wastefulness and extravagance of such expenditure. However, unlike the legal and regulatory audit, which is obligatory on the part of the CAG, the propriety audit is discretionary.

The secret service expenditure is a limitation on the auditing role of the CAG. In this regard, the CAG cannot call for particulars of expenditure incurred by the executive agencies, but has to accept a certificate from the competent administrative authority that the expenditure has been so incurred under his authority.

The Constitution of India visualises the CAG to be Comptroller as well as Auditor General. However, in practice, the CAG is fulfilling the role of an Auditor-General only and not that of a Comptroller. In other words, 'the CAG has no control over the issue of money from the consolidated fund and many departments are authorised to draw money by issuing cheques without specific authority from the CAG, who is concerned only at the audit stage when the expenditure has already taken place'[4]. In this respect, the CAG of India differs totally from the CAG of Britain who has powers of both Comptroller as well as Auditor General. In other words, in Britain, the executive can draw money from the public exchequer only with the approval of the CAG.

CAG AND CORPORATIONS

The role of CAG in the auditing of public corporations is limited. Broadly speaking, his relationship with the public corporations falls into the following three categories:

(i) Some corporations are audited totally and directly by the CAG, for example, Damodar Valley Corporation, Oil and Natural Gas Commission, Air India, Indian Airlines Corporation, and others.

(ii) Some other corporations are audited by private professional auditors who are appointed by the Central Government in consultation with the CAG. If necessary, the CAG can conduct supplementary audit. The examples are, Central Warehousing Corporation, Industrial Finance Corporation, and others.

(iii) Some other corporations are totally subjected to private audit. In other words, their audit is done exclusively by private professional auditors and the CAG does not come into the picture at all. They submit their annual reports and accounts directly to the Parliament. Examples of such corporations are Life Insurance Corporation of India, Reserve Bank of India, State Bank of India, Food Corporation of India, and others.

The role of the CAG in the auditing of Government companies is also limited. They are audited by private auditors who are appointed by the Government on the advise of the CAG. The CAG can also undertake supplementary audit or test audit of such companies.

In 1968, an Audit Board was established as a part of the office of CAG to associate outside specialists and experts to handle the technical aspects of audit of specialised enterprises like engineering, iron and steel, chemicals and so on. This board was established on the recommendations of the Administrative Reforms Commission of India. It consists of a Chairman and two members appointed by the CAG.

APPLEBY'S CRITICISM

Paul H Appleby, in his two reports on Indian Administration, was very critical of the role of CAG and attacked the significance of his work[5]. He also suggested that the CAG should be relieved of the responsibility of audit. In other words, he recommended the abolition of the office of CAG. His points of criticism of Indian audit are as follows:

1. The function of the CAG in India, is in a large measure, an inheritance from the colonial rule.

2. The CAG is today a primary cause of widespread and paralysing unwillingness to decide and to act. Auditing has a repressive and negative influence.

3. The Parliament has a greatly exaggerated notion of the importance of auditing to Parliamentary responsibility, and so has failed to define the functions of the CAG as the Constitution contemplated it would do.

4. The CAG's function is not really a very important one. Auditors do not know and cannot be expected to know very much about good administration; their prestige is highest with others who do not know much about administration.

5. Auditors know what is auditing, which is not administration; it is a necessary, but a highly pedestrian function with a narrow perspective and a very limited usefulness.

6. A deputy secretary in the department knows more about the problems in his department than the CAG and his entire staff.

Table 45.1   *Articles Related to Comptroller and Auditor-General of India at a Glance*

Article No.	Subject-matter
148.	Comptroller and Auditor-General of India
149.	Duties and powers of the Comptroller and Auditor-General
150.	Form of accounts of the Union and of the States
151.	Audit reports

NOTES AND REFERENCES

1. The Indian Audit and Accounts Department was created during the British rule in 1753.
2. *Constituent Assembly Debates*, Volume VIII, p. 405.
3. In 2009, the salary of a judge of the Supreme Court had been fixed at Rs 90,000 per month.
3a. Wattal, P.K., Parliamentary Financial Control in India, Second Edition. Bombay : Minerva Book Shop, 1962, P. 235.
4. D D Basu, *Introduction to the Constitution of India,* Wadhwa, 19th Edition, 2001, p. 198.
5. The two reports are : Public Administration in India (1953) and Re-examination of India's Administrative System, 1956.

Attorney General of India

The Constitution (Article 76) has provided for the office of the Attorney General for India[1]. He is the highest law officer in the country.

APPOINTMENT AND TERM

The Attorney General (AG) is appointed by the president. He must be a person who is qualified to be appointed a judge of the Supreme Court. In other words, he must be a citizen of India and he must have been a judge of some high court for five years or an advocate of some high court for ten years or an eminent jurist, in the opinion of the president.

The term of office of the AG is not fixed by the Constitution. Further, the Constitution does not contain the procedure and grounds for his removal. He holds office during the pleasure of the president. This means that he may be removed by the president at any time. He may also quit his office by submitting his resignation to the president. Conventionally, he resigns when the government (council of ministers) resigns or is replaced, as he is appointed on its advice.

The remuneration of the AG is not fixed by the Constitution. He receives such remuneration as the president may determine.

DUTIES AND FUNCTIONS

As the chief law officer of the Government of India, the duties of the AG include the following:

1. To give advice to the Government of India upon such legal matters, which are referred to him by the president.
2. To perform such other duties of a legal character that are assigned to him by the president.
3. To discharge the functions conferred on him by the Constitution or any other law.

The president has assigned the following duties to the AG[2]:

1. To appear on behalf of the Government of India in all cases in the Supreme Court in which the Government of India is concerned.
2. To represent the Government of India in any reference made by the president to the Supreme Court under Article 143 of the Constitution.
3. To appear (when required by the Government of India) in any high court in any case in which the Government of India is concerned.

RIGHTS AND LIMITATIONS

In the performance of his official duties, the Attorney General has the right of audience in all courts in the territory of India. Further, he has the right to speak and to take part in the proceedings of both the Houses of Parliament or their joint sitting and any committee of the Parliament of which he may be named a member, but without a right to vote. He enjoys all the privileges and immunities that are available to a member of Parliament.

Following limitations are placed on the Attorney General in order to avoid any complication and conflict of duty:

1. He should not advise or hold a brief against the Government of India.
2. He should not advise or hold a brief in cases in which he is called upon to advise or appear for the Government of India.
3. He should not defend accused persons in criminal prosecutions without the permission of the Government of India.
4. He should not accept appointment as a director in any company or corporation without the permission of the Government of India.

However, the Attorney General is not a full-time counsel for the Government. He does not fall in the category of government servants. Further, he is not debarred from private legal practice.

Solicitor General of India

In addition to the AG, there are other law officers of the Government of India. They are the solicitor general of India and additional solicitor general of India. They assist the AG in the fulfilment of his official responsibilities. It should be noted here that only the office of the AG is created by the Constitution. In other words, Article 76 does not mention about the solicitor general and additional solicitor general.

The AG is not a member of the Central cabinet. There is a separate law minister in the Central cabinet to look after legal matters at the government level[3].

Table 46.1 *Articles Related to Attorney-General of India at a Glance*

Article No.	Subject-matter
76.	Attorney-General of India
88.	Rights of Attorney-General as respects the Houses of Parliament and its Committee
105.	Powers, privileges and immunities of Attorney-General

Notes and References

1. Article 76 of Chapter 1 (The Executive) in Part V (The Union) of the Constitution deals with the office of the Attorney General of India. This is the only Article dealing with this office.
2. Notification No. F. 43-50C, 26 January 1950, *Gazette of India,* Extraordinary, Volume VII, p. 33–34.
3. During the prime ministership of Jawaharlal Nehru, a proposal was put forward by the Central government that the office of the Attorney General be merged with the office of the law minister. It did not materialise.

Advocate General of the State

The Constitution (Article 165) has provided for the office of the advocate general for the states.[1] He is the highest law officer in the state. Thus he corresponds to the Attorney General of India.

APPOINTMENT AND TERM

The advocate general is appointed by the governor. He must be a person who is qualified to be appointed a judge of a high court. In other words, he must be a citizen of India and must have held a judicial office[2] for ten years or been an advocate of a high court for ten years[3].

The term of office of the advocate general is not fixed by the Constitution. Further, the Constitution does not contain the procedure and grounds for his removal. He holds office during the pleasure of the governor. This means that he may be removed by the governor at any time. He may also quit his office by submitting his resignation to the governor. Conventionally, he resigns when the government (council of ministers) resigns or is replaced, as he is appointed on its advice.

The remuneration of the advocate general is not fixed by the Constitution. He receives such remuneration as the governor may determine.

DUTIES AND FUNCTIONS

As the chief law officer of the government in the state, the duties of the advocate general include the following:

1. To give advice to the government of the state upon such legal matters which are referred to him by the governor.
2. To perform such other duties of a legal character that are assigned to him by the governor.
3. To discharge the functions conferred on him by the Constitution or any other law.

In the performance of his official duties, the advocate general is entitled to appear before any court of law within the state. Further, he has the right to speak and to take part in the proceedings of both the Houses of the state legislature or any committee of the state legislature of which he may be named a member, but without a right to vote. He enjoys all the privileges and immunities that are available to a member of the state legislature.

Table 47.1 *Articles Related to Advocate-General of the state at a Glance*

Article No.	Subject-matter
165.	Advocate-General of the State
177.	Rights of Advocate-General as respects the Houses of State Legislature and its Committee
194.	Powers, privileges and immunities of Advocate-General

Table 47.2   *Articles Related to Constitutional Bodies at a Glance*

Article No.	Constitutional Bodies
76.	Attorney-General of India
148.	Comptroller and Auditor-General of India
165.	Advocate-General of the State
243-I.	State Finance Commission
243-K.	State Election Commission
243ZD.	District Planning Committee
243ZE.	Metropolitan Planning Committee
263.	Inter-State Council
280.	Finance Commission
307.	Inter-State Trade and Commerce Commission
315.	Union Public Service Commission and State Public Service Commission
324.	Election Commission
338.	National Commission for Scheduled Castes
338A.	National Commission for Scheduled Tribes
339.	Scheduled Areas and Scheduled Tribes Commission
340.	Backward Classes Commission
344.	Official Language Commission and Official Language Committee of Parliament
350B.	Special Officer for Linguistic Minorities

NOTES AND REFERENCES

1. Article 165 of Chapter 2 (The Executive) in Part VI (The States) of the Constitution deals with the office of the advocate general of the state. This is the only article dealing with this office.

2. Judicial office means an office within the judicial service of the state.

3. Unlike the Supreme Court, the Constitution makes no provision for appointment of an eminent jurist as a judge of high court.

P ART VIII

N ON-C ONSTITUTIONAL B ODIES

Planning Commission

The Planning Commission was established in March 1950 by an executive resolution of the Government of India, (i.e., union cabinet) on the recommendation of the Advisory Planning Board constituted in 1946, under the chairmanship of K C Neogi. Thus, the Planning Commission is neither a constitutional body nor a statutory body. In other words, it is a non-constitutional or extra-constitutional body (i.e., not created by the Constitution) and a non-statutory body (not created by an act of Parliament). In India, it is the supreme organ of planning for social and economic development.

FUNCTIONS

The functions of the Planning Commission include the following:

1. To make an assessment of material, capital and human resources of the country and investigate the possibilities of augmenting them.
2. To formulate a plan for the most effective and balanced utilisation of the country's resources.
3. To determine priorities and to define stages in which the plan should be carried out.
4. To indicate the factors that retard economic development.
5. To determine the nature of the machinery required for successful implementation of the plan in each stage.
6. To appraise, from time to time, the progress achieved in execution of the plan and to recommend necessary adjustments.

7. To make appropriate recommendations for facilitating the discharge of its duties, or on a matter referred to it for advice by Central or state governments.

The Allocation of Business Rules have assigned the following matters (in addition to the above) to the Planning Commission:

1. Public Co-operation in National Development
2. Specific programmes for area development notified from time to time
3. Perspective Planning
4. Institute of Applied Manpower Research
5. Unique Identification Authority of India (UIDAI)
6. All matters relating to National Rainfed Area Authority (NRAA)

Earlier, the National Informatics Centre was also under the Planning Commission. Later, it was brought under the Ministry of Information Technology.

The Unique Identification Authority of India (UIDAI) has been constituted in January, 2009 as an attached office under aegis of Planning Commission.

With the transfer of National Rainfed Area Authority (NRAA) from Ministry of Agriculture to the Planning Commission, all matters relating to the NRAA will henceforth be looked after by Planning Commission.

It should be noted that the Planning Commission is only a staff agency—an advisory body and has no executive responsibility. It is not responsible for taking and implementing decisions. This responsibility rests with the Central and state governments.

COMPOSITION

The following points can be noted in context of the composition (membership) of the Planning Commission:

1. The prime minister of India has been the chairman of the commission. He presides over the meetings of the commission.
2. The commission has a deputy chairman. He is the *de facto* executive head (i.e., full-time functional head) of the commission. He is responsible for the formulation and submission of the draft Five-Year Plan to the Central cabinet. He is appointed by the Central cabinet for a fixed tenure and enjoys the rank of a cabinet minister. Though he is not a member of cabinet, he is invited to attend all its meeting (without a right to vote).
3. Some Central ministers are appointed as a part-time members of the commission. In any case, the finance minister and planning minister are the *ex-officio* (by virtue of) members of the commission.
4. The commission has four to seven full-time expert members. They enjoy the rank of a minister of state.
5. The commission has a member-secretary. He is usually a senior member of IAS.

The state governments are not represented in the commission in any way. Thus, the Planning Commission is wholly a Centre-constituted body.

INTERNAL ORGANISATION

The Planning Commission has the following three organs:

1. Technical Divisions
2. House keeping Branches
3. Programme Advisors

Technical Divisions The technical divisions are the major functional units of Planning Commission. They are mainly concerned with plan formulation, plan monitoring and plan evaluation. These fall under two broad categories, that is, general divisions (concerned with aspects of the entire economy) and subject divisions (concerned with specified fields of development)[1].

Housekeeping Branches The Planning Commission has the following housekeeping branches:

1. General administration branch.
2. Establishment branch.
3. Vigilance branch.
4. Accounts branch.
5. Personal training branch.

Programme Advisors The post of programme advisors were created in the Planning Commission in 1952 to act as a link between the Planning Commission and the states of Indian Union in the field of planning.

They perform the following functions:

(i) To make an assessment of the implementation of development programmes in states
(ii) To keep the Planning Commission and Union Ministries informed about the progress of Centre-aided schemes as well as centre-sponsored schemes
(iii) To advise the Planning Commission on the proposals received from states for their five year and annual plans

PERSONNEL

The internal organisation of Planning Commission has dual hierarchy—administrative and technical. The administrative hierarchy is headed by the Secretary of the Planning Commission who is assisted by Joint Secretaries, Deputy Secretaries, Under Secretaries and other administrative and clerical staff. These functionaries are drawn from the Indian Administrative Service, Indian Revenue Service, Central Secretariat Service, Indian Audit and Accounts Service and the other non-technical Central services.

The technical hierarchy, on the other hand, is headed by the Advisor who is assisted by Chiefs, Directors, Joint Directors and other technical staff. These functionaries are drawn from the Indian Economic Service, Indian Statistical Service, Central Engineering Service and other Central technical services. The Advisor is head of the technical division and enjoys the rank of either an Additional Secretary or a Joint Secretary.

PROGRAMME EVALUATION ORGANISATION

The Programme Evaluation Organisation (PEO) was established in 1952 as an independent unit of the Planning Commission. However, it functions under the general guidance and direction of the Planning Commission.

The PEO is headed by a Director / Chief who is assisted by Joint Directors, Deputy Directors, Assistant Directors and other staff.

The PEO has seven regional offices at Chennai, Hyderabad, Mumbai, Lucknow, Chandigarh, Jaipur and Kolkata. Each regional evaluation office of PEO is headed by a Deputy Director.

The PEO undertakes an assessment of the implementation of development programmes and plans as contained in Five-Year Plans to provide, from time to time, feedback to the Planning Commission and executive agencies. It also provides technical advice to state evaluation organisations.

CRITICAL EVALUATION

The Planning Commission was originally established as a staff agency with advisory role but in the course of time it has emerged as a powerful and directive authority whereby its recommendations are considered both by the Union and states. The critics have described it as a 'Super Cabinet', an 'Economic Cabinet', a 'Parallel Cabinet', the 'Fifth Wheel of the Coach' and so on.

The following observations are made on the domineering role played by the Planning Commission.

1. Administrative Reforms Commission (ARC) of India

The ARC observed: 'Under the Constitution, the ministers, whether in the Centre or the states, are in effect, the ultimate executive authorities. Unfortunately, the Planning Commission has, in some measures, earned the reputation of being a Parallel Cabinet and sometimes, a Super Cabinet'[2].

2. D R Gadgil

D R Gadgil, the former Deputy Chairman of Planning Commission, also criticised the role of Planning Commission and concluded that it has failed in its task. He said: 'The root of the failure lies in the process by which the Planning Commission, essentially only an advisory body, has come to mix itself with the actual process of the formation of public policies even in matters other than of development . . . The misdirection has been helped largely by membership of the prime minister and the finance minister in the planning commission, which appears to have vested the Planning Commission and its decisions with an unnatural kind of prestige and importance'[3].

3. Ashok Chanda

This eminent administrative analyst said, 'The undefined position of the commission and its wide terms of reference have gradually led to its growth as the economic cabinet not merely for the Union but also for the states'.

He continued, 'The Commission has seized upon this position and extended the scope of its activities to embrace the functions and responsibilities which must both traditionally and otherwise belong to the constituted government.' He further observed, 'the position of pre-eminence accorded to the Planning Commission is inconsistent with the conception of a cabinet form of government'[4].

4. K Santhanam

This eminent constitutional expert stated that, 'Planning has superseded the federation and our country is functioning like a unitary system in many respects'[5].

5. P V Rajamannar

Rajamannar, the Chairman of the Fourth Finance Commission, highlighted the overlapping of functions and responsibilities between the Planning Commission and Finance Commission in federal fiscal transfers[6].

6. P.P. Agarwal

He observed, "Though Planning Commission is an advisory organ of the government, it has come to exercise significant influence over the formation of public policies even in matters other than of development, and its advisory role, in a way, extends over the entire administration."[7]

7. Estimates Committee

The committee opined that "The time has come when a review of entire position regarding the formal association of Cabinet Ministers of the Central Government with the Planning Commission should be made."[8]

Table 48.1   *Technical Divisions of the Planning Commission*[9]

General Divisions		Subject Divisions	
1.	Development Policy and Perspective Planning Division	1.	Agriculture Division
2.	Financial Resources Division	2.	Social Justice and Social Welfare Division
3.	International Economics Division	3.	Communication, IT & Information Division
4.	Labour, Employment and Manpower Division	4.	Human Resources Development Division
5.	Plan Coordination Division	5.	Environment and Forests Division (including climate changes)
6.	Project Appraisal and Management Division	6.	Health, Family Welfare & Nutrition Division
7.	Socio-Economic Research Unit	7.	Housing & Urban Affairs Division
8.	State Plan Division (including Island Development authority Cell)	8.	Industries Division
9.	Decentralised Planning Division, Panchayati Raj and Special Area Programmes (Including Western Ghat Sectt).	9.	Minerals Division
10.	Infrastructure Division	10.	Power & Energy Division
		11.	Rural Development Division
		12.	Science & Technology Division
		13.	Women & Child Development Division
		14.	Transport & Tourism Division
		15.	Village & Small Enterprises Division
		16.	Voluntary Action Cell
		17.	Water Resources Division

NOTES AND REFERENCES

1. See Table 48.1 at the end of this chapter.
2. *Interim Report on the Machinery for Planning,* 1967, Para 15.
3. Vide his *Laski Memorial Lecture,* 1958 (Harold Laski Institute of Political Science, Ahmedabad), p. 26.
4. Ashok Chanda, *Indian Administration,* George Allen and Unwin, 1958, p. 92.
5. K. Santhanam, *Union–State Relations in India,* Asia Publishing House, 1960, p. 70.
6. *Report of the Fourth Finance Commission,* New Delhi, Government of India, 1965, p 88 90. See 'Impact of Planning Commission' in Chapter 41.
7. Agarwal. P.P., "The Planning Commission", in The Indian Journal of Public Administration, Oct.-Dec. 1957.
8. Estimates Committee, 1957-58, Twenty-First Report (Second Lok Sabha), Para 22.
9. Annual Report 2011-12, Planning Commission, Government of India, P. 3.

National Development Council

The National Development Council (NDC) was established in August 1952 by an executive resolution of the Government of India on the recommendation of the first five year plan (draft outline). Like the Planning Commission, it is neither a constitutional body nor a statutory body[1].

COMPOSITION

The NDC is composed of the following members.
1. Prime minister of India (as its chairman/head).
2. All Union cabinet ministers (since 1967)[2].
3. Chief ministers of all states.
4. Chief ministers/administrators of all union territories.
5. Members of the Planning Commission.

The secretary of the Planning Commission acts as the secretary to the NDC. It (NDC) is also provided with administrative and other assistance for its work by the Planning Commission.

OBJECTIVES

The NDC was established with the following objectives.
1. To secure cooperation of states in the execution of the Plan.
2. To strengthen and mobilise the efforts and resources of the nation in support of the Plan.
3. To promote common economic policies in all vital spheres.

4. To ensure balanced and rapid development of all parts of the country.

FUNCTIONS

To realise the above objectives, the NDC is assigned with the following functions:
1. To prescribe guidelines for preparation of the national Plan.
2. To consider the national Plan as prepared by the Planning Commission.
3. To make an assessment of the resources that are required for implementing the Plan and to suggest measures for augmenting them.
4. To consider important questions of social and economic policy affecting national development.
5. To review the working of the national Plan from time to time.
6. To recommend measures for achievement of the aims and targets set out in the national Plan.

The Draft Five-Year Plan prepared by the Planning Commission is first submitted to the Union cabinet. After its approval, it is placed before the NDC, for its acceptance. Then, the Plan is presented to the Parliament. With its approval, it emerges as the official Plan and published in the official gazette.

Therefore, the NDC is the highest body, below the Parliament, responsible for policy matters with regard to planning for social and economic development. However, it is listed as an advisory body to the Planning Commission and its recommendations are not binding. It makes its recommendations to the Central and state governments and should meet at least twice every year.

CRITICAL EVALUATION

The first and foremost function of NDC is to act as a bridge and link between the Central government, the state governments and the Planning Commission, especially in the field of planning, to bring about coordination of policies and programmes of plans. It has been, to a large extent successful in this regard. Besides, it has also served as a forum for Centre–state deliberations on matters of national importance, and also as a device for sharing responsibility between them in the federal political system.

However, two diamentrically opposite views have been expressed on its working. On one hand, it has been described as a 'Super Cabinet' due to its wide and powerful composition, though its recommendations are only advisory and not binding, and can hardly be ignored as they are backed by a national mandate. On the other hand, it has been described as a mere 'rubber stamp' of the policy decisions already taken by the Union government. This is mainly due to the Congress Party rule both at the Centre and states for a long period. However, due to the emergence of regional parties in various states, the NDC is steadily acquiring its federal character and thus providing a greater say to the states in the preparation of national plans.

The following observations are made by eminent people on the working of NDC.

1. **M Brecher:** This biographer of Nehru remarked: 'The NDC was established as a supereme administrative and an advisory body on planning—it lays down policy directives invariably approved by the cabinet. Since their inception, the NDC and its standing committee have virtually relegated the Planning Commission to the status of a research arm'[3].

2. **H M Patel:** This former Finance Minister observed : 'Among the advisory bodies to the Planning Commission is included the NDC. This is surely inaccurate, as is clear from its composition. The NDC is a body obviously superior to the Planning Commission. It is, indeed, a policy-making body and its recommendations cannot but be regarded as policy decisions and not merely as advisory suggestions'[4].

3. **K. Santhanam:** This eminent Constitutional expert stated: 'The position of the NDC has come to approximate to that of a super cabinet of the entire Indian federation, a cabinet functioning for the Government of India and the governments of all states'[5].

4. **A P Jain:** This ex-Food Minister commented: 'The NDC encroaches upon functions that constitutionally belong to the council of ministers at the Central and state levels and sometimes approves the raised targets without prior consultation with the ministry concerned. The NDC, neither by law, nor by the nature of its composition, is a body competent to take decisions on issues at the national level. It is suited to talk, debate and advise. But it must leave the decisions to cabinets at the Centre and the states'[6].

NOTES AND REFERENCES

1. The Sarkaria Commission on Centre–State Relations (1983–1987) recommended that the NDC should be given a constitutional status under Article 263 of the Constitution and should be renamed as National Economic and Development Council.
2. Before 1967, only selected cabinet ministers like Home, Finance, Defence, External Affairs and so on were members of the NDC.

3. M Brecher, *Nehru—A Political Biography*, Oxford, 1959, p. 521.
4. *The Indian Journal of Public Administration*, October–December, 1959, p. 460.
5. K. Santhanam, *Union–State Relations in India*, Asia Publishing House, 1960, p. 47.
6. AP Jain, 'Food Problem and the NDC', *Times of India*, 6 May, 1959. He was a Food Minister in the Union cabinet.

National Human Rights Commission

ESTABLISHMENT OF THE HUMAN RIGHTS COMMISSION

The National Human Rights Commission is a statutory (and not a constitutional) body. It was established in 1993 under a legislation enacted by the Parliament, namely, the Protection of Human Rights Act, 1993[1]. This Act was amended in 2006.

The commission is the watchdog of human rights in the country, that is, the rights relating to life, liberty, equality and dignity of the individual guaranteed by the Constitution or embodied in the international covenants[2] and enforceable by courts in India.

The specific objectives of the establishment of the commission are[3] :
(a) To strengthen the institutional arrangements through which human rights issues could be addressed in their entirety in a more focussed manner;
(b) To look into allegations of excesses, independently of the government, in a manner that would underline the government's commitment to protect human rights; and
(c) To complement and strengthen the efforts that have already been made in this direction.

COMPOSITION OF THE COMMISSION

The commission is a multi-member body consisting of a chairman and four members. The chairman should be a retired chief justice of India, and members should be serving or retired judges of the Supreme Court, a serving or retired chief justice of a high court and two persons having knowledge or practical experience with respect to human rights. In addition to these full-time members, the commission also has four ex-officio members—the chairmen of the National Commission for Minorities, the National Commission for SCs, the National Commission for STs and the National Commission for Women.

The chairman and members are appointed by the president on the recommendations of a six-member committee consisting of the prime minister as its head, the Speaker of the Lok Sabha, the Deputy Chairman of the Rajya Sabha, leaders of the Opposition in both the Houses of Parliament and the Central home minister. Further, a sitting judge of the Supreme Court or a sitting chief justice of a high court can be appointed only after consultation with the chief justice of India.

The chairman and members hold office for a term of five years or until they attain the age of 70 years, whichever is earlier. After their tenure, the chairman and members are not eligible for further employment under the Central or a state government.

The president can remove the chairman or any member from the office under the following circumstances:
(a) If he is adjudged an insolvent; or
(b) If he engages, during his term of office, in any paid employment outside the duties of his office; or
(c) If he is unfit to continue in office by reason of infirmity of mind or body; or

(d) If he is of unsound mind and stand so declared by a competent court; or

(e) If he is convicted and sentenced to imprisonment for an offence.

In addition to these, the president can also remove the chairman or any member on the ground of proved misbehaviour or incapacity. However, in these cases, the president has to refer the matter to the Supreme Court for an inquiry. If the Supreme Court, after the inquiry, upholds the cause of removal and advises so, then the president can remove the chairman or a member.

The salaries, allowances and other conditions of service of the chairman or a member are determined by the Central government. But, they cannot be varied to his disadvantage after his appointment.

All the above provisions are aimed at securing autonomy, independence and impartiality in the functioning of the Commission.

Functions of the Commission

The functions of the Commission are:

(a) To inquire into any violation of human rights or negligence in the prevention of such violation by a public servant, either *suo motu* or on a petition presented to it or on an order of a court.

(b) To intervene in any proceeding involving allegation of violation of human rights pending before a court.

(c) To visit jails and detention places to study the living conditions of inmates and make recommendation thereon.

(d) To review the constitutional and other legal safeguards for the protection of human rights and recommend measures for their effective implementation.

(e) To review the factors including acts of terrorism that inhibit the enjoyment of human rights and recommend remedial measures.

(f) To study treaties and other international instruments on human rights and make recommendations for their effective implementation.

(g) To undertake and promote research in the field of human rights.

(h) To spread human rights literacy among the people and promote awareness of the safe-

guards available for the protection of these rights.

(i) To encourage the efforts of non-governmental organisations (NGOs) working in the field of human rights.

(j) To undertake such other functions as it may consider necessary for the promotion of human rights.

Working of the Commission

The commission's headquarters is at Delhi and it can also establish offices at other places in India. It is vested with the power to regulate its own procedure. It has all the powers of a civil court and its proceedings have a judicial character. It may call for information or report from the Central and state governments or any other authority subordinate thereto.

The commission has its own nucleus of investigating staff for investigation into complaints of human rights violations. Besides, it is empowered to utilise the services of any officer or investigation agency of the Central government or any state government for the purpose. It has also established effective cooperation with the NGOs with first-hand information about human rights violations.

The commission is not empowered to inquire into any matter after the expiry of one year from the date on which the act constituting violation of human rights is alleged to have been committed. In other words, it can look into a matter within one year of its occurrence[4].

The commission may take any of the following steps during or upon the completion of an inquiry:

(a) it may recommend to the concerned government or authority to make payment of compensation or damages to the victim;

(b) it may recommend to the concerned government or authority the initiation of proceedings for prosecution or any other action against the guilty public servant;

(c) it may recommend to the concerned government or authority for the grant of immediate interim relief to the victim;

(d) it may approach the Supreme Court or the high court concerned for the necessary directions, orders or writs.

ROLE OF THE COMMISSION

From the above, it is clear that the functions of the commission are mainly recommendatory in nature. It has no power to punish the violators of human rights, nor to award any relief including monetary relief to the victim. Notably, its recommendations are not binding on the concerned government or authority. But, it should be informed about the action taken on its recommendations within one month. In this context, a former member of the Commission observed[5]: 'The government cannot wash away the recommendations made by the Commission. The commission's role may be recommendatory, advisory, yet the Government considers the cases forwarded by it. It is, therefore, improper to say that the commission is powerless. It enjoys great material authority and no government can ignore its recommendation'.

Moreover, the commission has limited role, powers and jurisdiction with respect to the violation of human rights by the members of the armed forces[6]. In this sphere, the commission may seek a report from the Central government and make its recommendations. The Central government should inform the Commission of the action taken on the recommendations within three months.

The commission submits its annual or special reports to the Central government and to the state government concerned. These reports are laid before the respective legislatures, along with a memorandum of action taken on the recommendations of the commission and the reasons for non-acceptance of any of such recommendations.

PERFORMANCE OF THE COMMISSION

The various human rights issues taken up by the Commission are as follows:

1. Abolition of Bonded Labour
2. Functioning of the Mental Hospitals at Ranchi, Agra and Gwalior
3. Functioning of the Government Protective Home (Women), Agra
4. Issues Concerning Right to Food
5. Review of the Child Marriage Restraint Act, 1929
6. Protocols to the Convention on the Rights of the Child
7. Preventing Employment of Children by Government Servants: Amendment of Service Rules
8. Abolition of Child Labour
9. Guidebook for the Media on Sexual Violence against Children
10. Trafficking in Women and Children: Manual for the Judiciary for Gender Sensitisation
11. Sensitisation Programme on Prevention of Sex Tourism and Trafficking
12. Maternal Anemia and Human Rights
13. Rehabilitation of Destitute Women in Vrindavan
14. Combating Sexual Harassment of Women at the Work Place
15. Harassment of Women Passengers in Trains
16. Abolition of Manual Scavenging
17. Dalits Issues including Atrocities Perpetrated on them
18. Problems Faced by Denotified and Nomadic Tribes
19. Rights of the Disabled Persons
20. Issues Related to Right to Health
21. Rights of Persons Affected by HIV / AIDS
22. Relief Work for the Victims of 1999 Orissa Cyclone
23. Monitoring of Relief Measures undertaken after Gujarat Earthquake (2001)
24. District Complaints Authority
25. Population Policy – Development and Human Rights
26. Review of Statutes, including Terrorist & Disruptive Activities Act, and (Draft) Prevention of Terrorism Bill, 2000
27. Protection of Human Rights in Areas of Insurgency and Terrorism
28. Guidelines to Check Misuse of the Power of Arrest by the Police
29. Setting up of Human Rights Cells in the State / City Police Headquarters
30. Steps to Check Custodial Deaths, Rape and Torture
31. Accession to the Convention against Torture
32. Discussion on Adoption of a Refugee Law for the Country
33. Systemic Reforms of Police, Prisons and other Centers of Detention
34. Review of Laws, Implementation of Treaties, and the International Instruments on Human Rights

35. Promotion of Human Rights Literacy and Awareness in the Educational System
36. Human Rights Training for the Armed Forces and Police, Public Authorities and Civil Society

HUMAN RIGHTS (AMENDMENT) ACT, 2006

The Parliament has passed the Protection of Human Rights (Amendment) Act, 2006. The main amendments carried out in the Protection of Human Rights Act, 1993, relate to the following issues:

1. Reducing the number of members of State Human Rights Commissions (SHRCs) from five to three
2. Changing the eligibility condition for appointment of member of SHRCs
3. Strengthening the investigative machinery available with Human Rights Commissions
4. Empowering the Commissions to recommend award of compensation, etc. even during the course of enquiry
5. Empowering the NHRC to undertake visits to jails even without intimation to the state governments
6. Strengthening the procedure for recording of evidence of witnesses
7. Clarifying that the Chairpersons of NHRC and SHRCs are distinct from the Members of the respective Commission
8. Enabling the NHRC to transfer complaints received by it to the concerned SHRC
9. Enabling the Chairperson and members of the NHRC to address their resignations in writing to the President and the Chairperson and members of the SHRCs to the Governor of the state concerned
10. Clarifying that the absence of any member in the Selection Committee for selection of the Chairperson and member of the NHRC or the SHRCs will not vitiate the decisions taken by such Committees
11. Providing that the Chairperson of the National Commission for the Scheduled Castes and the Chairperson of the National Commission for the Scheduled Tribes shall be deemed to be members of the NHRC
12. Enabling the Central Government to notify future international covenants and conventions to which the Act would be applicable

NOTES AND REFERENCES

1. The president promulgated the Protection of Human Rights Ordinance on September 28, 1993. Subsequently, the Protection of Human Rights Bill, 1993, was passed by both the Houses of Parliament and received the assent of the President on January 8, 1994. The act came into force with restrospective effect from September 28, 1993.
2. 'International covenants' means the International Covenant on Civil and Political Rights and the International Covenant on Economic, Social and Cultural Rights adopted by the General Assembly of the United Nations on December 16, 1966 and such other Covenant or Convention adopted by the General Assembly of the UN as the Central Government may specify. The Indian government acceded to these two International Covenants on April 10 1979.

3. T K Thommen, 'Human Rights Commission', *Cochin University Law Review*, Vol. XVII, nos. 1 and 2, March–June 1993, p. 67–68.
4. A M Ahmadi Committee set up by the Commission recommended that the Commission should be empowered to inquire into any matter after the expiry of one year, if there is sufficient reason for not filing the complaint within the said period.
5. Justice V S Malimath, 'Role of Human Rights Commission', *Human Rights in India: Problems and Perspectives*, BP Singh Sehgal (ed.), Deep Publications, 1995, p. 17–20.
6. Under the Act, 'armed forces' means the naval, military and air forces and includes any other armed forces of the Union. A M Ahmadi Committee set up by the commission recommended that the definition of the 'armed forces' should be changed in a way that it includes only navy, army and air force, not para-military forces.

State Human Rights Commission

The Protection of Human Rights Act of 1993 provides for the creation of not only the National Human Rights Commission but also a State Human Rights Commission at the state level[1]. Accordingly, twenty three states have constituted the State Human Rights Commissions through Official Gazette Notifications[2].

A State Human Rights Commission can inquire into violation of human rights only in respect of subjects mentioned in the State List (List-II) and the Concurrent List (List-III) of the Seventh Schedule of the Constitution. However, if any such case is already being inquired into by the National Human Rights Commission or any other Statutory Commission, then the State Human Rights Commission does not inquire into that case.

COMPOSITION OF THE COMMISSION

The State Human Rights Commission is a multi-member body consisting of a chairperson and two members[3]. The chairperson should be a retired Chief Justice of a High Court and members should be a serving or retired judge of a High Court or a District Judge in the state with a minimum of seven years experience as District Judge and a person having knowledge or practical experience with respect to human rights.

The chairperson and members are appointed by the Governor on the recommendations of a committee consisting of the chief minister as its head, the speaker of the Legislative Assembly, the state home minister and the leader of the opposition in the Legislative Assembly. In the case of a state having Legislative Council, the chairman of the Council and the leader of the opposition in the Council would also be the members of the committee. Further, a sitting judge of a High Court or a sitting District Judge can be appointed only after consultation with the Chief Justice of the High Court of the concerned state.

The chairperson and members hold office for a term of five years or until they attain the age of 70 years, whichever is earlier[4]. After their tenure, the chairperson and members are not eligible for further employment under a state government or the Central government.

Although the chairperson and members of a State Human Rights Commission are appointed by the governor, they can be removed only by the President (and not by the governor). The President can remove them on the same grounds and in the same manner as he can remove the chairperson or a member of the National Human Rights Commission. Thus, he can remove the chairperson or a member under the following circumstances:

(a) If he is adjudged an insolvent; or
(b) If he engages, during his term of office, in any paid employment outside the duties of his office; or
(c) If he is unfit to continue in office by reason of infirmity of mind or body; or
(d) If he is of unsound mind and stands so declared by a competent court; or

(e) If he is convicted and sentenced to imprisonment for an offence.

In addition to these, the president can also remove the chairperson or a member on the ground of proved misbehaviour or incapacity. However, in these cases, the President has to refer the matter to the Supreme Court for an inquiry. If the Supreme Court, after the inquiry, upholds the cause of removal and advises so, then the President can remove the chairperson or a member.

The salaries, allowances and other conditions of service of the chairman or a member are determined by the state government. But, they cannot be varied to his disadvantage after his appointment.

All the above provisions are aimed at securing autonomy, independence and impartiality in the functioning of the Commission.

FUNCTIONS OF THE COMMISSION

The functions of the Commission are:

(a) To inquire into any violation of human rights or negligence in the prevention of such violation by a public servant, either *suo motu* or on a petition presented to it or on an order of a court.

(b) To intervene in any proceeding involving allegation of violation of human rights pending before a court.

(c) To visit jails and detention places to study the living conditions of inmates and make recommendation thereon.

(d) To review the constitutional and other legal safeguards for the protection of human rights and recommend measures for their effective implementation.

(e) To review the factors including acts of terrorism that inhibit the enjoyment of human rights and recommend remedial measures.

(f) To undertake and promote research in the field of human rights.

(g) To spread human rights literacy among the people and promote awareness of the safeguards available for the protection of these rights.

(h) To encourage the efforts of non-governmental organizations (NGOs) working in the field of human rights.

(i) To undertake such other functions as it may consider necessary for the promotion of human rights.

WORKING OF THE COMMISSION

The Commission is vested with the power to regulate its own procedure. It has all the powers of a civil court and its proceedings have a judicial character. It may call for information or report from the state government or any other authority subordinate thereto.

The Commission is not empowered to inquire into any matter after the expiry of one year from the date on which the act constituting violation of human rights is alleged to have been committed. In other words, it can look into a matter within one year of its occurrence.

The Commission may take any of the following steps during or upon the completion of an inquiry :

(a) it may recommend to the state government or authority to make payment of compensation or damages to the victim;

(b) it may recommend to the state government or authority the initiation of proceedings for prosecution or any other action against the guilty public servant;

(c) it may recommend to the state government or authority for the grant of immediate interim relief to the victim;

(d) it may approach the Supreme Court or the state high court for the necessary directions, orders or writs.

From the above, it is clear that the functions of the commission are mainly recommendatory in nature. It has no power to punish the violators of human rights, nor to award any relief including monetary relief to the victim. Notably, its recommendations are not binding on the state government or authority. But, it should be informed about the action taken on its recommendations within one month.

The Commission submits its annual or special reports to the state government. These reports are laid before the state legislature, along with a memorandum of action taken on the recommendations of the Commission and the reasons for non-acceptance of any of such recommendations[5].

HUMAN RIGHTS COURTS

The Protection of Human Rights Act (1993) also provides for the establishment of Human Rights Court in every district for the speedy trial of violation of human rights. These courts can be set up by the state government only with the concurrence of the Chief Justice of the High Court of that state. For every Human Rights Court, the state government specifies a public prosecutor or appoints an advocate (who has practiced for seven years) as a special public prosecutor.

NOTES AND REFERENCES

1. This Act was amended in 2006.
2. These are (in 2013): Assam, Andhra Pradesh, Bihar, Chhattisgarh, Gujarat, Goa, Himachal Pradesh, Jammu and Kashmir, Kerala, Karnataka, Madhya Pradesh, Maharashtra, Manipur, Odisha, Punjab, Rajasthan, Tamil Nadu, Uttar Pradesh, West Bengal, Jharkhand, Sikkim, Uttarakhand and Haryana.
3. The 2006 Amendment reduced the number of members of State Human Rights Commission from five to three and also changed the eligibility condition for appointment of member of the Commission.
4. A member is eligible for re-appointment for another term of five years subject to the age limit of 70 years.
5. Before each House of State Legislature where it consists of two Houses, or where such Legislature consists of one House, before that House.

Central Information Commission

The Central Information Commission was established by the Central Government in 2005. It was constituted through an Official Gazette Notification under the provisions of the Right to Information Act (2005). Hence, it is not a constitutional body.

The Central Information Commission is a high-powered independent body which inter alia looks into the complaints made to it and decide the appeals. It entertains complaints and appeals pertaining to offices, financial institutions, public sector undertakings, etc., under the Central Government and the Union Territories.

COMPOSITION

The Commission consists of a Chief Information Commissioner and not more than ten Information Commissioners[1]. They are appointed by the President on the recommendation of a committee consisting of the Prime Minister as Chairperson, the Leader of Opposition in the Lok Sabha and a Union Cabinet Minister nominated by the Prime Minister[2]. They should be persons of eminence in public life with wide knowledge and experience in law, science and technology, social service, management, journalism, mass media or administration and governance. They should not be a Member of Parliament or Member of the Legislature of any State or Union Territory. They should not hold any other office of profit or connected with any political party or carrying on any business or pursuing any profession.

TENURE AND SERVICE CONDITIONS

The Chief Information Commissioner and an Information Commissioner hold office for a term of 5 years or until they attain the age of 65 years, whichever is earlier. They are not eligible for reappointment[3].

The President can remove the Chief Information Commissioner or any Information Commissioner from the office under the following circumstances :

(a) if he is adjudged an insolvent; or
(b) if he has been convicted of an offence which (in the opinion of the President) involves a moral turpitude; or
(c) if he engages during his term of office in any paid employment outside the duties of his office; or
(d) if he is (in the opinion of the President) unfit to continue in office due to infirmity of mind or body; or
(e) if he has acquired such financial or other interest as is likely to affect prejudicially his official functions.

In addition to these, the President can also remove the Chief Information Commissioner or any Information Commissioner on the ground of proved misbehaviour or incapacity[4]. However, in these cases, the President has to refer the matter to the Supreme Court for an enquiry. If the Supreme Court, after the enquiry, upholds the cause of removal and advises so, then the President can remove him.

The salary, allowances and other service conditions of the Chief Information Commissioner are similar to those of the Chief Election Commissioner and that of the Information Commissioner are similar to those of an Election Commissioner. But, they cannot be varied to his disadvantage during service.

POWERS AND FUNCTIONS

The powers and functions of the Central Information Commission are:

1. It is the duty of the Commission to receive and inquire into a complaint from any person:
   (a) who has not been able to submit an information request because of non-appointment of a Public Information Officer;
   (b) who has been refused information that was requested;
   (c) who has not received response to his information request within the specified time limits;
   (d) who thinks the fees charged are unreasonable;
   (e) who thinks information given is incomplete, misleading or false; and
   (f) any other matter relating to obtaining information.
2. The Commission can order inquiry into any matter if there are reasonable grounds (suo-moto power).
3. While inquiring, the Commission has the powers of a civil court in respect of the following matters:
   (a) summoning and enforcing attendance of persons and compelling them to give oral or written evidence on oath and to produce documents or things;
   (b) requiring the discovery and inspection of documents;
   (c) receiving evidence on affidavit;
   (d) requisitioning any public record from any court or office;
   (e) issuing summons for examination of witnesses or documents; and
   (f) any other matter which may be prescribed.
4. During the inquiry of a complaint, the Commission may examine any record which is under the control of the public authority and no such record may be withheld from it on any grounds. In other words, all public records must be given to the Commission during inquiry for examination.
5. The Commission has the power to secure compliance of its decisions from the public authority. This includes:
   (a) providing access to information in a particular form;
   (b) directing the public authority to appoint a Public Information Officer where none exists;
   (c) publishing information or categories of information;
   (d) making necessary changes to the practices relating to management, maintenance and destruction of records;
   (e) enhancing training provision for officials on the right to information;
   (f) seeking an annual report from the public authority on compliance with this Act;
   (g) requiring the public authority to compensate for any loss or other detriment suffered by the applicant;
   (h) imposing penalties under this Act[5]; and
   (i) rejecting the application.
6. The Commission submits an annual report to the Central Government on the implementation of the provisions of this Act. The Central Government places this report before each House of Parliament.
7. When a public authority does not conform to the provisions of this Act, the Commission may recommend (to the authority) steps which ought to be taken for promoting such conformity.

Table 52.1   *National Commissions / Central Bodies and the Related Ministries*

Sl. No.	Commission / Body	Falls Under
1.	Central Information Commission	Ministry of Personnel
2.	Finance Commission	Ministry of Finance

(Contd.)

Sl. No.	Commission / Body	Falls Under
3.	Union Public Service Commission	Ministry of Personnel
4.	Inter-State Council	Ministry of Home Affairs
5.	Staff Selection Commission	Ministry of Personnel
6.	National Commission for SCs	Ministry of Social Justice & Empowerment
7.	National Commission for STs	Ministry of Tribal Affairs
8.	Central Vigilance Commission	Ministry of Personnel
9.	Zonal Councils	Ministry of Home Affairs
10.	Central Bureau of Investigation	Ministry of Personnel
11.	National Investigation Agency	Ministry of Home Affairs
12.	Commissioner for Linguistic Minorities	Ministry of Minority Affairs
13.	National Commission for Protection of Child Rights	Ministry of Women and Child Development
14.	National Commission for Backward Classes	Ministry of Social Justice & Empowerment
15.	Central Commissioner for Disabled Persons	Ministry of Social Justice & Empowerment
16.	Central Social Welfare Board	Ministry of Women and Child Development
17.	North Eastern Council	Ministry of Development of the North Eastern Region
18.	Central Administrative Tribunal	Ministry of Personnel
19.	National Commission for Minorities	Ministry of Minority Affairs
20.	National Human Rights Commission	Ministry of Home Affairs
21.	National Commission for Women	Ministry of Women and Child Development

NOTES AND REFERENCES

1. The Commission, when constituted initially, had five Commissioners including the Chief Information Commissioner. The Government has subsequently strengthened the Commission and it has now eight Information Commissioners headed by the Chief Information Commissioner.
Annual Report 2011-2012, Ministry of Personnel, Government of India, P.138.

2. Where the Leader of Opposition in the Lok Sabha has not been recognized as such, the Leader of the single largest group in opposition of the Government in the Lok Sabha shall be deemed to be the Leader of the Opposition.

3. The Information Commissioner is eligible for appointment as Chief Information Commissioner but cannot hold office for more than a total of five years including his term as Information Commissioner.

4. He is deemed to be guilty of misbehaviour, if he is concerned or interested in any contract or agreement made by the Central Government or participates in any way in the profit of such contract or agreement or in any benefit or emolument arising there from otherwise than as a member and in common with the other members of an incorporated company.

5. The Commission can impose a penalty on the Public Information Officer at the rate of ₹250 per day upto a maximum of ₹25,000. It can also recommend for disciplinary action against the errant official.

State Information Commission

The Right to Information Act of 2005 provides for the creation of not only the Central Information Commission but also a State Information Commission at the state level. Accordingly, all the states have constituted the State Information Commissions through Official Gazette Notifications.

The State Information Commission is a high-powered independent body which interalia looks into the complaints made to it and decide the appeals. It entertains complaints and appeals pertaining to offices, financial institutions, public sector undertakings, etc., under the concerned state government.

COMPOSITION

The Commission consists of a State Chief Information Commissioner and not more than ten State Information Commissioners[1]. They are appointed by the Governor on the recommendation of a committee consisting of the Chief Minister as Chairperson, the Leader of Opposition in the Legislative Assembly and a State Cabinet Minister nominated by the Chief Minister[2]. They should be persons of eminence in public life with wide knowledge and experience in law, science and technology, social service, management, journalism, mass media or administration and governance. They should not be a Member of Parliament or Member of the Legislature of any State or Union Territory. They should not hold any other office of profit or connected with any political party or carrying on any business or pursuing any profession.

TENURE AND SERVICE CONDITIONS

The State Chief Information Commissioner and a State Information Commissioner hold office for a term of 5 years or until they attain the age of 65 years, whichever is earlier. They are not eligible for reappointment[3].

The Governor can remove the State Chief Information Commissioner or any State Information Commissioner from the office under the following circumstances:

(a) if he is adjudged an insolvent; or
(b) if he has been convicted of an offence which (in the opinion of the Governor) involves a moral turpitude; or
(c) if he engages during his term of office in any paid employment outside the duties of his office; or
(d) if he is (in the opinion of the Governor) unfit to continue in office due to infirmity of mind or body; or
(e) if he has acquired such financial or other interest as is likely to affect prejudicially his official functions.

In addition to these, the Governor can also remove the State Chief Information Commissioner or any State Information Commissioner on the ground of proved misbehaviour or incapacity[4]. However, in these cases, the Governor has to refer the matter to the Supreme Court for an enquiry. If the Supreme Court, after the enquiry, upholds the cause of removal and advises so, then the Governor can remove him.

The salary, allowances and other service conditions of the State Chief Information Commissioner are similar to those of an Election Commissioner and that of the State Information Commissioner are similar to those of the Chief Secretary of the state government. But, they cannot be varied to his disadvantage during service.

POWERS AND FUNCTIONS

The powers and functions of the State Information Commission are:

1. It is the duty of the Commission to receive and inquire into a complaint from any person:
   (a) who has not been able to submit an information request because of non-appointment of a Public Information Officer;
   (b) who has been refused information that was requested;
   (c) who has not received response to his information request within the specified time limits;
   (d) who thinks the fees charged are unreasonable;
   (e) who thinks information given is incomplete, misleading or false; and
   (f) any other matter relating to obtaining information.

2. The Commission can order inquiry into any matter if there are reasonable grounds (suomoto power).

3. While inquiring, the Commission has the powers of a civil court in respect of the following matters:
   (a) summoning and enforcing attendance of persons and compelling them to give oral or written evidence on oath and to produce documents or things;
   (b) requiring the discovery and inspection of documents;
   (c) receiving evidence on affidavit;

(d) requisitioning any public record from any court or office;
(e) issuing summons for examination of witnesses or documents; and
(f) any other matter which may be prescribed.

4. During the inquiry of a complaint, the Commission may examine any record which is under the control of the public authority and no such record may be withheld from it on any grounds. In other words, all public records must be given to the Commission during inquiry for examination.

5. The Commission has the power to secure compliance of its decisions from the public authority. This includes :
   (a) providing access to information in a particular form;
   (b) directing the public authority to appoint a Public Information Officer where none exists;
   (c) publishing information or categories of information;
   (d) making necessary changes to the practices relating to management, maintenance and destruction of records;
   (e) enhancing training provision for officials on the right to information;
   (f) seeking an annual report from the public authority on compliance with this Act;
   (g) requiring the public authority to compensate for any loss or other detriment suffered by the applicant;
   (h) imposing penalties under this Act[5]; and
   (i) rejecting the application.

6. The Commission submits an annual report to the State Government on the implementation of the provisions of this Act. The State Government places this report before the State Legislature.

7. When a public authority does not conform to the provisions of this Act, the Commission may recommend (to the authority) steps which ought to be taken for promoting such conformity.

NOTES AND REFERENCES

1. The number of State Information Commissioners varies from one state to another state.
2. Where the Leader of Opposition in the Legislative Assembly has not been recognized as such, the Leader of the single largest group in opposition of the Government in the Legislative Assembly shall be deemed to be the Leader of the Opposition.
3. The State Information Commissioner is eligible for appointment as State Chief Information Commissioner but cannot hold office for more than a total of five years including his term as State Information Commissioner.
4. He is deemed to be guilty of misbehaviour, if he is concerned or interested in any contract or agreement made by the State Government or participates in any way in the profit of such contract or agreement or in any benefit or emolument arising there from otherwise than as a member and in common with the other members of an incorporated company.
5. The Commission can impose a penalty on the Public Information Officer at the rate of ₹250 per day up to a maximum of ₹25,000. It can also recommend for disciplinary action against the errant official.

Central Vigilance Commission

The Central Vigilance Commission (CVC) is the main agency for preventing corruption in the Central government. It was established in 1964 by an executive resolution of the Central government. Its establishment was recommended by the Santhanam Committee on Prevention of Corruption[1] (1962–64).

Thus, originally the CVC was neither a constitutional body nor a statutory body. Recently, in September 2003, the Parliament enacted a law conferring statutory status on the CVC[2].

In 2004, the Government of India authorised the CVC as the "Designated Agency" to receive written complaints for disclosure on any allegation of corruption or misuse of office and recommend appropriate action[2a].

The CVC is conceived to be the apex vigilance institution, free of control from any executive authority, monitoring all vigilance activity under the Central Government and advising various authorities in Central Government organisations in planning, executing, reviewing and reforming their vigilance work.

COMPOSITION

The CVC is a multi-member body consisting of a Central Vigilance Commissioner (chairperson) and not more than two vigilance commissioners. They are appointed by the president by warrant under his hand and seal on the recommendation of a three-member committee consisting of the prime minister as its head, the Union minister of home affairs and the Leader of the Opposition in the Lok Sabha. They hold office for a term of four years or until they attain the age of sixty five years, whichever is earlier. After their tenure, they are not eligible for further employment under the Central or a state government.

The president can remove the Central Vigilance Commissioner or any vigilance commissioner from the office under the following circumstances:

(a) If he is adjudged an insolvent; or
(b) If he has been convicted of an offence which (in the opinion of the Central government) involves a moral turpitude; or
(c) If he engages, during his term of office, in any paid employment outside the duties of his office; or
(d) If he is (in the opinion of the president), unfit to continue in office by reason of infirmity of mind or body; or
(e) If he has acquired such financial or other interest as is likely to affect prejudicially his official functions.

In addition to these, the president can also remove the Central Vigilance Commissioner or any vigilance commissioner on the ground of proved misbehaviour or incapacity. However, in these cases, the president has to refer the matter to the Supreme Court for an enquiry. If the Supreme Court, after the enquiry, upholds the cause of removal and advises so, then the president can remove him. He is deemed to be guilty of misbehaviour, if he (a) is concerned or interested in any contract or agreement made by the Central government, or (b) participates in any way in the profit of such contract or agreement or in any benefit or emolument arising therefrom otherwise than as a member and in common with the other members of an incorporated company

The salary, allowances and other conditions of service of the Central Vigilance Commissioner are similar to those of the Chairman of UPSC and that of the vigilance commissioner are similar to those of a member of UPSC. But they cannot be varied to his disadvantage after his appointment.

ORGANISATION

The CVC has its own Secretariat, Chief Technical Examiners' Wing (CTE) and a wing of Commissioners for Departmental Inquiries (CDIs).

Secretariat: The Secretariat consists of a Secretary, Joint Secretaries, Deputy Secretaries, Under Secretaries and office staff.

Chief Technical Examiners' Wing: The Chief Technical Examiners' Organisation constitutes the technical wing of the CVC. It consists of Chief Engineers (designated as Chief Technical Examiners) and supporting engineering staff. The main functions assigned to this organisation are as follows:

(i) Technical audit of construction works of Government organisations from a vigilance angle

(ii) Investigation of specific cases of complaints relating to construction works

(iii) Extension of assistance to CBI in their investigations involving technical matters and for evaluation of properties in Delhi

(iv) Tendering of advice / assistance to the CVC and Chief Vigilance Officers in vigilance cases involving technical matters

Commissioners for Departmental Inquiries: The CDIs function as Inquiry Officers to conduct oral inquiries in departmental proceedings initiated against public servants.

FUNCTIONS

The functions of the CVC are:

1. To inquire or cause an inquiry or investigation to be conducted on a reference made by

the Central government wherein it is alleged that a public servant being an employee of the Central government or its authorities[3], has committed an offence under the Prevention of Corruption Act, 1988.

2. To inquire or cause an inquiry or investigation to be conducted into any complaint against any official belonging to the below mentioned category of officials wherein it is alleged that he has committed an offence under the Prevention of Corruption Act, 1988:

   (a) Members of all-India services[4] serving in the Union and Group 'A' officers of the Central government; and

   (b) Specified level of officers of the authorities of the Central government.

3. To exercise superintendence over the functioning of Delhi Special Police Establishment (which is a part of Central Bureau of Investigation) in so far as it relates to the investigation of offences alleged to have been committed under the Prevention of Corruption Act, 1988. The Delhi Special Police Establishment is required to obtain the prior approval of the Central government before conducting any inquiry or investigation into an offence committed by officers of the rank of joint secretary and above in the Central government and its authorities.

4. To give directions to the Delhi Special Police Establishment for the purpose of discharging the responsibility entrusted to it under the Delhi Special Police Establishment Act, 1946.

5. To review the progress of investigations conducted by the Delhi Special Police Establishment into offences alleged to have been committed under the prevention of Corruption Act, 1988.

6. To review the progress of applications pending with the competent authorities for sanction of prosecution under the Prevention of Corruption Act, 1988.

7. To tender advise to the Central government and its authorities on such matters as are referred to it by them.

8. To exercise superintendence over the vigilance administration in the ministries of the Central government or its authorities.

9. To undertake or cause an inquiry into complaints received under the Public Interest Disclosure and Protection of Informers' Resolution and recommend appropriate action.

10. The Central Government is required to consult the CVC in making rules and regulations governing the vigilance and disciplinary matters relating to the members of Central Services and All-India Services.

11. The Central Vigilance Commissioner is also the Chairperson of the two Committees, on whose recommendations the Central Government appoints the Director of the Delhi Special Police Establishment and the Director of Enforcement.

12. The Committee concerned with the appointment of the Director of CBI is also empowered to recommend, after consultation with the Director (CBI), appointment of officers to the posts of the level of SP and above in DSPE.

13. The Committee concerned with the appointment of the Director of Enforcement is also empowered to recommend, after consultation with the Director of Enforcement, appointment of officers to the posts of the level of Deputy Director and above in the Directorate of Enforcement.

JURISDICTION

The jurisdiction of the CVC extends to the following:

1. Members of All India Services serving in connection with the affairs of the Union and Group A officers of the Central Government.
2. Officers of the rank of Scale V and above in the Public Sector Banks.
3. Officers in Grade D and above in Reserve Bank of India, NABARD and SIDBI.
4. Chief Executives and Executives on the Board and other officers of E-8 and above in Schedule 'A' and 'B' Public Sector Undertakings.
5. Chief Executives and Executives on the Board and other officers of E-7 and above in Schedule 'C' and 'D' Public Sector Undertakings.
6. Managers and above in General Insurance Companies.
7. Senior Divisional Managers and above in Life Insurance Corporation.

8. Officers drawing salary of ₹8700/- p.m. and above on Central Government D.A. pattern, as on the date of the notification and as may be revised from time to time in Societies and other Local Authorities.

WORKING

The CVC conducts its proceedings at its headquarters (New Delhi). It is vested with the power to regulate its own procedure. It has all the powers of a civil court and its proceedings have a judicial character. It may call for information or report from the Central government or its authorities so as to enable it to exercise general supervision over the vigilance and anti-corruption work in them.

The CVC, on receipt of the report of the inquiry undertaken by any agency on a reference made by it, advises the Central government or its authorities as to the further course of action. The Central government or its authorities shall consider the advice of the CVC and take appropriate action. However, where the Central government or any of its authorities does not agree with the advice of the CVC, it shall communicate the reasons (to be recorded in writing) to the CVC.

The CVC has to present annually to the President a report on its performance. The President places this report before each House of Parliament.

All ministries/departments in the Union Government have a Chief Vigilance Officer (CVO) who heads the Vigilance Division of the organisation concerned, assisting and advising the Secretary or Head of Office in all matters pertaining to vigilance. He also provides a link between his organisation and the Central Vigilance Commission on the one hand and his organisation and the Central Bureau of Investigation on the other. Vigilance functions performed by the CVO include

(i) Collecting intelligence about corrupt practices of the employees of his organisation

(ii) Investigating verifiable allegations reported to him

(iii) Processing investigation reports for further consideration of the disciplinary authority concerned

(iv) Referring matters to the Central Vigilance Commission for advice wherever necessary[5]

Notes and References

1. The Committee on Prevention of Corruption with parliamentarian K.Santhanam as the Chairman, four other MPs and two senior officers as members, was appointed by the Government of India in 1962.
2. The Central Vigilance Commission Bill having been passed by both the Houses of Parliament received the assent of the president on 11 September 2003. It came on the statute Book as the Central Vigilance Commission Act, 2003.
2a. Vide GOI Resolution on "Public Interest Disclosure and Protection of Informers" dated April 2004.

3. The authorities of the Central government include a corporation established by or under any Central act and government company, society and any local authority owned or controlled by the Central government.
4. The All-India Services include Indian Administrative Service (IAS), Indian Police Service (IPS) and Indian Forest Service (IFS).
5. Report on Ethics in Governance, January 2007, Second Administrative Reforms Commission, Government of India, P.106.

Central Bureau of Investigation

ESTABLISHMENT OF CBI

The Central Bureau of Investigation (CBI) was set up in 1963 by a resolution of the Ministry of Home Affairs. Later, it was transferred to the Ministry of Personnel and now it enjoys the status of an attached office[1]. The Special Police Establishment (which looked into vigilance cases) setup in 1941 was also merged with the CBI.

The establishment of the CBI was recommended by the Santhanam Committee on Prevention of Corruption (1962-1964). The CBI is not a statutory body. It derives its powers from the Delhi Special Police Establishment Act, 1946.

The CBI is the main investigating agency of the Central Government. It plays an important role in the prevention of corruption and maintaining integrity in administration. It also provides assistance to the Central Vigilance Commission.

MOTTO, MISSION AND VISION OF CBI

Motto: Industry, Impartiality and Integrity

Mission: To uphold the Constitution of India and law of the land through in-depth investigation and successful prosecution of offences; to provide leadership and direction to police forces and to act as the nodal agency for enhancing inter-state and international cooperation in law enforcement

Vision: *Based on its motto, mission and the need to develop professionalism, transparency, adaptability to change and use of science and technology in its working, the CBI will focus on*

1. Combating corruption in public life, curbing economic and violent crimes through meticulous investigation and prosecution
2. Evolving effective systems and procedures for successful investigation and prosecution of cases in various law courts
3. Helping fight cyber and high technology crime
4. Creating a healthy work environment that encourages team-building, free communication and mutual trust
5. Supporting state police organisations and law enforcement agencies in national and international cooperation, particularly relating to enquiries and investigation of cases
6. Playing a lead role in the war against national and transnational organised crime
7. Upholding human rights, protecting the environment, arts, antiques and heritage of our civilisation
8. Developing a scientific temper, humanism and the spirit of inquiry and reform
9. Striving for excellence and professionalism in all spheres of functioning so that the organisation rises to high levels of endeavor and achievement.

Organisation of CBI

At present (2013), the CBI has the following divisions[2]:

1. Anti-Corruption Division
2. Economic Offences Division
3. Special Crimes Division
4. Policy and International Police Cooperation Division
5. Administration Division
6. Directorate of Prosecution
7. Central Forensic Science Laboratory

Composition of CBI

The CBI is headed by a Director. He is assisted by a special director or an additional director. Additionally, it has a number of joint directors, deputy inspector generals, superintendents of police and all other usual ranks of police personnel. In total, it has about 5000 staff members, about 125 forensic scientists and about 250 law officers.

The Director of CBI as Inspector-General of Police, Delhi Special Police Establishment, is responsible for the administration of the organisation. With the enactment of CVC Act, 2003, the superintendence of Delhi Special Police Establishment vests with the Central Government save investigations of offences under the Prevention of Corruption Act, 1988, in which, the superintendence vests with the Central Vigilance Commission. The Director of CBI has been provided security of two-year tenure in office by the CVC Act, 2003. The CVC Act also provides the mechanism for the selection of the Director of CBI and other officers of the rank of SP and above in the CBI[3].

The Director of the CBI is appointed by the Central Government on the recommendation of a committee consisting of the Central Vigilance Commissioner as Chairperson, the Vigilance Commissioners, the Secretary to the Government of India in-charge of the Ministry of Home Affairs and the Secretary (Coordination and Public Grievances) in the Cabinet Secretariat.

Functions of CBI

The functions of CBI are:

(i) Investigating cases of corruption, bribery and misconduct of Central government employees

(ii) Investigating cases relating to infringement of fiscal and economic laws, that is, breach of laws concerning export and import control, customs and central excise, income tax, foreign exchange regulations and so on. However, such cases are taken up either in consultation with or at the request of the department concerned.

(iii) Investigating serious crimes, having national and international ramifications, committed by organised gangs of professional criminals

(iv) Coordinating the activities of the anti-corruption agencies and the various state police forces

(v) Taking up, on the request of a state government, any case of public importance for investigation

(vi) Maintaining crime statistics and disseminating criminal information.

The CBI is a multidisciplinary investigation agency of the Government of India and undertakes investigation of corruption-related cases, economic offences and cases of conventional crime. It normally confines its activities in the anti-corruption field to offences committed by the employees of the Central Government and Union Territories and their public sector undertakings. It takes up investigation of conventional crimes like murder, kidnapping, rape etc., on reference from the state governments or when directed by the Supreme Court/High Courts.

The CBI acts as the "National Central Bureau" of Interpol in India. The Interpol Wing of the CBI coordinates requests for investigation-related activities originating from Indian law enforcement agencies and the member countries of the Interpol.

CBI vs. State Police

The role of the Special Police Establishment (a division of CBI) is supplementary to that of the state police forces. Along with state police forces, the

Special Police Establishment (SPE) enjoys the concurrent powers of investigation and prosecution for offences under the Delhi Police Establishment Act, 1946. However, to avoid duplication and overlapping of cases between these two agencies, the following administrative arrangements have been made:

   (i) The SPE shall take up such cases which are essentially and substantially concerned with the Central Government's affairs or employees, even if they also involve certain state government employees.

  (ii) The state police force shall take up such cases which are substantially concerned with the state government's affairs or employees, even if they also involve certain Central Government employees.

 (iii) The SPE shall also take up cases against employees of public undertakings or statutory bodies established and financed by the Central Government.

CBI ACADEMY

The CBI Academy is located at Ghaziabad, Uttar Pradesh and started functioning in 1996. Earlier, training programmes were being conducted at the CBI Training Centre, New Delhi.

The vision of the CBI Academy is "Excellence in Training in the Fields of Crime Investigation, Prosecution and Vigilance Functioning" and its mission is to train the human resources of CBI, state police and the vigilance organisations to become professional, industrious, impartial, upright and dedicated to the service of the nation.

The academy is the focal point of training activities within the organisation and is responsible for identification of suitable training programmes, regulation of nominations of trainees and preparation of the annual training calendar.

Beside the CBI Academy at Ghaziabad, there are three regional training centres imparting training at regional levels at Kolkata, Mumbai and Chennai.

There are two kinds of training courses which are being conducted in the CBI Academy:

   (i) **Short Term In-service Courses:** For officers of the CBI, state police, central para-military forces and central government undertakings

  (ii) **Long Term Basic Courses:** For directly recruited deputy superintendents of police, sub-inspectors and constables of CBI.[4]

NOTES AND REFERENCES

1. The CBI comes under the administrative control of the Department of Personnel and Training (DoPT) of the Ministry of Personnel.
2. Annual Report 2011-2012, Ministry of Personnel, Government of India, p.106.
3. *Ibid*, p.107.
4. Annual Report 2012, Central Bureau of Investigation, Government of India, pp. 92-93.

Lokpal and Lokayuktas

GLOBAL SCENARIO

Modern democratic states are characterised by a welfare orientation. Hence, the government has come to play an important role in the socio-economic development of a nation. This has resulted in the expansion of bureaucracy and the multiplication of administrative process, which in turn increased the administrative power and discretion enjoyed by the civil servants at different levels of the government. The abuse of this power and discretion by civil servants opens up scope for harassment, malpractices, maladministration and corruption. Such a situation gives rise to citizens' grievances against administration[1].

The success of democracy and the realisation of socio-economic development depends on the extent to which the citizens' grievances are redressed. Therefore, the following institutional devices have been created in different parts of the world to deal with the redressal of these grievances:

1. The Ombudsman System
2. The Administrative Courts System
3. The Procurator System

The earliest democratic institution created in the world for the redressal of citizens' grievance is the Scandinavian institution of Ombudsman. Donald C. Rowat, an international authority on the Ombudsman, calls it a "uniquely appropriate institution for dealing with the average citizens' complaints about unfair administrative actions."

The institution of Ombudsman was first created in Sweden in 1809. 'Ombud' is a Swedish term and refers to a person who acts as the representative or spokesman of another person. According to Donald C. Rowat, Ombudsman refers to "an officer appointed by the legislature to handle complaints against administrative and judicial action."

The Swedish Ombudsman deals with the citizens' grievances in the following matters:

(i) Abuse of administrative discretion, that is, misuse of official power and authority
(ii) Maladministration, that is, inefficiency in achieving the targets
(iii) Administrative corruption, that is, demanding bribery for doing things
(iv) Nepotism, that is supporting one's own kith and kin in matters like providing employment
(v) Discourtesy, that is, misbehaviour of various kinds, for instance, use of abusive language.

The Swedish Ombudsman is appointed by the Parliament for a term of four years. He can be removed only by the Parliament on ground of its loss of confidence in him. He submits his annual report to the Parliament and hence, is also known as 'Parliamentary Ombudsman.' But he is independent of the Parliament (legislature) as well as the executive and judiciary.

The Ombudsman is a constitutional authority and enjoys the powers to supervise the compliance of laws and regulations by the public officials, and see that they discharge their duties properly. In other words, he keeps a watch over all public officials—

civil, judicial and military—so that they function impartially, objectively and legally, that is, in accordance with the law. However, he has no power to reverse or quash a decision and has no direct control over administration or the courts.

The Ombudsman can act either on the basis of a complaint received from the citizen against unfair administrative action or *suo moto* (i.e. on his own initiative). He can prosecute any erring official including the judges. However, he himself cannot inflict any punishment. He only reports the matter to the higher authorities for taking the necessary corrective action.

In sum, the characteristics of the Swedish institution of Ombudsman are as follows:

(i) Independence of action from the executive

(ii) Impartial and objective investigation of complaints

(iii) *Suo moto* power to start investigations

(iv) Uninterrupted access to all the files of administration

(v) Right to report to the Parliament as opposed to the executive; the institution of ombudsman is based on the doctrine of administrative accountability to legislature.

(vi) Wide publicity given to its working in press and other media

(vii) Direct, simple, informal, cheap and speedy method of handling complaints

From Sweden, the institution of Ombudsman spread to other Scandinavian countries—Finland (1919), Denmark (1955) and Norway (1962). New Zealand is the first Commonwealth country in the world to have adopted the Ombudsman system in the form of a Parliamentary Commissioner for Investigation in 1962. The United Kingdom adopted Ombudsman-like institution called Parliamentary Commissioner for Administration in 1967. Since then, more than 40 counties of the world have adopted Ombudsman-like institutions with different nomenclature and functions. The Ombudsman in India is called Lokpal/Lokayukta. Donald. C. Rowat says that the institution of Ombudsman is a "bulwark of democratic government against the tyranny of officialdom." While Gerald E. Caiden described the Ombudsman as "institutionalised public conscience."

Another unique institutional device created for the redressal of citizens' grievances against administrative authorities, is the French system of Administrative Courts. Due to its success in France, the system has gradually spread to many other European and African countries like Belgium, Greece and Turkey.

The socialist countries like the former USSR (now Russia), China, Poland, Hungary, Czechoslovakia and Romania have created their own institutional device for the redressal of citizens' grievances. It is called 'Procurator System' in these countries. It should be noted here that the office of the Procurator-General is still functioning in Russia. He is appointed for a tenure of seven years.

Position in India

The existing legal and institutional framework to check corruption and redress citizens' grievances in India consists of the followings:

1. Public Servants (Enquiries) Act, 1850
2. Indian Penal Code, 1860
3. Special Police Establishment, 1941
4. Delhi Police Establishment Act, 1946
5. Prevention of Corruption Act, 1988
6. Commissions of Inquiry Act, 1952 (against political leaders and eminent public men)
7. All-India Services (Conduct) Rules, 1968
8. Central Civil Services (Conduct) Rules, 1964
9. Railway Services (Conduct) Rules, 1966
10. Vigilance organisations in ministries / departments, attached and subordinate offices and public undertakings
11. Central Bureau of Investigation, 1963
12. Central Vigilance Commission, 1964
13. State Vigilance Commissions, 1964
14. Anti corruption bureaus in states
15. Lokayukta (Ombudsman) in states
16. Divisional Vigilance Board
17. District Vigilance Officer
18. National Consumer Disputes Redressal Commission
19. National Commission for SCs
20. National Commission for STs
21. Supreme Court and High Courts in states
22. Administrative Tribunals (quasi-judicial bodies)
23. Directorate of Public Grievances in the Cabinet Secretariat, 1988
24. Parliament and its committees

25. 'File to Field' programme in some states like Kerala; in this innovative scheme, the administrator goes to the village/area and hears public grievances and takes immediate action wherever possible.

LOKPAL

The Administrative Reforms Commission (ARC) of India (1966–1970) recommended the setting up of two special authorities designated as 'Lokpal' and 'lokayukta' for the redressal of citizens' grievances[2]. These institutions were to be set up on the pattern of the institution of Ombudsman in Scandinavian countries and the parliamentary commissioner for investigation in New Zealand. The Lokpal would deal with complaints against ministers and secretaries at Central and state levels, and the lokayukta (one at the Centre and one in every state) would deal with complaints against other specified higher officials. The ARC kept the judiciary outside the purview of Lokpal and lokayukta as in New Zealand. But, in Sweden the judiciary is within the purview of Ombudsman.

According to the ARC, the Lokpal would be appointed by the president after consultation with the chief justice of India, the Speaker of Lok Sabha and the Chairman of the Rajya Sabha.

The ARC also recommended that the institutions of Lokpal and lokayukta should have the following features:

1. They should be demonstratively independent and impartial.
2. Their investigations and proceedings should be conducted in private and should be informal in character.
3. Their appointment should be, as far as possible, non-political.
4. Their status should compare with the highest judicial functionaries in the country.
5. They should deal with matters in the discretionary field involving acts of injustice, corruption or favouritism.
6. Their proceedings should not be subject to judicial interference.
7. They should have the maximum latitude and powers in obtaining information relevant to their duties.

8. They should not look forward to any benefit or pecuniary advantage from the executive government.

The Government of India accepted the recommendations of ARC in this regard. So far, ten official attempts have been made to bring about legislation on this subject. Bills were introduced in the Parliament in the following years:

1. In May 1968, by the Congress Government headed by Indira Gandhi.
2. In April 1971, again by the Congress Government headed by Indira Gandhi.
3. In July 1977, by the Janata Government headed by Morarji Desai.
4. In August 1985, by the Congress Government headed by Rajiv Gandhi.
5. In December 1989, by the National Front Government headed by VP Singh.
6. In September 1996, by the United Front Government headed by Deve Gowda.
7. In August 1998, by the BJP-led coalition Government headed by AB Vajpayee.
8. In August 2001, by the NDA government headed by A B Vajpayee.
9. In August 2011, by the UPA government headed by Manmohan Singh.
10. In December 2011, by the UPA government headed by Manmohan Singh.

However, none of the bills mentioned above were passed by the Parliament due to one or the other reasons. The first four bills lapsed due to the dissolution of Lok Sabha, while the fifth one was withdrawn by the government. The sixth and seventh bills also lapsed due to the dissolution of the 11th and 12th Lok Sabha. Again, the eight bill (2001) lapsed due to the dissolution of the 13th Lok Sabha in 2004. The ninth bill (2011) was withdrawn by the government. The latest tenth bill (2011) is pending in the Parliament. Hence, the institution of Lokpal has not yet come into existence in our country, though its need was felt long ago.

Status of 2011 Lokpal Bills

In order to meet a long standing demand to establish a mechanism for dealing complaints on corruption against public functionaries, including corruption at high places, the Government had constituted a Joint

Drafting Committee on 8th April, 2011, consisting of five nominee ministers from the Government of India and five nominees of Anna Hazare (including Hazare himself), to prepare a draft of the Lokpal Bill. Based on the deliberations of the Committee, and on the basis of inputs received from Chief Ministers of states and political parties, the Government prepared a revised Lokpal Bill, 2011 which was introduced in the Lok Sabha on 4th August, 2011.

The said Bill was referred to the Department Related Parliamentary Standing Committee on Personnel, Public Grievances, Law and Justice on 8th August, 2011 for examination and report. The Department Related Parliamentary Standing Committee, after extensive discussion with all the stakeholders has, in its 48th Report, made a number of recommendations suggesting major amendments in the Bill, both as regards the scope and content of the Bill, including that necessary provisions be made in the Union legislation for establishment of Lokayuktas in the states, so as to provide leverage to the states where no such institution exists, and to bring uniformity in the laws relating to state Lokayuktas which are already in existence in a number of states. The Committee also recommended that Lokpal and Lokayuktas should be conferred Constitutional status.

Upon consideration of the recommendations of the Department Related Parliamentary Standing Committee, the Government withdrew the Lokpal Bill, 2011 pending in the Lok Sabha and introduced a new comprehensive Lokpal and Lokayuktas Bill, 2011 in the Lok Sabha on 22.12.2011 to establish the institution of Lokpal at the Centre and Lokayukta at the level of states. The Bill provides a uniform vigilance and anti corruption road map for the nation, both at Centre and states. The Bill also institutionalises separation of investigation from prosecution and thereby removes conflict of interest as well as increases the scope of professionalism and specialisation. Also, keeping in mind the recommendations of the Standing Committee that the Lokpal and Lokayuktas may be made Constitutional bodies, the Government also introduced the Constitution 116th Amendment Bill, 2011 to provide for the Constitutional status to these bodies.

These Bills were taken up for consideration by the Lok Sabha on 27th December, 2011. The Lokpal and Lokayuktas Bill, 2011 was passed with certain amendments whereas the Constitution 116th Amendment Bill, 2011 could not be passed with the requisite majority required for Constitutional amendments. The Lokpal and Lokayuktas Bill, 2011 was taken up for discussion and passing in the Rajya Sabha on 29th December 2011. The discussion remained inconclusive and the Lokpal and Lokayuktas Bill, 2011 is yet to be passed by the Rajya Sabha[3].

Lokpal and Lokayuktas Bill, 2011

The Bill seeks to provide for the establishment of a body of Lokpal for the Union and Lokayukta for states to inquire into allegations of corruption against certain public functionaries and for matters connected therewith or incidental thereto. The salient features of the Bill are enumerated here.

(i) Lokpal to consist of a Chairperson and upto eight members and not less than 50% of the members to be from SCs, STs, OBCs, minorities and women

(ii) Provision for Selection Committee for selection of the Chairperson and the members and a Search Committee of at least seven members not less than 50% of whom to be from SCs, STs, OBCs, minorities and women

(iii) Lokpal to have jurisdiction over public functionary who is or has been the Prime Minister (with subject matter exclusion and some other safeguards); Minister of the Union; Member of Parliament; Public Servant as defined under the Prevention of Corruption Act, 1988 belonging to Group 'A', 'B', 'C' or 'D'; functionary of any body or board or corporation or authority or company or society or trust or autonomous body established by an Act of Parliament or wholly or partly financed by the Central Government or controlled by it; functionary of such bodies or organisations aided by the Government the annual income of which exceeds an amount notified by the Central Government; functionary of such bodies or organisations in receipt of donation from public and their annual income exceeding an amount notified by the Central Government or where such bodies / organisations receive donation from any foreign source under FCRA in excess of Rs. 10 lakh in a year

(iv) Lokpal to have under it an independent Inquiry and Prosecution Wing

(v) Separation of investigation from prosecution thereby, removing conflict of interest and increasing scope for professionalism and specialisation

(vi) Lokpal to have power of superintendence and directions over any investigation agency including the CBI, for cases referred to them by the Lokpal

(vii) No prior sanction required for launching prosecution in cases inquired by Lokpal or initiated on the direction and with the approval of the, Lokpal

(viii) Provision for attachment and confiscation of property acquired by corrupt means even while prosecution is pending

(ix) Appointment of Director, CBI to be on the recommendations of a high-powered committee chaired by the Prime Minister

(x) Specific timelines for preliminary inquiry, investigation and trial

(xi) Enhancement of minimum and maximum punishment under the Prevention of Corruption Act from six months to two years and from seven years to ten years, respectively

(xii) Lokpal to have powers to recommend transfer or suspension of public servants connected with allegations of corruption

(xiii) Lokpal empowered to constitute sufficient number of special courts

(xiv) To provide for Lokayuktas in the States on similar lines.

LOKAYUKTAS

While the Central government is still debating the establishment of the institution of Lokpal, many states have already set up the institution of lokayuktas.

It must be noted here that the institution of lokayukta was established first in Maharashtra in 1971. Although Odisha had passed the Act in this regard in 1970, it came into force only in 1983.

Till now (2013), 18 states and 1 Union Territory (Delhi) have established the institution of Lokyuktas. The details in this regard are mentioned below in Table 56.1.

Table 56.1 *Establishment of Lokayukta in States (Chronological Order)*

Sl. No.	States	Created in (enacted in)
1.	Odisha	1970
2.	Maharashtra	1971
3.	Rajasthan	1973
4.	Bihar	1974
5.	Uttar Pradesh	1975
6.	Madhya Pradesh	1981
7.	Andhra Pradesh	1983
8.	Himachal Pradesh	1983
9.	Karnataka	1985
10.	Assam	1985
11.	Gujarat	1986
12.	Punjab	1995
13.	Delhi	1995
14.	Kerala	1999
15.	Jharkhand	2001
16.	Chattisgarh	2002
17.	Haryana	2002
18.	Uttarakhand	2002
19.	Goa	2011

The states which have not created the institution of Lokayuktas are Arunachal Pradesh, Jammu and Kashmir, Manipur, Meghalaya, Mizoram, Nagaland, Sikkim, Tamil Nadu, Tripura and West Bengal.

The various aspects of the institution of lokayukta are:

Structural Variations

The structure of the lokayukta is not same in all the states. Some States like Rajasthan, Karnataka, Andhra Pradesh and Maharashtra have created the lokayukta as well as upalokayukta, while some others like Bihar, Uttar Pradesh and Himachal Pradesh have created only the lokayukta. There are still other states like Punjab and Orissa that have designated officials as Lokpal. This pattern was not suggested by the ARC in the states.

Appointment

The lokayukta and upalokayukta are appointed by the governor of the state. While appointing, the governor in most of the states consults (a) the chief justice of the state high court, and (b) the leader of Opposition in the state legislative assembly[4].

Qualifications

Judicial qualifications are prescribed for the lokayukta in the States of Uttar Pradesh, Himachal Pradesh, Andhra Pradesh, Gujarat, Orissa, Karnataka and Assam. But no specific qualifications are prescribed in the states of Bihar, Maharashtra and Rajasthan.

Tenure

In most of the states, the term of office fixed for lokayukta is of 5 years duration or 65 years of age, whichever is earlier. He is not eligible for reappointment for a second term.

Jurisdiction

There is no uniformity regarding the jurisdiction of lokayukta in all the states. The following points can be noted in this regard:

(a) The chief minister is included within the jurisdiction of lokayukta in the states of Himachal Pradesh, Andhra Pradesh, Madhya Pradesh and Gujarat, while he is excluded from the purview of lokayukta in the states of Maharashtra, Uttar Pradesh, Rajasthan, Bihar and Orissa.

(b) Ministers and higher civil servants are included in the purview of lokayukta in almost all the states. Maharashtra has also included former ministers and civil servants.

(c) Members of state legislatures are included in the purview of lokayukta in the States of Andhra Pradesh, Himachal Pradesh, Gujarat, Uttar Pradesh and Assam.

(d) The authorities of the local bodies, corporations, companies and societies are included in the jurisdiction of the lokayukta in most of the states.

Investigations

In most of the states, the lokayukta can initiate investigations either on the basis of a complaint received from the citizen against unfair administrative action or *suo moto*. But he does not enjoy the power to start investigations on his own initiative (*suo moto*) in the States of Uttar Pradesh, Himachal Pradesh and Assam.

Scope of Cases Covered

The lokayukta can consider the cases of 'grievances' as well as 'allegations' in the States of Maharashtra, Uttar Pradesh, Assam, Bihar and Karnataka. But, in Himachal Pradesh, Andhra Pradesh, Rajasthan and Gujarat, the job of lokayuktas is confined to investigating allegations (corruption) and not grievances (maladministration).

Other Features

1. The lokayukta presents, annually, to the governor of the state a consolidated report on his performance. The governor places this report along with an explanatory memorandum before the state legislature. The lokayukta is responsible to the state legislature.

2. He takes the help of the state investigating agencies for conducting inquiries.

3. He can call for relevant files and documents from the state government departments.

4. The recommendations made by the lokayukta are only advisory and not binding on the state government.

NOTES AND REFERENCES

1. According to the Chambers Dictionary, grievance means 'a ground of complaint; a condition felt to be oppressive or wrongful'.

2. The ARC headed by Morarji Desai submitted a special interim report on the 'Problems of Redressal of Citizens' Grievances' in 1966.

3. Annual Report 2011-2012, Ministry of Personnel, Government of India, P.101-102.
4. But, in Andhra Pradesh, the leader of the Opposition in the state legislative assembly is not required to be consulted in this regard. In Karnataka, on the other hand, the Chairman of the state legislative council, the Speaker of the state legislative assembly and the leader of Opposition in the state legislative council are also required to be consulted on this matter.

PART IX

OTHER CONSTITUTIONAL DIMENSIONS

Co-operative Societies

The 97th *Constitutional Amendment Act* of 2011 gave a constitutional status and protection to co-operative societies. In this context, it made the following three changes in the constitution:

1. It made the right to form co-operative societies a fundamental right (Article 19[1]).
2. It included a new Directive Principle of State Policy on promotion of co-operative societies (Article 43-B[2]).
3. It added a new Part IX-B in the Constitution which is entitled "The Co-operative Societies" (Articles 243-ZH to 243-ZT).

CONSTITUTIONAL PROVISIONS

Part IX-B of the constitution contains the following provisions with respect to the co-operative societies:

Incorporation of Co-operative Societies: The state legislature may make provisions for the incorporation, regulation and winding-up of co-operative societies based on the principles of voluntary formation, democratic member-control, member-economic participation and autonomous functioning.

Number and Term of Members of Board and its Office Bearers: The board shall consist of such number of directors as may be provided by the state legislature.[3] But, the maximum number of directors of a co-operative society shall not exceed twenty-one.

The state legislature shall provide for the reservation of one seat for the Scheduled Castes or the Scheduled Tribes and two seats for women on the board of every co-operative society having members from such a category of persons.

The term of office of elected members of the board and its office bearers shall be five years from the date of election.[4]

The state legislature shall make provisions for co-option of persons having experience in the field of banking, management, finance or specialisation in any other related field, as members of the board. But, the number of such co-opted members shall not exceed two (in addition to twenty-one directors). Further, the co-opted members shall not have the right to vote in any election of the co-operative society or be eligible to be elected as office bearers of the board.

The functional directors of a co-operative society shall also be the members of the board and such members shall be excluded for the purpose of counting the total number of directors (that is, twenty-one).

Election of Members of Board: The election of a board shall be conducted before the expiry of the term of the board so as to ensure that the newly elected members assume office immediately on the expiry of the term of the office of members of the outgoing board.

The superintendence, direction and control of the preparation of electoral rolls and the conduct of elections to a co-operative society shall vest in such body, as may be provided by the state legislature.

Supersession and Suspension of Board and Interim Management: No board shall be superseded or kept under suspension for a period exceeding six months.[5] The board may be superseded or kept under suspension in case

(i) Of its persistent default

(ii) Of negligence in the performance of its duties

(iii) Of committing any act prejudicial to the interests of the co-operative society or its members

(iv) Of there being a stalemate in the constitution or functions of the board

(v) Of the election body having failed to conduct elections in accordance with the provisions of the State Act.

However, the board of any such co-operative society shall not be superseded or kept under suspension where there is no Government shareholding or loan or financial assistance or any guarantee by the Government.

In case of supersession of a board, the administrator appointed to manage the affairs of such a co-operative society shall arrange for conduct of elections within the period of six months and handover the management to the elected board.

Audit of Accounts of Co-operative Societies: The state legislature may make provisions for the maintenance of accounts by the co-operative societies and the auditing of such accounts at least once in each financial year. It shall lay down the minimum qualifications and experience of auditors and auditing firms that shall be eligible for auditing the accounts of the co-operative societies.

Every co-operative society shall be audited by an auditor or auditing firm, appointed by the general body of the co-operative society. But, such an auditor or auditing firm shall be appointed from a panel approved by the State Government or a body authorised by the State Government on this behalf.

The accounts of every co-operative society shall be audited within six months of the close of the financial year.

The audit report of the accounts of an apex co-operative society shall be laid before the state legislature.

Convening of General Body Meetings: The state legislature may provide that the annual general body meeting of every co-operative society shall be convened within a period of six months of the close of the financial year.

Right of a Member to Get Information: The state legislature may provide for access to every member of a co-operative society to the books, information and accounts of the co-operative society. It may also make provisions to ensure the participation of members in the management of the co-operative society. Further, it may provide for co-operative education and training for its members.

Returns: Every co-operative society shall file returns, within six months of the close of every financial year, to the authority designated by the State Government. These returns shall include the following matters:

(a) Annual report of its activities

(b) Its audited statement of accounts

(c) Plan for surplus disposal as approved by the general body of the co-operative society

(d) List of amendments to the by-laws of the co-operative society

(e) Declaration regarding date of holding of its general body meeting and conduct of elections when due

(f) Any other information required by the Registrar in pursuance of any of the provisions of the State Act.[6]

Offences and Penalties: The state legislature may make provisions for the offences relating to the co-operative societies and penalties for such offences. Such a law shall include the commission or omission of the following acts as offences:

(a) A co-operative society wilfully makes a false return or furnishes false information

(b) Any person wilfully disobeys any summon, requisition or order issued under the State Act

(c) Any employer who, without sufficient cause, fails to pay to a co-operative society the amount deducted from its employee within a period of fourteen days

(d) Any officer who wilfully fails to handover custody of books, accounts, documents, records, cash, security and other property belonging to a co-operative society to an authorised person

(e) Any person who adopts corrupt practices before, during or after the election of members of the board or office bearers.

Application to Multi-state Co-operative Societies: The provisions of this part shall apply to the multi-state co-operative societies subject to the modification that any reference to the "State Legislature", "State Act" or "State Government" shall be construed as a reference to "Parliament", "Central Act" or "Central Government" respectively.

Application to Union Territories: The provisions of this part shall apply to the Union territories. But, the President may direct that the provisions of this part shall not apply to any Union territory or part thereof as he may specify in the notification.

Continuance of Existing Laws: Any provision of any law relating to co-operative societies in force in a state immediately before the commencement of the Constitution (Ninety-seventh Amendment) Act, 2011, which is inconsistent with the provisions of this part, shall continue to be in force until amended or repealed or until the expiration of one year from such commencement, whichever is less.[7]

REASONS FOR THE 97ᵀᴴ AMENDMENT

The reasons for adding the above provisions in the Constitution by the 97ᵗʰ Constitutional Amendment Act of 2011 are as follows:

1. The co-operative sector, over the years, has made significant contribution to various sectors of national economy and has achieved voluminous growth. However, it has shown weaknesses in safeguarding the interests of the members and fulfilment of objects for which these institutions were organised. There have been instances where elections have been postponed indefinitely and nominated office bearers or administrators have remained in-charge of these institutions for a long time. This reduces the accountability in the management of co-operative societies to their members. Inadequate professionalism in management in many of the co-operative institutions has led to poor services and low productivity. Co-operatives need to run on well established democratic principles and elections held on time and in a free and fair manner. Therefore, there was a need to initiate fundamental re-

forms to revitalise these institutions in order to ensure their contribution in the economic development of the country and to serve the interests of members and public at large and also to ensure their autonomy, democratic functioning and professional management.

2. The "co-operative societies" is a subject enumerated in Entry 32 of the state list of the Seventh Schedule of the Constitution and the state legislatures have accordingly enacted legislations on co-operative societies. Within the framework of State Acts, growth of co-operatives on large scale was envisaged as part of the efforts for securing social and economic justice and equitable distribution of the fruits of development. It has, however, been experienced that in spite of considerable expansion of co-operatives, their performance in qualitative terms has not been up to the desired level. Considering the need for reforms in the *Co-operative Societies Acts* of the States, consultations with the State Governments have been held at several occasions and in the conferences of state co-operative ministers. A strong need has been felt for amending the Constitution so as to keep the co-operatives free from unnecessary outside interferences and also to ensure their autonomous organisational set up and their democratic functioning.

3. The Central Government was committed to ensure that the co-operative societies in the country function in a democratic, professional, autonomous and economically sound manner. With a view to bring the necessary reforms, it was proposed to incorporate a new part in the Constitution so as to provide for certain provisions covering the vital aspects of working of co-operative societies like democratic, autonomous and professional functioning. It was expected that these provisions will not only ensure the autonomous and democratic functioning of co-operatives, but also ensure the accountability of management to the members and other stakeholders and shall provide for deterrence for violation of the provisions of the law.

Table 57.1 *Articles Related to Co-operative Societies at a Glance*

Article No.	Subject-matter
243ZH	Definitions
243ZI	Incorporation of Co-operative Societies
243ZJ	Number and Term of Members of Board and its Office Bearers
243ZK	Election of Members of Board
243ZL	Supersession and Suspension of Board and Interim Management
243ZM	Audit of Accounts of Co-operative Societies
243ZN	Convening of General Body Meetings
243ZO	Right of a Member to Get Information
243ZP	Returns
243ZQ	Offences and Penalties
243ZR	Application to Multi-state Co-operative Societies
243ZS	Application to Union Territories
243ZT	Continuance of Existing Laws

NOTES AND REFERENCES

1. In Part III of the Constitution, in Article 19, in clause (1), in sub-clause (c), the words "co-operative societies" were inserted.
2. In Part IV of the Constitution, a new Article 43-B was inserted, which says: "The state shall endeavour to promote voluntary formation, autonomous functioning, democratic control and professional management of co-operative societies".
3. The "board" means the board of directors or the governing body of a co-operative society, by whatever name called, to which the direction and control of the management of the affairs of a society is entrusted to.
4. An "office bearer" means a president, vice-president, chairperson, vice-chairperson, secretary or treasurer of a co-operative society and includes any other person to be elected by the board of any co-operative society.
5. In case of cooperative banks, other than multi-state cooperative banks, this period cannot exceed one year.
6. The "Registrar" means the Central Registrar appointed by the Central Government in relation to the multi-state co-operative societies and the Registrar for co-operative societies appointed by the state government under the law made by the legislature of a state in relation to co-operative societies.
7. February 15, 2012, is the date of commencement of the Constitution (Ninety-seventh Amendment) Act, 2011. The Centre has asked state governments to amend their respective *State Cooperative Society Act* in tune with the Constitution (97th Amendment) Act, 2011 before February 14, 2013.

Official Language

Part XVII of the Constitution deals with the official language in Articles 343 to 351. Its provisions are divided into four heads—Language of the Union, Regional languages, Language of the judiciary and texts of laws and Special directives.

LANGUAGE OF THE UNION

The Constitution contains the following provisions in respect of the official language of the Union.

1. Hindi written in *Devanagari* script is to be the official language of the Union. But, the form of numerals to be used for the official purposes of the Union has to be the international form of Indian numerals and not the *Devanagari* form of numerals.

2. However, for a period of fifteen years from the commencement of the Constitution (i.e., from 1950 to 1965), the English language would continue to be used for all the official purposes of the Union for which it was being used before 1950.

3. Even after fifteen years, the Parliament may provide for the continued use of English language for the specified purposes.

4. At the end of five years, and again at the end of ten years, from the commencement of the Constitution, the president should appoint a commission to make recommendations with regard to the progressive use of the Hindi language, restrictions on the use of the English language and other related issues[1].

5. A committee of Parliament is to be constituted to examine the recommendations of the commission and to report its views on them to the president[2].

Accordingly, in 1955, the president appointed an Official Language Commission under the chairmanship of BG Kher. The commission submitted its report to the President in 1956. The report was examined by a committee of Parliament constituted in 1957 under the chairmanship of Gobind Ballabh Pant. However, another Official Language Commission (as envisaged by the Constitution) was not appointed in 1960.

Subsequently, the Parliament enacted the Official Language Act in 1963. The act provides for the continued use of English (even after 1965), in addition to Hindi, for all official purposes of the Union and also for the transaction of business in Parliament. Notably, this act enables the use of English indefinitely (without any time-limit). Further, this act was amended in 1967 to make the use of English, in addition to Hindi, compulsory in certain cases[3].

REGIONAL LANGUAGES

The Constitution does not specify the official language of different states. In this regard, it makes the following provisions:

1. The legislature of a state may adopt any one or more of the languages in use in the state or Hindi as the official language of that state.

Until that is done, English is to continue as official language of that state.

Under this provision, most of the states have adopted the major regional language as their official language. For example, Andhra Pradesh has adopted Telugu, Kerala—Malayalam, Assam—Assamese, West Bengal—Bengali, Odisha—Odia. The nine northern states of Himachal Pradesh, Uttar Pradesh, Uttarakhand, Madhya Pradesh, Chhattisgarh, Bihar, Jharkhand, Haryana and Rajasthan have adopted Hindi. Gujarat has adopted Hindi in addition to Gujarati. Similarly, Goa has adopted Marathi in addition to Konkani Jammu and Kashmir has adopted Urdu (and not Kashmiri). On the other hand, certain north-eastern States like Meghalaya, Arunachal Pradesh and Nagaland have adopted English. Notably, the choice of the state is not limited to the languages enumerated in the Eighth Schedule of the Constitution.

2. For the time being, the official language of the Union (i.e., English) would remain the link language for communications between the Union and the states or between various states. But, two or more states are free to agree to use Hindi (instead of English) for communication between themselves. Rajasthan, Uttar Pradesh, Madhya Pradesh and Bihar are some of the states that have entered into such agreements. The Official Language Act (1963) lays down that English should be used for purposes of communication between the Union and the non-Hindi states (that is, the states that have not adopted Hindi as their official language). Further, where Hindi is used for communication between a Hindi and a non-Hindi state, such communication in Hindi should be accompanied by an English translation.

3. When the President (on a demand being made) is satisfied that a substantial proportion of the population of a state desire the use of any language spoken by them to be recognised by that state, then he may direct that such language shall also be officially recognised in that state. This provision aims at protecting the linguistic interests of minorities in the states.

LANGUAGE OF THE JUDICIARY AND TEXTS OF LAWS

The constitutional provisions dealing with the language of the courts and legislation are as follows:

1. Until Parliament provides otherwise, the following are to be in the English language only:
   (a) All proceedings in the Supreme Court and in every high court.
   (b) The authoritative texts of all bills, acts, ordinances, orders, rules, regulations and bye-laws at the Central and state levels[4].

2. However, the governor of a state, with the previous consent of the president, can authorise the use of Hindi or any other official language of the state, in the proceedings in the high court of the state, but not with respect to the judgements, decrees and orders passed by it. In other words, the judgements, decrees and orders of the high court must continue to be in English only (until Parliament otherwise provides).

3. Similarly, a state legislature can prescribe the use of any language (other than English) with respect to bills, acts, ordinances, orders, rules, regulations or bye-laws, but a translation of the same in the English language is to be published.

The Official Language Act of 1963 lays down that Hindi translation of acts, ordinances, orders, regulations and bye-laws published under the authority of the president are deemed to be authoritative texts. Further, every bill introduced in the Parliament is to be accompanied by a Hindi translation. Similarly, there is to be a Hindi translation of state acts or ordinances in certain cases.

The act also enables the governor of a state, with the previous consent of the president, to authorise the use of Hindi or any other official language of the state for judgements, decrees and orders passed by the high court of the state but they should be accompanied by an English translation. For example, Hindi is used in Uttar Pradesh, Madhya Pradesh, Bihar and Rajasthan for this purpose.

However, the Parliament has not made any provision for the use of Hindi in the Supreme Court. Hence, the Supreme Court hears only those who petition or appeal in English. In 1971, a petitioner insisted on arguing in Hindi a *habeas corpus* petition in the Supreme Court. But, the Court cancelled his petition on the ground that the language of the Court was English and allowing Hindi would be unconstitutional.

SPECIAL DIRECTIVES

The Constitution contains certain special directives to protect the interests of linguistic minorities and to promote the development of Hindi language. There are:

Protection of Linguistic Minorities

In this regard, the Constitution makes the following provisions:

1. Every aggrieved person has the right to submit a representation for the redress of any grievance to any officer or authority of the Union or a state in any of the languages used in the Union or in the state, as the case may be. This means that a representation cannot be rejected on the ground that it is not in the official language.

2. Every state and a local authority in the state should provide adequate facilities for instruction in the mother-tongue at the primary stage of education to children belonging to linguistic minority groups. The president can issue necessary directions for this purpose[5].

3. The president should appoint a special officer for linguistic minorities to investigate all matters relating to the constitutional safeguards for linguistic minorities and to report to him. The president should place all such reports before the Parliament and send to the state government concerned[6].

Development of Hindi Language

The Constitution imposes a duty upon the Centre to promote the spread and development of the Hindi language so that it may become the *lingua franca* of the composite culture of India[7].

Further, the Centre is directed to secure the enrichment of Hindi by assimilating the forms, style and expressions used in hindustani and in other languages specified in the Eighth Schedule and by drawing its vocabulary, primarily on sanskrit and secondarily on other languages.

At present (2013), the Eighth Schedule of the Constitution specifies 22 languages (originally 14 languages). These are Assamese, Bengali, Bodo, Dogri (Dongri), Gujarati, Hindi, Kannada, Kashmiri, Konkani, Mathili (Maithili), Malayalam, Manipuri, Marathi, Nepali, Odia[8], Punjabi, Sanskrit, Santhali, Sindhi, Tamil, Telugu and Urdu. Sindhi was added by the 21st Amendment Act of 1967; Konkani, Manipuri and Nepali were added by the 71st Amendment Act of 1992; and Bodo, Dongri, Maithili and Santhali were added by the 92nd Amendment Act of 2003.

In terms of the Constitution provisions, there are two objectives behind the specification of the above regional languages in the Eighth Schedule:

(a) the members of these languages are to be given representation in the Official Language Commission; and

(b) the forms, style and expression of these languages are to be used for the enrichment of the Hindi language.

Table 58.1 *Articles Related to Official Language at a Glance*

Article No.	Subject-matter
Language of the Union	
343.	Official language of the Union
344.	Commission and Committee of Parliament on official language
Regional Languages	
345.	Official language or languages of a state
346.	Official language for communication between one state and another or between a state and the Union
347.	Special provision relating to language spoken by a section of the population of a state

(Contd.)

Language of the Supreme Court, High Courts, etc.	
348.	Language to be used in the Supreme Court and in the High Courts and for Acts, Bills, etc.
349.	Special procedure for enactment of certain laws relating to language
Special Directives	
350.	Language to be used in representation for redress of grievances
350A.	Facilities for instruction in mother-tongue at primary stage
350B.	Special Officer for linguistic minorities
351.	Directive for development of the Hindi language

NOTES AND REFERENCES

1. The Commission was to consist of a chairman and other members representing the different languages specified in the Eighth Schedule of the Constitution.

2. The Committee was to consist of 30 members (20 from Lok Sabha and 10 from Rajya Sabha), to be elected in accordance with the system of proportional representation by means of the single transferable vote.

3. These include: (a) resolutions, general orders, rules, notifications, administrative or other reports or press communications issued by the Central government; (b) administrative and other reports and official papers laid before Parliament; and (c) contracts and agreements executed, licences, permits, notices, etc, issued by the Central government or by a corporation or a company owned by the Central government.

4. For language in Parliament and a state legislature, see the respective Chapters (i.e., 22 and 29).

5. This provision was added by the 7th Amendment Act of 1956 on the recommendation of the States Reorganisation Commission.

6. *Ibid.*

7. In 1976, the Supreme Court declared Tamil Nadu's pension scheme to anti-Hindi agitators as unconstitutional.

8. The 96th Amendment Act of 2011 substituted "Odia" for "Oriya".

Public Services

CLASSIFICATION OF SERVICES

The public services (civil services or government services) in India are classified into three categories—all-India services, Central services and state services. Their meaning and composition are explained below:

All-India Services

All-India services are those services which are common to both Central and state governments. The members of these services occupy top positions (or key posts) under both the Centre and the states and serve them by turns.

At present, there are three all-India services. They are:

1. Indian Administrative Service (IAS)
2. Indian Police Service (IPS)
3. Indian Forest Service (IFS)

In 1947, the Indian Civil Service (ICS) was replaced by IAS, and the Indian Police (IP) was replaced by IPS and were recognised by the Constitution as all-India services. In 1966, the Indian Forest Service was established as the third all-India service[1].

The All-India Services Act of 1951 authorised the Central government to make rules in consultation with the state governments for the regulation of recruitment and service conditions of the members of all-India services. The members of these services are recruited and trained by the Central government but are assigned to different states for work. They belong to different state cadres; the Centre having no cadre of its own

in this regard. They serve the Central government on deputation and after completing their fixed tenure they go back to their respective states. The Central government obtains the services of these officers on deputation under the well-known tenure system. It must be noted here that irrespective of their division among different states, each of these all-India services form a single service with common rights and status and uniform scales of pay throughout the country. Their salaries and pensions are met by the states.

The all-India services are controlled jointly by the Central and state governments. The ultimate control lies with the Central government while the immediate control is vested in the state governments. Any disciplinary action (imposition of penalties) against these officers can only be taken by the Central government.

Sardar Vallabhbhai Patel was the chief protagonist of all-India services in the Constituent Assembly. Hence, he came to be regarded as the 'Father of all-India Services'.

Central Services

The personnel of Central services work under the exclusive jurisdiction of the Central government. They hold specialised (functional and technical) positions in various departments of the Central government.

Before Independence, the Central services were classified into class-I, class-II, subordinate and inferior services. After Independence, the nomenclature of subordinate and inferior services was replaced by class-III and class-IV services. Again in 1974, the classification of Central services into class-I, class-

II, class-III and class-IV was changed to group A, group B, group C and group D, respectively[2].

At present, there are 58 group A Central services. Some of them are:

1. Central Engineering Service.
2. Central Health Service.
3. Central Information Service.
4. Central Legal Service.
5. Central Secretariat Service.
6. Indian Audit and Accounts Service.
7. Indian Defence Accounts Service.
8. Indian Economic Service.
9. Indian Foreign Service.
10. Indian Meteorogical Service.
11. Indian Postal Service.
12. Indian Revenue Service (Customs, Excise and Income Tax)
13. Indian Statistical Service.
14. Overseas Communication Service.
15. Railway Personnel Service.

Most of the above cadres of group A Central services have also corresponding group B services. The group C Central services consists of clerical personnel while group D consists of manual personnel. Thus group A and group B comprises of gazetted officers while group C and group D are non-gazetted.

Among all, the Indian Foreign Service (IFS) is the highest central service in terms of prestige, status, pay and emoluments. In fact, it (though a central service) competes with the all-India services in position, status and pay scales. It comes next to the IAS in ranking and its pay scale is higher than the IPS.

State Services

The personnel of state services work under the exclusive jurisdiction of the state government. They hold different positions (general, functional and technical) in the departments of the state government. However, they occupy lower positions (in the administrative hierarchy of the state) than those held by the members of the all-India services (IAS, IPS and IFS).

The number of services in a state differ from state to state. The services that are common to all the states are:

1. Civil Service.
2. Police Service.
3. Forest Service.
4. Agricultural Service.
5. Medical Service.
6. Veterinary Service.
7. Fisheries Service.
8. Judicial Service.
9. Public Health Service.
10. Educational Service.
11. Co-operative Service.
12. Registration Service.
13. Sales Tax Service.
14. Jail Service.
15. Service of Engineers.

Each of these services is named after the state, that is, name of the state is added as a prefix. For example, in Andhra Pradesh (AP), they are known as AP Civil Service, AP Police Service, AP Forest Service, AP Agricultural Service, AP Medical Service, AP Veterinary Service, AP Fisheries Service, AP Judicial Service, and so on. Among all the state services, the civil service (also known as the administrative service) is the most prestigious.

Like the Central services, the state services are also classified into four categories: class I (group I or group A), class II (group II or group B), class III (group III or group C) and class IV (group IV or group D).

Further, the state services are also classified into gazetted class and non-gazetted class. Usually, Class I (Group-A) and Class-II (Group-B) Services are gazetted classes while Class-III (Group-C) and Class-IV (Group-D) services are non-gazetted classes. The names of the members of gazetted class are published in the Government Gazette for appointment, transfer, promotion and retirement, while those of the non-gazetted are not published. Further, the members of the gazetted class enjoy some privileges which are denied to the members of non-gazetted class. Also, the members of the gazetted class are called 'officers' while those of non-gazetted are called 'employees'.

The All-India Services Act of 1951 specifies that senior posts not exceeding thirty-three and one third per cent in the Indian Administrative Service (IAS), Indian Police Service (IPS) and Indian Forest Service (IFS) are required to be filled in by promotion of officers employed in the state services. Such promotions are made on the recommendation of selection committee constituted for this purpose in each state. Such a committee is presided over by the Chairman or a member of UPSC.

Constitutional Provisions

Articles 308 to 314 in part XIV of the Constitution contain provisions with regard to all-India services, Central services and state services. Article 308 makes it clear that these provisions do not apply to the state of Jammu and Kashmir.

1. Recruitment and Service Conditions

Article 309 empowers the Parliament and the state legislatures to regulate the recruitment and the conditions of service of the persons appointed to public services and posts under the Centre and the states, respectively. Until such laws are made, the president or the governor can make rules to regulate these matters..

Recruitment includes any method provided for inducting a person in public service like appointment, selection, deputation, promotion and appointment by transfer.

The conditions of service of a public servant includes pay, allowances, periodical increments, leave, promotion, tenure or termination of service, transfer, deputation, various types of rights, disciplinary action, holidays, hours of work and retirement benefits like pension, provident fund, gratuity and so on.

Under this provision, the Parliament or the state legislature can impose 'reasonable' restrictions on the Fundamental Rights of public servants in the interests of integrity, honesty, efficiency, discipline, impartiality, secrecy, neutrality, anonymity, devotion to duty and so on. Such restrictions are mentioned in the conduct rules like Central Services (Conduct) Rules, Railway Services (Conduct) Rules and so on.

2. Tenure of Office

According to Article 310, members of the defence services, the civil services of the Centre and the all-India services or persons holding military posts or civil posts[3] under the Centre, hold office during the pleasure of the president. Similarly, members of the civil services of a state or persons holding civil posts under a state, hold office during the pleasure of the governor of the state.

However, there is an exception to this general rule of dismissal at pleasure. The president or the governor may (in order to secure the services of a person having special qualifications) provide for the payment of compensation to him in two cases: (i) if the post is abolished before the expiration of the contractual period, or (ii) if he is required to vacate that post for reasons not connected with misconduct on his part. Notably, such a contract can be made only with a new entrant, that is, a person who is not already a member of a defence service, a civil service of the Centre, an all-India service or a civil service of a state.

3. Safeguards to Civil Servants

Article 311 places two restriction on the above 'doctrine of pleasure'. In other words, it provides two safeguards to civil servants against any arbitrary dismissal from their posts:

(a) A civil servant cannot be dismissed or removed[4] by an authority subordinate to that by which he was appointed.

(b) A civil servant cannot be dismissed or removed or reduced in rank[5] except after an inquiry in which he has been informed of the charges against him and given a reasonable opportunity of being heard in respect of those charges.

The above two safeguards are available only to the members of the civil services of the Centre, the all-India services, the civil services of a state or to persons holding civil posts under the Centre or a state and not to the members of defence services or persons holding military posts.

However, the second safeguard (holding inquiry) is not available in the following three cases:

(a) Where a civil servant is dismissed or removed or reduced in rank on the ground of conduct which has led to his conviction on a criminal charge; or

(b) Where the authority empowered to dismiss or remove a civil servant or to reduce him in rank is satisfied that for some reason (to be recorded in writing), it is not reasonably practicable to hold such inquiry; or

(c) Where the president or the governor is satisfied that in the interest of the security of the state, it is not expedient to hold such inquiry.

Originally, the opportunity of being heard was given to a civil servant at two stages—at the inquiry stage, and at the punishment stage. But, the 42nd Amendment Act of 1976 abolished the provision for second opportunity (that is, the right of a civil servant to make representation against the punishment proposed as a result of the findings of the inquiry). Hence, the present position is that where it is proposed (after inquiry) to impose upon a civil servant the punishment of dismissal, removal or reduction in rank, it may be imposed on the basis of the evidence adduced at the inquiry without giving him any opportunity of making representation on the penalty proposed.

The Supreme Court held that the expression 'reasonable opportunity of being heard' envisaged to a civil servant (in the second safeguard mentioned above) includes:

(a) an opportunity to deny his guilt and establish his innocence which he can only do if he is told what the charges levelled against him are and the allegations on which such charges are based;

(b) an opportunity to defend himself by cross-examining the witnesses produced against him and by examining himself or any other witnesses in support of his defence; and

(c) the disciplinary authority must supply a copy of the inquiry officer's report to the delinquent civil servant for observations and comments before the disciplinary authority considers the report.

4. All-India Services

Article 312 makes the following provisions in respect of all-India services:

(a) The Parliament can create new all-India services (including an all-India judicial service), if the Rajya Sabha passes a resolution declaring that it is necessary or expedient in the national interest to do so. Such a resolution in the Rajya Sabha should be supported by two-thirds of the members present and voting.

This power of recommendation is given to the Rajya Sabha to protect the interests of states in the Indian federal system.

(b) Parliament can regulate the recruitment and conditions of service of persons appointed to all-India services. Accordingly, the Parliament has enacted the All-India Services Act, 1951 for the purpose.

(c) The services known at the commencement of the Constitution (that is, January 26, 1950) as the Indian Administrative Service and the Indian Police Service are deemed to be services created by Parliament under this provision.

(d) The all-India judicial service should not include any post inferior to that of a district judge[6]. A law providing for the creation of this service is not to be deemed as an amendment of the Constitution for the purposes of Article 368.

Though the 42nd Amendment Act of 1976 made the provision for the creation of all-India judicial service, no such law has been made so far.

5. Other Provisions

Article 312 A (inserted by the 28th Amendment Act of 1972) confers powers on the Parliament to vary or revoke the conditions of service of persons who were appointed to a civil service of the Crown in India before 1950. Article 313 deals with transitional provisions and says that until otherwise provided, all the laws in force before 1950 and applicable to any public service would continue. Article 314 which made provision for protection of existing officers of certain services was repealed by the 28th Amendment Act of 1972.

Table 59.1 *Articles Related to Public Services at a Glance*

Article No.	Subject-matter
308.	Interpretation
309.	Recruitment and conditions of service of persons serving the Union or a state
310.	Tenure of office of persons serving the Union or a state
311.	Dismissal, removal or reduction in rank of persons employed in civil capacities under the Union or a state
312.	All-India Services
312A.	Power of Parliament to vary or revoke conditions of service of officers of certain services
313.	Transitional provisions
314.	Provision for protection of existing officers of certain services (Repealed)

NOTES AND REFERENCES

1. In 1963, a provision was made for the creation of three more all-India services. They were Indian Forest Service, Indian Medical and Health Service and Indian Service of Engineers. However, out of these three, only the Indian Forest Service came into existence in 1966.

2. This was done on the recommendation of the Third Pay Commission (1970–1973) while the earlier change was done on the recommendation of the First Pay Commission (1946-1947).

3. A 'civil post' means an appointment or office or employment on the civil side of the administration as distinguished from the military side.

4. The difference between dismissal and removal is that the former disqualifies for future employment under the government while the latter does not disqualify for future employment under the government.

5. 'Reduction in rank' means reduction from a higher to a lower rank or post. It is a penalty imposed on a civil servant.

6. The expression 'district judge' includes judge of a city civil court, additional district judge, joint district judge, assistant district judge, chief judge of a small cause court, chief presidency magistrate, additional chief presidency magistrate, sessions judge, additional sessions judge and assistant sessions judge.

Tribunals

The original Constitution did not contain provisions with respect to tribunals. The 42nd Amendment Act of 1976 added a new Part XIV-A to the Constitution. This part is entitled as 'Tribunals' and consists of only two Articles—Article 323 A dealing with administrative tribunals and Article 323 B dealing with tribunals for other matters.

ADMINISTRATIVE TRIBUNALS

Article 323 A empowers the Parliament to provide for the establishment of administrative tribunals for the adjudication of disputes relating to recruitment and conditions of service of persons appointed to public services of the Centre, the states, local bodies, public corporations and other public authorities. In other words, Article 323 A enables the Parliament to take out the adjudication of disputes relating to service matters from the civil courts and the high courts and place it before the administrative tribunals.

In pursuance of Article 323 A, the Parliament has passed the Administrative Tribunals Act in 1985. The act authorises the Central government to establish one Central administrative tribunal and the state administrative tribunals. This act opened a new chapter in the sphere of providing speedy and inexpensive justice to the aggrieved public servants.

Central Administrative Tribunal (CAT)

The Central Administrative Tribunal (CAT) was set up in 1985 with the principal bench at Delhi and additional benches in different states. At present, it has 17 regular benches, 15 of which operate at the principal seats of high courts and the remaining two at Jaipur and Lucknow[1]. These benches also hold circuit sittings at other seats of high courts.

The CAT exercises original jurisdiction in relation to recruitment and all service matters of public servants covered by it. Its jurisdiction extends to the all-India services, the Central civil services, civil posts under the Centre and civilian employees of defence services. However, the members of the defence forces, officers and servants of the Supreme Court and the secretarial staff of the Parliament are not covered by it.

The CAT is a multi-member body consisting of a chairman and members. Earlier, the CAT consisted of a Chairman, Vice-Chairmen and members. With the amendment in Administrative Tribunals Act, 1985 in 2006, the members have been given the status of judges of High Courts. At present (2013), the sanctioned strength of the Chairman is one and sanctioned strength of the Members is 65. They are drawn from both judicial and administrative streams and are appointed by the president. They hold office for a term of five years or until they attain the age of 65 years, in case of chairman and 62 years in case of members, whichever is earlier.

The CAT is not bound by the procedure laid down in the Civil Procedure Code of 1908. It is guided by the principles of natural justice. These principles keep the CAT flexible in approach. Only a nominal fee of ₹50 is to be paid by the applicant. The applicant may appear either in person or through a lawyer.

Originally, appeals against the orders of the CAT could be made only in the Supreme Court and not in the high courts. However, in the *Chandra Kumar* case[2] (1997), the Supreme Court declared this restriction on the jurisdiction of the high courts as unconstitutional, holding that judicial review is a part of the basic structure of the Constitution. It laid down that appeals against the orders of the CAT shall lie before the division bench of the concerned high court. Consequently, now it is not possible for an aggrieved public servant to approach the Supreme Court directly against an order of the CAT, without first going to the concerned high court.

State Administrative Tribunals

The Administrative Tribunals Act of 1985 empowers the Central government to establish the State Administrative Tribunals (SATs) on specific request of the concerned state governments. So far (2013), the SATs have been set up in the nine states of Andhra Pradesh, Himachal Pradesh, Odisha, Karnataka, Madhya Pradesh, Maharashtra, Tamil Nadu, West Bengal and Kerala. However, the Madhya Pradesh, Tamil Nadu and Himachal Pradesh Tribunals have since been abolished. The Kerala Administrative Tribunal was set up with effect from 26th August, 2010.

Like the CAT, the SATs exercise original jurisdiction in relation to recruitment and all service matters of state government employees.

The chairman and members of the SATs are appointed by the president after consultation with the governor of the state concerned.

The act also makes a provision for setting up of joint administrative tribunal (JAT) for two or more states. A JAT exercises all the jurisdiction and powers exercisable by the administrative tribunals for such states.

The chairman and members of a JAT are appointed by the president after consultation with the governors of the concerned states.

TRIBUNALS FOR OTHER MATTERS

Under Article 323 B, the Parliament and the state legislatures are authorised to provide for the establishment of tribunals for the adjudication of disputes relating to the following matters:

(a) Taxation
(b) Foreign exchange, import and export
(c) Industrial and labour
(d) Land reforms
(e) Ceiling on urban property
(f) Elections to Parliament and state legislatures
(g) Food stuffs
(h) Rent and tenancy rights[3]

Articles 323 A and 323 B differs in the following three aspects:

1. While Article 323 A contemplates establishment of tribunals for public service matters only, Article 323 B contemplates establishment of tribunals for certain other matters (mentioned above).

2. While tribunals under Article 323 A can be established only by Parliament, tribunals under Article 323 B can be established both by Parliament and state legislatures with respect to matters falling within their legislative competence.

3. Under Article 323 A, only one tribunal for the Centre and one for each state or two or more states may be established. There is no question of hierarchy of tribunals, whereas under Article 323 B a hierarchy of tribunals may be created.

In *Chandra Kumar* case[4] (1997), the Supreme Court declared those provisions of these two articles which excluded the jurisdiction of the high courts and the Supreme Court as unconstitutional. Hence, the judicial remedies are now available against the orders of these tribunals.

Table 60.1 *Name and Jurisdiction of Benches of CAT*

Sl.No.	Bench	Territorial Jurisdiction of the Bench
1.	Principal Bench, Delhi	Delhi
2.	Allahabad Bench	Uttar Pradesh (except the districts covered by Lucknow Bench)
3.	Lucknow Bench	Uttar Pradesh (except the districts covered by the Allahabad Bench)

(Contd.)

Sl.No.	Bench	Territorial Jurisdiction of the Bench
4.	Cuttack Bench	Orissa
5.	Hyderabad Bench	Andhra Pradesh
6.	Bangalore Bench	Karnataka
7.	Madras Bench	Tamil Nadu and Puducherry
8.	Ernakulam Bench	Kerala and Lakshadweep
9.	Bombay Bench	Maharashtra, Goa, Dadra and Nagar Haveli, and Daman and Diu
10.	Ahmedabad Bench	Gujarat
11.	Jodhpur Bench	Rajasthan (except the districts covered by the Jaipur Bench)
12.	Jaipur Bench	Rajasthan (except the districts covered by the Jodhpur Bench)
13.	Chandigarh Bench	J&K, Haryana, Himachal Pradesh, Punjab and Chandigarh
14.	Jabalpur Bench	Madhya Pradesh
15.	Patna Bench	Bihar
16.	Calcutta Bench	West Bengal, Sikkim and Andaman and Nicobar Islands
17.	Guwahati Bench	Assam, Meghalaya, Manipur, Tripura, Nagaland, Mizoram and Arunachal Pradesh

Table 60.2 *Circuit Sittings of Benches of CAT*

Sl.No.	Bench	Circuit Sittings held at
1.	Allahabad Bench	Nainital
2.	Calcutta Bench	Port Blair, Gangtok
3.	Chandigarh Bench	Shimla, Jammu
4.	Madras Bench	Puducherry
5.	Guwahati Bench	Shillong, Itanagar, Kohima, Agartala, Imphal
6.	Jabalpur Bench	Indore, Gwalior, Bilaspur
7.	Bombay Bench	Nagpur, Aurangabad, Panaji
8.	Patna Bench	Ranchi

Table 60.3 *Articles Related to Tribunals at a Glance*

Article No.	Subject-matter
323A.	Administrative tribunals
323B.	Tribunals for other matters

NOTES AND REFERENCES

1. See Table 60.1 at the end of this chapter.
2. *L. Chandra Kumar v. Union of India,* (1997). Clause 2(d) of Article 323 A was declared as unconstitutional.
3. Added by the 75th Amendment Act of 1993.
4. *L. Chandra Kumar v. Union of India,* (1997). Clause 2(d) of Article 323 A and Clause 3(d) of Article 323 B were declared as unconstitutional.

Rights and Liabilities of the Government

Articles 294 to 300 in Part XII of the Constitution deal with the property, contracts, rights, liabilities, obligations and suits of the Union and the states. In this regard, the Constitution makes the Union or the states as juristic (legal) persons.

PROPERTY OF THE UNION AND THE STATES

1. Succession

All property and assets that were vested in the Dominion of India or a province or an Indian princely state, before the commencement of the present Constitution, became vested in the Union or the corresponding state.

Similarly, all rights, liabilities and obligations of the government of the dominion of India or a province or an Indian state would now be the rights, liabilities and obligations of the Government of India or the corresponding state.

2. Escheat, Lapse and *Bona Vacantia*

Any property in India that would have accrued to King of England or ruler of Indian state (princely) by escheat (death of a person inte-state without any heir), lapse (termination of rights through disuse or failure to follow appropriate procedures) or *bona vacantia* (property found without any owner) for want of a rightful owner, would now vest in the state if the property is situated there, and in the Union, in any other case. In all these three cases, the property accrues to the government as there is no rightful owner (claimant).

3. Sea-Wealth

All lands, minerals and other things of value under the waters of the ocean within the territorial waters of India, the continental shelf of India and the exclusive economic zone of India vests in the Union. Hence, a state near the ocean cannot claim jurisdiction over these things.

India's territorial waters extend to a distance of 12 nautical miles from the appropriate base line. Similarly, India's exclusive economic zone extends upto 200 nautical miles[1].

4. Compulsory Acquisition by Law

The Parliament as well as the state legislatures are empowered to make laws for the compulsory acquisition and requisitioning of private property by the governments. Further, the 44th Amendment Act (1978) has also abolished the constitutional obligation to pay compensation in this regard except in two cases: (a) when the government acquires the property of a minority educational institution; and (b) when the government acquires the land held by a person under his personal cultivation and the land is within the statutory ceiling limits[2].

5. Acquisition under Executive Power

The Union or a state can acquire, hold and dispose property under the exercise of its executive power.

Further, the executive power of the Union or a state extends to the carrying on any trade or business within and in other states also.

SUITS BY OR AGAINST THE GOVERNMENT

Article 300 of the Constitution deals with the suits by or against the Government in India. It lays down that the Government of India may sue or be sued by the name of the Union of India and government of a state may sue or be sued by the name of that state, eg, State of Andhra Pradesh or State of Uttar Pradesh and so on. Thus, the Union of India and states are legal entities (juristic personalities) for purposes of suits and proceedings, not the Government of the Union or government of states.

Regarding the extent of the governmental liability, the Constitution (Article 300) declares that the Union of India or states can sue or be sued in relation to their respective affairs in the like cases as the dominion of India and the corresponding provinces or Indian states might have sued or been sued before the Constitution. This provision is subject to any law made by Parliament or a state legislature. But, no such law has been enacted so far. Hence, at present, the position in this respect remains the same as it existed before the Constitution. In the pre-Constitution period (i.e., from the days of the East India Company up to the commencement of the Constitution in 1950), the government was suable for contracts but not for torts (wrongs committed by its servants) in respect of its sovereign functions. This is explained in detail as follows:

1. Liability for Contracts

Under the exercise of its executive power, the Union or a state can enter into contracts for the acquisition, holding and disposal of property, or to carry on any trade or business, or for any other purpose. But, the Constitution lays down three conditions which must be fulfilled by such contracts:

(a) They must be expressed to be made by the president or governor, as the case may be;

(b) They must be executed on behalf of the president or governor, as the case may be; and

(c) They must be executed by such person or in such manner as the president or governor may direct or authorise.

These conditions are mandatory and not merely directory in nature. Failure to comply with them nullifies the contracts and renders them void and unenforceable in the courts.

Further, the president or the governor is not personally liable in respect of any contract executed in his name. Similarly, the officer executing the contract is also not personally liable. This immunity is purely personal and does not immunize the government from a contractual liability, making the government suable in contracts. This means that the contractual liability of the Union government and the state governments is the same as that of an individual under the ordinary law of contract, which has been the position in India since the days of the East India Company.

2. Liability for Torts

In the beginning, the East India Company was only a trading body. Gradually, it acquired territories in India and became a sovereign authority. The Company was suable for its functions as a trader but not as a sovereign. This immunity of the Company in respect of its sovereign functions was based on the English Common Law maxim that the 'King can do no wrong', which means that the King was not liable for wrongs of his servants. This traditional immunity of the State (i.e., Crown) in Britain from any legal liability for any action has been done away by the Crown Proceedings Act (1947). However, the position in India still remains the same.

Therefore, the government (Union or states) in India can be sued for torts (civil wrongs) committed by its officials only in the exercise of its non-sovereign functions but not in the sovereign functions like administering justice, constructing a military road, commandering goods during war, etc. This distinction between the sovereign and non-sovereign functions of the Government in India and the immunity of the government in respect of its sovereign functions was established in the famous *P and O Steam Navigation Company* case[3] (1861). This was reaffirmed by the Supreme Court in the post-independence era in the *Kasturilal* case[4] (1965). However, after this case, the Supreme Court started giving a restrictive interpretation to sovereign functions of the government and awarded compensation to victims in a large number of cases.

In Nagendra Rao Case[4a] (1994), the Supreme Court criticised the doctrine of sovereign immunity of the State and adopted a liberal approach with respect to the tortuous liability of the State. It ruled that when a citizen suffers any damage due to the negligent act of the servants of the State, the State would be liable to pay compensation for it and the State cannot avoid this liability on the ground of sovereign immunity. It held that in the modern sense, the distinction between sovereign and non-sovereign functions does not exist. It laid down the proposition that barring a few functions, the State cannot claim any immunity. Its observations, in this case, are as follows:

1. No civilised system can permit an executive to play with the people of its country and claim that it is entitled to act in any manner as it is sovereign. The concept of public interest has changed with structural change in the society. No legal or political system today can place the State above law as it is unjust and unfair for a citizen to be deprived of his property illegally by negligent act of officers of the State without any remedy.

2. The modern social thinking of progressive societies and the judicial approach is to do away with archaic State protection and place the State or the Government at par with any other juristic legal entity. Any water-tight compartmentalisation of the functions of the State as "sovereign" and "non-sovereign" or "governmental" and "non-governmental" is not sound. It is contrary to modern jurisprudential thinking.

3. The need of the State, duty of its officials and right of the citizens are required to be reconciled so that the rule of law in a welfare State is not shaken. In a welfare State, the functions of the State are not only the defence of the country or administration of justice or maintaining law and order but it extends to regulating and controlling the activities of the people in almost every sphere—educational, commercial, social, economic, political and even marital.

4. The demarcating line between sovereign and non-sovereign powers for which no rational basis survives has largely disappeared. Therefore, barring functions such as administration of justice, maintenance of law and order and repression of crime etc., which are among the primary and inalienable functions of a constitutional Government, the State cannot claim any immunity.

In the above case, the Supreme Court did not overrule its judgement in the Kasturilal case (1965). However, it said that it is applicable to rare and limited cases.

In Common Cause Case[4b] (1999), the Supreme Court again examined the whole doctrine and rejected the sovereign immunity rule. The Court held that the rule of State liability as laid down in P. & O. Steam Navigation Company case is very outmoded. It said that in modern times when the State activities have been considerably increased it is very difficult to draw a line between its sovereign and non-sovereign functions. The increased activities of the State have made a deep impression on all facets of citizens' life, and therefore, the liability of the State must be made co-extensive with the modern concept of a welfare State. The State must be liable for all tortuous acts of its employees, whether done in exercise of sovereign or non-sovereign powers[4c]. Finally, the court observed that the efficacy of Kasturilal case as a binding precedent has been eroded.

In the Prisoner's Murder case[4d] (2000), the Supreme Court ruled that in the process of judicial advancement Kasturilal case has paled into insignifance and is no longer of any binding value.

SUITS AGAINST PUBLIC OFFICIALS

1. President and Governor

The Constitution confers certain immunities to the president of India and governor of states with regard to their official acts and personal acts. These are:

(a) Official Acts The president and the governors cannot be sued during the term of their office or thereafter, for any act done by them in the exercise and performance of their official powers and duties. However, the official conduct of the president can be reviewed by a court, tribunal or any other body authorised by either House of Parliament to investigate charges for impeachment. Further, the aggrieved person can bring appropriate proceedings against the Union of India instead of the president and the state instead of the Governor of that state.

(b) Personal Acts   No criminal proceedings can be started against the president and the governors in respect of their personal acts nor can they be arrested or imprisoned. This immunity is limited to the period of the term of their office only and does not extend beyond that. However, civil proceedings can be started against them during their term of office in respect of their personal acts after giving two months' advance notice.

2. Ministers

The Constitution does not grant any immunity to the ministers for their official acts. But, since they are not required to countersign (as in Britain) the official acts of the president and the governors, they are not liable in the courts for those acts[5]. Moreover, they are not liable for the official acts done by the president and the governors on their advice as the courts are debarred from inquiring into such advice. However, the ministers do not enjoy any immunity for their personal acts, and can be sued for crimes as well as torts in the ordinary courts like common citizens.

3. Judicial Officers

The judicial officers enjoy immunity from any liability in respect of their official acts and hence,

cannot be sued. The Judicial Officers Protection Act (1850) lays down that, 'no judge, magistrate, justice of peace, collector or other person acting judicially shall be liable to be sued in any civil court for any act done by him in the discharge of his official duty'.

4. Civil Servants

Under the Constitution, the civil servants are conferred personal immunity from legal liability for official contracts. This means that the civil servant who made a contract in his official capacity is not personally liable in respect of that contract but it is the government (Central or state) that is liable for the contract. But, if the contract is made without complying the conditions specified in the Constitution, then the civil servant who made the contract is personally liable. Further, the civil servants also enjoy immunity from legal liability for their tortious acts in respect of the sovereign functions of the government. In other cases, the liability of the civil servants for torts or illegal acts is the same as of any ordinary citizen. Civil proceedings can be instituted against them for anything done in their official capacity after giving a two months' advance notice. But, no such notice is required when the action is to be brought against them for the acts done outside the scope of their official duties. Criminal proceedings can be instituted against them for acts done in their official capacity, with the prior permission of the president or the governor, where necessary[6].

Table 61.1   *Articles Related to Rights and Liabilities of the Government at a Glance*

Article No.	Subject-matter
294.	Succession to property, assets, rights, liabilities and obligations in certain cases
295.	Succession to property, assets, rights, liabilities and obligations in other cases
296.	Property accruing by escheat or lapse or as *bona vacantia*
297.	Things of value within territorial waters or continental shelf and resources of the exclusive economic zone to vest in the Union
298.	Power to carry on trade, etc.
299.	Contracts
300.	Suits and proceedings
361.	Protection (immunities) of President and Governors

Notes and References

1. Under the Territorial Waters, Continental Shelf, Exclusive Economic Zone and other Maritime Zones Act, 1976, passed by the Parliament after the 40th Constitutional Amendment Act, 1976.

2. The first provision was added by the 44th Amendment Act (1978). This amendment abolished the Fundamental Right to property and made it a legal right. The second provision was added by the 17th Amendment Act (1964).

3. *Peninsular and Oriental Steam Navigation Company v. Secretary of State for India,* (1861).

4. *Kasturilal v. State of UP*, (1965).

4a. *N. Nagendra Rao & Co. v. State of Andhra Pradesh* (1994).

4b. *Common Cause, Registered Society v. Union of India* (1999).

4c. J.N. Pandey, *The Constitutional Law of India*, 49th Edition, Central Law Agency, P.682.

4d. *State of A.P.* v. *Challa Ramkrishna Reddy* (2000).

5. In Britain, the ministers are required to countersign the official acts of the crown and are held liable in the courts for those acts.

6. Criminal Procedure Code says—where a public servant who is not removable from his office save by or with the sanction of the Central or state government is accused of an offence, committed by him while acting or purporting to act in the discharge of his official duty, no court can take cognizance of such offence without the previous sanction of the Central government or the state government, as the case may be.

Authoritative Text of the Constitution in Hindi Language

CONSTITUTIONAL PROVISIONS

Originally, the Constitution of India did not make any provision with respect to an authoritative text of the Constitution in the Hindi language. Later, a provision in this regard was made by the 58th Constitutional Amendment Act of 1987[1]. This amendment inserted a new Article 394-A in the last part of the Constitution i.e., Part XXII[2]. This article contains the following provisions:

1. The President shall cause to be published under his authority :
   (i) The translation of the Constitution in Hindi language. The modifications which are necessary to bring it in conformity with the language, style and terminology adopted in the authoritative texts of the Central Acts in Hindi can be made in it. All the amendments of the Constitution made before such publication should be incorporated in it.
   (ii) The translation in Hindi of every amendment of the constitution made in English.
2. The translation of the Constitution and its every amendment published shall be construed to have the same meaning as the original text in English. If any difficulty arises in this matter, the President shall cause the Hindi text to be revised suitably.
3. The translation of the Constitution and its every amendment published shall be deemed to be, for all purposes, its authoritative text in Hindi.

REASONS FOR THE 58TH AMENDMENT

The reasons for adding the above provisions in the Constitution by the 58th Constitutional Amendment Act of 1987 are as follows:

The Constitution of India adopted by the Constituent Assembly on November 26, 1949, was in the English language. A Hindi translation of the Constitution, singed by the members of the Constituent Assembly, was also published in 1950 under the authority of the President of the Constituent Assembly[3]. There had been a general demand for the publication of an authoritative text of the Constitution in Hindi incorporating in it all the subsequent amendments. It has also been imperative to have an authoritative text of the Constitution in the Hindi language for facilitating its use in the legal process. Further, any Hindi version of the Constitution should not only conform to the Hindi translation published by the Constituent Assembly in 1950, but should also be in conformity with the language, style and terminology adopted in the authoritative texts of the Central Acts in Hindi. It was, therefore, proposed to amend the constitution so as to empower the President of India to publish under his authority the translation of the Constitution and its every amendment in Hindi language.

In pursuance of Article 394-A, the President published in the Gazzette of India, an authoritative text of the Constitution of India in the Hindi language.

NOTES AND REFERENCES

1. The 56th Constitutional Amendment Bill of 1987, after being passed by both the Houses of Parliament and assented by the President, finally emerged as the 58th Constitutional Amendment Act of 1987.
2. Part XXII is entitled as 'Short Title, Commencement, Authoritative Text in Hindi and Repeals'. Originally, this part consisted of three Articles only – Article 393 (short title), Article 394 (commencement) and Article 395 (repeals).
3. In accordance with a resolution adopted by the Constituent Assembly.

Special Provisions Relating to Certain Classes

RATIONALE OF SPECIAL PROVISIONS

In order to realise the objectives of equality and justice as laid down in the Preamble, the Constitution makes special provisions for the scheduled castes (SCs), the scheduled tribes (STs), the backward classes (BCs) and the Anglo-Indians. These special provisions are contained in Part XVI of the Constitution from Articles 330 to 342. *They are related to the following:*

1. Reservation in Legislatures
2. Special Representation in Legislatures
3. Reservation in Services and Posts
4. Educational Grants
5. Appointment of National Commissions
6. Appointment of Commissions of Investigation

These special provisions can be classified into the following broad categories:

(a) Permanent and Temporary — Some of them are a permanent feature of the Constitution, while some others continue to operate only for a specified period.

(b) Protective and Developmental — Some of them aim at protecting these classes from all forms of injustice and exploitation, while some others aim at promoting their socio-economic interests.

SPECIFICATION OF CLASSES

The Constitution does not specify the castes or tribes which are to be called the SCs or the STs. It leaves to the President the power to specify as to what castes or tribes in each state and union territory are to be treated as the SCs and STs. Thus, the lists of the SCs or STs vary from state to state and union territory to union territory. In case of the states, the President issues the notification after consulting the governor of the state concerned. But, any inclusion or exclusion of any caste or tribe from Presidential notification can be done only by the Parliament and not by a subsequent Presidential notification. Presidents have issued several orders specifying the SCs and STs in different states and union territories and these have also been amended by the Parliament.[1]

Similarly, the Constitution has neither specified the BCs nor used a single uniform expression to characterise the BCs.[2] The expression 'BCs' means such backward classes of citizens other than the SCs and the STs as may be specified by the Central Government. Thus the expression 'BCs' in this context means the 'Other Backward Classes' (OBCs) as the SCs and STs are also backward classes of citizens.

Unlike in the case of SCs, STs and OBCs, the Constitution has defined the persons who belong to the Anglo-Indian community. Accordingly, 'an Anglo-Indian means a person whose father or any of whose other male progenitors in the male line is or was of European descent but who is domiciled within the territory of India and is or was born within such territory of parents habitually resident therein and not established there for temporary purposes only'.

COMPONENTS OF SPECIAL PROVISIONS

1. *Reservation for SCs and STs and Special Representation for Anglo-Indians in Legislatures:* Seats are to be reserved for the SCs and STs in the Lok Sabha and the state legislative assemblies on the basis of population ratios.

   The President can nominate two members of the Anglo-Indian community to the Lok Sabha, if the community is not adequately represented. Similarly, the governor of a state can nominate one member of the Anglo-Indian community to the state legislative assembly, if the community is not adequately represented.

   Originally, these two provisions of reservation and special representation were to operate for ten years (i.e., up to 1960) only. But this duration has been extended continuously since then by ten years each time. Now, under the *95th Amendment Act* of 2009, these two provisions of reservation and special representation are to last until 2020.[3]

   The reason for this special representation to the Anglo-Indians is as follows: "Anglo-Indians constitute a religious, social, as well as a linguistic minority. These provisions were necessary, for, otherwise, being numerically an extremely small community, and being interspersed all over India, the Anglo-Indians could not hope to get any seat in any legislature through election".[4]

2. *Claims of SCs and STs to Services and Posts:* The claims of the SCs and STs are to be taken into consideration while making appointments to the public services of the Centre and the states, without sacrificing the efficiency of administration. However, the *82nd Amendment Act* of 2000 provides for making of any provision in favour of the SCs and STs for relaxation in qualifying marks in any examination or lowering the standards of evaluation, for reservation in matters of promotion to the public services of the Centre and the states.

3. *Special Provision in Services and Educational Grants for Anglo-Indians:* Before independence, certain posts were reserved for the Anglo-Indians in the railway, customs, postal and telegraph services of the Union. Similarly, the Anglo-Indian educational institutions were given certain special grants by the Centre and the states. Both the benefits were allowed to continue under the Constitution on a progressive diminution basis and finally came to an end in 1960.

4. *National Commissions for SCs and STs:* The President should set up a National Commission for the SCs to investigate all matters relating to the constitutional safeguards for the SCs and to report to him (Article 338). Similarly, the President should also set up a National Commission for the STs to investigate all matters relating to the Constitutional safeguards for the STs and to report to him (Article 338-A). The President should place all such reports before the Parliament, along with the action taken memorandum. Previously, the Constitution provided for a combined National Commission for SCs and STs. The *89th Amendment Act* of 2003 bifurcated the combined commission into two separate bodies.[5]

   The National Commission for SCs is also required to discharge similar functions with regard to the OBCs and the Anglo-Indian Community as it does with respect to the SCs. In other words, the commission has to investigate all matters relating to the Constitutional and other legal safeguards for the OBCs and the Anglo-Indian community and report to the President upon their working.[6]

5. *Control of the Union over the Administration of Scheduled Areas and the Welfare of STs:* The President is required to appoint a commission to report on the administration of the scheduled areas and the welfare of the STs in the states. He can appoint such a commission at any time but compulsorily after ten years of the commencement of the Constitution. Hence, a commission was appointed in the year 1960. It was headed by U. N. Dhebar and submitted its report in 1961. After four decades, the second commission was appointed in 2002 under the chairmanship of Dilip Singh Bhuria.

   Further, the executive power of the Centre extends to the giving of directions to a state with respect to the drawing up and execution of schemes for the welfare of the STs in the state.

6. ***Appointment of a Commission to Investigate the Conditions of BCs:*** The President may appoint a commission to investigate the conditions of socially and educationally backward classes and to recommend the steps to improve their condition. The report of the commission is to be placed before the Parliament, along with action taken memorandum.

Under the above provision, the President has appointed two commissions so far. The first backward classes commission was ap-

pointed in 1953 under the chairmanship of Kaka Kalelkar. It submitted its report in 1955. But, no action was taken on it as the recommendations were considered to be too vague and impractical and also there was a sharp division among the members on the criterion of backwardness.

The second Backward Classes Commission was appointed in 1979 with B.P. Mandal as chairman. It submitted its report in 1980. Its recommendations were also lying unattended till 1990 when the V.P. Singh Government declared reservation of 27 percent government jobs for the OBCs.[7]

Table 63.1 *Articles Related to Special Provisions for Certain Classes at a Glance*

Article No.	Subject-matter
330	Reservation of seats for scheduled castes and scheduled tribes in the House of the people
331	Representation of the Anglo-Indian community in the House of the people
332	Reservation of seats for scheduled castes and scheduled tribes in the legislative assemblies of the states
333	Representation of the Anglo-Indian community in the legislative assemblies of the states
334	Reservation of seats and special representation to cease after seventy years
335	Claims of scheduled castes and scheduled tribes to services and posts
336	Special provision for Anglo-Indian community in certain services
337	Special provision with respect to educational grants for the benefit of Anglo-Indian community.
338	National Commission for scheduled castes
338A	National Commission for scheduled tribes
339	Control of the Union over the administration of scheduled areas and the welfare of scheduled tribes
340	Appointment of a commission to investigate the conditions of backward classes
341	Scheduled castes
342	Scheduled tribes

NOTES AND REFERENCES

1. These are the Constitution (Scheduled Castes) Order, 1950; the Constitution (Scheduled Castes) (Union Territories) Order, 1951; the Constitution (Scheduled Tribes) Order, 1950; the Constitution (Scheduled Tribes) (Union Territories) Order, 1951 and so on. The Parliament modified the Presidential orders by

enacting the Scheduled Castes and Scheduled Tribes Orders (Amendment) Act in 1956, in 1976 and in the subsequent years.

2. The Constitution has used various expressions like 'socially and educationally backward classes of citizens' in Article 15, 'backward class of citizens' in Article 16, 'weaker sec-

tions of the people' in Article 46 and again 'socially and educationally backward classes' in Article 340.

3. The 8ᵗʰ *Amendment Act* of 1959 extended the period of ten years to twenty years, the 23ʳᵈ *Amendment Act* of 1969 to thirty years, the 45ᵗʰ *Amendment Act* of 1980 to forty years, the 62ⁿᵈ *Amendment Act* of 1989 to fifty years, the 79ᵗʰ *Amendment Act* of 1999 to sixty years and the 95ᵗʰ *Amendment Act* of 2009 to seventy years, that is, until the year 2020.

4. M.P. Jain, Indian Constitutional Law, Wadhwa, Fourth Edition, p. 756.

5. For complete details in this regard, see Chapters 42 and 43.

6. Even after the *89ᵗʰ Amendment Act* of 2003, this provision of Article 338 reads as follows: "In this article, reference to the Scheduled Castes shall be construed as including references to such other backward classes as the President may, on receipt of the report of a Commission appointed under clause (1) of article 340 by order specify and also to the Anglo-Indian community".

7. For complete details in this regard, see 'Mandal Commission and Aftermath' in Chapter 7.

PART X

POLITICAL DYNAMICS

Political Parties

MEANING AND TYPES

Political parties are voluntary associations or organised groups of individuals who share the same political views and who try to gain political power through constitutional means and who desire to work for promoting the national interest. There are four types of political parties in the modern democratic states, viz., (i) reactionary parties which cling to the old socio-economic and political institutions; (ii) conservative parties which believe in the status-quo; (iii) liberal parties which aim at reforming the existing institutions; and (iv) radical parties which aim at establishing a new order by overthrowing the existing institutions. In their classification of political parties on the basis of ideologies, the political scientists have placed the radical parties on the left and the liberal parties in the centre and reactionary and conservative parties on the right. In other words, they are described as the leftist parties, centrist parties and the rightist parties. In India, the CPI and CPM are the examples of leftist parties, the Congress of centrist parties and the BJP is an example of rightist parties.

There are three kinds of party systems in the world, viz., (i) one party system in which only one ruling party exists and no opposition is permitted, as for example, in the former communist countries like the USSR and other East European countries; (ii) two-party system in which two major parties exists, as for example, in USA and Britain[1]; and (iii) multi-party system in which there are a number of political parties leading to the formation of coalition governments, as for example, in France, Switzerland and Italy.

PARTY SYSTEM IN INDIA

The Indian party system has the following characteristic features:

Multi-Party System

The continental size of the country, the diversified character of Indian society, the adoption of universal adult franchise, the peculiar type of political process, and other factors have given rise to a large number of political parties. In fact, India has the largest number of political parties in the world. At present (2013), there are 6 national parties, 51 state parties and 1415 registered – unrecognised parties in the country[2]. Further, India has all categories of parties—left parties, centrist parties, right parties, communal parties, non-communal parties and so on. Consequently, the hung Parliaments, hung assemblies and coalition governments have become a common phenomena.

One-Dominant Party System

In spite of the multiparty system, the political scene in India was dominated for a long period by the Congress. Hence, Rajni Kothari, an eminent political analyst, preferred to call the Indian party system as 'one party dominance system' or the 'Congress system'[3]. The dominant position enjoyed by the

Congress has been declining since 1967 with the rise of regional parties and other national parties like Janata (1977), Janata Dal (1989) and the BJP (1991) leading to the development of a competitive multi-party system.

Lack of Clear Ideology

Except the BJP and the two communist parties (CPI and CPM), all other parties do not have a clear-cut ideology. They (i.e., all other parties) are ideologically closer to each other. They have a close resemblance in their policies and programmes. Almost every party advocates democracy, secularism, socialism and Gandhism. More than this, every party, including the so-called ideological parties, is guided by only one consideration—power capture. Thus, politics has become issue-based rather than the ideology and pragmatism has replaced the commitment to the principles.

Personality Cult

Quite often, the parties are organised around an eminent leader who becomes more important than the party and its ideology. Parties are known by their leaders rather than by their manifesto. It is a fact that the popularity of the Congress was mainly due to the leadership of Nehru, Indira Gandhi and Rajiv Gandhi. Similarly, the AIADMK in Tamil Nadu and TDP in Andhra Pradesh got identified with MG Ramachandran and NT Rama Rao respectively. Interestingly, several parties bear the name of their leader like Biju Janata Dal, Lok Dal (A), Congress (I) and so on. Hence, it is said that "there are political personalities rather than political parties in India".

Based on Traditional Factors

In the western countries, the political parties are formed on the basis of socio-economic and political programme. On the other hand, a large number of parties in India are formed on the basis of religion, caste, language, culture, race and so on. For example, Shiv Sena, Muslim League, Hindu Maha Sabha, Akali Dal, Muslim Majlis, Bahujan Samaj Party, Republican Party of India, Gorkha League and so on. These parties work for the promotion of communal and sectional interests and thereby undermine the general public interest.

Emergence of Regional Parties

Another significant feature of the Indian party system is the emergence of a large number of regional parties and their growing role. They have become the ruling parties in various states like BJD in Orissa, DMK or AIADMK in Tamil Nadu, Akali Dal in Punjab, AGP in Assam, National Conference in J&K, JD(U) in Bihar and so on. In the beginning, they were confined to the regional politics only. But, of late, they have come to play a significant role in the national politics due to coalition governments at the Centre. In the 1984 elections, the TDP emerged as the largest opposition party in the Lok Sabha.

Factions and Defections

Factionalism, defections, splits, mergers, fragmentation, polarisation and so on have been an important aspect of the functioning of political parties in India. Lust for power and material considerations have made the politicians to leave their party and join another party or start a new party. The practice of defections gained greater currency after the fourth general elections (1967). This phenomenon caused political instability both at the Centre and in the states and led to disintegration of the parties. Thus, there are two Janata Dals, two TDPs, two DMKs, two Communist Parties, two Congress, three Akali Dals, three Muslim Leagues and so on.

Lack of Effective Opposition

An effective Opposition is very essential for the successful operation of the parliamentary democracy prevalent in India. It checks the autocratic tendencies of the ruling party and provides an alternative government. However, in the last 50 years, an effective, strong, organised and viable national Opposition could never emerge except in flashes. The Opposition parties have no unity and very often adopt mutually conflicting positions with respect to the ruling party. They have failed to play a constructive role in the functioning of the body politic and in the process of nation building.

RECOGNITION OF NATIONAL AND STATE PARTIES

The Election Commission registers political parties for the purpose of elections and grants them recognition as national or state parties on the basis of their poll performance. The other parties are simply declared as *registered-unrecognised* parties.

The recognition granted by the Commission to the parties determines their right to certain privileges like allocation of the party symbols, provision of time for political broadcasts on the state-owned television and radio stations and access to electoral rolls.

Every national party is allotted a symbol exclusively reserved for its use throughout the country. Similarly, every state party is allotted a symbol exclusively reserved for its use in the state or states in which it is so recognised. A registered-unrecognised party, on the other hand, can select a symbol from a list of free symbols. In other words, the Commission specifies certain symbols as 'reserved symbols' which are meant for the candidates set up by the recognised parties and others as 'free symbols' which are meant for other candidates.

Conditions for Recognition as a National Party:

At present (2013), a party is recognised as a national party if any of the following conditions is fulfilled[4]:

1. If it secures six per cent of valid votes polled in any four or more states at a general election to the Lok Sabha or to the legislative assembly; and, in addition, it wins four seats in the Lok Sabha from any state or states; or

2. If it wins two per cent of seats in the Lok Sabha at a general election; and these candidates are elected from three states; or

3. If it is recognised as a state party in four states.

Conditions for Recognition as a State Party :

At present (2013), a party is recognised as a state party in a state if any of the following conditions is fulfilled[5]:

1. If it secures six per cent of the valid votes polled in the state at a general election to the legislative assembly of the state concerned; and, in addition, it wins 2 seats in the assembly of the state concerned; or

2. If it secures six per cent of the valid votes polled in the state at a general election to the Lok Sabha from the state concerned; and, in addition, it wins 1 seat in the Lok Sabha from the state concerned; or

3. If it wins three per cent of seats in the legislative assembly at a general election to the legislative assembly of the state concerned or 3 seats in the assembly, whichever is more; or

4. If it wins 1 seat in the Lok Sabha for every 25 seats or any fraction thereof allotted to the state at a general election to the Lok Sabha from the state concerned; or

5. If it secures eight per cent of the total valid votes polled in the state at a General Election to the Lok Sabha from the state or to the legislative assembly of the state. This condition was added in 2011.

The number of recognised parties keeps on changing on the basis of their performance in the general elections. At present (2013), there are 6 national parties, 51 state parties and 1415 registered-unrecognised parties in the country[6]. The national parties and state parties are also known as all-India parties and regional parties respectively.

Table 64.1 *Recognised National Parties and State Parties (First to Fifteenth General Elections)*

General Elections (Year)	Number of National Parties	Number of State Parties
First (1952)	14	39
Second (1957)	4	11
Third (1962)	6	11

(Contd.)

General Elections (Year)	Number of National Parties	Number of State Parties
Fourth (1967)	7	14
Fifth (1971)	8	17
Sixth (1977)	5	15
Seventh (1980)	6	19
Eighth (1984)	7	19
Ninth (1989)	8	20
Tenth (1991)	9	28
Eleventh (1996)	8	30
Twelfth (1998)	7	30
Thirteenth (1999)	7	40
Fourteenth (2004)	6	36
Fifteenth (2009)	7	40

Table 64.2 *Recognised National Parties and their Symbols (2013)*

Sl.No.	Name of the Party (Abbreviation)	Symbol Reserved
1.	Bahujan Samaj Party (BSP)	Elephant*
2.	Bharatiya Janata Party (BJP)	Lotus
3.	Communist Party of India (CPI)	Ears of Corn and Sickle
4.	Communist Party of India (Marxist) (CPM)	Hammer, Sickle and Star
5.	Indian National Congress (INC)	Hand
6.	Nationalist Congress Party (NCP)	Clock

* - In all States / U.T.s except in Assam, where its candidates will have to choose a symbol out of the list of free symbols specified by the Election Commission.

Table 64.3 *Recognised State Parties and their Symbols (2013)*

Sl. No.	Name of the State / Union Territory	Name of the State Party (Abbreviation)	Symbol Reserved
1.	Andhra Pradesh	1. Telangana Rashtra Samithi (TRS)	Car
		2. Telugu Desam (TDP)	Bicycle
2.	Arunachal Pradesh	1. All India Trinamool Congress (AITC)	Flowers and Grass
		2. People's Party of Arunachal (PPA)	Maize
3.	Assam	1. All India United Democratic Front (AUDF)	Lock and Key
		2. Asom Gana Parishad (AGP)	Elephant
		3. Bodoland People's Front (BPF)	Nangol
4.	Bihar	1. Janata Dal (United) (JD(U))	Arrow
		2. Lok Jan Shakti Party (LJSP)	Bungalow
		3. Rashtriya Janata Dal (RJD)	Hurricane Lamp

(Contd.)

Sl. No.	Name of the State / Union Territory	Name of the State Party (Abbreviation)	Symbol Reserved
5.	Goa	Maharashtrawadi Gomantak (MAG)	Lion
6.	Haryana	1. Haryana Janhit Congress (BL) (HJC(BL))	Tractor
		2. Indian National Lok Dal (INLD)	Spectacles
7.	Jammu & Kashmir	1. Jammu & Kashmir National Conference (JKNC)	Plough
		2. Jammu & Kashmir National Panthers Party (JKNPP)	Bicycle
		3. Jammu and Kashmir People's Democratic Party (JKPDP)	Ink Pot and Pen
8.	Jharkhand	1. All Jharkhand Students Union (AJSU)	Banana
		2. Jharkhand Mukti Morcha (JMM)	Bow and Arrow
		3. Jharkhand Vikas Morcha (Prajatantrik) (JVM(P))	Comb
		4. Rashtriya Janata Dal (RJD)	Hurricane Lamp
9.	Karnataka	Janata Dal (Secular) (JD(S))	A Lady Farmer carrying Paddy on her head
10.	Kerala	1. Janata Dal (Secular) (JD(S))	A Lady Farmer carrying Paddy on her head
		2. Kerala Congress (M) (KEC(M))	Two Leaves
		3. Indian Union Muslim League (IUML)	Ladder
11.	Maharashtra	1. Maharashtra Navnirman Sena (MNS)	Railway Engine
		2. Shiv Sena (SHS)	Bow and Arrow
12.	Manipur	1. All India Trinamool Congress (AITC)	Flower and Grass
		2. Manipur State Congress Party	Cultivator Cutting Crop
		3. Naga People's Front (NPF)	Cock
		4. People's Democratic Alliance	Crown
13.	Meghalaya	1. United Democratic Party (UDP)	Drum
		2. Hill State People's Democratic Party	Lion
14.	Mizoram	1. Mizo National Front (MNF)	Star
		2. Mizoram People's Conference (MPC)	Electric Bulb
		3. Zoram Nationalist Party (ZNP)	Sun (without rays)
15.	Nagaland	Naga People's Front (NPF)	Cock
16.	Orissa	Biju Janata Dal (BJD)	Conch
17.	Puducherry	1. All India Anna Dravida Munnetra Kazhagam (ADMK) or (AIADMK)	Two Leaves
		2. All India N.R. Congress	Jug
		3. Dravida Munnetra Kazhagam (DMK)	Rising Sun
		4. Pattali Makkal Katchi (PMK)	Mango
18.	Punjab	Shiromani Akali Dal (SAD)	Scales
19.	Sikkim	Sikkim Democratic Front (SDF)	Umbrella

(Contd.)

Sl. No.	Name of the State / Union Territory	Name of the State Party (Abbreviation)	Symbol Reserved
20.	Tamil Nadu	1. All India Anna Dravida Munnetra Kazhagam (ADMK) or (AIADMK)	Two leaves
		2. Dravida Munnetra Kazhagam (DMK)	Rising Sun
		3. Desiya Murpokku Dravida Kazhagam (DMDK)	Nagara
21.	Uttar Pradesh	1. Rashtriya Lok Dal (RLD)	Hand Pump
		2. Samajwadi Party (SP)	Bicycle
22.	West Bengal	1. All India Forward Bloc (AIFB)	Lion
		2. All India Trinamool Congress (AITC)	Flowers and Grass
		3. Revolutionary Socialist Party (RSP)	Spade and Stoker

Table 64.4 *Formation of Political Parties (Chronological Order)*

Sl. No.	Name of the Party (Abbreviation)	Year of Formation
1.	Indian National Congress (INC)	1885
2.	Shiromani Akali Dal (SAD)	1920
3.	Communist Party of India (CPI)	1925
4.	Jammu & Kashmir National Conference (JKNC)	1939
5.	All India Forward Bloc (AIFB)	1939
6.	Revolutionary Socialist Party (RSP)	1940
7.	Indian Union Muslim League (IUML)	1948
8.	Dravida Munnetra Kazhagam (DMK)	1949
9.	Mizo National Front (MNF)	1961
10.	Maharashtrawadi Gomantak Party (MAG)	1963
11.	Communist Party of India (Marxist) (CPM)	1964
12.	Shiv Sena (SHS)	1966
13.	Mizoram People's Conference (MPC)	1972
14.	Jharkhand Mukti Morcha (JMM)	1972
15.	All India Anna Dravida Munnetra Kazhagam (AIADMK)	1972
16.	Kerala Congress (M) (KEC (M))	1979
17.	Bharatiya Janata Party (BJP)	1980
18.	Telugu Desam Party (TDP)	1982
19.	Bahujan Samaj Party (BSP)	1984
20.	Asom Gana Parishad (AGP)	1985
21.	People's Party of Arunachal (PPA)	1987
22.	Samajwadi Party (SP)	1992
23.	Sikkim Democratic Front (SDF)	1993
24.	Rashtriya Lok Dal (RLD)	1996

(Contd.)

Sl. No.	Name of the Party (Abbreviation)	Year of Formation
25.	Zoram Nationalist Party (ZNP)	1997
26.	Rashtriya Janata Dal (RJD)	1997
27.	Biju Janata Dal (BJD)	1997
28.	All India Trinamool Congress (AITC)	1998
29.	Indian National Lok Dal (INLD)	1998
30.	Jammu and Kashmir People's Democratic Party (PDP)	1999
31.	Janata Dal (United) (JD (U))	1999
32.	Janata Dal (Secular) (JD(S))	1999
33.	Nationalist Congress Party (NCP)	1999
34.	Lok Jan Shakti Party (LJSP)	2000
35.	Telangana Rashtra Samithi (TRS)	2001
36.	Naga People's Front (NPF)	2002
37.	All India United Democratic Front (AUDF)	2004
38.	Desiya Murpokku Dravidar Kazhagam (DMDK)	2005
39.	Maharashtra Navnirman Sena (MNS)	2006

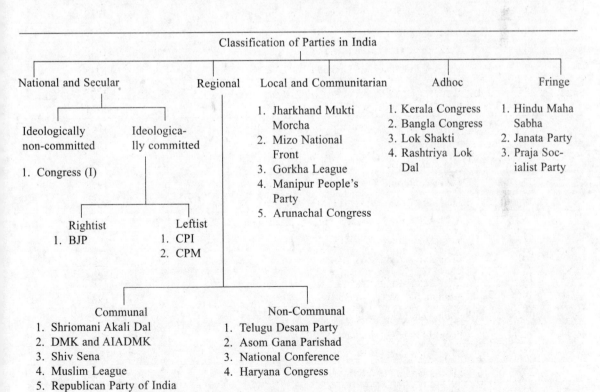

Classification of Parties in India

National and Secular | Regional | Local and Communitarian | Adhoc | Fringe

Local and Communitarian
1. Jharkhand Mukti Morcha
2. Mizo National Front
3. Gorkha League
4. Manipur People's Party
5. Arunachal Congress

Adhoc
1. Kerala Congress
2. Bangla Congress
3. Lok Shakti
4. Rashtriya Lok Dal

Fringe
1. Hindu Maha Sabha
2. Janata Party
3. Praja Socialist Party

National and Secular

Ideologically non-committed
1. Congress (I)

Ideologically committed

Rightist
1. BJP

Leftist
1. CPI
2. CPM

Communal
1. Shriomani Akali Dal
2. DMK and AIADMK
3. Shiv Sena
4. Muslim League
5. Republican Party of India

Non-Communal
1. Telugu Desam Party
2. Asom Gana Parishad
3. National Conference
4. Haryana Congress

Note: *Adopted from J. C. Johari: Indian Government and Politics, Vishal, 13th Edition (2001), P. 607.*

NOTES AND REFERENCES

1. The two parties in the US are Democratic and Republican, and in Britain are Conservative and Labour.
2. As per the Election Commission's notification dated January 18, 2013 and April 9, 2013.
3. Rajni Kothari: Congress System in India, Asian Survey, Volume 4, No. 12 (December, 1964), pp. 1–18.
4. The Election Symbols (Reservation and Allotment) Order, 1968, as amended from time to time. The latest amendment to this order was made in 2011.
5. Ibid.
6. See Reference 2 above.

Elections

ELECTORAL SYSTEM

Articles 324 to 329 in Part XV of the Constitution make the following provisions with regard to the electoral system in our country:

1. The Constitution (Article 324) provides for an independent Election Commission in order to ensure free and fair elections in the country. The power of super-tendence, direction and conduct of elections to the Parliament, the state legislatures, the office of the President and the office of the Vice-President is vested in the Commission[1]. At present, the commission consists of a chief election commissioner and two election commissioners[2].

2. There is to be only one general electoral roll for every territorial constituency for election to the Parliament and the state legislatures. Thus, the Constitution has abolished the system of communal representation and separate electorates which led to the partition of the country.

3. No person is to be ineligible for inclusion in the electoral roll on grounds only of religion, race, caste, sex or any of them. Further, no person can claim to be included in any special electoral roll for any constituency on grounds only of religion, race, caste or sex or any of them. Thus, the Constitution has accorded equality to every citizen in the matter of electoral franchise.

4. The elections to the Lok Sabha and the state assemblies are to be on the basis of adult franchise. Thus, every person who is a citizen of India and who is 18^3 years of age, is entitled to vote at the election provided he is not disqualified under the provisions of the Constitution or any law made by the appropriate legislature (Parliament or state legislature) on the ground of non-residence, unsound mind, crime or corrupt or illegal practice[4].

5. Parliament may make provision with respect to all matters relating to elections to the Parliament and the state legislatures including the preparation of electoral rolls, the delimitation of constituencies and all other matters necessary for securing their due constitution. In exercise of this power, the Parliament has enacted the following laws:

   (i) Representation of the People Act of 1950 which provides for the qualifications of voters, preparation of electoral rolls, delimitation of constituencies, allocation of seats in the Parliament and state legislatures and so on.

   (ii) Representation of the People Act of 1951 which provides for the actual conduct of elections and deals with administrative machinery for conducting elections, the poll, election offences, election disputes, by-elections, registration of political parties and so on.

   (iii) Delimitation Commission Act of 1952 which provides for the readjustment of seats, delimitation and reservation of territorial constituencies and other related matters.

6. The state legislatures can also make provision with respect to all matters relating to elections to the state legislatures including the preparation of electoral rolls and all other matters necessary for securing their due constitution. But, they can make provision for only those matters which are not covered by the Parliament. In other words, they can only supplement the parliamentary law and cannot override it.

7. The Constitution declares that the validity of any law relating to the delimitation of constituencies or the allotment of seats to such constituencies cannot be questioned in any court. Consequently, the orders issued by the Delimitation Commission become final and cannot be challenged in any court.

8. The Constitution lays down that no election to the Parliament or the state legislature is to be questioned except by an election petition presented to such authority and in such manner as provided by the appropriate legislature. Since 1966, the election petitions are triable by high courts alone. But, the appellate jurisdiction lies with the Supreme Court alone.

Article 323 B empowers the appropriate legislature (Parliament or state legislature) to establish a tribunal for the adjudication of election disputes. It also provides for the exclusion of the jurisdiction of all courts (except the special leave appeal jurisdiction of the Supreme Court) in such disputes. So far, no such tribunal has been established. It must be noted here that in *Chandra Kumar* case[5] (1997), the Supreme Court declared this provision as unconstitutional. Consequently, if at any time an election tribunal is established, an appeal from its decision lies to the high court.

Besides the three laws (mentioned above), the other laws and rules in respect of elections are:

(i) Presidential and Vice-Presidential Elections Act, 1952.

(ii) Government of Union Territories Act, 1963.

(iii) Government of the National Capital Territory of Delhi Act, 1991.

(iv) Chief Election Commissioner and other Election Commissioners (Conditions of Service) Act, 1991[6].

(v) Prohibition of Simultaneous Membership Rules, 1950.

(vi) Registration of Electors Rules, 1960.

(vii) Conduct of Elections Rules, 1961.

Further, the Election Commission has issued the Election Symbols (Reservation and Allotment) Order, 1968[7]. It is concerned with the registration and recognition of political parties, allotment of symbols and settlement of disputes among them.

ELECTION MACHINERY

Election Commission of India (ECI) Under Article 324 of the Constitution of India, the Election Commission of India is vested with the power of superintendence, direction and control of conducting the elections to the Lok Sabha and State Legislative Assemblies. The Election Commission of India is a three-member body, with one Chief Election Commissioner and two Election Commissioners. The President of India appoints the Chief Election Commissioner and the Election Commissioners.

Chief Electoral Officer (CEO) The Chief Electoral Officer of a state/ Union Territory is authorised to supervise the election work in the state/Union Territory subject to the overall superintendence, direction and control of the Election Commission. The Election Commission of India nominates or designates an Officer of the Government of the state / Union Territory as the Chief Electoral Officer in consultation with that State Government / Union Territory Administration.

District Election Officer (DEO) Subject to the superintendence, direction and control of the Chief Electoral Officer, the District Election Officer supervises the election work of a district. The Election Commission of India nominates or designates an officer of the state Government as the District Election Officer in consultation with the state government.

Returning Officer (RO) The Returning Officer of a Parliamentary or assembly constituency is responsible for the conduct of elections in the Parliamentary or assembly constituency concerned. The Election Commission of India nominates or designates an officer of the Government or a local authority as the Returning Officer for each of the assembly and parliamentary constituencies in consultation with the State Government / Union Territory

Administration. In addition, the Election Commission of India also appoints one or more Assistant Returning Officers for each of the assembly and Parliamentary constituencies to assist the Returning Officer in the performance of his functions in connection with the conduct of elections.

Electoral Registration Officer (ERO) The Electoral Registration Officer is responsible for the preparation of electoral rolls for a Parliamentary / assembly constituency. The Election Commission of India, in consultation with the state / UT government, appoints an officer of the government or the local authorities as the Electoral Registration Officer. In addition, the Election Commission of India also appoints one or more Assistant Electoral Registration Officers to assist the Electoral Registration Officer in the performance of his functions in the matter of preparation / revision of electoral rolls.

Presiding Officer The Presiding Officer with the assistance of polling officers conducts the poll at a polling station. The District Election Officer appoints the Presiding Officers and the Polling Officers. In the case of Union Territories, such appointments are made by the Returning Officers.

Observers The Election Commission of India nominates officers of Government as Observers (General Observers and Election Expenditure Observers) for Parliamentary and assembly constituencies. They perform such functions as are entrusted to them by the Commission. They report directly to the Commission.

ELECTION PROCESS

Time of Elections Elections for the Lok Sabha and every state Legislative Assembly have to take place every five years, unless called earlier. The President can dissolve Lok Sabha and call a General Election before five years is up, if the Government can no longer command the confidence of the Lok Sabha, and if there is no alternative government available to take over.

Schedule of Elections When the five-year limit is up, or the legislature has been dissolved and new elections have been called, the Election Commission puts into effect the machinery for holding an election. The Constitution states that there can be no longer than six months between the last session of the dissolved Lok Sabha and the recalling of the new House, so elections have to be concluded before then.

The Commission normally announces the schedule of elections in a major press conference a few weeks before the formal process is set in motion. The Model Code of Conduct for guidance of candidates and political parties comes immediately into effect after such announcement[8].

The formal process for the elections starts with the Notification or Notifications calling upon the electorate to elect Members of a House. As soon as Notifications are issued, candidates can start filing their nominations in the constituencies from where they wish to contest. These are scrutinised by the Returning Officer of the constituency concerned after the last date for the same is over after about a week. The validly nominated candidates can withdraw from the contest within two days from the date of scrutiny. Contesting candidates get at least two weeks for political campaign before the actual date of poll.

On account of the vast magnitude of operations and the massive size of the electorate, polling is held on a number of days for the national elections. A separate date for counting is fixed and the results declared for each constituency by the concerned Returning Officer.

The Commission compiles the complete list of members elected and issues an appropriate Notification for the due constitution of the House. With this, the process of elections is complete and the President, in case of the Lok Sabha, and the Governors of the concerned states, in case of State Assemblies, can then convene their respective Houses to hold their sessions.

Oath or Affirmation It is necessary for a candidate to make and subscribe an oath or affirmation before an officer authorised by the Election Commission[9]. For any particular election, the authorised persons are, principally, the Returning Officer and the Assistant Returning Officer for the constituency. In the case of a candidate confined in a prison or under preventive detention, the superintendent of the prison or commandant of the detention camp in which he is so confined or is under such detention is authorised to administer the oath. And in the case of a candidate confined to bed in a hospital or elsewhere owing to illness or any other cause, the medical superintendent in charge of the hospital or the medical practitioner attending on him is similarly authorised. If a candidate is outside India, the Indian Ambassador or High Commissioner or diplomatic consular authorised by him can also administer oath/affirmation. The candidate, in person, is required to make the oath or affirmation immediately after presenting his nomination papers and in any case not later than the day previous to the date of the scrutiny[10].

Election Campaign   The campaign is the period when the political parties put forward their candidates and arguments with which they hope to persuade people to vote for their candidates and parties. Candidates are given a week to put forward their nominations. These are scrutinised by the Returning Officers and if not found to be in order can be rejected after a summary hearing. Validly nominated candidates can withdraw within two days after nominations have been scrutinised. The official campaign lasts at least two weeks from the drawing up of the list of nominated candidates, and officially ends 48 hours before polling closes.

During the election campaign, the political parties and contesting candidates are expected to abide by a Model Code of Conduct evolved by the Election Commission on the basis of a consensus among political parties. The model code lays down broad guidelines as to how the political parties and candidates should conduct themselves during the election campaign. It is intended to maintain the election campaign on healthy lines, avoid clashes and conflicts between political parties or their supporters and to ensure peace and order during the campaign period and thereafter, until the results are declared. The model code also prescribes guidelines for the ruling party either at the Centre or in the state to ensure that a level field is maintained and that no cause is given for any complaint that the ruling party has used its official position for the purposes of its election campaign[11].

Once an election has been called, parties issue manifestos detailing the programmes they wish to implement if elected to government, the strengths of their leaders, and the failures of opposing parties and their leaders. Slogans are used to popularise and identify parties and issues, and pamphlets and posters distributed to the electorate. Rallies and meetings where the candidates try to persuade, cajole and enthuse supporters, and denigrate opponents, are held throughout the constituencies. Personal appeals and promises of reform are made, with candidates travelling the length and breadth of the constituency to try to influence as many potential supporters as possible.

Polling Days   Polling is normally held on a number of different days in different constituencies, to enable the security forces and those monitoring the election to keep law and order and ensure that voting during the election is fair.

Ballot Papers and Symbols   After nomination of candidates is complete, a list of competing candidates is prepared by the Returning Officer, and ballot papers are printed. Ballot papers are printed with the names of the candidates (in languages set by the Election Commission) and the symbols allotted to each of the candidates. Candidates of recognised parties are allotted their party symbols.

Voting Procedure   Voting is by secret ballot. Polling stations are usually set up in public institutions, such as schools and community halls. To enable as many electors as possible to vote, the officials of the Election Commission try to ensure that there is a polling station within two kilometres of every voter, and that no polling stations should have to deal with more than 1500 voters. Each polling station is open for at least eight hours on the day of the election.

On entering the polling station, the elector is checked against the electoral roll[12], and allocated a ballot paper. The elector votes by marking the ballot paper with a rubber stamp on or near the symbol of the candidate of his choice, inside a screened compartment in the polling station. The voter then folds the ballot paper and inserts it in a common ballot box which is kept in full view of the Presiding Officer and polling agents of the candidates. This marking system eliminates the possibility of ballot papers being surreptitiously taken out of the polling station or not being put in the ballot box.

Since 1998, the Commission has increasingly used Electronic Voting Machines (EMVs) instead of ballot boxes. In 2003, all state elections and by elections were held using EVMs. Encouraged by this, the Commission took a historic decision to use only EVMs for the Lok Sabha election in 2004. More than 1 million EVMs were used in this election.

Electronic Voting Machine An Electronic Voting Machine (EVM) is a simple electronic device used to record votes in place of ballot papers and boxes which were used earlier in conventional voting system. The advantages of the EVM over the traditional ballot paper / ballot box system are given here:

(i) It eliminates the possibility of invalid and doubtful votes which, in many cases, are the root causes of controversies and election petitions.

(ii) It makes the process of counting of votes much faster than the conventional system.

(iii) It reduces to a great extent the quantity of paper used thus saving a large number of trees making the process eco-friendly.

(iv) It reduces cost of printing (almost nil) as only one sheet of ballot paper is required for each Polling Station[13].

Supervising Elections The Election Commission appoints a large number of Observers to ensure that the campaign is conducted fairly, and that people are free to vote as they choose. Election expenditure Observers keeps a check on the amount that each candidate and party spends on the election.

Counting of Votes After the polling has finished, the votes are counted under the supervision of Returning Officers and Observers appointed by the Election Commission. After the counting of votes is over, the Returning Officer declares the name of the candidate, to whom the largest number of votes have been given, as the winner and as having been returned by the constituency to the concerned House.

Elections to the Lok Sabha are carried out using a first-past-the-post electoral system. The country is split up into separate geographical areas, known as constituencies, and the electors can cast one vote each for a candidate, the winner being the candidate who gets the maximum votes.

Elections to the State Assemblies are carried out in the same manner as for the Lok Sabha election, with the states and union territories divided into single-member constituencies, and the first-past-the-post electoral system used.

Media Coverage In order to bring as much transparency as possible to the electoral process, the media are encouraged and provided with facilities to cover the election, although subject to maintaining the secrecy of the vote. Media persons are given special passes to enter polling stations to cover the poll process and the counting halls during the actual counting of votes.

Election Petitions Any elector or candidate can file an election petition if he or she thinks there has been malpractice during the election. An election petition is not an ordinary civil suit, but treated as a contest in which the whole constituency is involved. Election petitions are tried by the High Court of the state involved, and if upheld can even lead to the restaging of the election in that constituency.

Table 65.1 *Results of Lok Sabha Elections*

General Elections (Year)	Elective Seats	Seats won by Parties (Major)
First (1952)	489	Congress 364, Communist 16, Socialist 12, KMPP 9, Jana Sangh 3.
Second (1957)	494	Congress 371, Communist 27, Praja Socialist 19, Jana Sangh 4.
Third (1962)	494	Congress 361, Communist 29, Swatantra 18, Jana Sangh 14, Praja Socialist 12, Socialists 6.
Fourth (1967)	520	Congress 283, Swatantra 44, Jana Sangh 35, CPI 23, CPM 19, Sanyukta Socialist 23, Praja Socialist 13.
Fifth (1971)	518	Congress 352, CPM 25, CPI 24, DMK 23, Jana Sangh 21, Swatantra 7, Socialist 5.

(Contd.)

General Elections (Year)	Elective Seats	Seats won by Parties (Major)
Sixth (1977)	542	Janata 298, Congress 154, CPM 22, CPI 7, AIADMK 18.
Seventh (1980)	542	Congress 353, Janata (Secular) 41, Janata 31, CPM 36, CPI 11, DMK 16.
Eight (1984)	542	Congress 415, TDP 28, CPM 22, CPI 6, Janata 10, AIADMK 12, BJP 2.
Ninth (1989)	543	Congress 197, Janata Dal 141, BJP 86, CPM 32, CPI 12, AIADMK 11, TDP 2.
Tenth (1991)	543	Congress 232, BJP 119, Janata Dal 59, CPM 35, CPI 13, TDP 13, AIADMK 11.
Eleventh (1996)	543	BJP 161, Congress 140, Janata Dal 46, CPM 32, TMCM 20, DMK 17, SP 17, TDP 16, SS 15, CPI 12, BSP 11.
Twelfth (1998)	543	BJP 182, Congress 141, CPM 32, AIADMK 18, TDP 12, SP 20, Samata 12, RJD 17.
Thirteenth (1999)	543	BJP 182, Congress 114, CPM 33, TDP 29, SP 26, JD (U) 20, SS 15, BSP 14, DMK 12, BJD 10, AIADMK 10.
Fourteenth (2004)	543	Congress 145, BJP 138, CPM 43, SP 36, RJD 24, BSP 19, DMK 16, Shiv Sena 12, BJD 11, CPI 10.
Fifteenth (2009)	543	Congress 206, BJP 116, SP 23, BSP 21, JD(U) 20, Trinamool 19, DMK 18, CPM 16, BJD 14, Shiv Sena 11, NCP 9, AIADMK 9, TDP 6, RLD 5, CPI 4, RJD 4, SAD 4.

Table 65.2 *Participation in Lok Sabha Elections*

General Elections (Year)	Number of Candidates	Electorate (Million)	Voter Turn-out (Percentage)	Number of Polling Stations
First (1952)	1,874	173.21	45.7	1,96,084
Second (1957)	1,519	193.65	45.74	2,20,478
Third (1962)	1,985	217.68	55.42	2,38,244
Fourth (1967)	2,369	274.60	61.33	2,67,255
Fifth (1971)	2,784	274.09	55.29	3,42,944
Sixth (1977)	2,439	321.17	60.49	3,58,208
Seventh (1980)	4,462	363.94	56.92	4,34,442
Eighth (1984)	5,493	400.10	64.1	5,05,751
Ninth (1989)	6,160	499.00	62.0	5,89,449
Tenth (1991)	8,699	514.00	61.0	5,94,797
Eleventh (1996)	13,952	592.57	57.94	7,66,462
Twelfth (1998)	4,750	605.58	61.97	7,73,494
Thirteenth (1999)	4,648	605.88	59.99	7,75,000
Fourteenth (2004)	5,435	671.00	57.86	6,87,402
Fifteenth (2009)	8,070	713.77	58.4	8,34,944

Table 65.3 *Women in Lok Sabha Elections*

General Elections (Year)	Contested	Elected
First (1952)	—	22
Second (1957)	45	27
Third (1962)	70	34
Fourth (1967)	67	31
Fifth (1971)	86	22
Sixth (1977)	70	19
Seventh (1980)	142	28
Eighth (1984)	164	44
Ninth (1989)	198	27
Tenth (1991)	325	39
Eleventh (1996)	599	40
Twelfth (1998)	274	43
Thirteenth (1999)	284	49
Fourteenth (2004)	355	45
Fifteenth (2009)	556	59

Table 65.4 *Cost of Lok Sabha Elections*

General Elections (Year)	Cost Borne by Election Commission (₹ In Crores)
First (1952)	10.45
Second (1957)	5.90
Third (1962)	7.81
Fourth (1967)	10.95
Fifth (1971)	14.43
Sixth (1977)	29.81
Seventh (1980)	37.07
Eighth (1984)	78.28
Ninth (1989)	110.00
Tenth (1991)	302.79
Eleventh (1996)	508.68
Twelfth (1998)	664.50
Thirteenth (1999)	880.00
Fourteenth (2004)	1,300.00
Fifteenth (2009)	1120.00

Table 65.5 *Largest and Smallest (Area-wise) Lok Sabha Constituencies in General Elections (2004)*

Sl. No.	Constituency	State/UT	Area (sq. km)
	I. LARGEST CONSTITUENCIES		
1.	Ladakh	Jammu & Kashmir	173266.37
2.	Barmer	Rajasthan	71601.24
3.	Kutch	Gujarat	41644.55
4.	Arunachal West	Arunachal Pradesh	40572.29
5.	Arunachal East	Arunachal Pradesh	39749.64
	II. SMALLEST CONSTITUENCIES		
1.	Chandni Chowk	NCT of Delhi	10.59
2.	Kolkata North West	West Bengal	13.23
3.	Mumbai South	Maharashtra	13.73
4.	Mumbai South Central	Maharashtra	18.31
5.	Delhi Sadar	NCT of Delhi	28.09

Table 65.6 *Articles Related to Elections at a Glance*

Article No.	Subject-matter
324.	Superintendence, direction and control of elections to be vested in an Election Commission
325.	No person to be ineligible for inclusion in, or to claim to be included in a special, electoral roll on grounds of religion, race, caste or sex
326.	Elections to the House of the People and to the Legislative Assemblies of states to be on the basis of adult suffrage
327.	Power of Parliament to make provision with respect to elections to Legislatures
328.	Power of Legislature of a state to make provision with respect to elections to such Legislature
329.	Bar to interference by courts in electoral matters
329A.	Special provision as to elections to Parliament in the case of Prime Minister and Speaker (Repealed)

NOTES AND REFERENCES

1. There is a separate state election commission to deal with elections to the panchayats and municipalities in the state.
2. For complete details regarding Election Commission, see Chapter 38.
3. The 61st Amendment Act of 1988 has reduced the voting age from 21 to 18 years. This came into force on March 28, 1989.
4. For more details in this regard, see 'universal adult franchise' in Chapter 3.
5. *L. Chandra Kumar V. Union of India* (1997). Clause 3(d) of Article 323 B was declared as unconstitutional.
6. Amended in 1993 with effect from January 4, 1994.
7. The latest amendment to this order was made in 2011.
8. For a complete text of the Model Code of Conduct, see Appendix-VIII.
9. For the form of oath or affirmation, see Appendix – IV.
10. General Elections 2009: Reference Handbook, Press Information Bureau, Government of India, P. 189.
11. The Model Code of Conduct was agreed to by all the political parties in 1968. The Election Commission first effectively put to use the Model Code of Conduct in the year 1991 to ensure fair elections and a level playing field.
12. The electoral roll is a list of all people in the constituency who are registered to vote in Indian elections. Only those people with their names on the electoral roll are allowed to vote. The electoral roll is normally revised every year to add the names of those who are to turn 18 on the 1st January of that year or have moved into a constituency and to remove the names of those who have died or moved out of a constituency.
13. General Elections 2009: Reference Handbook, Press Information Bureau, Government of India, P. 181.

Electoral Reforms

COMMITTEES RELATED TO ELECTORAL REFORMS

The various committees and commissions which have examined our electoral system, election machinery as well as election process and suggested reforms are mentioned here.

1. Tarkunde Committee was appointed in 1974 by Jaya Prakash Narayan (JP) during his "Total Revolution" movement. This unofficial committee submitted its report in 1975.
2. Dinesh Goswami Committee on Electoral Reforms (1990)[1]
3. Vohra Committee on the Nexus between Crime and Politics (1993)
4. Indrajit Gupta Committee on State Funding of Elections (1998)[2]
5. Law Commission of India Report on Reform of the Electoral Laws (1999)
6. National Commission to Review the Working of the Constitution (2000-2002)[3]. It was headed by M.N. Venkatachaliah.
7. Election Commission of India Report on Proposed Electoral Reforms (2004).
8. Second Administrative Reforms Commission of India Report on Ethics in Governance (2007). It was headed by Veerappa Moily.
9. Tankha Committee was appointed in 2010 to look into the whole gamut of the election laws and electoral reforms.

Based on the recommendations made by the above Committees and Commissions, various reforms have been introduced in our electoral system, election machinery and election process. These can be studied under the following four heads.

- Electoral reforms before 1996
- Electoral reforms of 1996
- Electoral reforms after 1996
- Electoral reforms since 2010

ELECTORAL REFORMS BEFORE 1996

Lowering of Voting Age The 61st Constitutional Amendment Act of 1988[4] reduced the voting age from 21 years to 18 years for the Lok Sabha as well as the assembly elections. This was done in order to provide to the unrepresented youth of the country an opportunity to express their feelings and help them become a part of political process.

Deputation to Election Commission In 1988[5], a provision was made that the officers and the staff engaged in preparation, revision and correction of electoral rolls for elections are deemed to be on deputation to the Election Commission for the period of such employment. These personnel, during that period, would be under the control, superintendence and discipline of the Election Commission.

Increase in Number of Proposers In 1988[6], the number of electors who are required to sign as proposers in nomination papers for elections to the Rajya Sabha and state legislative council has been increased to 10 per cent of the electors of the constituency or ten such electors, whichever is less. This was done in order to prevent non-serious candidates from contesting frivolously.

Electronic Voting Machines In 1989[7], a provision was made to facilitate the use of Electronic Voting Machines (EVMs) in elections. The EVMs were used for the first time in 1998 on experimental basis in selected constituencies in the elections to the Assemblies of Rajasthan, Madhya Pradesh and Delhi. The EVMs were used for the first time in the general elections (entire state) to the Assembly of Goa in 1999.

Booth Capturing In 1989[8], a provision was made for adjournment of poll or countermanding of elections in case of booth capturing. Booth capturing includes: (i) seizure of a polling station and making polling authorities surrender ballot papers or voting machines (ii) taking possession of polling station and allowing only one's own supporters to exercise their franchise (iii) threatening and preventing any elector from going to polling station and (iv) seizure of the place being used for counting of votes.

ELECTORAL REFORMS OF 1996

In 1990, the National Front Government headed by VP Singh appointed a committee on electoral reforms under the chairmanship of Dinesh Goswami, the then Law Minister. The Committee was asked to study the electoral system in detail and suggest measures for remedying the drawbacks within it. The Committee, in its report submitted in 1990 itself, made a number of proposals on electoral reforms. Some of these recommendations were implemented in 1996[9]. These are explained here.

Listing of Names of Candidates The candidates contesting elections are to be classified into three categories for the purpose of listing of their names. They are
 (i) Candidates of recognised political parties
 (ii) Candidates of registered-unrecognised political parties
 (iii) Other (independent) candidates
 Their names in the list of contesting candidates and in the ballot papers has to appear separately in the above order and in each category these have to be arranged in the alphabetical order.

Disqualification for Insulting the National Honour Act A person who is convicted for the following offences under the *Prevention of Insults to National Honour Act* of 1971 is disqualified to contest in the elections to the Parliament and state legislature for 6 years.
 (i) Offence of insulting the National Flag
 (ii) Offence of insulting the Constitution of India
 (iii) Offence of preventing the singing of National Anthem

Prohibition on the Sale of Liquor No liquor or other intoxicants are to be sold or given or distributed at any shop, eating place, hotel or any other place whether public or private within a polling area during the period of 48 hours ending with the hour fixed for the conclusion of poll. Any person who violates this rule is to be punished with imprisonment up to 6 months or with fine up to ₹2,000 or with both.

Number of Proposers The nomination of a candidate in a Parliamentary or assembly constituency should be subscribed by 10 registered electors of the constituency as proposers, if the candidate is not sponsored by a recognised political party. In the case of a candidate sponsored by a recognised political party, only one proposer is required. This was done in order to discourage non-serious people from contesting the elections.

Death of a Candidate Earlier, in case of death of a contesting candidate before the actual polling, the election used to be countermanded. Consequently, the election process had to start all over again in the concerned constituency. But now, the election would not be countermanded on the death of a contesting candidate before the actual polling. However, if the deceased candidate belonged to a recognised political party, the party concerned would be given an option to propose another candidate within seven days.

Time Limit for By-Elections Now, by-elections are to be held within six months of occurrence of the vacancy in any House of Parliament or a state legislature. But, this condition is not applicable in two cases:
 (i) Where the remainder of the term of the member whose vacancy is to be filled is less than one year; or

(ii) When the Election Commission in consultation with the Central Government, certifies that it is difficult to hold the by-elections within the said period.

Holiday to Employees on the Polling Day The registered voters employed in any trade, business, industry or any other establishment are entitled to a paid holiday on the polling day. This rule applies even to the daily wagers. Any employer who violates this rule is to be punished with a fine up to ₹500. However, this rule is not applicable in the case of a voter whose absence may cause danger or substantial loss in respect of the employment in which he is engaged.

Contestants Restricted to Two Constituencies A candidate would not be eligible to contest from more than two Parliamentary or assembly constituencies at a general election or at the by-elections which are held simultaneously. Similar restrictions are imposed for biennial elections and by-elections to the Rajya Sabha and the state legislative councils.

Prohibition of Arms Entering into the neighbourhood of a polling station with any kind of arms[10] is to be considered a cognizable offence. Such an act is punishable with imprisonment of up to two years or with fine or with both. Further, the arms found in possession of the offender are to be confiscated and the related licence is to be cancelled. But, these provisions are not applicable to the returning officer, presiding officer, any police officer or any other person appointed to maintain peace and order at the polling station.

Effective Campaigning Period Reduced The minimum gap between the last date for withdrawal of candidature and the polling date has been reduced from 20 to 14 days.

Electoral Reforms After 1996

Presidential and Vice Presidential Elections In 1997[11], the number of electors as proposers and seconders for contesting election to the office of the President was increased from 10 to 50 and to the office of the Vice President from 5 to 20. Further, the amount of security deposit was increased from ₹2,500 to ₹15,000 for contesting election to both the offices of President and Vice-President to discourage frivolous candidates.

Requisitioning of Staff for Election Duty In 1998[12], a provision was made whereby the employees of local authorities, nationalised banks, universities, LIC, government undertakings and other government-aided institutions can be requisitioned for deployment on election duty.

Voting through Postal Ballot In 1999[13], a provision was made for voting by certain classes of persons through postal ballot. Thus, any class of persons can be notified by the Election Commission, in consultation with the government, and the persons belonging to such notified class can give their votes by postal ballot, and not in any other manner, at elections in their constituency or constituencies.

Facility to Opt to Vote Through Proxy In 2003[14], the facility to opt to vote through proxy was provided to the service voters belonging to the Armed Forces and members belonging to a Force to which provisions of the Army Act apply. Such service voters who opt to vote through proxy have to appoint a proxy in a prescribed format and intimate the Returning Officer of the constituency.

Declaration of Criminal Antecedents, Assets, etc., by Candidates In 2003, the election Commission issued an order[15] directing every candidate seeking election to the Parliament or a State Legislature to furnish on his nomination paper the information on the following matters.

(i) Whether the candidate has been convicted or acquitted or discharged in any criminal offence in the past? Whether he/she was imprisoned or fined?

(ii) Prior to six months of filing nomination, whether the candidate is accused in any pending case, of any offence punishable with imprisonment for two years or more, and in which charges were framed or cognizance was taken by a court; if so, the details thereof

(iii) The assets (immovable, movable, bank balances, etc.) of a candidate and his/her spouse and that of dependents

(iv) Liabilities, if any, particularly whether there are any dues of any public financial institution or government dues

(v) The educational qualifications of the candidate

Furnishing of any false information in the affidavit is now an electoral offence punishable with imprisonment upto six months or fine or both.

Changes in Rajya Sabha Elections: In 2003, the following two changes were introduced with respect to elections to the Rajya Sabha[16]:

(i) Domicile or residency requirement of a candidate contesting an election to the Rajya Sabha was removed. Prior to this, a candidate had to be an elector in the state from where he was to be elected. Now, it would be sufficient if he is an elector in any parliamentary constituency in the country.

(ii) Introducing open ballot system, instead of secret ballot system, for elections to the Rajya Sabha. This was done to curb cross-voting and to wipe out the role of money power during Rajya Sabha elections. Under the new system, an elector belonging to a political party has to show the ballot paper after marking his vote to a nominated agent of that political party.

Exemption of Travelling Expenditure As per a provision of 2003[17], the traveling expenditure incurred by the campaigning leaders of a political party shall be exempted from being included in the election expenses of the candidate.

Free Supply of Electoral Rolls, etc. According to a 2003 provision[18], the Government should supply, free of cost, the copies of the electoral rolls and other prescribed material to the candidates of recognised political parties for the Lok Sabha and Assembly elections. Further, the Election Commission should supply specified items to the voters in the constituencies concerned or to the candidates set up by the recognised political parties.

Parties Entitled to Accept Contribution In 2003[19], the political parties were entitled to accept any amount of contribution from any person or company other than a government company. They have to report any contribution in excess of ₹20,000 to the Election Commission for making any claim to any income tax relief. Besides, the companies would get income tax exemption on the amount contributed.

Allocation of Time on Electronic Media Under a 2003 provision[20], the Election Commission should allocate equitable sharing of time on the cable television network and other electronic media during elections to display or propagate any matter or to address public. This allocation would be decided on the basis of the past performance of a recognised political party.

ELECTORAL REFORMS SINCE 2010

Restrictions Imposed on Exit Polls According to a 2009 provision[21], conducting exit polls and publishing results of exist polls would be prohibited during the election to Lok Sabha and State Legislative Assemblies. Thus, no person shall conduct any exit poll and publish or publicise by means of the print or electronic media or disseminate in any other manner, the result of any exit poll during the period notified by the Election Commission in this regard. Further, any person who contravenes this provision shall be punishable with imprisonment of upto two years or with fine or with both.

"Exit-poll" is an opinion survey regarding how electors have voted at an election or how all the electors have performed with regard to the identification of a political party or candidate in an election.

Time-Limit for Submitting a Case for Disqualification In 2009[22], a provision was made for the simplification of the procedure for disqualification of a person found guilty of corrupt practices. It provided for a three-month time-limit within which the specified authority will have to submit the case of a person found guilty of corrupt practice to the President for determination of the question of disqualification.

All Officials Included in Corrupt Practice In 2009[23], a provision was made for the inclusion of all officials, whether in the government service or not, appointed or deputed by the Election Commission in connection with the conduct of elections, within the scope of corrupt practice of obtaining any assistance by a candidate for the furtherance of the prospects of his election.

Increase in Security Deposit In 2009[24], the amount of security deposit to be paid by the candidates contesting elections to the Lok Sabha was increased from ₹10,000 to ₹25,000 for the general candidates and from ₹5,000 to ₹12,500 for SC and

ST candidates. Similarly, the security deposit in the case of elections to the state legislative assembly was increased from ₹5,000 to ₹10,000 for the general candidates and from ₹2,500 to ₹5,000 for the SC and ST candidates. This was done in order to check the multiplicity of non-serious candidates.

Appellate Authority within the District In 2009[25], a provision was made for appointment of an appellate authority within the district against the orders of the Electoral Registration Officers, instead of the Chief Electoral Officer of the state. Thus, an appeal against any order of the Electoral Registration Officer of a constituency (during continuous updation of the electoral roll) will now lie before the District Magistrate or Additional District Magistrate or Executive Magistrate or District Collector or an officer of equivalent rank. A further appeal against any order of the District Magistrate or Additional District Magistrate will now lie before the Chief Electoral Officer of the state.

Voting Rights to Citizens of India Living Abroad In 2010[26], a provision was made to confer voting rights to the citizens of India residing outside India due to various reasons. Accordingly, every citizen of India – (a) whose name is not included in the electoral roll (b) who has not acquired the citizenship of any other country (c) who is absent from his place of ordinary residence in India owing to his employment, education or otherwise outside India (whether temporarily or not) – shall be entitled to have his name registered in the electoral roll in the Parliamentary / Assembly constituency in which his place of residence in India as mentioned in his passport is located.

Ceiling on Election Expenditure Increased In 2011[27], the Central Government raised the maximum ceiling on election expenditure by candidates for a Lok Sabha seat in bigger states to ₹40 lakhs. In other states and union territories, it varies between ₹16 lakhs and ₹40 lakhs. Similarly, the limit for an Assembly seat in the bigger states was increased to ₹16 lakhs. In other states and union territories, it varies between ₹8 lakhs and ₹16 lakhs.

The state-wise and union territory-wise limits are mentioned below in Table 66.1.

Table 66.1 *Limit on Election Expenditure*

Sl. No.	Name of State or Union Territory	Maximum limit of election expenses in any one	
		Parliamentary Constituency	Assembly Constituency
	I. STATES	₹	₹
1.	Andhra Pradesh	40,00,000	16,00,000
2.	Arunachal Pradesh	27,00,000	10,00,000
3.	Assam	40,00,000	16,00,000
4.	Bihar	40,00,000	16,00,000
5.	Chhattisgarh	40,00,000	16,00,000
6.	Goa	22,00,000	8,00,000
7.	Gujarat	40,00,000	16,00,000
8.	Haryana	40,00,000	16,00,000
9.	Himachal Pradesh	40,00,000	11,00,000
10.	Jammu & Kashmir	40,00,000	—
11.	Jharkhand	40,00,000	16,00,000
12.	Karnataka	40,00,000	16,00,000
13.	Kerala	40,00,000	16,00,000
14.	Madhya Pradesh	40,00,000	16,00,000
15.	Maharashtra	40,00,000	16,00,000

(*Contd.*)

Sl. No.	Name of State or Union Territory	Maximum limit of election expenses in any one	
		Parliamentary Constituency	Assembly Constituency
	I. STATES	₹	₹
16.	Manipur	35,00,000	8,00,000
17.	Meghalaya	35,00,000	8,00,000
18.	Mizoram	32,00,000	8,00,000
19.	Nagaland	40,00,000	8,00,000
20.	Odisha	40,00,000	16,00,000
21.	Punjab	40,00,000	16,00,000
22.	Rajasthan	40,00,000	16,00,000
23.	Sikkim	27,00,000	8,00,000
24.	Tamil Nadu	40,00,000	16,00,000
25.	Tripura	40,00,000	8,00,000
26.	Uttarakhand	40,00,000	11,00,000
27.	Uttar Pradesh	40,00,000	16,00,000
28.	West Bengal	40,00,000	16,00,000
	II. UNION TERRITORIES		
1.	Andaman and Nicobar Islands	27,00,000	—
2.	Chandigarh	22,00,000	—
3.	Dadra and Nagar Haveli	16,00,000	—
4.	Daman and Diu	16,00,000	—
5.	Delhi	40,00,000	14,00,000
6.	Lakshadweep	16,00,000	—
7.	Puducherry	32,00,000	8,00,000

NOTES AND REFERENCES

1. See "Electoral Reforms of 1996", discussed later in this chapter.
2. In 1998, the BJP-led Government appointed an eight-member committee on state funding of elections under the chairmanship of Indrajit Gupta, a former Home Minister. The committee submitted its report in 1999. It upheld the argument for introduction of state funding of elections. It stated that state funding of elections is constitutionally and legally justified and is in public interest.
3. For recommendations of the commission in this regard, see Chapter 71.
4. This came into force on March 28, 1989. Consequently, amendments were also made in the *Representation of the People Act* of 1950 and 1951.
5. *Representation of the People (Amendment) Act* of 1988.
6. *Ibid.*
7. Amendment to the *Representation of the People Act* of 1951 with effect from March 15, 1989.
8. Section 58-A has been inserted in the *Representation of the People Act* of 1951 by Act 1 of 1989.
9. *Representation of the People (Amendment) Act*, 1996, with effect from August 1, 1996.
10. As defined in *Arms Act*, 1959.
11. *Presidential and Vice-Presidential Elections (Amendment) Act*, 1997.

12. *Representation of the People (Amendment) Act,* 1998.

13. *Representation of the People (Amendment) Act,* 1999.

14. *Election Laws (Amendment) Act,* 2003 and Conduct of Elections (Amendment) Rules, 2003.

15. Order dated March 27, 2003.

16. *Representation of the People (Amendment) Act,* 2003.

17. *Election and Other Related Laws (Amendment) Act,* 2003.

18. *Ibid.*

19. *Ibid.*

20. *Ibid.*

21. *Representation of the People (Amendment) Act,* 2009, with effect from February 1, 2010.

22. *Ibid.*

23. *Ibid.*

24. *Ibid.*

25. *Ibid*

26. *Representation of the People (Amendment) Act,* 2010, with effect from February 10, 2011.

27. Conduct of Election Rules, 1961, as amended in 2011, with effect from February 23, 2011.

Anti-Defection Law

The 52nd Amendment Act of 1985 provided for the disqualification of the members of Parliament and the state legislatures on the ground of defection from one political party to another. For this purpose, it made changes in four Articles[1] of the Constitution and added a new Schedule (the Tenth Schedule) to the Constitution. This act is often referred to as the 'anti-defection law'.

Later, the 91st Amendment Act of 2003 made one change in the provisions of the Tenth Schedule. It omitted an exception provision i.e., disqualification on ground of defection not to apply in case of split.

PROVISIONS OF THE ACT

The Tenth Schedule contains the following provisions with respect to the disqualification of members of Parliament and the state legislatures on the ground of defection:

1. Disqualification

Members of Political Parties: A member of a House belonging to any political party becomes disqualified for being a member of the House, (a) if he voluntarily gives up his membership of such political party; or (b) if he votes or abstains from voting in such House contrary to any direction issued by his political party without obtaining prior permission of such party and such act has not been condoned by the party within 15 days.

From the above provision it is clear that a member elected on a party ticket should continue in the party and obey the party directions.

Independent Members: An independent member of a House (elected without being set up as a candidate by any political party) becomes disqualified to remain a member of the House if he joins any political party after such election.

Nominated Members: A nominated member of a House becomes disqualified for being a member of the House if he joins any political party after the expiry of six months from the date on which he takes his seat in the House. This means that he may join any political party within six months of taking his seat in the House without inviting this disqualification.

2. Exceptions

The above disqualification on the ground of defection does not apply in the following two cases:

(a) If a member goes out of his party as a result of a merger of the party with another party. A merger takes place when two-thirds of the members of the party have agreed to such merger.

(b) If a member, after being elected as the presiding officer of the House, voluntarily gives up the membership of his party or rejoins it after he ceases to hold that office. This exemption has been provided in view of the dignity and impartiality of this office.

It must be noted here that the provision of the Tenth Schedule pertaining to exemption from disqualification in case of split by one-third members of legislature party has been deleted by the 91st Amendment Act of 2003. It means that the defectors have no more protection on grounds of splits.

3. Deciding Authority

Any question regarding disqualification arising out of defection is to be decided by the presiding officer of the House. Originally, the act provided that the decision of the presiding officer is final and cannot be questioned in any court. However, in *Kihoto Hollohan* case[2] (1993), the Supreme Court declared this provision as unconstitutional on the ground that it seeks to take away the jurisdiction of the Supreme Court and the high courts. It held that the presiding officer, while deciding a question under the Tenth Schedule, function as a tribunal. Hence, his decision like that of any other tribunal, is subject to judicial review on the grounds of *mala fides*, perversity, etc. But, the court rejected the contention that the vesting of adjudicatory powers in the presiding officer is by itself invalid on the ground of political bias[3].

4. Rule-Making Power

The presiding officer of a House is empowered to make rules to give effect to the provisions of the Tenth Schedule. All such rules must be placed before the House for 30 days. The House may approve or modify or disapprove them. Further, he may direct that any willful contravention by any member of such rules may be dealt with in the same manner as a breach of privilege of the House.

According to the rules made so, the presiding officer can take up a defection case only when he receives a complaint from a member of the House. Before taking the final decision, he must give the member (against whom the complaint has been made) a chance to submit his explanation. He may also refer the matter to the committee of privileges for inquiry. Hence, defection has no immediate and automatic effect.

EVALUATION OF THE ACT

The Tenth Schedule of the Constitution (which embodies the anti-defection law) is designed to prevent the evil or mischief of political defections motivated by the lure of office or material benefits or other similar considerations. It is intended to strengthen the fabric of Indian parliamentary democracy by curbing unprincipled and unethical political defections. Rajiv Gandhi, the then Prime Minister, described it as the 'first step towards cleaning-up public life'. The then Central law minister stated that the passing of the 52nd Amendment Bill (anti-defection bill) by a unanimous vote by both the Houses of Parliament was 'a proof, if any, of the maturity and stability of Indian democracy'.

Advantages

The following can be cited as the advantages of the anti-defection law:
 (a) It provides for greater stability in the body politic by checking the propensity of legislators to change parties.
 (b) It facilitates democratic realignment of parties in the legislature by way of merger of parties.
 (c) It reduces corruption at the political level as well as non-developmental expenditure incurred on irregular elections.
 (d) It gives, for the first time, a clear-cut constitutional recognition to the existence of political parties.

Criticism

Though the anti-defection law been hailed as a bold step towards cleansing our political life and started as new epoch in the political life of the country, it has revealed may lacunae in its operation and failed to prevent defections in toto. It came to be criticised on the following grounds:
 1. It does not make a differentiation between dissent and defection. It curbs the legislator's right to dissent and freedom of conscience. Thus, 'it clearly puts party bossism on a pedestral and sanctions tyranny of the party in the name of the party discipline'[4].
 2. Its distinction between individual defection and group defection is irrational. In other words, 'it banned only retail defections and legalised wholesale defections'[5].
 3. It does not provide for the expulsion of a legislator from his party for his activities outside the legislature.

4. Its discrimation between an independent member and a nominated member is illogical. If the former joins a party, he is disqualified while the latter is allowed to do the same.

5. Its vesting of decision-making authority in the presiding officer is criticised on two grounds. Firstly, he may not exercise this authority in an impartial and objective manner due to political exigencies. Secondly, he lacks the legal knowledge and experience to adjudicate upon the cases. In fact, two Speakers of the Lok Sabha (Rabi Ray—1991 and Shivraj Patil—1993) have themselves expressed doubts on their suitability to adjudicate upon the cases related to defections[6].

91ST AMENDMENT ACT (2003)

Reasons

The reasons for enacting the 91st Amendment Act (2003) are as follows:

1. Demands have been made from time to time in certain quarters for strengthening and amending the Anti-defection Law as contained in the Tenth Schedule, on the ground that these provisions have not been able to achieve the desired goal of checking defections. The Tenth Schedule has also been criticised on the ground that it allows bulk defections while declaring individual defections as illegal. The provision for exemption from disqualification in case of splits as provided in the Tenth Schedule has, in particular, come under severe criticism on account of its destabilising effect on the Government.

2. The Committee on Electoral Reforms (Dinesh Goswami Committee) in its report of 1990, the Law Commission of India in its 170th Report on "Reform of Electoral Laws" (1999) and the National Commission to Review the Working of the Constitution (NCRWC) in its report of 2002 have, *inter alia*, recommended omission of the provision of the Tenth Schedule pertaining to exemption from disqualification in case of splits.

3. The NCRWC was also of the view that a defector should be penalised for his action by debarring him from holding any public office as a minister or any other remunerative political post for at least the duration of the remaining term of the existing Legislature or until, the next fresh elections whichever is earlier.

4. The NCRWC has also observed that abnormally large Councils of Ministers were being constituted by various Governments at Centre and states and this practice had to be prohibited by law and that a ceiling on the number of ministers in a state or the Union Government be fixed at the maximum of 10% of the total strength of the popular House of the Legislature.

The 91st Amendment Act of 2003 has made the following provisions to limit the size of Council of Ministers, to debar defectors from holding public offices, and to strengthen the anti-defection law:

1. The total number of ministers, including the Prime Minister, in the Central Council of Ministers shall not exceed 15 per cent of the total strength of the Lok Sabha (Article 75).

2. A member of either House of Parliament belonging to any political party who is disqualified on the ground of defection shall also be disqualified to be appointed as a minister (Article 75).

3. The total number of ministers, including the Chief Minister, in the Council of Ministers in a state shall not exceed 15 per cent of the total strength of the Legislative Assembly of that state. But, the number of ministers, including the Chief Minister, in a state shall not be less than 12 (Article 164).

4. A member of either House of a state legislature belonging to any political party who is disqualified on the ground of defection shall also be disqualified to be appointed as a minister (Article 164).

5. A member of either House of Parliament or either House of a State Legislature belonging to any political party who is disqualified on the ground of defection shall also be disqualified to hold any remunerative political post. The expression "remunerative political post" means (i) any office under the Central

Government or a state government where the salary or remuneration for such office is paid out of the public revenue of the concerned government; or (ii) any office under a body, whether incorporated or not, which is wholly or partially owned by the Central Government or a state government and the salary or remuneration for such office is paid by such body, except where such salary or remuneration paid is compensatory in nature (Article 361-B).

6. The provision of the Tenth Schedule (anti-defection law) pertaining to exemption from disqualification in case of split by one-third members of legislature party has been deleted. It means that the defectors have no more protection on grounds of splits.

NOTES AND REFERENCES

1. These are Articles 101, 102, 190 and 191 which relate to the vacation of seats and disqualification from membership of Parliament and the state legislatures.
2. *Kihoto Hollohan* v. *Zachilhu*, (1993).
3. The court observed: 'The Chairmen or Speakers hold a pivotal position in the scheme of parliamentary democracy and are guardians of the rights and privileges of the House. They are expected to and do take far-reaching decisions in the functioning of parliamentary democracy. Vestiture of power to adjudicate questions under the Tenth Schedule in such constitutional functionaries should not be considered unexceptionable'.
4. Soli J Sorabjee, 'The Remedy should not be worse than the Disease', *The Times of India (Sunday Review),* February 1, 1985, p. 1.
5. Madhu Limaye, *Contemporary Indian Politics*, 1989, p. 190.
6. Speaker Shivraj Patil stated: 'The advantages in giving these cases to the judiciary are many. The Speaker or the Chairman may or may not be endowed with legal acumen and proficiency in law. It is more apt to have the cases decided by the Supreme Court or high court judges'.

Pressure Groups

MEANING AND TECHNIQUES

The term 'pressure group' originated in the USA. A pressure group is a group of people who are organised actively for promoting and defending their common interest. It is so called as it attempts to bring a change in the public policy by exerting pressure on the government. It acts as a liaison between the government and its members.

The pressure groups are also called *interest groups* or vested groups. They are different from the political parties in that they neither contest elections nor try to capture political power. They are concerned with specific programmes and issues and their activities are confined to the protection and promotion of the interests of their members by influencing the government.

The pressure groups influence the policy-making and policy-implementation in the government through legal and legitimate methods like lobbying, correspondence, publicity, propagandising, petitioning, public debating, maintaining contacts with their legislators and so forth. However, some times they resort to illegitimate and illegal methods like strikes, violent activities and corruption which damages public interest and administrative integrity.

According to Odegard, pressure groups resort to three different techniques in securing their purposes. First, they can try to place in public office persons who are favourably disposed towards the interests they seeks to promote. This technique may be labelled *electioneering*. Second, they can try to persuade public officers, whether they are initially favourably disposed toward them or not, to adopt and enforce the policies that they think will prove most beneficial to their interests. This technique may be labelled *lobbying*. Third, they can try to influence public opinion and thereby gain an indirect influence over government, since the government in a democracy is substantially affected by public opinion. This technique may be labelled *propagandizing*[1].

PRESSURE GROUPS IN INDIA

A large number of pressure groups exist in India. But, they are not developed to the same extent as in the US or the western countries like Britain, France, Germany and so on. The pressure groups in India can be broadly classified into the following categories:

1. Business Groups

The business groups include a large number of industrial and commercial bodies. They are the most sophisticated, the most powerful and the largest of all pressure groups in India. They include:

(i) Federation of Indian Chamber of Commerce and Industry (FICCI); major constituents are the Indian Merchants Chamber of Bombay, Indian Merchants Chamber of Calcutta and South Indian Chamber of Commerce of Madras. It broadly represents major industrial and trading interests.

(ii) Associated Chamber of Commerce and Industry of India (ASSOCHAM); major constituents are the Bengal Chamber of Commerce of Calcutta and Central Commercial Organisation of Delhi. ASSOCHAM represents foreign British capital.

(iii) Federation of All India Foodgrain Dealers Association (FAIFDA). FAIFDA is the sole representative of the grain dealers.

(iv) All-India Manufacturers Organisation (AIMO). AIMO raises the concerns of the medium-sized industry.

2. Trade Unions

The trade unions voice the demands of the industrial workers. They are also known as *labour groups*. A peculiar feature of trade unions in India is that they are associated either directly or indirectly with different political parties. They include:

(i) All-India Trade Union Congress (AITUC)—affiliated to CPI;

(ii) Indian National Trade Union Congress (INTUC)—affiliated to the Congress (I);

(iii) Hind Mazdoor Sabha (HMS)—affiliated to the Socialists;

(iv) Centre of Indian Trade Unions (CITU)—affiliated to the CPM;

(v) Bharatiya Mazdoor Sangh (BMS)—affiliated to the BJP;

(vi) All India Central Council of Trade Unions (Communist Party of India (Marxist-Leninist) Liberation);

(vii) All India United Trade Union Centre (Socialist Unity Centre of India (Communist));

(viii) New Trade Union Initiative (Independent from political parties, but left);

(ix) Labour Progressive Federation (Dravida Munnetra Kazhagam);

(x) Trade Union Coordination Committee (All India Forward Bloc);

(xi) United Trade Union Congress (Revolutionary Socialist Party);

(xii) All India Centre of Trade Unions (Marxist Communist Party of India (United));

(xiii) Anna Thozhil Sanga Peravai (All India Anna Dravida Munnetra Kazhagam);

(xiv) Bharatiya Kamgar Sena (Shiv Sena);

(xv) Hind Mazdoor Kisan Panchayat (Janata Dal (United));

(xvi) Indian Federation of Trade Unions (Communist Party of India Marxist-Leninist) New Democracy);

(xvii) Indian National Trinamool Trade Union Congress (All India Trinamool Congress);

(xviii) Pattali Trade Union (Pattali Makkal Katchi);

(ix) Swatantra Thozhilali Union (Indian Union Muslim League); and

(xx) Telugu Nadu Trade Union Council (Telugu Desam Party).

First Trade Union in India: All India Trade Union Congress (AITUC) was founded in 1920 with Lala Lajpat Rai as its first president. Upto 1945, Congressmen, Socialists and Communists worked in the AITUC which was the central trade union organisation of workers of India. Subsequently, the trade union movement got split on political lines.

3. Agrarian Groups

The agrarian groups represent the farmers and the agricultural labour class. They include:

(i) Bhartiya Kisan Union (under the leadership of Mahendra Singh Tikait, in the wheat belt of North India)

(ii) All India Kisan Sabha (the oldest and the largest agrarian group)

(iii) Revolutionary Peasants Convention (organised by the CPM in 1967 which gave birth to the Naxalbari Movement)

(iv) Bhartiya Kisan Sangh (Gujarat)

(v) R V Sangham (led by C N Naidu in Tamil Nadu)

(vi) Shetkhari Sanghatana (led by Sharad Joshi in Maharashtra)

(vii) Hind Kisan Panchayat (controlled by the Socialists)

(viii) All-India Kisan Sammelan (led by Raj Narain)

(ix) United Kisan Sabha (controlled by the CPM)

4. Professional Associations

These are associations that raise the concerns and demands of doctors, lawyers, journalists and teachers. Despite various restrictions, these associations pressurise the government by various methods including agitations for the improvement of their service conditions. They include:

(i) Indian Medical Association (IMA)

(ii) Bar Council of India (BCI)

(iii) Indian Federation of Working Journalists (IFWJ)

(iv) All India Federation of University and College Teachers (AIFUCT)

5. Student Organisations

Various unions have been formed to represent the student community. However, these unions, like the trade unions, are also affiliated to various political parties. These are:

(i) Akhila Bhartiya Vidyarthi Parishad (ABVP) (affiliated to BJP)

(ii) All India Students Federation (AISF) (affiliated to CPI)

(iii) National Students Union of India (NSUI) (affiliated to Congress (I))

(iv) Progressive Students Union (PSU) (affiliated to CPM)

6. Religious Organisations

The organisations based on religion have come to play an important role in Indian politics. They represent the narrow communal interest. They include:

(i) Rashtriya Swayam Sevak Sangh (RSS)

(ii) Vishwa Hindu Parishad (VHP)

(iii) Jamaat-e-Islami

(iv) Ittehad-ul-Mussalmeen

(v) Anglo-Indian Association

(vi) Associations of the Roman Catholics

(vii) All-India Conference of Indian Christians

(viii) Parsi Central Association

(ix) Shiromani Akali Dal

"The Shiromani Akali Dal should be regarded as more of a religious pressure group rather than a political party in view of the fact that it has been concerned more with the mission of saving the sikh community from being absorbed into the ocean of hindu society than with fighting for the cause of a sikh homeland"[2].

7. Caste Groups

Like religion, caste has been an important factor in Indian politics. The competitive politics in many states of the Indian Union is in fact the politics of caste rivalries: Brahmin versus Non-Brahmin in Tamil Nadu and Maharashtra, Rajput versus Jat in Rajasthan, Kamma versus Reddy in Andhra, Ahir versus Jat in Haryana, Baniya Brahmin versus Patidar in Gujarat.

Kayastha versus Rajput in Bihar, Nair versus Ezhava in Kerala and Lingayat versus Okkaliga in Karnataka[3]. Some of the caste-based organisations are:

(i) Nadar Caste Association in Tamil Nadu

(ii) Marwari Association

(iii) Harijan Sevak Sangh

(iv) Kshatriya Maha Sabha in Gujarat

(v) Vanniyakul Kshatriya Sangam

(vi) Kayastha Sabha

8. Tribal Organisations

The tribal organisations are active in MP, Chattisgarh, Bihar, Jharkhand, West Bengal and the North Eastern States of Assam, Manipur, Nagaland and so on. Their demands range from reforms to that of secession from India and some of them are involved in insurgency activities. The tribal organisations include:

(i) National Socialist Council of Nagaland (NSCN)

(ii) Tribal National Volunteers (TNU) in Tripura

(iii) People's Liberation Army in Manipur

(iv) All-India Jharkhand

(v) Tribal Sangh of Assam

(vi) United Mizo Federal Organisation

9. Linguistic Groups

Language has been so important factor in Indian politics that it became the main basis for the reorganisation of states. The language along with caste, religion and tribe have been responsible for the emergence of political parties as well as pressure groups. Some of the linguistic groups are:

(i) Tamil Sangh

(ii) Anjuman Tarraki-i-Urdu

(iii) Andhra Maha Sabha

(iv) Hindi Sahitya Sammelan

(v) Nagari Pracharani Sabha

(vi) Dakshina Bharat Hindi Prachar Sabha

10. Ideology Based Groups

In more recent times, the pressure groups are formed to pursue a particular ideology, i.e., a cause, a principle or a programme. These groups include:

(i) Environmental protection groups like Narmada Bachao Andolan, and Chipko Movement

(ii) Democratic rights organisations

(iii) Civil liberties associations

(iv) Gandhi Peace Foundation

(v) Woman rights organisations

11. Anomic Groups

Almond and Powell observed: "By anomic pressure groups we mean more or less a spontaneous break-through into the political system from the society such as riots, demonstrations, assassinations and the like. The Indian Government and bureaucratic elite, overwhelmed by the problem of economic development and scarcity of resources available to them,

inevitably acquires a technocratic and anti-political frame of mind, particularistic demands of whatever kinds are denied legitimacy. As a consequence inter-est groups are alienated from the political system"[4]. Some of the anomic pressure groups are:

(i) All-India Sikh Student's Federation.

(ii) Nava Nirman Samithi of Gujarat.

(iii) Naxalite Groups.

(iv) Jammu and Kashmir Liberation Front (JKLF).

(v) All Assam Student's Union.

(vi) United Liberation Front of Assam (ULFA).

(vii) Dal Khalsa.

NOTES AND REFERENCES

1. G A Almond and G B Coleman (eds), *The Politics of the Developing Areas,* Princeton, (1970), P. 185.

2. JC Johari: *Indian Government and Politics*, Vishal, Thirteenth Edition, P. 591.

3. Paul Kolenda: Caste in India since Independence (in *Social and Economic Development in India* by Basu and Sission, P. 110).

4. GA Almond and GB Powell: *Comparative Politics*, 1972, P. 75–76.

National Integration

India is a land of widespread diversities in terms of religion, language, caste, tribe, race, region and so on. Hence, the achievement of national integration becomes very essential for the all-around development and prosperity of the country.

Meaning of National Integration

Definitions and statements on national integration:

"National integration implies avoidance of divisive movements that would balkanise the nation and presence of attitudes throughout the society that give preference to national and public interest as distinct from parochial interests"[1] *Myron Weiner.*

"National integration is a socio-psychological and educational process through which a feeling of unity, solidarity and cohersion develops in the hearts of the people and a sense of common citizenship or feeling of loyalty to the nation is fostered among them"[2] *HA Gani.*

"National integration is not a house which could be built by mortar and bricks. It is not an industrial plan too which could be discussed and implemented by experts. Integration, on the contrary, is a thought which must go into the heads of the people. It is the consciousness which must awaken the people at large" *Dr S Radhakrishna.*

"National integrations means, and ought to mean, cohesion not fusion, unity but not uniformity, reconciliation but not merger, agglomeration but not assimilation of the discrete segments of the people constituting a political community or state"[3] *Rasheeduddin Khan.*

To sum-up, the concept of national integration involves political, economic, social, cultural and psychological dimensions and the inter-relations between them.

Obstacles to National Integration

Among the major obstacles to national integration include:

1. Regionalism

Regionalism refers to sub-nationalism and sub-territorial loyalty. It implies the love for a particular region or state in preference to the country as a whole. There is also sub-regionalism, that is, love for a particular region in preference to the state of which the region forms a part.

Regionalism is "a subsidiary process of political integration in India. It is a manifestation of those residual elements which do not find expression in the national polity and national culture, and being excluded from the centrality of the new polity, express themselves in political discontent and political exclusionism"[4].

Regionalism is a country-wide phenomenon which manifests itself in the following six forms:

(i) Demand of the people of certain states for secession from the Indian Union (like Khalistan, Dravid Nad, Mizos, Nagas and so on).

(ii) Demand of the people of certain areas for separate statehood (like Telengana, Bodoland, Uttarkhand, Vidharbha, Gorkhaland and so on).

(iii) Demand of people of certain Union Territories for full-fledged statehood (like Manipur, Tripura, Puducherry, Delhi, Goa, Daman and Diu and so on).

(iv) Inter-state boundary disputes (like Chandigarh and Belgaum) and river-water disputes (like Cauvery, Krishna, Ravi-Beas and so on).

(v) Formation of organisations with regional motives which advocates a militant approach in pursuing its policies and goals (like Shiv Sena, Tamil Sena, Hindi Sena, Sardar Sena, Lachit Sena and so on).

(vi) 'Sons of the soil theory' which advocates preference to local people in government jobs, private jobs, permits and so on. Their slogan will be Assam for Assamese, Maharashtra for Maharashtrians and so on.

2. Communalism

Communalism means love for one's religious community in preference to the nation and a tendency to promote the communal interest at the cost of the interest of other religious communities. It has its roots in the British rule where the 1909, 1919 and 1935 Acts had introduced communal representation for the Muslims, Sikhs and others.

The communalism got accentuated with the politicisation of religion. Its various manifestations are:

(i) Formation of political parties based on religion (like Akali Dal, Muslim League, Ram Rajya Parishad, Hindu Mahasabha, Shiv Sena and so on).

(ii) Emergence of pressure groups (non-political entities) based on religion (like RSS, Vishwa Hindu Parishad, Jamaat-e-Islami, Anglo-Indian Christians Association and so on).

(iii) Communal riots (between Hindus and Muslims, Hindus and Sikhs, Hindus and Christians and so on—Benaras, Lucknow, Mathura, Hyderabad, Allahabad, Aligarh, Amritsar, Moradabad and all other places are affected by communal violence).

(iv) Dispute over religious structures like temples, mosques and others (The dispute over Ram Janma Bhoomi in Ayodhya where the *kar sevaks* had demolished a disputed structure on December 6, 1992).

The reasons for the persistence of communalism include religious orthodoxy of muslims, role of Pakistan, hindu chauvinism, government's inertia, role of political parties and other groups, electoral compulsions, communal media, socio-economic factors and so on.

3. Casteism

Casteism implies love for one's own caste-group in preference to the general national interest. It is mainly an outcome of the politicisation of caste. Its various manifestations include:

(i) Formation of political parties on the basis of caste (like Justice Party in Madras, DMK, Kerala Congress, Republican Party, Bahujan Samaj Party and so on).

(ii) Emergence of pressure groups (non-political entities) based on caste (like Nadar Association, Harijan Sevak Sangh, Kshatriya Mahasabha and so on).

(iii) Allotment of party tickets during elections and the formation of council of ministers in the states on caste lines.

(iv) Caste conflicts between higher and lower castes or between dominant castes in various states like Bihar, Uttar Pradesh, Madhya Pradesh and so on.

(v) Violent disputes and agitations over the reservation policy.

B K Nehru observed: "The communal electorates (of the British days) in a vestigal form still remain in the shape of reservations for the Scheduled Castes and Scheduled Tribes. They serve to emphasise caste origin and make people conscious of the caste in which they were born. This is not conducive to national integeration"[5].

At the state level, the politics is basically a fight between the major caste groups like Kamma versus Reddy in Andhra Pradesh, Lingayat versus Vokaligga in Karnataka, Nayar versus Ezhava in Kerala, Bania versus Patidar in Gujarat, Bhumiar versus Rajput in Bihar, Jat versus Ahir in Haryana, Jat versus Rajput in Uttar Pradesh, Kalita versus Ahom in Assam and so on.

4. Linguism

Linguism means love for one's language and hatred towards other language-speaking people. The
phenomena of linguism, like that of regionalism,
communalism or casteism, is also a consequence
of political process. It has two dimensions: (a) the
reorganisation of states on the basis of language;
and (b) the determination of the official language
of the Union.

The creation of the first linguistic state of Andhra
out of the then Madras state in 1953 led to the coun-
trywide demand for the reorganisation of states on
the basis of language. Consequently, the states were
reorganised on a large-scale in 1956 on the basis of
the recommendations made by the States Reorganisation Commission[6] (1953–1955). Even after this,
the political map of India underwent a continuous
change due to the pressure of popular agitations
and the political conditions, which resulted in the
bifurcation of existing states like Bombay, Punjab,
Assam, and so on. By the end of 2000, the number
of states and union territories had reached 28 and 7
from that of 14 and 6 in 1956 respectively[7].

The enactment of the Official Language Act
(1963) making Hindi as the Official Language of the
Union led to the rise of anti-Hindi agitation in South
India and West Bengal. Then, the Central government
assured that English would continue as an 'associate'
official language so long as the non-Hindi speaking
states desire it. Moreover, the three-language formula (English, Hindi and a regional language) for
school system is still not being implemented in Tamil
Nadu[8]. Consequently, Hindi could not emerge as the
lingua franca of the composite culture of India as
desired by the framers of the Constitution.

The problem of linguism got accentuated with the
rise of some regional parties in recent times like the
TDP, AGP, Shiv Sena and so on.

NATIONAL INTEGRATION COUNCIL

The National Integration Council (NIC) was constituted in 1961, following a decision taken at a national conference on 'unity in diversity', convened by the
Central government, at New Delhi. It consisted of the
prime minister as chairman, central home minister,
chief ministers of states, seven leaders of political

parties, the chairman of the UGC, two educationists,
the commissioner for SCs and STs and seven other
persons nominated by the prime minister. The council was directed to examine the problem of national
integration in all its aspects and make necessary
recommendations to deal with it. The council made
various recommendations for national integration.
However, these recommendations remained only on
paper and no effort was made either by the Centre
or by the states to implement them.

In 1968, the Central government revived the
National Integration Council. Its size was increased
from 39 to 55 members. The representatives of industry, business and trade unions were also included
in it. The council met at Srinagar and adopted a
resolution condemning all tendencies that struck
at the root of national solidarity. It appealed to the
political parties, organisations and the press to mobilise the constructive forces of society in the cause
of national unity and solidarity. It also set up three
committes to report on regionalism, communalism
and linguism respectively. However, nothing tangible
was achieved.

In 1980, the Central government again revived the
National Integration Council which had become de-
funct. Its membership was made more broad-based.
It had three items on the agenda for discussion viz.,
the problem of communal harmony, unrest in the
north-eastern region and need for a new education
system. The council set up a standing committee to
keep a constant watch on the activities of communal and other divisive forces posing a threat to the
national unity.

In 1986, the NIC was reconstituted and its membership was further increased. It recognised terrorism
in Punjab as an attack on the unity, integrity and
secular ideals of the country. Accordingly, it passed
a resolution to fight terrorism in Punjab. The council
also set up a 21-member committee to function on a
continuing basis. The committee was asked to formulate both short-term as well as long-term proposals
for maintaining communal harmony and preserving
national integrity.

In 1990, the National Front Government headed
by VP Singh reconstituted the National Integration Council. Its strength was increased to 101. It
included prime minister as chairman, some Central
ministers, state chief ministers, leaders of national

and regional parties, representatives of women, trade and industry, academicians, journalists and public figures. It had various items on the agenda for discussion, viz., Punjab problem, Kashmir problem, violence by secessionists, communal harmony and Ram Janmabhomi-Babri Masjid problem at Ayodhya. But, there was no concrete result.

In 2005, the United Progressive Alliance (UPA) Government reconstituted the National Integration Council under the chairmanship of the Prime Minister, Manmohan Singh. The 103-member NIC was constituted after a gap of 12 years having held its meeting in 1992. Besides some central ministers, state and UT chief ministers and leaders of national and regional parties, the NIC included chairpersons of National Commissions, eminent public figures and representatives from business, media, labour and women. The NIC was to function as a forum for effective initiative and interaction on issues of national concern, review issues relating to national integration and make recommendations.

The 14th meeting of the NIC was held in 2008 in the backdrop of communal violence in various states like Orissa, Karnataka, Maharashtra, Jammu and Kashmir and Assam and so on. Promotion of education among minorities, scheduled castes and scheduled tribes; elements contributing to national integration; removal of regional imbalances, caste and identity divisions; prevention of extremism; promotion of communal harmony and security among minorities; and equitable development were some of the important items on the agenda of the meeting.

In April 2010, the United Progressive Alliance (UPA) Government again reconstituted the National Integration Council (NIC) under the chairmanship of the Prime Minister, Manmohan Singh. The NIC has 147 members, including Union Ministers, Leaders of the Opposition in the Lok Sabha and the Rajya Sabha, the Chief Ministers of all states and union territories with Legislatures. It also includes leaders of national and regional political parties, chairpersons of national commissions, eminent journalists, public figures, and representatives of business and women's organisations. It is chiefly aimed at suggesting means and ways to combat the menace of communalism, casteism and regionalism.

In October 2010, the Government also constituted a Standing Committee of the NIC. It consists of Union Home Minister as Chairman, four Union Ministers, nine Chief Ministers of various states and five co-opted members from NIC. It would finalise the agenda items for NIC meetings.

The 15th meeting of the NIC was held in September, 2011. The agenda for the meeting included measures to curb communalism and communal violence; approach to the Communal Violence Bill; measures to promote communal harmony; measures to eliminate discrimination, especially against minorities and scheduled tribes; how the state and the police should handle civil disturbances; and how to curb radicalisation of youth in the name of religion and caste.

Table 69.1 *Meetings of the National Integration Council*

Meeting Number	Held on
First Meeting	2nd and 3rd June, 1962
Second Meeting	20th to 22nd June, 1968
Third Meeting	12th November, 1980
Fourth Meeting	21st January, 1984
Fifth Meeting	7th April, 1986
Sixth Meeting	12th September, 1986
Seventh Meeting	11th April, 990
Eighth Meeting	22nd September, 1990
Ninth Meeting	2nd November, 1991
Tenth Meeting	31st December, 1991
Eleventh Meeting	18th July, 1992
Twelfth Meeting	23rd November, 1992
Thirteenth Meeting	31st August, 2005
Fourteenth Meeting	13th October, 2008
Fifteenth Meeting	10th September, 2011

NATIONAL FOUNDATION FOR COMMUNAL HARMONY

The National Foundation for Communal Harmony (NFCH) was set up in 1992. It is an autonomous body under the administrative control of the Union Home Ministry. It promotes communal harmony, fraternity and national integration.

The vision and mission of the NFCH are as follows:

Vision: India free from communal and all other forms of violence where all citizens especially children and youth live together in peace and harmony.

Mission: Promoting communal harmony, strengthening national integration and fostering unity in diversity through collaborative social action, awareness programs, reaching out to the victims of violence especially children, encouraging interfaith dialogue for India's shared security, peace and prosperity.

The activities undertaken by the NFCH are mentioned below:

1. To provide financial assistance to the child victims of societal violence for their care, education and training, aimed at their effective rehabilitation

2. To promote communal harmony and national integration by organising variety of activities either independently or in association with educational institutions, NGOs & other organisations

3. To conduct studies and grant scholarships to institutions / scholars for conducting studies

4. To confer awards for outstanding contribution to communal harmony and national integration

5. To involve Central / state governments / UT Administrations, industrial / commercial organisations, NGOs and others in promoting the objectives of the Foundation

6. To provide information services, publish monographs and books, etc. on the subject

NOTES AND REFERENCES

1. Myron Weiner: *Politics of Scarcity: Public Pressure and Political Response in India*, 1963.
2. HA Gani: *Muslim Political Issues and National Integration*, P. 3.
3. Rasheeduddin Khan: National Integration and Communal Harmony (in *National Integration of India*, Volume II, Edited by Sinha).
4. Kousar J. Azam: *Political Aspects of National Integration*, P. 82.
5. BK Nehru: The Indira Gandhi Memorial Lectures delivered at the University of Kerala in January, 1988.
6. It was a three-member commission headed by Fazl Ali. Its other two members were KM Panikkar and HN Kunzru.
7. In 2000, three more new states of Chhattisgarh, Uttarakhand and Jharkhand were created out the territories of Madhya Pradesh, Uttar Pradesh and Bihar respectively.
8. Tamil Nadu Government opposed the three language formula and continued to teach only two languages, that is, English and Tamil in the educational institutions of the state.

Foreign Policy

The foreign policy of India regulates India's relations with other states of the world in promoting its national interests. It is determined by a number of factors, viz., geography, history and tradition, social structure, political organisation, international milieu[1], economic position, military strength, public opinion and leadership.

PRINCIPLES OF INDIAN FOREIGN POLICY

1. Promotion of World Peace

India's foreign policy aims at the promotion of international peace and security. Article 51 of the Constitution (Directive Principles of State Policy) directs the Indian State to promote international peace and security, maintain just and honourable relations between nations, foster respect for international law and treaty obligations, and encourage settlement of international disputes by arbitration. Besides peace is necessary to promote the economic development of nations. Jawaharlal Nehru said: "Peace to us is not just a fervent hope; it is emergent necessity".

2. Anti-Colonialism

The foreign policy of India opposses colonialism and imperialism. India views that the colonialism and imperialism leads to exploitation of the weaker nations by the imperialist powers and affects the promotion of international peace. India advocated the liquidation of colonialism in all forms and supported the liberation movement in Afro-Asian countries like Indonesia, Malaya, Tunisia, Algeria, Ghana, Namibia and so on. Thus, India expressed her solidarity with the people of Afro-Asian nations in their struggle against colonial and imperialist forces like Britain, France, Holland, Portugal and so on. The present neo-colonialism and neo-imperialism is also opposed by India.

3. Anti-Racialism

Opposition to racialism in all its forms is an important aspect of Indian foreign policy. According to India, racialism (i.e., discrimination between people on the basis of race), like colonialism and imperialism, leads to exploitation of the blacks by the whites, social inequity and hinders the promotion of world peace. India strongly criticised the policy of apartheid (racial discrimination) being followed by the white minority racist regime of South Africa. It even snapped diplomatic relations with South Africa in 1954 as a protest against the policy of apartheid[2]. Similarly, India played an important role in the liberation of Zimbabwe (earlier Rhodesia) and Namibia from the white domination.

4. Non-Alignment

When India became independent in 1947, the world was divided into two blocs on ideological basis, namely, the capitalist bloc headed by USA and the communist bloc headed by the former USSR. In such a situation of 'cold war', India refused to join any of these two blocs and adopted a policy of non-alignment. In this context, Jawaharlal Nehru observed: "We propose to keep away from the power politics of groups, aligned against one another, which have led in the past to world wars and which may again lead to disasters on an even vaster scale. I feel that India can play a big part, and perhaps an effective part, in helping to avoid war. Therefore, it becomes all the more necessary that India should not be lined up with any group of power which for various reasons are full of fear of war and prepare for war".

"When we say that India follows a policy of non-alignment, it means (i) that India has no military alliances with countries of either bloc or indeed with any nation; (ii) India has an independent approach to foreign policy; and (iii) India attempts to maintain friendly relations with all countries"[3].

5. Panchsheel

Panchsheel implies the five principles of conduct in international relations. It was embodied in the Preamble of the Indo-China Treaty on Tibet, signed in 1954 by Jawaharlal Nehru and Chou-En-Lai, the Chinese Premier. The five principles were:

  (i) mutual respect for each other's territorial integrity and sovereignty;
 (ii) non-aggression;
(iii) non-interference in each other's internal affairs;
 (iv) equality and mutual benefit; and
  (v) peaceful co-existence.

"India perceived the 'Panchsheel' as productive of peaceful cooperation of sovereign nations instead of the balance of terror and the degrading cold war tensions, being brought about by the rival great power pacts and alliances. India explained it as based on the concept of universalism as against the concept of the balance of power"[4].

Panchsheel became very popular and many countries of the world like Burma, Yugoslavia, Indonesia and so on adopted it. Panchsheel and non-alignment are the greatest contributions of India to the theory and practice of international relations.

6. Afro-Asian Bias

Even though the foreign policy of India stands for maintaining friendly relations with all the countries of the world, it has always exhibited a special bias towards the Afro-Asian nations. It aims at promoting unity among them and tries to secure for them a voice and an influence in the international bodies. India has been seeking international assistance for the economic development of these countries. In 1947, India called the first Asian Relations Conference in New Delhi. In 1949, India brought together the Asian countries on the burning issue of Indonesian freedom. India played an active role in the Afro-Asian Conference at Bandung (Indonesia) in 1955. India also played an important role in the formation of Group of 77 (1964), Group of 15 (1990), Indian Ocean Rim Association for Regional Cooperation (1995), BIST Economic Cooperation (1997), and SAARC (1985). India earned the name of 'Big Brother' from many of the neighbouring countries.

7. Links with Commonwealth

In 1949 itself, India declared the continuation of her full membership of the Commonwealth of the Nations and the acceptance of the British Crown as the head of the Commonwealth. But, this extra-constitutional declaration does not affect India's sovereignty in any manner as the Commonwealth is a voluntary association of independent nations. It also does not affect India's republican character as India neither pays final allegiance to the British Crown nor the latter has any functions to discharge in relation to India.

India remained a member of the Commonwealth because of pragmatic reasons. It thought that the membership in the Commonwealth would be beneficial to her in the economic, political, cultural and other spheres. It has been playing an important role at the CHOGM (Commonwealth Heads of Governments Meet). India hosted the 24th Commonwealth Summit at New Delhi in 1983.

8. Support to the UNO

India became a member of the UNO in 1945 itself. Since then, it has been supporting the activities and programmes of UNO. It has expressed full faith in the objectives and principles of UNO. Some of the facets of India's role in UNO are:

  (i) It is through the UNO that India embarked on the policy of fighting against the colonialism, imperialism and racialism, and now neo-colonialism and neo-imperialism.

(ii) In 1953, Vijay Lakshmi Pandit of India was elected as the President of the UN General Assembly.

(iii) India actively participated in the UN Peace-keeping missions in Korea, Congo, El Salvador, Combodia, Angola, Somalia, Mozambique, Sierra Leone, Yugoslavia and so on.

(iv) India continued to participate actively in the open ended working groups of the UNO. India was the Co-chairman of the working group on the strengthening of the UN which submitted its report in 1997.

(v) Several times, India has been a non-permanent member of the UN Security Council. Now, India is demanding a permanent seat in the Security Council.

9. Disarmament

The foreign policy of India is opposed to arms race and advocates disarmament, both conventional and nuclear. This is aimed at promoting world peace and security by reducing or ending tensions between power blocs and to accelerate economic development of the country by preventing the unproductive expenditure on the manufacture of arms. India has been using the UNO platform to check the arms race and to achieve disarmament. India took the initiative of holding a six-nation summit at New Delhi in 1985 and made concrete proposals for nuclear disarmament.

By not signing the Nuclear Non-proliferation Treaty (NPT) of 1968 and the Comprehensive Test Ban Treaty (CTBT) of 1996, India has kept its nuclear options open. India opposses NPT and CTBT due to their discriminatory and hegemonistic nature. They perpetuate an international system in which only five nations (USA, Russia, China, UK and France) can legitimately posses nuclear weapons.

Objectives of Indian Foreign Policy

India's foreign policy is directed towards the realisation of the following objectives[5]:

1. To protect India's core national interests and concerns in a rapidly changing international environment by fostering support and understanding in the international community.

2. To preserve the autonomy of the decision making process and to play a pioneering role in the establishment of a stable, prosperous and secure global order.

3. To strengthen the international campaign against terrorism which is a global threat.

4. To build an international environment which is supportive of India's rapid economic growth including higher investments, trade, access to technology and strengthening India's energy security.

5. To work closely with P-5 countries and to build strategic ties with the major powers such as the USA, the EU, Japan, Russia, and China.

6. To intensify and strengthen ties with neighbours through mutually beneficial cooperation and by acknowledgement of each other's legitimate concerns.

7. To work for the realisation of SAARC as an economically integrated region at peace with itself and engaged with the world.

8. To ensure that cross-border terrorism is brought to an end and the entire infrastructure of terrorism operating from Pakistan is dismantled.

9. To further the gains from India's 'Look East' Policy and aspire for substantive progress in several areas of common interest to India and ASEAN.

10. To strengthen our ties with the countries of the Gulf region that has become home to over 4 million Indians and is a major source of supply of oil and gas.

11. To leverage economic growth through support to the activities of regional organisations like the Bay of Bengal Initiative for Multi-Sectoral Technical and Economic Cooperation (BIMSTEC), Mekong-Ganga Cooperation and trans-regional groupings like the India, Brazil and South Africa (IBSA) Initiative and Indian Ocean Rim Association for Regional Cooperation (IOR-ARC).

12. To continue to work closely with regional groupings like the EU and G-20 for furthering India's interests in the international arena.

13. To reform and restructure the UN Security Council and espouse multi-polarity in a world order that respects the principles of sovereignty and non-intervention.

14. To promote a more equitable equation between the developed and the developing world in the political, economic and technological domains.
15. To work towards the goal of global nuclear disarmament within a time-bound framework.
16. To closely interact with the Indian diaspora on a continuing basis in order to strengthen their bonds with India and to recognise their pivotal role in India's international relations.

LOOK EAST POLICY OF INDIA

India's 'Look East' Policy was first initiated in 1992 by the then Prime Minister P.V. Narasimha Rao. Since then, the policy has been one of the cornerstones of India's foreign policy.

The policy is a strategic shift in India's vision of the world and India's place in the evolving global economy. It lays emphasis on improving cooperation with India's neighbouring south-east and east Asian countries.

The policy is pursued in a multi-faceted manner in diverse areas such as improved connectivity, promotion of trade and investment and cultural exchanges. Some of the important developments of the policy, *interalia*, relate to initiating/resuming dialogue/trade with China, Bangladesh, Myanmar, Thailand and other countries of ASEAN.

The policy has also been pursued through constructive engagement with various regional groupings/organisations such as ASEAN, East Asia Summit, Bay of Bengal Initiative for Multi-Sectoral Technical and Economic Cooperation (BIMSTEC) and Mekong-Ganga Cooperation (MGC).

The policy, originally conceived as an economic initiative, has gained political, strategic and regional dimensions. It has renewed India's civilisational and historical ties with the Southeast and East Asian region on the strategic, military, political, economic, cultural and people-to-people level.

GUJRAL DOCTRINE OF INDIA

The Gujral Doctrine is a milestone in India's foreign policy. It was propounded and initiated in 1996 by I.K. Gujral, the then Foreign Minister in the Deve Gowda Government.

The doctrine advocates that India, being the biggest country in South Asia, should extend unilateral concessions to the smaller neighbours. In other words, the doctrine is formulated on India's accommodating approach towards its smaller neighbours on the basis of the principle of non-reciprocity. It recognises the supreme importance of friendly and cordial relations with India's neighbours.

The doctrine is a five-point roadmap to guide the conduct of India's foreign relations with its immediate neighbours. These five principles are as follows:

1. With the neighbous like Bangladesh, Bhutan, Maldives, Nepal and Sri Lanka, India should not ask for reciprocity, but give to them what it can in good faith.
2. No South Asian country should allow its territory to be used against the interest of another country of the region.
3. No country should interfere in the internal affairs of another country.
4. All South Asian countries should respect each other's territorial integrity and sovereignty.
5. All South Asian countries should settle all their disputes through peaceful bilateral negotiations.

Gujral himself explained: "The logic behind the Gujral Doctrine was that since we had to face two hostile neighbours in the north and the west, we had to be at 'total peace' with all other immediate neighbours in order to contain Pakistan's and China's influence in the region."

NUCLEAR DOCTRINE OF INDIA

India adopted its nuclear doctrine in 2003. The salient features of this doctrine are as follows:

1. Building and maintaining a credible minimum deterrent.
2. A posture of "No First Use" – nuclear weapons will only be used in retaliation against a nuclear attack on Indian territory or on Indian forces anywhere.
3. Nuclear retaliation to a first strike will be massive and designed to inflict unacceptable damage.
4. Nuclear retaliatory attacks can only be authorised by the civilian political leadership through the Nuclear Command Authority.

5. Non-use of nuclear weapons against non-nuclear weapon states.

6. However, in the event of a major attack against India, or Indian forces anywhere, by biological or chemical weapons, India will retain the option of retaliating with nuclear weapons.

7. A continuance of strict controls on export of nuclear and missile related materials and technologies, participation in the Fissile Material Cutoff Treaty negotiations, and continued observance of the moratorium on nuclear tests.

8. Continued commitment to the goal of a nuclear-weapon-free world, through global, verifiable and non-discriminatory nuclear disarmament.

The Nuclear Command Authority comprises a Political Council and an Executive Council. The Political Council is chaired by the Prime Minister. It is the sole body which can authorise the use of nuclear weapons.

The Executive Council is chaired by the National Security Advisor. It provides inputs for decision making by the Nuclear Command Authority and executes the directives given to it by the Political Council.

The Cabinet Committee on Security (CCS) reviewed the progress in the operationalising of India's nuclear doctrine. The CCS reviewed the existing command and control structures, the state of readiness, the targeting strategy for a retaliatory attack, and operating procedures for various stages of alert and launch. The CCS expressed satisfaction with the overall preparedness.

The CCS approved the appointment of a Commander-in-Chief, Strategic Forces Command, to manage and administer all Strategic Forces. The CCS also reviewed and approved the arrangements for alternate chains of command for retaliatory nuclear strikes in all eventualities.

NOTES AND REFERENCES

1. It includes world political climate, world public opinion and world organisations.

2. India again re-established full diplomatic relations with South Africa in 1994 when the policy of racial discrimination was finally given up and democratic government under Nelson Mandela came into existence.

3. AS Narang: *Indian Government and Politics*, Gitanjali, 2000 Edition, P. 602.

4. DN Mallik: *The Development of Non-Alignment in India's Foreign Policy*, P. 165.

5. *India 2009: A Reference Manual*, Publications Division, Government of India, p. 530.

PART XI

WORKING OF THE CONSTITUTION

71. National Commission to Review the Working of the Constitution

National Commission to Review the Working of the Constitution

The National Commission to Review the Working of the Constitution (NCRWC) was set up by a resolution of the Government of India in 2000[1]. The 11-member Commission was headed by M.N. Venkatachaliah, the former Chief Justice of India[2]. It submitted its report in 2002[3].

I. Terms of Reference of the Commission

According to the terms of reference, the commission was required to examine, in the light of the experience of the past fifty years, as to how far the existing provisions of the Constitution are capable of responding to the needs of efficient, smooth and effective system of governance and socio-economic development of modern India and to recommend changes, if any. The terms of reference clearly specified that the commission should recommend changes that are required to be made in the Constitution within the framework of parliamentary democracy and without interfering with the 'basic structure' or 'basic features' of the Constitution.

The commission clarified that its task was to review the working of the Constitution and not to rewrite it and its function was only recommendatory and advisory in nature. It was left to the Parliament to accept or reject any of the recommendations.

The commission had no agenda before it. On its own, it identified the eleven areas of study and proposed to examine them. They included the following[4]:

1. Strengthening of the institutions of parliamentary democracy (working of the Legislature, the Executive and the Judiciary; their accountability; problems of administrative, social and economic cost of political instability; exploring the possibilities of stability within the discipline of parliamentary democracy).
2. Electoral reforms; standards in political life.
3. Pace of socio-economic change and development under the Constitution (assurance of social and economic rights: how fair? how fast? how equal?).
4. Promoting literacy; generating employment; ensuring social security; alleviation of poverty.
5. Union-State relations.
6. Decentralization and devolution; empowerment and strengthening of Panchayati Raj Institutions.
7. Enlargement of Fundamental Rights.
8. Effectuation of Fundamental Duties.
9. Effectuation of Directive Principles and achievement of the Preambular objectives of the Constitution.
10. Legal control of fiscal and monetary policies; public audit mechanism.
11. Administrative system and standards in public life.

II. Fifty Years of Working of the Constitution

The observations made by the Commission on the working of the Constitution from 1950 to 2000 are as follows[5]:

What are our achievements and failures over the 50 years since Independence? How have each of the three organs of the State—the Legislature, the Executive and the Judiciary—redeemed the constitutional pledge of ushering in a social revolution? Has the dream of the founding fathers for a life of dignity to the vast millions through the process of socio-economic transformation been realized ? What then is the Balance Sheet ?

1. Political Accomplishments

1. India's democratic base has stabilized as a working federal polity. With the 73rd and 74th Constitutional amendments, the base of democratic debate has widened. There is greater push towards non-centralisation. General Elections have been held with regularity; and transfers of power consequent upon the results of elections have been orderly, peaceful and democratic.
2. The educational qualifications of the Members of Parliament and State Legislatures have shown marked improvements. The Parliament and State Legislatures are increasingly more representative of the composition of society. More and more members of the hitherto backward classes are moving up in the political ladder.

2. Economic Infrastructure—Impressive Performance

1. There has been marked expansion and diversification of production. New technologies and modern management techniques are increasingly employed. There are marked advances in Science, Technology, Medicine, Engineering and Information Technology.
2. Between 1950-2000, the index of agricultural production increased from 46.2 to 176.8.
3. Between 1960-2000, wheat production went up from 11 million tonnes to 75.6 million tonnes.

4. Between 1960-2000, rice production went up from 35 million tonnes to 89.5 million tonnes.
5. Impressive expansion of industrial and service sectors has taken place.
6. Index of industrial production went up from 7.9 in 1950-51 to 154.7 in 1999-2000.
7. Electricity generation has increased from 5.1 billion KWH in 1950-51 to 480.7 billion KWH in 1999-2000.
8. 6 to 8 per cent annual growth of GNP between 1994-2000 (except in 1997-98) was achieved.
9. Revenues from Information Technology industry have grown from $ 150 million in 1990 to $ 4 billion in 1999.
10. India's per capita Net National Product (NNP) in 1999-2000 was more than 2.75 times than what it was in 1951.

3. Social Infrastructure—Achievements

1. Between 1950 to 1998, infant mortality rate have halved to 72 births per 1000 births—down from 146.
2. Life expectancy at birth has grown up from 32 years in 1950-51 to 63 years in 2000.
3. A child born in Kerala today can expect to live longer than a child born in Washington.
4. Life expectancy of women in Kerala is now 75 years.
5. India has put in place an extensive system of Public Health Services and medical network. In 1951, the country had only 725 primary health centers. By 1995, this has increased to more than 1,50,000.
6. The number of primary schools has increased significantly between 1951 and 1995 from 2,10,000 to 5,90,000.
7. Nearly 95 per cent of the villages have a primary school within a walking distance of one kilometer.

4. Political Failures

1. The main cause and source of political-decay is the ineptness of the electoral process which has not been able to keep out criminal, anti-social and undesirable elements from participating in

and even dominating the political scene and polluting the electoral and parliamentary processes.

2. Though democratic traditions are stabilizing, however, democracy cannot be said to be an inclusive representative democracy. The pluralism and diversity of India is not reflected in and captured by its democratic institutions; likewise, participation of women in public affairs and decision-making processes is nowhere near proportionate to their numbers.

3. The enormity of the costs of elections and electoral corruption have been having a grievous deleterious effect on national progress and has led to the degradation of political processes to detriment of common good.

4. Political parties, which have a fair share of the criminal elements, handle enormous funds collected ostensibly for meeting party and electoral expenditure. Money-power and criminal elements have contributed to pervasive degeneration of standards in public life and have criminalized politics. This is reflected in the quality of governments and of the governing processes.

5. There are no legal instrumentalities or set of law regulating the conduct of the political parties, legitimacy of fund-raising, audit and account requirements and inner-party democracy.

6. National political parties are more divided on the definition of 'common national purpose' than ever before; the noble purposes of public life have degenerated than ever before into opportunistic and self-seeking politics of competitive personal gain.

7. 'Fraternity', the noble ideal of brotherhood of man, enshrined in the Preamble of the Constitution has remained unrealized. The people of India are more divided amongst themselves than at the time of the country's independence.

8. There is increasing criminalization and exploitation of the political climate and processes and an increasing criminals-politicians-bureaucratic nexus.

9. There is crisis of confidence. There is crisis of leadership. Political leaders, owing to narrow partisan and sectarian interests and desire for short-time political gains, are unable even to agree upon broad common national purposes.

5. Economic Failures

1. The richest top quintile of population has 85 per cent of the income. The poorest quintile has only 1.5 per cent of the country's income. The second, the third and the fourth quintile from top have respectively 8 per cent, 3.5 per cent and 2 per cent of the income.

2. 260 million people live below the poverty line.

6. Social Failures

1. India's maternal mortality rate in 1998 was 407 per 100,000 live births. These levels are more than 100 times the levels found in the West.

2. Some 53 per cent children (almost 60 million) under five remain malnourished—nearly twice the levels reported in many parts of sub-Saharan Africa.

3. The proportion of low birth weight babies born in India is 33 per cent. It is only 9 per cent in China and South Korea, 6 per cent in Thailand and 8 per cent in Indonesia.

4. India was a signatory to the Alma Ata Declaration in 1978 that assured 'health for all' by the year 2000. Only 42 per cent of the children between 12-23 months are fully immunized – 37 per cent in rural areas and 61 per cent in urban areas. The coverage is shockingly low in Bihar – 11 per cent and in Rajasthan – 17 per cent.

5. While per capita daily consumption of cereals has improved only marginally from 400 gms in 1950 to about 440 gms in 2000, the per capita pulses (protein intake) have over the 50 years decreased.

6. The promise of social revolution has remained unredeemed. There are 270 million Scheduled Castes and Scheduled Tribes and the measures for their welfare and uplift have not been implemented with sincerity.

7. There are 380 million children below the age of 14. Almost 100 million of them are Dalit children. No effective steps are taken to bring them to the level of the "core-mainstream".

8. Population control measures in the northern States have not succeeded. Fertility rates in Uttar Pradesh indicate that the State is almost a century behind Kerala.

7. Administrative Failures

1. Corruption, insensitivity and inefficiency of administration have resulted in extra-legal systems and parallel economies and even parallel governments. Bureaucratic corruption, which cause frustration in people in their daily lives, has pushed more and more people into extra-legal systems. The mal-administration has resulted in a lack of faith in and disenchantment with institutions of democracy.

2. There is an increasing non-accountability. Corruption has been pervasive. Public interest has suffered.

3. Constitutional protection for the Services under Article 311 has largely been exploited by dishonest officials to protect themselves from the consequences of their wrong-doings.

8. Gender Justice and Equality— Failures

1. The regional disparities in life expectancy is indicated by the fact that a woman born in Kerala can expect to live 18 years longer than one born in Madhya Pradesh.

2. In most countries life expectancy among women exceeds that of men by about 5 years. In all but a few countries of the world, there are typically 1005 women for every 1000 men. Men outnumber women only in societies where women are specifically and systematically discriminated. In India, there are only 933 women for every 1000 men. This is the phenomenon about 'missing' women.

3. Overall representation of women in public services is just 4.9 per cent.

4. Political participation of women indicates that in 1952 there were only 22 women in Łok Sabha against 499 seats (4.41 per cent). In 1991, this increased to 49 seats as against 544 seats (9.02 per cent).

5. Between 1995-2000, out of 503 judges of the High Court, only 15 were women.

9. Judicial System—Failures

1. Judicial system has not been able to meet even the modest expectations of the society. Its delays and costs are frustrating, its processes slow and uncertain.

2. People are pushed to seek recourse to extra-legal methods for relief.

3. Trial system both on the civil and criminal side has utterly broken down.

On an overall assessment, there are more failures than success stories, making the inference inescapable that the fifty years of the working of the Constitution is substantially a saga of missed opportunities.

III. Areas of Concern: Commission's Perception

The following are the important areas of concern according to the perception of the Commission[6] :

1. There is a fundamental breach of the constitutional faith on the part of Governments and their method of governance lies in the neglect of the people who are the ultimate source of all political authority. Public servants and institutions are not alive to the basic imperative that they are servants of the people meant to serve them. The dignity of the individual enshrined in the Constitution has remained an unredeemed pledge. There is, thus, a loss of faith in the Governments and governance. Citizens see their Governments besieged by uncontrollable events and are losing faith in institutions. Society is unable to cope up with current events.

2. The foremost area of concern is the present nature of the Indian State and its inability to anticipate and provide for the great global forces of change ushered in by the pace of scientific and technological developments.

3. The next and equally important dimension is the increasing cost of government and fiscal deficits which are alarming. In 1947, there was a deficit of ₹2 crores in the revenue budget; in 1997–98, it became ₹88,937 crores; in 2001-02, it is about ₹1,16,000 crores (4.8 per cent of GDP). India is on its way to a debt-trap.

4. There is pervasive impurity of the political climate and of political activity. Criminalisation of politics, political-corruption and the politician-criminal-bureaucratic nexus have reached unprecedented levels needing strong systemic changes.

5. Issues of national integrity and security have not received adequate and thoughtful attention. Mechanisms for the assessment of early warning symptoms of social unrest are absent. Mechanisms for adequate and immediate state responses to emergencies and disaster management are wholly inadequate. Administration, as a system for anticipating coming events and planning responses in advance, has failed. It has become un-coordinated and directionless amalgam of different departments often with over-lapping and even mutually conflicting jurisdictions, powers and responsibilities which merely acts as a reaction to problems. There are no clear-cut standards or basis for fixing responsibilities.

6. Though India's overall record and experience as a working democracy (despite many centrifugal forces) are worthy to mention and though the bases of democratic debate have widened with the 73rd and 74th Constitutional amendments, the working of the institutions of parliamentary democracy, however, have thrown-up serious fault-lines, which might, if unattended, prove destructive of the basic democratic values.

7. There is pervasive misuse of the electoral process and the electoral system is unable to prevent the entry of persons with criminal record into the portal of law-making institutions.

8. The Parliament and the State Legislatures, owing to the inherent weakness of the electoral system, have failed to acquire adequate representative character. The 13th Lok Sabha represents only 27.9 per cent of the total electorate and the Legislature of U.P. represents only 22.2 per cent of electorate respectively.

9. The increasing instability of the elected governments is attributable to opportunistic politics and unprincipled defections. The economic and administrative costs of political instability are unaffordably high and their impact on the polity is not clearly comprehended and realized. Though just four Prime Ministers ruled the country for 40 years out of the 54 years of independence and one political party alone was in power for 45 years, however, 1989 onwards the country saw five General Elections to the Lok Sabha. Costs of this political instability are simply colossal.

10. The state of the Indian economy is disturbing. The economy is gradually sinking into a debt-trap. Economic, fiscal and monetary policies, coupled with administrative inefficiency, corruption and wasteful expenditure are increasingly pushing the society into extra-legal systems, crime-syndicates, mob-rule and hoodlum out-fits. Black-money, parallel economy and even parallel governments are the overarching economic and social realities. Legitimate governments will, in due course, find it increasingly difficult to confront them. In course of time these illegal criminal out-fits will dictate terms to the legitimate governments.

11. Rural de-population, urbanization, urban-congestion and social unrest need immediate attention and solutions. Increasing unemployment will prove a serious threat to orderly government.

12. Future of society is increasingly knowledge-based and knowledge-driven. The quality of education and the higher research need urgent repair. The country is engaged in a unilateral and unthinking educational disarmament.

13. System of administration of justice in the country is another area of concern.

14. Criminal justice system is on the verge of collapse. The quality of investigations and prosecutions requires a strong second look. Law's delay and costs of litigation have become proverbial. Victimology, victim-protection and protection of witnesses in sensitive criminal-trials need institutional arrangements. Recruitment, training, refresher and continuing legal education for lawyers, judges and judicial administrators need immediate attention. The increasing utilization of alternative dispute resolution mechanisms such as mediation, conciliation and arbitration as well as mechanisms of auxiliary adjudicative services need to be stressed.

15. Communal and other inter-group riots in a country like India with its religious, social and cultural diversity cannot be treated as merely law and order problem. They are manifestations of collective behavioural disorders. Legal and administrative measures are required to be taken

to remove the insecurity felt by the minorities and for bringing them into the mainstream of the national fabric.

16. The state of social infrastructure is disturbing. There are 380 million children below the age of 14. The arrangements for their education, health and well-being are wholly inadequate both qualitatively and quantitatively. 96.4 per cent of the primary education budget goes for salaries alone.

17. Rates of infant mortality, blindness, maternal mortality, maternal-anemia, child malnutrition and child-immunization, despite significant progress achieved, yet remain at high and disconcerting levels.

18. Public health and hygiene have not received adequate attention. There is alarming increase of infectious diseases such as Tuberculosis, Malaria, Hepatitis, HIV etc.

IV. Recommendations of the Commission

In all, the commission made 249 recommendations. Of them, 58 recommendations involve amendments to the Constitution, 86 involve legislative measures and the remaining 105 recommendations could be accomplished through executive action.

The various recommendations of the commission are mentioned below in an area-wise manner[7] :

1. On Fundamental Rights

1. The scope of prohibition against discrimination (under Articles 15 and 16) should be extended to include 'ethnic or social origin, political or other opinion, property or birth'.

2. The freedom of speech and expression (under Article 19) should be expanded to include explicitly 'the freedom of the press and other media, the freedom to hold opinions and to seek, receive and impart information and ideas'.

3. The following should be added as new Fundamental Rights :
   (a) Right against torture, cruelty and inhuman treatment or punishment.
   (b) Right to compensation if a person is illegally deprived of his right to life or liberty.
   (c) Right to leave and to return to India.

   (d) Right to privacy and family life.
   (e) Right to rural wage employment for a minimum of 80 days in a year.
   (f) Right to access to courts and tribunals and speedy justice.
   (g) Right to equal justice and free legal aid[8].
   (h) Right to care and assistance and protection (in case of children).
   (i) Right to safe drinking water, prevention of pollution, conservation of ecology and sustainable development.

4. The right to education (under Article 21-A) should be enlarged to read as : 'Every child shall have the right to free education until he completes the age of fourteen years; and in the case of girls and members of the SCs and STs until they complete the age of eighteen years'.

5. Two changes should be made with respect to preventive detention (under Article 22), namely, (i) the maximum period of preventive detention should be six months; and (ii) the advisory board should consist of a chairman and two other members and they should be serving judges of any high court.

6. Sikhism, Jainism and Buddhism should be treated as religions separate from Hinduism and the provisions grouping them together (under Article 25) should be deleted. At present, the word 'Hindu' is defined to include these religions also.

7. The protection from judicial review afforded by Article 31-B to the Acts and Regulations specified in the Ninth Schedule should be restricted to only those which relate to (i) agrarian reforms, (ii) reservations, and (iii) the implementation of Directive Principles specified in clause (b) or (c) of Article 39.

8. No suspension of the enforcement of the Fundamental Rights under Articles 17, 23, 24, 25 and 32 in addition to those under Articles 20 and 21 during the operation of a national emergency (under Article 352).

2. On Right to Property

Article 300-A should be recast as follows:

1. Deprivation or acquisition of property shall be by authority of law and only for a public purpose.

2. There shall be no arbitrary deprivation or acquisition of property.

3. No deprivation or acquisition of agricultural, forest and non-urban homestead land belonging to or customarily used by the SCs and STs shall take place except by authority of law which provides for suitable rehabilitation scheme before taking possession of such land. In brief, a right to 'suitable rehabilitation' for the SCs and STs if their land is to be acquired.

3. On Directive Principles

1. The heading of Part-IV of the Constitution should be amended to read as 'Directive Principles of State Policy and Action'.

2. A new Directive Principle on control of population should be added.

3. An independent National Education Commission should be set-up every five years.

4. An Inter-Faith Commission should be established to promote inter-religious harmony and social solidarity.

5. There must be a body of high status to review the level of implementation of the Directive Principles.

6. A strategic Plan of Action should be initiated to create a large number of employment opportunities in five years.

7. Implementation of the recommendations contained in the Report of the National Statistical Commission (2001).

4. On Fundamental Duties

1. Consideration should be given to the ways and means by which Fundamental Duties could be popularized and made effective.

2. The recommendations of the Justice Verma Committee on operationalisation of Fundamental Duties should be implemented at the earliest[9].

3. The following new fundamental duties should be included in Article 51-A:

   (a) Duty to vote at elections, actively participate in the democratic process of governance and to pay taxes.

   (b) To foster a spirit of family values and responsible parenthood in the matter of education, physical and moral well-being of children.

   (c) Duty of industrial organizations to provide education to children of their employees.

5. On Parliament and State Legislatures

1. The privileges of legislators should be defined and delimited for the free and independent functioning of Parliament and state legislatures.

2. Article 105 may be amended to clarify that the immunity enjoyed by members under parliamentary privileges does not cover corrupt acts committed by them in connection with their duties in the House or otherwise. Further, no court would take cognizance of any offence arising out of a member's action in the House without prior sanction of the Speaker / Chairman. Article 194 may also be similarly amended in relation to the members of state legislatures.

3. The domiciliary requirement for eligibility to contest elections to Rajya Sabha from the concerned state should be maintained. This is essential to ensure the federal character of the Rajya Sabha.

4. The MP local area development scheme should be discontinued.

5. The Election Commission should be empowered to identify and declare the various offices under the central and state governments to be 'offices of profit' for the purposes of being chosen, and for being, a member of the appropriate legislature.

6. Immediate steps be taken to set up a Nodal Standing Committee on National Economy.

7. A Standing Constitution Committee of the two Houses of Parliament for a priori scrutiny of constitutional amendment proposals should be set up.

8. A new Legislation Committee of Parliament to oversee and coordinate legislative planning should be constituted.

9. The existing Parliamentary Committees on Estimates, Public Undertakings and Subordinate Legislation may not be continued.

10. The Parliamentarians must voluntarily place themselves open to public scrutiny through a parliamentary ombudsman.

11. The State Legislatures with less than 70 members should meet for at least 50 days in a year and other State Legislatures for at least 90 days. Similarly, the minimum number of days for sittings of Rajya Sabha and Lok Sabha should be fixed at 100 and 120 days respectively.
12. A Study Group outside Parliament for study of procedural reforms should be set up.

6. On Executive and Administration

1. In case of hung Parliament, the Lok Sabha may elect the leader of the House. He may then be appointed as the prime minister by the president. The same procedure could be followed at the state level also.
2. A motion of no-confidence against a prime minister must be accompanied by a proposal of alternative leader to be voted simultaneously. This is called as the 'system of constructive vote of no confidence'.
3. For a motion of no-confidence to be brought out against the government, at least 20 per cent of the total number of members of the House should give notice.
4. The practice of having oversized Council of Ministers should be prohibited by law. A ceiling on the number of Ministers in any State or the Union government be fixed at the maximum of 10 per cent of the total strength of the popular house of the legislature.
5. The practice of creating a number of political offices with the position, perks and privileges of a minister should be discouraged. Their number should be limited to 2 per cent of the total strength of the lower house.
6. The Constitution should provide for appointment of Lokpal keeping the prime minister outside its purview and the institution of lokayuktas in the states.
7. Lateral entry into government jobs above joint secretary level should be allowed.
8. Article 311 should be amended to ensure not only protection to the honest public servants but penalisation to dishonest ones.
9. The questions of personnel policy including placements, promotions, transfers and fast-track advancements should be managed by autonomous Civil Service Boards constituted under statutory provisions.
10. Officials, before starting their career, in addition to the taking of an oath of loyalty to the Constitution, should swear to abide by the principles of good governance.
11. Right to information should be guaranteed and the traditional insistence on secrecy should be discarded. In fact, there should be an oath of transparency in place of an oath of secrecy.
12. Public Interest Disclosure Acts (which are popularly called the Whistle-blower Acts) may be enacted to fight corruption and mal-administration.
13. A law should be enacted to provide for forfeiture of benami property of corrupt public servants as well as non-public servants.

7. On Centre-State and Inter-State Relations

1. The Inter-State Council Order of 1990 may clearly specify the matters that should form the parts of consultations.
2. Management of disasters and emergencies (both natural and manmade) should be included in the List III (Concurrent List) of the Seventh Schedule.
3. A statutory body called the Inter-State Trade and Commerce Commission should be established.
4. The president should appoint the governor of a state only after consultation with the chief minister of that state.
5. Article 356 should not be deleted, but it must be used sparingly and only as a remedy of the last resort.
6. The question whether the ministry in a state has lost the confidence of the assembly or not should be tested only on the floor of the House. The Governor should not be allowed to dismiss the ministry, so long as it enjoys the confidence of the House.
7. Even without the state being under a proclamation of emergency, President's Rule may be continued if elections cannot be held. Article 356 should be amended to this effect.

8. The State Assembly should not be dissolved before the proclamation issued under Article 356 has been laid before Parliament. Article 356 should be amended to ensure this.

9. River water disputes between States and / or the Centre should be heard and disposed by a bench of not less than three judges and if necessary, a bench of five judges of the Supreme Court for the final disposal of the suit.

10. Parliament should replace the River Boards Act of 1956 with another comprehensive enactment after consultation with all the states.

11. When the state bill is reserved for consideration of the President, there should be a time-limit (say of three months) within which the President should take a decision whether to give his assent or to return the bill.

8. On Judiciary

1. A National Judicial Commission under the Constitution should be established to recommend the appointment of judges of the Supreme Court. It should comprise the chief justice of India (as chairman), two senior most Judges of the Supreme Court, the Union law minister and one person nominated by the president.

2. A committee of the National Judicial Commission should examine complaints of deviant behaviour of the Supreme Court and high court judges.

3. The retirement age of the judges of high courts and Supreme Court should be increased to 65 and 68 respectively.

4. No court other than the Supreme Court and the High Courts should have the power to punish for contempt of itself.

5. Except the Supreme Court and the High Courts, no other court should have the power to declare the Acts of Parliament and State Legislatures as being unconstitutional or beyond legislative competence and so ultra-vires.

6. A National Judicial Council and Judicial Councils in States should be set up for the preparation of plans and annual budget proposals.

7. In the Supreme Court and the High Courts, judgements should ordinarily be delivered within 90 days from the conclusion of the case.

8. An award of exemplary costs should be given in appropriate cases of abuse of process of law.

9. Each High Court should prepare a strategic plan for time-bound clearance of arrears in courts within its jurisdiction. No case to remain pending for more than one year.

10. The system of plea-bargaining should be introduced as part of the process of decriminalization.

11. The hierarchy of the subordinate courts in the country should be brought down to a two-tier of subordinate judiciary under the High Court.

9. On Pace of Socio-Economic Change and Development

1. A way could and should be found to bring a reasonable number of SCs, STs and BCs on to the benches of the Supreme Court and high courts.

2. Social policy should aim at enabling the SCs, STs and BCs and with particular attention to the girls to compete on equal terms with the general category.

3. Appropriate new institutions should be established to ensure that the resources earmarked for the weaker sections are optimally used.

4. The Citizens' Charters be prepared by every service providing department / agency to enumerate the entitlements of the citizens specifically those of the SCs, STs and other deprived classes.

5. Reservation for SCs, STs and BCs should be brought under a statute covering all aspects of reservation including setting up of Arakshan Nyaya Adalats to adjudicate upon all disputes pertaining to reservation.

6. Residential schools for SCs, STs and BCs should be established in every district in the country.

7. All tribal areas governed by the Fifth Schedule of the Constitution should be transferred to the Sixth Schedule. Other tribal areas should also be brought under the Sixth Schedule.

8. Special courts exclusively to try offences under the SCs and STs (Prevention of Atrocities) Act, 1989, should be established.

9. Prevention of untouchability requires, inter alia, effective punitive action under the Protection of Civil Rights Act, 1955.

10. The Employment of Manual Scavengers and Construction of Dry Latrines (Prohibition) Act, 1993, should be strictly enforced.

11. Steps should be taken for improvement of educational standards as well as for increasing the political representation of the minority communities.

12. A fully empowered National Authority for the Liberation and Rehabilitation of bonded labour should be set up. Similar authorities should also be established at the state level.

13. As regards women, action covering reservation, development, empowerment, health and protection against violence should be taken.

10. On Decentralisation (Panchayats and Municipalities)

1. The Eleventh and Twelfth Schedules of the Constitution should be restructured in a manner that creates a separate fiscal domain for panchayats and municipalities.

2. State panchayat council should be established under the chairmanship of the chief minister.

3. Panchayats and Municipalities should be categorically declared to be 'institutions of self-government' and exclusive functions be assigned to them. For this purpose, Articles 243-G and 243-W should be suitably amended.

4. The Election Commission of India should have the power to issue directions to the State Election Commission for the discharge of its functions. The State Election Commission should submit its annual or special reports to the Election Commission of India and to the Governor. This requires the amendment of Articles 243-K and 243-ZA.

5. Article 243-E should be amended to the effect that a reasonable opportunity of being heard shall be given to a Panchayat before it is dissolved.

6. To ensure uniformity in the practice relating to audit of accounts, the CAG of India should be empowered to conduct the audit or lay down accounting standards for Panchayats.

7. Whenever a Municipality is superseded, a report stating the grounds for such dissolution should be placed before the State Legislature.

8. All provisions regarding qualifications and disqualifications for elections to local authorities should be consolidated in a single law.

9. The functions of delimitation, reservation and rotation of seats should be vested in a Delimitation Commission and not in the State Election Commission.

10. The concept of a distinct and separate tax domain for municipalities should be recognized.

11. On Institutions in North East India

1. Efforts are to be made to give all the States in this region the opportunities provided under the 73rd and 74th Constitutional Amendments. However, this should be done with due regard to the unique political traditions of the region.

2. The subjects given under the Sixth Schedule and those mentioned in the Eleventh Schedule could be entrusted to the Autonomous District Councils (ADCs).

3. Traditional forms of governance should be associated with self-governance because of the present dissatisfaction.

4. A National Immigration Council should be set up to examine a range of issues including review of the Citizenship Act, the Illegal Migrants Determination by Tribunal Act, the Foreigners Act and so on.

5. As regards Nagaland, the Naga Councils should be replaced by elected representatives of various Naga society groups with an intermediary tier at the district level.

6. As regards Assam, the Sixth Schedule should be extended to the Bodoland Autonomous Council and other Autonomous Councils be upgraded to Autonomous Development Councils.

7. As regards Meghalaya, a tier of village governance should be created for a village or a group of villages in the Autonomous District Councils.

8. As regards Tripura, the changes which may be made in respect of other Autonomous Councils should also apply in respect of the Autonomous District Councils.

9. As regards Mizoram, an intermediary elected tier should be developed at the district level in areas not covered by the Sixth Schedule.

10. As regards Manipur, the provisions of the Sixth Schedule should be extended to hill districts of the State.

12. On Electoral Processes

1. Any person charged with any offence punishable with imprisonment for a maximum term of five years or more, should be disqualified for being chosen as or for being a member of Parliament or Legislature of a State.

2. Any person convicted for any heinous crime like murder, rape, smuggling, dacoity, etc., should be permanently debarred from contesting for any political office.

3. Criminal cases against politicians pending before Courts either for trial or in appeal must be disposed of speedily, if necessary, by appointing Special Courts.

4. The election petitions should also be decided by special courts. In the alternative, special election benches may be constituted in the High Courts and earmarked exclusively for the disposal of election petitions and election disputes.

5. Any system of State funding of elections bears a close nexus to the regulation of working of political parties by law and to the creation of a foolproof mechanism under law with a view to implementing the financial limits strictly. Therefore, proposals for State funding should be deferred till these regulatory mechanisms are firmly in position.

6. Candidates should not be allowed to contest election simultaneously for the same office from more than one constituency.

7. The election code of conduct should be given the sanctity of law and its violation should attract penal action.

8. The Commission while recognizing the beneficial potential of the system of run off contest electing the representative winning on the basis of 50 per cent plus one vote polled, as against the present first-past-the-post system, for a more representative democracy, recommends that the Government and the Election Commission of India should examine this issue of prescribing a minimum of 50 per cent plus one vote for election in all its aspects.

9. An independent candidate who loses election three times consecutively should be permanently debarred from contesting election to the same office.

10. The minimum number of valid votes polled should be increased to 25 per cent from the current 16.67 per cent as a condition for the deposit not being forfeited.

11. The issue of eligibility of non-Indian born citizens or those whose parents or grandparents were citizens of India to hold high offices in the realm such as President, Vice-President, Prime Minister and Chief Justice of India should be examined in depth through a political process after a national dialogue[10].

12. The Chief Election Commissioner and the other Election Commissioners should be appointed on the recommendation of a body consisting of the Prime Minister, Leader of the Opposition in the Lok Sabha, Leader of the Opposition in the Rajya Sabha, the Speaker of the Lok Sabha and the Deputy Chairman of the Rajya Sabha. Similar procedure should be adopted in the case of appointment of State Election Commissioners.

13. On Political Parties

1. A comprehensive law regulating the registration and functioning of political parties or alliances of parties should be made. The proposed law should–

    (a) provide that political party or alliance should keep its doors open to all citizens irrespective of any distinctions of caste, community or the like.

    (b) make it compulsory for the parties to maintain accounts of the receipt of funds and expenditure in a systematic and regular way.

    (c) make it compulsory for the political parties requiring their candidates to declare their assets and liabilities at the time of filing their nomination.

    (d) provide that no political party should provide ticket to a candidate if he was convicted by any court for any criminal offence or if the courts have framed criminal charges against him.

(e) specifically provide that if any party violates the above provision , the candidate involved should be liable to be disqualified and the party deregistered and derecognized.

2. The Election Commission should progressively increase the threshold criterion for eligibility for recognition so that the proliferation of smaller political parties is discouraged.

3. A comprehensive legislation providing for regulation of contributions to the political parties and towards election expenses should be enacted by consolidating such laws. This new law should:

   (a) aim at bringing transparency into political funding;

   (b) permit corporate donations within higher prescribed limits;

   (c) make donations up to a specified limit tax exempt;

   (d) make both donors and donees of political funds accountable;

   (e) provide that audited political party accounts should be published yearly; and

(f) provide for de-recognition of the party and enforcement of penalties for filing false election returns.

14. On Anti-Defection Law

The provisions of the Tenth Schedule of the Constitution should be amended to provide the following:

1. All persons defecting (whether individually or in groups) from the party or the alliance of parties, on whose ticket they had been elected, must resign from their parliamentary or assembly seats and must contest fresh elections.

2. The defectors should be debarred to hold any public office of a minister or any other remunerative political post for at least the duration of the remaining term of the existing legislature or until the next elections whichever is earlier.

3. The vote cast by a defector to topple a government should be treated as invalid.

4. The power to decide questions regarding disqualification on ground of defection should vest in the Election Commission instead of in the Speaker / Chairman of the House concerned.

NOTES AND REFERENCES

1. The Ministry of Law and Justice (Department of Legal Affairs), vide its Resolution, dated the 22 February, 2000.

2. The other members of the Commission were : B.P. Jeevan Reddy (Chairman of the Law Commission), R.S. Sarkaria (former judge of the Supreme Court), K. Punnayya (former judge of the Andhra Pradesh High Court), Soli Sorabjee (Attorney–General of India), K. Parasaran (former Attorney–General of India), Subhash Kashyap (former Secretary–General of Lok Sabha), C.R. Irani (Chief Editor and MD of the Statesman), Abid Hussain (former Ambassador of India to the USA), Smt. Sumitra Kulkarni (former MP) and P.A. Sangma (former Speaker of the Lok Sabha). P.A. Sangma resigned three months before the submission of the report by the Commission.

3. The Commission was asked to complete its work and make recommendations within one

year. After three extensions, the Commission submitted its report on March 31, 2002. This report is a bulky one, containing 1,979 pages in two-volumes. Volume I contains its recommendations while Volume II (divided in Books 1, 2 and 3) consists of detailed consultation papers, background papers, details of deliberations and the report of its drafting and editorial committee.

4. Report of the Commission, Volume I, Chapter 1.

5. Report of the Commission, Volume I, Chapter 2.

6. Ibid.

7. Chapters 3 to 10 in Volume I of the Report of the Commission contains the detailed area-wise recommendations. The summary of recommendations is given in Chapter 11.

8. At present, it is a Directive Principle under Article 39-A.

9. The Government of India appointed the committee "to operationalise the suggestions to teach Fundamental Duties to the citizens of India" in the year 1998 under the chairmanship of Justice J.S. Verma. The Committee submitted its report in October 1999.

10. The Commission was deeply divided on this issue and because of this, P.A. Sangma left the Commission.

Appendix I

Articles of the Constitution (1–395)

UNION LIST (LIST-I)

1. Defence of India
2. Naval, military and air forces; any other armed forces of the Union
2A. Deployment of any armed force of the Union in any state in aid of the civil power
3. Cantonment areas and local self-government in such areas
4. Naval, military and air force works
5. Arms, firearms, ammunition, and explosives
6. Atomic energy and mineral resources necessary for its production
7. Defence industries
8. Central Bureau of Intelligence and investigation
9. Preventive detention for reasons connected with defence, foreign affairs, or the security of India
10. Foreign affairs
11. Diplomatic, consular and trade representation
12. United Nations Organisation
13. International conferences, associations and other bodies
14. Treaties, agreements and conventions with foreign countries
15. War and peace
16. Foreign jurisdiction
17. Citizenship, naturalisation and aliens
18. Extradition
19. Passports and visas
20. Pilgrimages to places outside India
21. Piracies and crimes committed on the high seas or in the air and offences against the law of nations.
22. Railways
23. National highways
24. Shipping and navigation on national waterways
25. Maritime shipping and navigation
26. Lighthouses for the safety of shipping and aircraft
27. Major ports
28. Port quarantine, seaman and marine hospitals
29. Airways; aircraft and air navigation; provision of aerodromes
30. Carriage of passengers and goods by railway, sea, air or national waterways
31. Posts and telegraphs; telephones, wireless, broadcasting and other like forms of communication
32. Property of the Union
33. (Omitted)
34. Courts of wards for the estates of rulers of Indian states
35. Public debt of the Union
36. Currency, coinage and legal tender; foreign exchange
37. Foreign loans
38. Reserve Bank of India
39. Post office savings bank
40. Lotteries organised by the Union or state
41. Trade and commerce with foreign countries
42. Inter-state trade and commerce
43. Trading corporations, including banking, insurance and financial corporations but not including co-operative societies
44. Corporations, whether trading or not, with objects not confined to one state
45. Banking
46. Bills of exchange, cheques, promissory notes and other like instruments
47. Insurance
48. Stock exchange and futures markets
49. Patents, inventions and designs; copyright; trademarks and merchandise marks

50. Establishment of standards of weight and measure
51. Establishment of standards of quality for goods to be exported out of India or transported from one state to another
52. Industries, the control of which by the Union is in the public interest
53. Oil fields and mineral oil resources; petroleum and petroleum products; other liquids and substances which are inflammable
54. Regulation of mines and mineral development in the public interest
55. Regulation of labour and safety in mines and oil fields
56. Regulation and development of inter-state rivers and river valleys
57. Fishing and fisheries beyond territorial waters
58. Manufacture, supply and distribution of salt by Union and other agencies
59. Cultivation and manufacture of opium and its export
60. Sanctioning of cinematograph films for exhibition
61. Industrial disputes concerning Union employees
62. National Library, the Indian Museum, the Imperial War Museum, the Victoria Memorial and the Indian War Memorial, and any other like institution of national importance
63. Benaras Hindu University, the Aligarh Muslim University and the Delhi University; any other institution of national importance
64. Scientific or technical education institutions of national importance
65. Union agencies and institutions for training, research or detection of crime
66. Standards in institutions for higher education or research and scientific and technical institutions
67. Ancient and historical monuments and records, and archaeological sites and remains of national importance
68. The Survey of India, the Geological, Botanical, Zoological and Anthropological Surveys of India; Meteorological organisations
69. Census
70. Union Public Services; All-India Services; Union Public Service Commission
71. Union pensions
72. Elections to Parliament, the legislatures of states and the offices of President and Vice-President; the Election Commission
73. Salaries and allowances of members and presiding officers of Parliament
74. Powers, privileges and immunities of each House of Parliament and of the members and the committees of each House
75. Emoluments and service conditions of the president, governors, the ministers for the Union and the Comptroller and Auditor General
76. Audit of the accounts of the Union and of the states
77. Organisation, jurisdiction and powers of the Supreme Court
78. Organisation of the high courts
79. Extension of the jurisdiction of a high court to any union territory
80. Extension of the powers and jurisdiction of members of a police force belonging to any state to any area outside that state
81. Inter-state migration; inter-state quarantine
82. Taxes on income other than agricultural income
83. Duties of customs including export duties
84. Duties of excise on tobacco and other goods except alcoholic liquors for human consumption and opium, Indian hamp and other narcotic drugs and narcotics, but including medicinal and toilet preparations containing alcohol
85. Corporation tax
86. Taxes on the capital value of the assets (exclusive of agricultural land) of individuals and companies; taxes on the capital of companies
87. Estate duty in respect of property other than agricultural land
88. Duties in respect of succession to property other than agricultural land
89. Terminal taxes on goods or passengers, carried by railway, sea or air; taxes on railway fares and freights
90. Taxes other than stamp duties on transactions in stock exchanges and futures markets
91. Rates of stamp duty in respect of bills of exchange, cheques, promissory notes, bills of lading, letters of credit, policies of insurance, transfer of shares, debentures, proxies and receipts
92. Taxes on the sale or purchase of newspapers and on advertisements published therein
92A. Taxes on the sale or purchase of goods other than newspapers, where such sale or purchase takes place in the course of inter-state trade or commerce
92B. Taxes on the consignment of goods in the course of inter-state trade or commerce
92C. Taxes on services
93. Offences against laws with respect to any of the matters in this list
94. Inquiries, surveys and statistics for the purpose of any of the matters in this list
95. Jurisdiction and powers of all courts (except the Supreme Court) with respect to any of the matters in this list; admiralty jurisdiction

96. Fees in respect of any of the matters in this list, but not including fees taken in any court
97. Any other matter not enumerated in List II or List III including any tax not mentioned in either of those lists

State List (list-II)

1. Public order
2. Police
3. Officers and servants of the high court
4. Prisons, reformatories, borstal institutions and other such institutions
5. Local government
6. Public health and sanitation
7. Pilgrimages, other than pilgrimages to places outside India
8. Intoxicating liquors
9. Relief of the disabled and unemployable
10. Burials and burial grounds
11. (Omitted)
12. Libraries, museums and other similar institutions; ancient and historical monuments and records other than those of national importance
13. Communications, that is, roads, bridges, ferries and other means of communication not specified in List I
14. Agriculture, including agricultural education and research
15. Preservation of stock and prevention of animal diseases
16. Pounds and the prevention of cattle trespass
17. Water, that is, water supplies, irrigation and canals, drainage and embankments, water storage and water power
18. Land, that is, right in or over land, land tenures and the collection of rents
19. (Omitted)
20. (Omitted)
21. Fisheries
22. Courts of wards
23. Regulation of mines and mineral development
24. Industries
25. Gas and gas-works
26. Trade and commerce within the state
27. Production, supply and distribution of goods
28. Markets and fairs
29. (Omitted)
30. Money-lending and money-lenders; relief of agricultural indebtedness
31. Inns and inn-keepers
32. Corporation, other than those specified in List I, and universities; unincorporated trading, literacy, scientific, religious and other societies and associations; co-operative societies
33. Theaters and dramatic performances; cinemas; sports, entertainments and amusements
34. Betting and gambling
35. Works, lands and buildings of the state
36. (Omitted)
37. Elections to the legislature of the state
38. Salaries and allowances of members and presiding officers of the legislature of the state
39. Powers, privileges and immunities of the legislature of the state and of the members and the committees thereof
40. Salaries and allowances of ministers for the state
41. States public services; State Public Service Commission
42. State pensions
43. Public debt of the state
44. Treasure trove
45. Land revenue, including maintenance of land records
46. Taxes on agricultural income
47. Duties in respect of succession to agricultural land
48. Estate duty in respect of agricultural land
49. Taxes on lands and buildings
50. Taxes on mineral rights
51. Duties of excise on alcoholic liquors for human consumption; opium, Indian hemp and other narcotic drugs and narcotics, but not including medicinal and toilet preparations containing alcohol
52. Taxes on the entry of goods into a local area
53. Taxes on the consumption or sale of electricity
54. Taxes on the sale or purchase of goods other than newspapers
55. Taxes on advertisements other than advertisements published in the newspapers and advertisements broadcast by radio or television
56. Taxes on goods and passengers carried by road or on inland waterways
57. Taxes on vehicles
58. Taxes on animals and boats
59. Tolls
60. Taxes on professions, trades, callings and employments
61. Capitation taxes
62. Taxes on luxuries, including taxes on entertainments, amusements, betting and gambling
63. Rates of stamp duty in respect of documents other than those specified in List I
64. Offences against laws with respect to any of the matters in this list

65. Jurisdiction and powers of all courts, except the Supreme Court, with respect to any of the matters in this list

66. Fees in respect of any of the matters in this list, but not including fees taken in any court

CONCURRENT LIST (LIST-III)

1. Criminal Law, including all matters included in the Indian Penal Code
2. Criminal procedure, including all matters included in the Code of Criminal Procedure
3. Preventive detention for reasons connected with the security of a state, the maintenance of public order, or the maintenance of supplies and services essential to the community
4. Removal from one state to another state of prisoners and accused persons
5. Marriage and divorce; infants and minors; adoption; wills, intestacy and succession; joint family and partition
6. Transfer of property other than agricultural land; registration of deeds and documents
7. Contracts
8. Actionable wrongs
9. Bankruptcy and insolvency
10. Trust and Trustees
11. Administrators-general and official trustees
11A. Administration of justice; constitution and organisation of all courts, except the Supreme Court and the high courts
12. Evidence and oaths; recognition of laws, public acts and records, and judicial proceedings
13. Civil procedure, including all matters included in the Code of Civil Procedure
14. Contempt of court, but not including contempt of the Supreme Court
15. Vagrancy; nomadic and migratory tribes
16. Lunacy and mental deficiency
17. Prevention of cruelty to animals
17A. Forests
17B. Protection of wild animals and birds
18. Adulteration of foodstuffs and other goods
19. Drugs and poisons
20. Economic and social planning
20A. Population control and family planning
21. Commercial and industrial monopolies, combines and trusts
22. Trade unions; industrial and labour disputes

23. Social security and social insurance; employment and unemployment
24. Welfare of labour including conditions of work, provident funds, employers' liability, workmen's compensation, invalidity and old age pensions and maternity benefits
25. Education, including technical education, medical education and universities
26. Legal, medical and other professions
27. Relief and rehabilitation of persons
28. Charitable institutions, religious endowments and religious institutions
29. Infectious or contagious diseases or pests affecting men, animals or plants
30. Vital statistics including registration of births and deaths
31. Ports other than major ports
32. Shipping and navigation on inland waterways
33. Trade and commerce in, and the production, supply and distribution of, foodstuffs, including edible oilseeds and oils; cattle fodder; raw cotton, and cotton seeds; and raw jute
33A. Weights and measures except establishment of standards
34. Price control
35. Mechanically propelled vehicles including the principles on which taxes on such vehicles are to be levied
36. Factories
37. Boilers
38. Electricity
39. Newspapers, books and printing presses
40. Archaeological sites and remains other than those of national importance
41. Evacuee property (including agricultural land)
42. Acquisition and requisitioning of property
43. Recovery in a state of claims in respect of taxes and other public demands
44. Stamp duties other than duties or fees collected by means of judicial stamps, but not including rates of stamp duty
45. Inquiries and statistics for the purposes of any of the matters specified in List II or List III
46. Jurisdiction and powers of all courts, except the Supreme Court, with respect to any of the matters in this list
47. Fees in respect of any of the matters in this list, but not including fees taken in any court

Appendix III

Table of Precedence

The Table of Precedence is related to the rank and order of the officials of the Union and State Governments. The present notification on this subject was issued on 26 July, 1979. This notification superseded all the previous notifications and was also amended many times. The updated version of the Table, containing all the amendments made therein so far (2013), is given below:

1. President
2. Vice-President
3. Prime Minister
4. Governors of states within their respective states
5. Former presidents
5A. Deputy Prime Minister
6. Chief Justice of India
   Speaker of Lok Sabha
7. Cabinet Ministers of the Union
   Chief Ministers of States within their respective States
   Deputy Chairman, Planning Commission
   Former Prime Ministers
   Leaders of Opposition in Rajya Sabha and Lok Sabha
7A. Holders of Bharat Ratna decoration
8. Ambassadors Extraordinary and Plenipotentiary and High Commissioners of Commonwealth countries accredited to India
   Chief Ministers of States outside their respective States
   Governors of States outside their respective States
9. Judges of Supreme Court
9A. Chairperson, Union Public Service Commission
   Chief Election Commissioner
   Comptroller & Auditor General of India
10. Deputy Chairman, Rajya Sabha

Deputy Chief Ministers of States
Deputy Speaker, Lok Sabha
Members of the Planning Commission
Ministers of State of the Union (and any other Minister in the Ministry of Defence for defence matters)

11. Attorney General of India
    Cabinet Secretary
    Lieutenant Governors within their respective Union Territories
12. Chiefs of Staff holding the rank of full General or equivalent rank
13. Envoys Extraordinary and Ministers Plenipotentiary accredited to India
14. Chairmen and Speakers of State Legislatures within their respective States
    Chief Justices of High Courts within their respective jurisdictions
15. Cabinet Ministers in States within their respective States
    Chief Ministers of Union Territories and Chief Executive Councillor, Delhi within their respective Union Territories
    Deputy Ministers of the Union
16. Officiating Chiefs of Staff holding the rank of Lieutenant General or equivalent rank
17. Chairman, Central Administrative Tribunal
    Chairman, Minorities Commission
    Chairperson, National Commission for Scheduled Castes
    Chairperson, National Commission for Scheduled Tribes
    Chief Justices of High Courts outside their respective jurisdictions

Puisne Judges of High Courts within their respective jurisdictions

18. Cabinet Ministers in States outside their respective States

    Chairmen and Speakers of State Legislatures outside their respective States

    Chairman, Monopolies and Restrictive Trade Practices Commission

    Deputy Chairmen and Deputy Speakers of State Legislatures within their respective States

    Ministers of State in States within their respective States

    Ministers of Union Territories and Executive Councilors, Delhi, within their respective Union Territories

    Speakers of Legislative Assemblies in Union Territories and Chairman of Delhi Metropolitan Council within their respective Union Territories

19. Chief Commissioners of Union Territories not having Councils of Ministers, within their respective Union Territories

    Deputy Ministers in States within their respective States

    Deputy Speakers of Legislative Assemblies in Union Territories and Deputy Chairman of Metropolitan Council, Delhi, within their respective Union Territories

20. Deputy Chairmen and Deputy Speakers of State Legislatures, outside their respective States

    Ministers of State in States outside their respective States

    Puisne Judges of High Courts outside their respective jurisdictions

21. Members of Parliament

22. Deputy Ministers in States outside their respective States

23. Army Commanders / Vice-Chief of the Army Staff or equivalent in other services

    Chief Secretaries to State Governments within their respective States

    Commissioner for Linguistic Minorities

    Commissioner for Scheduled Castes and Scheduled Tribes

    Members, Minorities Commission

    Members, National Commission for Scheduled Castes

    Members, National Commission for Scheduled Tribes

    Officers of the rank of full General or equivalent rank

    Secretaries to the Government of India (including officers holding this office ex-officio)

Secretary, Minorities Commission

Secretary, Scheduled Castes Commission

Secretary, Scheduled Tribes Commission

Secretary to the President

Secretary to the Prime Minister

Secretary, Rajya Sabha/Lok Sabha

Solicitor General

Vice-Chairman, Central Administrative Tribunal

24. Officers of the rank of Lieutenant General or equivalent rank

25. Additional Secretaries to the Government of India

    Additional Solicitor General

    Advocate Generals of States

    Chairman, Tariff Commission

    Charge d' Affairs and Acting High Commissioners a pied and ad interim

    Chief Ministers of Union Territories and Chief Executive Councillor, Delhi, outside their respective Union Territories

    Chief Secretaries of State Governments outside their respective States

    Deputy Comptroller and Auditor General

    Deputy Speakers of Legislative Assemblies in Union Territories and Deputy Chairman, Delhi Metropolitan Council, outside their respective Union Territories

    Director, Central Bureau of Investigation

    Director General, Border Security Force

    Director General, Central Reserve Police

    Director, Intelligence Bureau

    Lieutenant Governors outside their respective Union Territories

    Members, Central Administrative Tribunal

    Members, Monopolies and Restrictive Trade Practices Commission

    Members, Union Public Service Commission

    Ministers of Union Territories and Executive Councillors, Delhi, outside their respective Union Territories

    Principal Staff Officers of the Armed Forces of the rank of Major General or equivalent rank

    Speakers of Legislative Assemblies in Union Territories and Chairman of Delhi Metropolitan Council, outside their respective Union Territories

26. Joint Secretaries to the Government of India and officers of equivalent rank.

    Officers of the rank of Major-General or equivalent rank

NOTES

Note 1   The order in this Table of Precedence is meant for State and Ceremonial occasions and has no application in the day-to-day business of Government.

Note 2   Persons in the Table of Precedence will take rank in order of the number of the articles. The entries in the same article are arranged alphabetically. Those included in the same article will take precedence inter se according to date of entry into that article. However, where the dignitaries of different States and Union Territories included in the same article are present at a function outside their States or Union Territories and there is difficulty in ascertaining their dates of entry, they may be assigned precedence inter se in the alphabetical order of the name of States and Union Territories concerned after those whose precedence is determined according to date of entry into that article.

Note 3   In Article 7, former Prime Ministers will take precedence over the Cabinet Ministers of the Union and the Leaders of Opposition in the Rajya Sabha and the Lok Sabha. The Chief Ministers of States within their respective States will take precedence over the Cabinet Ministers of the Union in official functions held in the respective States.

Note 4   In Article 8:-
(a) Ambassadors Extraordinary and Plenipotentiary and High Commissioners of Commonwealth countries accredited to India will en bloc rank above Governors of States outside their respective States;
(b) Governors of States outside their respective States will en bloc rank above Chief Ministers of States outside their respective States.

Note 5   The Ministry of External Affairs may assign appropriate ranks to foreign dignitaries and Indian Ambassadors, High Commissioners and Ministers Plenipotentiary during their visit to India.

Note 6   Notwithstanding the procedure laid down in Note 2, the rank inter se and precedence of the persons in Article 10 shall be assigned in the following order:-
(1) Deputy Chairman, Rajya Sabha.
(2) Deputy Speaker, Lok Sabha.

(3) Ministers of State of the Union and any other Minister in the Ministry of Defence for defence matters.
(4) Deputy Chief Ministers of States.
(5) Members of Planning Commission.
However, the Deputy Chief Ministers of States outside their respective States will always rank below all other dignitaries figuring in this article.

Note 7   The Chairmen of State Legislative Councils will rank above the Speakers of Legislative Assemblies in cases where they were elected on the same date.

Note 8   When Members of Parliament are invited en bloc to major State functions, the enclosures reserved for them should be next to the Chief Justice, Speaker of the Lok Sabha, Ambassadors etc.

Note 9   Speakers of Legislative Assemblies in Union Territories and Chairman of Delhi Metropolitan Council will take precedence over Ministers and Executive Councillors, included in the same article.

Note 10   In Article 23:-
(a) Secretaries in the Ministry of External Affairs other than the Foreign Secretary, between themselves, will take precedence in the order of their seniority in Grade-I of the Indian Foreign Service and both of them will take precedence after the Foreign Secretary;
(b) Members of the Minorities Commission, the Scheduled Castes Commission and the Schedule Tribes Commission will always take precedence over the Secretaries of these Commissions;
(c) In official functions held at Delhi / New Delhi, Army Commanders / Vice-Chief of the Army Staff or equivalent in other Services will always rank after Secretaries to the Government of India.

Note 11   In Article 25:-
(a) Additional Secretaries in the Ministry of External Affairs, among themselves, will take precedence in the order of their seniority in Grade-II of the Indian Foreign Service;
(b) Additional Solicitor General will take precedence above the Advocate General of States;
(c) Lieutenant Governors will take precedence over the Chief Ministers and Chief Executive Councillor, Delhi, and the latter will take

precedence over Speakers of Legislative Assemblies and Chairman, Metropolitan Council, Delhi;

(d) Deputy Speakers of Legislative Assemblies of Union Territories and Deputy Chairman of Delhi Metropolitan Council will take precedence after Ministers of Union Territories and Executive Councillors, Delhi.

Note 12 For the purpose of Article 26, the posts equivalent to the posts of Joint Secretaries to the Government of India will be determined by the Ministry of Home Affairs.

Appendix IV

Oath by the Constitutional and other Authorities

1. OATH OR AFFIRMATION BY THE PRESIDENT

Every President and every person acting as President or discharging the functions of the President shall, before entering upon his office, make and subscribe in the presence of the Chief Justice of India or, in his absence, the senior most Judge of the Supreme Court available, an oath or affirmation in the following form, that is to say—

"I, A.B., do $\frac{\text{swear in the name of God}}{\text{solemnly affirm}}$ that I will faithfully execute the office of President (or discharge the functions of the President) of India and will to the best of my ability preserve, protect and defend the Constitution and the law and that I will devote myself to the service and well-being of the people of India".

2. OATH OR AFFIRMATION BY THE VICE-PRESIDENT

Every Vice-President shall, before entering upon his office, make and subscribe before the President, or some person appointed in that behalf by him, an oath or affirmation in the following form, that is to say –

"I, A.B., do $\frac{\text{swear in the name of God}}{\text{solemnly affirm}}$ that I will bear true faith and allegiance to the Constitution of India as by law established and that I will faithfully discharge the duty upon which I am about to enter".

3. OATH OR AFFIRMATION BY THE UNION MINISTERS

Before a Union Minister enters upon his office, the President shall administer to him the oath of office and oath of secrecy in the following two separate forms—

(i) Form of Oath of Office

"I, A.B., do $\frac{\text{swear in the name of God}}{\text{solemnly affirm}}$ that I will bear true faith and allegiance to the Constitution of India as by law established, that I will uphold the sovereignty and integrity of India, that I will faithfully and conscientiously discharge my duties as a Minister for the Union and that I will do right to all manner of people in accordance with the Constitution and the law, without fear or favour, affection or ill-will".

(ii) Form of Oath of Secrecy

"I, A.B., do $\frac{\text{swear in the name of God}}{\text{solemnly affirm}}$ that I will not directly or indirectly communicate or reveal to any person or persons any matter which shall be brought under my consideration or shall become known to me as a Minister for the Union except as may be required for the due discharge of my duties as such Minister."

4. OATH OR AFFIRMATION BY A CANDIDATE FOR ELECTION TO PARLIAMENT

A person shall not be qualified to be chosen to fill a seat in Parliament unless he makes and subscribes before some person authorised in that behalf by the Election Commission an oath or affirmation in the following form:

"I, A.B., having been nominated as a candidate to fill a seat in the Council of States (or the House of the People), do $\frac{\text{swear in the name of God}}{\text{solemnly affirm}}$ that I will bear true faith and allegiance to the Constitution of India as by law established and that I will uphold the sovereignty and integrity of India".

5. OATH OR AFFIRMATION BY MEMBERS OF THE PARLIAMENT

Every member of either House of Parliament shall, before taking his seat, make and subscribe before the President, or some person appointed in that behalf by him, an oath or affirmation in the following form :

"I, A.B., having been elected (or nominated) a member of the Council States (or the House of the People), do $\frac{\text{swear in the name of God}}{\text{solemnly affirm}}$ that I will bear true faith and allegiance to the Constitution of India as by law established, that I will uphold the sovereignty and integrity of India and that I will faithfully discharge the duty upon which I am about to enter".

6. OATH OR AFFIRMATION BY THE JUDGES OF THE SUPREME COURT

Every person appointed to be a Judge of the Supreme Court shall, before he enters upon his office, make and subscribe before the President, or some person appointed in that behalf by him, an oath or affirmation in the following form :

"I, A.B., having been appointed Chief Justice (or a Judge) of the Supreme Court of India, do $\frac{\text{swear in the name of God}}{\text{solemnly affirm}}$ that I will bear true faith and allegiance to the Constitution of India as by law established, that I will uphold the sovereignty and integrity of India, that I will duly and faithfully and to the best of my ability, knowledge and judgment perform the duties of my office without fear or favour, affection or ill-will and that I will uphold the Constitution and the laws".

7. OATH OR AFFIRMATION BY THE COMPTROLLER AND AUDITOR-GENERAL OF INDIA

Every person appointed to be the Comptroller and Auditor-General of India shall, before he enters upon his office, make and subscribe before the President, or some person appointed in that behalf by him, an oath or affirmation in the following form:

"I, A.B., having been appointed Comptroller and Auditor-General of India, do $\frac{\text{swear in the name of God}}{\text{solemnly affirm}}$ that I will bear true faith and allegiance to the Constitution of India as by law established, that I will uphold the sovereignty and integrity of India, that I will duly and faithfully and to the best of my ability, knowledge and judgment perform the duties of my office without fear or favour,

affection or ill-will and that I will uphold the Constitution and the laws".

8. OATH OR AFFIRMATION BY THE GOVERNOR

Every Governor and every person discharging the functions of the Governor shall, before entering upon his office, make and subscribe in the presence of the Chief Justice of the High Court exercising jurisdiction in relation to the State, or, in his absence, the senior most Judge of that court available, an oath or affirmation in the following form, that is to say—

"I, A.B., do $\frac{\text{swear in the name of God}}{\text{solemnly affirm}}$ that I will faithfully execute the office of Governor (or discharge the functions of the Governor) of ... (name of the State) and will to the best of my ability preserve, protect and defend the Constitution and the law and that I will devote myself to the service and well-being of the people of ... (name of the State)."

9. OATH OR AFFIRMATION BY THE STATE MINISTERS

Before a State Minister enters upon his office, the Governor shall administer to him the oath of office and oath of secrecy in the following two separate forms—

(i) Form of Oath of Office

"I, A.B., do $\frac{\text{swear in the name of God}}{\text{solemnly affirm}}$ that I will bear true faith and allegiance to the Constitution of India as by law established, that I will uphold the sovereignty and integrity of India, that I will faithfully and conscientiously discharge my duties as a Minister for the State of ... and that I will do right to all manner of people in accordance with the Constitution and the law without fear or favour, affection or ill-will".

(ii) Form of Oath of Secrecy

"I, A.B., do $\frac{\text{swear in the name of God}}{\text{solemnly affirm}}$ that I will not directly or indirectly communicate or reveal to any person or persons any matter which shall be brought under my consideration or shall become known to me as a Minister for the State of ... except as may be required for the due discharge of my duties as such Minister."

10. OATH OR AFFIRMATION BY A CANDIDATE FOR ELECTION TO THE STATE LEGISLATURE

A person shall not be qualified to be chosen to fill a seat in the Legislature of a State unless he makes and subscribes before some person authorized in that behalf by the Election Commission an oath or affirmation in the following form:

"I, A.B., having been nominated as a candidate to fill a seat in Legislative Assembly (or Legislative Council), do $\frac{\text{swear in the name of God}}{\text{solemnly affirm}}$ that I will bear true faith and allegiance to the Constitution of India as by law established and that I will uphold the sovereignty and integrity of India."

11. Oath or Affirmation by Members of the State Legislature

Every member of the Legislative Assembly or the Legislative Council of a State shall, before taking his seat, make and subscribe before the Governor, or some person appointed in that behalf by him, an oath or affirmation in the following form:

"I, A.B., having been elected (or nominated) a member of the Legislative Assembly (or Legislative Council), do $\frac{\text{swear in the name of God}}{\text{solemnly affirm}}$ that I will bear true faith and allegiance to the Constitution of India as by law established, that I will uphold the sovereignty and integrity of India and that I will faithfully discharge the duty upon which I am about to enter."

12. Oath or Affirmation by the Judges of High Courts

Every person appointed to be a Judge of a High Court shall, before he enters upon his office, make and subscribe before the Governor of the State, or some person appointed in that behalf by him, an oath or affirmation in the following form:

"I, A.B., having been appointed Chief Justice (or a Judge) of the High Court at (or of) ..., do $\frac{\text{swear in the name of God}}{\text{solemnly affirm}}$ that I will bear true faith and allegiance to the Constitution of India as by law established, that I will uphold the sovereignty and integrity of India, that I will duly and faithfully and to the best of my ability, knowledge, and judgment perform the duties of my office without fear or favour, affection or ill-will and that I will uphold the Constitution and the laws."

13. Oath or Affirmation by the Central Vigilance Commissioner or Vigilance Commissioner

The Central Vigilance Commissioner or a Vigilance Commissioner shall, before he enters upon his office, make and subscribe before the President, or some other person appointed in that behalf by him, an oath or affirmation in the following form:

"I, A.B., having been appointed Central Vigilance Commissioner (or Vigilance Commissioner) of the Central Vigilance Commission, do $\frac{\text{swear in the name of God}}{\text{solemnly affirm}}$ that I will bear true faith and allegiance to the Constitution of India as by law established, that I will uphold the sovereignty and integrity of India, that I will duly and faithfully and to the best of my ability, knowledge and judgment perform the duties of my office without fear or favour, affection or ill-will and that I will uphold the Constitution and the laws."

14. Oath or Affirmation by the Chief Information Commissioner/The Information Commissioner

The Chief Information Commissioner or an Information Commissioner shall, before he enters upon his office, make and subscribe before the President or some other person appointed by him in that behalf, an oath or affirmation in the following form:

"I, ..., having been appointed Chief Information Commissioner/Information Commissioner, do $\frac{\text{swear in the name of God}}{\text{solemnly affirm}}$ that I will bear true faith and allegiance to the Constitution of India as by law established, that I will uphold the sovereignty and integrity of India, that I will duly and faithfully and to the best of my ability, knowledge and judgment perform the duties of my office without fear or favour, affection or ill-will and that I will uphold the Constitution and the laws."

15. Oath or Affirmation by the State Chief Information Commissioner/The State Information Commissioner

The State Chief Information Commissioner or a State Information Commissioner shall, before he enters upon his office, make and subscribe before the Governor or some other person appointed by him in that behalf, an oath or affirmation in the following form:

"I, ..., having been appointed State Chief Information Commissioner/State Information Commissioner, do $\frac{\text{swear in the name of God}}{\text{solemnly affirm}}$ that I will bear truth faith and allegiance to the Constitution of India as by law established, that I will uphold the sovereignty and integrity of India, that I will duly and faithfully and to the best of my ability, knowledge and judgment perform the duties of my office without fear or favour, affection or ill-will and that I will uphold the Constitution and the laws."

Definitions Under the Constitution

Article 366 contains the definitions of various terms used in different provisions of the constitution. These are mentioned below:

1. **Agricultural Income** means agricultural income as defined for the purposes of the enactments relating to Indian income-tax.

2. **Anglo-Indian** means a person whose father or any of whose other male progenitors in the male line is or was of European descent but who is domiciled within the territory of India and is or was born within such territory of parents habitually resident therein and not established there for temporary purposes only.

3. **Article** means an article of this Constitution.

4. **Borrow** includes the raising of money by the grant of annuities, and "loan" shall be construed accordingly.

5. **Clause** means a clause of the article in which the expression occurs.

6. **Corporation Tax** means any tax on income, so far as that tax is payable by companies and is a tax in the case of which the following conditions are fulfilled:-

   (a) that it is not chargeable in respect of agricultural income;

   (b) that no deduction in respect of the tax paid by companies is, by any enactments which may apply to the tax, authorised to be made from dividends payable by the companies to individuals;

   (c) that no provision exists for taking the tax so paid into account in computing for the purposes of Indian income-tax the total income of individuals receiving such dividends, or in computing the Indian income-tax payable by, or refundable to, such individuals.

7. **Corresponding Province**, "corresponding Indian State" or "corresponding State" means in cases of doubt such Province, Indian State or State as may be determined by the President to be the corresponding Province, the corresponding Indian State or the corresponding State, as the case may be, for the particular purpose in question.

8. **Debt** includes any liability in respect of any obligation to repay capital sums by way of annuity and any liability under any guarantee, and "debt charges" shall be construed accordingly.

9. **Estate Duty** means a duty to be assessed on or by reference to the principal value, ascertained in accordance with such rules as may be prescribed by or under laws made by Parliament or the Legislature of a State relating to the duty, of all property passing upon death or deemed, under the provisions of the said laws, so to pass.

10. **Existing Law** means any law, Ordinance, order, bye-law, rule or regulation passed or made before the commencement of this Constitution by any Legislature, authority or person having power to make such a law, Ordinance, order, bye-law, rule or regulation.

11. **Federal Court** means the Federal Court constituted under the Government of India Act, 1935.

12. **Goods** include all materials, commodities, and articles.

13. **Guarantee** includes any obligation undertaken before the commencement of this Constitution to make payments in the event of the profits of an undertaking falling short of a specified amount.

14. **High Court** means any Court which is deemed for the purposes of this Constitution to be a High Court for any State and includes –
    (a) any Court in the territory of India constituted or reconstituted under this Constitution as a High Court, and
    (b) any other Court in the territory of India which may be declared by Parliament by law to be a High Court for all or any of the purposes of this Constitution.

15. **Indian State** means any territory which the Government of the Dominion of India recognized as such a State.

16. **Part** means a Part of this Constitution.

17. **Pension** means a pension, whether contributory or not, of any kind whatsoever payable to or in respect of any person, and includes retired pay so payable, a gratuity so payable and any sum or sums so payable by way of the return, with or without interest thereon or any other addition thereto, of subscriptions to a provident fund.

18. **Proclamation of Emergency** means a Proclamation issued under clause (1) of article 352.

19. **Public Notification** means a notification in the Gazette of India, or, as the case may be, the Official Gazette of a State.

20. **Railway** does not include –
    (a) a tramway wholly within a municipal area, or
    (b) any other line of communication wholly situated in one State and declared by Parliament by law not to be a railway.

21. **Ruler** means the Prince, Chief or other person who, at any time before the commencement of the Constitution (Twenty-sixth Amendment) Act, 1971, was recognised by the President as the Ruler of an Indian State or any person who, at any time before such commencement, was recognised by the President as the successor of such Ruler.

22. **Schedule** means a Schedule to this Constitution.

23. **Scheduled Castes** means such castes, races or tribes or parts of or groups within such castes, races or tribes as are deemed under article 341 to be Scheduled Castes for the purposes of this Constitution.

24. **Scheduled Tribes** means such tribes or tribal communities or parts of or groups within such tribes or tribal communities as are deemed under article 342 to be Scheduled Tribes for the purposes of this Constitution.

25. **Securities** include stock.

26. **Sub-Clause** means a sub-clause of the clause in which the expression occurs.

27. **Taxation** includes the imposition of any tax or impost, whether general or local or special, and "tax" shall be construed accordingly.

28. **Tax on Income** includes a tax in the nature of an excess profits tax.

29. **Tax on the Sale or Purchase of Goods includes—**
    (a) a tax on the transfer, otherwise than in pursuance of a contract, of property in any goods for cash, deferred payment or other valuable consideration;
    (b) a tax on the transfer of property in goods (whether as goods or in some other form) involved in the execution of a works contract;
    (c) a tax on the delivery of goods on hire-purchase or any system of payment by installments;
    (d) a tax on the transfer of the right to use any goods for any purpose (whether or not for a specified period) for cash, deferred payment or other valuable consideration;
    (e) a tax on the supply of goods by any unincorporated association or body of persons to a member thereof for cash, deferred payment or other valuable consideration;
    (f) a tax on the supply, by way of or as part of any service or in any other manner whatsoever, of goods, being food or any other article for human consumption or any drink (whether or not intoxicating), where such supply or service, is for cash, deferred payment or other valuable consideration;
    And such transfer, delivery or supply of any goods shall be deemed to be a sale of those goods by the person making the transfer, delivery or supply and a purchase of those goods by the person to whom such transfer, delivery or supply is made.

30. **Union Territory** means any Union territory specified in the First Schedule and includes any other territory comprised within the territory of India but not specified in that Schedule.

Constitutional Amendments at a Glance

Amendment Number and Year	Amended Provisions of the Constitution
First Amendment Act, 1951	1. Empowered the state to make special provisions for the advancement of socially and economically backward classes. 2. Provided for the saving of laws providing for acquisition of estates, etc. 3. Added Ninth Schedule to protect the land reform and other laws included in it from the judicial review. 4. Added three more grounds of restrictions on freedom of speech and expression, viz., public order, friendly relations with foreign states and incitement to an offence. Also, made the restrictions 'reasonable' and thus, justiciable in nature. 5. Provided that state trading and nationalisation of any trade or business by the state is not to be invalid on the ground of violation of the right to trade or business.
Second Amendment Act, 1952	Readjusted the scale of representation in the Lok Sabha by providing that one member could represent even more than 7,50,000 persons.
Third Amendment Act, 1954	Empowered the Parliament to control the production, supply and distribution of the foodstuffs, cattle fodder, raw cotton, cotton seed and raw jute in the public interest.
Fourth Amendment Act, 1955	1. Made the scale of compensation given in lieu of compulsory acquisition of private property beyond the scrutiny of courts. 2. Authorised the state to nationalise any trade. 3. Included some more Acts in the Ninth Schedule. 4. Extended the scope of Article 31 A (savings of laws).
Fifth Amendment Act, 1955	Empowered the president to fix the time-limit for the state legislatures to express their views on the proposed Central legislation affecting the areas, boundaries and names of the states.
Sixth Amendment Act, 1956	Included a new subject in the Union list i.e., taxes on the sale and purchase of goods in the course of inter-state trade and commerce and restricted the state's power in this regard.
Seventh Amendment Act, 1956	1. Abolished the existing classification of states into four categories i.e., Part A, Part B, Part C and Part D states, and reorganised them into 14 states and 6 union territories. 2. Extended the jurisdiction of high courts to union territories. 3. Provided for the establishment of a common high court for two or more states. 4. Provided for the appointment of additional and acting judges of the high court.

(Contd.)

Amendment Number and Year	Amended Provisions of the Constitution
Eight Amendment Act, 1960	Extended the reservation of seats for the SCs and STs, and special representation for the Anglo-Indians in the Lok Sabha and the state legislative assemblies for a period of ten years (i.e., up to 1970).
Ninth Amendment Act, 1960	Facilitated the cession of Indian territory of Berubari Union (located in West Bengal) to Pakistan as provided in the Indo-Pakistan Agreement (1958).
Tenth Amendment Act, 1961	Incorporated Dadra and Nagar Haveli in the Indian Union.
Eleventh Amendment Act, 1961	1. Changed the procedure of election of the vice-president by providing for an electoral college instead of a joint meeting of the two Houses of Parliament. 2. Provided that the election of the president or vice-president cannot be challenged on the ground of any vacancy in the appropriate electoral college.
Twelfth Amendment Act, 1962	Incorporated Goa, Daman and Diu in the Indian Union.
Thirteenth Amendment Act, 1962	Gave the status of a state to Nagaland and made special provisions for it.
Fourteenth Amendment Act, 1962	1. Incorporated Puducherry in the Indian Union. 2. Provided for the creation of legislatures and council of ministers for the Union Territories of Himachal Pradesh, Manipur, Tripura, Goa, Daman and Diu, and Puducherry.
Fifteenth Amendment Act, 1963	1. Enabled the high courts to issue writs to any person or authority even outside its territorial jurisdiction if the cause of action arise within its territorial limits. 2. Increased the retirement age of high court judges from 60 to 62 years. 3. Provided for appointment of retired judges of the high courts as acting judges of the same court. 4. Provided for compensatory allowance to judges who are transferred from one high court to another. 5. Enabled the retired judge of a high court to act as adhoc judge of the Supreme Court. 6. Provided for the procedure for determining the age of the Supreme Court and high court judges.
Sixteenth Amendment Act, 1963	1. Empowered the state to impose further restriction on the rights to freedom of speech and expression, to assemble peaceably and to form associations in the interests of sovereignty and integrity of India. 2. Included sovereignty and integrity in the forms of oaths or affirmations to be subscribed by contestants to the legislatures, members of the legislatures, ministers, judges and CAG of India.
Seventeenth Amendment Act, 1964	1. Prohibited the acquisition of land under personal cultivation unless the market value of the land is paid as compensation. 2. Included 44 more Acts in the Ninth Schedule.
Eighteenth Amendment Act, 1966	Made it clear that the power of Parliament to form a new state also includes a power to form a new state or union territory by uniting a part of a state or a union territory to another state or union territory.
Nineteenth Amendment Act, 1966	Abolished the system of Election Tribunals and vested the power to hear election petitions in the High Courts.
Twentieth Amendment Act, 1966	Validated certain appointments of district judges in the UP which were declared void by the Supreme Court.

(Contd.)

Amendment Number and Year	Amended Provisions of the Constitution
Twenty-First Amendment Act, 1967	Included sindhi as the 15th language in the Eight Schedule.
Twenty-Second Amendment Act, 1969	Facilitated the creation of a new autonomous State of Meghalaya within the State of Assam.
Twenty-Third Amendment Act, 1969	Extended the reservation of seats for the SCs and STs, and special representation for the Anglo-Indians in the Lok Sabha and the state legislative assemblies for a further period of ten years (i.e., up to 1980).
Twenty-Fourth Amendment Act, 1971	1. Affirmed the power of Parliament to amend any part of the Constitution including fundamental rights. 2. Made it compulsory for the president to give his assent to a Constitutional Amendment Bill.
Twenty-Fifth Amendment Act, 1971	1. Curtailed the fundamental right to property. 2. Provided that any law made to give effect to the Directive Principles contained in Article 39 (b) or (c) cannot be challenged on the ground of violation of the rights guaranteed by Articles 14, 19 and 31.
Twenty-Sixth Amendment Act, 1971	Abolished the privy purses and privileges of the former rulers of princely states.
Twenty-Seventh Amendment, 1971	1. Empowered the administrators of certain union territories to promulgate ordinances. 2. Made certain special provisions for new Union Territories of Arunachal Pradesh and Mizoram. 3. Authorised the Parliament to create the legislative assembly and the council of ministers for the new state of Manipur.
Twenty-Eighth Amendment Act, 1972	Abolished the special privileges of ICS officers and empowered the Parliament to determine their service conditions.
Twenty-Ninth Amendment Act, 1972	Included two Kerala Acts on land reforms in the Ninth Schedule.
Thirtieth Amendment Act, 1972	Did away with the provision which allowed appeal to the Supreme Court in civil cases involving an amount of ₹20,000, and provided instead that an appeal can be filed in the Supreme Court only if the case involves a substantial question of law.
Thirty-First Amendment Act, 1972	Increased the number of Lok Sabha seats from 525 to 545.
Thirty-Second Amendment Act, 1973	Made special provisions to satisfy the aspirations of the people of the Telengana region in Andhra Pradesh.
Thirty-Third Amendment Act, 1974	Provided that the resignation of the members of Parliament and the state legislatures may be accepted by the Speaker/Chairman only if he is satisfied that the resignation is voluntary or genuine.
Thirty-Fourth Amendment Act, 1974	Included twenty more land tenure and land reforms acts of various states in the Ninth Schedule.
Thirty-Fifth Amendment Act, 1974	Terminated the protectorate status of Sikkim and conferred on it the status of an associate state of the Indian Union. The Tenth Schedule was added laying down the terms and conditions of association of Sikkim with the Indian Union.
Thirty-Sixth Amendment Act, 1975	Made Sikkim a full-fledged State of the Indian Union and omitted the Tenth Schedule.
Thirty-Seventh Amendment Act, 1975	Provided legislative assembly and council of ministers for the Union Territory of Arunachal Pradesh.

(Contd.)

Amendment Number and Year	Amended Provisions of the Constitution
Thirty-Eighth Amendment Act, 1975	1. Made the declaration of emergency by the president non-justiciable. 2. Made the promulgation of ordinances by the president, governors and administrators of union territories non-justiciable. 3. Empowered the president to declare different proclamations of national emergency on different grounds simultaneously.
Thirty-Ninth Amendment Act, 1975	1. Placed the disputes relating to the president, vice-president, prime minister and Speaker beyond the scope of the judiciary. They are to be decided by such authority as may be determined by the Parliament. 2. Included certain Central acts in the Ninth Schedule.
Fortieth Amendment Act, 1976	1. Empowered the Parliament to specify from time to time the limits of the territorial waters, the continental shelf, the exclusive economic zone (EEZ) and the maritime zones of India. 2. Included 64 more Central and state laws, mostly relating to land reforms, in the Ninth Schedule.
Forty-First Amendment Act, 1976	Raised the retirement age of members of State Public Service Commission and Joint Public Service Commission from 60 to 62.
Forty-Second Amendment Act, 1976 (The most comprehensive amendment made so far to the Constitution; it is known as 'Mini-Constitution'; it gave effect to the recommendations of *Swaran Singh Committee*.)	1. Added three new words (i.e., socialist, secular and integrity) in the Preamble. 2. Added Fundamental Duties by the citizens (new Part IV A). 3. Made the president bound by the advise of the cabinet. 4. Provided for administrative tribunals and tribunals for other matters (Added Part XIV A). 5. Froze the seats in the Lok Sabha and state legislative assemblies on the basis of 1971 census till 2001. 6. Made the constitutional amendments beyond judicial scrutiny. 7. Curtailed the power of judicial review and writ jurisdiction of the Supreme Court and high courts. 8. Raised the tenure of Lok Sabha and state legislative assemblies from 5 to 6 years. 9. Provided that the laws made for the implementation of Directive Principles cannot be declared invalid by the courts on the ground of violation of some Fundamental Rights. 10. Empowered the Parliament to make laws to deal with anti-national activities and such laws are to take precedence over Fundamental Rights. 11. Added three new Directive Principles viz., equal justice and free-legal aid, participation of workers in the management of industries and protection of environment, forests and wild life. 12. Facilitated the proclamation of national emergency in a part of territory of India. 13. Extended the one-time duration of the President's rule in a state from 6 months to one year. 14. Empowered the Centre to deploy its armed forces in any state to deal with a grave situation of law and order. 15. Shifted five subjects from the state list to the concurrent list, viz, education, forests, protection of wild animals and birds, weights and measures and administration of justice, constitution and organisation of all courts except the Supreme Court and the high courts. 16. Did away with the requirement of quorum in the Parliament and the state legislatures. 17. Empowered the Parliament to decide from time to time the rights and privileges of its members and committees. 18. Provided for the creation of the All-India Judicial Service. 19. Shortened the procedure for disciplinary action by taking away the right of a civil servant to make representation at the second stage after the inquiry (i.e., on the penalty proposed).

(Contd.)

Amendment Number and Year	Amended Provisions of the Constitution
Forty-Third Amendment Act, 1977 *(Enacted by the Janata Government to nullify some of the distortions introduced by the 42nd Amendment Act of 1976)*	1. Restored the jurisdiction of the Supreme Court and the high courts in respect of judicial review and issue of writs. 2. Deprived the Parliament of its special powers to make laws to deal with anti-national activities.
Forty-Fourth Amendment Act, 1978 *(Enacted by the Janata Government mainly to nullify some of the other distortions introduced by the 42nd Amendment Act, 1976)*	1. Restored the original term of the Lok Sabha and the state legislative assemblies (i.e., 5 years)." 2. Restored the provisions with regard to quorum in the Parliament and state legislatures. 3. Omitted the reference to the British House of Commons in the provisions pertaining to the parliamentary privileges. 4. Gave constitutional protection to publication in newspaper of true reports of the proceedings of the Parliament and the state legislatures. 5. Empowered the president to send back once the advice of cabinet for reconsideration. But, the reconsidered advice is to be binding on the president. 6. Deleted the provision which made the satisfaction of the president, governor and administrators final in issuing ordinances. 7. Restored some of the powers of the Supreme Court and high courts. 8. Replaced the term 'internal disturbance' by 'armed rebellion' in respect of national emergency. 9. Made the President to declare a national emergency only on the written recommendation of the cabinet. 10. Made certain procedural safeguards with respect to national emergency and President's rule. 11. Deleted the right to property from the list of Fundamental Rights and made it only a legal right. 12. Provided that the fundamental rights guaranteed by Articles 20 and 21 cannot be suspended during a national emergency. 13. Omitted the provisions which took away the power of the court to decide the election disputes of the president, the vice-president, the prime minister and the Speaker of the Lok Sabha.
Forty-Fifth Amendment Act, 1980	Extended the reservation of seats for the SCs and STs and special representation for the Anglo-Indians in the Lok Sabha and the state legislative assemblies for a further period of ten years (i.e., up to 1990).
Forty-Sixth Amendment Act, 1982	1. Enabled the states to plug loopholes in the laws and realise sales tax dues. 2. Brought about some uniformity in tax rates on certain items.
Forty-Seventh Amendment Act, 1984	Included 14 land reforms Acts of various states in the Ninth Schedule.
Forty-Eighth Amendment Act, 1984	Facilitated the extension of President's rule in Punjab beyond one year without meeting the two special conditions for such extension.
Forty-Ninth Amendment Act, 1984	Gave a constitutional sanctity to the Autonomous District Council in Tripura.
Fiftieth Amendment Act, 1984	Empowered the Parliament to restrict the Fundamental Rights of persons employed in intelligence organisations and telecommunication systems set up for the armed forces or intelligence organisations.
Fifty-First Amendment Act, 1984	Provided for reservation of seats in the Lok Sabha for STs in Meghalaya, Arunachal Pradesh, Nagaland and Mizoram as well as in the Legislative Assemblies of Meghalaya and Nagaland.

(Contd.)

Amendment Number and Year	Amended Provisions of the Constitution
Sixty-First Amendment Act, 1989	Reduced the voting age from 21 years to 18 years for the Lok Sabha and state legislative assembly elections.
Sixty-Second Amendment Act, 1989	Extended the reservation of seats for the SCs and STs and special representation for the Anglo-Indians in the Lok Sabha and the state legislative assemblies for the further period of ten years (i.e., up to 2000).
Sixty-Third Amendment Act, 1989	Repealed the changes introduced by the 59th Amendment Act of 1988 in relation to Punjab. In other words, Punjab was brought at par with the other states in respect of emergency provisions.
Sixty-Fourth Amendment Act, 1990	Facilitated the extension of the President's rule in Punjab upto a total period of three years and six months.
Sixty-Fifth Amendment Act, 1990	Provided for the establishment of a multi-member National Commission for SCs and STs in the place of a Special Officer for SCs and STs.
Sixty-Sixth Amendment Act, 1990	Included 55 more land reforms Acts of various states in the Ninth Schedule.
Sixty-Seventh Amendment Act, 1990	Facilitated the extension of the President's rule in Punjab up to a total period of four years.
Sixty-Eight Amendment Act, 1991	Facilitated the extension of the President's rule in Punjab up to a total period of five years.
Sixty-Ninth Amendment Act, 1991	Accorded a special status to the Union Territory of Delhi by designing it as the National Capital Territory of Delhi. The amendment also provided for the creation of a 70-member legislative assembly and a 7-member council of ministers for Delhi.
Seventieth Amendment Act, 1992	Provided for the inclusion of the members of the Legislative Assemblies of National Capital Territory of Delhi and the Union Territory of Puducherry in the electoral college for the election of the president.
Seventy-First Amendment Act, 1992	Included konkani, manipuri and nepali languages in the Eight Schedule. With this, the total number of scheduled languages increased to 18.
Seventy-Second Amendment Act, 1992	Provided for reservation of seats for the STs in the Legislative Assembly of Tripura.
Seventy-Third Amendment Act, 1992	Granted constitutional status and protection to the panchayati raj institutions. For this purpose, the Amendment has added a new Part-IX entitled as 'the panchayats' and a new Eleventh Schedule containing 29 functional items of the panchayats.
Seventy-Fourth Amendment Act, 1992	Granted constitutional status and protection to the urban local bodies. For this purpose, the Amendment has added a new Part IX-A entitled as 'the municipalities' and a new Twelfth Schedule containing 18 functional items of the municipalities.
Seventy-Fifth Amendment Act, 1994	Provided for the establishment of rent tribunals for the adjudication of disputes with respect to rent, its regulation and control and tenancy issues including the rights, title and interest of landlords and tenants.
Seventy-Sixth Amendment Act, 1994	Included the Tamil Nadu Reservation Act of 1994 (which provides for 69 per cent reservation of seats in educational institutions and posts in state services) in the Ninth Schedule to protect it from judicial review. In 1992, the Supreme Court ruled that the total reservation should not exceed 50 per cent.
Seventy-Seventh Amendment Act, 1995	Provided for reservation in promotions in government jobs for SCs and STs. This amendment nullified the Supreme Court ruling with regard to reservation in promotions.

(Contd.)

Amendment Number and Year	Amended Provisions of the Constitution
Seventy-Eighth Amendment Act, 1995	Included 27 more land reforms Acts of various states in the Ninth Schedule. With this, the total number of Acts in the Schedule increased to 282. But, the last entry is numbered 284.
Seventy-Ninth Amendment Act, 1999	Extended the reservation of seats for the SCs and STs and special representation for the Anglo-Indians in the Lok Sabha and the state legislative assemblies for a further period of ten years (i.e., up to 2010).
Eightieth Amendment Act, 2000	Provided for an 'alternative scheme of devolution' of revenue between the Centre and states. This was enacted on the basis of the recommendations of the Tenth Finance Commission which has recommended that out of the total income obtained from Central taxes and duties, twenty-nine per cent should be distributed among the states.
Eighty-First Amendment Act, 2000	Empowered the state to consider the unfilled reserved vacancies of a year as a separate class of vacancies to be filled up in any succeeding year or years. Such class of vacancies are not to be combined with the vacancies of the year in which they are being filled up to determine the ceiling of 50 per cent reservation on total number of vacancies of that year. In brief, this amendment ended the 50 per cent ceiling on reservation in backlog vacancies.
Eighty-Second Amendment Act, 2000	Provided for making of any provision in favour of the SCs and STs for relaxation in qualifying marks in any examination or lowering the standards of evaluation, for reservation in matters of promotion to the public services of the Centre and the states.
Eighty-Third Amendment Act, 2000	Provided that no reservation in panchayats need be made for SCs in Arunachal Pradesh. The total population of the state is tribal and there are no SCs.
Eighty-Fourth Amendment Act, 2001	Extended the ban on readjustment of seats in the Lok Sabha and the state legislative assemblies for another 25 years (i.e., up to 2026) with the same objective of encouraging population limiting measures. In other words, the number of seats in the Lok Sabha and the assemblies are to remain same till 2026. It also provided for the readjustment and rationalisation of territorial constituencies in the states on the basis of the population figures of 1991 cesus.
Eighty-Fifth Amendment Act, 2001	Provided for 'consequential seniority' in the case of promotion by virtue of rule of reservation for the government servants belonging to the SCs and STs with retrospective effect from June 1995.
Eighty-Sixth Amendment Act, 2002	1. Made elementary education a fundamental right. The newly-added Article 21-A declares that "the State shall provide free and compulsory education to all children of the age of six to fourteen years in such manner as the State may determine". 2. Changed the subject matter of Article 45 in Directive Principles. It now reads—"The State shall endeavour to provide early childhood care and education for all children until they complete the age of six years". 3. Added a new fundamental duty under Article 51-A which reads—"It shall be the duty of every citizen of India who is a parent or guardian to provide opportunities for education to his child or ward between the age of six and fourteen years".
Eighty-Seventh Amendment Act, 2003	Provided for the readjustment and rationalisation of territorial constituencies in the states on the basis of the population figures of 2001 census and not 1991 census as provided earlier by the 84th Amendment Act of 2001.
Eighty-Eighth Amendment Act, 2003	Made a provision for service tax (Article 268-A). Taxes on services are levied by the Centre. But, their proceeds are collected as well as appropriated by both the Centre and the states in accordance with the principles formulated by parliament.

(Contd.)

Amendment Number and Year	Amended Provisions of the Constitution
Eighty-Ninth Amendment Act, 2003	Bifurcated the erstwhile combined National Commission for Scheduled Castes and Scheduled Tribes into two separate bodies, namely, National Commission for Scheduled Castes (Article 338) and National Commission for Scheduled Tribes (Article 338-A). Both the Commissions consist of a Chairperson, a Vice-Chairperson and three other members. They are appointed by the President.
Ninetieth Amendment Act, 2003	Provided for maintaining the erstwhile representation of the Scheduled Tribes and non- Scheduled Tribes in the Assam legislative assembly from the Bodoland Territorial Areas District (Article 332 (6)).
Ninety-First Amendment Act, 2003	Made the following provisions to limit the size of Council of Ministers, to debar defectors from holding public offices, and to strengthen the anti-defection law: 1. The total number of ministers, including the Prime Minister, in the Central Council of Ministers shall not exceed 15% of the total strength of the Lok Sabha (Article 75(1A)). 2. A member of either house of Parliament belonging to any political party who is disqualified on the ground of defection shall also be disqualified to be appointed as a minister (Article 75(1B)). 3. The total number of ministers, including the Chief Minister, in the Council of Ministers in a state shall not exceed 15% of the total strength of the legislative Assembly of that state. But, the number of ministers, including the Chief Minister, in a state shall not be less than 12 (Article 164(1A)). 4. A member of either House of a state legislature belonging to any political party who is disqualified on the ground of defection shall also be disqualified to be appointed as a minister (Article 164(1B)). 5. A member of either House of Parliament or either House of a State Legislature belonging to any political party who is disqualified on the ground of defection shall also be disqualified to hold any remunerative political post. The expression "remunerative political post" means (i) any office under the central government or a state government where the salary or remuneration for such office is paid out of the public revenue of the concerned government; or (ii) any office under a body, whether incorporated or not, which is wholly or partially owned by the central government or a state government and the salary or remuneration for such office is paid by such body, except where such salary or remuneration paid is compensatory in nature (Article 361-B). 6. The provision of the Tenth Schedule (anti-defection law) pertaining to exemption from disqualification in case of split by one-third members of legislature party has been deleted. It means that the defectors have no more protection on grounds of splits.
Ninety-Second Amendment Act, 2003	Included four more languages in the Eighth Schedule. They are Bodo, Dogri (Dongri), Mathilli (Maithili) and Santhali. With this, the total number of constitutionally recognised languages increased to 22.
Ninety-Third Amendment Act, 2005	Empowered the state to make special provisions for the socially and educationally backward classes or the Scheduled Castes or the Scheduled Tribes in educational institutions including private educational institutions (whether aided or unaided by the state), except the minority educational institutions (clause (5) in Article 15). This Amendment was enacted to nullify the Supreme Court judgement in the Inamdar case (2005) where the apex court ruled that the state cannot impose its reservation policy on minority and non-minority unaided private colleges, including professional colleges. The court declared that reservation in private, unaided educational institutions was unconstitutional.

(Contd.)

Amendment Number and Year	Amended Provisions of the Constitution
Ninety-Fourth Amendment Act, 2006	Freed Bihar from the obligation of having a tribal welfare minister and extended the same provision to Jharkhand and Chhattisgarh. This provision will now be applicable to the two newly formed states and Madhya Pradesh and Orissa, where it has already been in force (Article 164(1)).
Ninety-Fifth Amendment Act, 2009	Extended the reservation of seats for the SCs and STs and special representation for the Anglo-Indians in the Lok Sabha and the state legislative assemblies for a further period of ten years i.e., upto 2020 (Article 334).
Ninety-Sixth Amendment Act, 2011	Substituted "Odia" for "Oriya". Consequently, the "Oriya" language in the Eighth Schedule shall be pronounced as "Odia".
Ninety-Seventh Amendment Act, 2011	Gave a constitutional status and protection to co-operative societies. In this context, it made the following three changes in the constitution: 1. It made the right to form co-operative societies a fundamental right (Article 19). 2. It included a new Directive Principle of State Policy on promotion of co-operative societies (Article 43-B). 3. It added a new Part IX-B in the constitution which is entitled as "The Co-operative societies" (Articles 243-ZH to 243-ZT).
Ninety-Eighth Amendment Act, 2012	Provided for special provisions for the Hyderabad-Karnataka region of the State of Karnataka. The special provisions aim to establish an institutional mechanism for equitable allocation of funds to meet the development needs over the region, as well as to enhance human resources and promote employment from the region by providing for local cadres in service and reservation in educational and vocational training institutions (Article 371-J).

Appendix
VII

Allied Amending Acts at a Glance

Name and Year of the Act	Amended Provisions of the Constitution
Assam (Alteration of Boundaries) Act, 1951	Altered the boundaries of the state of Assam by ceding a strip of territory comprised in that state to Bhutan
Andhra State Act, 1953	Formed the first linguistic state, known as the state of Andhra, by taking out the Telugu speaking areas from the state of Madras; Kurnool was the capital of Andhra state and the state high court was established at Guntur
Lushai Hills District (Change of Name) Act, 1954	Renamed the Lushai Hills District as the Mizo District; the Lushai Hills District was one of the six autonomous districts in the tribal areas of Assam specified in the Sixth Schedule of the Constitution
Himachal Pradesh and Bilaspur (New State) Act, 1954	Formed the new state of Himachal Pradesh by uniting the existing states of Himachal Pradesh and Bilaspur
Chandernagore (Merger) Act, 1954	Merged the territory of Chandernagore (a former enclave of French India) into the state of West Bengal
States Reorganisation Act, 1956	Made extensive changes in the boundaries of various states for the purpose of meeting the linguistic, regional and local demands; it created 14 states and 6 union territories. The states were: Andhra Pradesh, Assam, Bihar, Bombay, Jammu and Kashmir, Kerala, Madhya Pradesh, Madras, Mysore, Orissa, Punjab, Rajasthan, Uttar Pradesh and West Bengal. The union territories were: Andaman and Nicobar Islands, Delhi, Himachal Pradesh, Laccadive, Minicoy and Amindivi Islands, Manipur and Tripura. It established the new state of Kerala by merging the Travancore-Cochin state with the Malabar district of Madras state and the Kasargode of South Canara (Dakshina Kannada). It merged the Telugu-speaking areas of Hyderabad state with the Andhra State to create the Andhra Pradesh state. Further, it merged the Madhya Bharat state, Vindhya Pradesh state and Bhopal state into the Madhya Pradesh state. Similarly, it merged the Saurashtra state and Kutch state into that of the Bombay state; the Coorg state into that of Mysore state; the Patiala and East Punjab states Union (Pepsu) into that of Punjab state; and the Ajmer state into that of Rajasthan state. Moreover, it created the new union territory of Laccadive, Minicoy and Amindivi Islands from the territory detached from the Madras state.
Bihar and West Bengal (Transfer of Territories) Act, 1956	Provided for the transfer of certain territories from the state of Bihar to the state of West Bengal

(Contd.)

Name and Year of the Act	*Amended Provisions of the Constitution*
Rajasthan and Madhya Pradesh (Transfer of Territories) Act, 1959	Provided for the transfer of certain territories from the state of Rajasthan to the state of Madhya Pradesh
Andhra Pradesh and Madras (Alteration of Boundaries) Act, 1959	Provided for the alteration of boundaries of the states of Andhra Pradesh and Madras
Bombay Reorganisation Act, 1960	Formed the new state of Gujarat (15th state) by taking out the Gujarati speaking areas from the state of Bombay and renamed the other part of the Bombay state as Maharashtra state. The city of Ahmedabad was made the capital of Gujarat.
Acquired Territories (Merger) Act, 1960	Provided for the merger into the states of Assam, Punjab and West Bengal of certain territories acquired from Pakistan under the agreements entered into between the Governments of India and Pakistan, in 1958 and 1959.
State of Nagaland Act, 1962	Formed the new state of Nagaland (16th state) by taking out the Naga Hills – Tuensang area from the state of Assam; the Naga Hills – Tuensang area was a tribal area of Assam specified in the Sixth Schedule of the Constitution.
Punjab Reorganisation Act, 1966	Formed the new state of Haryana (17th state) by taking out the Hindi speaking areas from the state of Punjab; it also made Chandigarh a new union territory as well as a common capital for both Punjab and Haryana.
Bihar and Uttar Pradesh (Alteration of Boundaries) Act, 1968	Provided for the alteration of boundaries of the states of Bihar and Uttar Pradesh
Andhra Pradesh and Mysore (Transfer of Territory) Act, 1968	Provided for the transfer of certain territory from the state of Mysore to the state of Andhra Pradesh
Madras State (Alteration of Name) Act, 1968	Changed the name of the state of Madras to that of state of Tamil Nadu.
West Bengal Legislative Council (Abolition) Act, 1969	Provided for the abolition of the Legislative Council of the state of West Bengal
Punjab Legislative Council (Abolition) Act, 1969	Provided for the abolition of the Legislative Council of the state of Punjab
Assam Reorganisation (Meghalaya) Act, 1969	Formed an autonomous state (sub-state) known as Meghalaya, within the state of Assam
State of Himachal Pradesh Act, 1970	Elevated the territory of Himachal Pradesh to the status of a state (18th state)
North-Eastern Areas (Reorganisation) Act, 1971	Elevated the two union territories of Manipur and Tripura to the status of states (19th state and 20th state respectively). It also conferred full statehood to Meghalaya (21st state), which was previously a sub-state within the state of Assam. Further, it formed the two union territories of Mizoram and Arunachal Pradesh out of the territories of Assam
Government of Union Territories (Amendment) Act, 1971	Amended the Sixth Schedule of the constitution to include certain provisions with respect to the autonomous districts and autonomous regions of the union territory of Mizoram
Mysore State (Alteration of Name) Act, 1973	Changed the name of the state of Mysore to that of the state of Karnataka
Laccadive, Minicoy and Amindivi Islands (Alteration of Name) Act, 1973	Changed the name of the union territory of the Laccadive, Minicoy and Amindivi Islands to that of the Union Territory of Lakshadweep
Repealing and Amending Act, 1974	Repealed certain enactments and amended certain other enactments; it also substituted the words "cattle pounds" for "cattle ponds" in the Sixth Schedule of the Constitution.

(Contd.)

Name and Year of the Act	Amended Provisions of the Constitution
Fifth Schedule to the Constitution (Amendment) Act, 1976	Empowered the President of India: (i) to increase the area of any Scheduled Area in a state after consultation with the Governor of that state; and (ii) to rescind any order made for the designation of an area in any state to be a Scheduled Area, or in consultation with the Governor of the State concerned, make fresh order redefining the area which is to be a Scheduled Area
Haryana and Uttar Pradesh (Alteration of Boundaries) Act, 1979	Provided for the alteration of boundaries of the states of Haryana and Uttar Pradesh
Andhra Pradesh Legislative Council (Abolition) Act, 1985	Provided for the abolition of the Legislative Council of the state of Andhra Pradesh
State of Mizoram Act, 1986	Elevated the union territory of Mizoram to the status of a state (23rd state)
Tamil Nadu Legislative Council (Abolition) Act, 1986	Provided for the abolition of the Legislative Council of the state of Tamil Nadu
State of Arunachal Pradesh Act, 1986	Elevated the union territory of Arunachal Pradesh to the status of a state (24th state)
Goa, Daman and Diu Reorganisation Act, 1987	Formed the new state of Goa (25th state) by separating the territory of Goa from the union territory of Goa, Daman and Diu
Sixth Schedule to the Constitution (Amendment) Act, 1988	Included certain modifications in the Sixth Schedule of the Constitution in its application to the states of Tripura and Mizoram; these (i) provided that the Governors shall act in their discretion in the discharge of some of their functions (ii) made provisions relating to the application of Acts of Parliament and the state legislatures to autonomous districts and autonomous regions and (iii) provided for a time-limit in making over the share of royalties to the district councils
Sixth Schedule to the Constitution (Amendment) Act, 1995	Included certain modifications in the Sixth Schedule of the Constitution in its application to the state of Assam: these (i) provided that the District Council constituted for the North Cachar Hills District shall be called the North Cachar Hills Autonomous Council and the District Council constituted for the Karbi-Anglong District shall be called the Karbi-Anglong Autonomous Council (ii) made provisions for the additional powers of the North Cachar Hills Autonomous Council and the Karbi-Anglong Autonomous Council to make laws and (iii) made it mandatory for the Governor to consult the North Cachar Hills Autonomous Council or the Karbi-Anglong Autonomous Council, as the case may be, in the exercise of his discretionary powers
Madhya Pradesh Reorganisation Act, 2000	Formed the new state of Chhattisgarh (26th state) out of the territories of the State of Madhya Pradesh
Uttar Pradesh Reorganisation Act, 2000	Created the new state of Uttaranchal (27th state) by carving out its territory from that of the territories of the state of Uttar Pradesh
Bihar Reorganisation Act, 2000	Established the new state of Jharkhand (28th state) by separating its territory from the territories of the state of Bihar
Sixth Schedule to the Constitution (Amendment) Act, 2003	Included certain modifications in the Sixth Schedule of the Constitution in its application to the state of Assam; this was done to meet the aspirations of the Bodos in Assam and in pursuance of the Memorandum of Settlement signed between the Central Government, the Government of Assam and Bodo Liberation Tigers (BLT) on 10-02-2003 for a durable solution to the Bodo issues. In this context, the Act made the following provisions: (i) specified the Bodoland Territorial Areas District in the list of the tribal areas of the State of Assam (ii) created an autonomous self-governing body known as the Bodoland Territorial Council (BTC) within the state of Assam (iii) vested the council with legislative, administrative and financial powers in respect of specified subjects and (iv) provided for adequate safeguards for the non-tribals in the BTC area

(Contd.)

Name and Year of the Act	Amended Provisions of the Constitution
Andhra Pradesh Legislative Council Act, 2005	Provided for the creation of Legislative Council for the state of Andhra Pradesh
Uttaranchal (Alteration of Name) Act, 2006	Changed the name of the state of Uttaranchal to that of the state of Uttarakhand
Pondicherry (Alteration of Name) Act, 2006	Renamed the union territory of Pondicherry as the union territory of Puducherry
Tamil Nadu Legislative Council Act, 2010	Provided for the creation of Legislative Council for the state of Tamil Nadu
Orissa (Alteration of Name) Act, 2011	Changed the name of the state of Orissa to that of the state of Odisha.

Model Code of Conduct Relating to Elections

Given here is the complete text of the *"Model Code of Conduct for the Guidance of Political Parties and Candidates"*, formulated by the Election Commission of India.

I. GENERAL CONDUCT

(1) No party or candidate shall indulge in any activity which may aggravate existing differences or create mutual hatred or cause tension between different castes and communities, religious or linguistic.

(2) Criticism of other political parties, when made, shall be confined to their policies and programmes, past record and work. Parties and candidates shall refrain from criticism of all aspects of private life, not connected with the public activities of the leaders or workers of other parties. Criticism of other parties or their workers based on unverified allegations or distortions shall be avoided.

(3) There shall be no appeal to caste or communal feelings for securing votes. Mosques, churches, temples or other places of worship shall not be used as forum for election propaganda.

(4) All parties and candidates shall avoid scrupulously all activities which are "corrupt practices" and offences under the election law, such as bribing of voters, intimidation of voters, impersonation of voters, canvassing within 100 meters of polling stations, holding public meetings during the period of 48 hours ending with the hour fixed for the close of the poll, and the transport and conveyance of voters to and from polling station.

(5) The right of every individual for peaceful and undisturbed home-life shall be respected, however much the political parties or candidates may resent his political opinions or activities. Organising demonstrations or picketing before the houses of individuals by way of protesting against their opinions or activities shall not be resorted to under any circumstances.

(6) No political party or candidate shall permit its or his followers to make use of any individual's land, building, compound wall etc., without his permission for erecting flag-staffs, suspending banners, pasting notices, writing slogans, etc.

(7) Political parties and candidates shall ensure that their supporters do not create obstructions in or break up meetings and processions organised by other parties. Workers or sympathisers of one political party shall not create disturbances at public meetings organised by another political party by putting questions orally or in writing or by distributing leaflets of their own party. Processions shall not be taken out by one party along places at which meetings are held by another party. Posters issued by one party shall not be removed by workers of another party.

II. MEETINGS

(1) The party or candidate shall inform the local police authorities of the venue and time of any proposed meeting well in time so as to enable the police to make necessary arrangements for controlling traffic and maintaining peace and order.

(2) A party or candidate shall ascertain in advance if there are any restrictive or prohibitory orders in force in the place proposed for the meeting. If such orders exist, they shall be followed strictly. If any exemption is required from such orders, it shall be applied for and obtained well in time.

(3) If permission or license is to be obtained for the use of loudspeakers or any other facility in connection with any proposed meeting, the party or candidate shall apply to the authority concerned well in advance and obtain such permission or license.

(4) Organisers of a meeting shall invariably seek the assistance of the police on duty for dealing with persons disturbing a meeting or otherwise attempting to create disorder. Organisers themselves shall not take action against such persons.

III. PROCESSIONS

(1) A party or candidate organising a procession shall decide before hand the time and place of the starting of the procession, the route to be followed and the time and place at which the procession will terminate. There shall ordinarily be no deviation from the programme.

(2) The organisers shall give advance intimation to the local police authorities of the programme so as to enable the latter to make necessary arrangements.

(3) The organisers shall ascertain if any restrictive orders are in force in the localities through which the procession has to pass, and shall comply with the restrictions unless exempted specially by the competent authority. Any traffic regulations or restrictions shall also be carefully adhered to.

(4) The organisers shall take steps in advance to arrange for passage of the procession so that there is no block or hindrance to traffic. If the procession is very long, it shall be organised in segments of suitable lengths, so that at convenient intervals, especially at points where the procession has to pass road junctions, the passage of held up traffic could be allowed by stages thus avoiding heavy traffic congestion.

(5) Processions shall be so regulated as to keep as much to the right of the road as possible and the direction and advice of the police on duty shall be strictly complied with.

(6) If two or more political parties or candidates propose to take processions over the same route or parts thereof at about the same time, the organisers shall establish contact well in advance and decide upon the measures to be taken to see that the processions do not clash or cause hindrance to traffic. The assistance of the local police shall be availed of for arriving at a satisfactory arrangement. For this purpose the parties shall contact the police at the earliest opportunity.

(7) The political parties or candidates shall exercise control to the maximum extent possible in the matter of processionists carrying articles which may be put to misuse by undesirable elements especially in moments of excitement.

(8) The carrying of effigies purporting to represent members of other political parties or their leaders, burning such effigies in public and such other forms of demonstration shall not be countenanced by any political party or candidate.

IV. POLLING DAY

All political parties and candidates shall

(i) Co-operate with the officers on election duty to ensure peaceful and orderly polling and complete freedom to the voters to exercise their franchise without being subjected to any annoyance or obstruction.

(ii) Supply to their authorised workers suitable badges or identity cards.

(iii) Agree that the identity slip supplied by them to voters shall be on plain (white) paper and shall not contain any symbol, name of the candidate or the name of the party.

(iv) Refrain from serving or distributing liquor on polling day and during the twenty-four hours preceding it.

(v) Not allow unnecessary crowd to be collected near the camps set up by the political parties and candidates near the polling booths so as to avoid confrontation and tension among workers and sympathisers of the parties and the candidates.

(vi) Ensure that the candidate's camps shall be simple. They shall not display any posters, flags, symbols or any other propaganda material. No eatable shall be served or crowd allowed at the camps.

(vii) Co-operate with the authorities in complying with the restrictions to be imposed on the plying of vehicles on the polling day and obtain permits for them which should be displayed prominently on those vehicles.

V. POLLING BOOTHS

Excepting the voters, no one without a valid pass from the Election Commission shall enter the polling booths.

VI. OBSERVERS

The Election Commission appoints Observers. If the candidates or their agents have any specific complaint or problem regarding the conduct of elections, they may bring the same to the notice of the Observer.

VII. PARTY IN POWER

The party in power whether at the Centre or in the state or states concerned, shall ensure that no cause is given for any complaint that it has used its official position for the purposes of its election campaign and in particular

(i) (a) The Ministers shall not combine their official visit with electioneering work and shall not also make use of official machinery or personnel during the electioneering work

    (b) Government transport including official air-crafts, vehicles, machinery and personnel shall not be used for furtherance of the interest of the party in power

(ii) Public places such as *maidans* etc., for holding election meetings, and use of helipads for air-flights in connection with elections shall not be monopolised by itself. Other parties and candidates shall be allowed the use of such places and facilities on the same terms and conditions on which they are used by the party in power.

(iii) Rest houses, *dak bungalows* or other Government accommodation shall not be monopolised by the party in power or its candidates and such accommodation shall be allowed to be used by other parties and candidates in a fair manner but no party or candidate shall use or be allowed to use such accommodation (including premises appertaining thereto) as a campaign office or for holding any public meeting for the purposes of election propaganda.

(iv) Issue of advertisement at the cost of public exchequer in the newspapers and other media and the misuse of official mass media during the election period for partisan coverage of political news and publicity regarding achievements with a view to furthering the prospects of the party in power shall be scrupulously avoided.

(v) Ministers and other authorities shall not sanction grants/payments out of discretionary funds from the time elections are announced by the Commission.

(vi) From the time elections are announced by the Commission, ministers and other authorities shall not

    (a) Announce any financial grants in any form or promises thereof

    (b) (Except civil servants) lay foundation stones etc., of projects or schemes of any kind

    (c) Make any promise of construction of roads, provision of drinking water facilities, etc.

    (d) Make any *ad-hoc* appointments in government, public undertakings, etc.

which may have the effect of influencing the voters in favour of the party in power.

Note: The Commission shall announce the date of any election which shall be a date ordinarily not more than three weeks prior to the date on which the notification is likely to be issued in respect of such elections.

(vii) Ministers of Central or state governments shall not enter any polling station or place of counting except in their capacity as a candidate or voter or authorised agent.

Appendix IX

Flag Code of India

There is universal affection and respect for, and loyalty to, the national flag. Yet, a perceptible lack of awareness is often noticed, not only amongst people but also in the organisations / agencies of the government, with regard to laws, practices and conventions that apply to the display of the national flag. Apart from non-statutory instructions issued by the Government from time to time, the display of the national flag is governed by the provisions of the *Emblems and Names (Prevention of Improper Use) Act*, 1950 and the *Prevention of Insults to National Honour Act*, 1971. The **Flag Code of India, 2002**, is an attempt to bring together all such laws, conventions, practices and instructions for the guidance and benefit of all concerned.

For the sake of convenience, the Flag Code of India, 2002, has been divided into three parts. Part I of the code contains a general description of the national flag. Part II of the code is devoted to the display of the national flag by members of public, private organisations, educational institutions, etc. Part III of the code relates to display of the national flag by Central and state governments and their organisations and agencies.

The Flag Code of India, 2002, took effect from January 26, 2002 and superseded the "Flag Code-India" as it existed earlier.

PART I–GENERAL DESCRIPTION OF THE NATIONAL FLAG

1.1 The national flag shall be a tri-colour panel made up of three rectangular panels or sub-panels of equal widths. The colour of the top panel shall be India saffron (*kesari*) and that of the bottom panel shall be India green. The middle panel shall be white, bearing at its centre the design of *Ashoka Chakra* in navy blue colour with 24 equally spaced spokes. The *Ashoka Chakra* shall preferably be screen printed or otherwise printed or stenciled or suitably embroidered and shall be completely visible on both sides of the flag in the centre of the white panel.

1.2 The national flag of India shall be made of hand spun and hand woven wool/cotton/silk *khadi* bunting.

1.3 The national flag shall be rectangular in shape. The ratio of the length to the height (width) of the flag shall be 3:2.

1.4 The standard sizes of the national flag shall be as follows:

Flag Size No.	Dimensions in mm
1	6300 × 4200
2	3600 × 2400
3	2700 × 1800
4	1800 × 1200
5	1350 × 900
6	900 × 600
7	450 × 300
8	225 × 150
9	150 × 100

1.5 An appropriate size should be chosen for display. The flags of 450 × 300 mm size are intended for aircrafts on VVIP flights, 225 × 150 mm size for motor-cars and 150 × 100 mm size for tables.

PART II–HOISTING/DISPLAY/USE OF NATIONAL FLAG BY MEMBERS OF PUBLIC, PRIVATE ORGANISATIONS, EDUCATIONAL INSTITUTIONS, ETC.

Section I

2.1 There shall be no restriction on the display of the national flag by members of general public, private organisations, educational institutions, etc., except to the extent provided in the *Emblems and Names (Prevention of Improper Use) Act*, 1950 and the *Prevention of Insults to National Honour Act*, 1971 and any other law enacted on the subject. Keeping in view the provisions of the aforementioned Acts

(i) The flag shall not be used for commercial purposes in violation of the *Emblems and Names (Prevention of Improper Use) Act*, 1950

(ii) The flag shall not be dipped in salute to any person or thing

(iii) The flag shall not be flown at half-mast except on occasions on which the flag is flown at half-mast on public buildings in accordance with the instructions issued by the Government

(iv) The flag shall not be used as a drapery in any form whatsoever, including private funerals

(v) The flag shall not be used as a portion of costume or uniform of any description nor shall it be embroidered or printed upon cushions, handkerchiefs, napkins or any dress material

(vi) Lettering of any kind shall not be put upon the flag

(vii) The flag shall not be used as a receptacle for receiving, delivering, holding or carrying anything:
Except that there shall be no objection to keeping flower petals inside the flag before it is unfurled as part of celebrations on special occasions and on national days like the Republic Day and the Independence Day;

(viii) When used on occasions like unveiling of a statue, the flag shall be displayed distinctly and separately and it shall not be used as a covering for the statue or monument

(ix) The flag shall not be used to cover a speaker's desk nor shall it be draped over a speaker's platform

(x) The flag shall not be intentionally allowed to touch the ground or the floor or trail in water

(xi) The flag shall not be draped over the hood, top, sides or back of a vehicle, train, boat or an aircraft

(xii) The flag shall not be used as a covering for a building

(xiii) The flag shall not be intentionally displayed with its saffron portion downwards

2.2 A member of public, a private organisation or an educational institution may hoist/display the national flag on all days and occasions, ceremonial or otherwise. Consistent with the dignity and honour of the national flag

(i) Whenever the national flag is displayed, it should occupy the position of honour and should be distinctly placed

(ii) A damaged or dishevelled flag should not be displayed

(iii) The flag should not be flown from a single masthead simultaneously with any other flag or flags

(iv) The flag should not be flown on any vehicle except in accordance with the provisions contained in Section IX of Part III of this code

(v) When the flag is displayed on a speaker's platform, it should be flown on the speaker's right as he faces the audience or flat against the wall, above and behind the speaker

(vi) When the flag is displayed flat and horizontal on a wall, the saffron band should be upper most and when displayed vertically, the saffron band shall be on the right with reference to the flag (i.e., left to the person facing the flag)

(vii) To the extent possible, the flag should conform to the specifications prescribed in Part I of this code

(viii) No other flag or bunting should be placed higher than or above or side by side with the national flag; nor should any object including flowers or garlands or emblem be placed on or above the flag-mast from which the flag is flown

(ix) The flag should not be used as a festoon, rosette or bunting or in any other manner for decoration

(x) The flag made of paper may be waved by public on occasions of important national, cultural and sports events. However, such paper flags should not be discarded or thrown on the ground after the event. As far as possible, they should be disposed of in private consistent with the dignity of the flag

(xi) Where the flag is displayed in open, it should, as far as possible, be flown from sunrise to sunset, irrespective of weather conditions

(xii) The flag should not be displayed or fastened in any manner as may damage it

(xiii) When the flag is in a damaged or soiled condition, it shall be destroyed as a whole in private, preferably by burning or by any other method consistent with the dignity of the flag.

Section II

2.3 The national flag may be hoisted in educational institutions (schools, colleges, sports camps, scout camps, etc.) to inspire respect for the flag. A model set of instructions for guidance is given here.

(i) The school will assemble in open square formation with pupils forming the three sides and the flag-staff at the centre of the fourth side. The headmaster, the pupil leader and the person unfurling the flag (if other than the headmaster) will stand three paces behind the flag-staff.

(ii) The pupils will fall according to classes and in squads of ten (or other number according to strength). These squads will be arranged one behind the other. The pupil leader of the class will stand to the right of the first row of his class and the form master will stand three paces behind the last row of his class, towards the middle. The classes will be arranged along the square in the order of seniority with the senior most class at the right end.

(iii) The distance between each row should be at least one pace (30 inches) and the space between form and form should be the same.

(iv) When each form or class is ready, the class leader will step forward and salute the selected school pupil leader. As soon as all the forms are ready, the school pupil leader will step up to the headmaster and salute him. The headmaster will return the salute. Then, the flag will be unfurled. The school pupil leader may assist.

(v) The school pupil leader in charge of the parade (or assembly) will call the parade to attention, just before the unfurling, and he will call them to the salute when the flag flies out. The parade will keep at the salute for a brief interval, and then on the command "order", the parade will come to the attention position.

(vi) The flag salutation will be followed by the national anthem. The parade will be kept at the attention during this part of the function.

(vii) On all occasions when the pledge is taken, the pledge will follow the national anthem. When taking the pledge the assembly will stand to attention and the headmaster will administer the pledge ceremoniously and the assembly will repeat it after him.

(viii) In pledging allegiance to the national flag, the practice to be adopted in schools is as follows:

Standing with folded hands, all repeat together the following pledge:

"I pledge allegiance to the National Flag and to the Sovereign Socialist Secular Democratic Republic for which it stands."

PART III—HOISTING/DISPLAY OF THE NATIONAL FLAG BY THE CENTRAL AND STATE GOVERNMENTS AND THEIR ORGANISATIONS AND AGENCIES

Section I: Defence Installations/Heads of Missions/Posts

3.1 The provisions of this part shall not apply to defence installations that have their own rule for display of the national flag.

3.2 The national flag may also be flown on the headquarters and the residences of the heads of missions/posts abroad in the countries where it is customary for diplomatic and consular representatives to fly their national flags on the headquarters and their official residences.

Section II: Official Display

3.3 Subject to the provisions contained in Section I above, it shall be mandatory for all governments and their organisations/agencies to follow the provisions contained in this part.

3.4 On all occasions for official display, only the flag conforming to specifications laid down by the Bureau of Indian Standards and bearing their standard mark shall be used. On other occasions also, it is desirable that only such flags as of appropriate size are flown.

Section III: Correct Display

3.5 Wherever the flag is flown, it should occupy the position of honour and be distinctly placed.

3.6 Where the practice is to fly the flag on any public building, it shall be flown on that building on all days including Sundays and holidays and, except as provided in this code, it shall be flown from sun-rise to sun-set irrespective of weather conditions. The flag may be flown on such a building at night also but this should be only on very special occasions.

3.7 The flag shall always be hoisted briskly and lowered slowly and ceremoniously. When the hoisting and the lowering of the flag is accompanied by appropriate bugle calls, the hoisting and lowering should be simultaneous with the bugle calls.

3.8 When the flag is displayed from a staff projecting horizontally or at an angle from a windowsill, balcony, or front of a building, the saffron band shall be at the farther end of the staff.

3.9 When the flag is displayed flat and horizontal on a wall, the saffron band shall be upper most and when displayed vertically, the saffron band shall be to the right with reference to the flag, i.e., it may be to the left of a person facing it.

3.10 When the flag is displayed on a speaker's platform, it shall be flown on a staff on the speaker's right as he faces the audience or flat against the wall above and behind the speaker.

3.11 When used on occasions like the unveiling of a statue, the flag shall be displayed distinctly and separately.

3.12 When the flag is displayed alone on a motor car, it shall be flown from a staff, which should be affixed firmly either on the middle front of the bonnet or to the front right side of the car.

3.13 When the flag is carried in a procession or a parade, it shall be either on the marching right, i.e., the flag's own right, or if there is a line of other flags, in front of the centre of the line.

Section IV: Incorrect Display

3.14 A damaged or disheveled flag shall not be displayed.

3.15 The flag shall not be dipped in salute to any person or thing.

3.16 No other flag or bunting shall be placed higher than or above or, except as hereinafter provided, side by side with the national flag; nor shall any object including flowers or garlands or emblem be placed on or above the flag-mast from which the flag is flown.

3.17 The flag shall not be used as a festoon, rosette or bunting or in any other manner for decoration.

3.18 The flag shall not be used to cover a speaker's desk nor shall it be draped over a speaker's platform.

3.19 The flag shall not be displayed with the saffron portion downwards.

3.20 The flag shall not be allowed to touch the ground or the floor or trail in water.

3.21 The flag shall not be displayed or fastened in any manner as may damage it.

Section V: Misuse

3.22 The flag shall not be used as a drapery in any form whatsoever except in State/military/Central para-military forces funerals hereinafter provided.

3.23 The flag shall not be draped over the hood, top, sides or back of a vehicle, train or boat.

3.24 The flag shall not be used or stored in such a manner as may damage or soil it.

3.25 When the flag is in a damaged or soiled condition, it shall not be cast aside or disrespectfully disposed of but shall be destroyed as a whole in private, preferably by burning or by any other method consistent with the dignity of the flag.

3.26 The flag shall not be used as a covering for a building.

3.27 The flag shall not be used as a portion of a costume or uniform of any description. It shall not be embroidered or printed upon cushions, handkerchiefs, napkins or boxes.

3.28 Lettering of any kind shall not be put upon the flag.

3.29 The flag shall not be used in any form of advertisement nor shall an advertising sign be fastened to the pole from which the flag is flown.

3.30 The flag shall not be used as a receptacle for receiving, delivering, holding or carrying anything: Provided that there shall be no objection to keeping flower petals inside the Flag before it is unfurled, as part of celebrations on special occasions and on National Days like the Republic Day and the Independence Day.

Section VI: Salute

3.31 During the ceremony of hoisting or lowering the flag or when the flag is passing in a parade or in a review, all persons present should face the flag and stand at attention. Those present in uniform should render the appropriate salute. When the flag is in a moving column, persons present will stand at attention or salute as the flag passes them. A dignitary may take the salute without a head dress.

Section VII : Display with Flags of other Nations and of United Nations

3.32 When displayed in a straight line with flags of other countries, the national flag shall be on the extreme right, i.e., if an observer were to stand in the center of the row of the flags facing the audience, the national flag should be to his extreme right.

3.33 Flags of foreign countries shall proceed as from the national flag in alphabetical order on the basis of English versions of the names of the countries concerned. It would be permissible in such a case to begin and also to end the row of flags with the national flag and also to include the national flag in the normal country-wise alphabetical order. The national flag shall be hoisted first and lowered last.

3.34 In case flags are to be flown in an open circle, i.e., in an arc or a semi-circle, the same procedure shall be adopted as is indicated in the preceding clause of this section. In case flags are to be flown in a closed, i.e., complete circle, the national flag shall mark the beginning of the circle and the flags of other countries should proceed in a clockwise manner until the last flag is placed next to the national flag. It is not necessary to use separate national flags to mark the beginning and the end of the circle of flags. The national flag shall also be included in its alphabetical order in such a closed circle.

3.35 When the national flag is displayed against a wall with another flag from crossed staffs, the national flag shall be on the right, i.e., the flag's own right, and its staff shall be in front of the staff of the other flag.

3.36 When the United Nation's flag is flown along with the national flag, it can be displayed on either side of the national flag. The general practice is to fly the national flag on the extreme right with reference to the direction which it is facing (i.e., extreme left of an observer facing the masts flying the flags).

3.37 When the national flag is flown with flags of other countries, the flag masts shall be of equal size. International usage forbids the display of the flag of one nation above that of another nation in time of peace.

3.38 The national flag shall not be flown from a single mast-head simultaneously with any other flag or flags. There shall be separate mast-heads for different flags.

Section VIII: Display over Public Buildings/Official Residences

3.39 Normally the national flag should be flown only on important public buildings such as high courts, secretariats, commissioners' offices, collectorates, jails and offices of the district boards, municipalities and *zilla parishads* and departmental/public sector undertakings.

3.40 In frontier areas, the national flag may be flown on the border customs posts, check posts, out posts and at other special places where flying of the flag has special significance. In addition, it may be flown on the camp sites of border patrols.

3.41 The national flag should be flown on the official residences of the President, Vice-President, governors and lieutenant governors when they are at headquarters and on the building in which they stay during their visits to places outside the headquarters. The flag flown on the official residence should, however, be brought down as soon as the dignitary leaves the headquarters and it should be re-hoisted on that building as he enters the main gate of the building on return to the headquarters. When the dignitary is on a visit to a place outside the headquarters, the flag should be hoisted on the building in which he stays as he enters the main gate of that building and it should be brought down as soon as he leaves that place. However, the flag should be flown from sun-rise to sun-set on such official residences, irrespective of whether the dignitary is at headquarters or not on the Republic Day, Independence Day, Mahatama Gandhi's Birthday, National Week (6th to 13th April, in the memory of martyrs of Jalianwala Bagh), any other particular day of national rejoicing as may be specified by the Government of India or, in the case of a state, on the anniversary of formation of that state.

3.42 When the President, the Vice-President or the Prime Minister visits an institution, the national flag may be flown by the institution as a mark of respect.

3.43 On the occasions of the visit to India by foreign dignitaries, namely, President, Vice-President, Emperor/King or Heir Prince and the Prime Minister, the national flag may be flown along with the flag of the foreign country concerned in accordance with the rules contained in Section VII by such private institutions as are according reception to the visiting foreign dignitaries and on such public buildings as the foreign dignitaries intend to visit on the day of visit to the institution.

Section IX: Display on Motor Cars

3.44 The privilege of flying the national flag on motor cars is limited to the
(1) President
(2) Vice-President
(3) Governors and Lieutenant Governors
(4) Heads of Indian missions/posts abroad in the countries to which they are accredited
(5) Prime Minister and other Cabinet Ministers
Ministers of State and Deputy Ministers of the Union
Chief Minister and other Cabinet Ministers of a State or Union Territory
Ministers of State and Deputy Ministers of a State or Union Territory
(6) Speaker of the Lok Sabha
Deputy Chairman of the Rajya Sabha
Deputy Speaker of the Lok Sabha
Chairmen of Legislative Councils in States
Speakers of Legislative Assemblies in States and Union Territories
Deputy Chairmen of Legislative Councils in States
Deputy Speakers of Legislative Assemblies in States and Union Territories
(7) Chief Justice of India
Judges of Supreme Court
Chief Justice of High Courts
Judges of High Courts

3.45 The dignitaries mentioned in Clauses (5) to (7) of Paragraph 3.44 may fly the national flag on their cars, whenever they consider it necessary or advisable.

3.46 When a foreign dignitary travels in a car provided by government, the national flag will be flown on the right side of the car and the flag of the foreign country will be flown on the left side of the car.

Section X: Display on Trains/Aircrafts

3.47 When the President travels by special train within the country, the national flag should be flown from the driver's cab on the side facing the platform of the station from where the train departs. The flag should be flown only when the special train is stationary or when coming into the station where it is going to halt.

3.48 The national flag will be flown on the aircraft carrying the President, the Vice-President or the Prime Minister on a visit to a foreign country. Alongside the national flag, the flag of the country visited should also be flown but, when the aircraft lands in countries *enroute*, the national flags of the countries touched would be flown instead, as a gesture of courtesy and goodwill.

3.49 When the President goes on tour within India, the national flag will be displayed on the side by which the President will embark the aircraft or disembark from it.

Section XI: Half-masting

3.50 In the event of the death of the following dignitaries, the national flag shall be half-masted at the places indicated against each on the day of the death of the dignitary.

Dignitary	Place or Places
President Vice-President Prime Minister	Throughout India
Speaker of the Lok Sabha Chief Justice of India	Delhi
Union Cabinet Minister	Delhi and State Capitals
Minister of State or Deputy Minister of the Union	Delhi
Governor Lt. Governor Chief Minister of a State Chief Minister of a Union territory	Throughout the State or Union Territory concerned
Cabinet Minister in a State	Capital of the State concerned

3.51 If the intimation of the death of any dignitary is received in the afternoon, the flag shall be half-masted on the following day also at the place or places indicated above, provided the funeral has not taken place before sun-rise on that day.

3.52 On the day of the funeral of a dignitary mentioned above, the flag shall be half-masted at the place where the funeral takes place.

3.53 If State mourning is to be observed on the death of any dignitary, the flag shall be half-masted throughout the period of the mourning throughout India in the case of the Union dignitaries and throughout the state or union territory concerned in the case of a state or union territory dignitary.

3.54 Half-masting of the flag and, where necessary, observance of state mourning on the death of foreign dignitaries will be governed by special instructions which will issue from the ministry of Home Affairs in individual cases.

3.55 Notwithstanding the above provisions, in the event of a half-mast day coinciding with the Republic Day, Independence Day, Mahatma Gandhi's Birthday, National Week (6th to 13th April, in the memory of martyrs of Jalianwala Bagh), any other particular day of national rejoicing as may be specified by the Government of India or, in the case of a state, on the anniversary of formation of that state, the flags shall not be flown at half-mast except over the building where the body of the deceased is lying until such time it has been removed and that flag shall be raised to the full-mast position after the body has been removed.

3.56 If mourning were to be observed in a parade or procession where a flag is carried, two streamers of black crepe shall be attached to the spear head, allowing the streamers to fall naturally. The use of black crepe in such a manner shall be only by an order of the Government.

3.57 When flown at half-mast, the flag shall be hoisted to the peak for an instant, then lowered to the half-mast position, but before lowering the flag for the day, it shall be raised again to the peak.

Note: By half-mast is meant hauling down the flag to one half the distance between the top and the guy-line and in the absence of the guy-line, half of the staff.

3.58 On occasions of State/military/Central para-military forces' funerals, the flag shall be draped over the bier or coffin with the saffron towards the head of the bier or coffin. The flag shall not be lowered into the grave or burnt in the pyre.

3.59 In the event of death of either the Head of the State or Head of the Government of a foreign country, the Indian mission accredited to that country may fly the national flag at half-mast even if that event falls on Republic Day, Independence Day, Mahatma Gandhi's Birthday, National Week (6th to 13th April, in the memory of martyrs of Jalianwala Bagh) or any other particular day of national rejoicing as may be specified by the Government of India. In the event of death of any other dignitary of that country, the national flag should not be flown at half-mast by the missions except when the local practice or protocol (which should be ascertained from the Dean of the Diplomatic Corps, where necessary) require that the national flag of a foreign mission in that country should also be flown at half-mast.

Presidents, Vice-Presidents, Prime Ministers, etc.

A. PRESIDENTS OF INDIA

	Name	Tenure
1.	Dr. Rajendra Prasad	1950 – 1962
2.	Dr. Sarvepalli Radhakrishnan	1962 – 1967
3.	Dr. Zakir Husain	1967 – 1969 (Died)
4.	Varahagiri Venkatagiri	1969 – 1969 (Acting)
5.	Justice Mohammad Hidayatullah	1969 – 1969 (Acting)
6.	Varahagiri Venkatagiri	1969 – 1974
7.	Fakhruddin Ali Ahmed	1974 – 1977 (Died)
8.	B.D. Jatti	1977 – 1977 (Acting)
9.	Neelam Sanjiva Reddy	1977 – 1982
10.	Giani Zail Singh	1982 – 1987
11.	R. Venkataraman	1987 – 1992
12.	Dr. Shanker Dayal Sharma	1992 – 1997
13.	K.R. Narayanan	1997 – 2002
14.	Dr. A.P.J. Abdul Kalam	2002 – 2007
15.	Smt. Pratibha Patil	2007 – 2012
16.	Pranab Mukherjee	2012 – till date

B. VICE-PRESIDENTS OF INDIA

	Name	Tenure
1.	Dr.Sarvepalli Radhakrishnan	1952 – 1962
2.	Dr. Zakir Husain	1962 – 1967
3.	Varahagiri Venkatagiri	1967 – 1969
4.	Gopal Swarup Pathak	1969 – 1974
5.	B.D. Jatti	1974 – 1979
6.	Justice Mohammad Hidayatullah	1979 – 1984

(Contd.)

	Name	Tenure
7.	R. Venkataraman	1984 – 1987
8.	Dr. Shanker Dayal Sharma	1987 – 1992
9.	K.R. Narayanan	1992 – 1997
10.	Krishan Kant	1997 – 2002 (Died)
11.	Bhairon Singh Shekhawat	2002 – 2007
12.	Mohammed Hamid Ansari	2007 – 2012
13.	Mohammed Hamid Ansari	2012 – till date

C. PRIME MINISTERS OF INDIA

	Name	Tenure
1.	Jawaharlal Nehru	1947 – 1964 (Died)
2.	Gulzari Lal Nanda	1964 – 1964 (Acting)
3.	Lal Bahadur Shastri	1964 – 1966 (Died)
4.	Gulzari Lal Nanda	1966 – 1966 (Acting)
5.	Indira Gandhi	1966 – 1977
6.	Morarji Desai	1977 – 1979
7.	Charan Singh	1979 – 1980
8.	Indira Gandhi	1980 – 1984 (Died)
9.	Rajiv Gandhi	1984 – 1989
10.	Vishwanath Pratap Singh	1989 – 1990
11.	Chandra Shekhar	1990 – 1991
12.	P.V. Narasimha Rao	1991 – 1996
13.	Atal Bihari Vajpayee	1996 – 1996 (For 16 Days)
14.	H.D. Deve Gowda	1996 – 1997
15.	I.K. Gujral	1997 – 1998
16.	Atal Bihari Vajpayee	1998 – 1999
17.	Atal Bihari Vajpayee	1999 – 2004
18.	Dr. Manmohan Singh	2004 – 2009
19.	Dr. Manmohan Singh	2009 – till date

D. DEPUTY PRIME MINISTERS

	Name	Tenure
1.	Sardar Vallabhbhai Patel	1947 – 1950
2.	Morarji Desai	1967 – 1969
3.	Charan Singh and Jagjivan Ram (jointly)	1979 – 1979
4.	Y.B. Chavan	1979 – 1980
5.	Devi Lal	1989 – 1990
6.	Devi Lal	1990 – 1991
7.	L.K. Advani	2002 – 2004

E. UNION FINANCE MINISTERS

	Name	Tenure
1.	R.K. Shanmukham Chetty	1947 – 1949
2.	John Mathai	1949 – 1951
3.	C.D. Deshmukh	1951 – 1957
4.	T.T. Krishnamachari	1957 – 1958
5.	Jawaharlal Nehru	1958 – 1959
6.	Morarji Desai	1959 – 1964
7.	T.T. Krishnamachari	1964 – 1966
8.	Sachindra Chowdhury	1966 – 1967
9.	Morarji Desai	1967 – 1970
10.	Indira Gandhi	1970 – 1971
11.	Y.B. Chavan	1971 – 1975
12.	C. Subramaniam	1975 – 1977
13.	H.M. Patel	1977 – 1978
14.	Charan Singh	1979 – 1980
15.	R. Venkataraman	1980 – 1982
16.	Pranab Mukherjee	1982 – 1985
17.	V.P. Singh	1985 – 1987
18.	N.D. Tiwari	1988 – 1989
19.	S.B. Chavan	1989 – 1990
20.	Madhu Dandavate	1990 – 1991
21.	Yashwant Sinha	1991 – 1991
22.	Manmohan Singh	1991 – 1996
23.	P. Chidambaram	1996 – 1998
24.	Yashwant Sinha	1998 – 2002
25.	Jaswant Singh	2002 – 2004
26.	P. Chidambaram	2004 – 2008
27.	Pranab Mukherjee	2009 – 2012
28.	P. Chidambaram	2012 – till date

F. SPEAKERS OF THE LOK SABHA

	Name	Tenure
1.	Ganesh Vasudev Mavalankar	1952 – 1956 *(Died)*
2.	M. Ananthasayanam Ayyangar	1956 – 1962
3.	Hukam Singh	1962 – 1967
4.	Neelam Sanjiva Reddy	1967 – 1969 (Resigned)
5.	Gurdial Singh Dhillon	1969 – 1975 (Resigned)
6.	Bali Ram Bhagat	1976 – 1977
7.	Neelam Sanjiva Reddy	1977 – 1977 (Resigned)
8.	K.S. Hegde	1977 – 1980
9.	Bal Ram Jakhar	1980 – 1989
10.	Rabi Ray	1989 – 1991
11.	Shivraj V. Patil	1991 – 1996
12.	P.A. Sangma	1996 – 1998
13.	G.M.C. Balayogi	1998 – 2002 (Died)
14.	Manohar Gajanan Joshi	2002 – 2004
15.	Somnath Chatterjee	2004 – 2009
16.	Ms. Meira Kumar	2009 – till date

G. CHIEF JUSTICES OF INDIA

	Name	Tenure
1.	Harilal J. Kania	1950 – 1951
2.	M. Patanjali Sastri	1951 – 1954
3.	M.C. Mahajan	1954 – 1954
4.	B.K. Mukherjea	1954 – 1956
5.	S.R. Das	1956 – 1959
6.	B.P. Sinha	1959 – 1964
7.	P.B. Gajendragadkar	1964 – 1966
8.	A.K. Sarkar	1966 – 1966
9.	K. Subba Rao	1966 – 1967
10.	K.N. Wanchoo	1967 – 1968
11.	M. Hidayatullah	1968 – 1970
12.	J.C. Shah	1970 – 1971
13.	S.M. Sikri	1971 – 1973
14.	A.N. Ray	1973 – 1977
15.	M.H. Beg	1977 – 1978
16.	Y.V. Chandrachud	1978 – 1985
17.	P.N. Bhagwati	1985 – 1986
18.	R.S. Pathak	1986 – 1989
19.	E.S. Venkataramaiah	1989 – 1989
20.	S. Mukherjee	1989 – 1990
21.	Ranganath Mishra	1990 – 1991
22.	K.N. Singh	1991 – 1991
23.	M.H. Kania	1991 – 1992
24.	L.M. Sharma	1992 – 1993
25.	M.N. Venkatachalaiah	1993 – 1994
26.	A.M. Ahmadi	1994 – 1997
27.	J.S. Verma	1997 – 1998
28.	M.M. Punchhi	1998 – 1998

(Contd.)

(Contd.)

	Name	Tenure
29.	A.S. Anand	1998 – 2001
30.	S.P. Bharucha	2001 – 2002
31.	B.N. Kirpal	2002 – 2002
32.	G.B. Pattanaik	2002 – 2002
33.	V.N. Khare	2002 – 2004
34.	S. Rajendra Babu	2004 – 2004
35.	R.C. Lahoti	2004 – 2005
36.	Y.K. Sabharwal	2005 – 2007
37.	K.G. Balakrishnan	2007 – 2010
38.	S.H. Kapadia	2010 – 2012
39.	Altamas Kabir	2012 – till date

H. CHIEF ELECTION COMMISSIONERS OF INDIA

	Name	Tenure
1.	Sukumar Sen	1950 – 1958
2.	K.V.K. Sundaram	1958 – 1967
3.	S.P. Sen Verma	1967 – 1972
4.	Dr. Nagendra Singh	1972 – 1973
5.	T. Swaminathan	1973 – 1977
6.	S.L. Shakdhar	1977 – 1982
7.	R.K. Trivedi	1982 – 1985
8.	R.V.S. Peri Sastri	1986 – 1990
9.	Smt. V.S. Rama Devi	1990 – 1990
10.	T.N. Seshan	1990 – 1996
11.	M.S. Gill	1996 – 2001
12.	J.M. Lyngdoh	2001 – 2004
13.	T.S. Krishna Murthy	2004 – 2005
14.	B.B. Tandon	2005 – 2006
15.	N. Gopalaswamy	2006 – 2009
16.	Naveen Chawla	2009 – 2010
17.	S.Y. Quraishi	2010 – 2012
18.	V.S. Sampath	2012 – till date

I. CHAIRMEN OF THE UPSC

	Name	Tenure
1.	Sir Ross Barker	1926 – 1932
2.	Sir David Petrie	1932 – 1936
3.	Sir Eyre Gorden	1937 – 1942
4.	Sir F.W. Robertson	1942 – 1947
5.	H.K. Kripalani	1947 – 1949
6.	R.N. Banerjee	1949 – 1955
7.	N. Govindarajan	1955 – 1955
8.	V.S. Hejmadi	1955 – 1961
9.	B.N. Jha	1961 – 1967
10.	K.R. Damle	1967 – 1971
11.	R.C.S. Sarkar	1971 – 1973

(Contd.)

	Name	Tenure
12.	Dr. A.R. Kidwai	1973 – 1979
13.	Dr. M.L. Shahare	1979 – 1985
14.	H.K.L. Capoor	1985 – 1990
15.	J.P. Gupta	1990 – 1992
16.	Smt. R.M. Bathew (Kharbuli)	1992 – 1996
17.	S.J.S. Chhatwal	1996 – 1996
18.	J.M. Qureshi	1996 – 1998
19.	Lt. Gen. (Retd.) Surinder Nath	1998 – 2002
20.	P.C. Hota	2002 – 2003
21.	Mata Prasad	2003 – 2005
22.	Dr. S.R. Hashim	2005 – 2006
23.	Gurbachan Jagat	2006 – 2007
24.	Subir Dutta	2007 – 2008
25.	D.P. Agrawal	2008 – till date

J. COMPTROLLER AND AUDITOR-GENERALS OF INDIA

	Name	Tenure
1.	V. Narhari Rao	1948 – 1954
2.	A.K. Chanda	1954 – 1960
3.	SH. A.K. Roy	1960 – 1966
4.	S. Ranganathan	1966 – 1972
5.	A. Baksi	1972 – 1978
6.	Gian Prakash	1978 – 1984
7.	T.N. Chaturvedi	1984 – 1990
8.	C.G. Somiah	1990 – 1996
9.	V.K. Shunglu	1996 – 2002
10.	V.N. Kaul	2002 – 2008
11.	Vinod Rai	2008 – 2013
12.	Shashi Kant Sharma	2013 – till date

K. ATTORNEY – GENERALS OF INDIA

	Name	Tenure
1.	M.C. Setalvad	1950 – 1963
2.	C.K. Daphtary	1963 – 1963
3.	Niren De	1968 – 1977
4.	S.V. Gupte	1977 – 1979
5.	L.N. Sinha	1979 – 1983
6.	K. Parasaran	1983 – 1989
7.	Soli J.Sorabjee	1989 – 1990
8.	G. Ramaswamy	1990 – 1992
9.	Milon K. Banerjee	1992 – 1996
10.	Ashok K. Desai	1996 – 1998
11.	Soli J. Sorabjee	1998 – 2004
12.	Milon K. Banerjee	2004 – 2009
13.	Goolam E. Vahanvati	2009 – till date

Appendix XI

UPSC Questions on Indian Polity (General Studies–Prelims)

1. The only instance when the President of India exercised his power of veto related to
   (a) the Hindu Code Bill
   (b) the PEPSU Appropriation Bill
   (c) the Indian Post Office (Amendment) Bill
   (d) the Dowry Prohibition Bill

2. The Chief Minister of a State in India is NOT eligible to vote in the Presidential election if
   (a) he himself is a candidate
   (b) he is yet to prove his majority on the floor of the Lower House of the State legislature
   (c) he is a member of the Upper House of the State Legislature
   (d) he is a caretaker Chief Minister

3. The abolition of the I.A.S. and the I.P.S. has been recommended by the
   (a) Dhebar Commission
   (b) Kalekar Commission
   (c) Kher Commission
   (d) Rajamannar Commission

4. Among the four pairs given below which one consists of a correct combination of dignitaries who became Vice-Presidents after having held diplomatic posts like Ambassadors and High Commissioners ?
   (a) Dr. S. Radhakrishnan and G.S. Pathak
   (b) Dr. S. Radhakrishnan and V.V. Giri
   (c) Dr. Zakir Hussain and K.R. Narayanan
   (d) B.D. Jatti and K.R. Narayanan

5. Which one of the following statements is correct?
   (a) Neither the Finance Commission nor the Planning Commission is a constitutional body
   (b) The scope of the Finance Commission is limited to a review of the revenue segment of the budget while the Planning Commission takes an overall review embracing both capital and revenue requirements of the States
   (c) No one can be a member of both the Finance Commission and the Planning Commission at the same time
   (d) There is no overlapping of work and responsibility of the Finance Commission and those of the Planning Commission.

6. The Swaran Singh Committee considered the question of
   (a) more autonomy to Punjab on the model of Jammu and Kashmir
   (b) the suitability of the Presidential form of government for India
   (c) the precedence of the Directive Principles over Fundamental Rights
   (d) administrative reforms

7. Which one of the following is a feature common to both the Indian Federation and the American Federation ?
   (a) A single citizenship
   (b) Three lists in the Constitution
   (c) Dual judiciary
   (d) A federal supreme court to interpret the Constitution

8. Which one of the following is in the Concurrent List in the Constitution of India ?
   (a) Population control and family planning
   (b) Public health and sanitation
   (c) Capitation taxes
   (d) Treasure trove

9. Which one of the following statements regarding the office of the Speaker is correct ?
   (a) He holds office during the pleasure of the President

(b) He need not be a member of the House at the time of his election but has to become a member of the House within six months from the date of his election.

(c) He loses his office if the House is dissolved before the end of its normal tenure

(d) If he intends to resign the letter of his resignation is to be addressed to the Deputy Speaker

10. Which one of the following comes under the jurisdiction of both the High Court and the Supreme Court ?

    (a) Disputes between the Centre and the States

    (b) Disputes between the States inter se

    (c) Protection of the Fundamental Rights

    (d) Protection against the violation of the Constitution

11. The Anti-Defection Law was enacted as early as 1979 in

    (a) Kerala

    (b) Jammu and Kashmir

    (c) West Bengal

    (d) Tamil Nadu

12. Which one of the following is INCORRECT in respect of Parliamentary control over the Budget?

    (a) Parliament has no say in the preparation of the budget

    (b) Parliament has the power to increase expenditure charged on the Consolidated Fund

    (c) Parliament has no power to impose a tax without the President's recommendation

    (d) Parliament has no power to increase a tax without the President's recommendation

13. Match List I with List Ii and select the correct answer by using the codes given below the lists :

List-I (Features of the Indian Constitution)	List-II (Borrowed from)
A. Fundamental Rights	1. U.K.
B. Parliamentary system of government	2. U.S.A.
C. Emergency provisions	3. Ireland
D. Directive Principles of State Policy	4. German Reich
	5. Canada

Codes :

	A	B	C	D
(a)	2	4	5	1
(b)	5	1	3	4
(c)	2	1	4	3
(d)	1	2	4	3

14. Which of the following statements regarding the Constituent Assembly are true ?

    1. It was not based on adult franchise.

    2. It resulted from direct elections.

    3. It was a multi-party body.

    4. It worked through several committees.

Select the correct answer from the codes given below:

    (a) 1 and 2

    (b) 2 and 3

    (c) 1 and 4

    (d) 1, 2, 3 and 4

1994 TEST PAPER

1. Which of the following statements regarding the advisory jurisdiction of the Supreme Court are correct?

    1. It is binding on the Supreme Court to give its opinion on any matter referred to it by the President.

    2. The full bench of the Supreme Court hears any reference made to it under its power of advisory jurisdiction.

    3. The opinion given by the Supreme Court on a reference under advisory jurisdiction is not binding on the government.

    4. Not more than one reference at a time can be made to the Supreme Court under its power of advisory jurisdiction.

Select the correct answer from the codes given below:

    (a) 1 and 2

    (b) 1 and 3

    (c) 2 and 3

    (d) 2 and 4

2. Which one of the following statements is correct?

    (a) All the members of the Rajya Sabha are elected by State Legislative Assemblies

    (b) As the Vice-president is the ex-officio Chairman of the Rajya Sabha, only a member of the Rajya Sabha can contest for the office of the Vice-president

    (c) A point of difference between the Lok Sabha and the Rajya Sabha is that while a candidate to the Lok Sabha can contest from any State in India, a candidate to the Rajya Sabha should ordinarily be a resident of the State from where he is contesting

    (d) The Constitution of India explicitly prohibits the appointment of a nominated member of the Rajya Sabha to the post of a minister

3. Freedom of the press in India

    (a) is specially provided in Article 19(1)(a) of the Constitution

    (b) is implied in the wider freedom of expression guaranteed by Article 19(1)(a) of the constitution

    (c) is guaranteed under the provisions of Article 361A of the Constitution

    (d) emanates from the operation of the Rule of Law in the country

4. In which respect have the Centre-State relations been specifically termed as 'municipal relations'?
   - (a) Centre's control of the State in legislative sphere
   - (b) Centre's control of the State in financial matters
   - (c) Centre's control of the State in the administrative sector
   - (d) Centre's control of the State in the planning process

5. Which one of the following statements regarding 'Exit Poll' is correct ?
   - (a) 'Exit Poll' is a term used to denote a post-election survey of voters regarding the candidate in whose favour they had exercised their franchise
   - (b) 'Exit Poll' and 'Opinion Poll' are one and the same
   - (c) 'Exit Poll' is device through which results of voting can be most exactly predicted
   - (d) 'Exit Poll' is an administrative device made recently by the Chief Election Commissioner to prevent impersonation

6. Who among the following became the Prime Minister of India without being earlier the Chief Minister of a State ?
   1. Morarji Desai
   2. Charan Singh
   3. V.P. Singh
   4. Chandrashekhar
   5. P.V. Narasimha Rao

   Select the correct answer from the codes given below:
   Codes:
   - (a) 1, 2 and 4
   - (b) 2, 3 and 5
   - (c) 2 only
   - (d) 4 only

7. Given below are two statements, one labelled as Assertion (A) and the other labelled as Reason (R):

   Assertion (A): In India, the political parties which formed the governments represented the majority of seats secured in the elections to the House of the People at the Centre and the Legislative Assemblies in the States but not the majority of votes.

   Reason (R): The elections based on the majority-vote-system decide the result on the basis of relative majority of votes secured.

   In the context of the above two statements, which one of the following is correct ?
   - (a) Both A and R are true and R is the correct explanation of A
   - (b) Both A and R are true, but R is not a correct explanation of A
   - (c) A is true, but R is false
   - (d) A is false, but R is true

8. Which of the following is/are among the functions of the Election Commission of India ?
   1. Conduct of election for the posts of the Speaker and the Deputy Speaker, Lok Sabha and the Deputy Chairman, Rajya Sabha
   2. Conduct of election to the Corporations and Municipalities
   3. Deciding on all doubts and disputes arising out of elections

   Select the correct answer from the codes given below:
   Codes:
   - (a) 1 and 2
   - (b) 1 and 3
   - (c) 2 and 3
   - (d) None

9. Which of the following electoral systems have been adopted for various elections in India?
   1. System of direct election on the basis of adult suffrage
   2. System of proportional representation by means of the single transferable vote
   3. List system of proportional representation
   4. Cumulative system of indirect elections

   Select the correct answer from the codes given below:
   Codes:
   - (a) 1 and 2
   - (b) 1 and 3
   - (c) 1, 2 and 3
   - (d) 2, 3 and 4

10. Which of the following taxes is/are levied by the Union and collected and appropriated by the States?
    - (a) Stamp duties
    - (b) Passenger and goods tax
    - (c) Estate duty
    - (d) Taxes on Newspapers

11. Which one of the following determines that the Indian Constitution is federal ?
    - (a) A written and rigid Constitution
    - (b) An independent Judiciary
    - (c) Vesting of residuary powers with the Centre
    - (d) Distribution of powers between the Centre and the States

12. Given below are voting percentages of a political party secured in three successive elections to the Lok Sabha:

Years	1984	1989	1991
Percentages of Votes	7.4	11.4	22.4

The party which secured these percentages of votes was
- (a) Congress (I)
- (b) Bahujan Samaj Party
- (c) Bharatiya Janata Party
- (d) Communist Party of India (Marxist)

13. Who among the following are appointed by the President of India ?
    1. The Chairman, Finance Commission
    2. The Deputy Chairman, Planning Commission
    3. The Chief Minister of a Union Territory

    Choose the correct answer from the codes given below:
    Codes:
    (a) 1 only
    (b) 1 and 2 only
    (c) 1 and 3 only
    (d) 2 and 3 only

14. The basic structure theory of the Constitution of India implies that
    (a) certain features of the Constitution are so essential to it that they cannot be abrogated
    (b) fundamental rights cannot be abridged or taken away
    (c) the Constitution cannot be amended except in accordance with the procedure prescribed in Art. 368
    (d) the Preamble of the Constitution cannot be amended for it is not part of the Constitution and at the same time represents its real spirit

1995 TEST PAPER

1. The Dinesh Goswami Committee was concerned with
   (a) de-nationalisation of banks
   (b) electoral reforms
   (c) steps to put down insurgency in the north east
   (d) the problem of the chakmas

2. Which one of the following is not explicitly stated in the Constitution of India but followed as a convention?
   (a) The Finance Minister is to be a Member of the Lower House
   (b) The Prime Minister has to resign if he loses majority in the Lower House
   (c) All the parts of India are to be represented in the Council of Ministers
   (d) In the event of both the President and the Vice-President demitting office simultaneously before the end of their tenure the Speaker of the Lower House of the Parliament will officiate as the President.

3. Which of the following are the States in which the Lok Ayukta Act includes the Chief Minister in its ambit ?
   (a) West Bengal and Kerala
   (b) Gujarat and Maharashtra
   (c) Madhya Pradesh and Orissa
   (d) Rajasthan and Karnataka

4. Which one of the following is incorrect in respect of Local Government in India ?
   (a) According to the Indian Constitution, local government is not an independent tier in the federal system
   (b) 30% of the seats in local bodies are reserved for women
   (c) Local government finances are to be provided by a Commission
   (d) Elections to local bodies are to be determined by a Commission.

5. Which of the following political parties is/are national political parties ?
   1. Muslim League
   2. Revolutionary Socialist Party
   3. All India Forward Block
   4. Peasants and Workers Party of India

   Choose the correct answer from the codes given below:
   Codes:
   (a) 1, 2 and 3
   (b) 2 and 4
   (c) 3 only
   (d) None

6. If in an election to a State Legislative Assembly the candidate who is declared elected loses his deposit, it means that
   (a) the polling was very poor
   (b) the election was for a multi-member constituency
   (c) the elected candidate's victory over his nearest rival was very marginal
   (d) a very large number of candidates contested the election

7. Which one of the following is correct in respect of the commencement of the election process in India ?
   (a) The recommendation for election is made by the government and the notification for election is issued by the Election Commission
   (b) The recommendation for election is made by the Election Commission and the notification for election is issued by the Home Ministry at the Centre and Home Departments in the States
   (c) The recommendation for election is made by the Election Commission and the notification for election is issued by the President and Governors of the States concerned
   (d) Both the exercises of making a recommendation for election and that of issuing a notification in respect of it are done by the Election Commission

8. Which of the following is/are extra-constitutional and extra-legal device(s) for securing cooperation and coordination between the States in India ?

1. The National Development Council
2. The Governor's Conference
3. Zonal Councils
4. The Inter-State Council

Choose the correct answer from the codes given below:

Codes:
- (a) 1 and 2
- (b) 1, 3 and 4
- (c) 3 and 4
- (d) 4 only

9. Which of the following are matters on which a constitutional amendment is possible only with the ratification of the legislatures of not less than one-half of the States ?
   1. Election of the President
   2. Representation of States in Parliament
   3. Any of the Lists in the 7th Schedule
   4. Abolition of the Legislative Council of a State

   Choose the correct answer from the codes given below:

   Codes:
   - (a) 1, 2 and 3
   - (b) 1, 2 and 4
   - (c) 1, 3 and 4
   - (d) 2, 3 and 4

10. Consider the table given below:

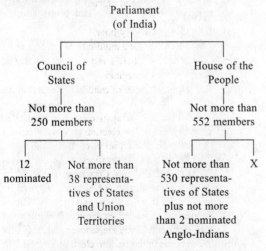

Parliament (of India)

Council of States — Not more than 250 members — 12 nominated, Not more than 38 representatives of States and Union Territories

House of the People — Not more than 552 members — Not more than 530 representatives of States plus not more than 2 nominated Anglo-Indians, X

Which one of the following will fit in the place marked 'X'?
- (a) Ministers who are not members of Parliament but who have to get themselves elected to either House of Parliament within six months after assuming office
- (b) Not more than 20 nominated members
- (c) Not more than 20 representatives of Union Territories

(d) The Attorney General who has the right to speak and take part in the proceedings of either House of Parliament.

11. Who among the following have the right to vote in the elections to both the Lok Sabha and the Rajya Sabha?
    - (a) Elected members of the Lower House of the Parliament
    - (b) Elected Members of the Upper House of the Parliament
    - (c) Elected members of the Upper House of the State Legislature
    - (d) Elected members of the Lower House of the State Legislature

12. Which one of the following States of India does not have a Legislative Council so far even though the Constitution (Seventh Amendment) Act, 1956 provides for it ?
    - (a) Maharashtra
    - (b) Bihar
    - (c) Karnataka
    - (d) Madhya Pradesh

13. In the interim government formed in 1946 the Vice-President of the Executive Council was
    - (a) Jawaharlal Nehru
    - (b) Dr. S. Radhakrishnan
    - (c) C. Rajagopalachari
    - (d) Dr. Rajendra Prasad

14. Article 156 of the Constitution of India provides that a Governor shall hold office for a term of five years from the date on which he enters upon his office. Which of the following can be deduced from this?
    1. No Governor can be removed from office till the completion of his term.
    2. No Governor can continue in office beyond a period of five years.

    Select the correct answer from the codes given below:

    Codes:
    - (a) 1 only
    - (b) 2 only
    - (c) Both 1 and 2
    - (d) Neither

15. Prohibition of discrimination on grounds of religion etc. (Article 15 of the Constitution of India) is a Fundamental Right classifiable under
    - (a) the Right to Freedom of Religion
    - (b) the Right against Exploitation
    - (c) the Cultural and Educational Rights
    - (d) the Right to Equality

16. Corporation tax
    - (a) is levied and appropriated by the States

(b) is levied by the Union and collected and appropriated by the States

(c) is levied by the Union and shared by the Union and the States

(d) is levied by the Union and belongs to it exclusively

17. Agricultural income tax is assigned to the State governments by
    (a) the Finance Commission
    (b) the National Development Council
    (c) the Inter-State Council
    (d) the Constitution of India

1996 Test Paper

1. If the number of seats allocated to a state in the Lok Sabha is 42, then the number of seats reserved for the Scheduled Castes in that state will be
   (a) 21   (b) 14   (c) 7   (d) 6

2. The power of the Supreme Court of India to decide disputes between the Centre and the States falls under its
   (a) advisory jurisdiction
   (b) appellate jurisdiction
   (c) original jurisdiction
   (d) constitutional jurisdiction

3. Given below are two statements, one labelled as Assertion (A) and the other labelled as Reason (R):
   Assertion (A): The British sovereignty continued to exist in free India.
   Reason (R): The British sovereign appointed the last Governor General of free India.
   In the context of the above two statements, which one of the following is correct ?
   (a) Both A and R are true and R is the correct explanation of A
   (b) Both A and R are true, but R is not a correct explanation of A
   (c) A is true, but R is false
   (d) A is false, but R is true

4. When the Chief Justice of a High Court acts in an administrative capacity, he is subject to
   (a) the writ jurisdiction of any of the other judges of the High Court
   (b) special control exercised by the Chief Justice of India
   (c) discretionary powers of the Governor of the state
   (d) special powers provided to the Chief Minister in this regard

5. According to the Constitution of India, the term 'District Judge' shall not include
   (a) chief presidency magistrate
   (b) sessions judge

(c) tribunal judge

(d) chief judge of a small cause court

6. Which one of the following is part of the electoral college for the election of the President of India but does not form part of the forum for his impeachment?
   (a) Lok Sabha
   (b) Rajya Sabha
   (c) State Legislative Councils
   (d) State Legislative Assemblies

7. What is the system of governance in the Panchayati Raj set-up ?
   (a) Single tier structure of local self-government at the village level
   (b) Two tier system of local self-government at the village and block levels
   (c) Three tier structure of local self-government, at the village, block and district levels
   (d) Four tier system of local self-government at the village, block, district and state levels

8. Consider the following statements:
   No one can be compelled to sing the National Anthem since
   1. it will be violative of the Right to freedom of speech and expression.
   2. it will be violative of the Right to freedom of conscience and practice and propagation of religion.
   3. there is no provision obliging anyone to sing the National Anthem.
   Of these statements:
   (a) 1 and 2 are correct
   (b) 2 and 3 are correct
   (c) 1, 2 and 3 are correct
   (d) none is correct

9. Which one of the following statements is correct?
   The prime minister of India
   (a) is free to choose his ministers only from among those who are members of either House of the Parliament
   (b) can choose his cabinet colleagues after due counselling by the President of India in this regard
   (c) has full discretion in the choice of persons who are to serve as ministers in his cabinet
   (d) has only limited powers in the choice of his cabinet colleagues because of the discretionary powers vested with the President of India

10. Given below are two statements, one labelled as Assertion (A) and the other labelled as Reason (R):
    Assertion (A): The world 'minority' is not defined in the Constitution of India.
    Reason (R): The Minorities Commission is not a constitutional body.

In the context of the above two statements, which one of the following is correct ?

(a) Both A and R are true and R is the correct explanation of A

(b) Both A and R are true, but R is not a correct explanation of A

(c) A is true, but R is false

(d) A is false, but R is true

1997 Test Paper

1. In the Presidential election in India, every elected member of the Legislative Assembly of a State shall have as many votes as there are multiples of one thousand in the quotient obtained by dividing the population of the State by the total number of the elected members of the Assembly. As at present (1997) the expression "Population" here means the population as ascertained by the

(a) 1991 Census   (b) 1981 Census

(c) 1971 Census   (d) 1961 Census

2. Which of the following are/is stated in the Constitution of India ?

1. The President shall not be a member of either Houses of Parliament.

2. The Parliament shall consist of the President and two Houses.

Choose the correct answer from the codes given below:

Codes:

(a) Neither 1 nor 2   (b) Both 1 and 2

(c) 1 alone   (d) 2 alone

3. Match List I with List II and select the correct answer by using the codes given below the lists :

List-I (Functionaries)	List-II (Oaths or affirmations)
A. President of India	1. Secrecy of Information
B. Judges of the Supreme Court	2. Faithful Discharge of Duties
C. Members of Parliament	3. Faith and Allegiance to the Constitution of India
D. Ministers for the Union	4. Upholding the Constitution and the law

Codes:

	A	B	C	D
(a)	3	4	1	2
(b)	4	3	2	1
(c)	3	4	2	1
(d)	4	3	1	2

4. In the following quotation,

"WE, THE PEOPLE OF INDIA,

having solemnly resolved to constitute India into a Sovereign Socialist Secular Democratic Republic and to secure to all its citizens: JUSTICE, social, economic and political; LIBERTY of thought, expression, belief, faith and worship; EQUALITY of status and of opportunity; and to promote among them all FRATERNITY assuring the dignity of the individual and the unity and integrity of the Nation; In our Constituent Assembly this 'X' – do hereby adopt, enact and give to ourselves this Constitution", 'X' stands for

(a) twenty-sixth day of January, 1950

(b) twenty-sixth day of November, 1949

(c) twenty-sixth day of January, 1949

(d) None of the above

5. Given below are two statements, one labelled as Assertion (A) and the other labeled as Reason (R):

Assertion (A): Wilful disobedience or non-compliance of Court orders and use of derogatory language about judicial behaviour amounts to Contempt of Court.

Reason (R): Judicial activism cannot be practiced without arming the judiciary with punitive powers to punish contemptuous behaviour.

In the context of the above two statements, which one of the following is correct ?

(a) Both A and R are true and R is the correct explanation of A

(b) Both A and R are true, but R is not a correct explanation of A

(c) A is true, but R is false

(d) A is false, but R is true

6. The Dinesh Goswami Committee recommended

(a) the constitution of state level election commissions

(b) List system of election to the Lok Sabha

(c) governmental funding of parliamentary elections

(d) a ban on the candidature of independent candidates in the parliamentary elections

7. Which one of the following is NOT a principle of "Panchsheel" ?

(a) Non-alignment

(b) Peaceful Co-existence

(c) Mutual respect for each other's territorial integrity and sovereignty

(d) Mutual non-interference in each other's internal affairs

8. Which one of the following was NOT proposed by the 73rd Constitutional Amendment in the area of Panchayati Raj ?

(a) Thirty per cent seats in all elected rural local bodies will be reserved for women candidates at all levels

(b) The States will constitute their Finance commissions to allocate resources to Panchayati Raj institutions

(c) The Panchayati Raj elected functionaries will be disqualified to hold their offices if they have more than two children

(d) The elections will be held in six months time if Panchayati Raj bodies are superseded or dissolved by the State government

9. Proportional representation is NOT necessary in a country where

(a) there are no reserved constituencies

(b) a two-party system has developed

(c) the first-past-post system prevails

(d) there is a fusion of Presidential and Parliamentary forms of government

10. The concept of Public Interest Litigation originated in

(a) the United Kingdom

(b) Australia

(c) the United States

(d) Canada

11. If the Prime Minister of India belonged to the Upper House of Parliament

(a) he will not be able to vote in his favour in the event of a no-confidence motion

(b) he will not be able to speak on the budget in the Lower House

(c) he can make statements only in the Upper House

(d) he was to become a member of the Lower House within six months after being sworn in as the Prime Minister

12. Given below are two statements, one labelled as Assertion (A) and the other labelled as Reason (R):

Assertion (A): The reservation of thirty-three per cent of seats for women in Parliament and State legislatures does not require Constitutional amendment.

Reason (R): Political parties contesting elections can allocate thirty-three per cent of seats they contest to women candidates without any Constitutional amendment.

In the context of the above two statements, which one of the following is correct ?

(a) Both A and R are true and R is the correct explanation of A

(b) Both A and R are true, but R is not a correct explanation of A

(c) A is true, but R is false

(d) A is false, but R is true

1998 TEST PAPER

1. Which one of the following schedules of the Constitution of India contains provisions regarding anti-defection Act ?

(a) Second Schedule (b) Fifth Schedule

(c) Eighth Schedule (d) Tenth Schedule

2. The Indian parliamentary system is different from the British parliamentary system in that India has

(a) both a real and a nominal executive

(b) a system of collective responsibility

(c) bicameral legislature

(d) the system of judicial review

3. Panchayat Raj was first introduced in India in October, 1959 in

(a) Rajasthan (b) Tamil Nadu

(c) Kerala (d) Karnataka

4. Economic Survey in India is published officially, every year by the

(a) Reserve Bank of India

(b) Planning Commission of India

(c) Ministry of Finance, Govt. of India

(d) Ministry of Industries, Govt. of India

5. Which of the following Parties were not a part of the United Front which was in power during 1996-97 ?

1. Bahujana Samaj Party.

2. Samata Party

3. Haryana Vikas Party

4. Asom Gana Parishad

Select the correct answer using the codes given below:

Codes:

(a) 1, 2, 3 and 4 (b) 1, 2 and 3

(c) 3 and 4 (d) 1 and 2

1999 TEST PAPER

1. Which one of the following statements is correct?

(a) Kacchativu and Tin Bigha were territories acquired by the Indian Republic from the French

(b) Kacchativu and Tin Bigha are territories handed over to Sri Lankan and Bangladeshi sovereignty respectively by the Government of India

(c) Kacchativu and Tin Bigha are areas that were annexed by the Chinese in the 1962 Sino-Indian War

(d) Kacchativu and Tin Bigha are enclaves which are transferred to India by lease arrangements with Sri Lanka and Pakistan respectively.

2. A British citizen staying in India cannot claim Right to

(a) Freedom of trade and profession

(b) Equality before the law

(c) Protection of life and personal liberty

(d) Freedom of religion

3. Consider the following statements regarding the National Human Rights Commission of India:
   1. Its Chairman must be a retired Chief Justice of India
   2. It has formations in each state as State Human Rights Commission
   3. Its powers are only recommendatory in nature
   4. It is mandatory to appoint a woman as a member of the Commission

   Which of the above statements are correct ?
   (a) 1, 2, 3 and 4   (b) 2 and 4
   (c) 2 and 3   (d) 1 and 3

4. The most short-lived of all of Britain's constitutional experiments in India was the
   (a) Indian Councils Act of 1861
   (b) Indian Councils Act of 1892
   (c) Indian Councils Act of 1909
   (d) Government of India Act of 1919

5. The Constitution of India recognises
   (a) only religious minorities
   (b) only linguistic minorities
   (c) religious and linguistic minorities
   (d) religious, linguistic and ethnic minorities

6. In the new Panchayati Raj Bill enacted in 1993, there are several fresh provisions deviating from the past. Which one of the following is not one such provision?
   (a) A number of added responsibilities in the area of agriculture, rural development, primary education and social forestry among others.
   (b) Elections being made mandatory for all posts at the time they are due
   (c) A statutory representation for women in the panchayats, up to a third of the strength
   (d) Regular remuneration to the panchayat members, so as to ensure their punctuality and accountability.

7. Consider the following statements :
   An amendment to the Constitution of India can be initiated by the
   1. Lok Sabha
   2. Rajya Sabha
   3. State Legislatures
   4. President

   Which of the above statements is/are correct ?
   (a) 1 alone   (b) 1, 2 and 3
   (c) 2, 3 and 4   (d) 1 and 2

8. Consider the following statements about the recent amendments to the Election Law by the Representation of the People (Amendment) Act 1996:
   1. Any conviction for the offence of insulting the Indian National Flag or the Constitution of India shall entail disqualification for contesting

elections to Parliament and State Legislatures for six years from the date of conviction.
   2. There is an increase in the security deposit which a candidate has to make to contest the election to the Lok Sabha.
   3. A candidate cannot now stand for election from more than one Parliamentary constituency.
   4. No election will now be countermanded on the death of a contesting candidate.

   Which of the above statements are correct ?
   (a) 2 and 3   (b) 1, 2 and 4
   (c) 1 and 3   (d) 1, 2, 3 and 4

9. Which one of the following statements regarding the levying, collecting and distribution of Income Tax is correct ?
   (a) The Union levies, collects and distributes the proceeds of income tax between itself and the states
   (b) The Union levies, collects and keeps all the proceeds of income tax to itself
   (c) The Union levies and collects the tax but all the proceeds are distributed among the states
   (d) Only the surcharge levied on income tax is shared between the Union and the states

2000 Test Paper

1. The Speaker can ask a member of the House to stop speaking and let another member speak. This phenomenon is known as
   (a) decorum
   (b) crossing the floor
   (c) interpellation
   (d) yielding the floor

2. Consider the following statements about the Attorney General of India:
   1. He is appointed by the President of India.
   2. He must have the same qualifications as are required for a Judge of the Supreme Court.
   3. He must be a member of either House of Parliament.
   4. He can be removed by impeachment by Parliament.

   Which of these statements are correct ?
   (a) 1 and 2   (b) 1 and 3
   (c) 2, 3 and 4   (d) 3 and 4

3. Consider the following functionaries :
   1. Cabinet Secretary
   2. Chief Election Commissioner
   3. Union Cabinet Ministers
   4. Chief Justice of India

   Their correct sequence, in the Order of Precedence is
   (a) 3, 4, 2, 1   (b) 4, 3, 1, 2
   (c) 4, 3, 2, 1   (d) 3, 4, 1, 2

4. The primary function of the Finance Commission in India is to
   (a) distribute revenue between the Centre and the States
   (b) prepare the Annual Budget
   (c) advise the President on financial matters
   (d) allocate funds to various ministries of the Union and State Governments

5. The state which has the largest number of seats reserved for the Scheduled Tribes in the Lok Sabha is
   (a) Bihar
   (b) Gujarat
   (c) Uttar Pradesh
   (d) Madhya Pradesh

6. A college student desires to get elected to the Municipal Council of his city. The validity of his nomination would depend on the important condition, among others, that
   (a) he obtains permission from the Principal of his college
   (b) he is a member of a political party
   (c) his name figures in the Voters' List
   (d) he files a declaration owing allegiance to the Constitution of India

7. Match List I with List Ii and select the correct answer by using the codes given below the lists:

List-I (Local bodies)	List-II (States as in 1999)
A. Zilla Parishads at the sub-divisional level	1. Andhra Pradesh
B. Mandal Praja Parishad	2. Assam
C. Tribal Councils	3. Mizoram
D. Absence of Village Panchayats	4. Meghalaya

   Codes:

	A	B	C	D
(a)	2	1	4	3
(b)	1	2	4	3
(c)	3	2	1	4
(d)	2	1	3	4

8. Which one of the following statements is incorrect ?
   (a) Goa attained full statehood in 1987
   (b) Diu is an island in the Gulf of Khambhat
   (c) Daman and Diu were separated from Goa by the 56th Amendment of the Constitution of India
   (d) Dadra and Nagar Haweli were under French colonial rule till 1954.

9. The Parliament can make any law for the whole or any part of India for implementing International treaties
   (a) with the consent of all the States
   (b) with the consent of the majority of States
   (c) with the consent of the States concerned
   (d) without the consent of any State

10. Which one of the following is NOT a feature of the Government of India Act of 1935 ?
    (a) Diarchy at the Centre as well as in the provinces
    (b) A bicameral legislature
    (c) Provincial autonomy
    (d) An All-India Federation

11. Which one of the following statements about a Money Bill is not correct ?
    (a) A Money Bill can be tabled in either House of Parliament
    (b) The Speaker of Lok Sabha is the final authority to decide whether a Bill is a Money Bill or not
    (c) The Rajya Sabha must return a Money Bill passed by the Lok Sabha and send it for consideration within 14 days
    (d) The President cannot return a Money Bill to the Lok Sabha for reconsideration

12. The 73rd Constitution Amendment Act 1992 refers to the
    (a) generation of gainful employment for the un-employed and the under-employed men and women in rural area.
    (b) generation of employment for the able bodies adults who are in need and desirous of work during the lean agricultural season.
    (c) laying the foundation for strong and vibrant Panchayati Raj Institutions in the country.
    (d) guarantee of right to life, liberty and security of person, equality before law and equal protection without discrimination.

2001 Test Paper

1. Which Article of the Constitution provides that it shall be the endeavour of every state to provide adequate facility for instruction in the mother tongue at the primary stage of education ?
   (a) Article 349   (b) Articld 350
   (c) Article 350 A   (d) Article 351

2. The Supreme Court of India tenders advice to the President on a matter of law or fact
   (a) on its own initiative
   (b) only if he seeks such advice
   (c) only if the matter relates to the Fundamental Rights of citizens
   (d) only if the issue poses a threat to the unity and integrity of the country

3. Which one of the following duties is NOT performed by the Comptroller and Auditor General of India ?
   (a) To audit and report on all expenditure from the Consolidated Fund of India

   (b) To audit and report on all expenditure from the Contingency Funds and Public Accounts

   (c) To audit and report on all trading, manufacturing, profit and loss accounts

   (d) To control the receipt and issue of public money, and to ensure that the public revenue is lodged in the exchequer

4. Which one of the following statements correctly describes the Fourth Schedule of the Constitution of India?

   (a) It lists the distribution of powers between the Union and the states.

   (b) It contains the languages listed in the Constitution.

   (c) It contains the provisions regarding the administration of tribal areas.

   (d) It allocates seats in the Council of States.

5. In what way does the Indian Parliament exercise control over the administration ?

   (a) Through Parliamentary Committees

   (b) Through Consultative Committees of various ministries

   (c) By making the administrators send periodic reports

   (d) By compelling the executive to issue writs

6. Consider the following statements about the minorities in India:

   1. The Government of India has notified five communities, namely, Muslims, Sikhs, Christians, Buddhists and Zoroastrians as Minorities.

   2. The National Commission for Minorities was given statutory status in 1993.

   3. The smallest religious minority in India are the Zoroastrians.

   4. The Constitution of India recognizes and protects religious and linguistic minorities.

Which of these statements are correct ?

   (a) 2 and 3   (b) 1 and 4

   (c) 2, 3 and 4   (d) 1, 2 and 4

7. In which one of the following areas does the State Government NOT have control over its local bodies?

   (a) Citizens' grievances   (b) Financial

   (c) Legislation   (d) Personnel matters

8. Consider the following statements regarding the High Courts in India:

   1. There are eighteen High Courts in the country.

   2. Three of them have jurisdiction over more than one state.

   3. No Union Territory has a High Court of its own.

   4. Judges of the High Court hold office till the age of 62.

Which of these statements is/are correct ?

   (a) 1, 2 and 4   (b) 2 and 3

   (c) 1 and 4   (d) 4 only

9. Match List I with List II and select the correct answer by using the codes given below the lists :

List-I (Amendments to the Constitution)		List-II (Contents)	

Codes:

	A	B	C	D
(a)	5	1	4	2
(b)	1	5	3	4
(c)	5	1	3	4
(d)	1	5	4	2

10. If a new state of the Indian Union is to be created, which one of the following schedules of the Constitution must be amended ?

   (a) First   (b) Second

   (c) Third   (d) Fifth

11 Consider the following statements regarding the political parties in India:

   1. The Representation of the People Act, 1951 provides for the registration of political parties.

   2. Registration of political parties is carried out by the Election Commission.

   3. A national level political party is one which is recognised in four or more states.

   4. During the 1999 general elections, there were six national and 48 state level parties recognised by the Election Commission.

Which of these statements are correct ?

   (a) 1, 2 and 4   (b) 1 and 3

   (c) 2 and 4   (d) 1, 2, 3 and 4

12. Match List I with List II and select the correct answer by using the codes given below the lists :

List-I (Articles of the Constitution)	List-II (Content)
A. Article 54	1. Election of the President of India
B. Article 75	2. Appointment of the Prime Minister And Council of Ministers
C. Article 155	3. Appointment of the Governor of a state
D. Article 164	4. Appointment of the Chief Minister and Council of Ministers of a state
	5. Composition of Legislative Assemblies

Codes:

	A	B	C	D
(a)	1	2	3	4
(b)	1	2	4	5
(c)	2	1	3	5
(d)	2	1	4	3

2002 TEST PAPER

1. Match List I (Article of Indian Constitution) with List II (Provisions) and select the correct answer using the codes given below the lists :

List-I (Article of Indian Constitution)	List-II (Provisions)
A. Article 16(2)	1. No person shall be deprived of his property save by the authority of law
B. Article 29(2)	2. No person can be discriminated against in the matter of public appointment on the ground of race, religion or caste
C. Article 30(1)	3. All minorities whether based on religion or language shall have the fundamental right to establish and administer educational institutions of their choice
D. Article 31(1)	4. No citizen shall be denied admission into any educational institution maintained by the State, or receiving State aid, on grounds of religion, race, caste, language or any of them.

   Codes:

	A	B	C	D
(a)	2	4	3	1
(b)	3	1	2	4
(c)	2	1	3	4
(d)	3	4	2	1

2. The salaries and allowances of the Judges of the High Court are charged to the
   - (a) Consolidated Fund of India
   - (b) Consolidated Fund of the State
   - (c) Contingency Fund of India
   - (d) Contingency Fund of the State

3. The members of the Constituent Assembly which drafted the Constitution of India were
   - (a) nominated by the British Parliament
   - (b) nominated by the Governor General
   - (c) elected by the Legislative Assemblies of various provinces
   - (d) elected by the Indian National Congress and Muslim League

4. The purpose of the inclusion of Directive Principles of State Policy in the Indian Constitution is to establish
   - (a) political democracy
   - (b) social democracy
   - (c) Gandhian democracy
   - (d) social and economic democracy

5. The real intention of the British to include the princely states in the Federal Union proposed by the India Act of 1935 was to
   - (a) exercise more and direct political and administrative control over the princely states
   - (b) involve the princes actively in the administration of the colony
   - (c) finally effect the complete political and administrative take-over of all the princely states by the British
   - (d) use the princes to counter-balance the anti-imperialist doctrines of the nationalist leaders

6. Which one of the following Articles of the Directive Principles of State Policy deals with the promotion of international peace and security ?
   - (a) 51   (b) 48 A
   - (c) 43 A   (d) 41

7. Which one of the following rights was described by Dr. B.R. Ambedkar as the heart and soul of the Constitution ?
   - (a) Right to freedom of religion
   - (b) Right to property
   - (c) Right to equality
   - (d) Right to Constitutional remedies

8. Match List I (Article of Colonial Government of India) with List II (Provisions) and select the correct answer using the codes given below the lists:

List-I (Acts of Colonial Government of India)	List-II (Provisions)
A. Charter Act, 1813	1. Set up a Board of Control in Britain to fully regulate the East India Company's affairs in India
B. Regulating Act	2. Company's trade monopoly in India was ended
C. Act of 1858	3. The power to govern was transferred from the East India Company to the British Crown
D. Pitt's India Act	4. The Company's directors were asked to

present to the British government all correspondence and documents pertaining to the administration of the company

Codes:

	A	B	C	D
(a)	2	4	3	1
(b)	1	3	4	2
(c)	2	3	4	1
(d)	1	4	3	2

9. Which one of the following Acts of British India strengthened the Viceroy's authority over his executive council by substituting "portfolio" or departmental system for corporate functioning ?
   (a) Indian Councils Act, 1861
   (b) Government of India Act, 1858
   (c) Indian Councils Act, 1892
   (d) Indian Councils Act, 1909

10. Consider the following statements with reference to India:
    1. The Chief Election Commissioner and other Election Commissioners enjoy equal powers but receive unequal salaries.
    2. The Chief Election Commissioner is entitled to the same salary as is provided to a judge of the Supreme Court.
    3. The Chief Election Commissioner shall not be removed from his office except in like manner and on like grounds as a judge of the Supreme Court.
    4. The term of office of the Election Commissioner is five years from the date he assumes his office or till the day he attains the age of 62 years, whichever is earlier.
    Which of these statements are correct ?
    (a) 1 and 2   (b) 2 and 3
    (c) 1 and 4   (d) 2 and 4

11. The Consultative Committee of Members of Parliament for Railway Zones is constituted by the
    (a) President of India
    (b) Ministry of Railways
    (c) Ministry of Parliamentary Affairs
    (d) Ministry of Transport

12. Five Year Plan in India is finally approved by
    (a) Union Cabinet
    (b) President on the advice of Prime Minister
    (c) Planning Commission
    (d) National Development Council

13. Which one of the following authorities recommends the principles governing the grants-in-aid of the revenues to the states out of the Consolidated Fund of India?
    (a) Finance Commission
    (b) Inter-State Council
    (c) Union Ministry of Finance
    (d) Public Accounts Committee

14. With reference to Indian Polity, which one of the following statements is correct ?
    (a) Planning Commission is accountable to Parliament
    (b) President can make ordinance only when either of the two Houses of Parliament is not in session
    (c) The minimum age prescribed for appointment as a Judge of the Supreme Court is 40 years
    (d) National Development Council is constituted of Union Finance Minister and the Chief Ministers of all the States

15. In the Indian Constitution, the Right to Equality is granted by five Articles. They are
    (a) Article 16 to Article 20
    (b) Article 15 to Article 19
    (c) Article 14 to Article 18
    (d) Article 13 to Article 17

16. Which one of the following amendments to the Indian Constitution empowers the President to send back any matter for reconsideration by the Council of Ministers?
    (a) 39th   (b) 40th
    (c) 42nd   (d) 44th

17. The term of the Lok Sabha
    (a) cannot be extended under any circumstances
    (b) can be extended by six months at a time
    (c) can be extended by one year at a time during the proclamation of emergency
    (d) can be extended for two years at a time during the proclamation of emergency

18. In the case of election to the Lok Sabha, the amount of Security deposited for general category candidates and SC/ST category candidates respectively is
    (a) Rs. 5,000 and Rs. 2,500
    (b) Rs. 10,000 and Rs. 2,500
    (c) Rs. 10,000 and Rs. 5,000
    (d) Rs. 15,000 and Rs. 7,500

19. The 93rd Constitutional Amendment Bill deals with the
    (a) continuation of reservation for backward classes in government employment
    (b) free and compulsory education for all children between the age of 6 and 14 years
    (c) reservation of 30 percent posts for women in government recruitments
    (d) allocation of more number of parliamentary seats for recently created States

2003 TEST PAPER

1. Consider the following statements :
   In the electoral college for Presidential Election in India,
   1. the value of the vote of an elected Member of Legislative Assembly equals

   $$\frac{\text{State Population}}{\text{Number of elected MLAs of the State}} \times 100$$

   2. the value of the vote of an elected Member of Parliament equals

   $$\frac{\text{Total value of the votes of all elected MLAs}}{\text{Total number of elected MPs}}$$

   3. there were more than 5000 members in the latest election.

   Which of these statement is/are correct ?
   (a) 1 and 2   (b) Only 2
   (c) 1 and 3   (d) Only 3

2. Which of the following Constitutional Amendments are related to raising the number of Members of Lok Sabha to be elected from the States ?
   (a) 6th and 22nd (b) 13th and 38th
   (c) 7th and 31st (d) 11th and 42nd

3. Which one of the following provisions was NOT made in the Charter Act of 1833 ?
   (a) The trading activities of the East India Company were to be abolished
   (b) The designation of the supreme authority was to be changed as the Governor-General of India in Council
   (c) All law-making powers to be conferred on Governor-General in Council
   (d) An Indian was to be appointed as a Law Member in the Governor-General's Council

4. Consider the following statements :
   The function(s) of the Finance Commission is/are
   1. to allow the withdrawal of money out of the Consolidated Fund of India.
   2. to allocate between the States the shares of proceeds of taxes.
   3. to consider applications for grants-in-aid from States.
   4. to supervise and report on whether the Union and State governments are levying taxes in accordance with the budgetary provisions.
   Which of these statements is/are correct ?
   (a) Only 1   (b) 2 and 3
   (c) 3 and 4   (d) 1, 2 and 4

5. Which one of the following statements is correct?
   (a) Only the Rajya Sabha and not the Lok Sabha can have nominated members
   (b) There is a constitutional provision for nominating two members belonging to the Anglo-Indian community to the Rajya Sabha
   (c) There is no constitutional bar for a nominated member to be appointed as a Union minister
   (d) A nominated member can vote both in the Presidential and Vice Presidential elections

6. The power to enlarge the jurisdiction of the Supreme Court of India with respect to any matter included in the Union List of Legislative Powers rests with
   (a) The President of India
   (b) The Chief Justice of India
   (c) The Parliament
   (d) The Union Ministry of Law, Justice and Company Affairs

7. Which one of the following High Courts has the Territorial Jurisdiction over Andaman and Nicobar Islands ?
   (a) Andhra Pradesh   (b) Calcutta
   (c) Madras   (d) Orissa

8. Under which Article of the Indian Constitution did the President make a reference to the Supreme Court to seek the Court's opinion on the Constitutional validity of the Election Commission's decision on deferring the Gujarat Assembly elections (in the year 2002) ?
   (a) Article 142
   (b) Article 143
   (c) Article 144
   (d) Article 145

9. Consider the following statements :
   1. While members of the Rajya Sabha are associated with Committees on Public Accounts and Public Undertakings, members of Committee on Estimates are drawn entirely from Lok Sabha.
   2. The Ministry of Parliamentary Affairs works under the overall direction of Cabinet Committee on Parliamentary Affairs.
   3. The Minister of Parliamentary Affairs nominates Members of Parliament on Committees, Councils, Boards and Commissions etc., set up by the Government of India in the various ministries.
   Which of these statements are correct ?
   (a) 1 and 2   (b) 2 and 3
   (c) 1 and 3   (d) 1, 2 and 3

10. As per Indian Protocol, who among the following ranks highest in the order of precedence ?
    (a) Deputy Prime Minister

(b) Former President

(c) Governor of a State within his State

(d) Speaker of Lok Sabha

11. Which one of the following schedules of the Indian Constitution lists the names of states and specifies their territories ?

(a) First   (b) Second

(c) Third   (d) Fourth

12. The Ninth Schedule to the Indian Constitution was added by

(a) First Amendment

(b) Eighth Amendment

(c) Ninth Amendment

(d) Forty Second Amendment

13. Who headed the Interim Cabinet formed in the year 1946 ?

(a) Rajendra Prasad

(b) Jawaharlal Nehru

(c) Sardar Vallabhbhai Patel

(d) Rajagopalachari

14. Consider the following statements :

1. The joint sitting of the two houses of the Parliament in India is sanctioned under Article 108 of the Constitution.

2. The first joint sitting of Lok Sabha and Rajya Sabha was held in the year 1961.

3. The second joint sitting of the two Houses of Indian Parliament was held to pass the Banking Service Commission (Repeal) Bill.

Which of these statements are correct ?

(a) 1 and 2   (b) 2 and 3

(c) 1 and 3   (d) 1, 2 and 3

15. Under which Article of the Indian Constitution did the President give his assent to the ordinance on electoral reforms when it was sent back to him by the Union Cabinet without making any changes (in the year 2002) ?

(a) Article 121   (b) Article 122

(c) Article 123   (d) Article 124

16. Which one of the following Articles of the Indian Constitution provides that 'It shall be the duty of the Union to protect every State against external aggression and internal disturbance' ?

(a) Article 215   (b) Article 275

(c) Article 325   (d) Article 355

17. Consider the following statements:

In India, stamp duties on financial transactions are

1. levied and collected by the State Government

2. appropriated by the Union Government.

Which of these statements is/are correct ?

(a) Only 1   (b) Only 2

(c) Both 1 and 2   (d) Neither 1 nor 2

18. Match List I (Item in the Indian Constitution) with List II (Country from which it was derived) and select the correct answer using the codes given below the lists :

List-I (Item in the Indian Constitution)	List-II (Country from which it was derived)
A. Directive Principles of State Policy	1. Australia
B. Fundamental Rights	2. Canada
C. Concurrent List in Union-State Relations	3. Ireland
D. India as a Union of States with greater powers to the Union	4. United Kingdom
	5. United States of America

Codes:

	A	B	C	D
(a)	5	4	1	2
(b)	3	5	2	1
(c)	5	4	2	1
(d)	3	5	1	2

19. Which one of the following Bills must be passed by each House of the Indian Parliament separately, by special majority ?

(a) Ordinary Bill

(b) Money Bill

(c) Finance Bill

(d) Constitution Amendment Bill

2004 TEST PAPER

1. With reference to Indian Public Finance, consider the following statements:

1. Disbursements from Public Account of India are subject to the Vote of Parliament.

2. The Indian Constitution provides for the establishment of a Consolidated Fund, a Public Account and a Contingency Fund for each State.

3. Appropriations and disbursements under the Railway Budget are subject to the same form of parliamentary control as other appropriations and disbursements.

Which of these statements are correct ?

(a) 1 and 2   (b) 2 and 3

(c) 1 and 3   (d) 1, 2 and 3

2. Consider the following statements:

Some of the main features of the Government of India Act, 1935 were the

1. abolition of diarchy in the Governor's provinces

2. power of the Governors to veto legislative action and to legislate on their own

3. abolition of the principle of communal representation

Which of the statements given above is/are correct ?

(a) 1 only   (b) 1 and 2

(c) 2 and 3   (d) 1, 2 and 3

3. Which one of the following statements is correct?

(a) The Constituent Assembly of India was elected by the Provincial Assemblies in the year 1946

(b) Jawaharlal Nehru, M.A. Jinnah and Sardar Vallabhbhai Patel were members of the Constituent Assembly of India

(c) The First Session of the Constituent Assembly of India was held in January, 1947

(d) The Constitution of India was adopted on 26th January, 1950

4. Consider the following statements:

1. The highest criminal court of the district is the Court of District and Sessions Judge.

2. The District Judges are appointed by the Governor in consultation with the High Court.

3. A person to be eligible for appointment as a District Judge should be an advocate or a pleader of seven years' standing or more, or an officer in judicial service of the Union or the State.

4. When the Sessions Judge awards death sentence, it must be confirmed by the High Court before it is carried out.

Which of the statements given above are correct ?

(a) 1 and 2   (b) 2, 3 and 4

(c) 3 and 4   (d) 1, 2, 3 and 4

5. Consider the following statements:

1. The Speaker of Lok Sabha has the power to adjourn the House sine die but, on prorogation, it is only the President who can summon the House.

2. Unless sooner dissolved or there is an extension of the term, there is an automatic dissolution of the Lok Sabha by efflux of time, at the end of the period of five years, even if no formal order of dissolution is issued by the President.

3. The Speaker of Lok Sabha continues in office even after the dissolution of the House and until 'immediately before the first meeting of the House'.

Which of the statements given above are correct ?

(a) 1 and 2   (b) 2 and 3

(c) 1 and 3   (d) 1, 2 and 3

6. Which one of the following statements is not correct?

(a) In Lok Sabha, a no – confidence motion has to set out the grounds on which it is based

(b) In the case of a no – confidence motion in Lok Sabha, no conditions of admissibility have been laid down in the Rules

(c) A motion of no – confidence once admitted, has to be taken up within ten days of the leave being granted

(d) Rajya Sabha is not empowered to entertain a motion of no – confidence

7. Which one of the following statements correctly describes the Fourth Schedule of the Constitution of India?

(a) It contains the scheme of the distribution of powers between the Union and the States

(b) It contains the languages listed in the Constitution

(c) It contains the provisions regarding the administration of tribal areas

(d) It allocates seats in the Council of States

8. The Montagu-Chelmsford Report formed the basis of

(a) the Indian Councils Act, 1909

(b) the Government of India Act, 1919

(c) the Government of India Act, 1935

(d) the Indian Independence Act, 1947

9. The resolution for removing the Vice-President of India can be moved in the

(a) Lok Sabha alone

(b) Either House of Parliament

(c) Joint Sitting of Parliament

(d) Rajya Sabha alone

10. With reference to the Constitution of India, which one of the following pairs is not correctly matched?

(a) Forests   :   Concurrent List

(b) Stock Exchanges   :   Concurrent List

(c) Post Office   :   Union List
Savings Bank

(d) Public Health   :   State List

11. Consider the following tasks:

1. Superintendence, direction and conduct of free and fair elections

2. Preparation of electoral rolls for all elections to the Parliament, State Legislatures and the Office of the President and the Vice-President

3. Giving recognition to political parties and allotting election symbols to political parties and individuals contesting the election

4. Proclamation of final verdict in the case of election disputes

Which of the above are the functions of the Election Commission of India?

(a) 1, 2 and 3   (b) 2, 3 and 4

(c) 1 and 3   (d) 1, 2 and 4

12. Consider the following statements:

1. The highest deciding body for planning in India is the Planning Commission of India.

2. The Secretary of the Planning Commission of India is also the Secretary of National Development Council.

3. The Constitution includes economic and social planning in the Concurrent List in the Seventh Schedule of the Constitution of India.

Which of the statements given above is/are correct ?

(a) 1 and 2   (b) 2 and 3
(c) 2 only   (d) 3 only

13. With reference to Indian Parliament, which one of the following is not correct ?

(a) The Appropriation Bill must be passed by both the Houses of Parliament before it can be enacted into law

(b) No money shall be withdrawn from the Consolidated Fund of India except under the appropriation made by the Appropriation Act

(c) Finance Bill is required for proposing new taxes but no another Bill/Act is required for making changes in the rates of taxes which are already under operation

(d) No Money Bill can be introduced except on the recommendation of the President

14. Which one of the following Articles of the Constitution of India says that the executive power of every State shall be so exercised as not to impede or prejudice the exercise of the executive power of the Union?

(a) Article 257   (b) Article 258
(c) Article 355   (d) Article 356

15. Match List I (Articles of the Constitution of India) with List II (Provision) and select the correct answer using the codes given below the lists :

List-I (Articles of the Constitution of India)	List-II (Provision)
A. Article 14	1. The State shall not discriminate against any citizen on grounds only of religion, race, caste, sex, place of birth or any of them
B. Article 15	2. The State shall not deny to any person equality before the law or the equal protection of laws within the territory of India
C. Article 16	3. 'Untouchability' is abolished and its practice in any form is forbidden
D. Article 17	4. There shall be equality of opportunity for all citizens in matters relating to employment or appointment to any office under the State

Codes:

	A	B	C	D
(a)	2	4	1	3
(b)	3	1	4	2
(c)	2	1	4	3
(d)	3	4	1	2

16. Given below are two statements, one labelled as Assertion (A) and the other labelled as Reason (R):

Assertion (A): The Central Rural Sanitation Programme was launched in 1986 to improve the quality of life of rural people in India.

Reason (R): Rural sanitation is a subject in the Concurrent List in the Constitution of India.

In the context of the above two statements, which one of the following is correct ?

(a) Both A and R are individually true and R is the correct explanation of A

(b) Both A and R are individually true, but R is not a correct explanation of A

(c) A is true, but R is false

(d) A is false, but R is true

17. Which Article of the Constitution of India says, 'No child below the age of fourteen years shall be employed to work in any factory or mine or engaged in any other hazardous employment' ?

(a) Article 24   (b) Article 45
(c) Article 330   (d) Article 368

18. According to the National Human Rights Commission Act, 1993, who amongst the following can be its Chairman ?

(a) Any serving Judge of the Supreme Court

(b) Any serving Judge of the High Court

(c) Only a retired Chief Justice of India

(d) Only a retired Chief Justice of a High Court

19. Who among the following was never the Lok Sabha Speaker ?

(a) K.V.K. Sundaram   (b) G.S. Dhillon
(c) Baliram Bhagat   (d) Hukum Singh

20. Which of the following pairs is correctly matched?

Departments	Ministry of the Government of India
1. Department of Women and Child Development	: Ministry of Health and Family Welfare
2. Department of Official Language	: Ministry of Human Resource Development
3. Department of Drinking Water Supply	: Ministry of Water Resources

Select the correct answer using the codes given below:

(a) 1   (b) 2
(c) 3   (d) None

21. Consider the following events:
    1. Fourth general elections in India
    2. Formation of Haryana State
    3. Mysore named as Karnataka State
    4. Meghalaya and Tripura become full States

    Which one of the following is the correct chronological order of the above?

    (a) 2 – 1 – 4 – 3   (b) 4 – 3 – 2 – 1

    (c) 2 – 3 – 4 – 1   (d) 4 – 1 – 2 – 3

22. Which one of the following is the correct sequence in the descending order of precedence in the warrant of precedence ?

    (a) Attorney General of India – Judges of the Supreme Court – Members of Parliament – Deputy Chairman of Rajya Sabha

    (b) Judges of the Supreme Court – Deputy Chairman of Rajya Sabha – Attorney General of India – Members of Parliament

    (c) Attorney General of India – Deputy Chairman of Rajya Sabha – Judges of the Supreme Court – Members of Parliament

    (d) Judges of the Supreme Court – Attorney General of India – Deputy Chairman of Rajya Sabha – Members of Parliament

2005 TEST PAPER

1. Consider the following:
    1. Disputes with mobile cellular companies
    2. Motor accident cases
    3. Pension cases

    For which of the above are Lok Adalats held ?

    (a) 1 only   (b) 1 and 2

    (c) 2 only   (d) 1, 2 and 3

2. Consider the following statements:
    1. Part IX of the Constitution of India contains provisions for Panchayats and was inserted by the Constitution (73rd Amendment) Act, 1992.
    2. Part IX–A of the Constitution of India contains provisions for municipalities and the Article 243–Q envisages two types of municipalities – a Municipal Council and a Municipal Corporation for every State.

    Which of the statements given above is/are correct ?

    (a) 1 only   (b) 2 only

    (c) Both 1 and 2   (d) Neither 1 nor 2

3. Consider the following statements:
    1. Articles 371–A to 371–I were inserted in the Constitution of India to meet regional demands of Nagaland, Assam, Manipur, Andhra Pradesh, Sikkim, Mizoram, Arunachal Pradesh and Goa.
    2. Constitutions of India and the United States of America envisage a dual polity (The Union and the States) but a single citizenship.

3. A naturalized citizen of India can never be deprived of his citizenship.

    Which of the statements given above is/are correct ?

    (a) 1, 2 and 3   (b) 1 and 3

    (c) 3 only   (d) 1 only

4. Consider the following statements:
    1. Article 301 pertains to the Right to Property.
    2. Right to Property is a legal right but not a Fundamental Right.
    3. Article 300–A was inserted in the Constitution of India by the Congress Government at the Centre by the 44th Constitutional Amendment.

    Which of the statements given above is/are correct ?

    (a) 2 only   (b) 2 and 3

    (c) 1 and 3   (d) 1, 2 and 3

5. The Constitution (98th Amendment) Bill is related to:

    (a) Empowering the Centre to levy and appropriate service tax

    (b) The constitution of the National Judicial Commission

    (c) Readjustment of electoral constituencies on the basis of the Population Census 2001

    (d) The demarcation of new boundaries between States.

6. Consider the following statements:
    1. The Constitution of India has 20 parts.
    2. There are 390 Articles in the Constitution of India in all.
    3. Ninth, Tenth, Eleventh and Twelfth Schedules were added to the Constitution of India by the Constitution (Amendment) Acts.

    Which of the statements given above is/are correct ?

    (a) 1 and 2   (b) 2 only

    (c) 3 only   (d) 1, 2 and 3

7. Who among the following was the Chairman of the Union Constitution Committee of the Constituent Assembly ?

    (a) B.R. Ambedkar

    (b) J.B. Kripalani

    (c) Jawaharlal Nehru

    (d) Alladi Krishnaswami Ayyar

8. Consider the following statements :

    The Government of India Act, 1935 provided for
    1. the provincial autonomy
    2. the establishment of Federal Court
    3. All India Federation at the centre

    Which of the statements given above are correct ?

    (a) 1 and 2   (b)   2 and 3

    (c) 1 and 3   (d)   1, 2 and 3

9. Consider the following statements :
    1. The Parliament cannot enlarge the jurisdiction of the Supreme Court of India as its jurisdiction is limited to that conferred by the Constitution.

2. The officers and servants of the Supreme Court and High Courts are appointed by the concerned Chief Justice and the administrative expenses are charge on the Consolidated Fund of India.

Which of the statements given above is/are correct ?

(a) 1 only   (b) 2 only

(c) Both 1 and 2   (d) Neither 1 nor 2

10. Consider the following statements :

1. There are 25 High Courts in India
2. Punjab, Haryana and the Union Territory of Chandigarh have a common High Court.
3. National Capital Territory of Delhi has a High Court of its own.

Which of the statements given above is/are correct ?

(a) 2 and 3   (b) 1 and 2

(c) 1, 2 and 3   (d) 3 only

2006 TEST PAPER

1. Which one of the following subjects is under the Union List in the Seventh Schedule of the Constitution of India ?

(a) Regulation of labour and safety in mines and oilfields

(b) Agriculture

(c) Fisheries

(d) Public health

2. Consider the following statements :

1. There is no provision in the Constitution of India to encourage equal pay for equal work for both men and women.
2. The Constitution of India does not define backward classes.

Which of the statements given above is/are correct ?

(a) 1 only   (b) 2 only

(c) Both 1 and 2   (d) Neither 1 nor 2

3. Consider the following statements :

1. The Rajya Sabha alone has the power to declare that it would be in national interest for the Parliament to legislate with respect to a matter in the State List.
2. Resolutions approving the Proclamation of Emergency are passed only by the Lok Sabha.

Which of the statements given above is/are correct ?

(a) 1 only   (b) 2 only

(c) Both 1 and 2   (d) Neither 1 nor 2

4. *Assertion* (A): In India, every state has a High Court in its territory.

Reason (R): The Constitution of India provides for a High Court in each state.

Codes:

(a) Both A and R are individually true and R is the correct explanation of A

(b) Both A and R are individually true, but R is not the correct explanation of A

(c) A is true, but R is false

(d) A is false, but R is true

5. What does the 104th Constitution Amendment Bill relate to ?

(a) Abolition of Legislative Councils in certain States

(b) Introduction of dual citizenship for persons of Indian origin living outside India

(c) Providing quota to socially and educationally backward classes in private educational institutions

(d) Providing quota for religious minorities in the services under the Central Government

6. Which one among the following Commissions was set up in pursuance of a definite provision under an Article of the Constitution of India ?

(a) University Grants Commission

(b) National Human Rights Commission

(c) Election Commission

(d) Central Vigilance Commission

7. Which portfolio was held by Dr. Rajendra Prasad in the Interim Government formed in the year 1946?

(a) Defence

(b) External Affairs and Commonwealth Relations

(c) Food and Agriculture

(d) None

8. Consider the following statements :

1. A person who has held office as a permanent Judge of a High Court cannot plead or act in any court or before any authority in India except the Supreme Court.
2. A person is not qualified for appointment as a Judge of a High Court in India unless he has for at least five years held a judicial office in the territory of India.

Which of the statements given above is/are correct ?

(a) 1 only   (b) 2 only

(c) Both 1 and 2   (d) Neither 1 nor 2

9. Which one of the following pairs is not correctly matched ?

(a) States Reorganization Act : Andhra Pradesh

(b) Treaty of Yandabu : Assam

(c) State of Bilaspur : Himachal Pradesh

(d) Year 1966 : Gujarat becomes a State

10. Consider the following statements :

1. Free and compulsory education to the children of 6-14 years age group by the State was made a Fundamental Right by the 76th Amendment to the Constitution of India.

2. Sarva Shiksha Abhiyan seeks to provide computer education even in rural areas.

3. Education was included in the Concurrent List by the 42nd Amendment, 1976 to the Constitution of India.

Which of the statements given above are correct ?

(a) 1, 2 and 3   (b) 1 and 2 only
(c) 2 and 3 only   (d) 1 and 3 only

11. Which one of the following is the correct statement? Service tax is a/an

(a) direct tax levied by the Central Government.
(b) indirect tax levied by the Central Government.
(c) direct tax levied by the State Government.
(d) indirect tax levied by the State Government.

12. Who was the Chief Justice of India when public interest litigation (PIL) was introduced to the Indian judicial system ?

(a) M. Hidayatullah   (b) A.M. Ahmadi
(c) A.S. Anand   (d) P.N. Bhagwati

13. Consider the following statements :

1. The Charter Act 1853 abolished East India Company's monopoly of Indian trade.

2. Under the Government of India Act 1858, the British Parliament abolished the East India Company altogether and undertook the responsibility of ruling India directly.

Which of the statements given above is/are correct ?

(a) 1 only   (b) 2 only
(c) Both 1 and 2   (d) Neither 1 nor 2

2007 TEST PAPER

1. Consider the following statements:

1. Jawaharlal Nehru was in his fourth term as the Prime Minister of India at the time of his death.

2. Jawaharlal Nehru represented Rae Bareilly constituency as a Member of Parliament.

3. The first non-Congress Prime Minister of India assumed the Office in the year 1977.

Which of the statements given above is/are correct ?

(a) 1 and 2   (b) 3 only
(c) 1 only   (d) 1 and 3

2. Consider the following statements:

1. Robert Clive was the first Governor-General of Bengal.

2. William Bentinck was the first Governor-General of India.

Which of the statements given above is/are correct ?

(a) 1 only   (b) 2 only
(c) Both 1 and 2   (d) Neither 1 nor 2

3. Who was the Speaker of the First Lok Sabha ?

(a) Hukam Singh   (b) G.V. Mavalankar
(c) K.M. Munshi   (d) U.N. Dhebar

4. Which one of the following pairs is not correctly matched ?

(a) T.S. Krishna Murthy : Former Chief Election Commissioner of India
(b) K.C. Pant : Chairman, Tenth Finance Commission of India
(c) A.M. Khusro : Former Chairman, Union Public Service Commission
(d) R.C. Lahoti : Former Chief Justice of India

5. Who among the following have been the Union Finance Ministers of India?

1. V.P. Singh   2. R. Venkataraman
3. Y.B. Chavan   4. Pranab Mukherjee

Select the correct answer using the code given below:

(a) 1, 2 and 3 only   (b) 1, 3 and 4 only
(c) 2 and 4 only   (d) 1, 2, 3 and 4

6. *Assertion* (A): The Council of Ministers in the Union of India is collectively responsible both to the Lok Sabha and the Rajya Sabha.

Reason (B): The Members of both the Lok Sabha and the Rajya Sabha are eligible to be the Ministers of the Union Government.

Codes :

(a) Both A and R are individually true and R is the correct explanation of A
(b) Both A and R are individually true but R is not the correct explanation of A
(c) A is true but R is false
(d) A is false but R is true

7. Consider the following statements :

1. The Judges (Inquiry) Bill 2006 contemplates to establish a Judicial Council which will receive complaints against Judges of the Supreme Court including the Chief Justice of India, High Court Chief Justices and Judges.

2. Under the Protection of Women from Domestic Violence Act, 2005, a woman can file a petition before a 1st Class Judicial Magistrate.

Which of the statements given above is/are correct ?

(a) 1 only   (b) 2 only
(c) Both 1 and 2   (d) Neither 1 nor 2

8. Consider the following statements:

1. The Chairman of the Committee on Public Accounts is appointed by the Speaker of the Lok Sabha.

2. The Committee on Public Accounts comprises Members of Lok Sabha, Members of Rajya Sabha and a few eminent persons of industry and trade.

Which of the statements given above is/are correct ?

(a) 1 only   (b) 2 only

(c) Both 1 and 2   (d) Neither 1 nor 2

9. Which of the following Constitution Amendment Acts seeks that the size of Councils of Ministers at the Centre and in a State must not exceed 15 per cent of the total number of members in the Lok Sabha and the total number of members of the Legislative Assembly of that State, respectively?

(a) 91st (b) 93rd

(c) 95th (d) 97th

10. Consider the following statements in respect of financial emergency under Article 360 of the Constitution of India :

1. A Proclamation of financial emergency issued shall cease to operate at the expiration of two months, unless before the expiration of that period it has been approved by the resolutions of both Houses of Parliament.

2. If any Proclamation of financial emergency is in operation, it is competent for the President of India to issue directions for the reduction of salaries and allowances of all or any class of persons serving in connection with the affairs of the Union but excluding the Judges of the Supreme Court and the High Courts.

Which of the statements given above is/are correct ?

(a) 1 only   (b) 2 only

(c) Both 1 and 2   (d) Neither 1 nor 2

11. Consider the following statements :

1. The mode of removal of a Judge of a High Court in India is same as that of removal of a Judge of the Supreme Court.

2. After retirement from the office, a permanent Judge of a High Court cannot plead or act in any court or before any authority in India.

Which of the statements given above is/are correct ?

(a) 1 only   (b) 2 only

(c) Both 1 and 2   (d) Neither 1 nor 2

12. Which one of the following is the correct chrono-logical order of the formation of the following as full States of the Indian Union ?

(a) Sikkim – Arunachal Pradesh – Nagaland – Haryana

(b) Nagaland – Haryana – Sikkim – Arunachal Pradesh

(c) Sikkim – Haryana – Nagaland – Arunachal Pradesh

(d) Nagaland – Arunachal Pradesh – Sikkim - Haryana

2008 Test Paper

1. What is the number of spokes in the Dharmachakra in the National Flag of India?

(a) 16   (b) 18

(c) 22   (d) 24

2. How many High Courts in India have jurisdiction over more than one State (Union Territories not included)?

(a) 2   (b) 3

(c) 4   (d) 5

3. Who among the following have held the office of the Vice-President of India ?

1. Mohammad Hidayatullah

2. Fakhruddin Ali Ahmed

3. Neelam Sanjiva Reddy

4. Shankar Dayal Sharma

Select the correct answer using the code given below :

(a) 1, 2, 3 and 4   (b) 1 and 4 only

(c) 2 and 3 only   (d) 3 and 4 only

4. Which was the Capital of Andhra State when it was made a separate State in the year 1953 ?

(a) Guntur   (b) Kurnool

(c) Nellore   (d) Warangal

5. Match List-I with List-II and select the correct answer using the code given below the Lists:

List-I (Person)	List-II (Position)
A. Nagender Singh	1. Chief Election Commissioner of India
B. A.N. Ray	2. President, International Court of Justice
C. R.K. Trivedi	3. Chief Justice of India
D. Ashok Desai	4. Attorney General of India

Codes:

	A	B	C	D
(a)	1	4	2	3
(b)	2	3	1	4
(c)	1	3	2	4
(d)	2	4	1	3

6. Which one of the following is the largest (areawise) Lok Sabha constituency ?

(a) Kangra   (b) Ladakh

(c) Kachchh   (d) Bhilwara

7. Consider the following statements:

1. Justice V.R. Krishna Iyer was the Chief Justice of India

2. Justice V.R. Krishna Iyer is considered as one of the progenitors of public interest litigation (PIL) in the Indian judicial system

Which of the statements given above is / are correct?

(a) 1 only   (b) 2 only

(c) Both 1 and 2   (d) Neither 1 nor 2

8. Under which one of the following Constitution Amendment Acts, four languages were added to the languages under the Eighth Schedule of the Constitution of India, thereby raising their number to 22?

(a) Constitution (Ninetieth Amendment) Act

(b) Constitution (Ninety-first Amendment) Act

(c) Constitution (Ninety-second Amendment) Act

(d) Constitution (Ninety-third Amendment) Act

9. Consider the following statements:

The Constitution of India provides that

1. the Legislative Assembly of each State shall consist of not more than 450 members chosen by direct election from territorial constituencies in the State

2. a person shall not be qualified to be chosen to fill a seat in the Legislative Assembly of a State if he / she is less than 25 years of age

Which of the statements given above is/are correct ?

(a) 1 only   (b) 2 only

(c) Both 1 and 2   (d) Neither 1 nor 2

10. Which of the following is/are included in the Directive Principles of State Policy?

1. Prohibition of traffic in human beings and forced labour

2. Prohibition of consumption except for medicinal purposes of intoxicating drinks and of other drugs which are injurious to health

Select the correct answer using the code given below :

(a) 1 only   (b) 2 only

(c) Both 1 and 2   (d) Neither 1 nor 2

11. Which Schedule of the Constitution of India contains special provisions for the administration and control of Scheduled Areas in several States ?

(a) Third   (b) Fifth

(c) Seventh   (d) Ninth

12. Department of Border Management is a Department of which one of the following Union Ministries ?

(a) Ministry of Defence

(b) Ministry of Home Affairs

(c) Ministry of Shipping, Road Transport and Highways

(d) Ministry of Environment and Forests

13. For which one of the following reforms was a Commission set up under the Chairmanship of Veerappa Moily by the Government of India ?

(a) Police Reforms

(b) Tax Reforms

(c) Reforms in Technical Education

(d) Administrative Reforms

2009 TEST PAPER

1. Among the following Presidents of India, who was also the Secretary General of Non-Aligned Movement for some period ?

(a) Dr. Sarvepalli Radhakrishnan

(b) Varahagiri Venkatagiri

(c) Giani Zail Singh

(d) Dr. Shanker Dayal Sharma

2. Under the administration of which one of the following is the Department of Atomic Energy ?

(a) Prime Minister's Office

(b) Cabinet Secretariat

(c) Ministry of Power

(d) Ministry of Science and Technology

3. In India, who is the Chairman of the National Water Resources Council ?

(a) Prime Minister

(b) Minister of Water Resources

(c) Minister of Environment and Forests

(d) Minister of Science and Technology

4. During which Five Year Plan was the Emergency clamped, new elections took place and the Janata Party was elected ?

(a) Third   (b) Fourth

(c) Fifth   (d) Sixth

5. If a Panchayat is dissolved, elections are to be held within

(a) 1 month   (b) 3 months

(c) 6 months   (d) 1 year

6. Consider the following statements :

1. The Governor of Punjab is concurrently the Administrator of Chandigarh.

2. The Governor of Kerala is concurrently the Administrator of Lakshadweep.

Which of the above statements is / are correct ?

(a) 1 only   (b) 2 only

(c) Both 1 and 2   (d) Neither 1 nor 2

7. Consider the following statements :

1. The Advocate General of a State in India is appointed by the President of India upon the recommendation of the Governor of the concerned State.

2. As provided in Civil Procedure Code, High Courts have original, appellate and advisory jurisdiction at the State level.

Which of the statements given above is/are correct ?

(a) 1 only   (b) 2 only

(c) Both 1 and 2   (d) Neither 1 nor 2

8. In India, the first Municipal Corporation was set up in which one among the following ?

(a) Calcutta   (b) Madras

(c) Bombay   (d) Delhi

9. With reference to Lok Adalats, consider the following statements:
   1. An award made by a Lok Adalat is deemed to be a decree of a civil court and no appeal lies against thereto before any court.
   2. Matrimonial/Family disputes are not covered under Lok Adalat.

   Which of the statements given above is/are correct ?
   (a) 1 only   (b) 2 only
   (c) Both 1 and 2   (d) Neither 1 nor 2

10. With reference to Union Government, consider the following statements :
    1. The Constitution of India provides that all Cabinet Ministers shall be compulsorily the sitting members of Lok Sabha only.
    2. The Union Cabinet Secretariat operates under the direction of the Ministry of Parliamentary Affairs.

    Which of the statements given above is/are correct ?
    (a) 1 only   (b) 2 only
    (c) Both 1 and 2   (d) Neither 1 nor 2

11. Which one of the following Constitutional Amendments states that the total number of Ministers, including the Prime Minister, in the Council of Ministers shall not exceed fifteen percent of the total number of members of the House of the People ?
    (a) 90th (b) 91st
    (c) 92nd (d) 93rd

12. Consider the following statements :
    1. Central Administrative Tribunal (CAT) was set up during the Prime Ministership of Lal Bahadur Shastri.
    2. The Members for CAT are drawn from both judicial and administrative streams.

    Which of the statements given above is/are correct?
    (a) 1 only   (b) 2 only
    (c) Both 1 and 2   (d) Neither 1 nor 2

13. With reference to Union Government, consider the following statements :
    1. The number of Ministries at the Centre on 15th August 1947 was 18.
    2. The number of Ministries at the Centre at present is 36.

    Which of the statements given above is/are correct ?
    (a) 1 only   (b) 2 only
    (c) Both 1 and 2   (d) Neither 1 nor 2

14. With reference to Union Government, consider the following statements :
    1. The Ministries/Departments of the Government of India are created by the Prime Minister on the advice of the Cabinet Secretary.
    2. Each of the Ministries is assigned to a Minister by the President of India on the advice of the Prime Minister.

Which of the statements given above is/are correct ?
(a) 1 only   (b) 2 only
(c) Both 1 and 2   (d) Neither 1 nor 2

2010 TEST PAPER

1. With reference to the Constitution of India, consider the following:
   1. Fundamental Rights
   2. Fundamental Duties
   3. Directive Principles of State Policy

   Which of the above provisions of the Constitution of India is/are fulfilled by the National Social Assistance Programme launched by the Government of India?
   (a) 1 only   (b) 3 only
   (c) 1 and 3 only   (d) 1, 2 and 3

2. Consider the following statements:
   The Supreme Court of India tenders advice to the President of India on matters of law or fact
   1. on its own initiative (on any matter of larger public interest).
   2. if he seeks such an advice.
   3. only if the matters relate to the Fundamental Rights of the citizens.

   Which of the statements given above is/are correct?
   (a) 1 only   (b) 2 only
   (c) 3 only   (d) 1 and 2

3. With reference to Lok Adalats, which of the following statements is correct?
   (a) Lok Adalats have the jurisdiction to settle the matters at pre-litigative stage and not those matters pending before any court
   (b) Lok Adalats can deal with matters which are civil and not criminal in nature
   (c) Every Lok Adalat consists of either serving or retired judicial officers only and not any other person
   (d) None of the statements given above is correct

4. The "Instrument of Instructions" contained in the Government of India Act 1935 have been incorporated in the Constitution of India in the year 1950 as
   (a) Fundamental Rights
   (b) Directive Principles of State Policy
   (c) Extent of executive power of State
   (d) Conduct of business of the Government of India

5. Who of the following shall cause every recommendation made by the Finance Commission to be laid before each House of Parliament?
   (a) The President of India
   (b) The Speaker of Lok Sabha
   (c) The Prime Minister of India
   (d) The Union Finance Minister

6. Which one of the following is responsible for the preparation and presentation of Union Budget to the Parliament?
   (a) Department of Revenue
   (b) Department of Economic Affairs
   (c) Department of Financial Services
   (d) Department of Expenditure

7. With reference to the National Rehabilitation and Resettlement Policy, 2007, consider the following statements:
   1. This policy is applicable only to the persons affected by the acquisition of land for projects and not to the involuntary displacement due to any other reason.
   2. This policy has been formulated by the Ministry of Social Justice and Empowerment.
   Which of the statements given above is/are correct?
   (a) 1 only
   (b) 2 only
   (c) Both 1 and 2
   (d) Neither 1 nor 2

8. With reference to the Consumer Disputes Redressal at district level in India, which one of the following statements is not correct?
   (a) A State Government can establish more than one District Forum in a district if it deems fit
   (b) One of the members of the District Forum shall be a woman.
   (c) The District Forum entertains the complaints where the value of goods or services does not exceed rupees fifty lakhs
   (d) A complaint in relation to any goods sold or any service provided may be filed with a District Forum by the State Government as a representative of the interests of the consumers in general

9. Which one of the following authorities makes recommendation to the Governor of a State as to the principles for determining the taxes and duties which may be appropriated by the Panchayats in that particular State?
   (a) District Planning Committees
   (b) State Finance Commission
   (c) Finance Ministry of that State
   (d) Panchayati Raj Ministry of that State

10. Consider the following statements:
    In India, taxes on transactions in Stock Exchanges and Futures Markets are
    1. levied by the Union
    2. collected by the States
    Which of the statements given above is/are correct?
    (a) 1 only
    (b) 2 only
    (c) Both 1 and 2
    (d) Neither 1 nor 2

2011 TEST PAPER

1. The Constitution (Seventy-Third Amendment) Act, 1992, which aims at promoting the Panchayati Raj Institutions in the country, provides for which of the following?
   1. Constitution of District Planning Committees.
   2. State Election Commissions to conduct all panchayat elections.
   3. Establishment of State Finance Commissions.
   Select the correct answer using the codes given below:
   (a) 1 only
   (b) 1 and 2 only
   (c) 2 and 3 only
   (d) 1, 2 and 3

2. In India, if a religious sect/community is given the status of a national minority, what special advantages it is entitled to?
   1. It can establish and administer exclusive educational institutions.
   2. The President of India automatically nominates a representative of the community to Lok Sabha.
   3. It can derive benefits from the Prime Minister's 15-Point Programme.
   Which of the statements given above is/are correct?
   (a) 1 only
   (b) 2 and 3 only
   (c) 1 and 3 only
   (d) 1, 2 and 3

3. India is home to lakhs of persons with disabilities. What are the benefits available to them under the law?
   1. Free schooling till the age of 18 years in government-run schools.
   2. Preferential allotment of land for setting up business.
   3. Ramps in public buildings.
   Which of the statements given above is/are correct?
   (a) 1 only
   (b) 2 and 3 only
   (c) 1 and 3 only
   (d) 1, 2 and 3

4. The authorization for the withdrawal of funds from the Consolidated Fund of India must come from
   (a) The President of India
   (b) The Parliament of India
   (c) The Prime Minister of India
   (d) The Union Finance Minister

5. All revenues received by the Union Government by way of taxes and other receipts for the conduct of Government business are credited to the
   (a) Contingency Fund of India
   (b) Public Account
   (c) Consolidated Fund of India
   (d) Deposits and Advances Fund

6. With reference to "Look East Policy" of India, consider the following statements:

1. India wants to establish itself as an important regional player in the East Asian affairs.
2. India wants to plug the vacuum created by the termination of Cold War.
3. India wants to restore the historical and cultural ties with its neighbours in Southeast and East Asia.

Which of the statements given above is/are correct?

(a) 1 only   (b) 1 and 3 only
(c) 3 only   (d) 1, 2 and 3

7. When the annual Union Budget is not passed by the Lok Sabha,
   (a) the Budget is modified and presented again
   (b) the Budget is referred to the Rajya Sabha for suggestions
   (c) the Union Finance Minister is asked to resign
   (d) the Prime Minister submits the resignation of Council of Ministers

8. Under the Constitution of India, which one of the following is not a fundamental duty?
   (a) To vote in public elections
   (b) To develop the scientific temper
   (c) To safeguard public property
   (d) To abide the Constitution and respect its ideals

9. With reference to the Finance Commission of India, which of the following statements is correct?
   (a) It encourages the inflow of foreign capital for infrastructure development
   (b) It facilitates the proper distribution of finances among the Public Sector Undertakings
   (c) It ensures transparency in financial administration
   (d) None of the statements (a), (b) and (c) given above is correct in this context

10. Consider the following:
    1. Right to education.
    2. Right to equal access to public service.
    3. Right to food.

    Which of the above is/are Human Right/Human Rights under "Universal Declaration of Human Rights"?

    (a) 1 only   (b) 1 and 2 only
    (c) 3 only   (d) 1, 2 and 3

11. Consider the following statements:
    In India, a Metropolitan Planning Committee
    1. is constituted under the provisions of the Constitution of India.
    2. prepares the draft development plans for metropolitan area.
    3. has the sole responsibility for implementing Government sponsored schemes in the metropolitan area.

Which of the statements given above is/are correct?

(a) 1 and 2 only   (b) 2 only
(c) 1 and 3 only   (d) 1, 2 and 3

12. What is the difference between "vote-on-account" and "interim budget"?
    1. The provision of a "vote-on-account" is used by a regular Government, while an "interim budget" is a provision used by a caretaker Government.
    2. A "vote-on-account" only deals with the expenditure in Government's budget, while an "interim budget" includes both expenditure and receipts.

Which of the statements given above is/are correct?

(a) 1 only   (b) 2 only
(c) Both 1 and 2   (d) Neither 1 nor 2

2012 TEST PAPER

1. The distribution of powers between the Centre and the States in the Indian Constitution is based on the scheme provided in the
   (a) Morley-Minto Reforms, 1909
   (b) Montagu-Chelmsford Act, 1919
   (c) Government of India Act, 1935
   (d) Indian Independence Act, 1947

2. In the areas covered under the Panchayat (Extension to the Scheduled Areas) Act, 1996, what is the role/power of Gram Sabha?
   1. Gram Sabha has the power to prevent alienation of land in the Scheduled Areas.
   2. Gram Sabha has the ownership of minor forest produce.
   3. Recommendation of Gram Sabha is required for granting prospecting licence or mining lease for any mineral in the Scheduled Areas.

Which of the statements given above is/are correct?

(a) 1 only   (b) 1 and 2 only
(c) 2 and 3 only   (d) 1, 2 and 3

3. In the Parliament of India, the purpose of an adjournment motion is
   (a) to allow a discussion on a definite matter of urgent public importance
   (b) to let opposition members collect information from the ministers
   (c) to allow a reduction of specific amount in demand for grant
   (d) to postpone the proceedings to check the inappropriate or violent behaviour on the part of some members

4. The National Green Tribunal Act, 2010 was enacted in consonance with which of the following provisions of the Constitution of India?

1. Right to healthy environment, construed as a part of Right to life under Article 21
2. Provision of grants for raising the level of administration in the Scheduled Areas for the welfare of Scheduled Tribes under Article 275(1)
3. Powers and functions of Gram Sabha as mentioned under Article 243(A)

Select the correct answer using the codes given below:

(a) 1 only   (b) 2 and 3 only

(c) 1 and 3 only   (d) 1, 2 and 3

5. Consider the following provisions under the Directive Principles of State Policy as enshrined in the Constitution of India:
    1. Securing for citizens of India a uniform civil code
    2. Organizing village Panchayats
    3. Promoting cottage industries in rural areas
    4. Securing for all the workers reasonable leisure and cultural opportunities

    Which of the above are the Gandhian Principles that are reflected in the Directive Principles of State Policy?

    (a) 1, 2 and 4 only   (b) 2 and 3 only

    (c) 1, 3 and 4 only   (d) 1, 2, 3 and 4

6. Consider the following statements:
    1. Union Territories are not represented in the Rajya Sabha.
    2. It is within the purview of the Chief Election Commissioner to adjudicate the election disputes.
    3. According to the Constitution of India, the Parliament consists of the Lok Sabha and the Rajya Sabha only.

    Which of the statements given above is/are correct?

    (a) 1 only   (b) 2 and 3

    (c) 1 and 3   (d) None

7. With reference to consumers' rights / privileges under the provisions of law in India, which of the following statements is/are correct?
    1. Consumers are empowered to take samples for food testing.
    2. When a consumer files a complaint in any consumer forum, no fee is required to be paid.
    3. In case of death of a consumer, his/her legal heir can file a complaint in the consumer forum on his/her behalf.

    Select the correct answer using the codes given below:

    (a) 1 only   (b) 2 and 3 only

    (c) 1 and 3 only   (d) 1, 2 and 3

8. Regarding the office of the Lok Sabha Speaker, consider the following statements:
    1. He/She holds the office during the pleasure of the President.

2. He/She need not be a member of the House at the time of his/her election but has to become a member of the House within six months from the date of his/her election.
3. If he/she intends to resign, the letter of his/her resignation has to be addressed to the Deputy Speaker.

Which of the statements given above is/are correct?

(a) 1 and 2 only   (b) 3 only

(c) 1, 2 and 3   (d) None

9. Which of the following are included in the original jurisdiction of the Supreme Court?
    1. A dispute between the Government of India and one or more States
    2. A dispute regarding elections to either House of the Parliament or that of Legislature of a State
    3. A dispute between the Government of India and a Union Territory
    4. A dispute between two or more States

    Select the correct answer using the codes given below:

    (a) 1 and 2   (b) 2 and 3

    (c) 1 and 4   (d) 3 and 4

10. Which of the following is/are the principal feature(s) of the Government of India Act, 1919?
    1. Introduction of diarchy in the executive government of the provinces
    2. Introduction of separate communal electorates for Muslims
    3. Devolution of legislative authority by the centre to the provinces

    Select the correct answer using the codes given below:

    (a) 1 only   (b) 2 and 3 only

    (c) 1 and 3 only   (d) 1, 2 and 3

11. Which of the following special powers have been conferred on the Rajya Sabha by the Constitution of India?

    (a) To change the existing territory of a State and to change the name of a State

    (b) To pass a resolution empowering the Parliament to make laws in the State List and to create one or more All India Services

    (c) To amend the election procedure of the President and to determine the pension of the President after his/her retirement

    (d) To determine the functions of the Election Commission and to determine the number of Election Commissioners

12. Which of the following are the methods of Parliamentary control over public finance in India?
    1. Placing Annual Financial Statement before the Parliament

2. Withdrawal of moneys from Consolidated Fund of India only after passing the Appropriation Bill
3. Provisions of supplementary grants and vote-on-account
4. A periodic or at least a mid-year review of programme of the Government against macroeconomic forecasts and expenditure by a Parliamentary Budget Office
5. Introducing Finance Bill in the Parliament

Select the correct answer using the codes given below:
(a) 1, 2, 3 and 5 only
(b) 1, 2 and 4 only
(c) 3, 4 and 5 only
(d) 1, 2, 3, 4 and 5

13. Which of the following provisions of the Constitution of India have a bearing on Education?
1. Directive Principles of State Policy
2. Rural and Urban Local Bodies
3. Fifth Schedule
4. Sixth Schedule
5. Seventh Schedule

Select the correct answer using the codes given below:
(a) 1 and 2 only
(b) 3, 4 and 5 only
(c) 1, 2 and 5 only
(d) 1, 2, 3, 4 and 5

14. In India, other than ensuring that public funds are used efficiently and for intended purpose, what is the importance of the office of the Comptroller and Auditor General (CAG)?
1. CAG exercises exchequer control on behalf of the Parliament when the President of India declares national emergency / financial emergency
2. CAG reports on the execution of projects or programmes by the ministries are discussed by the Public Accounts Committee.
3. Information from CAG reports can be used by investigating agencies to press charges against those who have violated the law while managing public finances.
4. While dealing with the audit and accounting of government companies, CAG has certain judicial powers for prosecuting those who violate the law.

Which of the statements given above is/are correct?
(a) 1, 3 and 4 only
(b) 2 only
(c) 2 and 3 only
(d) 1, 2, 3 and 4

15. The Prime Minister of India, at the time of his/her appointment
(a) need not necessarily be a member of one of the Houses of the Parliament but must become a member of one of the Houses within six months

(b) need not necessarily be a member of one of the Houses of the Parliament but must become a member of the Lok Sabha within six months
(c) must be a member of one of the Houses of the Parliament
(d) must be a member of the Lok Sabha

16. With reference to the Delimitation Commission, consider the following statements:
1. The orders of the Delimitation Commission cannot be challenged in a Court of Law.
2. When the orders of the Delimitation Commission are laid before the Lok Sabha or State Legislative Assembly, they cannot effect any modifications in the orders.

Which of the statements given above is/are correct?
(a) 1 only
(b) 2 only
(c) Both 1 and 2
(d) Neither 1 nor 2

17. According to the Constitution of India, it is the duty of the President of India to cause to be laid before the Parliament which of the following?
1. The Recommendations of the Union Finance Commission
2. The Report of the Public Accounts Committee
3. The Report of the Comptroller and Auditor General
4. The Report of the National Commission for Scheduled Castes

Select the correct answer using the codes given below:
(a) 1 only
(b) 2 and 4 only
(c) 1, 3 and 4 only
(d) 1, 2, 3 and 4

18. A deadlock between the Lok Sabha and the Rajya Sabha calls for a joint sitting of the Parliament during the passage of
1. Ordinary Legislation
2. Money Bill
3. Constitution Amendment Bill

Select the correct answer using the codes given below:
(a) 1 only
(b) 2 and 3 only
(c) 1 and 3 only
(d) 1, 2 and 3

19. Which of the following is/are among the Fundamental Duties of citizens laid down in the Indian Constitution?
1. To preserve the rich heritage of our composite culture
2. To protect the weaker sections from social injustice
3. To develop the scientific temper and spirit of inquiry
4. To strive towards excellence in all spheres of individual and collective activity

Select the correct answer using the codes given below:
(a) 1 and 2only
(b) 2 only
(c) 1, 3 and 4 only
(d) 1, 2, 3 and 4

20. What is the provision to safeguard the autonomy of the Supreme Court of India?
    1. While appointing the Supreme Court Judges, the President of India has to consult the Chief Justice of India.
    2. The Supreme Court Judges can be removed by the Chief Justice of India only.
    3. The salaries of the Judges are charged on the Consolidated Fund of India to which the legislature does not have to vote.
    4. All appointments of officers and staff of the Supreme Court of India are made by the Government only after consulting the Chief Justice of India.

    Which of the statements given above is/are correct?
    (a) 1 and 3 only   (b) 3 and 4 only
    (c) 4 only   (d) 1, 2, 3 and 4

2013 TEST PAPER

1. Who among the following constitute the National Development Council?
   1. The Prime Minister
   2. The Chairman, Finance Commission
   3. Ministers of the Union Cabinet
   4. Chief Ministers of the States

   Select the correct answer using the codes given below:
   (a) 1, 2 and 3 only   (b) 1, 3 and 4 only
   (c) 2 and 4 only   (d) 1, 2, 3 and 4

2. Consider the following statements:
   The Parliamentary Committee on Public Accounts
   1. consists of not more than 25 Members of the Lok Sabha
   2. scrutinizes appropriation and finance accounts of the Government
   3. examines the report of the Comptroller and Auditor General of India

   Which of the statements given above is/are correct?
   (a) 1 only   (b) 2 and 3 only
   (c) 3 only   (d) 1, 2 and 3

3. In the context of India, which of the following principles is/are implied institutionally in the parliamentary government?
   1. Members of the Cabinet are Members of the Parliament.
   2. Ministers hold the office till they enjoy confidence in the Parliament.
   3. Cabinet is headed by the Head of the State.

   Select the correct answer using the codes given below.
   (a) 1 and 2 only   (b) 3 only
   (c) 2 and 3 only   (d) 1, 2 and 3

4. Consider the following statements:
   1. The Council of Ministers in the Centre shall be collectively responsible to the Parliament.

2. The Union Ministers shall hold the office during the pleasure of the President of India.
3. The Prime Minister shall communicate to the President about the proposals for legislation.

Which of the statements given above is/are correct?
(a) 1 only   (b) 2 and 3 only
(c) 1 and 3 only   (d) 1, 2 and 3

5. Consider the following statements:
   1. National Development Council is an organ of the Planning Commission.
   2. The Economic and Social Planning is kept in the Concurrent List in the Constitution of India.
   3. The Constitution of India prescribes that Panchayats should be assigned the task of preparation of plans for economic development and social justice.

   Which of the statements given above is/are correct?
   (a) 1 only   (b) 2 and 3 only
   (c) 1 and 3 only   (d) 1, 2 and 3

6. Consider the following statements:
   1. The Chairman and the Deputy Chairman of the Rajya Sabha are not the members of that House.
   2. While the nominated members of the two Houses of the Parliament have no voting right in the presidential election, they have the right to vote in the election of the Vice President.

   Which of the statements given above is/are correct?
   (a) 1 only   (b) 2 only
   (c) Both 1 and 2   (d) Neither 1 nor 2

7. With reference to National Legal Services Authority, consider the following statements:
   1. Its objective is to provide free and competent legal services to the weaker sections of the society on the basis of equal opportunity.
   2. It issues guidelines for the State Legal Services Authorities to implement the legal programmes and schemes throughout the country.

   Which of the statements given above is/are correct?
   (a) 1 only   (b) 2 only
   (c) Both 1 and 2   (d) Neither 1 nor 2

8. Under the Scheduled Tribes and Other Traditional Forest Dwellers (Recognition of Forest Rights) Act, 2006, who shall be the authority to initiate the process for determining the nature and extent of individual or community forest rights or both?
   (a) State Forest Department
   (b) District Collector / Deputy Commissioner
   (c) Tahsildar / Block Development Officer / Mandal Revenue Officer
   (d) Gram Sabha

9. 'Economic Justice' as one of the objectives of the Indian Constitution has been provided in

(a) the Preamble and the Fundamental Rights

(b) the Preamble and the Directive Principles of State Policy

(c) the Fundamental Rights and the Directive Principles of State Policy

(d) None of the above

10. According to the Constitution of India, which of the following are fundamental for the governance of the country?

(a) Fundamental Rights

(b) Fundamental Duties

(c) Directive Principles of State Policy

(d) Fundamental Rights and Fundamental Duties

11. What will follow if a Money Bill is substantially amended by the Rajya Sabha?

(a) The Lok Sabha may still proceed with the Bill, accepting or not accepting the recommendations of the Rajya Sabha

(b) The Lok Sabha cannot consider the Bill further

(c) The Lok Sabha may send the Bill to the Rajya Sabha for reconsideration

(d) The President may call a joint sitting for passing the Bill

12. Which one of the following statements is correct?

(a) In India, the same person cannot be appointed as Governor for two or more States at the same time

(b) The Judges of the High Court of the States in India are appointed by the Governor of the State just as the Judges of the Supreme Court are appointed by the President

(c) No procedure has been laid down in the Constitution of India for the removal of a Governor from his/her post

(d) In the case of a Union Territory having a legislative setup, the Chief Minister is appointed by the Lt. Governor on the basis of majority support

13. With reference to Indian History, the Members of the Constituent Assembly from the Provinces were

(a) directly elected by the people of those Provinces

(b) nominated by the Indian National Congress and the Muslim League

(c) elected by the Provincial Legislative Assemblies

(d) selected by the Government for their expertise in constitutional matters

14. Consider the following statements:

1. An amendment to the Constitution of India can be initiated by an introduction of a bill in the Lok Sabha only.

2. If such an amendment seeks to make changes in the federal character of the Constitution, the amendment also requires to be ratified by the legislature of all the States of India.

Which of the statements given above is/are correct?

(a) 1 only   (b) 2 only

(c) Both 1 and 2   (d) Neither 1 nor 2

15. Consider the following statements:

Attorney General of India can

1. take part in the proceedings of the Lok Sabha

2. be a member of a committee of the Lok Sabha

3. speak in the Lok Sabha

4. vote in the Lok Sabha

Which of the statements given above is/are correct?

(a) 1 only   (b) 2 and 4 only

(c) 1, 2 and 3   (d) 1 and 3 only

16. Which of the following bodies does not/do not find mention in the Constitution?

1. National Development Council

2. Planning Commission

3. Zonal Councils

Select the correct answer using the codes given below.

(a) 1 and 2 only   (b) 2 only

(c) 1 and 3 only   (d) 1, 2 and 3

17. The Parliament can make any law for whole or any part of India for implementing international treaties

(a) with the consent of all the States

(b) with the consent of the majority of States

(c) with the consent of the States concerned

(d) without the consent of any State

18. The Government enacted the Panchayat Extension to Scheduled Areas (PESA) Act in 1996. Which one of the following is not identified as its objective?

(a) To provide self-governance

(b) To recognize traditional rights

(c) To create autonomous regions in tribal areas

(d) To free tribal people from exploitation

Answers

1993 TEST PAPER

1. **b**	2. **c**	3. **d**	4. **c**	5. **b**	6. **b**
7. **d**	8. **a**	9. **d**	10. **c**	11. **c**	12. **b**
13. **c**	14. **c**				

1994 TEST PAPER

1. **c**	2. **c**	3. **b**	4. **d**	5. **a**	6. **d**
7. **c**	8. **d**	9. **a**	10. **a**	11. **d**	12. **c**
13. **a**	14. **a**				

1995 TEST PAPER

1. **b**	2. **b**	3. **b**	4. **a**	5. **d**	6. **d**
7. **a**	8. **a**	9. **a**	10. **c**	11. **d**	12. **d**
13. **a**	14. **b**	15. **d**	16. **d**	17. **d**	

1996 TEST PAPER

1. d   2. c   3. d   4. b   5. c   6. d
7. c   8. c   9. c   10. b

1997 TEST PAPER

1. c   2. b   3. b   4. b   5. b   6. c
7. a   8. c   9. b   10. c   11. a   12. d

1998 TEST PAPER

1. d   2. d   3. a   4. c   5. b

1999 TEST PAPER

1. b   2. a   3. d   4. c   5. c   6. d
7. d   8. b   9. a

2000 TEST PAPER

1. d   2. a   3. c   4. a   5. d   6. c
7. a   8. d   9. d   10. a   11. a   12. c

2001 TEST PAPER

1. c   2. b   3. d   4. d   5 a   6. d
7. a   8. a   9. a   10. a   11. d   12. a

2002 TEST PAPER

1. a   2. b   3. c   4. d   5. d   6. a
7. d   8. a   9. a   10. b   11. c   12. d
13. a   14. b   15. c   16. d   17. c   18. c
19. b

2003 TEST PAPER

1. b   2. c   3. d   4. b   5. c   6. c
7. b   8. b   9. d   10. c   11. a   12. a
13. b   14. d   15. c   16. d   17. d   18. d
19. d

2004 TEST PAPER

1. b   2. b   3. a   4. d   5. d   6. a
7. d   8. b   9. d   10. b   11. a   12. b
13. c   14. a   15. c   16. c   17. a   18. c
19. a   20. d   21. a   22. b

2005 TEST PAPER

1. d   2. a   3. d   4. a   5. b   6. c
7. c   8. d   9. b   10. a

2006 TEST PAPER

1. a   2. b   3. a   4. d   5. c   6. c
7. c   8. d   9. d   10. c   11. b   12. d
13. b

2007 TEST PAPER

1. d   2. b   3. b   4. c   5. d   6. d
7. b   8. a   9. a   10. a   11. a   12. b

2008 TEST PAPER

1. d   2. b   3. b   4. b   5. b   6. b
7. b   8. c   9. b   10. b   11. b   12. b
13. d

2009 TEST PAPER

1. c   2. a   3. a   4. c   5. c   6. a
7. d   8. b   9. a   10. d   11. b   12. b
13. a   14. b

2010 TEST PAPER

1. b   2. b   3. d   4. b   5. a   6. b
7. d   8. c   9. b   10. a

2011 TEST PAPER

1. c   2. c   3. d   4. b   5. c   6. b
7. d   8. a   9. d   10. d   11. a   12. b

2012 TEST PAPER

1. c   2. d   3. a   4. a   5. b   6. d
7. c   8. b   9. c   10. c   11. b   12. a
13. c   14. c   15. c   16. c   17. c   18. a
19. c   20. a

2013 TEST PAPER

1. b   2. b   3. a   4. b   5. b   6. b
7. c   8. d   9. b   10. c   11. a   12. c
13. c   14. d   15. c   16. d   17. d   18. c

Practice Questions on Indian Polity (General Studies—Prelims)

1. Which article of the Indian Constitution deals with the suability of the State of India?
   (a) Article 100   (b) Article 200
   (c) Article 300   (d) Article 330

2. The Chairman of which of the following parliamentary committees is invariably from the members of ruling party?
   (a) Committee on Public Undertakings
   (b) Public Accounts Committee
   (c) Estimates Committee
   (d) Committee on Delegated Legislation

3. Which of the following is not a formally prescribed device available to the members of Parliament?
   (a) Question Hour
   (b) Zero Hour
   (c) Half-an-hour discussion
   (d) Short duration discussion

4. Which of the following is exclusively a committee of the Lower House:
   (a) Committee on Assurances
   (b) Committee on Delegated Legislation
   (c) Committee on Public Undertakings
   (d) Estimates Committee

5. Which one of the following devices calls the attention of minister towards a matter of public importance?
   (a) Half-an-hour discussion
   (b) Calling attention notice
   (c) Short duration discussion
   (d) Adjournment motion

6. Central Vigilance Commission was set up on the recommendation of:
   (a) Administrative Reforms Commission of India
   (b) Gorwala Report
   (c) Kripalani Committee
   (d) Santhanam Committee

7. The institution of Lokayukta was created for the first time by the state of:
   (a) Orissa   (b) Bihar
   (c) Pubjab   (d) Maharashtra

8. The institution of Lokayukta was created first in Maharashtra in:
   (a) 1970   (b) 1972
   (c) 1973   (d) 1971

9. The correct statements about zero hour includes:
   1. It is the first hour of every sitting in both the houses of Parliament.
   2. It is mentioned in the Rules of Business of the houses of Parliament.
   3. During this time, matters are raised without any prior notice.
   4. It is the time immediately following the Question Hour in both the houses of Parliament.
   5. It is an Indian innovation in parliamentary procedure since 1964.
      (a) 2, 3 and 4   (b) 3 and 4
      (c) 1, 2 and 5   (d) 2, 3 and 5

10. The correct statements about calling attention notice are:
    1. It is a device of calling the attention of a minister to a matter of urgent public importance.
    2. Its main purpose is to seek an authoritative statement from the minister.
    3. It does not involve any censure against government.
    4. It is an Indian innovation in the parliamentary procedure since 1952.
    5. It is not mentioned in the Rules of Business and Procedure.
       (a) 1, 2, 3 and 4   (b) 4 and 5
       (c) 1, 2, 3 and 5   (d) 1, 2 and 3

11. Which of the following statements are true of Adjournment Motion?
    1. It is an extraordinary procedure which sets aside the normal business of the House.
    2. Its main object is to draw the attention of the House to a recent matter of urgent public importance.
    3. The Rajya Sabha can make use of this procedure.
    4. It must be supported by not less than 50 members for introduction.
    5. It involves an element of censure against government.
       - (a) 1, 2, 4 and 5
       - (b) 2, 3 and 5
       - (c) 2, 3 and 4
       - (d) 1, 2 and 4

12. Which of the following statements are incorrect about the difference between the writ jurisdiction of the Supreme Court and high courts in India?
    1. The Supreme Court can issue writs not only for the purpose of enforcement of Fundamental Rights but also for any other purpose, whereas high courts can issue writs only for the purpose of enforcement of Fundamental Rights.
    2. High courts can issue the writ of Injunction, whereas the Supreme Court cannot issue the writ of Injunction.
    3. The Supreme Court can issue writs only in the case of appeal, whereas high courts can issue writs only when the party directly approaches it.
    4. High courts can issue writs not only for the purpose of enforcement of Fundamental Rights but also for any other purpose, whereas the Supreme Court can issue writs only for the purpose of enforcement of Fundamental Rights.
       - (a) 1 and 2
       - (b) 1, 2 and 3
       - (c) 2 and 3
       - (d) 4 only

13. In parliamentary countries, like India, the legislative control over administration is considerably reduced and restricted in effectiveness due to which of the following reasons?
    1. The expansion in the volume and variety of administrative work.
    2. Frequent use of Guillitone.
    3. The large size of the legislature.

4. The members of the legislature are laymen.
5. The financial committees do post mortem work.
   - (a) 1, 2 and 5
   - (b) 2, 3 and 4
   - (c) 2, 3, 4 and 5
   - (d) 1, 2, 3, 4 and 5

14. No-confidence Motion, to be admitted in the Lok Sabha, needs the support of:
    - (a) 80 Members
    - (b) 140 Members
    - (c) 160 Members
    - (d) 50 Members

15. Which of the following statements are incorrect about unstarred question?
    1. It is distinguished by an asterisk mark.
    2. Answer to such a question is given orally.
    3. Answer to such a question is not followed by supplementary questions.
    4. It does not carry an asterisk mark.
    5. Answer to such a question is given in a written form.
       - (a) 2 and 3
       - (b) 3, 4 and 5
       - (c) 1 and 2
       - (d) 2, 3 and 4

16. In which of the following stated years, the Lokpal Bill was not introduced in the Parliament?
    - (a) 1968
    - (b) 1971
    - (c) 1978
    - (d) 1985

Assertion (A) and Reason (R) Pattern

Answer the following questions by using the codes given below.
- (a) Both A and R are true and R is the correct explanation of A.
- (b) Both A and R are true but R is not a correct explanation of A.
- (c) A is true but R is false.
- (d) A is false but R is true.

17. Assertion: The writ jurisdiction of the Supreme Court and high courts in India is same.
    Reason: Both, the Supreme Court and the High Court can issue the writs of Habeas Corpus, Mandamus, Prohibition, Certiorari and Quo warranto.

18. Assertion: In democracy, the ultimate responsibility of administration is to the people.
    Reason: The democratic government is based on the principle of popular sovereignty.

Matching Pattern

Match List-I with List-II and select correct answer by using the codes given below the lists.

19.

List-I	List-II
A. Short duration discussion	1. 1964
B. Calling attention notice	2. 1962
C. Zero Hour	3. 1953
D. Committee on Public Undertakings	4. 1954

Codes:	A	B	C	D
(a)	4	3	1	2
(b)	3	4	2	1
(c)	4	2	1	3
(d)	3	2	4	1

20. List-I (Writs)
    A. Mandamus
    B. Habeas Corpus
    C. Quo warranto
    D. Certiorari

    List-II (Literal meanings)
    1. 'By what warrant or authority'
    2. 'We command'
    3. 'To be certified'
    4. 'You may have the body' or 'To have the body of'

Codes:	A	B	C	D
(a)	2	3	4	1
(b)	2	4	3	1
(c)	1	4	2	3
(d)	2	4	1	3

21. List-I
    (Provisions)
    A. Writ jurisdiction of the Supreme Court
    B. Suits against government
    C. Writ jurisdiction of the High Court
    D. Source of the power of judicial review

    List-II
    (Contained in)
    1. Article 13
    2. Article 226
    3. Article 300
    4. Article 32
    5. Article 166

Codes:	A	B	C	D
(a)	4	3	5	1
(b)	3	4	2	5
(c)	4	3	2	1
(d)	5	4	3	2

22. The final work of UPSC in recruitment process is:
    (a) Selection   (b) Appointment
    (c) Certification   (d) Placement

23. The conditions of service of members of All-India Services are determined by:
    (a) President of India
    (b) Constitution of India
    (c) Parliament of India
    (d) Union Public Service Commission

24. Constitutional safeguards to civil servants are ensured by:
    (a) Art. 310   (b) Art. 315
    (c) Art. 312   (d) Art. 311

Assertion (A) and Reason (R) Pattern

Answer the following questions by using the codes given below.
(a) Both A and R are true and R is the correct explanation of A.
(b) Both A and R are true but R is not a correct explanation of A.
(c) A is true but R is false.
(d) A is false but R is true.

25. Assertion: India has imposed severe restrictions on the political activities of civil servants.
    Reason: The civil servants in India enjoy the right to vote.

26. Assertion: A member of All-India Service can appeal against the order of a State Government to the President of India.

Reason: Article 311 of the Constitution says that a civil servant cannot be removed or dismissed by any authority which is subordinate to the authority by which he was appointed.

27. The Vote on Account is passed:
    (a) After the voting of demands
    (b) Before the general discussion
    (c) After the general discussion
    (d) Either after the voting of the demands or after the general discussion.

28. Arrange the following stages in the enactment of budget in proper order:
    1. General discussion
    2. Appropriation Bill
    3. Finance Bill
    4. Voting of the demands for grant
    5. Presentation to legislature
       (a) 1, 2, 3, 4, 5   (b) 5, 1, 4, 2, 3
       (c) 5, 1, 4, 3, 2   (d) 5, 1, 3, 4, 2

29. Which of the following documents are presented to the legislature along with the budget?
    1. An explanatory memorandum on the budget
    2. A summary of demands for grants
    3. An Appropriation Bill
    4. A Finance Bill
    5. The economic survey
       (a) 1, 3 and 5   (b) 1, 2 and 3
       (c) 2, 3 and 5   (d) 1, 2, 3 and 4

30. Which of the following is not a condition of admissibility of cut motions in the Parliament?

(a) It should not make suggestions for the amendment of existing laws.
(b) It should not relate to expenditure charged on the Consolidated Fund of India.
(c) It should relate to more than one demand.
(d) It should not raise a question of privilege.

31. The ultimate responsibility of taking due action on the comments of the C & AG vests with:
(a) President of India
(b) Supreme Court
(c) Parliament
(d) National Development Council

32. The number of demands in the General Budget for civil expenditures is:
(a) 109 (b) 106
(c) 103 (d) 102

33. The word 'Budget' is mentioned in which of the following Articles of the Constitution of India:
(a) Art. 266 (b) Art. 112
(c) Art. 265 (d) None

34. The budget was formally introduced in India in:
(a) 1860 (b) 1947
(c) 1950 (d) 1868

35. Which of the following statements are incorrect?
1. Rajya Sabha can reject a Money Bill.
2. Rajya Sabha can make recommendations on a Money Bill.
3. Rajya Sabha cannot reject a Money Bill.
4. Rajya Sabha should return the Money Bill to the Lok Sabha within 14 days.
5. Rajya Sabha can amend a Money Bill.
(a) 2, 3 and 4 (b) 1, 2 and 5
(c) 1 and 5 (d) only 1

36. Which of the following expenditures are charged upon the Consolidated Fund of India?
1. Allowances of the Chairman of Lok Sabha.
2. Expenditure relating to the raising of loans and the service and redemption of debt.
3. Pensions of the judges of High Courts.
4. Any sum required to satisfy the award of any arbitration tribunal.
5. Administrative expenses of the office of the Comptroller and Auditor-General
(a) 2 and 5 (b) 1, 2 and 5
(c) 2, 3 and 4 (d) 1, 2, 3, 4 and 5

37. The correct statements about Public Account of India are:
1. The public account is the fund to which all public moneys received by or on behalf of the government are credited.
2. No legislative appropriation is required for payments from the Public Account of India.
3. Legislative appropriation is required for payments from the Public Account of India.
4. All public moneys, other than those credited to the Consolidated Fund of India, which are received by or on behalf of the government are credited to the Public Account of India.
5. It is operated by executive action.
(a) 1, 2 and 5 (b) 1, 3 and 5
(c) 2, 4 and 5 (d) 2 and 4

38. Which of the following statements are incorrect?
1. Appropriation Bill cannot be amended while the Finance Bill can be amended.
2. Finance Bill cannot be amended while Appropriation Bill can be amended.
3. Same procedure governs both the Appropriation Bill and the Finance Bill.
4. Appropriation Bill and the Finance Bill are governed by different procedures.
5. Appropriation Bill cannot be rejected by the Rajya Sabha while Finance Bill can be rejected by it.
(a) 2 and 4 (b) 2, 4 and 5
(c) 1 and 3 (d) 1, 3 and 5

Matching Pattern

Match List-I with List-II and select the correct answer by using the codes given below the lists.

39.

List-I
A. Token Cut Motion
B. Economy Cut Motion
C. Policy Cut Motion

List-II
1. "That the amount of the demand be reduced by a specified amount."
2. "That the amount of the demand be reduced by Re 1."
3. "That the amount of the demand be reduced by Rs 100."
4. "That the amount of the demand be reduced to Re 1."
5. "That the amount of the demand be reduced to Rs 100."

Codes:

	A	B	C
(a)	5	1	2
(b)	5	3	1
(c)	3	1	4
(d)	3	5	2

40.   List-I (Principles)

A. No tax shall be levied or collected
    except by authority of law.
B. No bill imposing tax can be introduced
    in the Parliament except on the
    recommendation of the President.
C. No expenditure can be incurred except
    with the sanction of the legislature.
D. No Demand for grant of any money
    for expenditure can be made except on
    the recommendation of the President.

List-II (Provided by)

1. Article 117
2. Article 113
3. Article 265
4. Article 112
5. Article 266

Codes:

	A	B	C	D
(a)	5	4	2	3
(b)	3	1	5	2
(c)	4	5	2	1
(d)	3	2	4	1

41.   List-I (Terms)

A. Consolidated Fund of India
B. Money Bill
C. Annual Financial Statement
D. Contingency Fund of India

List-II (Defined by)

1. Article 110
2. Article 267
3. Article 266
4. Article 265
5. Article 112

Codes:

	A	B	C	D
(a)	4	1	5	3
(b)	2	1	5	4
(c)	4	1	5	2
(d)	3	1	5	2

Assertion (A) and Reason (R) Pattern

Answer the following questions by using the codes given below.
  (a) Both A and R are true and R is the correct explanation of A.
  (b) Both A and R are true but R is not a correct explanation of A.
  (c) A is true but R is false.
  (d) A is false but R is true.

42. Assertion: Budget is a secret document and should not be leaked out before being presented to the Parliament.
Reason: India has adopted the parliamentary form of government.

43. Assertion: The budget makes a distinction between the expenditure 'charged' on the Consolidated Fund of India and the expenditure 'made' from the Consolidated Fund of India.
Reason: The expenditure 'charged' on the Consolidated Fund of India is not subject to the vote of Parliament.

44. Assertion: No expenditure can be incurred without the approval of the Parliament.
Reason: Our democratic government, like that of Britain, is based on the concept of sovereignty of the parliament.

45. Assertion: The Rajya Sabha has less powers in financial matters.
Reason: The Lok Sabha alone votes the demands for grants.

46. Assertion: The budget is placed in the Upper House (Rajya Sabha) at the end of the Finance Minister's Budget Speech in the Lok Sabha.
Reason: The budget is presented to the Lok Sabha on the last working day of February.

47. Assertion: The expenditure 'charged' on the Consolidated Fund of India is not subject to the vote of Parliament.
Reason: It is in the nature of obligatory payment.

48. Assertion: The Constitution of India has authorised the parliament to create a Contingency Fund of India.
Reason: The Contingency Fund enables the government to meet any unforeseen expenditure.

49. Assertion: Audit in India is equally concerned with the legal and technical as well as the propriety aspects of expenditure.
Reason: The provision under which the audit is performed by CAG says that he has "to ascertain whether the moneys shown in the accounts as having been disbursed were legally available for and applicable

to the purpose to which they had been applied and whether the expenditure conforms to the authority which governs it."

50. The Finance Commission does not recommend on:
    (a) The distribution of net proceeds of taxes between the union and the states.
    (b) The principles to be followed by the centre while giving grants-in-aid to the states out of the consolidated Fund of India.
    (c) The amount of money to be allocated to the states from Public Account of India.
    (d) Any other matter referred to the Commission by President in the interest of sound finance.

51. The National Development Council consists of:
    (a) The Prime Minister, the Chief Ministers of all the states and the members of the Planning Commission.
    (b) The Prime Minister, the Chief Ministers of all the states, the Central Cabinet Ministers and the Members of the Planning Commission.
    (c) The Prime Minister, the Chief Ministers of all the states, Selected Central Cabinet Ministers, Administrators of union territories and the members of the Planning Commission.
    (d) The Prime Minister, all Union Cabinet Ministers, Chief Ministers of all the states, Administrators of union territories and the members of the Planning Commission.

52. Which of the following statements about President's ordinance-making power is not correct?
    (a) It is co-extensive with legislative power of Parliament.
    (b) Laid down in Article 123.
    (c) Shall cease to operate on expiry of six weeks from the reassembly of the Parliament.
    (d) Cannot be withdrawn at any time by the President.

53. The salient features of the Government of India Act, 1935 are:
    1. All India Federation
    2. Provincial Autonomy
    3. Dyarchy at the Centre
    4. Abolition of Dyarchy in the states
        (a) 1 and 2   (b) 1, 2 and 3
        (c) 2, 3 and 4   (d) 1, 2, 3 and 4

54. The accounts of the Union and of the States shall be kept in such form as prescribed by:
    (a) Finance Minister of India in consultation with CAG of India.
    (b) CAG of India with the approval of Planning Commission.
    (c) CAG of India with the approval of the President.
    (d) President of India in consultation with CAG of India

55. The Planning Commission is described as the "Economic Cabinet" by:
    (a) P.P. Agarwal   (b) Ashok Chanda
    (c) D.R. Gadgil   (d) Santhanam

56. Which of the following acts introduced the principle of election in India.
    (a) Indian Councils Act of 1861
    (b) Indian Councils Act of 1892
    (c) Indian Councils Act of 1909
    (d) Indian Councils Act of 1919

57. Which of the following enjoys the constitutional status:
    1. Finance Commission
    2. Planning Commission
    3. Zonal Councils
    4. National Development Council
    5. Election Commission
    6. University Grants Commission
        (a) 1, 3 and 5   (b) 1 and 5
        (c) 1, 2, 5 and 6   (d) 1, 3, 5 and 6

58. The features of Indian federal system are:
    1. Division of powers
    2. Separation of powers
    3. Independent judiciary
    4. Leadership of the Prime Minister
    5. A written Constitution
        (a) 2, 3 and 5   (b) 1, 4 and 5
        (c) 1, 2 and 5   (d) 1, 3 and 5

59. Which of the following is not a department under the Ministry of Home Affairs?
    (a) Department of Internal Security
    (b) Department of Home
    (c) Department of States
    (d) Department of Law and Order

60. Which of the following is not correct about Finance Commission?
    (a) Constituted at the expiration of every fifth year.
    (b) Recommends the distribution of proceeds of taxes between Centre and states.
    (c) Consists of a Chairman and four other members.
    (d) Its advice is binding on the Government.

61. Which of the following is correctly matched?
    (a) 1909 Act   – Principle of election
    (b) 1919 Act   – Provincial autonomy
    (c) 1935 Act   – Dyarchy in states
    (d) 1947 Act   – Responsible government

62. The CAG of India can be removed from the office only in like manner and on like grounds as:
    (a) Chairman of the UPSC
    (b) Supreme Court Judge
    (c) Attorney General of India
    (d) Speaker of Lok Sabha

63. Discretionary grants are given to states by the Centre on the recommendation of:

(a) Finance Commission

(b) National Development Council

(c) Finance Ministry

(d) Planning Commission

64. Statutory recognition to the portfolio system was accorded by:

(a) Indian Councils Act of 1892

(b) Indian Councils Act of 1871

(c) Indian Councils Act of 1861

(d) Indian Councils Act of 1882

65. Dyarchy was introduced by:

(a) Indian Councils Act of 1909

(b) Government of India Act of 1919

(c) Government of India Act of 1935

(d) Independence Act of 1947

66. Which of the following is not a feature of Government of India Act of 1935?

(a) Dyarchy at the Centre

(b) All-India Federation

(c) Provincial autonomy

(d) Dyarchy in the provinces

67. Which one of the following amendments to the Constitutions, for the first time, made it obligatory for the President to act on the advice of the council of ministers?

(a) 24th amendment   (b) 42nd amendment

(c) 44th amendment   (d) 54th amendment

68. The Indian federation is based on the pattern of:

(a) Switzerland   (b) USA

(c) Russia   (d) Canada

69. Who said the "Indian Constitution established a unitary state with subsidiary federal features rather than federal state with subsidiary unitary features?"

(a) Granville Austin   (b) Ivor Jennings

(c) B.R. Ambedker   (d) K.C. Wheare

70. Which of the following are not correct about CAG of India?

1. He is appointed by the President for a period of five years.

2. His salary and conditions of service are determined by President.

3. He shall vacate office on attaining the age of 60 years.

4. He can be removed by the President on his own.

5. He is responsible for maintaining the accounts of Central and state governments.

(a) 1, 4 and 5   (b) 2, 3 and 4

(c) 1, 2, 3, 4 and 5   (d) 3, 4 and 5

71. Which of the following are correct about Deputy Chairman of Planning Commission?

1. He is appointed by the Prime Minister.

2. He enjoys the status of a Cabinet-rank minister.

3. He is a member of the Union cabinet.

4. He attends all Cabinet meetings.

5. He is the de facto executive head of the Commission.

(a) 1, 2, 4 and 5   (b) 2, 3, 4 and 5

(c) 2, 4 and 5   (d) 1, 2, 3 and 5

72. The correct statements about the Directive Principles of State Policy are:

1. They are borrowed from the Irish Constitution.

2. They are incorporated in Part V of the Constitution.

3. They seek to provide social and economic base to democracy.

4. The state must compulsorily implement them.

5. All of them are Gandhian in nature.

(a) 1, 2, 3 and 5   (b) 1, 3 and 5

(c) 1, 3, 4 and 5   (d) 1 and 3

73. The Governor-General of Bengal became the Governor-General of India by:

(a) Government of India Act of 1858

(b) Indian Councils Act of 1861

(c) Pitts India Act of 1784

(d) Charter Act of 1833

74. Which is incorrectly matched?

(a) Prohibition of Discrimination—Article 15

(b) Right to Association—Article 19.

(c) Right to Protection of Life—Article 20.

(d) Right to Constitutional Remedies—Article 32.

75. Who characterises Indian Union as "a federation with a centralising tendency?"

(a) B.R. Ambedker   (b) K.C. Wheare

(c) Ivor Jennings   (d) Granville Austin

76. Which act provided for direct control of Indian affairs by the British Government?

(a) Charter Act of 1858

(b) Regulating Act of 1773

(c) Pitts India Act of 1784

(d) Charter Act of 1833

77. The correct statements about Fundamental Rights are:

1. They are enforceable in the court of law.

2. These rights are absolute.

3. They can be suspended during national emergency, except some.

4. They are available only to Indian citizens.

5. They are contained in Part IV of the Constitution.

(a) 1, 3, 4 and 5   (b) 1, 2, 3 and 5

(c) 1 and 3   (d) 1, 3 and 5

78. The words 'socialist' and 'secular' were added to the Preamble by:

(a) 41st amendment   (b) 44th amendment

(c) 46th amendment   (d) 42nd amendment

79. No demand for a grant is to be made except on the recommendation of:

(a) Prime Minister

(b) President

(c) Finance Minister

(d) Comptroller and Auditor-General

80. Which of the following are not the departments of Finance Ministry?
   1. Department of Expenditure
   2. Department of Economic Affairs
   3. Department of Banking
   4. Department of Revenue
   5. Department of Budget
      (a) 2 and 3   (b) 3 and 4
      (c) 3 and 5   (d) 2 and 5

81. The features of Government of India Act of 1858 includes:
   1. Replacement of Company rule by the Crown rule.
   2. Establishment of a Board of Control over the Court of Directors.
   3. Reaffirmation of the system of open competition.
   4. Separating the legislative and executive functions of the Governor-General.
   5. Creation of a new office of the Secretary of State for India.
      (a) 1, 3 and 4   (b) 1, 2 and 4
      (c) 1 and 5   (d) 1, 3 and 5

82. Which of the following are not the federal features of Indian Constitution?
   1. Supremacy of Constitution
   2. All-India services
   3. Single citizenship
   4. Independent judiciary
   5. Bicameral legislature
   6. Integrated judiciary
      (a) 1, 4 and 5   (b) 1, 5 and 6
      (c) 2, 3 and 6   (d) 2, 3 and 4

83. The features of Indian parliamentary system are:
   1. Independent judiciary.
   2. Collective responsibility of the executive to the legislature.
   3. A written Constitution.
   4. Presence of de jure and de facto executives.

5. Individual responsibility of the executive to the legislature.
      (a) 2, 3 and 4   (b) 1, 2 and 4
      (c) 2, 4 and 5   (d) 1, 2, 4 and 5

84. Which is correctly matched?
   (a) Amendment procedure – Article 268
   (b) Duties of Prime Minister – Article 74
   (c) President's rule   – Article 365
   (d) Inter-State Council   – Article 264

85. The President of India is elected by an electoral college consisting of:
   (a) Members of Parliament and state legislatures
   (b) Elected members of Parliament and state legislatures
   (c) Elected members of Parliament and state legislative assemblies
   (d) Elected members of Lok Sabha and members of Rajya Sabha and state Legislative Assemblies

86. The ex-officio members of the Planning Commission are:
   1. Home Minister
   2. Finance Minister
   3. Defence Minister
   4. Human Resources Minister
   5. Planning Minister
   6. Agriculture Minister
      (a) 1, 2 and 5   (b) 2, 3, 5 and 6
      (c) 1, 2, 4 and 5   (d) 2 and 5

87. Which of the following acts laid the foundation of Central administration?
   (a) Charter Act of 1833
   (b) Regulating Act of 1773
   (c) Charter Act of 1853
   (d) Pitts India Act of 1784

88. Planning Commission was set up on the recommendation of:
   (a) National Planning Committee
   (b) Gorwala Report
   (c) Planning Advisory Board
   (d) Constituent Assembly

Matching Pattern

Match List I with List II and select the correct answers by using codes given below the lists.

89.

List-I	List-II
A. Board of Control	1. Regulating Act of 1773
B. Central Administration	2. Government of India Act of 1858
C. Governor-General of India	3. Pitts India Act of 1784
D. Secretary of state for India	4. Charter Act of 1833

Codes:	A	B	C	D
(a)	4	2	3	1
(b)	3	1	4	2
(c)	1	2	3	4
(d)	3	1	2	4

90. List-I

A. Bicameral system
B. Legislative devolution
C. Separate electorate
D. Provincial autonomy

List-II

1. Government of India Act of 1935
2. Indian Councils Act of 1861
3. Montagu-Chelmsford Reforms
4. Indian Councils Act of 1892
5. Minto-Morely Reforms.

Codes:	A	B	C	D
(a)	5	2	3	1
(b)	3	4	5	1
(c)	3	2	5	1
(d)	5	4	3	1

91. List-I

A. Equality in Public employment
B. Minorities rights
C. Right to personal liberty
D. Right against exploitation

List-II

1. Article 29
2. Article 21
3. Article 23
4. Article 16
5. Article 25

Codes:	A	B	C	D
(a)	4	3	1	2
(b)	3	4	2	1
(c)	4	2	1	3
(d)	4	1	2	3

92. List-I

A. Withholding of assent
B. Overriden by an ordinary majority
C. Taking no action on the bill
D. Overriden by a higher majority

List-II

1. Qualified veto
2. Pocket veto
3. Absolute veto
4. Suspensive veto
5. Majority veto

Codes:	A	B	C	D
(a)	3	5	2	1
(b)	4	3	2	5
(c)	5	3	1	2
(d)	3	4	2	1

93. List-I

A. Third Schedule
B. Ninth Schedule
C. Fourth Schedule
D. Tenth Schedule

List-II

1. Allocation of seats in Upper House
2. Disqualification on Grounds of defection
3. Validation of certain acts
4. Languages
5. Forms of affirmations

Codes:	A	B	C	D
(a)	1	3	4	2
(b)	5	3	1	2
(c)	5	4	2	1
(d)	1	4	2	3

Assertion (A) and Reason (R) Pattern

Answer the following questions by using the codes given below.

(a) Both A and R are true and R is the correct explanation of A.

(b) Both A and R are true but R is not a correct explanation of A.

(c) A is true but R is false.

(d) A is false but R is true.

94. Assertion: India has adopted the parliamentary form of government.

Reason: The President is the titular head of the state while the council of ministers headed by the Prime Minister is the real executive authority.

95. Assertion: Article 149 of the Indian Constitution lays down the provisions with regard to the appointment and service conditions of the Comptroller and Auditor-General of India.
    Reason: He cannot function independently unless he enjoys the constitutional protection.

96. Assertion: A person who holds, or who has held, office as President shall not be eligible for re-election to that office.
    Reason: No person shall be eligible for election as a President unless he is qualified for election as a member of the House of People.

97. Assertion: All doubts and disputes arising out of or in connection with the election of a President or Vice-President shall be inquired into and decided by the Supreme Court whose decision shall be final.
    Reason: Parliament may, by law, regulate any matter relating to or connected with the election of a President or a Vice-President.

98. Assertion: There shall be a council of ministers with the Prime Minister at the head to aid and advise the President who shall, in the exercise of his functions, act in accordance with such advice.
    Reason: The question whether any, and if so what, advice was tendered by ministers to the President shall not be inquired into in any court.

99. A new All-India Service can be created by:
    (a) A resolution of the Rajya Sabha
    (b) An act of Parliament
    (c) An order of the President
    (d) A resolution of the UPSC

100. The Central Administrative Tribunal deals with:
    (a) Recruitment matters
    (b) Promotion matters
    (c) Disciplinary matters
    (d) Recruitment and all service matters

101. Which of the following can provide for the appointment of a Joint Public Service Commission?
    (a) President of India
    (b) Parliament of India
    (c) UPSC
    (d) State Governors

102. The origins of UPSC can be traced to:
    (a) 1909 Act   (b) 1919 Act
    (c) 1930 Act   (d) 1947 Act

103. The functions of the UPSC can be extended by:
    (a) President
    (b) Prime Minister
    (c) Ministry of Personnel
    (d) Parliament

104. The UPSC derives its functions from which of the following sources?
    1. Constitution
    2. Parliamentary laws

    3. Executive rules and orders
    4. Conventions
        (a) 1 only   (b) 1 and 2
        (c) 1 and 3   (d) 1, 2, 3 and 4

105. The personnel system of any local authority, corporate body or public institution can be placed within the jurisdiction of the UPSC by:
    (a) President of India
    (b) Central Ministry of Personnel
    (c) Parliament
    (d) Supreme Court

106. The Chairman and members of the UPSC hold office for a term of:
    (a) Three years   (b) Four years
    (c) Five years   (d) Six years

107. Who is regarded as the "Father of All-India Services?"
    (a) Lord Macaulay   (b) Lord Cornwallis
    (c) B.R. Ambedker   (d) Sardar Patel

108. A Joint Public Service Commission can be created by:
    (a) An order of the President
    (b) A resolution of the Rajya Sabha
    (c) An act of Parliament
    (d) A resolution of the concerned state legislatures

109. Which of the following statements are correct?
    1. The Constitution does not fix the number of members of the UPSC.
    2. One-half of the members of the UPSC should be persons who have held office under the Government of India or of a state atleast for five years.
    3. The Chairman and members of the UPSC hold office for a term of five years or until they attain the age of 60 years.
    4. The salaries and allowances of the members of the UPSC are determined by the Parliament.
    5. The entire expanses of UPSC are charged on the Consolidated Fund of India.
        (a) 2, 4 and 5   (b) 1 and 5
        (c) 2, 3 and 4   (d) 1, 4 and 5

110. Which of the follwing statements are correct with regard to the prohibition as to the holding of offices by members of Public Service Commissions on ceasing to be such members?
    1. The Chairman of the UPSC shall be ineligible for further employment either under the Government of India or under the government of a state.
    2. The Chairman of a SPSC shall be eligible for appointment as Chairman or any other member of the UPSC or as Chairman of any other SPSC, but not for any other employment either under the Government of India or under the government of a state.
    3. A member other than Chairman of the UPSC shall be eligible for appointment as Chairman of the UPSC or as Chairman of a SPSC, but not for any

other employment, either under the Government of India or under the government of a state.

4. A member other than Chairman of the SPSC shall be eligible for appointment as Chairman or any other member of the UPSC or as Chairman of that or any other SPSC, but not for any other employment either under the Government of India or under the government of a state.

(a) 1 only   (b) 2 and 4

(c) 1 and 3   (d) 1, 2, 3 and 4

111. Which of the following statements related to the Central Administrative Tribunal are correct?

1. It is a statutory body.

2. Its members are drawn from administrative background only.

3. It is not bound by the procedure prescribed in the code of civil procedure.

4. Its jurisdiction covers the members of All India Services as well as Central Services and Central Government posts.

5. It was setup in 1985.

(a) 2, 3 and 5   (b) 1 and 4

(c) 1, 3, 4 and 5   (d) 2 and 3

Assertion (A) and Reason (R) Pattern

Answer the following questions by using the codes given below

(a) Both A and R are true and R is the correct explanation of A.

(b) Both A and R are true but R is not the correct explanation of A.

(c) A is true but R is false.

(d) A is false but R is true.

112. Assertion: All-India Services are instruments of national integration.

Reason: Its members are appointed by President of India.

113. Assertion: Chairman and members of the UPSC are appointed by President.

Reason: The UPSC is a constitutional body.

114. Assertion: The Rajamannar Committee recommended the abolition of the IAS and IPS.

Reason: The IAS and IPS violate the principles of federalism and ministerial responsibility at the state level.

115. Assertion: The UPSC makes recruitment to Group A and Group B services.

Reason: The Staff Selection Commission makes recruitment to Group C services.

116. Assertion: The members of All-India Services can give independent and impartial advise to political executives in the states.

Reason: They enjoy constitutional safeguards with regard to security of service.

117. Assertion: The salaries and allowances of members of the UPSC are charged on the consolidated Fund of India.

Reason: Under the provisions of the Constitution, additional functions may be conferred on the Commission by President.

118. Assertion: The salaries of the members of the UPSC cannot be changed to their disadvantage during their tenure.

Reason: The independence of the Public Service Commission has to be maintained.

119. Assertion: The Constitution has not fixed the number of members of the UPSC.

Reason: The Chairman and members of the UPSC are appointed by President.

Matching Pattern

Match List-I with List-II and select the correct answer by using the codes given below the lists.

120.   List-I (Provisions)

A. Tenure of office of persons serving the Union or a state.

B. Public Service Commissions for the Union and for the states.

C. Recruitment and conditions of service of persons serving the Union or a state.

D. Dismissal, removal or reduction in rank of persons employed in civil capacities under the Union or a state.

List–II (Contained in)

1. Article 315

2. Article 310

3. Article 312

4. Article 309

5. Article 311

Codes:	A	B	C	D
(a)	4	1	5	2
(b)	4	5	2	3
(c)	2	1	4	5
(d)	2	1	5	4

121. Which of the following statements are true about the Governor of a state?
    1. The executive power of the state is vested in him.
    2. He must have attained 35 years of age.
    3. He holds office during the pleasure of the President.
    4. The grounds for his removal are laid down in the Constitution.
       (a) 1, 2, and 4   (b) 1, 2 and 3
       (c) 1, 3 and 4   (d) 1, 2, 3 and 4

122. The recommendations of the Ashok Mehta Committee on Panchayati Raj are:
    1. Creation of a two-tier system
    2. Reservation of seats for SCs and STs
    3. Compulsory powers of taxation to Panchayati Raj institutions
    4. Open participation of political parties in Panchayati Raj affairs
    5. If superceded, elections must be held within one year
       (a) 1, 3 and 4   (b) 1, 2, 4 and 5
       (c) 1, 2, 3 and 4   (d) 1, 3, 4 and 5

123. District Judges are appointed by:
    (a) The Chief Justice of High Court
    (b) The State Public Service Commission
    (c) The Chief Minister of state
    (d) The Governor of state

124. Money bill can be introduced in the state legislature only on the recommendation of:
    (a) Speaker   (b) Finance Minister
    (c) Chief Minister   (d) Governor

125. According to the Balwantray Mehta Committee, the District Collector should be:
    (a) Kept out of the Zila Parishad
    (b) A non-voting member of the Zila Parishad
    (c) A member of the Zila Parishad with the right to vote
    (d) The Chairman of the Zila Parishad

126. The Balwantray Mehta Committee was a committee on:
    (a) Democratic-decentralisation
    (b) Panchayati Raj institutions
    (c) Administrative arrangements for rural development
    (d) Community development programme

127. Panchayati Raj form of rural local government was adopted first by (in the order):
    (a) Rajasthan and Madhya Pradesh
    (b) Andhra Pradesh and West Bengal
    (c) Rajashtan and Andhra Pradesh
    (d) Andhra Pradesh and Rajasthan

128. The District and sessions Judge works directly under the control of:
    (a) District Collector
    (b) Governor of the state

(c) Law Minister of the state
(d) High Court of the state

129. Which of the following is a committee on Panchayati Raj institutions?
    (a) Balwantray Mehta Committee
    (b) G.V.K. Rao Committee
    (c) L.M. Singhvi Committee
    (d) Ashok Mehta Committee

130. "The state shall take steps to organise village Panchayats and endow them with such powers as may be necessary to enable them to function as units of self-government." This provision is mentioned in:
    (a) Part I of the Constitution
    (b) Part IV-A of the Constitution
    (c) Part III of the Constitution
    (d) Part IV of the Constitution

131. A President's rule can be imposed in a state under the provisions of:
    1. Article 356   2. Article 360
    3. Article 352   4. Article 365
       (a) only 1   (b) 1 and 3
       (c) 1 and 4   (d) 1 and 2

132. Which of the following Constitutional Amendment act provided for the appointment of the same person as Governor for two or more states?
    (a) 4th Amendment   (b) 7th Amendment
    (c) 11th Amendment   (d) 24th Amendment

133. Article 154 states that the Governor can exercise his executive authority either directly or through officers subordinate to him. The word subordinates includes:
    (a) All the ministers and the Chief Minister
    (b) All the ministers except the Chief Minister
    (c) Only the Chief Minister and the Deputy Chief Minister
    (d) Only the Cabinet Ministers

134. In the event of declaration of constitutional emergency in the state, the President can:
    1. Assume to himself all the functions of the state government including the High Court.
    2. Declare that the powers of the state legislature shall be exercisable under the authority of the Governor.
    3. Assume to himself all the functions of the state government except the High Court.
    4. Declare that the powers of the state legislature shall be exercisable under the authority of the parliament.
    Of the above, the correct statements are:
       (a) 1 and 2   (b) 2 and 3
       (c) 3 and 4   (d) 1 and 4

135. The correct statements about ordinance making power of the Governor are:
    1. It is laid down in Article 213.
    2. It can be issued by him after the advice of the President or state council of ministers.

3. It is co-extensive with the legislative power of the state legislature.

4. It can be issued only during the recess of State Legislative Assembly and not the Legislative Council.

5. It can not be withdrawn by him anytime.

(a) 2, 3 and 4   (b) 1, 3 and 5
(c) 1, 2 and 3   (d) 2, 4 and 5

136. Panchayati Raj is a system of:
(a) Local government
(b) Local administration
(c) Local self-government
(d) Rural local self-government

137. The correct statements about cantonment boards are:
1. This system of municipal administration is a British legacy in our country.
2. They are set up under the resolutions passed by the Ministry of Defence.
3. The Ministry of Defence exercises direct administrative control over them.
4. It consists of elected members only.
5. The executive officer of the board is appointed by the President of the board.

(a) 1, 3 and 5   (b) 2, 3 and 4
(c) 1 and 3   (d) 3, 4 and 5

138. Which of the following are the features of 74th Amendment Act on municipalities?
1. Reservation of seats for SCs and STs in proportion of their population (to the total population) in municipal Area.
2. Mandatory periodic elections every 5 years.
3. The procedure for maintenance of accounts and audit would be decided by the State Governor.
4. Constitution of Nagar Panchayats for smaller urban area.
5. One-third of the seats shall be reserved for women, excluding the number of seats reserved for SC and ST women.

(a) 1, 2 and 4   (b) 2, 3 and 5
(c) 3, 4 and 5   (d) 1 and 2

Assertion (A) and Reason (R) Pattern

Answer the following questions by using the codes given below:
(a) Both A and R are true and R is the correct explanation of A.

Matching Pattern

Match List-I with List-II and select the correct answer by using the codes given below the lists.

(b) Both A and R are true but R is not a correct explanation of A.
(c) A is true but R is false.
(d) A is false but R is true.

139. **Assertion:** Under the Constitution, the Chief Minister holds office till the pleasure of the Governor.
Reason: The Chief Minister is appointed by the Governor.

140. **Assertion:** Lord Ripon's Resolution of 1882 was hailed as the 'Magna Carta' of local government.
Reason: Lord Ripon is regarded as the 'father of local self-government in India.'

141. **Assertion:** The 73rd amendment to the Constitution gives a constitutional status to the Gram Sabha.
Reason: The Balvantray Mehta Committee report made a formal mention of the Gram Sabha.

142. **Assertion:** The Governor of a state is a nominal (titular) executive head.
Reason: The Constitution has provided for a parliamentary government in the states.

143. **Assertion:** No person shall be eligible for appointment as a Governor unless he is a citizen of India and has completed the age of thirty years.
Reason: The Governor shall not hold any other office of profit.

144. **Assertion:** The Governor shall hold office during the pleasure of the President.
Reason: The Governor of a state shall be appointed by the President India.

145. **Assertion:** The emoluments and allowances of the Governor shall not be diminished during his term of office.
Reason: Where the same person is appointed as Governor of two or more states, the emoluments and allowances payable to the Governor shall be allocated among the states in such proportion as the President may by order determine.

146. **Assertion:** There shall be a council of ministers with the Chief Minister at the head to aid and advise the Governor in the exercise of his functions, except in so far he is by or under the Constitution, required to exercise his functions, or any of them in his discretion.
Reason: The Chief Minister shall be appointed by the Governor and other ministers shall be appointed by the Governor on the advice of the Chief Minister.

147.	List-I	List-II
	A. Governor	1. Article 167
	B. Counil of ministers	2. Article 169
	C. Duties of Chief Minister	3. Article 155
	D. Legislative Council	4. Article 163

Codes:

	A	B	C	D
(a)	1	2	3	4
(b)	4	3	2	1
(c)	3	2	4	1
(d)	3	4	1	2

148.

List-I	List-II
A. Deliberative organisation	1. Commissioner
B. Formal head	2. Standing Committee
C. Management	3. Mayor
D. Executive body	4. Council

Codes:

	A	B	C	D
(a)	4	2	3	1
(b)	3	2	1	4
(c)	2	3	1	4
(d)	4	3	2	1

149.

List-I (States)	List-II (Governor's special responsibilities)
A. Madhya Pradesh	1. Law and order
B. Gujarat	2. Administration of tribal areas
C. Nagaland	3. Development of backward areas
D. Assam	4. Minister for Tribal Welfare
	5. Hill Areas Committee working

Codes:

	A	B	C	D
(a)	3	4	2	5
(b)	2	1	4	3
(c)	4	3	1	2
(d)	5	3	2	4

150.

List I	List II
A. Article 156	1. Executive authority of Governor
B. Article 154	2. Tenure of Governor
C. Article 153	3. Appointment of Governor
D. Article 155	4. Office of Governor
	5. Discretionary power of Governor.

Codes:

	A	B	C	D
(a)	3	4	5	1
(b)	2	1	4	3
(c)	5	2	3	4
(d)	2	3	4	1

151.

List I (Committees)	List II (Setup on)
A. G.V.K. Rao Committee	1. Panchayati Raj institutions
B. Balvantray Mehta Committee	2. Revitalisation of PRIs for democracy and development
C. L.M. Singhvi Committee	3. Existing administrative arrangments for Rural Development and Poverty Alleviation Programmes.
D. Ashok Mehta Committee	4. Community Development Programme and National Extension Service.
	5. Panchayati Raj elections

Codes:

	A	B	C	D
(a)	4	3	1	2
(b)	4	3	2	1
(c)	3	4	2	1
(d)	3	4	1	2

152. The Governor of a state:
    1. Possesses executive, legislative and judicial powers analogous to the President.
    2. Has to act with the aid and advice of the council of ministers always.
    3. Has the power to appoint and remove the members of State Public Service Commission.
    4. Has the power to allocate business of the government among the various ministers.
       Of the above, the correct statements are:
       (a) 1 and 2   (b) 2, 3 and 4
       (c) 1 and 4   (d) 1, 3 and 4

153. The Constitution says that the state council of ministers hold office during the pleasure of the Governor. The words "during the pleasure of the Governor" in reality means:
    (a) Pleasure of the President
    (b) Pleasure of the Prime Minister
    (c) Pleasure of the Chief Minister
    (d) Pleasure of the Legislative Assembly

154. The main objective of the National Development Council is:
    (a) To promote common economic policies in all vital spheres.
    (b) To strengthen and mobilise the efforts and resources of the nation in support of the plan.
    (c) To ensure balanced and rapid development of all parts of the country.
    (d) To secure cooperation of states in execution of the plan.

155. Which of the following factors have led to the decline of Indian Parliament?
    1. Growth of delegated legislation.
    2. Low level of attendance in the Parliament.
    3. Frequent promulgation of ordinances.
    4. Frequent amendment of the Constitution.
    5. Setback in Parliamentary behaviour and ethics.
       (a) 1, 2, 3 and 5   (b) 1, 3, 4 and 5
       (c) 2, 3 and 4   (d) 1, 3 and 5

156. The term 'Cabinet' is mentioned in which of the following articles of the Constitution?
    (a) Article 74
    (b) Article 75
    (c) Article 352
    (d) Not mentioned in the Constitution

157. Which of the following statements with regard to the Planning Commission are correct?
    1. It was constituted on 15th March, 1950.
    2. It has representation from the state governments.
    3. It acts as a kind of a bridge between Union Government, National Development Council and state governments.

4. It is a collegiate body.
    (a) 2, 3 and 4   (b) 1, 2 and 3
    (c) 1 and 4   (d) 2 and 4

158. Which of the following statements with regard to the CAG are correct?
    1. He is responsible only to the Parliament.
    2. He certifies the net proceeds of any tax.
    3. He compiles and maintains the accounts of state governments.
    4. He has control over the issue of money from the Consolidated Fund of India.
       (a) 2 and 4   (b) 1, 3 and 4
       (c) 1, 2 and 3   (d) 2, 3 and 4

159. Which of the following statements are correct about the difference between a censure motion and a no-confidence motion?
    1. A censure motion should state the reasons for its adoption whereas a no-confidence motion need not state the reasons for its adoption.
    2. A no-confidence motion can be moved only against the council of ministers, whereas a censure motion can be moved against the council of ministers or an individual minister or a group of ministers.
    3. The Government must resign if a no-confidence motion is passed, whereas the Government need not resign if a censure motion is passed.
    4. A censure motion can be moved in both, the Lok Sabha and the Rajya Sabha, whereas no-confidence motion can be moved only in the Lok Sabha.
       (a) 1, 3 and 4   (b) 2, 3 and 4
       (c) 2, 3 and 4   (d) 1, 2 and 3

160. While appointing a Lokayuka, the Governor in most of the states consults:
    1. President of India
    2. Speaker of the Legislative Assembly
    3. Leader of the opposition in the Legislative Assembly
    4. Chief Justice of the State High Court
    5. Leader of the Opposition in the Legislative Council.
       (a) 1, 4 and 5   (b) 1, 2 and 4
       (c) 3, 4 and 5   (d) 3 and 4

161. The first Lokpal Bill was introduced in the Parliament in:
    (a) 1971   (b) 1967
    (c) 1968   (d) 1972

162. The Central Vigilance Commission was set up by:
    (a) Constitutional provision
    (b) Act of the Parliament
    (c) Resolution of the Santhanam Committee
    (d) Executive resolution

163. The functions of Estimates Committee include:
    1. To suggest alternative policies in order to bring out efficiency and economy in administration.
    2. To see that the expenditure conforms to the authority which governs it.
    3. To examine whether the money is well laid out within the limits of the policy implied in the estimates.
    4. To suggest the form in which estimates shall be presented to the Parliament.
    Of the above, the correct statements are:
    (a) 1 and 2   (b) 1, 3 and 4
    (c) 1, 2 and 4   (d) 1, 2, 3 and 4

164. The recommendations of Balwantray Mehta Committee includes:
    1. Open participation of political parties in Panchayati Raj affairs.
    2. Genuine transfer of power and responsibility to the Panchayati Raj institutions.
    3. Constitutional protection for Panchayati Raj.
    4. District Collector should be the Chairman of the Zila Parishad.
    5. Panchayat Samiti to be the executive body.
    (a) 1, 2 and 5   (b) 2, 4 and 5
    (c) 2, 3 and 4   (d) 1, 3 and 4

165. Which of the following statements is incorrect?
    (a) Adjournment means an interruption in normal business of the Assembly.
    (b) Prorogation means the end of the Assembly.
    (c) Dissolution means the end of the Assembly.
    (d) Proroagation means end of a session of the Assembly.

166. Which of the following are the compulsory provisions of the 73rd Amendment Act on Panchayati Raj?
    1. Indirect elections of the chairpersons of Panchayats at the intermediate and district levels.
    2. Fresh elections within six months in case of dissolution.
    3. Provision for reservation of seats for backward classes.
    4. Giving representation to MPs and MLAs in Panchayats.
    (a) 1, 3 and 4   (b) 2 and 4
    (c) 1 and 2   (d) 2, 3 and 4

167. Consider the following statements about municipal corporations:
    1. They are established in the states by the acts of the concerned state legislatures.
    2. They are established in the union territories by an order of the Chief Administrator.
    3. They work under direct control and supervision of state governments.

4. Their deliberative functions are separated from the executive functions.
    Of the above, the correct statements are:
    (a) 1 and 3   (b) 1, 3 and 4
    (c) 1, 2 and 3   (d) 1, 2, 3 and 4

168. Which of the following is not correct about a cantonment board?
    (a) It is created by an executive resolution.
    (b) It works under the administrative control of the Union Defence Ministry.
    (c) It is established for municipal administration for civilian population in the cantonment area.
    (d) It is a statutory body.

169. Consider the following statements with regard to All-India Services:
    1. Article 312 of the Constitution specifies the procedure for their creation.
    2. The All-India Services Act was enacted in 1950.
    3. Indian Forest Service is managed by the Ministry of Forests and Environment.
    4. A new All-India Service can be created by the Rajya Sabha.
    Of the above, the incorrect statements are:
    (a) 2 and 4   (b) 1 and 4
    (c) 1, 3 and 4   (d) 2 and 3

170. Under which of the following conditions, the UPSC can serve the needs of a state?
    1. When requested by the President
    2. When requested by the Governor
    3. With the approval of Parliament
    4. With the approval of President
    5. With the approval of the concerned sate legislature.
    (a) 1 and 3   (b) 2 and 5
    (c) 2 and 4   (d) 1 and 5

Assertion (A) and Reason (R) Pattern

Answer the following questions by using the codes given below:
    (a) Both A and R are true and R is the correct explanation of A.
    (b) Both A and R are true but R is not a correct explanation of A.
    (c) A is true but R is false.
    (d) A is false but R is true.

171. Assertion: A minister at the Central level can be dismissed by the Prime Minister.
    Reason: A minister is appointed by President only on the advice of Prime Minister.

172. Assertion: The Finance Commission facilitates the maintenance of financial balance between the Union and the states in the Indian federal system.
    Reason: The Constitution of India has given more financial powers to the Union Government.

173. Assertion: The duty of CAG is not merely to ensure the legality of expenditure but also its propriety.
Reason: He has to uphold the Constitution and the laws of Parliament in the field of financial administration.

174. Assertion: The UPSC is the Central recruiting agency in India.
Reason: It is an independent constitutional body.

175. Assertion: The Governor is dejure head of state administration.
Reason: The Chief Minister is de-facto head of state administration.

176. Assertion: The Rajya Sabha has no power to vote on the demands-for-grants.
Reason: A money bill or finance bill dealing with taxation cannot be introduced in the Rajya Sabha.

Matching Pattern

Match List-I with List-II and select the correct answer by using the codes given below.

177.   List-I (Meaning of writs)   List-II (Name of writs)

A. It is a command issued by the court to a public official asking him to perform his official duties.   1. Injunction

B. It is issued by a higher court to a lower court when the latter exceeds its jurisdiction.   2. Mandamus

C. It is issued by the courts to enquire into the legality of claim of a person to a public office.   3. Certiorari

D. It is issued by the court asking a person to do a thing or refrain from doing a thing.   4. Prohibition

5. Quo-warranto

Codes:

	A	B	C	D
(a)	3	4	5	1
(b)	5	3	4	2
(c)	2	4	5	1
(d)	4	5	2	3

178.   List-I (Committees)   List-II (Function)

A. Public Accounts Committee   1. Examines whether the promises made by the ministers on the floor of the house have been fulfilled.

B. Committee on Subordinate Legislation   2. Examines the CAG's report on the appropriation accounts and ascertains whether the funds voted by Parliament are spent within the scope of the demand.

C. Committee on Public Undertakings   3. Examines whether the powers to make rules and regulations delegated by the Parliament are properly exercised by the executive.

D. Committee on Government Assurances.   4. Examines the reports and accounts of the public undertakings and finds out whether their affairs are being managed in accordance with sound business principles and prudent commercial practices.

Codes:

	A	B	C	D
(a)	4	3	1	2
(b)	2	3	4	1
(c)	1	4	3	2
(d)	2	4	1	3

179.   List-I   List-II

A. Token grant   1. It is granted for meeting an unexpected demand whose details cannot be stated.

B. Exceptional grant   2. It is voted by the Lok Sabha before the end of the financial year.

C. Vote of credit

D. Excess grant

3. It is voted by the Lok Sabha after the end of the financial year.

4. It forms no part of the current service of any financial year.

5. It is granted when funds to meet proposed expenditure on a new service can be made available by reappropriation.

Codes:

		A	B	C	D
	(a)	4	3	5	2
	(b)	5	4	1	3
	(c)	3	4	2	1
	(d)	5	3	1	4

180. List-I (Schedules in the Constitution)

A. Sixth Schedule

B. Second Schedule

C. Twelfth Schedule

D. Fifth Schedule

List-II (Provisions)

1. Administration and control of scheduled areas and scheduled tribes.

2. Administration of tribal areas in states of Assam, Meghalya, Tripura and Mizoram.

3. Provisions as to the Speaker and Deputy Speaker of state Legislative Assemblies.

4. Powers, authority and responsibilities of municipalities.

5. Powers, authority and responsibilities of Panchayats.

Codes:

		A	B	C	D
	(a)	1	3	4	2
	(b)	1	2	5	3
	(c)	2	3	4	1
	(d)	2	3	5	1

181. List-I

A. Taxes levied by the Union but collected and appropriated by the states.

B. Taxes levied and collected by the Union but assigned to the states.

C. Taxes levied by the Union and collected and appropriated by the Union and the states.

D. Taxes and duties for purposes of the Union.

List-II

1. Surcharges on taxes and duties

2. Taxes on services.

3. Stamp duties on bills of exchange.

4. Income tax

5. Taxes on the consignment of goods in the course of inter-state trade or commerce.

Codes:

		A	B	C	D
	(a)	5	3	1	4
	(b)	5	4	2	3
	(c)	3	1	5	2
	(d)	3	5	2	1

182. Which of the following is not correctly matched?

(a) Article 153 — Office of the Governor

(b) Article 156 — Term of the Governor

(c) Article 154 — Executive authority of Governor

(d) Article 155 — Removal of Governor

183. The most important Legislative power of the Governor is:

(a) Nominating members to the state legislature.

(b) Issuing ordinances

(c) Assenting bills passed by the state legislature

(d) Dissolving the state legislative Assembly

184. Assertion: The Chief Minister is the channel of communication between the Governor and the council of ministers.

Reason: The Chief Minister is the head of the state council of ministers.

Select the correct code:

(a) Both A and R are true and R is the correct explanation of A.

(b) Both A and R are true but R is not a correct explanation of A.

(c) A is true but R is false.

(d) A is false but R is true.

185. Which of the following statements are correct?
    1. Balwantray Mehta Committee was appointed in 1957.
    2. Ashok Mehta Committee submitted its report in 1977.
    3. G.V.K. Rao Committee submitted its report in 1986.
    4. L.M. Singhvi Committee submitted its report in 1987.
    (a) 1, 2 and 3   (b) 1, 2 and 4
    (c) 1, 3 and 4   (d) 1 and 4

186. Which of the following are the voluntary provisions of the 73rd Amendment Act on Panchayati Raj?
    1. Making provision for reservation to the backward classes.
    2. Authorising the Panchayats to prepare plans for economic development.
    3. Organisation of Gram Sabhas.
    4. Conferring financial powers on Panchayats with regard to taxes, fees and so on.
    5. Setting up of a State Election Commission to conduct elections to the Panchayats.
    (a) 1, 2, 3 and 4   (b) 1, 2 and 5
    (c) 1, 2 and 4   (d) 1, 2, 4 and 5

187. Assertion: The UPSC's function is not to decide but to advise.
    Reason: UPSC is a constitutional body
    Select the correct code:
    (a) Both A and R are true and R is the correct explanation of A.
    (b) Both A and R are true but R is not a correct explanation of A.
    (c) A is true but R is false.
    (d) A is false but R is true.

188. Which of the following are true of the Central Administrative Tribunal?
    1. It was established under the provisions of Article 312-A of the Constitution.
    2. It was set up by an order of the President of India.
    3. It was set up in 1985.
    4. It was set up by an Act of Parliament.
    (a) 1, 2 and 3   (b) 1, 3 and 4
    (c) 3 and 4   (d) 2, 3 and 4

189. Which of the following audit is discretionary and not obligatory on the part of CAG?
    (a) Audit of Accountancy
    (b) Audit of Authority
    (c) Audit of Appropriation
    (d) Audit of Propriety

190. "The state shall strive to promote the welfare of people by securing and protecting as effectively as it may, a social order in which justice—social, economic and political—shall inform all the institutions of the national life." This provision is contained in which of the following articles of the Indian Constitution?
    (a) Article 39   (b) Article 46
    (c) Article 38   (d) Article 37

191. Which of the following will be the consequences of the proclamation of Financial Emergency by the President?
    1. The President can give directions to the states to observe the principles of financial propriety.
    2. The President can reduce the salaries and allowances of government employees excluding the judges of Supreme Court and High Courts.
    3. All money bills and other financial bills passed by a state legislature can be reserved for the consideration of the President.
    4. The Parliament can authorise the President to sanction expenditure from the Consolidated Fund of the state.
    (a) 1, 2 and 3   (b) 1, 2, 3 and 4
    (c) 1 and 3   (d) 1, 3 and 4

192. If any question arises as to the age of a judge of a High Court, the question shall be decided by the President after consultation with:
    (a) The Chief Justice of the concerned High Court
    (b) The Governor of the concerned state
    (c) The Attorney-General of India
    (d) The Chief Justice of India

193. Which of the following articles of the Constitution broadly govern the relationship between the Prime Minister and the President?
    1. Article 75   2. Article 73
    3. Article 78   4. Article 76
    5. Article 74
    (a) 1, 2, 3 and 5   (b) 1, 3 and 5
    (c) 1, 3, 4 and 5   (d) 1, 2, 3, 4 and 5

194. Which of the following distinguishes the audit of the CAG from the audit made by professional auditors?
    (a) Audit of Authority
    (b) Audit of Appropriation
    (c) Audit of Accountancy
    (d) Audit of Propriety

195. Who/which of the following has called the Planning Commission as "The Economic Cabinet, not merely for the Union but also for the states"?
    (a) K. Santhanam
    (b) O.R. Gadgil
    (c) Administrative Reforms Commission
    (d) Ashok Chanda

196. Match the following:

List-I (Statements on NDC)	List-II (Made by)
A. "Among the advisory bodies to the Planning Commission is included the NDC. This is surely incorrect as is clear from its composition. The NDC is a body obviously superior to the Planning Commission."	1. K. Santhanam
B. The NDC was established as a supreme administrative and advisory body on planning ... since their inception the NDC and its standing Committee have virtually relegated the Planning Commission to the status of a research arm."	2. A. P. Jain
C. "The NDC infringes upon functions which under the Constitution, are assigned to other bodies and attempts to do what the council of ministers at the central and the states' levels should do."	3. M. Brecher
D. "The position of NDC has come to approximate to that of a Super Cabinet of the entire Indian federation, a Cabinet functioning for the Government of India and the government of all the states."	4. Ashok Chanda
	5. H.M. Patel

Codes:

	A	B	C	D
(a)	2	3	4	1
(b)	2	4	3	5
(c)	5	3	2	1
(d)	5	3	4	1

197. Which of the following are the functions of Planning Commission?
1. To formulate development plans of state governments.
2. To secure public cooperation in national development.
3. To consider important questions of social and economic policy affecting development.
4. To provide secretarial assistance to the NDC.
 (a) 1, 2, 3 and 4   (b) 2, 3 and 4
 (c) 1, 2 and 4   (d) 2 and 4

198. In which of the following respects, the Finance Commission differs from the Planning Commission?
1. Legal status   2. Composition
3. Tenure   4. Form of organisation
5. Functions
 (a) 1, 2 and 5   (b) 1, 2, 3 and 5
 (c) 1, 2, 4 and 5   (d) 1, 2, 3, 4 and 5

199. The need for a separate parliamentary committee on public undertakings was first visualised by:
 (a) Ashok Mehta
 (b) G.V. Mavalankar
 (c) Lanka Sundaram
 (d) Krishna Menon Committee

200. Match the following:

List-I	List-II
A. Executive authority of President	1. Article 56
B. Tenure of President	2. Article 55
C. Election of President	3. Article 61
D. Impeachment of President	4. Article 53
	5. Article 54

Codes:

	A	B	C	D
(a)	4	1	2	3
(b)	4	1	5	3
(c)	4	5	2	3
(d)	4	2	5	3

201. Assertion: Parliamentary control over public expenditure is diminished by the creation of the Contingency Fund of India.
Reason: The Contingency Fund of India is operated by the President of India.
Select the correct code:
 (a) Both A and R are true and R is the correct explanation of A.
 (b) Both A and R are true but R is not a correct explanation of A.
 (c) A is true but R is false.
 (d) A is false but R is true.

202. Which of the following pairs are incorrectly matched?

1. Vote on account	— To allow enough time for legislative scrutiny and discussion of the budget.
2. Charged items	— Not submitted to the Parliament.
3. Vote of credit	— Blanck cheque given to the executive.
4. Excess grant	— Submitted directly to the Lok Sabha for its approval

(a) 1 and 3   (b) 1, 2 and 4

(c) 2 and 4   (d) 3 and 4

203. Which of the following expenditures are charged on the Consolidated Fund of India?
    1. Salaries of the Supreme Court judges
    2. Pensions of the Chairman of UPSC
    3. Debt charges for which the Government of India is liable
    4. Emoluments and allowances of the Prime Minister
       (a) 1, 2 and 3   (b) 1, 2, 3 and 4
       (c) 1, 3 and 4   (d) 1, 2 and 4

204. Which of the following are the functions of the Public Accounts Committee of Parliament?
    1. To examine, in the light of CAG's report, the accounts showing the appropriation of sums granted by the Parliament.
    2. To examine, in the light of CAG's report, the statement of accounts of state corporations, trading and manufacturing projects except of those as are allotted to the committee on public undertakings.
    3. To examine the statement of accounts of autonomous and semi-autonomous bodies, the audit of which is conducted by the CAG.
    4. To examine if any money has been spent on any service during a financial year in excess of the amount granted by house of people for that purpose.
       (a) 1, 2 and 4   (b) 1, 2, 3 and 4
       (c) 1, 2 and 3   (d) 1, 3 and 4

205. Assertion: The device of Adjournment Motion is not used by the Rajya Sabha.
    Reason: An Adjournment Motion does not result in removing the Government from office.
    Select the correct code:
    (a) Both A and R are true and R is the correct explanation of A.
    (b) Both A and R are true but R is not the correct explanation of A.
    (c) A is true but R is false.
    (d) A is false but R is true.

206. Which of the following Lokpal Bills had Prime Minister in their jurisdiction?
    1. The Lokpal Bill of 1968
    2. The Lokpal Bill of 1971
    3. The Lokpal Bill of 1977
    4. The Lokpal Bill of 1985
    5. The Lokpal Bill of 1990
       (a) 1, 3 and 5   (b) 2, 3 and 5
       (c) 3 and 5   (d) 3, 4 and 5

207. Which of the following are true of Central Vigilance Commission?
    1. It was set up in 1964.
    2. It is a statutory body.

3. Its functions are advisory in the same sense as those of UPSC.
4. Its mode of receiving complaints is similar to that of the Parliamentary Commissioner for Administration in UK.
   (a) 1, 2, 3 and 4   (b) 1, 3 and 4
   (c) 1, 2 and 3   (d) 1 and 3

208. Which of the following statements related to UPSC are correct?
    1. It derives its functions only from the Constitution.
    2. It is not consulted on matters related to the reservation of posts for the BCs, SCs and STs.
    3. The President can exclude posts, services and matters from the purview of consultation with UPSC.
    4. The President can place the personnel system of any local authority, corporate body or public institution within the jurisdiction of UPSC.
       (a) 2 and 3   (b) 1, 2 and 3
       (c) 2, 3 and 4   (d) 1, 2 and 4

209. The executive officer of the cantonment board is appointed by the:
    (a) President of the board
    (b) Defence Secretary
    (c) Chief Secretary of the state
    (d) President of India

210. The correct statements about municipalities include:
    1. They are known by various other names in different states.
    2. They are controlled by the state governments.
    3. Vesting of the executive authority in the Chairman.
    4. They are statutory bodies.
       (a) 1, 2 and 4   (b) 1, 2, 3 and 4
       (c) 1 and 2   (d) 1, 2 and 3

211. The 73rd Amendment Act does not apply to the states of:
    1. Nagaland
    2. Mizoram
    3. Jammu and Kashmir
    4. Meghalaya
       (a) 1 and 2   (b) 1, 2 and 4
       (c) 1, 2, 3 and 4   (d) 2 and 3

212. The first municipal corporation in India was set up at Madras in:
    (a) 1767   (b) 1687
    (c) 1667   (d) 1678

213. Who/which of the following can abolish a State Legislative Council.
    (a) Parliament   (b) President
    (c) Governor   (d) State Assembly

214. In which of the following recommendations, the Ashok Mehta Committee differed from Balwantray Mehta Committee?

1. Two-tier system of Panchayati Raj.
2. Official participation of political parties at all levels of Panchayat elections.
3. Zila Parishad as the executive body.
4. Entrusting development functions to the Zila Parishad.
   - (a) 1, 2 and 4
   - (b) 1, 2 and 3
   - (c) 1 and 2
   - (d) 1, 3 and 4

215. Under which of the following circumstances, the Governor can reserve a state bill for the consideration of the President?
   1. If it is ultra vires.
   2. If it is opposed to the Directive Principles of State Policy.
   3. If it endangers the position of the state High Court.
   4. If it is dealing with the compulsory acquisition of property under Article 31A.
   - (a) 1, 2 and 3
   - (b) 1, 2, 3 and 4
   - (c) 2, 3 and 4
   - (d) 1, 3 and 4

216. Which of the following expenditures are 'charged' on the Consolidated Fund of India?
   1. Salaries and allowances of Chairman of Council of States.
   2. Salaries and allowances of Comptroller and Auditor-General.
   3. Any sum required to satisfy any judgement of any arbitral tribunal.
   4. Salaries and allowances of Deputy Speaker.
   - (a) 2 and 3
   - (b) 1, 2 and 3
   - (c) 1, 2, 3 and 4
   - (d) 2 and 4

217. The Railway budget has:
   - (a) 36 demands
   - (b) 34 demands
   - (c) 42 demands
   - (d) 32 demands

218. Which of the following must be approved by the Public Accounts Committee before being submitted to the Lok Sabha for voting?
   - (a) Additional grant
   - (b) Exceptional grant
   - (c) Token grant
   - (d) Excess grant

219. Which of the following is not involved in the preparation of budget?
   - (a) Finance Ministry
   - (b) Planning Commission
   - (c) Comptroller and Auditor-General
   - (d) Finance Commission

220. According to Administrative Reforms Commission, the Lokpal would be appointed by the President after consultation with the:
   1. Chief Justice of India
   2. Leader of opposition in the Lok Sabha
   3. Speaker of the Lok Sabha
   4. Chairman of the Rajya Sabha
   - (a) 1, 2, 3 and 4
   - (b) 1, 2 and 3
   - (c) 1, 3 and 4
   - (d) 2, 3 and 4

221. Which of the following categories of bills require prior consent of the President before their introduction?
   1. Bills to reorganise states.
   2. Bills affecting taxes in which the states are interested.
   3. State bills imposing restrictions on freedom of trade.
   4. Bills involving expenditure from the Consolidated Fund of India.
   - (a) 1, 2 and 4
   - (b) 1, 2, 3 and 4
   - (c) 2, 3, and 4
   - (d) 1, 2, 3

222. The Inter-State Council consists of
   1. Prime Minister
   2. Chief Ministers of all states
   3. Chief Ministers of union territories with legislatures
   4. Eight Union Cabinet Ministers
   5. Administrators of union territories with legislatures
   - (a) 1, 2, 3, 4 and 5
   - (b) 1, 2, 3 and 4
   - (c) 1, 2 and 3
   - (d) 1, 2, 3 and 5

223. Which of the following Cabinet Committees is not chaired by the Prime Minister?
   - (a) Political Affairs Committee
   - (b) Appointments Committee
   - (c) Committee on Parliamentary Affairs
   - (d) Economic Affairs Committee

224. "Since their inception, the NDC and its standing committee have virtually relegated the Planning Commission to the status of a research arm." This statement is associated with:
   - (a) K. Santhanam
   - (b) M. Brecher
   - (c) H.M. Patel
   - (d) Ashok Chanda

225. On which of the following items, the Finance Commission makes recommendations to the President?
   1. The distribution between the Union and the states of the net proceeds of taxes and the allocation between the states of the respective shares of such proceeds.
   2. The principles which should govern the grants-in-aid of the revenues of the states out of the Consolidated Fund of India.
   3. The measures needed to augment the Consolidated Fund of a state to supplement the resources of the municipalities in the state on the basis of the recommendations made by the Finance Commission of the state.
   4. Any other matter referred to it by the President in the interests of sound finance.
   - (a) 1, 2 and 4
   - (b) 1, 2, 3 and 4
   - (c) 1 and 2
   - (d) 1, 2 and 3

226. Fundamental Duties were incorporated in the Constitution on the recommendation of:
    (a) Shah Commission
    (b) Administrative Reforms Commission
    (c) Santhanam Committee
    (d) Swaran Singh Committee

227. Which of the following are the provisions of Article 75 of the Constitution?
    1. Ministers shall be appointed by the President on the advice of Prime Minister.
    2. The council of ministers shall be collectively responsible to the House of People.
    3. The question whether any, and if so what, advice was tendered by ministers to the President shall not be inquired into in any court.
    4. The salaries and allowances of ministers shall be determined by Parliament.
        (a) 1, 2 and 3   (b) 1, 2 and 4
        (c) 2, 3 and 4   (d) 2 and 4

228. The composition of National Development Council includes:
    1. Chief Ministers of all the states
    2. All Union Cabinet Ministers
    3. Prime Minister
    4. Administrators of union territories
    5. Selected Union Cabinet Ministers
    6. Members of Planning Commission
        (a) 1, 2, 3 and 6
        (b) 1, 2, 3, 4 and 6
        (c) 1, 2, 3, 5 and 6
        (d) 1, 3, 4, 5 and 6

Assertion (A) and Reason (R) Pattern

Answer the following questions by using the codes given below.
    (a) Both A and R are true and R is the correct explanation of A.
    (b) Both A and R are true but R is not a correct explanation of A.
    (c) A is true but R is false.
    (d) A is false but R is true

229. Assertion: The Estimates Committee has been described as a 'continuous economy committee'.
    Reason: It is a means of legislative control over administration.

230. Assertion: The President of India can be impeached for the violation of the Constitution.
    Reason: The Constitution lays down the procedure for impeachment of the President.

231. Assertion: The 73rd Amendment Act is a significant landmark in the evolution of grassroots democratic institutions in the country.

Reason: The Act has brought the Panchayati Raj institutions under the purview of justiciable part of the the Constitution.

232. Consider the following statements about the Governor:
    1. He submits his resignation letter to the Chief Justice of the state.
    2. He should have completed 35 years of age.
    3. His emoluments, allowances and privileges are determined by the President.
    4. No criminal proceedings can be instituted against him.
    Of the above, the incorrect statements are:
        (a) 1 and 3   (b) 2, 3 and 4
        (c) 1, 3 and 4   (d) 2 and 4

233. How many members are nominated to the State Legislative Council by the Governor?
        (a) One-third   (b) One-twelfth
        (c) One-eighth   (d) One-sixth

234. Assertion: A minister at the state level continues in office till he enjoys the confidence of the Chief Minister.
    Reason: The Chief Minister can ask him to resign or advise the Governor to dismiss him in case of difference of opinion.
    Select the correct code:
        (a) Both A and R are true and R is the correct explanation of A.
        (b) Both A and R are true but R is not a correct explanation of A.
        (c) A is true but R is false.
        (d) A is false but R is true.

235. Which of the following are true of the recommendations of Ashok Mehta Committee on Panchayati Raj?
    1. Creation of Mandal Panchayat covering a population of 10,000 to 15,000.
    2. The state legislature to have a committee on Panchayati Raj to look after the needs of weaker sections.
    3. If Panchayati Raj institutions are superseded, elections must be held within one year.
    4. Nyaya Panchayats should be presided over by the village development officer.
        (a) 1, 2 and 4   (b) 2 and 4
        (c) 1, 2 and 3   (d) only 2

236. Which of the following are true of the provisions of the 74th Amendment Act on municipalities?
    1. Wards Committees, for wards with population of two lakhs.
    2. The state Governor may authorise them to levy, collect and appropriate taxes.
    3. A Municipal council for smaller Urban area.
    4. The Twelfth Schedule contains 20 functional items for the municipalities.

(a) 1, 3 and 4   (b) 1, 2 and 4

(c) 3 only   (d) 3 and 4

237. Assertion: The number of members of UPSC is determined by the President.

Reason: The members of the UPSC are appointed by the President.

Select the correct code:

(a) Both A and R are true and R is the correct explanation of A.

(b) Both A and R are true and R is not a correct explanation of A.

(c) A is true but R is false.

(d) A is false but R is true.

238. Assertion: The members of All-India Services work in the Central Government, state governments and union territories.

Reason: They are selected and recruited on the basis of all-India competitive examinations conducted by the UPSC.

Select the correct code:

(a) Both A and R are true and R is the correct explanation of A.

(b) Both A and R are true but R is not a correct explanation of A.

(c) A is true but R is false.

(d) A is false but R is true.

239. Which of the following are true of the Staff Selection Commission?

1. It was set up in 1976.

2. It enjoys the status of a subordinate office of Ministry of Personnel.

3. It was created by executive resolution.

4. It recruits personnel to non-technical Class III posts in the Secretariat, the attached offices and the subordinate offices in the Central Government.

(a) 1, 2 and 4   (b) 2, 3 and 4

(c) 3 and 4   (d) 2 and 4

240. Which of the following pairs are correctly matched?

1. Article 266 – No tax shall be levied or collected except by authority of law.

2. Article 117 – No tax can be imposed unless asked for by the executive government.

3. Article 113 – No expenditure can be sanctioned unless asked for by the executive government.

4. Article 265 – No expenditure can be incurred except with the authorisation of the legislature.

(a) 1, 2, 3 and 4   (b) 2, 3 and 4

(c) 1, 3 and 4   (d) 2 and 3

241. Which of the following are true of the Contingency Fund of India.

1. It was created under the provisions of Article 267.

2. It was created in 1951.

3. It is held by the Finance Secretary on behalf of the President.

4. Its amount will be determined by the President.

(a) 1 and 3   (b) 1, 3 and 4

(c) 2, 3 and 4   (d) 3 and 4

242. Assertion: The principle of the rule of lapse leads to 'rush of expenditure' towards the end of a financial year.

Reason: The unspent voted expenditure would lapse by the end of the financial year.

Select the correct code:

(a) Both A and R are true and R is the correct explanation of A.

(b) Both A and R are true but R is not a correct explanation of A.

(c) A is true but R is false.

(d) A is false but R is true.

243. Match the following:

List-I (Parliamentary committees)	List-II (Created in)
A. Committee on Government Assurances	1. 1923
B. Committee on Public Undertakings	2. 1953
C. Committee on Subordinate Legislation	3. 1921
D. Public Accounts Committee	4. 1953
	5. 1964

Codes:	A	B	C	D
(a)	4	5	1	3
(b)	2	5	4	1
(c)	4	5	2	1
(d)	2	5	4	3

244. Which of the following are true of Central Vigilance Commission?

1. It was set up on the recommendation of Santhanam Committee.

2. It does not exercise superintendence over the functioning of CBI.

3. It is set up by an executive resolution of the Government of India.

4. It consists of a chairman and three members.

(a) 1, 2 and 4   (b) 1, 3 and 4

(c) 1 and 3   (d) 1 and 4

245. Which of the following will be the consequences of declaration of national emergency by the President?

1. The President can issue directives to the state executives.

2. The President can extend the normal tenure of the Lok Sabha.

3. The President can suspend all the Fundamental Rights of citizens.

4. The President can modify the distribution pattern of financial resources between Centre and states.
   - (a) 1, 3 and 4
   - (b) 1and 4
   - (c) 1, 2, 3 and 4
   - (d) 1, 2 and 3

246. Which one of the following pairs is correctly matched?
   - (a) 1919 Act — Dyarchy at the Centre
   - (b) 1861 Act — Portfolio system
   - (c) 1935 Act — Bicameralism
   - (d) 1853 Act — Governor-General of India

247. Which of the following are true of the President's ordinance making power?
   1. It is laid down in Article 123.
   2. Its ambit is coextensive with the legislative power of Parliament.
   3. He can promulgate an ordinance only when the Lok Sabha is not in session.
   4. It is a discretionary power of the President.
   - (a) 1, 2, 3 and 4
   - (b) 1, 2 and 4
   - (c) 1 and 2
   - (d) 1, 2, and 3

248. Assertion: The Prime Minister's Office influences the formulation of plans.
   Reason: The PM is the Chairman of the Planning Commission
   Select the correct code:
   - (a) Both A and R are true and R is the correct explanation of A.
   - (b) Both A and R are true but R is not a correct explanation of A.
   - (c) A is true but R is false.
   - (d) A is false but R is true.

249. Match the following:

List-I	List-II
A. The council of ministers shall be collectively responsible to the House of People.	1. Article 74
B. Duties of the Prime Minister towards the President.	2. Article 77
C. Council of ministers to aid and advise the President.	3. Article 76
D. All executive action of the Government of India shall be taken in the name of the President.	4. Article 75
	5. Article 78

Codes:

	A	B	C	D
(a)	4	5	1	3
(b)	3	2	4	1
(c)	4	5	1	2
(d)	3	4	1	2

250. Which of the following are the limitations on the sovereignty of Indian Parliament?

1. Fundamental Rights
2. Judicial Review
3. Federalism
4. Written Constitution
   - (a) 1, 3 and 4
   - (b) 1, 2 and 3
   - (c) 1 and 2
   - (d) 1, 2, 3 and 4

251. Assertion: Under the Government of India Act of 1935, the Residuary powers were vested in the Central Legislature.
   Reason: The Government of India Act of 1935 divided the subjects into three lists viz. the federal, provincial and concurrent.
   Select the correct code:
   - (a) Both A and R are true and R is the correct explanation of A.
   - (b) Both A and R are true but R is not a correct explanation of A.
   - (c) A is true but R is false.
   - (d) A is false but R is true.

252. Which of the following are the federal features of the Indian Constitution?
   1. Rigid Constitution
   2. Bicameral legislature
   3. Office of the CAG
   4. Collective responsibility
   5. Office of the Governor
   - (a) 1, 2 and 3
   - (b) 1, 2 and 5
   - (c) 1, 2, 3 and 4
   - (d) 1 and 2

253. "The position of pre-eminence, accorded to Planning Commission, is inconsistent with the conception of a Cabinet form of Government." The above state-ment is associated with:
   - (a) Ashok Chanda
   - (b) K. Santhanam
   - (c) Estimates Committee
   - (d) Administrative Reforms Commission

254. Which of the following are the objectives of the National Development Council?
   1. To promote common economic policies in all vital spheres.
   2. To secure the cooperation of states in the execution of the Plan.
   3. To review the working of the Plan from time to time.
   4. To consider important questions of social and economic policy affecting develo-pment.
   - (a) 1 and 2
   - (b) 1, 2, 3 and 4
   - (c) 1, 2 and 4
   - (d) 1, 2 and 3

255. Assertion: The President of India determines the qualifications of the Chairman and members of the Finance Commisson.
   Reason: The Chairman and members of the Finance Commission are appointed by the President of India.

Select the correct code:

(a) Both A and R are true and R is the correct explanation of A.

(b) Both A and R are true but R is not a correct explanation of A.

(c) A is true but R is false.

(d) A is false but R is true.

256. The correct statements about Finance Commission are:

1. It is to act as the balancing wheel of Indian fiscal federalism

2. It consists of a chairman and three other members.

3. Qualifications of the members of the Commission are determined by the President.

4. It is constituted under the provisions of Article 280.

(a) 2, 3 and 4   (b) 2 and 3

(c) 1 and 4   (d) 1, 2 and 3

257. The Indian President's veto power is a combination of:

1. Pocket veto   2. Absolute veto

3. Suspensive veto   4. Qualified veto

(a) 2 and 3   (b) 1, 3 and 4

(c) 2, 3 and 4   (d) 1, 2 and 3

258. The functions of National Development Council includes:

1. To consider the national plan as formulated by the Planning Commission.

2. To secure the cooperation of states in the execution of the plan.

3. To review the working of the plan from time to time.

4. To consider questions of social and economic policy affecting development.

(a) 1, 2 and 3   (b) 2 and 3

(c) 1, 3 and 4   (d) 2 and 4

259. The present relationship between the President and the council of ministers is governed by the provisions of:

(a) 42nd Amendment Act

(b) 48th Amendment Act

(c) 54th Amendment Act

(d) 44th Amendment Act

260. The Zonal Councils have been established by:

(a) Article 263 of the Constitution

(b) States reorganisation Act

(c) Zonal Councils Act

(d) An order of the President of India

261. Which of the following statements are correct?

1. Parliament can increase a tax.

2. Parliament cannot reduce a tax.

3. Parliament can abolish a tax.

4. Parliament cannot increase a tax.

5. Parliament can reduce a tax.

(a) 1, 3 and 5   (b) 3, 4 and 5

(c) 2, 3 and 4   (d) 3 and 4

262. Which of the following statements are correct with regard to the expenditure charged upon the Consolidated Fund of India?

1. It is subject to the vote of Parliament.

2. It is subject to the discussion in Parliament.

3. It is subject to the vote of Lok Sabha only.

4. It is not subject to the vote of Parliament.

(a) 1 and 2   (b) 2 and 3

(c) 2 and 4   (d) 1 and 4

263. The correct statements regarding the difference between the pardoning powers of President and Governor are:

1. The Governor can pardon sentences inflicted by court martial while the President cannot.

2. The President can pardon death sentence while Governor cannot.

3. The Governor can pardon death sentence while the President cannot.

4. The President can pardon sentences inflicted by court martial while the Governor cannot.

(a) 1 and 2   (b) 2 and 4

(c) 1 and 3   (d) 3 and 4

264. Which of the following statements are correct regarding the powers of a Governor to reserve a bill for the consideration of the President?

1. It is laid down in Article 200.

2. It is not a discretionary power of the Governor.

3. It is compulsory, if the bill endangers the position of High Court.

4. He can reserve any bill passed by the state legislature.

(a) 1, 2 and 3   (b) 3 and 4

(c) 1 and 3   (d) 2, 3 and 4

265. Which of the following is not correctly matched?

(a) Central Bureau of Investigation—1963

(b) Special Police Establishment—1942

(c) Prevention of Corruption Act—1947

(d) Central Vigilance Commission—1964

266. The incorrect statements about Central Vigilance Commission are:

1. It was set up on the recommendations of Administrative Reforms Commission.

2. It is headed by the Central Vigilance Commissioner appointed by the Prime Minister.

3. Its functions, in certain cases, overlap with the functions of the UPSC.

4. It is certainly a substitute for an Ombudsman.

5. It receives complaints directly from aggrieved persons.

(a) 1, 4 and 5   (b) 1, 2 and 4

(c) 3 and 4   (d) 3, 4 and 5

267. Which of the following civil services find mention in the Constitution?

1. Indian Administrative Service

2. Indian Forest Service

3. Indian Police Service
4. All-India Judicial Service
5. Indian Foreign Service
    (a) 1 and 3   (b) 1, 2 and 3
    (c) 1, 3 and 5   (d) 1, 3 and 4

268. In which of the following circumstances the President can remove a member of the UPSC without referring the matter to the Supreme Court?

1. If he engages, during his term of office, in any paid employment outside the duties of his office.
2. If he is adjudged an insolvent.
3. If he is unfit to continue in office by reason of infirmity of mind or body.

4. If he becomes, in any way, concerned or interested in any contract or agreement made by or on behalf of the Government of India or the government of a state.
    (a) 2 and 3   (b) 4 only
    (c) 1 only   (d) 1, 2 and 3

269. Which of the following are not the concerns of the UPSC?

1. Classification of services
2. Promotion
3. Training
4. Disciplinary matters
5. Talent hunting
    (a) 2, 4 and 5   (b) 1, 3 and 4
    (c) 1 and 3   (d) 1 and 4

Matching Pattern

Match List-I with List-II and select the correct answer by using the codes given below the respective lists.

270.

List-I	List-II
A. Tax belonging to the state exclusively.	1. Excise duties on medicinal preparations
B. Duties levied as well as collected by the Union, but assigned to the states.	2. Surcharge on taxes
C. Tax belonging to the Centre exclusively.	3. Taxes on the sale of goods in the course of inter-state trade.
D. Duties levied by the Union but collected and appropriated by the states.	4. Taxes on non-agricultural income
	5. Sales Tax.

Codes:	A	B	C	D
(a)	5	4	2	3
(b)	4	3	5	2
(c)	5	3	2	1
(d)	2	4	5	1

271.

List-I (Acts)	List-II (Provisions)
A. Indian Councils Act of 1861.	1. Introduced Dyarchy
B. Government of India Act of 1919	2. Placed Indian affairs under the direct control of the British Government.
C. Indian Councils Act of 1892	3. Introduced representative institutions.
D. Pitts India Act of 1784	4. Introduced provincial autonomy.
	5. Introduced the principle of election.

Codes:	A	B	C	D
(a)	5	1	3	2
(b)	5	4	2	3
(c)	3	4	2	5
(d)	3	1	5	2

Assertion (A) and Reason (R) Pattern

Answer the following questions by using the codes given below:

    (a) Both A and R are true and R is the correct explanation of A.
    (b) Both A and R are true but R is not a correct explanation of A.
    (c) A is true but R is false.
    (d) A is false but R is true.

272. Assertion: Planning Commission is neither a statutory body nor a constitutional body.
Reason: It is established by an executive resolution of the Union Cabinet.

273. Assertion: The Constitution of India in quasi-federal.
Reason: It has given more powers to the Central Government than to the state governments.

274. Assertion: The Chief Minister can dismiss a minister of state government.
Reason: The Chief Minister is the head of the state council of ministers.

275. Which of the following are correct with regard to the functions of the UPSC?
   1. To conduct examinations for appointments to the services of the Union.

2. To assist states, if requested, in framing and operating schemes of joint recruitment for any services for which candidates possessing special qualifications are required.

3. To advise the Union and state governments on all matters relating to methods of recruitment to civil services and for civil posts.

4. To present, annually, to the President a report as to the work done by it.
   (a) 1, 2 and 3   (b) 1, 3 and 4
   (c) 1, 2 and 4   (d) 1, 2, 3 and 4

276. Which of the following writs is not specifically provided in the Constitution of India?
   (a) Prohibition   (b) Mandamus
   (c) Quowarranto   (d) Injunction

Answers

1. c	2. c	3. b	4. d	5. b	6. d	7. d	8. d	9. b	10. d
11. a	12. b	13. d	14. d	15. c	16. c	17. d	18. a	19. b	20. d
21. c	22. c	23. c	24. d	25. b	26. a	27. c	28. b	29. d	30. c
31. c	32. c	33. d	34. a	35. c	36. d	37. c	38. b	39. c	40. b
41. d	42. a	43. a	44. c	45. a	46. b	47. a	48. a	49. d	50. c
51. d	52. d	53. d	54. d	55. b	56. b	57. b	58. d	59. d	60. d
61. d	62. b	63. d	64. c	65. b	66. d	67. b	68. d	69. d	70. c
71. c	72. d	73. d	74. c	75. c	76. c	77. c	78. d	79. b	80. c
81. d	82. c	83. c	84. c	85. c	86. d	87. b	88. c	89. b	90. c
91. d	92. d	93. b	94. a	95. d	96. d	97. b	98. b	99. b	100. d
101. b	102. b	103. d	104. d	105. c	106. d	107. d	108. c	109. b	110. d
111. c	112. a	113. a	114. a	115. b	116. a	117. c	118. a	119. b	120. c
121. b	122. c	123. d	124. d	125. d	126. d	127. c	128. d	129. d	130. d
131. c	132. b	133. a	134. c	135. c	136. d	137. c	138. d	139. a	140. b
141. c	142. a	143. d	144. a	145. b	146. b	147. d	148. d	149. c	150. b
151. c	152. c	153. d	154. d	155. a	156. c	157. c	158. c	159. d	160. d
161. c	162. d	163. b	164. b	165. b	166. c	167. b	168. a	169. a	170. c
171. d	172. a	173. a	174. b	175. a	176. b	177. c	178. b	179. b	180. c
181. d	182. d	183. b	184. a	185. c	186. c	187. b	188. c	189. b	190. c
191. c	192. d	193. b	194. d	195. d	196. c	197. c	198. b	199. c	200. b
201. d	202. c	203. a	204. b	205. b	206. c	207. c	208. a	209. d	210. b
211. c	212. b	213. a	214. b	215. b	216. a	217. d	218. d	219. d	220. c
221. b	222. c	223. c	224. b	225. b	226. d	227. b	228. b	229. b	230. b
231. a	232. a	233. d	234. a	235. d	236. c	237. b	238. b	239. c	240. d
241. a	242. a	243. d	244. c	245. b	246. b	247. c	248. a	249. c	250. d
251. d	252. d	253. a	254. a	255. d	256. c	257. d	258. c	259. d	260. b
261. b	262. c	263. b	264. c	265. b	266. b	267. d	268. d	269. c	270. c
271. d	272. a	273. a	274. d	275. c	276. d				

UPSC Questions on Indian Polity (General Studies—Mains)

1993 Test Paper

1. (a) What are the essentials of a true federation? Analyse the nature of the Indian federation. (About 250 words)   **40**

OR

   (b) Describe the powers and functions of the Council of States. Compare its powers with those of the House of the People. (About 250 words)

2. Answer any two of the following (Answer to each question should be in about 150 words):
                                                       20 + 20 = 40

   (a) What are the fundamental duties and their implications?
   (b) Describe the doctrine of colourable legislation.
   (c) Describe the composition and functions of the Election Commission of India.
   (d) Describe the composition and functions of the National Development Council.

3. Answer any three of the following (Answer to each question should be in about 25 words):
                                                       3 × 3 = 9

   (a) Distinguish between preventive detention and punitive detention.
   (b) What are the various writs available to the citizens of India?
   (c) When and why was the National Literacy Mission founded?
   (d) What is meant by 'equal protection of law'?
   (e) What is the content of the 10th Schedule of the Constitution of India?
   (f) What is the purpose of Article 24 of the Constitution of India?

1994 Test Paper

1. (a) "In India, though the Governor is the constitutional head of a state just as the President of the country, the former may be enjoying more powers than the latter." Do you agree? Give reasons. (About 250 words)   **40**

OR

   (b) Explain the role of the Planning Commission and the National Development Council in the formulation of public policy in India. (About 250 words)

2. Answer any two of the following (Answer to each question should be in about 150 words):
                                                       20 + 20 = 40

   (a) Explain the significance of the April 1994 Supreme Court judgement on the proclamation of President's rule.
   (b) Describe the emergence of Basic Structure concept in the Indian Constitution.
   (c) What are the major recommendations of the Swaminathan Committee's Draft National Population Policy, relating to gender issues?
   (d) Explain the position of the Election Commission with regard to the residential qualification of the members of the Council of States. What do you think about it?

3. Answer any three of the following (Answer to each question should be in about 25 words):
                                                       3 × 3 = 9

   (a) Differentiate between the 'due process of law' and 'the procedure established by law' in the context of deprivation of personal liberty in India.
   (b) Explain the meaning of ex post-facto legislation.

(c) What is Section 309 IPC about? Why was it in the news recently?

(d) What is our country's highest civilian award? Who are the two foreigners on whom the award was conferred?

(e) Indicate the provisions of Indian Constitution relating to Secularism.

(f) Four more languages were added to the 8th Schedule of the Constitution through two amendments. Give the names of these four languages as also the serial number of amendments.

1995 TEST PAPER

1. (a) Distinguish between Parliamentary and Presidential forms of Government. Do you think that changing over to presidential form will be a solution for better governance? Substantiate your answer. (About 250 words)   **40**

OR

(b) What is the position of the Supreme Court under the Constitution of India? Discuss its role as a guardian of the Constitution. (About 250 words)

2. Answer any two of the following (Answer to each question should be in about 150 words):

20 + 20 = 40

(a) Explain the functions of the Estimates Committee.

(b) Describe the non-federal features of the Council of States.

(c) What are the constitutional rights of the citizens of India? What do you think about the demand of the NRI's for dual citizenship?

(d) Describe the salient features of Anti-Defection Law.

3. Answer any three of the following (Answer to each question should be in about 25 words):   **3 × 3 = 9**

(a) Define Financial Emergency. How many times has this been proclaimed so far?

(b) What is the present status of the right to property as a Fundamental Right?

(c) Why is Article 32 considered as the cornerstone of the Constitution?

(d) What is a bicameral legislature? Mention the states that have a bicameral legislature in our country.

(e) Explain the scope of Article 331.

(f) Explain the status of the Ministers known as 'Ministers of State'.

1996 TEST PAPER

1. (a) What do you understand by the term 'Rule of Law'? How does the Constitution of India seek to establish it? (About 250 words)   **40**

OR

(b) Why does the Constitution of India contain different forms of Oath for the President, the Ministers, the Legislators and the members of the Judiciary? Discuss their significance. (About 250 words)

2. Answer any two of the following (Answer to each question should be in about 150 words):

20 + 20 = 40

(a) What is a Cut Motion? Discuss its significance.

(b) How are electoral constituencies delimited for Parliamentary elections in India?

(c) What is delegated legislation and which are the factors responsible for its increase?

(d) What are the Consolidated and Contingency Funds of India? How are the two operated?

3. Answer any three of the following (Answer to each question should be in about 25 words):

3 × 3 = 9

(a) What is the major recommendation of Dinesh Goswami Committee?

(b) What role can the Union Government play in settling inter-state water disputes?

(c) The Writ of Mandamus cannot be granted against certain persons. Who are they?

(d) What constitutional provisions make the office of the Comptroller and Auditor General of India independent?

(e) How do you distinguish between a Money Bill and a Finance Bill?

(f) What are the functions of the Human Rights Commission of India?

1997 TEST PAPER

1. (a) How are the President and the Vice-President of India elected? What are the constitutional issues involved in their election? (About 250 words) **40**

OR

(b) What is Social Justice? How can reservation of seats for women in Parliament contribute to the establishment of a socially just society in India? (About 250 words)

2. Answer any two of the following (Answer to each question should be in about 150 words):

20 + 20 = 40

(a) Present your views for and against the creation of an All India Judicial Service.

(b) Discuss the factors responsible for the rise of regionalism in India. How does it influence the political system?

(c) What, according to the Supreme Court, constituted 'The Basic Features' which is upheld in case known as

(i) Keshavanand Bharati v/s. State of Kerala (1990)

(ii) Minerva Mills v/s. Union of India (1990)?

(d) How does the Parliament control the financial system in India?

3. Answer any three of the following (Answer to each question should be in about 25 words):

$3 \times 3 = 9$

(a) What do Rule 184 and 193 in Parliamentary Procedure signify?

(b) What is meant by 'Gujral Doctrine'? Write its specific principles.

(c) Give a brief account of C.M.P. (Common Minimum Programme) of the United Front Government at the Centre.

(d) Write any four fundamental duties prescribed in the Constitution of India.

(e) What specific provisions exist in the Constitution of India about child labour?

(f) What is Article 356 in the Indian Constitution? Comment.

1998 Test Paper

1. (a) Briefly state the stages through which the present position of the Directive Principles vis-à-vis the Fundamental Rights has emerged. (About 250 words) **40**

OR

(b) Explain the concept of 'Prime Ministerial Government' and account for its decline in recent times in India.

2. Answer any two of the following (Answer to each question should be in about 150 words):

$20 + 20 = 40$

(a) Highlight the significance of the Seventy-Third Amendment to the Constitution of India?

(b) How are the new States formed in India? Why have the demands of separate states like those of Vidarbha, Telangana etc. not been considered by the Government recently?

(c) On what grounds the Legislative Councils are justified? How is it created or abolished in a State?

(d) Differentiate and state the significance of general election, mid-term election and by-election.

3. Answer any three of the following (Answer to each question should be in about 25 words): $3 \times 3 = 9$

(a) What is meant by 'Protem Speaker'?

(b) Point out the constitution and functions of the Central Vigilance Commission.

(c) State the amplitude of Article 21 of the Constitution.

(d) Which of the cases regarding disqualifications for Membership of either House of Parliament are decided by the President?

(e) Differentiate between Parliamentary Secretary and Lok Sabha Secretary.

(f) What is a Privilege Motion?

1999 Test Paper

1. (a) In what ways is the Rajya Sabha expected to play a special role in today's changing political scenario? (About 250 words) **40**

OR

(b) On what grounds does Article 15 of the Indian Constitution prohibit discrimination? Indicate the way the concept of 'special protection' has qualified this prohibition, and contributed to social change.

2. Answer any two of the following (Answer to each question should be in about 150 words):

$20 + 20 = 40$

(a) What is the importance of Directive Principles of State Policy? Mention which Directive Principles of State Policy have got primacy over the Fundamental Rights.

(b) Discuss the composition and functions of the National Security Council.

(c) Highlight the significance of the Twenty Fourth Amendment to the Constitution of India?

(d) Assess the importance of the role played by the Public Accounts Committee.

3. Answer any three of the following (Answer to each question should be in about 25 words): $3 \times 3 = 9$

(a) Who presides over the Joint-Session of the two Houses of the Indian Parliament over a non-money bill?

(b) Is there any provision to impeach the Governor of a State?

(c) In case of any dispute whether a bill is a money bill or not, whose decision is final?

(d) How is the Vice-President of India elected?

(e) What is the status of the Right to Property in the Indian Constitution?

(f) What is the maximum gap between two sessions of the Indian Parliament?

2000 Test Paper

1. Answer any ONE of the following (About 250 words): **30**

(a) Examine the need for the review of the Indian Constitution.

(b) Examine the demand for greater State-autonomy and also its impact on the smooth functioning of the Indian polity.

2. Answer any ONE of the following (About 250 words):   **30**
   - (a) How does Parliament control the Union Executive? How effective is its control?
   - (b) What constitutes the doctrine of 'basic features' as introduced into the Constitution of India by the Judiciary?

3. Answer any TWO of the following (About 150 words each):   **15 × 2 = 30**
   - (a) Identify the major electoral reforms which are necessary in the Indian Political System.
   - (b) Examine the role of Estimates Committee.
   - (c) Discuss the major extra-constitutional factors influencing the working of federal polity in India.

4. Answer the following (About 20 words each):   **5 × 2 = 10**
   - (a) What is vote on account?
   - (b) What is Caretaker Government?
   - (c) Do you justify the Prime Minister's entry into Parliament through the Rajya Sabha?
   - (d) What is a Privilege Motion?
   - (e) What is contempt of Parliament?

5. Answer any ONE of the following (About 250 words):   **30**
   - (a) Discuss the provisions of the Human Rights Protection Act (1993) relating to the following :
     - (i) Definition of human rights.
     - (ii) Composition of the National Human Rights Commission.
     - (iii) Functions of the Commission.
     - (iv) What suggestions have been made for amending the Act for making the role of the NHRC more effective?
   - (b) Discuss the propositions laid down by the Supreme Court of India in the context of Torture in Prisons and Human Dignity.

2001 Test Paper

1. Answer any ONE of the following (About 250 words):   **30**
   - (a) Discuss the administrative relations between the centre and the states in the light of recent controversies.
   - (b) Bring out the aberrations of the parliamentary system of government in India.

2. Answer any ONE of the following (About 250 words):   **30**
   - (a) What is the constitutional position of Directive Principles of State Policy? How has it been interpreted by the judiciary after the emergency in 1975-77?

   - (b) What are the main differences between the passage of a Constitution Amendment Bill and other Legislative Bills?

3. Answer any TWO of the following (About 150 words each):   **2 × 15 = 30**
   - (a) Comment on the nature of Ordinance-making power of the President of India. What safeguards are there against possible misuse?
   - (b) Distinguish between Cabinet Secretariat and Prime Minister's Secretariat. Which of these is more important?
   - (c) Discuss the constitutional provisions regarding the rights of children.

4. Answer the following (About 20 words each):   **5 × 2 = 10**
   - (a) Explain the Local Area Development Scheme of the Members of Parliament.
   - (b) What is Ethics Committee of Lok Sabha?
   - (c) Why is it said that the centre has absolute veto over state legislation?
   - (d) What is Call Attention Motion?
   - (e) When is the device of joint sitting of both the Houses of Parliament not available?

2002 Test Paper

1. Answer any ONE of the following (About 250 words):   **30**
   - (a) "The issue of a hung Parliament adversely affects the stability of Indian Government." Discuss the statement and point out how far changing over to the Presidential form of government will be a solution to this problem.
   - (b) Why does the Constitution of India provide different forms of Oaths for the President, the Ministers, the legislators and the members of the judiciary? Discuss their significance.

2. Answer any ONE of the following (About 250 words):   **30**
   - (a) What is the position of the Supreme Court under the Constitution of India? How far does it play its role as the guardian of the Constitution?
   - (b) How is the Constitution of India amended? Do you think that the procedure for amendment makes the Constitution a play-thing in the hands of the Centre?

3. Answer any TWO of the following (About 150 words each):   **2 × 15 = 30**
   - (a) Discuss the constitutional provisions relating to the non-justiciable directives binding upon the states.
   - (b) Describe the methods of delimiting constituencies for parliamentary elections in India.

(c) Explain the role of the Public Accounts Committee.

4. Answer the following (About 20 words each):
   $5 \times 2 = 10$
   (a) What is the importance of the 84th Amendment of the Indian Constitution?
   (b) Under what Article of the Constitution can the Union Government play its role in settling inter-state water disputes?
   (c) What is the role of the protem speaker?
   (d) What is meant by the 'lame-duck session' of the legislature?
   (e) What is meant by the 'fringe areas' in the sphere of local government in India?

5. Write on any ONE of the following (About 250 words):
   30
   (a) What is the composition of the Electoral College for the election of the President of the Indian Republic? How is the value of votes cast counted?

2003 TEST PAPER

1. Answer any ONE of the following (About 250 words):
   30
   (a) Discuss the question of death sentence and Presidential clemency.
   (b) Explain the discretionary powers of the Governor of a State.

2. Answer any ONE of the following (About 250 words):
   30
   (a) Discuss Parliamentary Control over the Executive.
   (b) Identify the major obstacles in the smooth functioning of Parliamentary democracy in India.

3. Answer any TWO of the following (About 150 words each):
   $2 \times 15 = 30$
   (a) Highlight the significance of Forty Fourth Amendment to the Constitution of India.
   (b) Identify the major Fundamental Duties.
   (c) Explain the relevance of Rajya Sabha as a second chamber in the federal set up of Indian Parliamentary System.

4. Answer the following (About 20 words each):
   $5 \times 2 = 10$
   (a) What is a point of order? When can it be raised?
   (b) What is a Privilege Motion?
   (c) State the difference between Council of Ministers and the Cabinet.
   (d) How is the Vice-President of India elected?
   (e) What is meant by 'sine-die' adjournment?

2004 TEST PAPER

1. Answer any ONE of the following (About 250 words):
   30

(a) What is the significance of a preamble to a constitution? Bring out the philosophy of the Indian polity as enshrined in the Preamble of the Indian Constitution.
   (b) Discuss the meaning of "breakdown of constitutional machinery". What are its effects?

2. Answer any ONE of the following (About 250 words):
   30
   (a) Discuss how the Constitution of India provides equal rights.
   (b) How does the Indian Constitution seek to maintain independence of the Public Service Commission?

3. Answer any TWO of the following (About 150 words each):
   $2 \times 15 = 30$
   (a) Define Money-bill. Discuss how it is passed in the Parliament.
   (b) What is a Finance Commission? Discuss the main functions of the State Finance Commission.
   (c) Discuss how state governments can exercise control over panchayats.

4. Answer the following (About 20 words each):
   $5 \times 2 = 10$
   (a) What is Habeas Corpus?
   (b) What are the constitutional restrictions imposed upon the power of borrowing of the state governments?
   (c) What is the special facility provided to the linguistic minorities under Article 350 A?
   (d) How can a judge of the Supreme Court be removed?
   (e) How is the Election Commission of India constituted?

2005 TEST PAPER

1. Answer any ONE of the following (About 250 words):
   30
   (a) Comment on the financial relations between the Union and the States in India. Has post-1991 liberlization in any way affected it?
   (b) Is it possible to distinguish between judicial review and judicial activism in India? Does the recent behaviour of the Indian judiciary partake more of judicial activism? Argue with suitable examples.

2. Answer any ONE of the following (About 250 words):
   30
   (a) Would you say that the implementation of the Panchayati System in the last ten years has led to a real restructuring of the Indian polity?
   (b) Give your views on the right to freedom of religion as enshrined in the Indian Constitution. Do they make India a secular State?

3. Answer any TWO of the following (About 150 words each):   **15 × 2 = 30**
   (a) What are the constitutional limitations on the free movements of Indians throughout the country?
   (b) How has the Indian State tackled the trade-off between environment and development?
   (c) What are the steps that the Election Commission may take if a recalcitrant State Government wants to put off Assembly Elections?

4. Answer the following (About 20 words each):   **2 × 5 = 10**
   (a) What is meant by 'double jeopardy'?
   (b) What are the protections afforded to Scheduled Tribes in the Fifth Schedule of the Indian Constitution?
   (c) In what ways can the President of India ascertain the views of the Supreme Court on a particular bill?
   (d) What is the common point between articles 14 and 226 of the Indian Constitution?
   (e) Who and what does the Indian Parliament consist of?

2006 TEST PAPER

1. Answer any ONE of the following (About 250 words):   **30**
   (a) What is right to life and personal liberty? How have the courts expanded its meaning in recent years?
   (b) On what grounds can a member be disqualified from either House of Parliament?

2. Answer any ONE of the following (About 250 words):   **30**
   (a) What is the 'strategic partnership' between India and United States of America? What are its implications for both the partners?
   (b) Discuss economic backwardness as a major challenge of Indian democracy. Can democracy and development go together smoothly?

3. Answer any TWO of the following (About 150 words):   **2 × 15 = 30**
   (a) How would you differentiate between the passage of a Constitution Amendment Bill and of an Ordinary Legislative Bill?
   (b) How does the Inter-State Council establish co-ordination between States?
   (c) Is the High Courts' power to issue 'writs' wider than that of the Supreme Court of India?

4. Answer the following (About 20 words each):   **5 × 2 = 10**
   (a) Explain the following terms :
      (i) Dissolution of the House
      (ii) Prorogation of the House
      (iii) Adjournment of the business of the House
   (b) What is Consolidated Fund of India?
   (c) To what extent can the President withhold his assent to a Bill already passed by the Parliament?
   (d) What is India's 'Look East' Policy?
   (e) What is meant by 'empowerment of women' in India?

2007 TEST PAPER

1. Answer any ONE of the following (About 250 words):   **30**
   (a) What is a Constitution? What are the main sources of the Indian Constitution?
   (b) Bring out the differences between the Fundamental Rights and the Directive Principles of State Policy. Discuss some of the measures taken by the Union and State Governments for the implementation of the Directive Principles of State Policy.

2. Answer any ONE of the following (About 250 words):   **30**
   (a) What is Regionalism? In which way regionalism has affected the Indian polity?
   (b) What are the main determinants of voting behaviour in India?

3. Answer any TWO of the following (About 150 words):   **15 × 2 = 30**
   (a) What are the exceptions when the President of India is not bound by the aid and advice of the Council of Ministers?
   (b) What is pro tem Speaker?
   (c) Under what circumstances, Parliament may legislate on State subjects?

4. Answer the following questions (About 20 words each):   **2 × 5 = 10**
   (a) What is criminalization of politics?
   (b) How is the President of India elected?
   (c) What is casting vote?
   (d) What is the difference between Council of Ministers and Cabinet?
   (e) What is the importance of Right to Constitutional Remedies?

2008 TEST PAPER

1. Answer any ONE of the following (About 250 words):   **30**
   (a) What is meant by 'Judicial Activism'? Evaluate its role in the context of the functioning of Indian polity.
   (b) Discuss the major extra-constitutional factors influencing the federal polity in India.

2. Answer any TWO of the following (About 150 words each): **15 × 2 = 30**
   (a) Enumerate the Fundamental Duties incorporated in the Constitution after the 42nd Amendment.
   (b) Examine the demand for greater state autonomy and its impact on the smooth functioning of Indian polity.
   (c) Discuss the composition and functions of the Union Public Service Commission.

3. Answer the following (About 20 words each): **2 × 5 = 10**
   (a) What is a Censure Motion?
   (b) Distinguish between the auditing and accounting functions of the CAG of India.
   (c) Distinguish between a starred question and an unstarred one asked in the Parliament.
   (d) What is contempt of Parliament?
   (e) What were the two major considerations to have the Governor appointed and not elected?

4. Answer any ONE of the following (About 250 words): **30**
   (a) What, in your opinion, are the causes of terrorism? Suggest suitable measures to deal with the threat of terrorism in India.
   (b) Do you think there is a need for a review of the Indian Constitution? Justify your view.

5. Answer any TWO of the following (About 150 words each): **15 × 2 = 30**
   (a) Examine the role of caste in Indian politics.
   (b) Discuss the problems in achieving National Integration in India.
   (c) Examine the impact of Regional Political Parties in Indian politics.

2009 Test Paper

1. Answer any two of the following (in about 150 words each): **15 × 2 = 30**
   (a) What are your views on the features and impact of the Domestic Violence Act, 2005?
   (b) Are the traditional determinants of voting behaviour in India changing? Examine in the context of the last General Elections.
   (c) Examine corruption as a serious development challenge in Indian Polity.

2. Answer the following (in about 150 words): **15**
   (a) In the changing context of governance in the country, what should be the role of the UPSC?

3. Answer the following (in about 150 words): **15**
   (a) 'As we live in a plural society we need the greatest freedom to express our opinions even if others find it offensive' – Do you agree? Discuss with reference to some recent incidents in the Indian context.

4. Write on the following (in about 20 words each): **2 × 3 = 6**
   (a) Significance of 26th November in the country's polity
   (b) Pocket Veto
   (c) PESA, 1996

2010 Test Paper

1. Answer the following (in about 250 words): **20**
   (a) "Disputes between the riparian states on sharing of river waters in post-Independence India are becoming increasingly complex." Objectively analyse the major disputes in this connection, with special reference to the Southern States.

2. Answer the following (in about 150 words): **12**
   (a) With respect to Cooperative Societies what are the salient features of the 106th and 111th Constitutional Amendment Bills as at present?

3. Answer the following (in about 150 words): **12**
   (a) What are the grounds of disqualification of a Member of Parliament from either House? Quote relevant provisions in your answer.

4. Write brief but precise note on the following. Your answer should not exceed 50 words. **5**
   (a) Legislative powers assigned to the Rajya Sabha under Art. 249 and Art. 312 of the Constitution.

5. Answer the following (in about 150 words): **12**
   (a) Bring out the powers and responsibilities attached to the office of the Speaker of the Lok Sabha.

6. Answer the following, briefly but precisely. Answer should be less than 50 words. **5**
   (a) How is disagreement between the Legislative Council and the Legislative Assembly of a State in passing of an ordinary Bill, resolved?

2011 Test Paper

1. Answer the following (in about 250 words each): **20 × 3 = 60**
   (a) 'Essentially all that is contained in Part IV – A of the Constitution is just a codification of tasks integral to the Indian way of life'. Critically examine this statement.
   (b) 'The exercise of executive clemency is not a privilege but is based on several principles, and discretion has to be exercised in public considerations.' Analyse this statement in the context of the judicial powers of the President of India.
   (c) Bring out the salient features of the PCPNDT Act, 1994, and the implications of its amendment in 2003.

2. Comment on the following (in about 150 words each): $12 \times 3 = 36$
   (a) Deendayal Disabled Rehabilitation Scheme (DDRS).
   (b) Evolution of 'Green Benches' in our higher judiciary.
   (c) Distinction between 'Department Related Parliamentary Standing Committees' and 'Parliamentary Forums'.
3. Comment on the following in NOT more than 50 words each: $5 \times 2 = 10$
   (a) Composition and functions of the National Executive Committee of the National Disaster Management Authority.
   (b) The Bihar Special Courts Act, 2009 and why it has been in the news recently?
4. Comment on the following in not more than 50 words: 5
   (a) E-governance initiatives by the Union Public Service Commission (UPSC).

2012 TEST PAPER

1. Answer the following (in about 150 words each): $15 \times 2 = 30$
   (a) The Union Cabinet recently cleared the proposal to rename and amend the Child Labour (Prohibition and Regulation) Act, 1986. What are the salient features of the proposed amendments?
   (b) What are the salient features of the Consumer Protection (Amendment) Bill, 2011 introduced in the Lok Sabha in December 2011?
2. Answer the following (in about 50 words each): $5 \times 3 = 15$
   (a) What is the 'Parivarik Mahila Lok Adalat'?
   (b) What are the Rights within the ambit of Article 21 of the Indian Constitution?
   (c) Comment on the significance of the Preamble contained in the Right to Information Act.
3. Comment on the following (in about 20 words): 2
   (a) Determining the 'value' assigned to the vote of a Member of a State Legislative Assembly and of a Member of Parliament in the Indian Presidential elections.

Practice Questions on Indian Polity (General Studies—Mains)

I. Long Answer Questions

Instructions: Answer the following questions. Answer to each question should be in about 250 words. Each question carries 30 Marks.

1. How does the parliament exercise control over the Union Executive? How can it be made more effective?
2. Explain the ways of acquiring and losing Indian Citizenship.
3. Explain the right to freedom of religion as envisaged in the Indian Constitution.
4. Evaluate the position of the President of India.
5. Discuss the features of the party system in India.
6. Describe the procedure for the amendment of the Indian Constitution. What are the criticisms levelled against it?
7. Critically examine the extent to which the Directive Principles of State Policy have been implemented. What measures do you suggest for their better implementation?
8. Explain the principles of Indian foreign policy.
9. Critically examine the emergency powers of the Indian President.
10. Describe the relative roles of the Rajya Sabha and the Lok Sabha in the Indian Political System.
11. Explain the jurisdiction and powers of the Supreme Court.
12. The 80th and 88th Amendments have changed the centre-state financial relations. Explain the present position in this regard.
13. "The Indian Constitution is federal in form but unitary in spirit". Discuss.
14. What is the need for promoting National Integration in India? What measures do you suggest in this regard?
15. Describe the various constitutional provisions for the protection and development of women and children in India.
16. What has been the controversy regarding the amendability of Fundamental Rights? What constitutes the 'basic structure' of the Constitution?
17. Explain the constitutional position of Jammu & Kashmir and its relationship with the Indian Union.
18. Describe the various changes made in the Constitution by the 42nd and 44th Amendment Acts.
19. What are the anti-defection provisions under the Constitution? What are the recommendations of the National Commission to Review the Working of the Constitution in this regard?
20. What is a coalition government? What has been its experience in India at the central level?

II. Short Answer Questions

Instructions: Answer the following questions. Answer to each question should be in about 150 words. Each question carries 15 Marks.

1. Describe the composition of the Constituent Assembly of India.
2. What are the constitutional provisions with respect to the reorganization of states?
3. How does the writ jurisdiction of the Supreme Court differ from that of a High Court?
4. How the Directive Principles differ from the Fundamental Rights?
5. Explain the role of regional parties in Indian Politics.
6. Describe the composition and functions of a State Public Service Commission.
7. Explain the ideals contained in the Preamble of the Indian Constitution.

8. Examine the functioning of Judicial Review in the Indian Political System.
9. "India is a secular state". Explain.
10. Explain the six freedoms guaranteed under Article 19 of the Constitution.
11. What is meant by President's Rule? Explain.
12. Critically examine the discretionary powers of a State Governor.
13. Describe the composition and functions of the National Commission for Women.
14. What are the unitary features of the Indian Constitution?
15. Explain the procedure for the impeachment of the President.
16. What are the functions of the Vice-President of India? How does he differ from the American Vice-President?
17. What are the special powers enjoyed by the Rajya Saba? What is its utility?
18. Describe the powers and functions of the Speaker of Lok Sabha.
19. What is a 'cut motion'? What are its different kinds? What is its significance?
20. How is the State Legislative Assembly supreme over the State Legislative Council?
21. What is the composition of the Finance Commission? What are its functions?
22. Describe the features of the new Panchayati Raj System as introduced by the 73rd Amendment Act.
23. What is public opinion? Explain the agencies for its formation.
24. What is meant by 'Martial Law'? What are the constitutional provisions in this regard?
25. What are the circumstances under which the Parliament can legislate on the State List subjects?
26. What is 'Sovereignty of Parliament'? Is Indian Parliament a sovereign body?
27. What are the constitutional provisions with respect to the joint sitting of the two Houses of Parliament?
28. Describe the ordinance-making power of the President of India?
29. Who are linguistic minorities? What are the constitutional safeguards for them?
30. Describe the composition and functions of the National Commission for Protection of Child Rights.

1. What is meant by 'Gujral Doctrine'?
2. What is the concept of 'National Government'?
3. What is the significance of Article 355 of the Constitution of India?
4. What is the purpose of the Lok Adalats?
5. Distinguish between police custody and judicial custody.
6. What is meant by the 'Doctrine of Pith and Substance'?
7. Why Rajya Sabha is known as a Permanent House?
8. What is meant by 'Non-Alignment'?
9. Is the Constitution of India flexible or rigid?
10. What is the present position of the Right to Property?
11. Write the Directive Principles that were added by the Forty-Second Constitutional Amendment Act.
12. Who do not participate in the election of the President of India?
13. How is the Vice-President of India elected?
14. What are the different categories of ministers at the Union level?
15. What is meant by 'Cabinet Dictatorship'?
16. What are the changes made in the constitution by the 42nd and 44th Amendment Acts with respect to the powers of the President in relation to the Central Council of Ministers?
17. What is the meaning of 'Guillotine'?
18. Distinguish between Public Bill and Private Bill.
19. What are the qualifications of the judges of State High Courts?
20. What is meant by 'Residuary Powers'?
21. What is the purpose of Family Courts?
22. What are the various types of elections held in India?
23. What is meant by 'All-India Services'?
24. What is 'Panchasheel'?
25. What are the functions of the Attorney-General of India?
26. What is meant by 'Point of Order'?
27. What are the functions of the Zonal Councils?
28. What is first-past-the-post-system?
29. What is meant by 'Money Bill'?
30. Describe the composition of the National Development Council.

III. Very Short Answer Questions

Instructions: Answer the following questions. Answer to each question should be in about 20 words. Each question carries 2 Marks.